THE
WEST

THE
WEST

A COLLECTION FROM

HARPER'S MAGAZINE

GALLERY BOOKS

Gallery Books
an imprint of W.H. Smith Publishers, Inc.
112 Madison Avenue
New York, New York 10016

This volume first published in 1990 by

The Octopus Group Limited
Michelin House, 81 Fulham Road, London SW3 6RB

This edition published in 1990 by Gallery Books
an imprint of W.H. Smith Publishers Inc.
112 Madison Avenue, New York 10016

ISBN 0 8317 4254 2

Printed in Great Britain by the Bath Press

CONTENTS

ACROSS ARIZONA

IF there be anything disrupting in mere topography, the section below the range which closes in the Los Angeles and Riverside country should also, in its turn, clamor to be admitted as a separate State. It should clamor at any rate to be joined to Arizona, with the climatic system of which it is inseparably connected. Arizona and the portion of California southeast of the low San Gorgonio Pass have the same seasons as Mexico, that is to say, the rains fall in the summer, while northward they fall in the winter and spring. The thunder-storms on each side of the mountains are plainly visible to the other, but never pass this limit. I myself have seen, from the Arizona side, in December, being under hot, clear sunshine at the time, the murky clouds billowing up above this range, and lightnings playing in them, and have found Los Angeles, on presently returning thither, drenched with its first showers.

There is but one reason why the inhabitants of the section described should not raise such a clamor, or rather there is this excellent reason, that it does not possess at present any inhabitants worth mentioning. For one hundred and fifty miles from the pass, to the Arizona frontier at Yuma, the railroad hardly knows what local traffic is. Its route is over the much-talked-of "Colorado Desert," in comparison with which the deserts we have seen hitherto, though by no means unimposing in their way, are of small dimensions. There are various stopping-places, with designations on the map, but these are rarely more than signal stations and points where the locomotive stops to drink at the artesian wells.

The plain is not of vast extent laterally. Black and purplish mountains are always in sight, and spurs of them cross the course. Bowlders and pebbles are scattered thickly on the surface at first, among patches of bunch-grass; then the jaws of the black and purple mountains open, near Seven Palms, and show the genuine white sand desert, strewn with bowlders still, but bare of vegetation, and varied with dunes and large hills of clean sand. One expects a glimpse of blue water between the dunes at every moment, as if riding to Coney Island or Long Branch. We traverse a singular depression, which is below the level of the sea for a hundred miles, at its lowest point nearly three hundred feet. At Dos Palmas, in the very bottom of the pit, a board shanty saloon, covered with inscriptions in an amateurish lettering, stands alone at a little distance from the track. Surely the keeper of it must consume his own drinks, and lead a melancholy existence unprecedented among barkeepers. No; a horseman in Mexican accoutrements dashes across the plain— though where he should dash from, and how he should be riding anything but the mummy of a dolphin or a sea-horse here in the very bottom of the sea itself, is a mystery—and pulls up there, and enters. And it further appears that from this place a stage starts every other day for points on the Colorado River, and for Prescott, the remote capital of Arizona Territory. This is but a faint survival of a bustle which once reigned before the day of the railroad, when the route of the southern overland mail was hither, and long trains of immigrant and freight wagons, carrying water in casks for two and three days' supply, passed continually over these wastes east and west.

Nothing would appear more depressing on general principles than such a country, but as a matter of fact it is entertaining instead. It is a stimulus to the curiosity, and ends by having a real fascination. One would not wish to be abandoned alone in it without resources, it is true, but he does not tire of looking at it from a car window. Its blazing dryness is in its favor. It is disinfectant and preservative. Perhaps there can never be the most poignant extreme of sadness in scenes without the element of decay by dampness. It is chemical and not botanical processes that are principally going on. Wonders of almost any sort may be expected. Phantoms might flit about over it, hiding among the frequent mirages.

A considerable part of Arizona as well is of the same character, but it is estimated by competent authority that with irrigation thirty-seven per cent. can be redeemed for agriculture, and sixty per cent. for pasturage. It may be called to mind that even the apparently hopeless bottom of the Colorado Desert, below the level of the sea, is also below the level of the Colorado River, and that water from this copious stream might be spared for it, and spread over it with comparative ease. The truly patriotic resident of Arizona is by no means ashamed of his encompassing desert, and with reason. It is in reality a laboratory of useful products. Paper is made from the yucca, or Spanish-bayonet, which abounds in certain parts of it.

more accessible, have given the Territory the fame it enjoys.

Our train runs out upon a long wooden draw-bridge, across the Colorado River, and we arrive at Yuma. The company has placed here the first of its series of hotels of uniform pattern. It is both station and hotel. Such provision on an equal scale of comfort would hardly have been judicious as an investment yet for private persons. These structures therefore become not only a typical feature of the scenery, but an indication as well of the extent to which the railroad has had to, and has been able to, by reason of its ample resources, take this bare new country in hand. They are of the usual reddish-brown, two stories in height, and surrounded by piazzas of generous width — an indispensable adjunct under the dazzling light and heat of the country.

The heat of Yuma has become traditional. Great heat, nevertheless, is not equally formidable everywhere. It is well attested that there is no sunstroke here, and no such suffering results as from a much lower degree of temperature in moister climates. Distinct sanitary properties are even claimed for this well-baked air. So

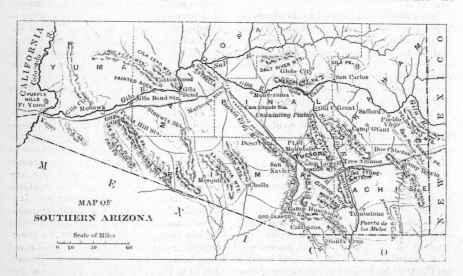

MAP OF
SOUTHERN ARIZONA

Scale of Miles

There are tracts of salt, borax, gypsum, sulphur, asbestos, and kaolin, and quarries of pumice-stone, only waiting for shipment. It is maintained also that it has deposits of the same precious metals which, mined in places where water is

near the sea-level, it is said to be less rarefied, and to comprise, therefore, a greater quantity of oxygen to a given bulk than that of mountain districts which in purity and dryness it resembles. It is thought to be beneficial in lung troubles. Yuma

NORTON'S LANDING, ON THE COLORADO RIVER.

among its arid sand-hills has aspirations to be a sanitarium, whither civilized people shall resort to engage in a sensible sort of sun-worship, to bask in the genial warmth, and then plunge into the river, as the resident Indians now do, making for themselves a kind of natural Turkish bath of it.

A transition state often has its disadvantages, even when it is a step toward something better. Yuma has now its railroad, and is to have a shipping port by the construction of another to Port Ysabel, on the Gulf of California; but it laments the decline of the greater activity it once enjoyed as the chief distributing point for the mines and the upper river towns. It expects the Port Ysabel Railroad, which is a portion of a through line chartered to Guaymas, in Mexico, to have the effect of doubling its population in two years. It will not be a stupendous population even then, as it is now only fifteen hundred.

The town is a collection of inferior adobes, but a few of the very best being altered from the natural mud-color by a coating of whitewash. The poorer part of it resembles more the tropical hamlets on the trail to Acapulco than even the ordinary villages of Mexico. The houses consist of a frame-work of cottonwood or ocotilla wattles, plastered with mud inside and out, so as to make a wall two or three inches thick. The roof is thatch, the floor the bare ground. Around them are generally high palisades of more ocotilla sticks, and, adjoining, corrals of the same.

The waiters in a Yuma hotel are of a highly miscellaneous character. We were served in the same dining-room by Mexicans, Chinamen, Irish, Americans, and a tame Apache Indian. One and all had a certain astounded air, ending in confirmed depression, on finding that we were to remain, and could dine somewhat at leisure, instead of having the dishes shot at us as if out of a catapult, as is done for the benefit of ordinary travellers who pause the allotted half-hour in passing through. But one does not expect too much of his waiter in Arizona.

The Colorado at Yuma makes about the same impression as to width as the Sacramento at the place of the same name, the Ohio at Pittsburgh, or the Connecticut at Hartford. It is a turbulent yellow stream. It cuts into high sand bluffs on the Arizona side, and spreads out their contents in wide bars on that of California. It is without wharves, the few light-draught, high-decked steamboats or barges visible, of those that ply up and down the interminable reaches of the much-celebrated river, being tied up to the banks. Mountains of a jagged eccentric formation follow its general course to the northward. Peaks impressively counterfeiting human design — Castle Dome, Chimney Peaks, Cargo Muchacho, or Freight Boy, and Picacho, simply the Peak—loom at various points around the horizon, a fitting fore-

PASQUAL, THE YUMA CHIEF.

taste of the marvels naturally to be expected in Arizona.

It was immediately at the close of the late Indian war that our visit was made. It had been reported in rumors, which proved much exaggerated, that the whole white civilization of the Territory was in danger from the outbreak, and troops—who were but just now on their return—had been hastened hither from all sides. The first view of Indians, therefore, at Yuma was an event of double importance. They were not Apaches, it is true, but a subsequent acquaintance with the general field proved them to be even more picturesque. They are of that satisfactory type of savages who wear little clothing, and none of this European. They are to be seen in numbers about the railway station by the casual passenger on the train. The railroad is still new to them, and they have not satiated their curiosity. They take friends who visit them to see the draw-bridge, and describe how it swings, and how the cars are switched from one track to another.

They are met with coming across this bridge from the patch of river-bottom near the fort on the California side, where their principal settlement is. The young men run or stride at great speed, so as to throw out behind them a long red sash or band, depending from the breech-cloth, which makes an important part of their attire. Their costume for the rest, in winter, consists of a close-fitting gray or crimson under-shirt. They wear their thick coal-black hair "banged" low over their foreheads, and long and bushy upon their necks. The effect at a little distance is curiously "æsthetic," like that of the Boccaccio period at Florence, when men wore jerkins and hose fitting them like their skins, and just such bushy locks, except that instead of going bare-headed, they crowned them with jaunty velvet caps.

The fort is without guns, other than a howitzer for firing salutes, and has no strength, as it no longer needs to have, except from its position on a commanding bluff. The military policy of the government now is to station its troops along a railroad or other easy line of communication, where they can be quickly massed to one another's support. All the Arizona posts—Camp Lowell, with its grassy parade and fine avenue of cottonwoods, on the level; Camp Grant, on its elevated table-land (*mesa*); Camp Apache, at the junction of two charming trout streams, in the White River Cañon; and the others—have only this strategic importance instead of intrinsic strength. The barracks at Yuma consist of a series of comfortable, large, adobe houses, plastered and painted green, surrounding an oblong plaza. They have in front of them a peculiar screen-work of green blinds, which shuts out the glare from the yellow ground, and makes both a cool promenade and sleeping apartments for the summer.

The principal chief of the band upon whose habitations the fort looks down chooses his sub-chiefs, but is himself appointed by the military commandant. The last investiture with this distinction was made as long ago as 1852, by General, then Major, Heintzelman. He conferred it upon the now wrinkled and decrepit Pasqual, who was described at the time as a tall, fine-looking man, of an agreeable disposition. Pasqual's people cultivate little patches of vegetables and hay in the river-bottom after it has been fertilized by the annual overflow. Their principal sustenance, however, is a sweet bean resembling that of the locust, from a variety of the mesquit-tree. This they pound in mortars into a kind of flour. Sometimes, on the move, they float their hay across the river on rafts, which they push before them, swimming; and they propel the small children in the same way, putting them into the large Egyptian-looking *ollas*, or water jars.

The crop of mesquit beans was so large one year as to be beyond their own un-aided capacity of consumption. They therefore hospitably invited in their friends the Pimas, but with undesirable results. Old Pasqual describes with graph-ic gestures how haggard and lank these visitors were on their arrival, and what an unctuous corpulence they had attained when, after nearly eating their hosts them-selves out of house and home, they were only got rid of at last by force.

Well, we are bowling along that now actually constructed Southern Pacific Railroad which is discoursed of in the musty debates in the *Congressional Globe* for the year 1852 (and who knows how much earlier?) with a sagacity that great-ly increases one's respect for ancestors he may have thought rather commonplace. We reach Stanwix with its lava beds, Painted Rock, named from its mysterious-ly decorated huge bowlders, Casa Grande, from its architectural ruins of the Toltecs, and Tucson. Adopting the policy of leav-

ing this last to be examined on the return, we push on to the extreme end of the Ter-ritory, to the eccentrically named Tomb-stone silver district. Benson, the point of departure from the railroad for Tomb-stone, is 1024 miles from San Francisco.

Tombstone is the very latest and liveli-est of those mushroom civilizations in un-likely places which have been so often seen to gather helter-skelter around a "find" of the precious metals. They live at a headlong pace while they go; draw around them wild and lawless spirits; con-fer great fortunes here, the suicide's grave or that of the victim of violence there. A school of literature, in Bret Harte and his followers, has arisen to celebrate their ex-traordinary doings. And with the rapid advance of population and conventional ideas they must shortly disappear from sight as absolutely as the dodo of tradition. While things go well with them, prices of commodities are hardly considered. No-body haggles. The most expensive is that which is most wanted. "Diamonds—two-hundred-dollar watches and chains—Lord! we couldn't hand 'em out fast enough," says an ex-jeweller, describing his experi-ence at one of these camps in its halcyon days. "Champagne wasn't good enough

YUMA INDIANS AT HOME.

TOMBSTONE.

for me then," says a seedy customer, recalling his doings after his discovery and sale of a rich mine, and sighing for a repetition of the event, not to make provision for his old age, but that he may have one more such glorious "spree" before he dies. Sometimes this rush of life departs even more quickly than it came. One fine day the lead is exhausted, there is no more treasure in the mine, away fly the heterogeneous elements, and the town, be it never so well built, is left vacant and desolate as Tadmor of the Wilderness. In a Nevada mining town, once having some thousands of inhabitants, Indians are living in abandoned rows of good brick houses, which they have adapted to their purposes as far as possible by knocking out the doors and windows and punching holes in the roofs.

A six-horse Concord coach carried us, not too speedily, over the twenty-five miles of dusty road to Tombstone. It was called the "Grand Central," after a prosperous mine. A rival line was the "Sandy Bob," from its proprietor, who preferred to be thus known, instead of by a conventional family name, such as might be found in a directory. We should certainly have taken the "Sandy Bob," for its greater suggestiveness, in the line of the Bret Harte romances, except that it was just coming down when we wanted to go up, and coming up when we were going down. However, our own proved to have a good deal of suggestiveness too. A guard got up with a Winchester rifle, and posted himself by the Wells-Fargo Express box. The driver began to relate robber stories. This stage had been stopped and "gone through" twice within the past six months. The experience was enlivened on one occasion by a runaway and turnover, and on the other by the shooting and killing of the driver. Of this last feature his successor spoke with a disgust not unnatural. He would have the line drawn at drivers. He respected a person who took to the road and robbed those who could afford it. At least he considered it more honorable than borrowing money of a friend which you knew you could never repay, or gobbling up the earnings of the poor, received on deposit, like a certain large firm lately suspended in Pima County. But as to shooting a driver, even in mistake for somebody else, he had no words to express his sense of the meanness of it.

He threw stones at his horses, as is done in Mexico, that is, at the leaders, which were beyond the reach of his long lash. A single stone was made to "carom," such was his skill, and served for both. Long teams of mules or of Texas steers, sixteen to a team, drawing ore wagons—three usually tackled together—were strung interminably along the road. The Mexican-looking drivers trudged beside them in the deep yellow dust, cracking huge "black-snakes" at the animals. Mesquit bushes, and a long grass dried to hay—said not to be as good as it looked—covered portions of the surface; the rest was stony and bare. We rode for a certain distance beside the branch railroad in course of construction between Benson and Tombstone. A series of lateral valleys along the tributaries branching from the Gila, both north and south, as the Santa Cruz, the Salt River, the San Carlos, San Pedro, and San Simon, not only afford excellent stock ranges, and promise of a flourishing agriculture in time, but easy routes for tributary railways. They have begun already to be utilized, as the San Pedro for the Southern Pacific branch mentioned, and the Santa Cruz for the Arizona Southern, from the centre of the Territory at Florence, on the Atlantic and Pacific, to connect with the Mexican system at Calabasas. The transcontinental road—or roads, when the Atlantic and Pacific shall be built—will draw trade through these tributary valleys as the Gila draws its waters, and particularly from the northern States of Mexico, where mining enterprise, in which Americans play conspicuous part, is making great headway.

The route began to be up-hill. We changed horses and lunched at Contention City. One naturally expected a certain belligerency of such a place, but none appeared on the surface during our stay. There were plenty of saloons—the "Dew-drop," the "Head-light," and the like—and at the door of one of them a Spanish señorita smoked her cigarette and showed her white teeth.

Contention City was the seat of stamp-mills for crushing ore brought to it from Tombstone, the latter place being without a water-power, though the defect has probably since been remedied. The stamps are rows of heavy beams dropping upon the mineral, on the mortar and pestle plan, with a continuous dull roar, by night as well as by day. The route grew steeper yet. On the few wayside fences were painted such announcements as, "Go To Bangley and Schlagenstein's. They Are The Bosses, You Bet." Then over the edge of bare hills appeared the outline of Tombstone itself.

A large circular water-tank loomed up the most conspicuous object in front, recalling, except for being painted with a mammoth advertisement, one of the chain of bold round forts crowning the heights above Verona.

At the beginning of the year 1878 there was not so much as a tent at Tombstone. "Ed" Schieffelin and brother started thither prospecting. It was supposed to be an adventure full of dangers. At the Santa Rita silver mines, in the Santa Cruz Valley, for instance, by no means so far away, three superintendents had been murdered by Indians in rapid succession. Friends therefore said, "Better take your coffin with you, Ed; you will find your tombstone, and nothing else." But Ed Schieffelin—a young man yet, who has not discarded a picturesque way of dress-

"ED" SCHIEFFELIN.

ing of which he was fond, nor greatly altered his habits otherwise—found instead the Tough Nut and Contention mines, made a great fortune out of them, and was so pleased with the difference between

MISSION CHURCH OF SAN XAVIER DEL BAC, NEAR TUCSON.

what had really happened and the prediction that he conferred the name of Tombstone upon the place itself.

One of the two well-printed and very creditable daily papers now existing has assumed the correspondingly dismal title of the *Epitaph*. The unreliability of epitaphs—if the remark may be safely ventured at this distance—is proverbial. Nevertheless, they may occasionally tell the truth; and from appearances it would seem that this was one of those occasions, and that almost any laudation of its sub-ject by this particular *Epitaph* was justifiable. The small city, two years old at the date of this journey, had attained to a population of 2000, and a property valuation, apart from the mines, of $1,050,980. A desirable lot of 30 by 80 feet, on Allen Street, between Fourth and Sixth—such was the business-like nomenclature used already in this settlement of yesterday— was worth $6000. A shanty that cost $50 to build rented for $15 a month. A nucleus of many blocks at the centre consisted of substantial, large-sized buildings—hotels, banks, Schieffelin Hall, for meetings and amusements, and stores stocked with goods of more than the average excellence for even older towns.

The mining claims run under the city itself. From the roof of the Grand Hotel you looked down at the shafts, the hoist works, and heaps of extracted ore of the Vizina, the Gilded Age (close by the Palace Lodging-House), the Mountain Maid, and other mines opening strangely in the very midst of the buildings. This circumstance has given rise to disputes of ownership, so that whoever would be safe purchases all the conflicting titles both aboveground and below. On a commanding hill close by, to the southward, were the

with common sheds and poorer appliances of every kind. About them all lie heaps of a blackish material, resembling inferior coal mixed with slate, which is the silver ore in its native condition. A laborer above-ground earned $3.50, and belowground $4, for a "shift" of eight hours' work; and the work went on night and day, Sundays and all.

The outskirts consisted still of huts and tents. A burly miner could be seen stretched upon his cot in his windowless cabin barely large enough to contain it. There were small tents provided with wooden doors and adobe chimneys. New as it was, the business portion of the place had been swept out of existence at one time.

THE SHERIFF OF TOMBSTONE AND HIS CONSTITUENTS.

Tough Nut and Contention, with above them many others discovered later. The larger mines have extensive buildings of wood, painted Indian red, with handsome draughting and assay rooms within, and regularly educated scientists, ex-college professors and the like, in charge. The lesser are fain to put up in the beginning

A devastating fire had originated from a characteristic incident—the explosion of a whiskey barrel at the Oriental Saloon. But in fourteen days all had been rebuilt much better than before. I took the pains to remark the number of establishments in a single short block of Allen Street at which intoxicating beverages could be had. There were the bar-rooms of two principal hotels, the Eagle Brewery, Can-can Chop-House, French Rôtisserie, Alhambra, Maison Doré, City of Paris, Brown's Saloon, Fashion Saloon, Miners' Home, Kelly's Wine-House, the Grotto, the Tivoli, and two saloons besides apparently unnamed. At all these places gambling goes on without let or hinderance. The absence of savings-banks or of other opportunities for depositing money in these wild new communities, and the consequent temptation of having it always under the eye, no doubt has something to do with the general passion for gambling. From the hygienic point of view, whiskey and cold lead are mentioned as the leading diseases at Tombstone. What with the leisure that seems to prevail, the constant drinking and gambling at the saloons, and the universal practice of carrying deadly weapons, there is but one source of astonishment, and that is that the cold-lead disease should claim so few victims. Casualties are very infrequent considering the amount of vaporish talk indulged in, and the imminent risks that are constantly run; and the small cemetery over toward Contention Hill is still comparatively virgin ground.

A further element, in addition to the silver mines, adds to the exceptional liveliness of Tombstone. It has attained a certain fame already for the doings of its "Cow-boys." The term cow-boys was at first applied to persons engaged in the cattle business indiscriminately, but while still including the honest sort, has been narrowed down so as to mean particularly a class who have become stealers of cattle, at first over the Mexican frontier, then at home, and terrorists generally in their day and generation. Exceptional despera-

APACHE PRISONERS AT CAMP LOWELL.

AN ARIZONA WATERING-PLACE.

does of this class, such as "Billy the Kid," "Curly Bill," and "Russian George," have been scourges of whole districts in Colorado, New Mexico, and Arizona, and have had their memories embalmed in yellow-covered literature. I bought on the train a crimson pamphlet purporting to contain an account of the exploits of Billy the Kid. He had committed a score at least of horrid murders. "So many cities have claimed the honor of giving him birth," my pamphlet began, "that it is difficult to locate with any accuracy the locality where he passed his youth." It appeared, however, to have been New York, and it was on the Bowery that his mates "learned to love him for his daring and prowess, and delighted to refer to him as Billy the Kid." This promising life was cut off at the age of twenty-two. Curly Bill was also young, and so was Man-killer Johnson. I remarked upon this peculiarity of their youth to a philosophic new ac-

quaintance of the region. "Yes," said he, "they *don't* live to be very old; that's so."

The recipe for long life for persons of an active habit in this country, it appears, is to be very quick and to "get the drop" on an antagonist, that is to say, to be ready to shoot first. It is not the custom to shoot unless it is likely that this can be done, but even to put up with some ignominious abuse, and wait for another opportunity.

The cow-boys frequenting Tombstone at this time were generally from ranches in the San Pedro and San Simon valleys. There were said to be strongholds in the San Simon Valley for concealing stolen cattle, until rebranded and prepared for market, where no officer of the law ever ventured. The running off of stock from Mexico was possibly looked upon only as a more dashing form of smuggling, although it was marked by frequent tragedies on both sides. Not to fix upon all the wickedness of the few, we no doubt saw on Tombstone streets plenty of cow-boys of the legitimate sort, whose only faults were an occasional boisterousness and a too free throwing about of their money.   There appeared to be something of a standing feud between the miners and the cow-boys.   An irregular faction of "town cow-boys" besides was organized against the country cow-boys.

The leading cattle-men had a Southern cut and accent, and were apt to have hailed from Missouri or Texas.   Some few appeared in full suits of broadcloth.   The wide felt sombrero was invariably worn.   The landlord of the hotel described them as "perfect gentlemen, some good at the bar for $20 and $25 a day."

The great object in life of various factions, or of individuals who from time to time arise in search of a brilliant notoriety, is to "run the town."   This seems to consist largely of the privilege of blustering the loudest in the saloons, whooping (with an occasional pistol-shot or two, if thought good) in the streets, and a moderate security from arrest for casual doings that might bring them under the cognizance of the law. The privilege is secured by inspiring in all who might be disposed to object a salutary dread of their prowess.

This is necessarily a very insecure domination.   New aspirants and rebels against it would be continually piqued into showing themselves whenever it seemed attained.   Our visit happened to be timed upon the heels of a conflict making the most tragic page yet written in the annals of Tombstone.   Official opinions were evenly divided about it, the sheriff extending his sympathy to one party, the city marshal, who was, in fact, its leader, to the other. City Marshal Earp, with his two brothers, and one "Doc" Holliday, a gambler, came down the street armed with rifles and opened fire on the two Clanton brothers and the two McLowry brothers.   The latter party had been practically disarmed by the sheriff, who had feared such a meeting, and meant to disarm the others as well.   Three of them fell, and died on the spot.   "Ike" Clanton alone escaped.   The slayers were imprisoned, but released on bail. The Grand Jury was now in session, and hearing the evidence in the case.   It was rumored that the town party, for such were the Earps, would be able to command sufficient influence to go free of indictment.   The country cow-boys, on the other hand, were flocking into town, and on one quiet Sunday in particular things wore an ominous look.   It was said that should justice fail to be done, the re-

CACTI.

STREET VIEW IN TUCSON.

vengeful, resolute-looking men conferring together darkly at the edges of the sidewalk would attempt to take the matter into their own hands.

The night journey on the return to Benson by the stage was whiled away with shooting stories. We heard especially of the doings of the late Brazelton of Tucson —a bugaboo indeed, as I saw his photograph presently, taken in his mask and general paraphernalia after death. He robbed stages unaided for years while apparently working quietly all the time as a hostler in a corral, and was finally tracked through some peculiar mark of the horse he rode. One of the narrators had himself just recovered sufficiently from wounds received in a fight with a Mexican—whom he had killed—over cards at Bisbee to be able, with the stimulus of frequent doses of morphine, to resume his journey toward New Mexico, where his home was. The train men at Benson were found chary of carrying the usual lanterns about the depot yard, a habit having arisen with the

cow-boys of trying to snuff them out with revolvers from a distance.

There seemed a certain tameness even in the Apaches after this wild product of the higher civilization of the whites. The principal group of prisoners taken after the attempted massacre of General Carr's command was found in confinement at Camp Lowell, nine miles north of Tucson. There were forty-two of them, including Sanchez, their chief. They were of fairly regular features, and of expressions, now that the war-paint was off, almost amiable. They were handcuffed together in couples, and had manacles on their legs. They wore now gray army under-shirts and cotton drawers, the rags in which they came in having been taken from them. Their long black hair hung about their ears, not frowzy like that of the Yumas, but smoothly parted in the middle, and brushed back. A number had red bands or handkerchiefs around their heads. These figures, seen half-obscurely in the chief prison-room by the side light of a grated window, had a certain resemblance now to *sans culottes* of 1793, now to Greek insurgents, and now to the wild Vendean peasants who fought in 1793 also, under Rochejaquelein and Jean Chouan, for religion and the king. The captives were taken out by way of airing in the mornings, and allowed to squat on their blankets in the sun at the edge of the pleasant parade, with its avenue and shady row of officers' dwellings. Their rising, it appears, was the result of a delusion of fanaticism. One of their medicine-men had persuaded them that he had received the mission to drive all the whites from the land. As soon as the corn was ripe, he said, all their brethren long since dead would arise and take arms also to aid them in carrying out the decree of Heaven He had, as prophets often have not, the courage of his professions. Though taken in charge himself by the troops, he gave the signal for the massacre to begin, and called to his people not to be concerned for his fate, since he should come to life and join them again in three days.

The bluff Arizonians themselves are apt to indulge in a derisive way of speaking of the army and its relation to the savages. Judging from the short shrift they would possibly give these latter, if they took the business into their own hands, they imply that the army does not really wish to kill off, or even wholly put down, the Indians, but to preserve them as a gentle stimulus to public dread, in order to keep itself in occupation and quicken promotions, and for those interested in profitable supply contracts. However this may have been, it would seem that after the repression of the late revolt, and with the penetration of railroads into the Territory, Indians need no longer be a deterring influence with the intending settler in Arizona. This old historic source of apprehension is as good as abolished from its last stronghold.

Eight miles further to the northward brought us to a ranch called Fuller's Hot Springs, one of the few places where a beginning of systematic cultivation has been made, and interesting besides as a typical Arizona summer resort. There was a young orchard of twenty-five acres, sheltered by a wind-break of three rows of ash-trees, doing very well in an alkali soil. The buildings were a number of unpainted adobe houses, each consisting of a single large comfortable room, and roofed over with strips of cactus. A "summer dining-room" was made of ocotilla sticks, the intervals left open; a " winter dining-room" had tight walls, and a fire-place, in which a wood fire was burned mornings and evenings. The hot spring, a clear pleasant water said to resemble the English Harrowgate water, ran out from below a patched canvas tent, which was used as a bath-house. It became below a pretty brook, a pond for the cattle, and a source of supply for irrigating the orchard. The mountains behind the place, the Santa Catalinas, are like the Sierra Madres behind Los Angeles, of the same sharp fracture, and allurement to exploration, but higher yet and grander, and jutting up into as perfect castles, here and there, as Harlech, or the Trostberg, or Ehrenbreitstein. There are forests of pines of large dimensions among their summits. To the south and southwest across the wide plain show the Rincons and the silver-bearing Santa Ritas.

There was a fascination in the opportunity to at last examine the strange growths of the plain, and not merely to know of them flying past the windows. We made haste especially to cut down an example of the enormous saguaras, the organ-cactus, which, sometimes rising to a height of sixty feet, bristle over the landscape like masts or columns, and if with branches, like the seven-branched candlestick of the Mosaic law. Inside it consists of a white juicy pulp, imbedding as a skeleton long wands, which, when dried, serve a number of useful purposes. It has a palatable fruit, which the Indians collect in August with long forked sticks. The ocotilla is simply a wattle of sticks, fifteen and twenty together, waiting to be cut down and turned into palings. The bisnaga is a thorny cactus like an immense watermelon set on end. One need never die of thirst where it is found. The cholla is one mass of spines, barbed on the fish-hook principle. It is considered particularly funny to hear of somebody's having fallen into a cholla. The "deer brush" resembles horns. The palo verde ("green stick") grows as large as an apple-tree, but is more like a mammoth sea-weed. The "grease-wood" is a large bush which is said to burn just as well green as dry. Most of this vegetation is leafless, or rather the plant seems a leaf itself, having the usual chlorophyll and tender structure distributed throughout. There are homely legends and superstitions about these plants of the desert which it would be interesting to follow up. A certain kind poisons a white spot it may happen to touch in a horse, but has no effect on other colors. Another, if eaten by horses, renders them fat and imbecile; while the loco, or rattleweed, met with also in California, drives them raving crazy.

Tucson, seen from a distance in early morning or late afternoon, level, square-edged, and brown, with the mellow sunshine upon it and upon the castellated mountains behind it, and in the foreground some lazy ox-wains, a prospector with his pots and kettles, or a mounted Mexican towing a bull, which ducks its head in vain

resistance, is thoroughly foreign, and of an attractive promise. There is something of a Dead Sea apple experience in the investigation of this promise. If the theory of Ruskin be correct, that a building should be of the general color of the soil on which it stands, Tucson has great merit. It is entirely made of adobe bricks, which are left to their natural mud-color, since violent storms occur, and paint and kalsomine can not be counted upon for long duration.

Tucson has great antiquity as a corporate existence, having been founded by some one of the Spanish expeditions that came up the Santa Cruz Valley in quest

INTERIOR OF MISSION CHURCH OF SAN XAVIER DEL BAC.

of the reputed treasures of the Aztecs in "the land of Cibola," but this has left no visible trace upon it. If there were ever any monuments of importance, they have effectually vanished. Even the church is new. Such foreignness as there is is simply a provincial Mexican squalor. The items of interest about it are of a purely commonplace bearing, such as how it is to be paved, drained, lighted, provided with an adequate water-supply (instead of paying four cents a bucket for water, as at present); how it is to get rid of its malarial fevers and shabby rookeries, and prepare to become that seat of learning and that Alexandria of the desert of which prediction has been made.

It is the commercial centre of the Southern mining district, and has an eligible position for future development. It has derived profit in the past from supplying the army, and from smuggling into Mexico—the goods being taken out by teams, then packed over the passes to Altar and Magdalena on donkeys. That part of Sonora traversed both by stage line and the new railroad to Guaymas is cactus-covered and sterile. The traders at Tucson, as throughout the Southwest generally, are largely Jewish. A certain kind of "life" prevails here as at Tombstone. Roulette, faro, and the other games of chance are played openly in a large way in the leading saloons, while the poor Mexicans gamble for small stakes at their own *fondas* under the aegis of some wretched portrait of Hidalgo, or General Zaragoza, the hero of Puebla. There is lacking, however, the choleric, dangerous air of Tombstone. People make way for you to pass, and are not exclusively preoccupied with looking for somebody to tread on the tails of their coats.

If Tucson be without historic remains of its own, it has one of the loveliest possible in its immediate vicinity, in the old mission church of San Xavier del Bac. San Xavier del Bac, on the reservation of the Christian Papago Indians, in the Santa Cruz Valley, ten miles to the southward, creates a new sensation even for him who arrives from Mexico with an impression that he has thoroughly gone through everything belonging to the peculiar school. It is not surpassed either in Mexico or elsewhere for the kind of quaintness, the qualities of form and color, and the gentle sentiment of melancholy that appeal to the artistic sense. The tread of

Father Time has fallen heavily on the wooden balconies of the front, broken out their floors, and left parts of them dangling, with bits of the railings. The old bells, of a sweet tone, still hang in one of the towers. The space, terminating in a scrolled gable, between, is enriched with escutcheons, rampant lions wreathed in foliage, niches containing broken statues, and complicated pilasters flanking the doorway—all formed in stucco upon a basis of moulded brick.

The designer, whoever he may have been, was inspired by Venetian-Byzantine traditions. The interior, with numerous simple domes and half domes, frescoed with angels and evangelists, especially the chancel end, almost covered with gilding, now stained and battered, and the painted and gilded lions on the chancel rails, recall to the least observant Saint Mark's at Venice. This style is not consistently carried out, however. A rococo decoration, so exuberant that it might be taken for the vagaries of East Indian work, mingles with and overrides it. A Henri II. faience candlestick might give a certain idea of the fashion of the interior columns. The date has disappeared from the church itself, but it is believed that it should be about 1768, and that the present edifice was built upon the ruins of a former one, going back much nearer to the year 1654, when the mission to the Papagos was begun. Large angels holding bannerets, with draperies formed in *papier-maché* or gummed muslin, are attached to the main chancel piers; and a painted and gilded Virgin, with a long face, and hair brushed back from a high forehead, in the manner of the French Jean Goujon, looks down from a high central niche.

All this, within, is of the true mediæval richness and obscurity. Without, in the broad sunshine, is the peaceful Papago hamlet, where a few old men trudge about their bake-ovens and water jars and strings of dried squash, and some women pass carrying tall loads of hay or other produce in a queer contrivance of sticks and netting fastened on their backs, which they call the *kijo*. Nobody concerns himself about the visitors, except the foolishly smiling boy Domingo, who has brought us the key. To be at San Xavier del Bac, and to have come to it from that spasm of aggressive modernism, Tombstone, could contrast further go?

THE LOG OF A FORTY-NINER

Extracts from the Journal of William Ives Morgan, of Bristol, Connecticut, who on May 26, 1849, sailed in the barque *J. Walls, Jr.*, with "The Brothers Mining and Trading Company," for California, *viâ* Cape Horn. He arrived in San Francisco Bay, January 1, 1850. These extracts are published by permission of Mr. Morgan's family, and through the courtesy of his son, William C. Morgan.

OFF Florida, June, 1849—a month after sailing—Morgan writes:
"The Barque does not move. Four of us went on board the first American vessel we have seen; a hard pull of 20 miles. Got papers up to June 5. Going back was compelled to steer by the stars: did not get off our course. Bells, guns, drums, horns, were sounded, and lights set in diferent parts of the riggen. Caught a turtle that weighed about 100 pounds; will make a meal of flesh."

July 4.—"The Boys began to feel independent quite early," with flags, salutes, and "three things called Orations." The "Company's" doings caused "a regular growl" aboard, and Morgan "moved into the forecastle out of cabbin" society.

"Spoke an English Man-o'-War; 5 women aboard; looked some good; gave her three cheers. Sailor went overboard after Mr. Clemmen's cap. Received 1.00 reward. The word of God was preached to-day."

July 13.—"Put upon water allowance —one quart a day. Heavy shower. All hands stripped and had a fine wash.

"Crowded sail, with drums, fifes, and guns, after a French brigantine, which mistook us for pirates, or anything but peaceable Yankees."

Off St. Roque their first death occurred. "We committed his body to the deep with services from the Church Book. He was sewn up in canvass, bricks to his feet, and slid from a plank into the sea. The weather makes some of the Boys feel homesick."

August 1.—Out of sight of land fifty-six days. Made Rio de Janeiro. He describes adobe huts on mountainsides, tropic fruits, gardens, theatres, native festas, and sailor sprees in squalid streets. He admits his share with frank amusement: "The 30th being my birthday, *I got drunk!*"

September 18 they sailed. Two days out, "a slave that we stole and stowed away unbeknown to the Captain came on deck, also a white chap that ran away from an English ship.

"Making tall tracks for Cape Horn. Our female is dead—the only one on board. Death felt all over the ship— *it was the cat.* Put on sugar allowance. Who would not sell a farm and go to sea! Saw penguins and four right whales. Man lowered boat to lance one, but only got laughed at. Doctor says I have scurvy, but I *don't.*"

October 6.—Sighted snow-capped Terra del Fuego. Next day "the long-looked-for and dreaded Cape Horn is in sight. I am putting it down on paper—a very good picture.

"The Barque is taking water over both rails; everything on deck breaking loose; man hurt from beef-barrel rolling on him. Vessel heaved to, under close-reefed mainsail, and riggen covered with ice. Only one sail for company on this tempest of waters."

The ship made Valparaiso in forty-two days, "quickest passage but two on record." They remained two weeks, hunting, fishing, playing ball, horse-racing. "Had a little time with a thing that calls himself a man, for calling me a liar; have cured him of such bad habits."

Nearing California, he records: "The Boys smell gold. Independence Day, My Birthday, Thanksgiving, Christmas, and a good chance of New-Years" on board. A heavy gale. "Cruising down the coast, looking for the Golden Gate. All hands in good spirits. Ship like bedlam."

January 1, 1850.—"Came to anchor in harbor about 4 bells this afternoon. Shore green and beautiful. San Francisco not so extensive as I expected; is about half tents. Mud two to four feet deep. Many murders reported. Fully 400 vessels here, and every day swells the list."

January 29.—Still in harbor. Sailors deserted, taking their best boat and provisions. Morgan turned cook. "Waldo, Tom, Tuttle, Wallace, and Nettleton" started after a boat to go up the Sacramento, Morgan being detained by illness. Long search failed to find "*those that went out.* Rather solemn on board. We fear they are drifted out to sea. To die by this climate is bad enough, but they were all healthy and in good spirits." They never returned.

Soon after they started up the Sacramento in the same bark with which they had rounded the Horn—afterward sold for $4000 to pay "Company's depts. We go just far enough to change the scenery daily. Collided with the *Senator*—no damage."

There was much sickness. They took "slow ways of going to the Diggens,"— "warping," "kegging," or towing the bark, shifting cargo, waiting on wind or tide—thirty-three men working the boat, while others scanned the shore for elk, antelope, deer, ducks, or other "fresh," so welcome after "raw pork and hard bread. One does not know luxury unless he takes a trip round the Horn.

"Can see New York (a mining town), 5 small huts, 3 tents, five vessels, and some stakes to tie up cattle."

Nearing Sacramento.—"Altogether I do not think it is a bad country after one gets into it. Splendid view. A few buildings that look very well; a mile of vessels along the bank. Went ashore. Paid $1.00 for a piece of pie and cake."

Many stopped at Sacramento; more "rushed to Yuba River." Morgan remained aboard, hoping to "get something from the Company" which refused to settle.

"Captain demands security for our

passage . . . darned fool! Plenty of room now; after being penned together for months in 100 feet by 17. Lonesome as the Devel. A man can appreciate friends after a trip round the Horn. Have been on board 9 months this day noon. A year since I have earned a cent." Going ashore, farther up the river, he paid seventy-five cents per pound for shot, and brought down three ducks.

"I do think I can beat half the girls in old Bristol cooking. Feel as I do at home after Thanksgiving Dinner!

"Burned my fingers — am through cooking. Gave a bit for a segar and thought about home."

After two lonely weeks, with sudden resolve he rowed back to "the Boys' camp," Sacramento. "Slept sound, 5 in a bed."

Next day he found his first scale of gold, with a "butcher-knife," and earned $5 working. "Risked at monté and made ten; bet again and lost all but $1.10, which I intend to lose soon. Reckon if I was home, would never leave it for this tarnal hole.

"Barque of 500 tons sold for $37.00. Five of us earned $50.00 to-day. Langdon earned $6.00 setting up 6 clocks. Walter is sick—gave him lobelia to bring the kinks out. Many are sick in other Companys; fever very common. Costs $10.00 per day for medical attendance— a hard country! Saw New York paper's account of San Francisco's fire; which is not true."

March 27.—"Start for Mines *Manyaner*,* and shall sleep sound thinking of the goodly tramp. Burned extra clothing.

"Started for Diggens through flowers plenty as grass and timber oak; passed a deserted Spanish doby house. Walked in stockings—feet very sore. Slept on ground."

They pitched tent at Beal's Bar, a beautiful hill between ravines, the Rio de los Americanos dashing below. "Caught about 300 fish in 2 hours. To-day makes me think of home— the New England Spring. Air light and sweet."

April 1.—"Folly to have any of us April-fooled. That bump is very promi-

* *Mañana,* Spanish, "to-morrow."

nent in us all! Found a small quantity of the root of evil—not enough to hurt, with poor molasses $5.00 per gallon! Hope to do better when river lowers. *It is no use* being discouraged.

"No gold here; all hands blue; boys gone prospecting. Provisions nearly gone; nothing but good looks to get more with. Am poisoned again, down sick, no medicine, no bed but the ground. I wish I could have some chicken broth, or some such thing that I could get at home. Bought some sugar at $1.00 per lb., butter at $2.50, and the best wine I could buy for $3.50. Can hardly stand; can lift tent-flaps and get fresh air— also mosquitoes, flies, bugs, and ants. I am used up; would die if I were home.

"Another fire in San Francisco, city half destroyed. Bread is thirty-five cents a small loaf; milk seventy-five cents per quart. Saw Downs to-day; tough and hearty. That pays me for a good deal."

They talked matters over with Downs, and went out again to the mines, tramping thirty-six miles in two days, over dusty plains, hills, woodland. "My hammock fell from the branch, near broke my tarnel neck. Was very tired, slept where I fell. We are in the Southern Diggens (Amadore). Some Indians near; made about $50.00 in an hour."

When he found his first large specimen: "It set the rest crazy; they started out with knives to try their luck."

Soon they were taking out considerable gold, which they weighed and reduced to dollars. This was short-lived, and they went prospecting. Then Downs gave up a claim to them—going in for merchandise himself.

May 26.—"Just one year since we left Connecticut. Many have gone a longer journey than they thought. All the gold I have is $75.00—but *it is gold.*"

Sundays he washed, mended ("enlarged my *trowsers* to-day"), greased his boots, cooked "for the week," wrote letters to mother, sister, and others.

Their luck varied:—"five dollars, forty, ten, half an ounce; fifty cents, not a spec, poor luck! No tarnal fortune here." When they had $461, and had paid hospital bills, they "declared dividend, leaving $61.00 in treasury, with *one ounce missing.* Think I shall not

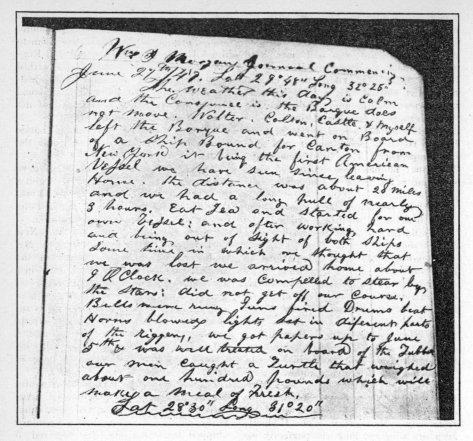

MANUSCRIPT PAGE OF WILLIAM IVES MORGAN'S JOURNAL—1849

work in company with a thief but little longer.

"H—— picks up all the large pieces and puts them in his pocket as the proceeds of private enterprise. Walter is playing monté with the Indians; not a very good plan, I think."

Finally their company of four dissolved, Langdon and Morgan working "under our own management."—"Made $361.00 this week, living costs $20.00. Took out $55.00 in ten minutes—doing well. Our pan of dust stood near. I threw a stone, and the loss was about $15.00. Broke the best shovel ever was in Amadore. Washed 150 buckets of dirt—made $30.00. Little *Oro* this day, —claim sort o' caved in—signed over! Start prospecting *Manyaner*.

"Tried digging—a rod from cabin; took out $25.00. So it goes! Passed balance of day shooting mice, got four with four successive shots. Read home letters for the last time untill I get fresh ones."

August 29.—"I shall be 23 years Old *Manyaner*, if I live—and come near it if I don't. Should work contented at 5 dollars per day.

"An Indian pounded on my door last night. I fired my revolver and told him to vamose, but he only laughed. So I knocked him down, and then assisted him to leave by taking my foot away from the seat of his pants as fast as I could."

October.—Morgan "took the job of putting up a House at Rancheria for Hanford and Downs—for 50 Dollars." In five days he "hired a man to finish it, for four Dollars."

He greatly appreciated the "ten

American women in Amadore with little white responsibilitys squalling. A man with a perfect tiger of a wife claims our cabbin; she will have hard work to make me leave my *Home*."

They constantly tried new claims. Some dirt yielded only a "bit" a pan. Once they hired a man to dig, paying " 3.00 per day and we board him."

"Picked up $3.75—enough to pay our help! He is a schoolmaster and Son of Temperance. Has lived among the Mormons; he has been telling of their spiritual wifes. Not a bad place, barring the wifes."

The "Diggens were darned poor," even with hose for washing, cradle, and "other fixens." "Hope to find *oro poco tiempo soon.*"

December.—"As runs calculations in this country, to-day is Christmas." To celebrate properly, Morgan went horseback ten miles to see a bull and bear fight. "Grizzly, surrounded by horsemen, declined to play. . . . Not a very Merry Christmas for Wm I Morgan."

January, 1851.—He began storekeeping for Hanford and Downs in Volcano, "throwing dirt" between trades.

"Fitted up counters in log store. Sold $100.00 first day. Got pay for an ounce's worth of oysters, in cakes from city. Man asked *whar* I should keep my whiskey, and was perfectly astonished when I said I should not keep any. Slept on upper side of a pine plank—my counter. No cooking utensils yet. Crackers are good enough if one can't do better. Picked up $2.00 going to store.

"A white man, his squaw wife, white pappoose, 9 dogs and 7 hens are my neighbors. Big row below. Thought of Jackson and Battle of Orleans. Man with Bowie and revolver, a good deal excited, insisted on paying me $2.00. His revolver being Allen's, I did not care; but did not like the way he handled his knife, swearing he would cut my damned head off. Took his warlike instruments and sent him home."

Gold being struck near store, immediately fifty men were staking claims "anxious as office-seekers." One claim dispute was "settled by a game of ucre."

"Could not get rid of 16 five-cent pieces by fair means, so put them on monté card. Played a chap to see if he should give me $1.00 for one pound onions, or whether I should give them to him. He paid. Played poker for English walnuts—made 5 lbs. Came within $2.00 of breaking a monté bank—dealer's hand shook bad, but he got all back. Rained like the Devel. One end of my store fell down; good light now.

"Twelve inches of snow and all hands snowballing. Most fun since I left the States."

May.—"Some chaps going home gave 15 of us an oyster supper. One is going to Vermont — another to New York. Would send letters, but have not had one for six months. Have wrote a dozen.

"Sent $1000.00 home by two New York friends. Sent some letters by Mr. Dudley: he goes by my home on the cars. Fixed up 54 ounces of gold dust to send home by Jones McGregor of Maine. A man left about $3000.00 here to-day for me to keep for him. Was invited to a Party, had peaches and strawberries. There was one woman and 8 fellows. Nobody drunk. Danced with a white girl. It seemed kinder natural, *it did!*"

June.—" San Francisco burned again, loss 15 Millions. Stockton burned. Auburn in ashes. Weather cool, hot, calm, windy, clear, and foggy. Saw a Spaniard whipped for stealing — he received 3 dozen. Saw nigger whipped for fighting his Master. Saw man yesterday worth $5000.00; to-day not five cts. Bought a horse for $30.00. Am doctoring him to sell.

"A fellow said Langdon took something from his cabin. I told him he was a liar, and slapped his face, which cooled him off some."

He became deeply interested in politics. "I am some pumpkins on election in California and have started a Candidate for Justice. Done my best and got beat by five majority—the grog-hole did it."

He is Democratic delegate to Yuba convention—jeers at a speech and balloon ascension in the interests of "smart Whiggery," and is proud to meet the miner who was Democratic nominee.

"The Fourth" they had dinner, wine, and cigars, and "told stories about home." "A rather independent chap"

AN OLD SEVENTY-FOUR-GUN FRIGATE
(From a sketch made by William Ives Morgan on a page of his book)

fell off a store box; "two fellows put him on my back, and I carried him home."

Mining was never neglected. "The Quartz Mountain excitement is raging." He caught the fever and joined a prospecting company. He later valued his stock at $5000.

August 30.—"Am 24 years old today. Got $6.00 out of one dipperfull of dirt. Somebody stole our rocker, dipper, and scoop."

September.—"Have a new store—20× 24 feet—built since yesterday."

On account of lameness he decided in October to go to the Sandwich Islands "on a speculation trip after hogs."

He reached San Francisco in three days. "Went to the theatre. Bought coat, pants, boots, socks, and cravat for $2.50. Saw Girls dressed Bloomer style—Sorter *odd.* Loafed around 24 hours looking for my vessel," and October 16 began his unprofitable seven months' Pacific voyage.

His "rather unlucky" trip ended May 25, 1852, the ship "laying where

I was the 1 day of January, 1849. Expect to hear a lot of news soon. Owe $224.00 for my passage from Sandwich Islands." Fare to Sacramento, $10 by steamer, twenty-six hours. Here Hanford loaned him $100.

"Hanford's wife has come—a first-rate woman. I think a good deal of her—the second White Lady I have spoken to in 3 years. They have a nice little girl."

Back in Volcano. "Thought *the Boys* would shake me to pieces."

July and August.—"Have got 7 chaps to go home with me, if Hanford will let me off."

Hanford objecting, he loyally stood by, but packed a lot of relics to send—walrus-tusks, shells, Chinese curiosities.

"I had my Dagueratype taken, and sat up all night writing letters for the Boys to take home. Found my name on a keepsake a girl gave me; first time I had seen it; done me good! Can get an ounce for one of my kittens any time; but 25 dollars would not buy one. Second white boy on record here just born. There is one little Connecticut Yankee girl—a truly great country!

"Emigrants from Connecticut arrived. Let them have provisions. The new chaps would not buy anything Sunday. Gave $5.50 for the New Emigrant Road from the Plains, and had the honor to be the first man to treat the first 4 men who came over it. They christened it The Pennsylvania Cut-off.

"Hot enough to roast eggs. Think some of taking matters in hand myself to get houses for destitute familys."

He again represented Volcano Democracy at the convention, and worked hard; but "too much wire-pulling and log-rolling" disgusted him. Defeated, he "went to bed at 3 a little excited. Shall go the Independent Ticket if it suits me. Cost me $50.00." Later, his favorite speaker gave "the Great, Noble, and Self-denying Whig party, including Gen. Scott, a good, sound, intelligent drubbing. The Whigs tryed to organize, but dissolved in a Dog fight. Later he was appointed "Judge of Election" in Volcano.

"Very large Eastern Mails—2 bushell flimsy 'Lifes of Gen. Scott' franked at Uncle Samuel's expense; trying to run Scott in on the strength of an un-Holy and God-abhorred War. Forelorn hope! Have bet 20 dollars on election. Paid $1.75 for two pie-plant pies."

Pending election, his ball came off: "Town full of people, buying shirts and shoes." Thirty ladies and forty gentlemen were present—big success. Morgan escorted Mrs. Hanford, "the most of a Lady I have seen in California."

August 31, 1852.—"Am now in my 26th year, getting old fast. Large train came in, with 15 wagons, 10 women, and lots of children."

September.—"Went out of the store a few minutes. Came back and found about 10 ounces of gold gone from my box. Shut the door and searched everybody; did not find it, but strongly suspect a man."

This must have been some trusted friend, for Morgan dwells upon "peculiar circumstances" which worked upon his feeling till "I was nearly crazy and could have killed him." He lay awake long, brooding; then, declining a search-warrant, took his knife, went to the man's room, wakened him, and demanded his gold. It was finally produced. "I told him he better leave town as soon as possible. I never experienced such feelings in my life before."

Sacramento was burned, and Morgan hustled about to corner flour "before it is found out." In three weeks: "Sacramento City is about built up again."

Wherever he lived, he had a pathetic way of naming the place "home." Coming back from his old store, with shelf and counter tools, he was glad to be "safely home."

December 7.—He went to Volcano afoot to buy potatoes, pork, and barley; and valiantly refrained from "getting drunk on news of Peirce's election."

"Am manager of a Christmas Ball in Volcano, without my consent. Sha'n't go.

"Could make a thousand dollars trading if weather was good. Flour is 75 cts a pound. Mined one afternoon to buy a loaf of bread. Just made it—$2.25."

Christmas eve, reduced to "a few potatoes," the boys started out to steal a pig, but failed. "Think some of going Home. Intend to go next Spring anyhow; can't do anything here this weather."

December 30.—"Potatoes nearly gone. Washed a *sirrapha to wear Home.*"

January 1—5, 1853.—He sold his $400 worth of goods at cost. "Started for Sacramento, with poisen or smallpox breaking out on my face. Mud to my knees in city."

January 15.—Left San Francisco for the States, in sailing-steamer *Independence.* He slept, from choice, on deck, without cover.

February 1.—"Landed at San Juan, Central America." He crossed Central America to Greytown, where he finally took ship for New York.

February 13.—"Arrived at Quarantine, New York, 1 O Clock Sunday morning. On shore about 9. Took coach to Franklin House—29 days from San Francisco." Here ends the Journal.

He married the following June. In 1859 he returned to California for a time, holding a political office near Volcano. After his second home-coming he was Selectman and Representative. He died at Bristol, 1869, bravely, as he had always lived.

THE COLUMBIA RIVER

THE early completion of the Northern Pacific Railroad from its eastern connections across the Territories to its western terminus on the Pacific Ocean will establish for tourists and travellers rapid communication with the northwestern corner of the United States—Oregon and Washington Territory. The Columbia River will then become known to others than the student of geography as the largest river emptying into the Pacific Ocean from the American continent, and second only to the Mississippi in length and volume. Some writer has aptly called this the Achilles of rivers; and judging by its vigorous beauty and strength, the appellation is well bestowed, and as that ancient hero of history and song was vulnerable only in the heel, the weak point of the Columbia is said to be at its mouth. The fountains of the Yellowstone region, or National Park, give birth to the triad of great rivers of the United States—the Missouri, Columbia, and Colorado. The mountain-bound lakes of the Kootenay region of British America supply the Clarke's Fork, or main Columbia, with its pellucid waters; and the crooked, tortuous Snake drains the rills and springs of Northern Nevada, and collects the melting snows of the highest peaks of Utah and Wyoming.

The great plain of the Columbia, now a vast grain and grass growing country, received all these waters, and before the Columbia forced its passage through the enormous rent or chasm across the Cascade Mountains, was the bed of an inland lake or sea. These mountains, a continuation of the Sierra Nevada chain, bound this plain on the west, and the Bitter Root and Blue mountains encircle the eastern and southern horizons. The great plain of the Columbia is a vast grazing and farming country. Its natural garment is bunch-grass, the most nutritious of the wild grasses, which grows in the greatest luxuriance and abundance on level ground and steepest slopes alike. This domain of forty thousand square miles belongs to the people of the United States— and the Northern Pacific Railroad. The settler can select a farm, not for the asking, but for the filing, or by purchase of the railroad on easy terms.

Timber there is none except on the mountain ranges; a few willows and cottonwoods fringe the banks of watercourses, the bottoms of gulches, and ravines. Westward from the Cascade Mountains, as far as the eye can reach toward the coast, is a wilderness of forest, covering a broken and diversified country. Snake River has cut its channel deep down through the hard basaltic walls, and its course is impeded by many rocky rapids. After reaching the Columbia, the traveller can enjoy all the comforts of modern travel by rail or on well-appointed steamboats. The navigation of the Upper Columbia and Snake rivers is difficult but not dangerous, though to one unaccustomed to swift water it seems perilous and well-nigh impossible to control a steamboat threading the narrow channel of wild, whirling waters among the black and threatening rocks. Our stern-wheel boat creeps along up stream close to the banks, taking advantage of every eddy, now shooting across to an eddy on the opposite shore, then boldly attacks the rapids. Presently the swiftest water is reached, the race of the rapid. Now commences what Western steamboat men call "bucking"; the wheel flies round fast enough, and there is a great kicking up of water behind, and a tremendous exhaust of steam. But the boat stands still, then draws back inch by inch, and we hold our breath with suspense. But a steady hand and nerve at the wheel

CASTLE ROCK.

hold her balanced in the flying current like a bird poised on the wing, and soon a rapid feeding of the voracious furnace furnishes the required power. The steam index goes up five, ten, fifteen pounds, and inch by inch the rapid is passed, and we relieve our feelings by a long breath.

Until a few years since stock-raising was the principal industry of the great treeless region of Eastern Oregon and Washington; but it has now been demonstrated that wheat of the best quality can be surely and successfully grown over a large area of the country, and that, too, as cheaply as anywhere in the world. The bunch-grass, unlike the prairie-grass of the Western States, forms no sod or turf, does not need "breaking," and the first ploughing will produce a crop.

We ask if it is profitable. Hitherto transportation charges consequent upon the many handlings at the different portages have not left much margin of profit to the producer. The Columbia, open on a tidal level from the ocean to the Cascades, is there obstructed by the first cataract, a fall of twenty-five or thirty feet, which is passed by a railroad portage of six miles, necessitating the handling of grain twice, from boat to car. Another stretch of river reaches to the Dalles, the second cataract, passed by a rail portage fifteen miles long, requiring again the twice handling of grain, making, with the transfer at each end from warehouse to ship, at least six handlings. The expense of these numerous transshipments is being

rapidly reduced. The Oregon Railway and Navigation Company have already completed a line of rails from the Dalles to Walla Walla, and are constructing feeders in all directions from the main artery to tap the grain-growing country. They are also rapidly building from the Dalles down to the Cascades, and preparing their line from the latter place down the river to Portland. The Northern Pacific are also pushing with great energy their continental line from the mouth of Snake River eastward toward Lake Pend Oreille and the pass of the Bitter Root Mountains. The great need of all new countries, the railroad, will soon supply the rapid transportation of all that a new country wants. Transportation charges have already been reduced where railroad connections have cheapened the handling, and the whole farming and grain-growing interest has brightened up at the encouraging prospects of the near future. One is astonished to see the immense numbers of farming and harvesting implements and machinery, in all their glory of fresh red and green paint, crowding the boats and trains on their way to the front of civilization.

And yet this country has barely been wrested from the control of the Indian, and he still makes spasmodic attempts to check the overpowering flood of whites. Let us not suppose that all the advantages are on the side of the farmer, for there are some drawbacks and disadvantages which prevent a man from being an optimist. To enumerate some of these, we will find that water is not abundant, and often of poor quality, and the absence of forest growth makes lumber expensive.

The winds blow with great force in the summer months, and carry clouds of sand and dust flying through the air. The nights on the highest lands are cool, and occasional frosts are liable to occur. Nothing, however, seems to prevent the growth of wheat, one season's crop often taxing the carrying capacity of boats and trains to the utmost.

Walla Walla has been formerly the centre of the grain-farming interest, and private enterprise constructed a narrow-gauge railroad from there to the Columbia, thirty-five miles. This road has been changed to the standard gauge. We find Walla Walla a thriving, busy town of several thousand inhabitants, its streets thronged with wagons and horses. The stage still dashes along the dusty street under the tall poplar-trees, and the prairie schooner, or large lumbering freight wagon, unknown to Eastern residents, looms cavalry, and is one of the handsomest frontier posts in the West. The services of the army are still needed to subdue the insurrections of the Indian tribes; the war

BASALTIC CLIFFS ABOVE CATHLAMET, ON THE COLUMBIA RIVER.

up in the distance of the country roads. The fort, or military post, of the same name as the town, is on a pretty little elevated plateau a short distance from the village, and the regimental band can be heard playing every evening at sunset. The post is garrisoned by one regiment of with the Bannocks and Nez Percé tribes, the flying settlers, devastated homes, herds and flocks ruthlessly slaughtered, with pursuing troopers following fast over mountain and plain, attest the necessity of a strong military force for the protection of the pioneer. Since the completion

GRAIN PIPE ON SNAKE RIVER.

the steepest slopes. Long trains of Indians, driving their ponies and dragging their camps, file along the perilous trails high up the frowning cliffs. The general surface of the country being so high above the river level, it is not practicable to construct roads except at certain points. At one point is seen a novel expedient in shipping grain. From the summit of a hill twelve or fifteen hundred feet high a wooden pipe has been constructed down the steep slope of the hill for a thousand feet or more, to a point below where a road can be brought. The grain is deposited in bulk at the mouth of this tube, and pours into a bin at the bottom, where it is sacked and hauled to the river.

At many points on the river we pass the ferries — flat-bottomed scows decked over, propelled across the rapid current by the water acting diagonally against the side of the boat. A twisted wire cable is suspended from shore to shore, sometimes over high tripods, and again from the solid rocky banks. Sheaves run along this cable, to which the boat is secured by blocks and tackle. They are quite expeditious and effective, but not very safe unless carefully and skillfully handled.

The scenery soon ceases to interest us by the constant repetition of similar forms along a hundred miles of river. It would puzzle any one but a steamboat pilot to make out from the landscape in what particular part of the river he happened to be. Our attention is called to a large open-mouthed cave in the face of the cliffs on the south bank of the river, and noticing a row of children seated against the walls, we are surprised to learn that the cave is utilized as a summer school-house—Na-

of the railroad from the Dalles to Walla Walla, but few steamboats ply upon the Upper Columbia and Snake rivers. The head of navigation on the Columbia is Priest's Rapids, forty-five miles above its confluence with the Snake. Lewiston, at the junction of the Clearwater and Snake, is the head of navigation on that stream, three hundred and fifty miles from the ocean. The scenery on the river is grand and peculiar, perpendicular or terraced walls of reddish-brown basalt, carved by the elements into architectural forms of great regularity and beauty, like the mullions and flying-buttresses of some great Gothic temple, tower upward a thousand feet above the water's edge. The rounded summits are covered with bunch-grass and the ubiquitous sage; cattle and sheep can barely be discerned, clinging like ants to

ture's temple of learning. The land bordering the Upper Columbia is nearly worthless, sand and gravel forming the soil, while, strange as it may seem, the best soil is on the highest hills and rolling ridges.

The Dalles of the Columbia, as named by the old French voyageurs and trappers, is a remarkable place, and will well repay us to stop and examine it. The whole volume of water flows through a narrow channel of unknown depth, across which one can easily throw a stone. It justifies the saying that the river goes through the Dalles edgewise. There is every evidence here before our eyes that in former geological times a permanent barrier or cataract existed, the rocks across the whole basin of the

are submerged with water, and to account for this forest of broken stumps we are forced to take either the hypothesis that the land sank below the water-level, or that the obstruction at the Cascades has been raised, perhaps by an immense avalanche of rocks from the mountain-sides of the gorge. The Cascades are formed by a great ledge of solid rock with large bowlders obstructing the current which it has not the power to remove. The mountain-sides along the Cascades are a wilder-

A SUMMER SCHOOL-HOUSE ON SNAKE RIVER.

river high above the highest water level being stripped of soil, and gullied by the action of rapid water. After the river has passed the Dalles, it flows onward as serenely as though all its troubles were over. For forty-five miles, to the upper Cascades, it resembles more a long, placid lake, and from the strange appearance of a forest of large fir stumps several miles above the Cascades standing broken off in the water, it is apparent that the river stands at a higher level than at no very distant day past. It is well known that the Douglas fir will die when its roots

ness of broken crags to the summits, three thousand feet high. The unbroken forest which extends over Western Oregon crosses the Cascade Mountains, gradually becoming thinner, until at the Dalles, the eastern base of the mountains, the great army of pines is represented only by outposts, pickets, and skirmishers. The two portions of Oregon and Washington lying respectively east and west of the Cascade range are as dissimilar in all distinctive features of climate and character as can be conceived : the former, hot, dry, sandy, and entirely barren of forest growth, ex-

MOUNT HOOD AND THE COLUMBIA RIVER BOTTOM.

cept on the mountain-summits; the latter, cool, moist, and densely covered with coniferous forests and deciduous trees from the mountain-top to the water's edge. In the former, trees must be planted and raised with care; in the latter, when a clearing is made, constant vigilance is required to prevent the encroachments of the primeval forest from which it has been wrested. Undoubtedly the abundance of timber in one section will compensate for the poverty in the other. West of the mountains the settler looks upon a fir-tree as his natural enemy; when he has cut it down, his troubles have commenced. The settler on the plains would regard it as a friend in need.

If the Upper Columbia is barren of beauty to lovers of picturesque scenery, the passage of the river from the Dalles to Vancouver, through the heart of the Cascade Mountains, is a panorama of magnificent pictures. The grand towering peak of Mount Hood, its icy slopes and glaciers glistening in the sun, pierces the blue vault over the southern horizon. Our gaze constantly returns to his hoary summit, and we find ourselves silently worshipping, overpowered with a sense of littleness in contemplating his enormous bulk. Rising from the summit of the mountain range, with majestic sweeping outlines gradually growing steeper and steeper toward the apex of the cone, like a silhouette his form is set against the empyrean blue. The morning sun, rising behind his vast bulk, casts the whole mountain in one unbroken tint of tender, pearly gray; the early mists around his base enhance the beauties they conceal. At midday, when the clouds born in the gorges round his feet have risen, their shadows chase each other across his face, now dark against the glistening fields of snow, now lost in the shadow of some gloomy gorge. At sunset, when the sky takes on the gold and purple haze, the mountain glows in hues of gold and carmine like a ruby in the eastern sky. Ever-changing, sometimes sad and cold, sometimes bright and airy, like the different moods of woman, but always grand and glorious, we turn our gaze reluctantly away, to feel, in the words of the prophet, "What is man that thou art mindful of him?" Opposite Mount Hood stands Mount Adams, looming up against the northern sky; both stretch out their long mountain ridges, like arms, to bar the passage of the river.

The Columbia, at the Cascades, narrowed to half its width, dashes down the rapids in a rush of wild waters, resembling in a manner the rapids of Niagara. The river approaches the lip of the cataract as placid and calm as a lake, its surface dotted here and there with many a tufted rocky islet. Our steamboat approaches at full speed, and swings round to her moorings with the greatest confidence, while a few hundred yards below the angry water is lashing its rocky shores

and leaping high over the submerged rocks. The government is building locks on the Oregon side to enable steamboats to pass up to the Dalles.

As we pass up and down the river in the early part of May, the scene is a succession of grand and lovely surprises. The cottonwoods along the shores have just donned their spring vesture of tender green; the delicate quaking aspens stand in groups and fringes, their round leaves quivering with the lightest breath of air.

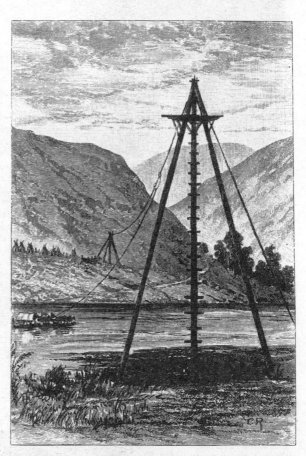

WIRE-ROPE FERRY ON SNAKE RIVER.

Above, the forests of pines and firs with sombre foliage fill the ravines, and stand boldly out on every peak and crag. The tops of the precipitous cliffs are lost in the fleecy clouds, while gleams of sunshine here and there bring out with vivid whiteness the snow still lingering on the north-

MULTNOMAH FALL.

ern slopes. Crystal cascades come leaping boldly over the lip of some towering cliff, or thread the face of the dark basaltic rock with lines of inlaid silver.

In autumn months, when frost has lighted the flame of the maples on the hills, the red and golden hues are blended by the smoke and haze of Indian summer in dreamy contrast to the blackness of the pines. We are subdued by beauty; our hearts are full, but our lips are silent. We long for the magic brush of a Turner to transfer this beauty to our own possession. The views through the highlands of the Columbia can not be effaced from the memory; the chambers of the imagination are haunted by their shapes, and the heart swells with rapture and contentment that the sense of perfect beauty has been fully gratified.

We must leave these scenes and hasten on our journey, but not before having a nearer look at the beautiful cascade called the Multnomah Fall. This fairy-like veil of water, which seems born in the sky, comes leaping sheer over its precipice of seven or eight hundred feet to the pool below, scarcely to be seen through the spray, which supports a trembling rainbow. Giant pines lift their tapering shafts and sturdy columns around the pool, and the banks are clothed with dense green shrubbery and beds of wild flowers.

Cascades, as the village is named, was a fortified post during the early Indian wars with the Cayuse tribe, and the old log block-houses are still standing. Here the famous cavalry commander General Phil Sheridan passed some of his early military days, dreaming, perhaps, of some Winchester so many leagues away. General Grant was a young lieutenant at Fort Vancouver, and many excursions to various points, and amusing incidents connected therewith, are still remembered and related by his early associates. Fort Vancouver is the head-quarters of the Military Department of the Columbia, and is the most attractive post on the west coast. It is only eighteen miles from Portland, and boats run often to and fro. The honorable Hudson Bay Company established the post as their main trading station, and their lumbering bateau and the clipper-shaped

CHINOOK INDIAN AND CANOE.

HIGHLANDS OF THE COLUMBIA.

canoe of the Chinook Indian were the only craft that plied the waters of the Columbia in early days. Now swift and noble steam-ships, of three thousand tons burden, arrive and depart with the punctuality of a ferry. The Lower Columbia is open to the influence of the tides from the sea to Portland and the Cascades. Ships of large draft are towed up the river to Portland to load wheat at the wharves for the English market. To appreciate the rapid development of the grain-growing interest, we have but to remember that only as far back as 1868 the first cargo of Oregon wheat was shipped by an enterprising merchant of Portland to Sydney, merely as an experiment. In the following year a vessel was dispatched to Liverpool, and it was not until 1870 that Oregon became known as a wheat-producing State. The yearly shipments of wheat from the Columbia are steadily and rapidly increasing. In 1879 the exports of wheat were 1,932,080 centals, valued at $3,611,240. Flour exports for the same year amounted to 209,098 barrels, of the value of $1,143,523; and the shipments to San Francisco for the same period were—wheat, 112,155 centals, and flour, 92,016 barrels. Most of this grain has been shipped from Portland, and the largest portion was grown in the Umpqua and Willamet valleys. While farmers living beyond a very few miles from the rivers or railroads in Eastern Oregon can raise fields of grain producing fifty or sixty bushels to the acre, and a volunteer crop of twenty-five, and

feed it all to their hogs for lack of cheap transportation, the bulk of the exports will come from west of the mountains. But the time has nearly arrived when, as I have said, cheaper transportation will bring down the Columbia an amount of wheat truly astonishing.

Wool is also one of the great staples of this new country, large areas of which are well adapted to sheep husbandry. In 1879 the shipments of wool amounted to over 26,000 sacks.

The Lower Columbia has no distinctive valley, but flows between its encircling hills, which pitch directly down to the water's edge, or are bordered on either side by low-lying islands flooded in June or July by the annual rise from melting snows.

The lowlands are intersected by an intricate net-work of ponds and sloughs, long vistas of green meadows lying between, affording abundant grazing when the water is off. The resources of Oregon and Washington in timber and lumber are practically inexhaustible, the whole country from the ocean to the Cascade Mountains, except the Willamet and other smaller valleys, being covered by a forest of fir, spruce, cedar, and pine. It is true, fires have ravaged these virgin forests over large areas, and the hoary and blackened trunks on many a mountain-side bear witness to the ghastly devastation: but where fire has not consumed the humus or mould, the Douglas fir, like the phœnix, springs triumphant from its ashes. When the timber shall have been

A SALMON-CANNING ESTABLISHMENT.

cupy every little gulch and ravine. The sailor on the ascending ship, just arrived from the long voyage around the Horn, gazes on the placid waters of the river and the towering hills in wonder and delight.

On the first twenty-five miles of the river above its mouth we observe the large buildings of the salmon fisheries, and Astoria is the centre of that industry. From a small beginning in 1864 or 1865, it has arrived at the proportions of a great business, employing large capital and thousands of men. Salmon commence to run into the river to spawn in March or April, and ascend the different tributaries to their sources in the Rocky Mountains. The fish are taken by gill-nets, the size of the meshes being prescribed by law. The nets are several hundred fathoms long, and twelve or fifteen feet deep. When the water is quite muddy, fish may be taken in daytime, but most fishing is done at night. Each boat, being managed by two men, is cast rapidly across the current, and allow-

stripped from the pineries of Maine, Michigan, and Wisconsin, the magnificent fir forests of the northwest coast will prove a great source of supply. At many places on the lower river the hills come down to the water in beetling cliffs of columnar basalt, the forest overhanging the very edge. In earlier days, when vessels sailed up and down the river, their yards and rigging have become entangled in the limbs of overhanging trees. Bushes, moss, and lichens, in tropical profusion, cling to every projection where it is possible to obtain the slightest footing, and small cascades and trickling streams oc-

SALMON FISHING ON THE COLUMBIA.

ed to drift down a mile or two before being hauled in. Seals follow the salmon, and are so bold as to take them out of the nets, and are frequently caught along with their prey. The fishermen are a remarkably adventurous and reckless set of beings, in their zeal to outstrip their comrades fishing down to the bar of the river, where at ebb tide no boat can stem the current, and are frequently swept into the treacherous breakers. Very many lives have been lost in these fool-hardy efforts.

The salmon-canning establishments are large unsightly structures, constructed over the water on piles, and without the slightest concessions to architectural effect or taste. The labor employed is almost exclusively Chinese—a monotonous work for which they prove well fitted. On the arrival and departure of every steamboat, the heads (and tails) of John Chinaman fill every window, and their unintelligible gabble drowns all other noises. The products of these establishments have found their way to every market in the world, and salmon packed on the Columbia commands a higher price than any other. It is, indeed, a noble fish, and if means are taken to prevent the diminution of the run, will prove a source of wealth for many years to come. In 1876 the number of cases put up was 428,730, and in 1879 there were shipped to England 106,102 cases, and to San Francisco 238,500 cases. It is a beautiful sight at Astoria on a fair summer evening to look at the fishing-boats start off to take their stations for the night's work. The setting sun off the river's mouth casts its broad golden rays across the water, softly ruffled by a light breeze, and glints on the hundreds of white and tan-colored sails which look like a vast flock of white-winged birds. The cliffs and crags on the opposite shore of the bay are glorified by the beams of the departing orb; the forest of pines casts long dense shadows across the tumbling rugged hills and down the river toward Cape Hancock; the melting haze blends the whole scene in softest tints of ethereal purple. The ancient village

CAPE HORN.

CAPE DISAPPOINTMENT AND BAKER'S BAY.

of Astoria, situated on the south shore of the river or bay, fifteen miles from the ocean, looks to us like a very new wooden town, though really the first settlement on the northwest coast. As early as 1811 the Pacific Fur Company occupied the present site as a trading-post, and it became a bone of contention between the English and American companies, whose field of operations covered the same ground. A large part of the place is built on piles over the water, like the lake-dwellings of prehistoric man. It has always been a place of great expectations and tardy fulfillments; but the ancient Astorian will ever adduce the fact that as New York occupies a similar site at the mouth of a great river, *ergo* Astoria must become a great city. Vessels enter and clear at the Custom-house, and are towed over the bar by competent tug-boats. The only building constructed of other material than wood is the Custom-house—a neat structure of stone. During the fishing season in spring and summer the streets are thronged by a cosmopolitan population belonging to every nationality of Europe and the East. On each side of the river entrance is a fortified post, both of doubtful efficacy in resisting the entrance of a hostile fleet.

Fort Hancock is situated on the summit of Cape Disappointment, the high headland which forms the northern side of the entrance. The cape protects the secure harbor of Baker's Bay, the anchoring ground for pilot-boats and bar tugs and all bar-bound vessels.

The terrors of the Columbia bar have been grossly exaggerated. The statistics of losses which have occurred in passing the entrance prove that for the shipping entered and cleared it has a much better record than many other ports not discriminated against in insurance. Vasco de Gama, when he discovered the great ocean on the calm tropical shores of the Bay of Panama, named it the Pacific. The name does not hold good so far north as latitude 46°. The surf which breaks incessantly on the shores of the North Pacific is much heavier than on the Atlantic, and therefore breaks in much deeper water. Like every barred harbor which a great sea rolls across, it is best to cross it at the highest tide; and when proper precautions are taken, no unusual difficulty or danger is experienced in the passage.

At last our trip was over; and as we steamed swiftly down the channel on a falling tide, past the forts on either hand and close under the rock-ribbed walls of Cape Hancock, at the close of a beautiful day in June, the ship rose and fell to the vigorous pulsations of the broad Pacific, while the snow-clad dome of Mount St. Helen's rose higher and higher, and filled the broad gateway of the river.

UNDER THE SPELL OF THE GRAND CAÑON

THERE were ten of us when we started — three white men, one Navajo, two horses, one pony, one bronco, and two mules. We had been busy for several days padding pack-saddles, mending blankets, cleaning guns, and laying in our stock of food — flour, sugar, baking-powder, bacon, rice, oatmeal, and dried fruit.

"Adios!" "Good luck!" and we turned our faces westward. It was the Alamo Ranch at Mancos, in southwestern Colorado, the time July, and we were off for that glorious plateau country through which the great river of the West has cut a series of profound chasms and rough desolate valleys, known to the world as the Cañons of the Colorado.

Most people who go to see the Grand Cañon leave the Santa Fe Railroad at Flagstaff, and after an all-day stage ride over a shoulder of the San Francisco Mountain, across a small corner of the Painted Desert, and through the majestic pines of the Coconino Forest, alight, tired but expectant, in a little camp of tents close upon the brink of the cañon.

He who lingers here in the presence of this stupendous and yet beautiful and alluring episode in world-making sooner or later becomes conscious of a haunting desire to know what sort of a land it is of which he catches fitful glimpses across this bewildering, palpitating space. No sign of a human being ever comes across to you, it is much too far for sound, and you wonder whether the tiny greenish uplifts upon the farther brink can be more than saplings. And where does it come from, that broken streak of water shimmering between the cliffs, and now and then roaring up at you on the wind like the great mad river it really is, a mile beneath? It seems to come out of a red wall ten miles to your right. But over that and across a narrow gleam of desert rises a hazy line of rosy cliffs, with a faint blue mountain dome beyond. Close under this they tell you the great river is coming down, already buried deep between gigantic walls. You follow its course toward the west through a maze of gorgeous temples and pinnacles and towers, until these merge into the illimitable blue of the sky, or are lost in the fading tints of sunset clouds.

This, then, is why our faces are set westward. We want to see where the old Colorado comes from and where it goes. We want to pluck out the heart of its mystery in those hidden hundreds of miles of awesome gorges. We want to wander in the country beyond the river which the pioneers have told about, and where the geologists have conjured from the rocks such impressive secrets of the world's workshop. And we want to

TROUBLE AT DANDY CROSSING.

soak in Arizona sunshine and revel in Arizona skies, and sleep under the stars, which are so bright and clear that they cannot be very far away from Arizona.

The great plateau country lies between the high mountain ranges which run north and south across the State of Colo-rado and the imposing Wahsatch Range in Utah on the west. It stretches far up into Wyoming on the north, while to the south it broadens out over a large part of the upper half of Arizona and over the northwest corner of New Mexico. The higher of the great plateaus are more than eleven thousand feet above the sea, vast, level, timbered platforms bordered by winding cliffs.

A multitude of drainage channels traverse the plateaus in broad sweeps of sandy valley, or in complex systems of chasms and cañons cut from a few hundred to five or six thousand feet below the various surfaces. The streams which have worn and swept away the rocks over wide areas, leaving gullied buttes and mesas rising from monotonous stretches of sandy plain, are in these days mostly dry, except as now and then they become the temporary flood channels of the storm-swept uplands.

Obliquely across the northwestern segment of the great plateau runs the Colorado River, slicing off from the rest a long, rough tract which borders the desolate basin country farther west.

The Colorado River is formed by the junction of the Green and Grand in southeastern Utah. Its upper foaming stretch, running in the Cataract Cañon, is about fifty miles long, and from thirteen hundred to twenty-seven hundred feet deep. At the lower end of this the Fremont River comes in from the west. When Powell came down the Colorado in his memorable exploring expedition, his men were not pleased with this tributary, and named it the Dirty Devil, a name which in local parlance clings to it still. Here the walls of the cañon break away on either side, giving access to the Dandy Crossing.

Below this the walls close in again to form the Glen Cañon, one hundred and fifty miles long, but bordered by lower and more broken cliffs. Into this segment of the cañon the San Juan enters close at the base of Navajo Mountain. The Colorado can be crossed at three points along the Glen Cañon—at Hall's Crossing, near the mouth of the Escalante, at the Hole-in-the-Rock Crossing, near by, and at the Crossing of the Fathers—*El Vado de los Padres*—below the entrance of the San Juan.

These crossings are now little used, except by miners who pass here to reach placer beds along the stream.

At its lower end the Glen Cañon pierces the cliffs, the Colorado receives the Paria from the west, and runs for a mile or so sedately in the open. Here is Lee's Ferry, where a large boat carries across the few horsemen and teams which pass this way.

But the walls close in again, and for sixty-five miles the river is closely bordered by cliffs from two to three thousand feet high. This is the Marble Cañon. At its foot the Colorado Chiquito—the Little Colorado—enters from the east.

From this point until it sweeps out upon the desert, more than two hundred and eighteen miles away, the Colorado runs at the bottom of a great valley from four to twelve miles across, sunk from three-quarters of a mile to a mile and a quarter below the surface of the great plateau, and bordered by an endless succession of vast rock amphitheatres, with gorges and cañons reaching far back from the valley, while from its depths and along its sides rise graceful, majestic, tapering buttes in infinite variety. This rock-walled valley of amphitheatres and buttes, wonderful in color beyond all possibility of description, is called the Grand Cañon, or the Grand Chasm, of the Colorado.

Through the long reaches of its upper cañons the Colorado River holds a southwesterly course. But at the head of the Grand Cañon it turns westward in great sweeps, now northwest, then southwest, and again northwest, until it rolls out of its self-wrought prison and enters upon its six hundred miles of placid journey south to the Gulf of California.

We headed, by way of Bluff City on the San Juan River, for the Dandy Crossing.

One day in the saddle in the plateau country is much like another, save for the ever-changing scene and the mild adventures of the way. Before dawn the Indian is off to track and bring in the beasts, which have been turned adrift to forage for themselves through the night.

Now, one by one, jumpled heaps of blankets, scattered on the ground, heave and shift, and at length disclose each a man, who quickly satisfies the modest claims of the toilet, and at once gets to work at the breakfast. A fire is made, the biscuit are baked in an iron pot set upon coals, with a small fire alight upon the lid. The ground is seat and table. There is no dallying with the breakfast. The mules are packed early, for it gets hot right away after sunrise.

So the beasts get their last sip of water, the canteens are filled, and the caravan moves off in single file. The gait is usually a jog-trot or a walk. The distance covered in a day depends upon the situation of water along the route. The average is from twenty - five to thirty miles.

The march in summer is always strenuous in the Southwest, because of the burning sun. But in the high country refreshing breezes are almost always astir, and the vast sweep of the vision, the great masses of marvellous color in sand and cliff and butte, the matchless sky, and the glorious freedom of the life, banish all thought of hardship, and hide fatigue in the inspiration of a careless holiday.

You skirt the bases of gigantic cliffs, which, seen from near and far below, look like the sides of mountain ranges. You scramble up through rugged gullies to the top, and find that they are level plateaus scantily clad with soil, and broken by shrub and piñon and cedar. The Spanish-bayonet bristles and great scrawny cactuses stare at you as you pass. The eye wanders off to other uplands scored and furrowed by gorges of wildest form, and catches farther still away the shadowy uplift of mountain-peaks—the Henrys, the La Sals, the Blues, and the long dome of old Navajo, faint and tremulous through miles of shimmering space. Away off on the San Juan desert great sand pillars swirl upward on the wind and sway and crumble and fade, while the under surfaces of fleecy cloud banks sailing over its dreadful wastes are lurid from the hot reflection of the sand.

You swing across the plateau and slide and clamber down again. But with the descent of a few hundred feet you are in another world. The vision no longer revels in those upland spaces which raise the spirit into exultant mastery. It may be a desperate labyrinth of gorges along which now you fare, whose grotesque and threatening walls crowd in upon the way in stolid, brutal insistence. It may be a broad valley with dry, level, grassy bottom, and bordered by miles of majestic cliffs stretching away in broad panelled and buttressed sweeps, and beset with alcoves here and there, whose blissful shadows lure you from the way. But there is more than shade in these cool recesses, for it is only when you get well back in shadow, so that the eyes are released from the glare of the sun, that you realize the full richness and beauty of the great masses of simple color which dominate these wastes. Perhaps ahead of you the valley narrows, the buttressed cliffs form-

ing a gigantic colonnade down which you ride, while great rock pillars and colossal obelisks tower here and there above the walls, gleaming in gray or buff or pink or red against the rich blue background of the sky. Or the valley may open out upon a sweep of sandy plain, its buff and yellow stretches beset with billowy masses of the sage, now gray, now lilac-tinted through the shimmering air, with an elusive purple among the shadows of its leaves, which, as you rustle by them, fling a faint aroma on the air. You look across this tremulous stretch of lilac and purple and gold, like a brilliant restless sea struck motionless, with its waves abreak, to the far horizon upon which rise miles of gorgeous buttes—white, yellow, purple, orange, and brown—all alive with the intense shadows which come and go upon their rugged faces.

Now and then the hot quivering air plays strange tricks with the vision as you ride over the sandy reaches of the bottoms. The cliffs shoot up in wavering pinnacles, rock columns rise and hang in swaying, pointed masses above their real selves, then slowly dwindle and fade or draw upward and flash out of sight. A few times I have seen beautiful lakes suddenly appear across the pathway, with foam - tipped waves breaking in silence upon green shores, which glided along the burning sand to vanish in a breath.

From the high uplands you sometimes see scudding clouds shoot down long wavering shower slants, which vanish at the touch of the hot, dry air before they reach the earth. You may see afar, or encounter, brief veil-like showers, which are conjured into being with never a cloud in all the sky.

Although rainfall is infrequent upon the wide expanses of the plateau in summer, thunder-showers of terrific violence sometimes sweep across them. And I know of no more severe test of serenity of spirit than to face one of these in its unmitigated violence. If there were but a rock or tree or bush under which you could secure at least the moral support of a shelter, the strain would be less severe. But you may summon fortitude at last to face the rage and fury of the wind and rain, and even to exult in the flash and roar and clatter of the bolts which fall in quick succession all about you. When the demon of the storm is once in possession you lose all thought of danger, and are fairly regretful when at last, with a sudden swish, the last pulse of the downpour sweeps by, and the black chaos goes roaring off. But when, as not rarely happens in these violent showers, out of the seething alembic monstrous hailstones are hurled down upon you, neither serenity nor bravado is of much avail. You get black and blue welts upon your back and shoulders just the same, and your horses go wild with the terror and pain of the fiendish bombardment. These hailstones are often from half an inch to an inch in diameter, occasionally as large as a hen's egg. And I have assisted at one of these way-side dramas—my head and shoulders under a saddle which a relenting fate had thrown beside me on the ground—in which the larger missiles measured between three and four inches in their brutal diameters. But they lent enchanting beauty to the scene as, a few minutes later, we crunched our rueful way over them sparkling in the sun.

Here and there you come upon small ruins of the old cliff-dwellers, plastered on the faces of the cliffs, or atop of dizzy pinnacles of rock, or in sags of the hills, where trickling springs may still be found. Broken pottery in places litters the ground about these ruins, and the old burial-places tell in no doubtful fashion, to him who knows how to read the story, the age and populousness of these long-forgotten homes.

Your animals must be well cared for in the long arduous jaunts, no matter how man is neglected. Because, in these dry, desolate countries, to be left afoot is to face such hardships as few care to risk. Your horse is fed first, watered first, and first unburdened for his rest. How he will fare in the night forage is the last thing in your consciousness before you sleep. How he has fared, the first query of the morning. And all day long he is your comrade. Sharing thus the varied fortunes of the way, you fall into terms of intimacy and often affection. The animals of the Southwest country are wonted to long journeys and serious hardship. But that which most relentlessly saps the energy and daunts the spirit is lack of water. A horse or mule may now and then go on for two hot days and a night without it; but this may be his ruin, for he is apt to lose heart and give up if such demands like frequent. The men in a company like

ours can carry water enough for themselves in canteens and a small keg for two dry days. But dry camps are not cheerful, and you ought to be mighty certain of water of some sort before dark on the second night.

Now and then you ride forward for a chat with a comrade; you may beguile the way with a song. The Indian strikes up some weird refrain; then one shrieks at the pack-mules as they stray. But the order is mostly single file, and the trail is mostly silent. It is a dreamy, vacuous life which you slip away into as the hot hours pass. You are half conscious of the splendid sky and the lengthening shadows on cliff and plain as you jog on and on, but the vision of memory is often more vivid than the impression of the hour.

So at last you come to the camping-place. There are no tents to pitch, nothing necessary but forage for the horses, water, a little wood, and a few square feet of earth. The horses are turned adrift, supper is materialized, and if the night be at hand, hurriedly and sleepily despatched. Each man pre-empts a little patch of ground, which he levels off as best he can. The blankets are spread early, for the nights are always cool; and as the stars come out you may see here and there the gleam of pipes alight, as, half ensconced in his nest, the smoker wooes the last and sweetest solace of the day before he tastes oblivion. Then sunrise is at hand again. So the days go.

We had ridden steadily down the long reaches of the White Cañon for two days, skirting the brinks of dizzy cliffs, scrambling across gorges, and winding in and out among rocks and buttes and piñons, when a sudden turn of the trail brought us upon the crest of a low bluff, with the Colorado River, our goal for seven days, sweeping on to the south. This was the Dandy Crossing, and the first sign of humanity since we left Bluff City was a rough cabin on the far side of the river, here about one-eighth of a mile across. We drew up the caravan, fired a shot in the air, and waited. Presently three black-clad figures issued from the cabin, filed solemnly around in front, and squatted in a row upon the ground. Then we both waited.

The black row brooded motionless. We fired again. Presently we caught faintly, "What ye want?" "We want to get across; send over the boat." "They ain't no boat; ye can't git over." This was pleasant. The nearest other available crossing was ninety miles as the crow flies, and full thrice as far as mules must go. At last we gathered amid the roar, "They's a skiff somers upstream, and mebbe ye kin git 'er." So we scrambled for three or four miles along the shelving rocks at the river's brink, the cliffs towering a thousand feet over us, and then stopped, clinging as best we could to the last shelf upon a wall which rose sheer from the water. But we had sighted a miserable hovel on the other side, and presently hailed with joy a blessed woman, clad largely in a sunbonnet. She said, "They is an old boat yar, but I ain't strong enough to git 'er acrost." Night was at hand, so we turned back to a less precipitous place where our stock could forage, made camp, and sat in council.

The river is big, it is broad, it is muddy, it is swift, and even in its quieter places sullen and forbidding. Great smooth swirls come and go upon its surface; it swishes viciously past the rocks and bushes on the brink. And it has a bad reputation. It drowns people and it drowns stock. It often claimed, but fortunately lost, its tribute from Major Powell's plucky little company in 1869. Nothing short of human life appeased it when Colonel Stanton and his men went through the cañons twenty years later. The folks who know it best, the cattlemen and the miners, dread and hate it. "She's a durned, cussed, ugly devil, and ye'd best not monkey with 'er," said one of our native councillors who knew.

But we thought that we would make an attempt anyhow, so one of our number mounted our veteran horse and plunged in. There was splashing and turmoil in the water, horse and man disappeared, and when, in a few seconds, the rider was dragged ashore in grieved surprise, and the horse scrambled up the bank a hundred yards below, trembling and snorting, we were ready to concede that the task before us was not what in the juvenile vocabulary would be called a "cinch." Then we had supper, and slept upon the situation—and the rocks.

In the morning, one of us crawled around the cliff and along the rocks far up the bank, secured a stranded log, and floating and swimming with the current,

finally reached the other side. The boat was an old ramshackle, leaky, flat-bottomed, ten-foot skiff, with patched and clumsy oars, but in small loads we got our saddles and packs across, and then, after a careful reconnoissance of the banks on both sides for a safe entering-place and landing, we tackled the stock. None of our animals had been tried in deep and rapid streams before, and it was evident from our first attempts that if we pushed them off into deep water to take their chances, they would either scramble back again or drown. The only thing to do was to tow them over, one by one. This would have been a more agreeable undertaking if the oars had been less nondescript in form and less fragile, if the boat had leaked in fewer places and in less abandoned fashion, and if she hadn't threatened to fall to pieces every time the oarsman pulled unequally upon the sides.

It would make a long list if one were to set down all the surprising things which a horse or a mule will undertake to do when, with a rope around his neck, held in the boat a rod or so off shore, he is suddenly pushed off a steep bank into deep water. He tries to go to the bottom first, but he is too buoyant for success at that; then he tries to get back to the bank, but the rope pulling from the boat and shouting men ashore brandishing clubs discourage that. He surges right and left, he snorts, he splashes, he groans, and when at length he realizes that he can't possibly get ashore again, he concentrates all his hitherto diverse purposes into a fixed intention to get aboard the boat. He has now been hauled close astern, and has lost all notion of the shore. The oarsman meanwhile is pulling madly toward the other bank, the whole circus sweeping every second down the stream. With every lurch upon the rope the joints in the crazy craft open, and the Colorado River seems determined to get aboard along with the horse. Floundering up and down in the struggle to raise his fore feet over the stern, his knees thump against the outside of the boat. He swims first around one side, then around the other, as far as the short rope will let him go. He rolls on his side as a vicious whirl in the water catches him, and seems to lose his bearings. His eyes bulge, his breath grows short, he groans rather than snorts, and at last, when the man sitting astern with the rope raises his nose over

the thwart, with a great sigh he gives up
and swims along behind, blowing and
puffing and with strained eyes, but quietly
and smoothly. The fight is over. In
this lull in the panic we secure evident
recognition of words of cheer and encouragement with which, even in mid-
stream, we strive to re-establish claims
to friendliness and good-will so rudely
strained by the deep damnation of that
pushing off. Presently the boat begins
to slew around. The oarsman cannot
keep her on the course headed for a rocky
point far down the stream upon which
and nowhere else the landing must be
made, because of quicksand at every other
place. It is evident in an instant that
the beast has caught sight of the far
shore, and, regardless of the boat, is heading for it. So the rope is payed out and
let go, and he bears away gallantly for the
point.

It was fortunate that the first horse
which we piloted thus across let us drag
him nearly all the way, because we secured
for him the proper landing, where he and
the others, as one by one they joined him,
stood as landmarks for those which were
to follow. We had a distinct and variegated campaign with each animal, but the
lines of the story fall much the same in
all. At last we got them safely over,
and gratefully returned in one piece the
gallant craft which saved the day. We
had lost a few illusions about the ease of
primitive travel on the frontier, but we
had gained a distinct preference for
bridges, and we had conquered the Colorado.

Here upon a long sand bar we camp
and lie over a day to wash, dry, mend,
eat, and brace up for the next stage of
our journey. At night we make a huge
fire of river drift-wood. And here, if
ever, the grim walls looming far up on
either side, a clear-cut strip of starry sky
between, and the swirl and roar of the
river close at hand, is the time and place
for a story.

There are so many kinds of story
which a camp fire invites that one might
hesitate in choice. But the spirit of the
situation and the hour leads most directly
to a sober tale of world-making which
geologists have read out of the stone
story-book opened wider in this land of
the great plateaus than almost anywhere
else on earth.

I have upon my writing-table, holding

down a pile of unruly papers, the oldest
relic of America which human eyes have
ever rested on. It is a rough fragment
of rock which I broke off from a long,
low granite ridge, a part of which is now
called the Laurentian Hills in Canada—
the first land to emerge from that universal, shoreless sea which once swept
unhindered round the earth. After the
appearance of my paper-weight—the ava-
tar of the North American Continent—
some scattering rock islets and ridges got
their heads also into the sunlight here
and there, along the line of the Appala-
chian chain, among the tips of the Rockies, and over the central and northern regions of the future great republic.

Then these rock islands, and others
which the throes of the uneasy earth sent
up to join them, and the shallow bottoms
here and there, were pounded through
ages by resistless seas, and powdered and
weathered into bowlder, pebble, sand, and
silt. This wreckage filled in the borders
of the land, and slowly built up, layer by
layer, the bottoms of the interinsular
seas. This layered ruin of earlier rock
was then baked by plutonic fires into new
rock, and again became the sport of the
elements, and took new forms and places
in the earth's foundation. And so, after
never mind how many millions of years,
the continent of North America grew into
some semblance of its present form. But
for a long time the South Atlantic sea-
board was under water; Florida was not;
and what now we call the Gulf of Mexico sent a deep bay up the Mississippi half-
way to the Great Lakes; while a vast inland sea, the Mediterranean of early America, stretched northwestward from the
Gulf across the Rocky Mountain country,
over the region of our great plateaus, and
far on toward the Arctic Ocean.

Just here the sequence of events grows
dim as centuries file along. At any rate,
the great inland sea was gradually filled
by the wash from the shores and by the
water-borne wreckage of the hills in the
back country. Then it lost its connection with the sea, and became a vast fresh-
water lake, or chain of lakes, with rather
unstable bottoms, whose shores and depths
were haunted by strange living creatures.
Finally the whole basin got filled up and
dry, except for the water pouring down
out of the northern hills. Thus a great
new drainage area was formed, which
headed far in the crumpled mountains to

the north, and stretched off southwestward toward a mighty arm of the sea, of which the Gulf of California is the dwindling relic. This drainage area became in time the plateau country, and the new watercourse, the Colorado River, so noisily in evidence beside our camp, forswore its inherited fealty to the Atlantic, long maintained through the Gulf of Mexico, and henceforth paid loyal tribute to the Pacific. Please remember that I am just telling the story as I have gleaned it from the students of the rocks in book and lecture and in far-off camps among the hills. So if a million years or so should slip away unheeded in my tale, or if the shores of nameless, vanished seas should in my memory break in wider beach-lines, or a little farther inland than in fact they did, I claim the license of way-side narrative.

It is tiresome to try to conceive of the long reaches of time during which this great inland sea was filling up, and it is fortunate that the geologists who deal in such lordly, lavish fashion with the years, handling them in parcels of a few millions or a hundred millions or so, finally lump them together under *ages*—Carboniferous, Permian, Triassic, Jurassic, Cretaceous, etc., names which are not insistent in the suggestion that they were, after all, made up of hours and minutes, which only one by one have slipped away.

But if you go out into the plateau country five hundred miles from any ocean you will not doubt this inland sea. For you may ride for hours along shaly rock escarpments on which the ripples of the ancient shores are as plain and plenty as ever you saw them on the Jersey coast. You can pick up shells, too, which at least suggest clams, stone though they be to-day. In the northern part of the plateau country, now cut off from the rest by the Uintah Mountains, the bones of monkeys and crocodiles, of birds with teeth and three-toed horses, of sea-serpents—honor bright, I appeal to Marsh—and of a motley lot of named and nameless uncouth, ludicrous beasts, are piled pell-mell together in the washes, or half buried in banks and cliffs and weathered buttes which once were the shores and bottoms of our slowly shoaling inland sea.

It is a vivid memory which lingers with the writer, of an undergraduate summer spent in this region under the tutelage of Professor Marsh, who is so wise in the lore of these crumbling hills, and eager still, as the years pass, with the enthusiasm which led him then to share with the boys the toil and hardships of the bone-hunters in the fossil beds upon the northern segment of the great plateau. Most vivid of all, perhaps, is the recollection of a long hot week whose daylight hours were spent alone astride the shelving edge of a low weathered butte, with hammer and stone-chisel, pecking away the rock around the fossil head of a preposterous beast, something like a crocodile, I fancied, which once had floundered about in that old inland sea. Every day, as soon as the click of the chisel began, three huge gray wolves came peering over the edge of the bluff a hundred feet or so above me, and there they stood, alert, but silent and motionless, all through the hot day. A hallo and a sudden wave of the hand would send them scampering off, but presently they were there again, attentive as ever to the strange thing below. It was a far cry back from my contemporaries upon the bluff, who seemed to have very little business of their own on hand, to the old inhabitant at my feet; and though we hadn't much in common, we all got on very well together, and parted friends.

But I have lingered behind my story, for we have seen the old inland sea filled up, and a new great river, which will some day be the Colorado, sweeping down from the northern regions on its way to the Pacific. This stream bore great floods of water, and began to gather enormous quantities of eroded stuff from the lake-beds over which it passed. So that after this great basin, covering an area of considerably more than a hundred thousand square miles, had been filled in, layer by layer, some two or three miles deep, at such an inordinate cost in mountains and at such a reckless expenditure of time, and the stuff had all got nicely packed and settled into good solid earth crust, the whole thing began to wash out again, to make new land somewhere else. I don't know where it all went to, but in the later periods, at least, a vast amount went down the Colorado. But gone much of it is, especially of the upper strata, as you may see for yourself if you go over into southern Utah and northern Arizona, whither to-morrow we shall turn our faces.

We shall get up on top of some of the upper strata of the rock which filled the inland sea, now forming what are known as the High Plateaus of Utah, and then bear off south toward the river again, down a series of gigantic steps hundreds of feet high, each the edge of one of the old upper layers, left exposed in miles of gorgeous, fantastic cliffs by the wear and tear and wash of the centuries. When we get down from the remnants of the top layers we shall have descended over six thousand feet upon the lower level, whose surface has been exposed in huge patches over hundreds of square miles by the erosion of insatiate streams. Even then we shall not have reached the bottom of the inland sea. For we shall make our way southward for forty miles across a rough desert country, on the top of what our learned friends call the Carboniferous strata, until we come to the brink of the cañon at its grandest part, and nearly opposite to the camp of tents. If then we could descend the dizzy mile of Carboniferous cliffs and terraces to the level of the river, we should at last have reached the very bottom of our old inland sea, and gone a thousand feet into the ragged granite ledge beneath, which claims the kinship of age with my paperweight from the Laurentian Hills.

The secret of the great denudation and of this wonderful achievement of the Colorado in carving out of rock a series of cañons about five hundred miles long, and, in one place at least, more than a mile deep, with a multitude of tributary chasms and gorges, is very simple when you know it. *The old lake-bed slowly rose.* At first, the Colorado River and its tributaries, or some nameless monstrous ancestor of these, sweeping over the slowly rising surfaces, planed them down in most relentless fashion, and then began wearing out broad shallow stream-beds. But then the country rose more rapidly, and the water had to cut deeper channels in the rocks in order to get out and away to sea. Owing in part to the wear of the water itself, but more to the ceaseless bombardment of the suspended sand which it bore from the up country, or picked up as it went along, and to the thump of pebbles and bowlders which it swept on in flood-time, the river kept cutting down as the strata rose, until finally, when what was left of our inland sea-bottom got thrust up so

that, towering far above its erstwhile rocky shores, it had to be called a plateau, the Colorado and its auxiliaries found themselves at the bottom of a series of colossal cañons and gorges, where they are to-day.

Then, increasing the complexity of things hereabouts, the strata in the rising plateau got overstrained, and bent up in great swells or ridges, forming subsidiary tables or plateaus of great extent. In other places the strata broke in cracks, a hundred miles long sometimes. Along these cracks the rock layers on one side or the other often sank below or were pushed above the general level, forming those abrupt cliffs or escarpments which the wise ones call "faults."

So, thrust up hundreds of feet, over great areas, by resistless plutonic forces, losing large tracts of its upper strata by earlier floods and streams, gouged out by our Colorado and its tributaries, still existing or extinct, and withal crumpled and cracked and displaced in varied fashion when the earth's crust writhed, our old inland sea-bottom certainly has won through much tribulation the right to glory in its stupendous relics.

But, in addition to all the rest, a multitude of volcanoes and lava streams have at one time or another burst up through the tortured strata here and there, some of them not so very long ago, leaving imposing mountains, building cinder cones, and deluging the land with molten rock.

That is my story. Its plot in years is long indeed. It exploits the forces which build and sculpture worlds. And if it lack the human touch which lies at the heart of the best stories, one yet may link the present to the past if he realize that the swift turbid stream beside us, still as sand and silt, is bearing the mountains to the sea; that the click of pebble against pebble where the water rushes over shallows, and the beat of rock on rock along the deeper bottoms, are slowly wearing stone to sand; that the great river is cutting its channel deeper and wider year by year, while the shower gusts and the frost are yet at work shaping this wonderland into those forms of grace and majesty which are the heritage of millenniums. The great inland sea is gone, but the ripples are on its beaches still. The strange beasts have vanished, but their bones cumber the ground. The earth's crust has ceased to heave and crack, but the crumpled broken strata rise in- imposing hills and cliffs. The volcanoes are cold and silent, but the great cinder cones and lava beds even yet are sinister.

So at last we head away westward, up the nearly dry, rough wash of Crescent Creek or Lost Gulch, and are soon out upon the plateau again close under the eastern slope of the Henry Mountains. We skirt the northern spurs of the Henrys, entering the midreaches of the Fremont Valley among outlying Mormon settlements.

Now, day after day, the way leads west and south through great gashes in the ledges of the Water-pocket Fault, across the summits of lofty plateaus, past cliff-girt mountain vales, up the long stretches of the Sevier, until at last we climb the height which divides the waterways leading back to the salt-lake basins of Utah from the summit sources of the Kanab and the Virgen, children of the great Colorado.

As we cross the divide we are between two great tables which rise a thousand feet or more above us to the right and left. These are the Panságunt and the Markágunt plateaus, standing nine and ten thousand feet above the sea. From their southern crests you may look off upon a vast plain six thousand feet below, whither we are bound, and across which the Grand Cañon, now beyond the vision, in majestic winding sweeps, takes its westerly course.

The Kanab Creek has cut a rough winding gorge down through the cliffs and terraces which mark the descent from the high plateaus southward to the great bench of the Colorado. In this we clamber down the marvellous series of terraces, sloping upward to their edges, clearing at a leap ledges which it took a thousand or perhaps a hundred thousand years to build, and as many more, mayhap, to wash away again. How we and our mules flaunted our heels in the face of Time that day! If we were geologists, we should check the ledges off as we descend—Eocene, Cretaceous, Jurassic, Triassic, and out upon the Permian. But being just common folks, they may be for us the Pink Cliffs, White Cliffs, Vermilion Cliffs, Brown Cliffs. I will not try to describe their majesty, nor the weird forms and the gorgeous colors with which

in the lower series they are glorified. At last we come down upon the lowest of the terraces, the Vermilion Cliffs sweeping away right and left, and into the little hamlet of Kanab, the last Mormon outpost in southern Utah, close upon the northern line of Arizona.

The Grand and Marble cañons cut the northwestern corner of Arizona completely off from the rest of the Territory. Except by Lee's Ferry, and the long hot road which leads to it, or by a far western route, this corner is inaccessible from the south. It looks small enough on the map, but it is rather larger than the State of Connecticut, and, save for a few scattered cattle-shacks, has no human habitation.

For the next two weeks we wander over this stretch of the plateau which lies along the northern side of the Grand Cañon, under the guidance of one of the Saints, who, as sheep-herder and cow-puncher in summer and winter, has learned every turn and curve of the vast desolate surface, and, what is more to the point, every spring and water-pocket and possible mud puddle.

While from the terraces of the high plateaus this region looks almost flat, it is, in fact, very rough and broken. There are four tables, or subsidiary uplands, rising above the general level, each one a great plateau, and each in its way worthy of visit and description. But we can only name them here. Far to the west lies the Shiwitz Plateau, overlooking the miserable Desert Basin. Next eastward is the Uinkaret, with its volcanic cones and lava beds, Mount Trumbull sloping black and sinister above the rest. Still eastward, across the ancient valley of the Toroweap, is the Kanab Plateau, its southern end forming the northern wall of some twenty miles of the Grand Cañon. Finally, lying along the whole eastern side of the district, and forming a large part of the most imposing segment of the northern wall of the Grand Cañon and the eastern wall of the Marble Cañon esplanade, is the Kaibab Plateau, or Old Buckskin, as hereabouts it is familiarly called. It is the Kaibab which looms up before the tourist on the farther side of the Grand Cañon as he stands upon the brink at the camp of tents. It is from seven to nine thousand feet above sea-level, stretches a hundred miles north and south, and at its widest is somewhat more than thirty miles across.

Over the middle and western portions of this barren northern Colorado bench, where in five thousand square miles there may be a dozen springs and fickle water-pockets, bands of wild horses roam, defying pursuit, worrying more docile stock, and eating grass and drinking water which are none too plenty for cattle and for better-mannered horses. But a fine show these splendid creatures make of it when, from ten to fifty in a bunch, they catch sight of an outfit like ours and line out for a run.

We bear off to the southwest, over the long lava slopes and up the frowning crests of Mount Trumbull, thence southward along a broad shallow valley called the Toroweap; to our right a gloomy line of volcanoes perched upon the Uinkaret, with great black rivers of lava sweeping between them down into the valley close beside the trail, while to the left, marvellously buttressed and alcoved, the western edge of the Kanab Plateau journeys with us. Soon the farther wall of the Great Cañon looms up ahead, across the valley, two thousand feet high, and we ride out upon a broad esplanade opening east and west. The Toroweap, entering the valley of the great Colorado, swings us back among the centuries to a time after the Colorado Plateau had be-

A GLIMPSE DOWN THE BRIGHT ANGEL.

come cleared of its upper strata, and when, as a leisurely stream up in the sunlight, the great river swept down from the mountains, receiving here and there its tributaries, also leisurely and sun-loving, their burrowing capacities in check because the descent was slow and the channels free. Such a tributary to the Colorado River was the Toroweap. But there is no stream in the Toroweap Valley now, and the dry bed ends upon the dry bed of the old Colorado, which we have called its esplanade.

But what of the Colorado River? Has

it too gone dry? Let us see. We leave the animals and saunter on in the direction of the long cliff-line on the opposite side of the esplanade. But not far, for almost before we know it the bottom has fallen away, and we are peering over the edge of a chasm three thousand feet sheer down to a foaming rivulet, for such it seems, at the bottom. This chasm, about as wide as it is deep, stretches away to right and left, nearly in the axis of the esplanade on which we stand. This is the inner gorge of the Colorado.

What has happened to drop the Colorado three thousand feet through solid rock with this mockery of a river gaping down upon it?

The geologists say that this was due to a change of weather, the climate becoming arid while the plateau went on rising. Evidence of such a change is at hand all over this region in the form of shallow, ancient river-courses, dry like the Toroweap, which run toward the Colorado, their bottoms more or less covered now with the wash of the hills about them. These were relatively short streams, their drainage areas small, and including no mountains to wring moisture from the clouds or store the winter snows. But the parent stream, the Colorado, with its chief tributaries, heads in far high mountains, and so has continued to carry a large volume of water. Thus as the whole plateau slowly rose, bearing the dried-up channels upon its surface, the Colorado, narrowing its bed, cut its way deeper and deeper, forming the inner gorge upon whose brink we stand.

From whatever point in the western part of this district you gain an outlook, the eye is drawn to a long dark level uplift which wholly cuts off the world farther east. This is the Kaibab Plateau, and thither now we turn, for everybody has told us that it is a paradise up there in the forest. We struggle for four days across the desert, heading the Kanab Cañon and up the rough trails which lead to the summit. Here you may wander for days in an open forest of noble pines; or along exquisite glades, green-bottomed, where the quaking aspen cheers the eye, and edged with the delicate spires of spruce and fir. Bright flowers bloom in long forest-sequestered parks, and you may even hear water gurgle here and there among the rocks. Deer are plenty and very tame. We chased them among the trees as one might runaway cows. But as we were not out to kill things, we left them mostly to their own devices.

However pleasant it may be, after the hot weeks of strenuous travel in the open, to loiter under the pines and among the glades in the heart of the Kaibab, you cannot long resist those hazy glimpses caught here and there between the trees into far blue depths upon which shadowy outlines of temples and minarets, and nameless dreamy masses in soft rich colors, float and gleam. However deep in the forest or cozy beside your camp fire at the edge of one of those matchless glades, the spell of the great abyss hovers about you and lures you to its side. You ride for a day and crawl over upon a great peninsula of rock — Powell's Plateau, they name it — which looms above the heart of this under-world, and revel in the vision. It was from this commanding point that Thomas Moran caught the inspiration of color and of space which is translated upon his great canvas hanging in the Capitol at Washington. You ride and camp and ride again out and out for miles to the last rock pillar which stands poised on Point Sublime, and linger hour after hour in the thrall of a waking dream.

Then away you go again—for it makes you restless, this mighty thing of transcendent beauty—and after many miles reach a towering promontory around which the river makes a great curve as it emerges from the Marble Cañon and sweeps into the vast chambered space below. This is the vantage-ground, locally known as Greenland Point, infrequently visited by parties of the nearest Mormon villagers for a view of the Grand Cañon. Two projecting cliffs upon this point are known to the geologists as Cape Royal and Cape Final.

When Major Powell and his men came floating down the river they seemed a little remorseful for the mood in which the Dirty Devil had been named, and as they reached the mouth of a gorgeous side cañon a few miles below our Greenland Point, whence issues a sparkling brook, they were inspired to call it the Bright Angel. It was at a little spring close under the edge of the summit ledges in which this happily christened streamlet finds its source that we lingered longest in camp, loath to relinquish the shelter of the noble forest and lose the glimpses of wonderland down through the glowing corridor of cliffs and towers which the Bright Angel has fashioned in its mad rush to the bosom of the Colorado. But there are hundreds of hot miles between us and home, and so at last, after some days of forest wandering, we turn our faces toward the eastern façade of the Kaibab, heading for Lee's Ferry.

Here we secure a small boat and work our way toilsomely up into the lower boxes of the Glen Cañon, trying to realize, as we drift back again, the toils and dangers and recompense of those who have floated through all the long stretches of the cañons—Powell and Stanton with their parties, and twice in more recent years adventurous persons in rude skiffs, whose names I do not know. From the ferry crossing you look down the upper reaches of the Marble Cañon, its walls steadily rising until they close in perspective over gloomy depths.

It is a thirsty ride of seventy-five miles along the Echo Cliffs from Lee's Ferry to water at the trading-post at Willow Springs, whence the way leads on to the Mormon city of Tuba and to the Pueblo Indian ranches in the valley of the Moencopie.

I have not woven into my way-side narrative the human interests passing in and out through the story of the scarred, insistent earth which so inevitably dominated our waking hours. But we stopped beside forlorn hovels, whose Mormon inmates had memories clear enough of better times in other lands, and hopes pathetic and dim of a brighter day for the chosen. Cattle-men, weeks from the sight of other faces, were glad to leave their cabins under lonesome cliffs and ride for miles beside us to hear our story and to tell their own. Dusky forms, mostly of Pah Utes and Navajos, would dash out upon us or suddenly materialize at our camp fires in the remotest places, and in mutual stares and smokes and pantomime we always won our way to good fellowship and confidence.

From Tuba the way is not far to the eastern fringe of the Coconino Forest, and across the uplands to the camp of tents upon the southern brink of the Grand Cañon, where the stage route from Flagstaff ends. A large tract on both sides of the cañon in this region has been sequestered for a national park.

The Cataract. the Glen, and the Marble cañons, and that portion of the Grand Cañon which lies below the Toroweap, are gorges of overpowering grandeur, but they are perfectly comprehensible. When you have won your way along and across them, and now in sun and now in shadow have studied their sombre walls, you can easily enough describe them and recall better-known cañons and gorges which serve fairly well by comparison to illustrate their extent and majesty. But face to face with this other, comparisons are futile, and figures and estimates seem impertinent. Each change of season, each new day, and every passing hour reveals new elements of grandeur in the cliffs, fresh phases of transcendent beauty in their colors.

The great cañon is shy of the camera, and the marvellous blue haze, now luminous, now faint, now shot with purple as the light falls red upon it at sunset, is always there holding its reserve inviolate. Single cliffs and towers of rare strength and beauty you may secure upon your films, but the cañon never.

The outline panoramas sketched by Holmes for the geological survey recall some very striking forms and grouping of masses, and, simple as they are, convey, I think, better than photographs an impression of space and distance.

The first white men to look upon the Grand Cañon were some old Spaniards, who went out from the Moqui villages in 1541. A few of them scrambled down the cliffs a little way, and took a world of satisfaction, when they got back, in pointing out to their wiser comrades, who had staid above, some pinnacles of rock part way down apparently as large as a man, but which they triumphantly declared were bigger than the great tower of Seville.

Major Powell, who knows the Colorado well, says impressive things, in very charming fashion, about the Grand Cañon. But he finds the task perilously exacting, and at last, yielding to the frenzy of comparison, plucks up Mount Washington by the roots to the level of the sea, and drops it head-first into the abyss, calling you to witness that the waters still flow between the walls. Anon the Blue Ridge is plucked up and even hurled into the cañon; but there is room aplenty still. Mr. Warner, wearying of description, stows away the Yosemite in an inconspicuous side gorge, and defies you to find it. Then he summons dreams of the Orient, calls Babylon back across the years, fixes his eyes upon a far, aerial heaven which fades at last into visions of the New Jerusalem, and so, altogether, comes off with flying colors from his skilful, lusty tilt with the impossible.

The most wise and sympathetic, as well as learned description of the Grand Cañon and its adjacent country is, I think, that of Captain Dutton, unfortunately buried for most readers in a bulky report —Vol. II.—of the United States Geological Survey.

After all, one may be glad if he can win the conviction that in a world so strenuous with obvious duties and conscientious impulses no man has *got* to describe the Grand Cañon.

But if you would really know the cañon you must not hasten away. Many interesting journeys along its borders, afoot and ahorse, are feasible from the camp. You may ride northeastward for sixteen miles among the piñons of the Coconino Basin and peer into the shivery depths of the narrow gorge through which the Little Colorado sinks into the arms of its big brother from the scorching sands of the Painted Desert. You may visit a little group of cliff-houses in the gullies which lead from the basin up into the northern fringes of the forest. You can grope your way into limestone caves far down the ledges. You may wander for miles along the brink of the cañon, winding in and out to head the vast amphitheatres which face the abyss, picking up old arrow-heads and fragments of archaic pottery. Here and there small stone ruins of the ancient folk stand upon overhanging pinnacles and spurs; and if you know the Pueblo Indians, the descendants of the cliff-dwellers, you will not doubt that dusky forms have in the old days lingered motionless upon these commanding outlooks, enthralled by the sublime spectacle, and in close commune with those mysterious powers in earth and air which fashioned it. A ride of ninety miles southwestward will bring you to the bottom of the cañon of Cataract Creek, where a dwindling relic of the Supai Indians awaits extinction in poor wickieups among their meagre cornfields and melon-patches.

It is not easy, where every outlook is sublime, to select a single point upon the cañon's brink of which you can say, this is, after all, the best. Altogether, it has seemed to me that of all the places which I have visited on either side of the river the one which is most impressive is a long high spur, forest-clad at the base and bare at the end, on the south side, about forty miles below Hance's Camp. This looms far out over the deeps between two mighty gulfs, and commands a stretch of many miles of the broadest and profoundest sections of the Grand Cañon. It has been called Sentinel Point. There is water upon the plateau near the base of the spur.

Do not go before you have seen the great valley filled to the brim with seething billows of cloud, and watched their fading under the touch of the early sun. You must see a shower march across the vast spaces below, leaving trails of heightened color upon the streaming faces of the cliffs. From above you should see the night close in, and strain the eyes to catch the outline of familiar forms grown faint and far and strange. And when the moonlight falls full into the depths, say if you can that down there it is still a part of the earth you know.

You should scramble down the trails and learn that it is a real river foaming and tossing over the rocks. But you will not win your way to the inmost spirit of the place unless you spend a night alone down in those awesome chambers—as far out of the world as you can get, it seems, and still hold the link intact. The going out of the day from your seclusion and the splendor of the world's night far above you, the unearthly sweep of the moonlight across the faces of the awful cliffs which hem you in, and the coming of the morning, ushered in upon your solitude in mysterious fashion from some invisible source—these and the memory of a hundred weird happenings of the night, which I may not linger to set down, will seal the enchantment when, again stretched in the friendly shade of some gnarled old cedar close upon the brink, you let the hours slip by in dreamy visions which each moment weaves afresh out of the mass and color of cliff and pinnacle and gorge and their veil of ethereal blue.

So at last we have learned where the old Colorado comes from, and have seen it sweeping through dwindling gorges out to the desert of the far Southwest. We

have won from the great plateau a re-
hearsal of its eventful story. The mystery of the country beyond the river has
been merged in pictures of a summer holiday. We know that those tiny uplifts
over there upon the farther brink are not
the puny twiglets which they seem, but
gigantic pines, through whose swaying
tops the wind moans and sings. We
could even prove, "an we would," out of
its miles of splendid cliffs, that the Grand
Cañon is, indeed, the masterpiece of
world sculpture. But when the last is said,
the spirit, as at the first, is swayed most
of all by its elusive, unearthly beauty.
Perhaps Mr. Warner, after all, was wise
to drop halting phrases and turn to visions
of the New Jerusalem.

Our way homeward leads past the Moqui villages, where we linger through
the weird ceremonial of the snake-dance
at Walpi. Thence the hot trails lead us
for eight days over the wide stretches of the
Navajo reservation, through a forest ruin
turned to stone, around the western spur
of the Carriso Mountains, across the San
Juan River into the Montezuma Valley,
past the long foot of the Sierra El Late,
along the western front of the Mesa Verde.
in whose recesses the great cliff-dwellings
are concealed. And so we straggle into
the ranch. There still are ten of us, but
it is in part another ten. For of the six
sturdy, willing beasts which started on
the way, only two have weathered the
privations and hardships of the thirteen
hundred arid, toilsome miles which make
up the record of our summer wandering.

The hardships of the way are soon
forgotten, but in the lulls of busy life
the memory is fain to conjure back
the spell of those serene deeps, which
woven once, nor time nor space shall
ever break.

THE CITY OF DENVER

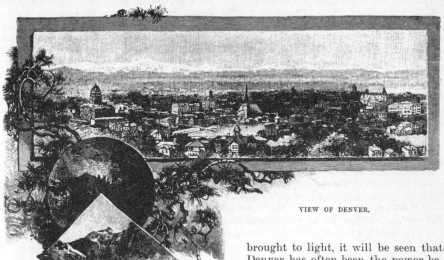

VIEW OF DENVER.

NEARLY six hundred miles west of the Missouri River, and almost in the shadow of the Rocky Mountain range, there has grown, from a small and insignificant settlement, a city that to-day is the largest and perhaps the most famous of any in the great middle West. No one would have dared claim for Denver, a quarter of a century ago, the proud position that it holds at this time. Then it was a mere village, without wealth, without influence, remote, and unsightly. Now it is a metropolis, a centre of refinement, a place rich in itself, influential, and the admiration of all beholders. More than keeping pace with the phenomenal growth of a region that is still in its infancy, so far as development is concerned, it has lost no opportunity, has neglected no chance. Active, keenly alive, progressive, and vigorous, it has turned to its own account the fortunes of the State of which it is the capital, and has secured for itself by every means in its power the reputation it to-day enjoys. When the history of the Far West is written, and the causes of that growth and development which we now applaud are analyzed and

brought to light, it will be seen that Denver has often been the power behind the throne. Her capital and her people have protected new ventures, kept alive the confidence in the future of the State. In the days when there were no railways across the plains, when the Indians, rebellious and deceitful, disputed the progress of every emigrant train, Denver never wavered, and her handful of settlers never lost heart. Through days of financial disaster, through all vicissitudes, there can be found no diminution of the faith that at last has been rewarded by the growth of a great city in close proximity to the region that as long ago as 1806 tempted the valiant Pike to cross the unknown plains lying beyond the muddy waters of the Missouri. Like a romance is the story of Colorado's growth, and not less so is that of the growth of Denver. We miss finding in its history the fanciful doings of Spanish adventurer and pious padre. No fierce wars were ever waged for its possession, no glittering pageants were ever held in the long wide streets, with their vista of mountains and plains. There was little that was poetical, but much that was practical. Still the story is as interesting as though there had been these well-worn episodes to draw upon and to magnify and render picturesque, for the tale is of how man came to a wilderness and lived down all trials and all disappointments; how he fought against great odds and battled with hardships, and came out victorious. And if we are not satisfied with the practical realities presented, and still desire some glitter of gold to lighten the narrative, we have but to turn to the mountains. In their wild fastnesses will be found the foundation of all the romance we wish.

At Denver Junction, a little more than half-way between Omaha and Denver, the Union Pacific sends a branch line southward to Denver. It is now that one begins to look eagerly westward for a sight of the Rocky Mountains. At last they appear. First the highest peaks, each white with snow, loom into view, and then one after another of the great blue-hued shoulders of the range is seen. At last the whole bulky wall lifts itself high above the level of the far-reaching plains, and one is face to face with the mountains that have tempted so vast an army across the six hundred miles of rolling plains. No pen can ever do justice to the beauties of the Rockies; no artist can paint them as they really are. They do not impress one at first as being mountains; they are more like islands, with the prairie as the ocean. Their coloring is exquisite—a deep rich blue, with here and there a bit of crimson and snowy white. It was well toward evening before we were near enough to define the contour or separate the foot-hills from the main range, and the shadows of night soon shut from sight all but the higher summits. They, however, were rosy red in the rays of sunset, and stood gleaming out of the gathering darkness like huge heaps of phosphorus.

In going westward from the Missouri one constantly gains a higher elevation, until at Denver he is nearly 6000 feet above the level of the sea. Each day the blueness of the Colorado sky becomes intensified. As we neared Denver the lights of that city blazed out at us from the top of the high poles from which they are suspended. It seemed almost impossible that the station we reached should be that of a place which so short a time ago was nothing more than a frontier town; and as we drove through the brilliantly lighted streets to our hotel, there was nothing to suggest that we were so far from home, and at last had reached the base of the Rocky Mountains.

It is not an easy matter to describe Denver. It is so similar to other cities, in many respects, that one feels doubtful about the propriety or the necessity of

mentioning many of its prominent features, and is in danger of forgetting that what may seem only ordinary, is in reality most extraordinary. If the city were less substantial in appearance than it is, if it possessed certain glaring peculiarities, it would be much easier to describe it. But it so belies its age, and seems so much older than it really is, that one falls to taking

CITY HALL.

for granted that which should be surprising. Wide, shaded, and attractive-looking streets, handsome residences surrounded by spacious grounds, noble public buildings, and the many luxuries of city life, tempt one to forget that Denver has gained all these excellencies in less than twenty-five years. Every tree that one sees has been planted and tended; every attractive feature is the result of good judgment and careful industry. Nature gave Denver the mountains which the city looks out upon; but beyond those hills and the bright sky and the limitless plains, she gave nothing to the place which one has only to see to admire. The site originally was a barren waste, dry and hilly. Never was it green, except perchance in early spring, and not a tree grew, save a few low bushes clinging to the banks of the river. Surrounded on the east, south, and north by the extended prairie lands, fast being converted into productive farms, and having on the west the mountains with their treasures of gold, silver, coal, iron, and lead, Denver is the natural concentrator of all the productions of Colorado. From it are sent forth the capital, the machinery, and the thousand and one other necessities of a constantly increasing number of people engaged in developing a new country.

From Capitol Hill, a rounded height formerly on the eastern outskirts of Denver, but now not far from its centre, is obtained the best view of the city. The scene is one that will never change. Rapid as the progress in the State has been, the mountains remain, as of old, high, stately, beautiful, their loftier summits capped with snow, and their wooded sides rich with coloring. At one's feet, however, the contrast between the present and the past is most marked. Gone are the sanded gardens with their weeds; the cabins of earlier days are nowhere to be found. A city lies grouped around the hill —a city of wide, shaded streets and stately buildings. From the height you can look down upon the score of church steeples and the flat roofs of business blocks. The murmur of the activity below creeps up to you, and in the distance lie the sea-like plains, no longer dry and brown, but dotted with farms and the bright new houses of those who have come to the West and accepted it as their home.

The history of Denver is interesting rather than eventful. It was born of the first Pike's Peak gold excitement in 1858-9, and in 1860 was simply a straggling camp of log cabins and tents. From this time the population of what is now Colorado increased with phenomenal rapidity. In August, 1860, there were as many as 60,000 people engaged in mining, and 175 quartz-mills had been erected, at a cost of $1,800,000. Denver during this era became the acknowledged base of supplies. The camp was centrally located, and was, moreover, a station on the Ben Holliday route across the continent. When the mining excitement subsided, as it had by 1865, Denver was too firmly established to be materially affected by the change in the fortunes of the State. Its population, indeed, was considerably larger than when the excitement ran highest. While many of the districts failed to meet the expectations once held regarding them, there were a few that proved richer than had been anticipated. Among these was the Clear Creek territory, forty miles west of Denver. The towns, or camps, in that district continued to hold their own, and were the main-stay of the settlement near the junction of Cherry Creek and the Platte. To Central City, Black Hawk, and Georgetown, Denver may be said to owe its continuance during that period when the future of Colorado was most uncertain. Had they failed, and had the mines there proved unproductive, it may well be doubted if Denver could have maintained its existence.

"The Queen City of the Plains," as the Denverites fondly call their much-admired city, has not escaped its trials and disappointments. In 1873 the financial shadow in the East swept across the plains and blackened many a Western project, and in '75 and '76 the grasshopper plague, by which all crops were destroyed, caused large sums of money to be drawn from Denver to pay for wheat and flour. The banks were seriously cramped during this unfortunate time, and all speculation ended. But the failures, after all, were few and unimportant, and the faithful only worked the harder to prove that Colorado was the centre of vast wealth.

In 1877 the cloud lifted. The harvest was abundant, the export of beeves was the largest ever known. More than $15,000,000 was added to the wealth of the miners, stockmen, and farmers. Speculation revived. Money became easy, and confidence wide-spread. Capital poured into the State, and there was a development of industries never known before. Leadville was born and flourished. Its fame was world-wide. Fortunes there were made in a day. He who had a dollar to invest sought Colorado securities. Railways fought for right of way to mining towns, and the plains were dotted with wagon trains again bearing people to the new El Dorado. For nearly six years the excitement continued unabated, and Denver, alive through all the activity to her own interests, which she carefully guarded and nourished, thrived as never before.

And then, in 1883, came the inevitable reaction. The pulse of trade and speculation had beat too rapidly. The pace could not be maintained. Some ventures failed, and others were abandoned because of these failures. The reckless suddenly became conservative. Investors hesitated to invest. Loans were called, and a de-

CLIMBING THE ROCKIES.

pression of values followed. But considering the advance that had been scored, the retrograde movement was immaterial. In the language of the stock exchanges, it was a "healthy reaction," and eventually did more good than harm. It enabled men to rest and to think. There was time given to study the situation. By the end of 1886 confidence slowly returned. In reviewing that year it was evident that the State had again entered upon a season of prosperity. And in sympathy more than re-established, and the population was nearly 70,000. It was found that the mines had produced a grand total of over $26,000,000 in 1886, and therefore mining received a new impetus. In 1885 permits for the erection of 403 new improvements in Denver were issued by the Building Inspector; in 1886 he issued 709 permits, the cost of the improvements being $2,000,661. In 1885 the total valuation of the State was $115,450,193 90; in 1886 it was $124,269,710 06; and in 1887 amounted to $141,314,329, the greatest gain being in Arapahoe County. Among the banks of Denver the year 1886 showed

Denver's sun shone once more, and its clouds were dispersed. By January, 1887, the tide had perceptibly turned. The activity in commercial circles became greater than ever. Old valuations were

the surplus funds and undivided profits had decreased $128,945 26 as compared with 1885, and the deposits had increased $2,107,633 02, or twenty-three per cent. The loans and overdrafts had also increased twenty-three per cent. The welcome facts giving assurance of progress, and which showed a more healthy condition of affairs in the various trades and mercantile institutions, afforded a promising outlook for the new year. Nor, as it proved, were the signs premature or misleading. The real-estate sales for 1887 amounted to $29,345,451 82, an increase of $18,324,242 91 over those for 1886. Six churches, three school-houses, nearly nine hundred dwellings, several new business blocks, and thirty-five miscellaneous buildings were erected. The total value of improvements in the city proper was $2,971,-770, and for Denver and its suburbs was nearly $5,000,000. The recently completed business blocks, among which are the Henry Lee, C. B. Patterson, Tritch, and Patterson and Thomas, are among the largest and best in the city. The new high-school was dedicated in 1887, and work on the Capitol was continued. Many large residences were completed on Capitol Hill and elsewhere, the condition of all banks materially improved, and the year was one of phenomenal activity.

Coming to a contemplation of the moral, social, and intellectual aspects that are presented for one's consideration, it is apparent that the city is again almost indescribable.

It would be untrue to say of Denver that it was "literary to the core," or that it was the "Athens of the West." So far as I know, it never claimed such distinction. It is not a literary centre, and yet it does not want for literature. A lecture on "Burns" might not prove so attractive as one on "Our Mines" or "Our Commerce," but because this is so the inference need not be drawn that a Denverite never reads, or that he does not know who Bobby Burns was. The people of Denver have not yet gotten over being practical. There never has been a Browning craze, and Oscar Wilde was caricatured in the streets. There are ripe scholars and diligent readers in Denver, as in other places of equal size. Indeed, the claim is made that there are more resident college graduates than in any other city of the same number of people. Therefore one may be safe in believing that the literary sense is keener than would casually appear to be the case. And yet in the sense that Boston is literary Denver is not. Perhaps in the daily papers there is evidence at times of a lack of careful attention to Addison. But when it comes to news-gathering, let the journals of the East take notice. The history of the world's doings is laid beside the plate of every Denverite in the morning, and no question of the day is too profound for the editor to discuss. The three leading Denver papers are the *News*, *Republican*, and *Times*, the last an evening publication. The *Republican* is

STATE CAPITOL.

FOURTEENTH STREET.

largely owned by ex-Senator Hill, and was established about ten years ago. The proprietor of the *Times* is F. S. Woodbury. The *News* was first published in 1859, its office being a rudely built log cabin. In 1866 the paper moved into quarters on Larimer Street, and remained there until 1880, when room was secured in the new Patterson and Thomas block. Closely identified with the history of Denver, it led an eventful life in the early days of lawlessness, and was more than once in danger of destruction by the calamities that threatened the young city. The present manager, editor, and largest owner of the *News* is Colonel John Arkins, a well-known journalist and an indefatigable worker.

Denver has not yet become so literary as to warrant the establishment of large publishing houses, but there are several wholesale and retail book-stores, and in one is a list of books as large as may be found in any New York book-store. This fact is not, perhaps, important in itself, but as evidence of the moral and intellectual growth of the city, it is. Denver is young in years, let us remember, and is the outcome of a place having little regard for things of a bookish nature. It is natural that many crudities should have been buried with the pioneers, and yet it is no less praiseworthy that Denver should so generally have accepted the more modern conditions of life.

Socially, Denver may be called a charming place. The security afforded by the active enforcement of good laws has drawn together a class of people such as is found in towns of a much more prosaic origin and greater age. Society, in the truest sense of the word, is cosmopolitan. There are constant arrivals and departures. No titled foreigner feels he has seen the "States" if he omits Denver, and our own countrymen endeavor to visit the city during their tour of the West. People of refinement make Denver their home for a season, and often adopt it for a lifetime. It is astonishing at times to notice the effect of Western life upon natures long accustomed to self contemplation and esteem. It is the air of Colorado, perhaps, that so often changes the Eastern man, and leads him to appreciate the truth of the phrase regarding general equality which the signers of the Declaration framed. Or, if not this, then something else works the transformation, and gives us, most fortunately, a whole-souled being who is glad to see you when you pay him a visit, and who does all in his power to render your stay delightful.

It must not be imagined, however, that, with all the good-fellowship, there is not the proper amount of conservatism. One is not waylaid upon the street and presented with the freedom of the houses he sees. Shoddyism exists—as where does it not?—and there is a manifest delight in certain quarters to make a lavish display of newly acquired wealth. But circles within the circle may be found, and those with the shortest diameter are the most agreeable as well as less conspicuous. Proper presentation means as much in Denver as it does in New York or Boston.

The best known social organization in the city is the Denver Club. Among its members are a majority of the leading men in law, politics, and business. Once a year the club gives a reception to "society," which is an event of the season.

Among those who have helped give Denver its present reputation, and who now rank among the prominent men of the city and State, may be mentioned the names of Henry Wolcott, once a candidate for Governor, and a lawyer of highest standing; Edward O. Wolcott, his brother, and the attorney for the Denver and Rio Grande Railway; D. H. Moffat, President of the Denver and Rio Grande Railway; H. A. W. Tabor, who represented his State in the Senate at Washington, owns many of the largest buildings in Denver, and was once Lieutenant - Governor; ex - Senator N. P. Hill, closely identified with the Argo Smelting-Works, and prominent in social and political life; Senator and ex-Secretary of the Interior Henry M. Teller; James Belford, the ex-Congressman; Governor Adams, the Chief Executive, and many others. All are self-made men; many are self-educated as well. Hon. H. A. W. Tabor enjoys the distinction of having had the most romantic career. A country store-keeper in the ante-Leadville days, and "grub-staking" a prospector who discovered the "Little Pittsburgh" mine, he now counts his wealth by the millions, and has done more for the welfare of Denver than any other one man. With a strangely contradictory character, his liberality has never been questioned, and his "good luck" is phenomenal.

The three great industries of Colorado, mining, agriculture, and stock-raising, are those from which Denver derives its chief support. As a mining region, Colorado has made an enviable record. The total yield of the State in gold and silver now exceeds $200,000,000. It is estimated that 100,000 lodes have been discovered, besides numerous placers. Silver was not found until 1870, but in 1886 the yield of that metal amounted to $16,450,921. Among the ores produced are gold, tellurium, copper, iron, and lead. At Denver is made much of the machinery used at the various camps, and to its furnaces and smelters is shipped a large proportion of the precious ores. Shipments from the Boston and Colorado Smelting-Works at Argo, on the outskirts of Denver, amounted in 1887 to $3,767,685, and those from the Omaha and Grant Smelter in 1886 to $8,053,143. Still another smelting company has been formed, which uses every modern appliance and improvement. These three concerns make Denver the largest smelting point outside of Leadville, and afford employment to a small army of men.

As an ore market, Denver is important. For 1887 there were 15,806 car loads of ore received in the city. Allowing 13½ tons to each car, the daily receipts amounted to 584 tons. The deposits at the Mint during 1887 had a value of $1,843,891 90, a gain over 1886 of 28 per cent. The modern practice of buying and selling ore through men known as public samplers is constantly growing in favor. The Denver Public Sampling-Works handled and sold in 1886 over 44,000,000 pounds, or nearly 22,000 tons, as against 13,433 tons in 1885. The value of the ore sold in 1886 was $1,243,360 84—an average of $56 59 per ton. The ore which is received comes not only from Colorado, but from New Mexico and old Mexico, Montana, Arizona, Idaho, Oregon, Nevada, and even from South America. The public sampler is a commission man. He receives ore from the miner, samples it, and gives a sealed sample to each of the buyers, who are the smelter and ore brokers. The buyers assay their sample, and make sealed bids for the lot of ore. On stated days these bids are opened, and the ore sold to whoever bids the highest. The owner of the ore may see it sampled, and is even furnished a sample. The smelters prefer buying of the public sampler to dealing directly with the miner, as they have a larger line of ore to select from, and are saved from dealing with a number of different men.

Agriculture in Colorado is comparatively in its infancy. Not until later days has the industry been given much attention. Now, however, by a system of irrigation that renders long-neglected lands productive, it is fairly launched. The area of farming land has been widely extended. Immense tracts of government land have been put under water and cultivation. Wherever it was possi-

GOVERNOR ALVA ADAMS.

HENRY M. TELLER.

ble, on the Arkansas, Rio Grande, San Juan, Dolores, Gunnison, and other rivers, canals for irrigation have been projected, and water taken out, to reclaim vast areas that were once considered worthless. In his surveys Professor Hayden estimated that Colorado contained not less than 6,000,000 acres of agricultural land. From reports made by the Land-office in Denver up to 1885, over 4,000,000 acres of that amount had been taken up. In 1885 nearly 900,000 more acres were added, and in 1886 fully 1,000,000 acres, thus making more than the original estimate. The crops for 1886 amounted to 2,100,000 bushels of wheat,

H. A. W. TABOR.

N. P. HILL.

600,000 bushels of oats, 250,000 bushels of barley, and 175,000 bushels of corn. The total value of the agricultural products does not fall much below $12,000,000 annually. Seed is purchased at the Denver markets, agricultural implements are made and sold there, and the cereals are returned to the flouring mills that have been built.

The third source of Denver's revenue is from cattle and sheep. The herds are

WHITTIER SCHOOL.

raised in nearly every part of the State, and millions of money are invested in the industry. For 1887 the State assessors estimated the number of animals and their valuation as follows:

	No.	Valuation.
Horses	148,027	$5,042,480
Mules	7,560	544,865
Sheep	685,725	877,913
Cattle	894,439	10,634,355
Hogs	15,833	51,573
Other animals	....	56,963

According to other estimates there are fully 1,500,000 sheep in Colorado, the wool clip from which would be not less than $1,500,000. Exact figures are hard to obtain. Cattle are being constantly improved by the introduction of "blooded" stock. In 1886 there were 122,678 cattle shipped from Colorado to eastern markets, as against 75,579 head shipped in 1885. Denver capital is largely invested in the industry, and the fortunes of many of her people have been made in it. The city is the chief hide, wool, and tallow market in the State, and several of the banks are founded on capital made in former years by the cattle kings.

In addition to these sources of wealth Denver has her home commerce, founder-

ies, street railway systems, and list of taxable property. The total revenue of the city for 1886 was $452,648 39, the item for taxes alone being $301,362 42. The assessed valuation of Arapahoe County, of which Denver is the seat, was $11,093,520 in 1878, $38,374,920 in 1886, and $47,037,574 in 1887. The rate of taxation in that time had been reduced from 20.9 mills to 9.7. The growth of Denver's manufacturing industries has been rapid. For 1887 the increase was between 20 and 25 per cent. In 1885 the total value of the product of manufactures in the city was $20,293,650. In 1886 the total value was $24,045,006. In 1886 Denver had 219 manufacturing establishments, employing 4056 men, the annual pay-roll being $2,100,998. As nearly as can be approximated, the statistics for 1887 will be as follows: number of establishments, 240; number of employés, 5000; amount of wages, $3,000,000; value of product, $30,000,000. The shops of the Denver and Rio Grande Railway at Denver employ 600 men, and the general offices of the road are in the city.

The water supply of Denver is more than abundant. In many instances water for drinking purposes is taken from artesian-wells, more than a hundred of which have been bored since 1883. Some are sunk to a depth of 1125 feet. The first flow was struck at 350 feet, the second at 525, the third at 555, and the fourth at 625. Six successful wells were bored in 1885, and eight in 1886. Water from these wells is deliciously pure and cold, and flows from the faucets with sparkling brilliancy.

For irrigation purposes water is brought by a system of ditches from a source twelve miles south of the city. For other uses it is taken from the Platte, and forced by the Holly system into every building. There are fifty miles of distributing mains, and the annual supply is seventeen hundred millions of gallons, an average of nearly 5,000,000 gallons per day. A company now proposes bringing water by gravity from Cherry Creek to a reservoir overlooking the city, thus obviating the necessity of pumping the needed supply.

The material at-
tractions of Den-
ver have not been
gained at the
expense of the
immaterial ones.
The city prides it-
self upon its many
churches, schools,
and public build-
ings. Gas and elec-
tricity are both in
use, and there is
an extended horse
railway system
that connects all
parts of the city
and reaches far
into the suburbs.
The property of
the Denver City
Railway now in-
cludes fifty run-
ning cars, four-

ST. JOHN'S CATHEDRAL.

teen extra cars, and three hundred and
fifty horses. One hundred and fifty men
are employed. The cars make 883 trips
per day, and there are twenty-four miles
of track inside the city limits. The Circle
Railway, narrow gauge, was built for the
purpose of increasing the value of suburban property. It reaches the southern
additions to the city and the outlying
parks and race-course. In the city proper, cable and electric roads have recently
been completed, thus giving Denver exceptionally good transportation facilities.
Still another home comfort is afforded by
a steam-heating company. Over one hundred thousand gallons of water are evaporated daily, and the steam is delivered
through five miles of mains and three
miles of service pipes.

As a city of churches, Denver ranks
next to Brooklyn. There are sixty-two,
all told, or one for every 1200 inhabitants.
A new Unitarian church is being erected,
which, with the land it occupies, will cost
$55,000; the design is Romanesque. The
Catholics propose to soon build a massive
cathedral; a corporation with a stock of
$50,000 has already been organized for
a cathedral fund. St. John's Cathedral
(Protestant Episcopal) is one of the prominent buildings of the city; the design of
the crucifixion in one of the windows is
said to be the largest in the world.

Next to her churches, the city is proud
of her schools. They are numerous and

ably managed. School district No. 1 includes that part of Denver lying east of
the Platte and Cherry Creek, and extends
four miles down the Platte and several
miles eastward to the plains. It is of an
independent character, and was chartered
before the adoption of the State Constitution. The property has an assessed valuation of about $29,000,000. A special tax
levy of four and a half mills is made for
school purposes, and from 5000 to 8000
children are in daily attendance. A new
High-School and Library building is now
being erected. It will cost $200,000. There
are fourteen schools in district No. 1, and
120 teachers are employed.

In West Denver are five school buildings
and nearly 2000 pupils. In North Denver
the several institutions have an enrolment
of about 1200 children. Besides the public schools there is the Denver University,
soon to have new quarters; Jarvis Hall, a
private school for boys; St. Mary's School,
under the direction of the Sisters of Lo-
retto; and Wolfe Hall, an advanced seminary for young ladies.

As a railroad centre, Denver is fast becoming as important as either Kansas
City or Omaha. The new Union Depot,
where centre the many tracks of the various roads now extended across the plains
to this seat of influence in the West, is one
of the largest and handsomest buildings
in Denver. It is built almost entirely of
native stone, and is 503 feet long by 69 feet

UNION DEPOT.

From 1876 to 1883 there was great activity in Colorado railway circles. More than one thousand miles of rails were laid over the mountains and through the valleys of the State. When Leadville was discovered, and a vast army of men surged toward that famous place, from which came daily tales of fabulous wide. The central tower is 165 feet high, and contains an illuminated clock. Two hundred thousand pieces of baggage were handled at the Union Station in 1886, and the passenger business was larger than ever before. The general passenger agent of the Denver and Rio Grande Railway, together with several other officials of the road, occupy one half of the second floor of the building, and in the other half are offices of the Union Pacific Company. The main floor is divided into spacious waiting, baggage, and dining rooms, and the grounds to the east of the depot are laid out in flower beds, lawns, and walks.

The first transcontinental railroad to reach Denver was the Union Pacific. It made its appearance in the year 1869, sending two lines across the plains, one from Omaha and one from Kansas City. The former was the first to arrive, and the latter followed the next year. Soon after the advent of the Union Pacific the Atchison, Topeka, and Santa Fe extended its system westward toward the Rocky Mountains as far as Pueblo, and was soon connected with Denver by the Rio Grande road, a narrow-gauge which was rapidly built southward along the base of the mountains. In 1883 the Chicago, Burlington, and Quincy Railroad, generally known in the West as the Burlington, pushed on past the Missouri, and taking a path between that followed by the Union Pacific and that of the Kansas Pacific, came into Denver. The city had now three direct routes to the East, and the fact that the traffic of the several roads more than repaid them for the expense of building, offers conclusive evidence of the commercial importance of the city at that period of its history.

wealth, the Atchison and the Rio Grande were both at Pueblo. From here there was only one known route through the mountains to Leadville. This was up the cañon of the Arkansas. Both roads claimed the right of way, and each disputed with the other which should have it. Excitement ran high, and the employés of the two companies were transformed into two contending armies. There were daily battles, some resulting in bloodshed, and all fought with earnestness and grim determination. At last the Rio Grande was declared victorious, and the work of laying tracks through the deep and narrow gorge was begun. The rate of progress was marvellous, considering the difficulties encountered, and while Leadville was still in the first flush of its sudden renown, the plucky little narrow-gauge was at its door.

By the completion of this one and only railroad to what was then the most famous mining camp in the world, Denver became the chief seat of supplies for the newly opened region. Leadville drew upon her unceasingly; and in meeting all demands the commerce of the city was greatly increased, and the merchants enriched. More than all, Denver profited by Leadville's wealth. Fortunes made in the one place were spent in the other. To-day, even, some of the richest Denverites are those who made their money in Leadville. In 1887 the Atchison, Topeka, and Santa Fe built its road from Pueblo to Denver, and gave the city a fourth line to the east. The new route closely parallels the Rio Grande road, and passes through Colorado Springs.

And it is now a settled fact that the Missouri Pacific will soon enter Colorado, and reach Denver over the Denver, Texas, and Gulf road, now built as far south as Pueblo, and once known as the Denver and New Orleans. How many other lines will in the future make Denver their objective point, time alone can tell. One may safely venture the prophecy, however, that both the St. Paul and the Northwestern will eventually enter it and strive for its business.

The railway communication which Denver has with the different districts of the State has been considerably extended by the new Colorado Midland road, extending from Colorado Springs, seventy-five miles south of Denver, to Leadville. The road passes through the heart of the State. When completed beyond its present terminus, it will enter Utah, and connect there with the Utah Midland, a proposed new line to the Pacific. The Colorado Midland now uses the newly laid track of the Atchison road between Denver and Colorado Springs. Eventually it will use the Denver, Texas, and Gulf track, or possibly become a part of the Missouri Pacific system. The road has an important bearing upon the future of Colorado, and gives an additional route from Denver to the productive sections of the State. Still another road of direct benefit to Denver is the Texas, Santa Fe, and Northern. It connects the Rio Grande and the Atchison at Santa Fe, New Mexico, and gives Denver a nearly direct route into the Southwest —old Mexico and the cities along the Gulf of Mexico and in Texas.

Besides its successful attempts to obtain control of the country lying south and west, Denver was not so blind to its interests as to neglect the productive territory of its northern surroundings. It is this district which the Union Pacific controls.

The Denver and South Park and the Colorado Central are both owned by the Union Pacific. The former extends westward to Leadville and the Gunnison country, and the latter to Idaho Springs, Breckinridge, and Georgetown. The two lines are important in their relation to Denver. As examples of engineering skill they are remarkable. The South Park crosses the mountains at an altitude of over 10,000 feet, and on the Central, near Georgetown, is the celebrated loop, where the road doubles upon itself in a manner which engineers never cease to admire. The favorite excursion for Denverites is over the Central. The road follows Clear Creek Cañon, a narrow gorge of wonderfully varied scenery, and places within easy reach of every lover of mountain scenery the famous health resorts of Idaho Springs and Estes Park. On the South Park road one gains an idea at least of the varied and picturesque beauty of Colorado. He sees its valleys and its mountains, and is made acquainted with the passes over which the emigrants of years ago used to drag their heavy wagons.

But it is not because of their scenic attractions alone that Denver is fortunate in being the centre of these two roads. The country of which they are the outlet

UNITED STATES COURT-HOUSE AND POST-OFFICE.

is the first that was developed in the State. The old placer claims there yielded fabulous sums of money, and to-day the mines in and around Georgetown have a yearly output that adds materially to the wealth of Colorado. No better illustration of this fact can be given, perhaps, than by taking the report of the United States Mint at Denver for 1886. The total operations of that concern for the year aggregated $1,500,000. Of this sum Colorado furnished $1,303,807 87, the several counties contributing as follows:

Arapahoe	$292 86
Boulder	20,771 46
Chaffee	65,602 81
Clear Creek	18,575 31
Dolores	379 05
Eagle	670 04
Gilpin	686,793 15
Gunnison	2,447 46
Huerfano	115 83
Jefferson	2,854 20
Lake	80,631 01
La Plata	193 08
Mesa	111 08
Montrose	285 10
Ouray	1,973 28
Park	54,552 81
Pitkin	13,603 96
Rio Grande	57,210 39
Routt	17,279 31
San Juan	8,707 00
San Miguel	54,813 60
Summit	149,686 28
Unknown	66,258 80
Total Colorado	$1,303,807 87

From this table the relative importance of Boulder, Chaffee, Clear Creek, and Gilpin counties, which the Union Pacific system reaches, is at once apparent.

The Mint at Denver is only used for assays, and not for coinage. Ore is received from nearly every mining State and Territory in the West, California sending $2821 11 in 1886, Idaho, $16,869 39, and New Mexico, $108,849 34.

The trade of Denver for 1886, including the product of her manufactories, amounted to over $72,000,000. Of this sum the smelters produced $10,000,000. The real estate sales, as recorded, were nearly $11,000,000. Property, compared with that in Kansas City, is not high. Prices are not within a fourth what they are there, are less than a third those of Omaha, one-half those in Los Angeles, and one-seventh those in Minneapolis. Following the depression of a few years ago has come no "boom" or unwarranted advance. The sales for 1886 were large, but were the result of an active and legitimate demand.

The business portion of Denver is continually expanding, and every year creeps eastward and toward the north. It seems reasonable to suppose that the centre of trade in the future will be near the County Court-house, and eventually surround that spacious structure. Lands that a few years ago were looked upon as far outside the city limits are no longer so regarded. Capitol Hill, which in 1882 contained not more than one or two houses, is now nearly covered with the largest and most expensive houses in the city. Residence streets have been rapidly absorbed by business interests, and there is a continual pressure away from the old centre down by the junction of the Platte and Cherry.

The streets, houses, and public buildings of Denver are most attractive. Bright red brick and yellow stone are the favorite materials of construction, and the effect of this combination gives the city a peculiarly pleasing appearance. The number of public buildings is still limited, but is being rapidly increased. The City Hall, Tabor Opera-house, Duff Block, County Court-house, and mercantile blocks would be a credit to any city. None of the streets are paved, and at times are uncomfortably muddy. In the residence quarter rows of trees line each thoroughfare, and there are streams of water coursing past them. In a majority of cases the houses are surrounded by lawns and gardens. Especially is this true of those on Capitol Hill.

Besides its County Court house, Denver will soon have the Capitol Building. It is now being constructed, and will cost a million of dollars. Ground for its reception was first broken on the 6th of July, 1886, and the foundations for the stonework were completed the following November. The Corinthian order of architecture has been adopted, and the stone for the front walls will be from the sandstone quarries of Gunnison County. Georgetown granite will be used in the foundations, and other portions of the building will be of stone obtained from the quarries at Stout, in Larimer County.

The Governor and other State officials will have apartments on the lower floor over the basement, and on the floors above will be the legislative halls, the Supreme Court rooms, and the private rooms of the judges. The legislative hall will occupy the west front, and will be 63 feet long, 52 wide, and 42 feet high. The building will be severely simple, having no dome or minarets, and will be 383 feet long and 313 feet wide. It is to stand on Capitol Hill, and overlook the entire city and its varied surroundings.

The climatic advantages of Denver, like those of Colorado in general, have often been described, and are now tolerably familiar to all. A clear, invigorating air, cool nights even in midsummer, mild days in winter, with now and then a season of extreme dry cold, are the chief characteristics of the highly favored place. One enjoying these blessings is loath to leave the city. Rarely is the sky obscured. Almost to a certainty one may plan for the pleasures of a week ahead. For sufferers from throat and lung troubles, Denver is a natural sanatorium, and now that it has every comfort of life, and has become staid, conservative, and stable, it will

OPERA-HOUSE.

add to its population every year, and tempt to itself those who no longer are able or willing to brave the discomforts of older but much less favored centres.

SAUNTERINGS IN UTAH

WHAT a strangely interesting city it is, this "Deseret" of the Latter-day Saints, which ordinary men and women who live outside the Utah Territory call Salt Lake City!

The Mormons would like to hear it always spoken of by its Reformed-Egyptian name—for Deseret means "the honey-bee" in Reformed-Egyptian (but what "Reformed-Egyptian" means probably only honey-bees know)—for the Mormons pride themselves upon their symbol of the hive, and are complacently content with their badge of the bee, the busy little insect that carries, as a Mormon hierarch has observed, both honey-bag and sting. While I was in Utah I sauntered about under a felt hat of Republic-of-the-Free dimensions, dispensing, unselfishly, a grateful shade wherever I passed. When walking in the noontide glare I could always invite a friend to come in out of the sun and share my shelter with me, and when seated, my hat, spread out on the ground, comfortably sufficed as a seat for two.

And very pleasant they were, those saunterings in the orchard-smothered settlements of the Mormon peasant-farmers, and in the trout-stream cañons that surround the Lucern Territory. Every State, I find, has a second name, and very picturesque some of them are, and if Utah ever arrives at similar dignities, I would suggest "the Lucern State." At any rate, it would be only common gratitude (by-the-way, what is "common" gratitude?) if the compliment were paid to that wonderful plant—the alfalfa of Southern Europe—for Utah would have found it as difficult to struggle into permanent existence without lucern as the early Briton without the traditional acorns, or the Piute Indian without crickets.

Speaking of crickets reminds me of an "idea" of which I am possessed, and which, if acted upon, might result in for-

tune. It is to prepare from crickets or grasshoppers a "patent food for Indians"! The raw material is absurdly cheap, and the Indian likes it. Where is the objection? Perhaps some needy capitalist may think the idea worth acting upon.

If he does, I can direct him where to go for the fattest and blackest crickets that have ever hopped under my personal observation. Throughout the whole Territory of Utah the cricket is one of the common objects of the country, but there are crickets and crickets, and it is just as well when in search of the best article to "see that you get it." For a consideration, therefore, I will put the speculator on the track of some of the grossest locusts that ever devoured green stuff—locusts, moreover, that *squeak* when pursued. Poets (American poets especially) are very partial to what they are pleased to call the cricket's merry chirp. But the poet's cricket is the insect of the domestic hearth, a pale-colored ghost of a thing, all voice, and with an irregular midnight appetite for the kitchen cloths that are hung out to dry before the stove. The Piutes' cricket is very much otherwise. It is the Jumbo of crickets, and just as black. It lives on the slopes of the Utah hills, among the sage-brush, and when alarmed tries invariably to jump down-hill. But being all stomach, and therefore top-heavy, so to speak, the ill-balanced insect invariably rolls head over heels, and every time it turns a somersault it squeaks dismally. To walk down the hill-side, driving a whole herd of these corpulent crickets before me, used to amuse me immoderately, for the spectacle of so many fat things simultaneously trying to jump down-hill, simultaneously rolling head over heels, and simultaneously squeaking, was mirthful enough to drive the dullest care away.

Apart from its substantial utility, the alfalfa is a very noticeable crop. For its sweet bloom attracts innumerable nations of winged insects, and these in their turn attract all the insect-eating tribes of birds. Nature works her wonders by methods that may seem roundabout, but the result somehow is always equilibrium. And so, though the lucern flower may nourish injurious insects, it also concentrates them for their easier destruction. In the mean time, the naturalist delights in the purple fields of blossom, and gathers in his treasures with little trouble.

"Have you got one of our horned toads yet?" asked a rustic one day as he saw me searching, after my fashion, for small game among the rose-bushes and yellow currants up the Logan Cañon.

"Horned toad!" I said. "Is there a horned toad to be got here?"

"Oh yes," was the reply. "There's quite a few about among the rocks."

And after that I always kept my eyes upon rocks in the hope of meeting with a horned toad. But in vain, until at last one day, wandering among the rocks that overlook Salt Lake, I caught sight of a frog-like object crawling across a slab of wrinkled gray-green stone. It looked like a wrinkled gray-green stone itself, but it was obviously alive. So I scrambled up to it, and the thing, as I approached, immediately squatted itself flat on the surface it was traversing, and with that instinctive assimilation to surroundings which is always so surprising, became at once indistinguishable from the stone it rested motionless upon. I stooped over it, and scrutinizing my captive, saw at once that this was the rustic's "horned toad."

Nor is the name altogether misapplied, for if ever there was a creature that succeeded in looking like what it wasn't it is this lizard—the *phrynosoma* of the scientific. I had never seen one before, but I recognized it from written descriptions. At the first glance I thought it was a frog, or a frog's brother-in-law, or something very german to a frog. But at the second I noticed that it had a short tail, and then (by experiment) I found it couldn't jump worth a cent, and then I turned it over on its back, and found its legs were all the same length, and so fact by fact I discovered that my new possession was a lizard—a very stumpy, truncated, spiny, horny, and knobby lizard, it was true, but still a lizard. So I picked it up and put it into my collecting case,

and when I got home I made it apartments out of a large millinery box, which I furnished handsomely, not to say luxuriously, with stones and sprigs of sage-brush. Inside it I hung up a piece of paper smeared with molasses, and then I put my horned toad in his cage out in the sun. The flies soon found out the molasses—and the "toad" soon found out the flies.

For straightforward, all-round ugliness I think I can safely commend the phrynosoma, but ugliness does not necessarily interfere with agility or other virtues, and the way in which this reptile managed to get outside of the flies showed that he was a professional.

Have you ever seen a "horned toad"? They are found, I am told, in several parts of the States, but are by no means common, so it is probable that the creature is a stranger to you. Imagine, then, a frog with four legs, all the same size, that end in long thin claws. Wrinkle or pinch up the skin on its back into ridges and sharp points and warts, till it looks as if the creature had been unskillfully stuffed with peas and tin tacks. Add a short stump of a tail to one end of the thing, and put on at the other end a head, all pimpled and peaky and spiny, to match the body. Finally, take a handful of dust and powder it all over. It is not a lovable object, is it?—not exactly the kind of animal to make a pet of? But all the same it is well worth watching; for whether in repose, pretending to be only another stone, or in motion when on the war-path after a fly, the "horned toad" is distinctly an "amoosin' cuss."

I was staying at the time on the shore of Salt Lake, and every morning after breakfast used to take a stroll with my pipe through the sage-brush that stretched from my door to the foot of the hills about a quarter of a mile off. I generally had my botanizing tin on my back, my insect forceps in my pocket, and a short alpenstock, fitted with a geological hammer, in my hand. Thus equipped, I was sauntering along one day, when I heard a soft rattling at my feet, and looking down, saw that I had brushed against a plant which bore a bunch of dry pods filled with ripe seeds. I stooped and picked it, and as I went along I kept rattling the pods in an idle way. All the time, too, I was birdnesting, for the sage-brush abounded in the nests of three species of birds, which from the eggs I knew to be of the linnet, pipit, and blackbird kinds. I used to find some every day, for not only have I been an expert from my youth up at birdnesting under any circumstances, but the ground here was particularly favorable. Your footsteps, as they fell upon the carpet of last year's sage leaves, were muffled, while the bird sitting on its nest could not see you, owing to the density of the sage-bushes, until you were close upon it. Sometimes, indeed, the hen bird would fly startled off her nest as I was actually stepping over the bush where her treasures were. So, as I went along, I was examining the roots of the sage-brush, and groping about with my hands among the leaves, picking up an insect here or a flower there, and, as I have said, rattling the seed-pods in my hand from time to time.

Suddenly I heard a responsive rattle, and looking down, found that I was walking through quite a cluster of the same plants. I picked a handful, thinking they would amuse my host's children, and soon after turned to saunter homeward. I had taken only a step or two when again I heard the same sound, and instinctively looking down, was just in time to see the last few inches of a dark-colored snake slipping under a tuft of sage-brush.

I turned back the tuft with my alpenstock, and as I did so the ominous rattle of the dangerous reptile sounded its warning, and there, curled up at the root of the bush, was the first rattlesnake I had ever seen, and the largest I have ever seen alive.

My experience of snakes of all kinds in Asia and Africa had long ago cured me of any superstitious dread of them, so I proceeded to experiment upon the "worm" before me. I gave it my alpenstock to strike at. The second time I did so it struck with such viciousness that one tooth pierced the wood, and I lifted the snake nearly off the ground by its imbedded fang. The tooth broke off, however (I cut out the tiny point afterward with my knife), and the rattlesnake re-coiled itself, and again sprang its rattle. In reply I rattled the seed-pods, and the snake responded immediately, attempting after each rattle to make its escape. But I jerked it back again, and continued my experiments, offering it my alpenstock to strike at. It struck at it seven times in succession, and then, exhausted, refused to be irritated into retaliation any more. During all the time the rattle was kept sounding without any intermission, though sometimes in a lower and lazier tone than at others, so that there seemed to be almost a regular cadence, a rise and fall, in the sound. But at last the snake grew weary of even rattling and hopeless of escape, and lay obstinately knotted up, with its head flat on the ground, peering up from under its coils.

I had half a mind to let the creature go with its life, such is my aversion to needless killing; but remembering how favorite a spot this was for pleasure-seekers from Salt Lake City, and what numbers of children are brought out on holidays to wander about among the sage-brush picking flowers, I killed the incautious reptile, and carried off the rattle—"twelve rattles and a button"—as a reminder for the future that all that rattles is not seed-pods.

How often, I wonder, during my walks had I innocently heard the snake at my feet and thought it was the plant? During my stay I killed thirteen rattlesnakes, and all near the same spot; so the chances are that I made the mistake more than once.

But, after all, the rattlesnake, from the very fact of its rattle, must be considered one of the least dangerous of the venomous reptiles. How many thousands of lives would be annually saved in India if the cobra had a rattle at the end of its tail! How immeasurably the terrors of the korait would be lessened if it only gave warning of its presence?

In the case of the rattlesnake there must be stupidity or deafness as a factor in every accident, for it is hardly possible to disregard so distinct a sound. While on the subject of snakes, it is worth saying, perhaps, that one of the most universally accepted superstitions in the world is that of the jumping snake. Wherever you go you are assured, even by so-called eye-witnesses, that snakes can leave the ground and leap up at the victim's face. In America I believe the error to be very wide-spread, for wherever conversation has turned upon the subject, and the company begins exchanging snake stories, the snake that "sprang from the ground" is sure to come to the front. Now, as a matter of fact, no snake can leave the ground to strike; indeed, it can only raise one-third of its total length off the ground at a time. A six-foot snake, therefore, has a striking radius of only two feet. At any point within that circle is probable death, but one inch beyond that circle is complete security. A six-foot snake of any venomous species is, however, a rarity, and though I have been often assured by those who thought they had seen them that six-foot cobras and ten-foot rattlesnakes exist, I believe in them no more than I do in that other persistent fiction, the ten-foot tiger. The largest rattlesnake I killed myself—and its rattles proved it to be an old one—was barely three feet in length. The largest cobra (and I have killed a considerable number) was four and a half, and none of my venomous acquaintances, whether cobra, korait, or rattlesnake, daboia, black-snake, whip-snake, coral-snake, or viper, has ever committed the colubrine impossibility of springing off the ground at me, although abundantly provoked to every species of irregularity by teasing before execution.

A singular superstition, to which I paid some little attention while I was in Utah, and which I find is still prevalent in many parts of America, is that of the water-witch. Rabdomancy, or divination by rods, is, of course, as old as history, and certainly therefore much older, and the very form of it which still flourishes, the discovery of subterranean springs · by means of a divining-rod, is known to have been in use in the earliest times of which any records have survived. The Bible, for instance, denounces its use more than once. Nevertheless, Christian bishops still carry it as the emblem of authority, and the divining-rod finds its professors and disciples in one form or another in every part of the world. All over Europe, in places remote from advanced intelligence, the magic twig is used for searching for water and for precious metals, and in France just now a professor of the science of rabdomancy has arisen in the person of Madame Cailhava, who claims not only the power of discovering hidden treasures, but the merit of having actually discovered them. In Australia the miners sometimes appeal to "the twig" for information, and I am told that in Colorado and in California the same belief in the mystic affinities of certain temperaments and certain metals is practically acted upon. However this may be, the location of water wells by the agency of the divining-rod is a matter of common usage in many parts of

the States, and notably in the West. Utah itself abounds in "water-witches" of varying degrees of local celebrity, but all held more or less in popular repute.

I found little difficulty, therefore, in making the acquaintance of professors of the art, and in their company I spent (I am half ashamed to say) many hours sauntering about with the water-finding fork in my hands. It worked with me without any difficulty, but the results very seldom coincided, I regret to say, with those of my companion's experiments. My twig and his were hardly ever *en rapport*, and the upshot, as a rule, of an hour or two's marching and countermarching was that there *ought* to be water under every few feet of the ground, and "indications" every few inches!

One man in particular has the reputation in the Territory of being a successful and trustworthy diviner, and there is no doubt of it that his reputation so far stands him in good stead that he is always in request, and always, therefore, at work. By trade he is a well-digger, but to this commonplace occupation he has added the more unusual profession of water-finder, and it is a curious fact that his claim to the occult properties involved in the second capacity is really the reason for his employment in the first. And this, too, not by silly, woolly-headed people, but by practical, hard-headed men of business. Thus he is locating for a local railway company all the wells along the new line which they are now constructing through the Piute country. He works invariably with his "twig," and as yet has not failed once. Yet who could say that Cedar Valley was a promising place or its approaches likely places for water?

Nor do his employers make any secret of their preference for a workman with a water-witch reputation. They laugh, of course, at his pretensions, but they employ him all the same. I have spoken to them frequently on the subject, and they admit not only the man's uniform success in placing wells in unlikely places, but their own belief that without the "twig" he would have been unable to locate them!

The instrument of divination is a forked twig, by preference in Europe a hazel, in Utah a mulberry. The prevalent idea that the rod must be cut from a tree that bears stoned fruit is therefore incorrect. Next to the mulberry in popularity is the peach, after that the pear, and after that anything. Even sage-brush is not rejected, and, as I know from personal experience, not without reason, for it turns in the hand almost as readily as any other vegetable.

For myself, after a careful experiment, I must confess I have no faith in the water-witch, and my reasons are these: that the twig has obstinately refused in my hands to dip over spots where it is *certain* there was water; that it has dipped in the course of an hour over nearly every yard of ground in a half-acre plot; that in the hands of a blindfolded person it will vary in its indications in such a way as to stultify itself completely.

The twig, in fact, will never say the same thing twice, and I refuse, therefore, to believe in such a very dubious oracle.

It is generally supposed, I find, that the simple fact of the declination of the twig is in itself remarkable.

"There!" says a person in triumph, as soon as the twig turns of its own accord, and against his will, in his hands. But, as a matter of fact, the wonder is when the twig does *not* turn. For the difficulty is to keep the angle of the forks perpendicular, and the most natural thing for it to do is to dip down, and the reason for this is almost obvious. The grasp clinches the forks tightly enough at first, and at first, therefore, the rod never dips, for the hands are dry, the muscles vigorous, and the will strong. But a very few minutes of such violent effort to keep the hands clinched suffices to make the fingers perspire, the muscles relax, and the will flag. The alteration is imperceptible to the performer; the languor comes on insensibly. But the twig detects it at once, and the instant that the force that keeps it rigidly perpendicular at first begins to lessen, it begins to decline. Once on the dip, it is more difficult than ever to keep the twig straight, and though spasms of muscular contraction may check it temporarily in its downward dip, the necessity for obedience to natural laws triumphs in the end, and the twig insists on ultimately having its heaviest point downward. Moreover, the very tightness of the grip has a tendency to accelerate the speed of the declination, on the simple principle that the tighter you squeeze a slippery object the harder it is to hold it, and also from the fact that as the twigs are not perfectly circular, the grip of the hand is not applied with equal force all round, and the unequal pressure

that results gives the twigs just the assistance they need.

Idling on the hill-side one spring morning, close to the city creek, I saw two hyacinth-like blades of green thrusting themselves up from the ground. "That is the sego," said my friend, "and it is good to eat. When we first came into the valley we used to consider the sego almost a staple of our food, and for myself I far preferred it to thistle root, which was about all I used to get to eat as a lad."

Thinking I should like to taste the original food of the primitive Mormon in the days before wheat and potatoes grew in the Salt Lake Valley, I dug up the root and ate it, and, as my friend had said, found it was good to eat. Indeed, cooked, I can understand its being a very agreeable and nutritious vegetable.

A few days later, being alone, I chanced again upon some sego plants, and proceeded to dig them up. The small boy who was carrying my botanizing tin and other apparatus seeing me at work, came up and contemplated me.

"That is the sego," said he. "It is deadly poison."

"Well, my friend," I replied, "I am proof against poison. I ate several the other day, and am still alive."

"Maybe," answered the lad, "you ate the *proper* sego. This 'ere's the poisonous sego. *That's* the proper sego," said he, pointing to another hyacinth leaf so nearly like the one I was digging up that I could see no difference between them.

But the boy was quite right. Had I eaten the other I should not probably have died—though deaths have not been infrequent among children—but I should certainly have been very ill indeed. The moral of this is, when you go eating sego, see that you eat "the *proper* sego."

Among the quests in which I busied myself when wandering among the Mormon settlements was that of Indian arrowheads. The central and southern portions of Utah were once favorite haunts of the red man; and hunting parties from the different tribes used often—when following game across the Utah valleys from the hill range on one side to that on the other—to meet on the Sevier and San Pete bottom lands, and there fight out their rival claims to antelope and bison. In later years, that is, since Mormon settlement, the Indians still continue to haunt the southern cañons, and again and again the settlers have had to abandon their infant colonies to the desolating Navajo. Nearly every mile of the country, therefore, from the Utah Lake southward, has its local tradition of Indian warfare, and nearly every river bend, willow bush, cedar clump, or isolated rock marks the scene of some tragic encounter.

A somewhat barbaric but very effective tobacco was also among my Indian experiences. I was on the extreme south of the Territory, on the frontier, in fact, of Arizona, when we came upon a lodge of friendly ("tickaboo") Indians pitched on the pine-covered slope of Long Valley, and I succeeded in accomplishing a long-cherished ambition, namely, smoking with Indians out of an Indian pipe some Indian tobacco.

My friends, being able to converse with the red men, gave them to understand that I wished to buy a pipe, and the assertion was confirmed by my producing from our wagon a number of cakes of tobacco, which I held out in the primitive attitude of bargaining. The gesture gave rise to much "how-howing" among the Lamanites (such is the name given to the Indians in the Book of Mormon), and eventually a pipe head was produced, and then a pipe stem, and after much grunting and ejaculation the one was fitted into the other and handed to me. Affecting to be a connoisseur in Indian pipes, I examined it with an assumption of critical preciseness, and then, putting on an air of only very moderate approbation, I offered two cakes of tobacco in exchange for it. A grunt of dissatisfaction was the only reply of the noble savage, upon which, as if after mature calculation, I put the pipe down on the ground with *three* cakes by its side, and assumed an expression of final determination. But they were not satisfied, and after some minutes of bargaining it was decided by my friends that I should *buy* the pipe for three cakes, but that I should "make a present" to the chief of three more. To this honorable compromise I gladly consented, and so the pipe became mine for seventy-five cents' worth of tobacco.

The bowl is fashioned out of a piece of a very heavy red limestone of such fine grain that it might almost be called "marble." It is three and a half inches long, with a bore about a third of an inch in diameter, the sides of the pipe being over a third of an inch thick. A second bowl, as it were,

projects at right angles from the first, the bore being nearly exactly the same, but this is intended for the insertion of the mouth-piece. There seems, however, to be no reason why either should not be used as the bowl, and, indeed, from examination of the bore, I am inclined to think that its late possessor used sometimes to use them indiscriminately. The mouth-piece is a flat lath of locust-wood an inch and a quarter wide, and pierced with a bore about as large as a 0.45 revolver barrel. One end of this is sharpened for inserting in the stone, the other for inserting in the mouth, a notch being cut about a couple of inches from each end for a bunch of blue-bird feathers.

Another cake of tobacco readily enlisted a red man to show me how to prepare Indian tobacco. We went together down to the stream and cut a handful or two of red willow twigs, while the boy who was with us picked a handful of sumac leaves, and another of wire-grass. Thus provided, we returned to the lodge, and the ashes of a cedar-charcoal fire being fanned into a red heat (with my hat, by-the-way, which one of the Indians unceremoniously took off my head for the purpose), the process commenced. The outer red bark of the willow twigs was first of all peeled off and thrown aside—it is generally supposed that the Indians smoke this bark, but this is a mistake—and then the under yellow bark was peeled upward in strips, but left attached to the twig at one end. As each twig was peeled it was stuck into the ground at the edge of the fire (sloping slightly over the embers), and the strips of yellow under-bark hanging down gradually curled up with the heat, crinkling themselves in a kind of rosette round the top of the twig. When they had shrivelled up as tightly as they could do the twig was pulled up, and the crisp bark crumbled off between the hands on to a clean spot prepared for it "on the hearth." The result was the "kinnikinic" of travellers, a pale yellow pile of stuff resembling "granulated" tobacco. Meanwhile the wire-grass had been roughly plaited into a little mat about the size of the palms of the two hands, and on this a layer of sumac leaves had been spread out. As soon as the latter began to wrinkle up with the heat they were turned over, and eventually, when they had ceased forming into blisters, and when, therefore, the moisture was all dried out, they were taken off and powdered between the hands, and the result mixed with the "kinnikinic."

I was now informed that the tobacco was ready; so, having cleaned my pipe as thoroughly as possible, and fastened my cigarette-holder over the mouth-piece, I filled Pukwana up to the muzzle with the Indian mixture, and smoked it. What was it like? Well, it was very like willow bark and sumac leaves, but not a bit like tobacco. It was neither narcotic nor stimulant, but rather pleasant, mild, and aromatic to the taste, giving out a profuse smoke of acrid smell.

My pipe finished, we exchanged howhows with our hosts, gave the chief half a box of matches, and went on our way down the valley.

We stopped in the afternoon by a sawmill, and while enjoying some delicious milk which was offered to us by the men in the shed, a strapping young fellow with a gun in his hand came up to me and asked me if I would like to have a shot at a "pine hen." I promptly accepted the chance, and taking the gun, followed my young Hercules into the pinetrees. After a while he stopped and "made a point." I approached, and looking up into the pine above us, saw sitting on a bough about twenty feet overhead a handsome red-wattled bird with rich plumage, brown, white, and gray, rather smaller than a caper-cailzie, but very much resembling it in shape and gestures. As it craned its head out to look down at us my guide said, "You won't get a better shot than that."

"But surely," I said, "you don't expect me to shoot that bird while it is sitting there?"

"If you don't," was the reply, "I guess it'll skin out."

"But," I argued, "can't you throw something at it to make it fly? Try a pine cone."

"It'll just go up the tree, that's all," said my guide, and, to prove himself right, he picked up a cone and threw it at the bird. And sure enough the "pine hen" immediately commenced hopping up from branch to branch farther into the tree. A little higher, and it would have been lost to sight altogether, so I tried the effect of a shot, firing well to one side of the bird. The result was immediately satisfactory, for the "pine hen," with a loud, horrified cluck, flung itself out of the tree,

and flopped across the cart-road, offering a mark when its wings were spread of quite four feet in width. To hit this at twenty yards was no great feat of marksmanship, and the noble fowl came down with a mighty thud at the second barrel.

A day or two later I should have been glad to have had a rifle in my hand, for in one of the cañons leading south to the Rio Colorado we came in sight, some two miles off, of "a mountain lion." By spending a whole day over it we might have stalked the beast with the certainty of getting a fair shot, but as it was, we could only look at it with impotent envy. Lighting my pipe, I sat down and leisurely contemplated this much-exaggerated cat as it sharpened its claws on the rocks and performed its toilet, and eventually strolled in an aimless, idle way out of sight.

How interesting it always is to watch a wild animal when it thinks itself unobserved, and is therefore thoroughly natural! At different times, in different countries, I have sat amused in the company of many wild things that never suspected my presence. Waiting, for instance, for a tiger to break cover before the advancing line of beaters, I have watched wolves and foxes, badgers, monkeys, wild-cat, and pea-fowl. Sitting out in the evening expecting bears, I have had hyenas and deer so close to me I could have hit them with my hat. Nor was our unconscious companion, the puma, less interesting than others. It stretched itself, and yawned, and washed its face with its paws, scratched its head with its hind-feet, and, unless my glasses did it an injustice, played with its own tail. But most of the time it was either on its hind-legs, clawing the rock as high as it could reach, or rolling on the ground with all its four feet up in the air.

In the Zoological Gardens in London the puma (or cougar, or American lion) looks a comparatively harmless and pleasing animal by the side of its neighbors, the true lion, the tiger, the panther, and the jaguar, and stands popularly classed with the smaller rather than with the larger carnivora, taking its place with the cheetah and ocelot and lynx rather than with the tyrants of Indian jungles and African solitudes. But in the Rocky Mountains the puma is "the lion," and I heard some wonderful stories in Colorado and elsewhere of the magnitude and ferocity of these animals, and of the prowess of the men who dared to attack them. Yet further from its home the American lion has only an indifferent reputation for personal courage.

There is (or was) a very fine specimen of the puma at one of the eating-houses on the Union Pacific line, I think Evanston, but even it, superior though it was to the average of its kind, seemed to me less formidable game than the leopards I had shot on foot in India, and utterly beneath notice as compared with the tiger; but in the West men have described to me very dangerous encounters in which they themselves took part—the danger, however, resulting, in one instance at any rate, from the assailants firing at the puma with small shot, a proceeding eminently calculated to irritate a beast of prey without seriously wounding it. I confess I should not care myself to face a puma in a cave after I had peppered it with quail shot!

Another Utah animal with which, in captivity, I made acquaintance was the wolverene. It was captured alive near Park City, in a prospector's hole into which it had incautiously descended (after some offal that had been thrown into it), and from which it was unable to escape. It took three men to drag the comparatively small but enormously powerful brute into the cage prepared for it, and the three weeks or so which it had already passed in durance vile had been spent by the amiable animal in gnashing its teeth and trying to tear its prison down with its claws and teeth. The wolverene, if I remember aright, is the State badge of Michigan.

Among the curiosities of Utah (and Utah, I take it, is the centre of one of the most marvellous regions in the whole world for natural eccentricities and wonders) ought certainly to be mentioned the freaks in the way of water with which the Territory abounds.

In the extreme north is a magnificent subterranean reservoir of first-class soda-water, which is forever bubbling and effervescing out of the ground in such quantities that, if bottled off, all America might be supplied. What a blessing such a spring would be in India! And what a delightful rendezvous it would make for a picnic party, every one bringing his own brandy flask!

In the extreme south is an exquisite circular lakelet that is always just full to the brim with water as clear and as green as beryl. And wherever the water overflows the lake's edge it incrusts the ground, and the grass and the fallen leaves upon it, with a fine coating of limestone, so that the brim is perpetually growing higher and higher with the imperceptible but certain growth of a coral reef, and in course of generations the lake will become a concreted basin.

Between these two points are scattered all over the country springs and pools of the strangest waters. In one place hot and cold run side by side out of the same bank. There is one pool only a foot deep, and situated at high altitudes, that refuses to freeze even in the severest winters. There is another that mysteriously replenishes itself with half-grown trout. One stream that I saw, though clear as crystal to the eye, and tasteless, stains all the vegetation it flows over a deep brown. A warm spring near Salt Lake City is the strongest sulphur water known in the world. A "hot spring," a few miles off, with waters so hot that you can hardly put your hand into them, and as bright as diamonds, is one of the most remarkable combinations of chemicals ever analyzed.

But, after all, is not Salt Lake a sufficient water-wonder by itself for any one State? I lived on its shores for nearly a month, and the mystery and beauty of the lake never palled. Its waters, which I had been told by some one who could never have seen them were dull and opaque, I found intensely, marvellously clear. The pattern on a plate lying twenty feet deep was almost as distinct as if in the hand, and as the bottom can never be disturbed (owing to the weight of the water), nothing that falls into the lake heavy enough to sink to the bottom is ever covered over. But there are not many things that fall into Salt Lake that are heavy enough to sink, and the novelty of finding myself afloat on water in which it was impossible to drown was a perpetual delight to me.

I rigged up a sailing apparatus, which acted admirably. There was a small block of wood (comfortably padded with bathing towels) for the head to rest upon, and another for the feet, and into each end of the latter I fixed an upright spar about a yard high, and stretched a towel between them. Attached to the top of each of the spars was a string, which I held in my hands, and so by shifting my feet as necessary, and working the strings, I could not only sail before the wind, but tack, my best speed being at the rate of a mile in twelve minutes. Laziness prevented my perfecting the apparatus; but it is easy enough to see that if the water is so buoyant as to support the human body, the human body might be treated by its owner exactly as if it were a boat. It could be fitted with sails and steering gear for sailing, or it could be outrigged for rowing, or even arranged for carrying freight. The body, in fact, could have this vast advantage over the boat, that it would be intelligent, and could therefore assist in its own navigation. And what a delightful spectacle it would be, a flotilla of such craft, with the parents hurricane-decked for carrying the younger members of the family! And think, too, of the annual regattas!

For in the water of Salt Lake a bather can lie on the surface of the water without any exertion whatever, or by passing a towel under his knees and holding the two ends he can remain in any depth of water kneeling, with the head and shoulders out of water, or by shifting it under the sole of the feet he can sit on the water. The one exertion, in fact, is to keep one's balance; none whatever is required to keep afloat. The only danger, therefore, arises from choking by accidentally swallowing some of the water, for the strength of the brine is so intense that the muscles of the throat are convulsed, and strangulation ensues. All the same, I have myself dived several times into Salt Lake, and have survived.

A fiction is current that nothing can live in the lake, but during the month of June I found two living things in its water, one an exquisite rotifer, the other a shrimp-like creature that was one of the liveliest and most interesting objects to watch that I ever had before me. Fresh-water killed them in two hours, but in the concentrated brine of Salt Lake they lead apparently lives of the most eccentric and determined gayety.

During the month of April, also, the beach of the lake was heaped in places for miles at a time with a drift, sometimes a foot thick, of a gelatinous animal matter, of which without a microscope it was impossible to settle the nature. But whatever it was, whether spawn or anything else, it proves the existence of such a quantity of animate matter of some kind or another as almost passes computation. In June this prodigious accumulation of jelly-like matter had been replaced by an equally astonishing accumulation of the empty pupa cases of some tiny winged insect. They lay in a bank six feet wide, and in some places nine inches deep. Mingled with them was such an immense débris of insect life of all kinds that entomologists could not do better than search the lake beach if they wish to arrive rapidly at a knowledge of the insect life of the surrounding country. Every wind that blows drives the winged things of the neighborhood into the water, and there they die at once, and at once are preserved in their natural colors by the antiseptic brine. The shingle, and in places the surface of the water, were covered with a myriad of small black dipterous flies, but having neither the leisure nor the apparatus, I was unable, to my eternal regret, to decide for myself whether the lively shrimp in the water, the empty chrysalis case on the beach, and the black fly in the air were or were not one and the same insect in the three stages of larva, pupa, and imago.

Nor was this all that I found in the lake, for I came one day upon an immense drift of small shells. I followed it for half a mile and more, and it showed no signs of decreasing. Filling a towel with the shells, I examined them at my leisure, and found three varieties of one species of spiralis—if such they really were—and one "cyclostoma." These may, of course, be fresh-water shells that have been washed down into the lake by one of the influent streams, and have drifted on to the beach where I saw them; but, on the other hand, they may *not*, and till some one proves the contrary, there is nothing to prevent the theory being held that somewhere or another in the lake there is a colony of shelled things living on the herbage which grows at the edge of the water. For there are several species of plants that grow within high-water line of the lake, and these, if anywhere in abundance, would suffice for the sustenance of these pickled mollusks.

Nor is the general impression of the great briny sea—that it is a Dead Sea, silent and avoided by birds and beast—at all in accord with the fact that at certain seasons of the year Egg Island is one of the busiest, liveliest spots on the whole earth, while at all times of the year wild fowl seek the refuge of its islands and waters at night. Egg Island during the nesting season is the haunt of innumerable gulls, of flocks of pelicans, and some cormorants and cranes, and it is one of the most remarkable facts of ornithology that the parents should, several times a day, make a journey of at least thirty miles each way to bring their nestlings the necessary food. Among the rocks and vegetation on the shores of the lake all kinds of bird and beast life find a place; the sage-brush is full of rabbits, gophers, "and small deer"; the brackish marsh-lands are the haunt of curlews, avocets, plovers, and other wading birds, while wild duck and geese (and sometimes swans) are found at times in great abundance on the very margin of the lake. Flowers of many beautiful kinds grow close to the margin, and attract a large variety of insect life.

Where have I not seen sunsets—by land and by sea—in Asia, Africa, Europe, and America? And where can I say I have ever seen more wondrous coloring, more electrifying effects, than in the great Salt Lake? They were too baffling in their splendor for any attempt at description, but it seemed, evening after evening, as if a whole world in flames lay on the other side of the craggy islands that stud the lake, and I shall carry in my memory forever and forever that terrible range of crimson peaks standing up from the water —that seemed all stained and streaked with crimson -- and then the gradual change from the hues of catastrophe, of conflagration, and carnage, to the loveliest shades of the loveliest colors, the daintiest pinks of the daintiest roses, and all the shifting charms of Alcinous's golden-gated cities in his kingdom of the clouds. It was a veritable Apocalypse of beauty and of power.

Needless to say, the lake is a place of legend and superstition. The Indians of all tribes agree in venerating this mysterious body of water, and their traditions have been handed down by the old trappers and hunters to the present day. The suddenness of storms upon the lake, and the extraordinary force of waves of such heavy water, the mere buoyancy of the water itself, filled the red man with awe, and the stern islands, rising so precipitously from the surface, were supposed to be the abodes of the spirits of the storms.

Nor are the other lakes of Utah exempt from the same superstitious associations.

The Utah Lake (a fresh-water lake south of Salt Lake City) has a legendary "monster" that inhabits it. Panguitch Lake is haunted by the ghosts of dead Navajo chiefs. But Bear Lake is perhaps preeminent for its mysterious reputation, inasmuch as there is abundant testimony on record—or the formally registered oath, moreover, of men whom I know from personal acquaintance to be incapable of willful untruth—of the actual existence at the present day of an immense aquatic animal of some species as yet unknown to science.

Now credulity is both a failing and a virtue—a failing when it arises from ignorance, a virtue when it arises from an intelligent recognition of possibilities. Any ignoramus, for instance, can believe in the existence of the sea-serpent. And Professor Owen, one of the very wisest of living men, is quite ready to accept testimony as to the existence of a monster of hitherto unrecorded dimensions. But while the former will take his monster in any shape it is offered to him, the professor, as he told me himself, will have nothing unless it is a seal or a cuttle-fish. In these two directions recent facts as to size go so far beyond previous data that it is within the scientific possibilities that still larger creatures of both species may be some day encountered, and until the end of time, therefore, the limit of size can never be positively said to have been reached.

With this preamble, let me say that I believe in the Bear Lake monster, and I have these reasons for the faith that is in me: that the men whose testimony is on record are trustworthy and agree as to their facts, and that their facts point to a very possible monster — in fact, a fresh-water seal or manatee. Driving along the shore of the lake one day, a party surprised the monster basking on the bank. They saw it go into the water with a great splash, and pursued it, one of the party firing at it with a revolver as it swam swiftly out toward the middle of the lake. The trail on the beach was afterward carefully examined, and the evidence of the party placed on record at once. Other men, equally credible, have also seen "the monster," but, *in my opinion*, the experience of the one party referred to above sufficiently substantiates the Indian legends, and establishes the existence of this aquatic nonpareil. Let the Smithsonian see to it.

SAN FRANCISCO

IT is the way of sea-coasts, as observed from the water, to maintain a close reserve. If they allow us to see a cliff or two, a suggestion of the green of forests, or a mountain in the background, it is as much as they do. They are in the habit of drawing in their horns. All their natural projections, from a steamer's deck, retire into a straight line. "You have chosen your element," the shore seems to say to the voyager sailing by, "and you shall not have the pleasures of both. If you can do without me, so can I without you, and until you take the pains to disembark upon me you shall know nothing of the attractions I purposely keep out of sight just over the line of my surf-whitened margin."

The coast of California seems of even especial moroseness in this respect. I came to it by sea from Mexico, having entered Mexico from the Atlantic side, and keeping the attractive journey across the continent to New York by the Pacific railroads for the return. We pass some large islands, and the inlets at San Diego and Wilmington, the Santa Barbara Channel, the bays of Santa Monica, San Luis, and Monterey, but for the most part the land of gold stretches on little broken. It is low, brown, and bare, and search is vain for any suggestion of orange or palm grove. It is a foreign-looking coast to one who arrives from the eastern shores of the United States. Lions might come prowling down over such slopes. It might be the dominions of the Emperor of Morocco, and we some other Crusoes escaped in the long-boat with the boy Xury from captivity under the Rover of Sallee, and afraid to land for the howlings of wild creatures at night. However this may be, if, in our great Pacific Mail steamer, we were discovering the country for the first time—as every new traveller really does discover a new country for himself, no matter what he may previously have heard of it—we should have tried along finding scarcely a safe harbor to put into for the six hundred miles or so from the Mexican frontier northward.

Then all at once occurs an opening through a bold mountainous range on the very water's edge, and we are at the far-famed "Golden Gate" of San Francisco. It is a mere eyelet slit of a strait, but gives access to a wide expanse of bay. So happy is the opening and so commodious the shelter that the reversal of churlish tradition by which the shore has been governed up to this point seems quite startling.

There is no room for doubt, when once the site is known, as to why San Francisco is located where it is. It has the only natural harbor between Astoria, Oregon, seven hundred miles to the north of it, and San Diego, six hundred miles to the southward. It has, with this advantage, such a relation to the resources of the country behind it that it could not escape a destiny of greatness if it would.

It is not simply a bay upon which we enter, but an inland sea with a commerce of its own. There are islands in front —round-backed Goat and Angel, islands like sea-monsters gone to sleep; and terraced Alcatraz, with its citadel as picturesque as a bit of Malta. Far vistas open beyond them on many sides, and there are gleams of light on white cities under lowlying areas of smoky atmosphere. San Francisco itself, close at hand, bristles up sharply from numerous hills. The waterfront is lined with shipping. A Mexican gun-boat and a French and Russian frigate or two are lying at anchor. Craft of all shapes and sizes cut across one another's tracks in the harbor. The lateen-sails

ALCATRAZ ISLAND.

of Genoese and Maltese fishermen and the junks of Chinese shrimp-catchers figure among them. Ferry-boats of a pattern much superior, as a rule, to anything of the same kind we are familiar with at the East, ply to the Brooklyn-like suburb of Oakland—already a city of fifty thousand people; to Alameda, with its esplanade of white bathing pavilions; to Berkeley, with its handsome university buildings and institution for the blind and deaf and dumb; and to rustic Saucelito and San Rafael, under the shade of dark Mount Tamalpais.

Yonder from Oakland projects the interminable pier of the Central Pacific Railway. It is a mile in length as it is, and but for being stopped by what was probably the short-sighted policy of opponents, it would have gone on to a junction with Goat Island, which would then have been made a city, and the terminus of overland journeys. Some patches of yellow soil on the right, under the Presidio, are taken by a novice for the "sand-lots," so famous in the late Kearneyite agitations. The Presidio, now a barrack, was a fort and mission at the time of the first settlement of the place by the Spaniards—to what very slight extent they ever settled it—in the year 1776. But the man who "has been there before" comes out strong on the arrival of a ship in port. This personage, planting himself squarely, with his legs well apart, and pulling his silk cap down on his forehead, points out that the sand-lots are not at the Presidio, but are the yard of the new, unfinished City Hall, in the centre of the town. But Kearneyism is dead and buried, he says—as the case, indeed, proves—and there will be no opportunity to see one of the traditional assemblages on them.

He points out, too, as we come up, the various hills, the Palace Hotel, the Market Street shot-tower, and the houses of the great millionaires who have made such a stir in their day and generation. Three or four of these, of great size, crown California Street, or "Nob" Hill, as it is called, with a prominence in keeping with their owners' station. They are chiefly those of the railroad kings, as Crocker, Stanford, and Hopkins, the Bonanza or mining kings having up to this time preferred to expend their principal building efforts in the country. "Nob" Hill is three hundred feet high, the more vulgar Telegraph Hill nearly as much, and Russian Hill, behind the first, also coming into favor as a precinct for fine residences, is three hundred and sixty. Murray Hill in New York is seventy-eight, and rises far more gradually. How in the world do these millionaires and the others get up to their imposing homes? All in good time! We shall see.

The city does not begin directly at the ocean, but a mile or two within it. It follows the inner shore of the long narrow peninsula which comes from the south to meet that coming from the north, and to form with it the strait and the inclosed bay. It is indeed an inland sea, this bay. You can go southward upon it thirty miles, northward as far, and thirty miles northeastward also to the Straits of Carquinez—with Benicia on one side, and Martinez, the point of departure for the ascent of the high peak of Mount Diablo, on the other—and through these straits into Suisun Bay, which receives the waters of the Sacramento and San Joaquin rivers, and is itself some twenty miles long in addition.

How strange it is, arriving from the other side of the world, to find the line of people waiting for us at the edge of the dock all dressed in the usual way, and chattering in the familiar speech, even to the latest bit of current slang! A China steamer, however, has come in just before us, and supplies a sufficient element of foreignness. The almond-eyed Celestials in blue blouses are swarming on her decks, and pouring down her sides. Groups of them are loaded into express wagons, and driven up town under the convoy of friends who have come down to meet them. Others trudge stoutly away on foot, with their effects deposited in a pair of wicker baskets, one at each end of a long bamboo rod supported on their shoulders. This is a way of carrying burdens constantly met with in the town, especially among the vegetable dealers, who hawk their wares from house to house. The figures thus equipped present exactly the aspect of those shown us in the cuts of the laborers in the tea fields. Nothing is more to the traveller's taste than the spice of foreignness. It is poor travelling when the curiosity alone and not the imagination is gratified, and San Francisco promises ample material for both.

The arrivals in the gold-hunting days of '49 landed some half-dozen blocks further inland than we of to-day, for by so much has the original water-front been extended, and built up into a solid commercial quarter. The 'Forty-niners found but a scanty strip of sand at the base of the steep hills. Why, then, did they stop here, where it must be such infinite trouble to build their city, instead of seeking some more convenient site elsewhere on the bay? There is—or was at the time—some serious objection to all other locations as well. At Oakland there was not sufficient depth of water. Saucelito, where whalers, Russian and other, had been accustomed to refit, was backed by Tamalpais, 2700 feet high,

instead of Telegraph Hill. Distant Benicia and Vallejo—the latter the naval station of the Pacific coast, and once for a brief space the capital of the State—were much too distant in those days. Steam was little in use then. The greater part of the ships that came in were under sail, and there were no tugs to pull them about. They must be able to get in and out with the greatest attainable facility.

Such ships as they were, according to the accounts we have of them! The most antiquated and dangerous hulks were furbished up to make this one more voyage. The freight of eager humanity they carried gave little heed to perils and discomforts, so it was but on the way to the goal to which all adventurous spirits turned. When the port was still but a beggarly scattering of huts and tents it mustered two hundred vessels, good and bad, at one time. Plenty of these never got out again. It was not on account of nautical difficulties, but partly because they had no return cargoes, and principally because their crews ran away from them to the mines the moment they set foot on shore. Certain of these vessels were beached and converted into dwellings; others, utilized for a time as warehouses, rotted at their moorings, and to-day form a part of the "made" ground. This remarkable young city, which had eight hundred and fifty people in 1848, twenty thousand in '49, has now, after an existence of thirty-four years, three hundred thousand.

The buildings on this level ground are generally on a foundation of piling. The practice prevails, too, of tying them well together with iron rods, against the jar of the occasional earthquake, which is among San Francisco's idiosyncrasies, with so many others. Along the water-front, which it is proposed to improve, in time, with a massive sea-wall, a portion of it being already built, are seen extensive yards of the attractive-looking redwood lumber, which resembles cedar; and warehouses for the storage of grain. The elevator system, owing to the lack of proper ships for carrying grain in bulk, is not in use in California.

Beyond, we pass through a precinct given up to a heavy traffic in the fruits and other produce of the country. Battery and Sansome streets are lined with large wholesale dry-goods houses similar to those seen in the greater Eastern cities. Montgomery Street shows stately office buildings, exchanges, and hotels. Kearney Street, above—all those named are parallel, and run north and south—has been the chief thoroughfare for dry-goods, clothing, jewelry, and the lighter articles, at retail. Its exclusive prerogative is passing, however, to the wide thoroughfare of Market Street, which is not unlike State Street in Chicago. Having unlimited room for extension in the direction of the trend of the peninsula, whereas the others named are contracted, Market Street is certain to be San Francisco's Broadway of the future.

The financial centre is the area of two blocks contained between California and Bush streets, north and south, and Sansome and Montgomery, east and west. Here are those great institutions whose immense transactions and singular histories are unknown now in but few parts of the earth. The Nevada Bank, the lever of the Bonanza kings, and the supposed emanating point of all the weightiest influences in mining matters, is found to be a four-story and Mansard-roof iron façade, decorated with the usual classic "orders." The Bank of California, whence the brilliant Ralston rushed forth in his trouble to drown himself in the bay, is two stories in height, of "blue stone," of a pleasant color, and an exceedingly sharp, agreeable cutting. The Merchants' Exchange, erected so long ago as 1867, is a very ornate, city-hall-looking building, of iron and stone, dark-colored, and with a clock tower in the centre. It is adjoined by the Safe Deposit Company's block, in similar style. A glimpse is had in the basement of this of a splendid steel vault, or treasure-chamber, decorated with a dozen life-size, gilded figures of men in armor.

The large and agreeably proportioned Stock Exchange, on Pine Street, is in gray granite, with numerous polished columns of the same. The board-room within is amphitheatre-shaped, and a bronze railing protects the circle of seats. With its agreeable illumination and bright neat furniture, which includes Axminster rugs in the central space, it presents a much more comfortable, home-like air than is the rule in such chambers. It is mining stocks exclusively that are dealt in. We find it quiet enough now. There is no lack of complaints of the evil times upon which we have fallen—complaints how that capitalists have withdrawn their millions to the East; that ships are coming only in ballast for grain, instead of

bringing valuable exchange cargoes, and are in consequence charging almost prohibitory rates; that there is not one "turn-out" on the Cliff House road where there were formerly a dozen; and how that real estate has shrunk fifty per cent., if in certain places it have any value at all.

But this board was once the theatre of a speculative movement which took hold upon the community like a madness. The aggregate value of the mining stocks which belonged to the list at the period of highest prices, in the year 1875, was, in round numbers, $282,000,000. The aggregate value of the same stocks in the summer of 1881 was but $17,000,000. There had occurred a shrinkage of $265,000,000, or more than fifteen times the amount of the total value surviving. What had happened? The "bottom had dropped out" of the famous "Comstocks," which had been during their productive period among the richest mines known to the history of the world. "Consolidated Virginia," which had been valued at $75,000,000, was now estimated as worth less than one. "Sierra Nevada" had fallen from $27,000,000 to $825,000. But the greatest shrinkage of all was in "California," which declined from $84,000,000 to $351,000. These figures alone explain a depression the vestiges of which, though the ruinous crisis is long past, still remain. The stock-gambling mania had possessed the community, hardly making a distinction of either age or sex, and when the bubble broke there was reason enough for gloom among those who had laid up their treasures in this kind of securities.

Some of the earlier buildings, which now appear of a flat, thin, unornamental sort, were obtained, nevertheless, at trouble and expense quite out of proportion to their plainness. The stone of which the old City Hall is made was brought expressly from Australia; that of Wells-Fargo's Express building, the Union Club, and others, from China; the granite of the fine Branch Mint was dressed in Oregon. The newer structures, however, exhibit all the modern varieties of form and color decoration carried out in excellent materials found in the State itself.

The idea of being upon a remote side of the world is kept before one by such signs as that of the New Zealand Insurance Company. It gives no mean idea of New Zealand itself, where a cannibal population were but lately eating mis-

"NOB" HILL, AS SEEN FROM THE BAY.

sionaries, that it should be able thus to send over and take an American city under its protection. Here are the Alaska Commercial Company, and the Bank of British Columbia; and here again, its inscription gilded in Chinese as well as in English, The Hong-Kong and Shanghai Banking Company. An occasional office building is noted without the usual doors, its main entrance and staircase, owing to the comparative mildness of the climate, being left as open as the street.

A system of alleys passing among the colossal business buildings is filled up with small refreshment resorts, such as "The Dividend Saloon," "Our Jacob," "The Comstock Exchange," and "The New Idea," to which the busy inmates repair in the intervals of their labors. The San Francisco boot-blacks seem quite a model to their class. They are neatly uniformed men instead of, as with us, ragged boys. Favored by the open climate, they establish their rows of easy-chairs upon platforms under neat canvas awnings which are not at all disagreeable to the sight.

The corner of California and Montgomery streets, in the quarter just described, may be considered one of the two focal points of San Francisco, the "Lotta Fountain" the other. The Lotta Fountain is a tawdry little cast-iron affair, which was presented to the city by the minor actress after whom it is named, and has been placed in a position of distinguished honor. Five important streets radiate from it, and its pedestal is a place where you seek refuge at need from the throng of vehicles coming along them. Market Street extends to the Oakland Ferry in one direction, and off (past the Mechanics' Institute Fair, and the popular pleasure resort known as Woodward's Garden) toward the distant Mission Hills in the other. Geary Street takes you by its cable road to Lone Mountain, around which all the cemeteries are grouped, and to the Golden Gate Park, which reaches westward to the ocean. Upon the top of

Lone Mountain stands up a dark cross, which recalls the Crucifixion. Third Street, a thoroughfare of the working-people, and abounding in small restaurants, markets, and "tin-type" galleries, leads to the water at a different angle from Market. Finally Kearney Street debouches here, and Montgomery terminates at but a few steps below the same point.

Parisian and fairy-like. A band plays twice a week, and the guests promenade in their several galleries or look down over the balustrades to the bottom of the court, where there are flowers, people in chairs, and carriages standing in a circular, asphalt-paved driveway.

Though the resident of San Francisco feels called upon to complain of its present comparative stagnation, the bare ex-

LONE MOUNTAIN.

The Palace Hotel, a vast drab-colored building of iron and stuccoed brick, looms up nine stories in height on Market Street, and closes in the vista at the end of Montgomery. It is so studded with bay-windows that it has the air of a mammoth bird-cage. The devoted San Franciscan, wherever met with, never fails to boast of this hotel as the most stupendous thing of its kind in the world. With the conviction that size is not the kind of improvement which all of our hotels, and our communities as well, most need, I should say at least that perfection in exterior design had not been reached. Within the glass-roofed court which occupies the centre the effect is more satisfactory. At night, when the electric light strikes upon the many tiers of columns as white as white paint can make them, it is even

istence of such a place strikes the new-comer with amazement. It has not an ephemeral air, but a fine massive gravity. Its shops are filled with costly goods, its streets with comely, beautifully dressed women. It has art and literature. The private galleries contain foreign pictures of the best class; a number of local artists have made for themselves much more than a local reputation, and there is a well-attended "School of Design," which has already graduated many pupils whose talent has been recognized abroad. Its "Mercantile Library" is the most handsomely appointed that I have seen in any American city. San Francisco "society," though a trifle bizarre in the use of its newly acquired wealth, has an understratum of unexceptionable refinement. Its most bizarre side, too, is certainly appreciated in Europe, where its magnates entertain kings at their garden parties, and their daughters are sought in marriage by titles of distinction.

The European traveller who has visited the land of Barnum and of Washington with literary intentions—though still capable, no doubt, of representing us as he thinks we should be, for some time to come—must be puzzled by what he finds here. Such a place particularly should be a vast motley camp, as it is known to European travellers that most American cities are. With its thirty-three years of existence and its heterogeneous elements, it should exhibit only a combination of squalor and mushroom splendor. The hovel should elbow the tawdry palace, a democratic boorishness of manners prevail, vulgarians blaze in diamonds, and the few refined natures that by chance have ventured into the midst shrink abashed to the wall. But alas! we live in an age of expeditious movement and labor-saving inventions, and with unlimited means such as are here enjoyed the work of years is condensed into months. Camp it is none, but a solid, luxurious city. There are Americans as well, not a few, who confine their interest in their own country to a small strip of its eastern seaboard. But, as it seems to me, those who will not see this original California, and on their way to it, the chain of cities across the continent, Chicago, Denver, Salt Lake, the Rocky Mountain chain, and the gold-bearing fastnesses of the Sierra Nevada, now that all has become so easy of access, are by no means living up to their privileges.

The association which perhaps comprises more than any other the best intelligence of San Francisco is the rather well-known Bohemian Club. It takes a special interest in literature and the arts —numbering the leading professionals and amateurs in these branches in its membership — welcomes distinguished strangers, and gives a monthly entertainment of a composite character, known as a "Jinks." Its grand festival of the year is a "High Jinks," which takes the form of an excursion into the country. The High Jinks has sometimes been given at night, in masquerade costume, among the Big Trees—the enormous redwoods of Sonoma County, to the northward. The ceremonies on this occasion are as wild and weird as the humorous invention of a

couple of hundred bright intellects can make them.

A population of three hundred thousand is not extraordinary, as populations go nowadays, but San Francisco is also cosmopolitan beyond its actual size. We are here in an entirely new commercial situation, which gives rise to what the French call a new *milieu*. San Francisco faces Asia, the great English-speaking colonies of Oceanica, and the islands of the sea; just as New York faces Europe. It enjoys already a trade with the Orient amounting to ten millions per annum in imports and eight millions in exports. The possibilities of the extension of this trade among the teeming populations in the cradle of the human race and of civilization, now that the circuit of the world has been completed, seem almost limitless. A way must be found sooner or later out of the imbroglio into which inexperience has plunged us on the Chinese question, and in the close intercommunication of nations which is at hand trade must flow unimpeded. Between countries separated by water, and demanding each other's productions, cities arise at the places of transfer and receipt, and with its situation San Francisco can not escape its destiny of greatness.

The Oriental trade is but a small item in the total as yet. The ships which sail out, besides those bound for the regular Eastern and European ports, are going to the British and Russian possessions in the North, to Mexico, Central and South America, to Tahiti, Feejee, Manila, the Sandwich, Navigator's, and Friendly islands— to all those far-off islands in the South Pacific, in short, which now in their turn promise to shine with the light of civilization, and become principalities and powers of the earth. Coals are burned at many a fireside—not of the most desirable quality, it must be confessed — which come from that far coast characterized by the poet in his line—

"The wolf's long howl on Oonalaska's shore."

Seventy million pounds of sugar a year are brought in from the Sandwich Islands, which slew Captain Cook, and are now a peaceful modern state. But it is particularly Australasia, and our coming relations toward it, that awaken admiring speculation. Melbourne has already more than 280,000 people, and Sydney 225,000, while along the coasts of that cannibal New Zealand which sends us its insurance companies are scattered also a line of flourishing cities like Dunedin, with 43,000, Auckland, with 40,000, Christchurch, with 32,000, Wellington, with 22,000, and I know not how many more.

Astoria and Portland in Oregon, San Diego, and no doubt, in time, ports to be created along the Mexican shores, will receive their share of these new influences arising in the world, but at San Francisco they touch us first and nearest.

There is a definite fascination in having arrived at the "jumping-off place," in being at the final verge of the last of the continents. An excellent situation to feel it in is lying in the brown heather at the last point of land above the Golden Gate—though it is a raw and gusty place too in which to lie too long—or looking down from the parapeted road or piazzas of the Cliff House. There is practically nothing between us and Japan but the Seal Rocks down there in the surf in front, with the sea-lions slipping and growling upon them.

"Ah! when a man has travelled," Thoreau takes upon himself to tell us, "when he has robbed the horizon of his native fields of its mystery, tarnished the blue of distant mountains with his feet, he may begin to think of another world." Very well! but travel has its compensations too. And as it may do a man no harm to come to think upon another world at some time, the reflectiveness may as well be aroused by this cause as another. At evening the Golden Gate is the gateway to the sunset. The orb of day settles into the sea, the size of a great cartwheel, at the end of the gleaming strait. It goes down precisely there where we have always figured it to ourselves as first arising in the morning. The circle is complete, and as the last extremes of every kind, even love and hate, are said to be identical in their essence, that old quiescent East has become the bounds of the impetuous new West.

What is the world to do, you say to yourself, when it has no longer a West? How is it to get on without that vague open region on its borders which has always been its safety-valve, the outlet for surplus population and for uneasy spirits? And when the race has quite arrived at this further shore, will it stop here? Or will it possibly go round the world once more, and yet many times more, starting

always at the highest pitch of perfection it has attained, and the weaker types dying out in front to make the necessary room, till it shall become in its march an army of dazzling light? Is the Millennium to be attained perchance in this way by a kind of cumulative motion, as the efficacy of a magnet is increased by the greatest number of turns of a helix around it?

The sentiment of gain, as is well known, has been the leading factor in drawing peoples around the globe. First it was sought in conquest, later in mines of the precious metals. Gold has been dangled like a bait before the eyes of the nations, or it has danced before them like Ariel or a will-o'-the-wisp. Tantalized and disappointed as a rule, after floundering on a certain way, they have paused to develop the new lands in which they found themselves. But now at length, when all the vacant spaces are full, and the need of subterfuge seems exhausted, the golden bait is cast down to be gorged by those who have found it. Never before the hegira of '49 were its followers rewarded with such an unstinted liberality. The treasures of the earth were piled up in the fastnesses of these far Pacific ranges. The yield since the year 1848 has been $2,100,000,000, and it is still going on at the rate of $80,000,000 a year.

Gold was scattered at first in the very sands, later it was washed out of high gravel-banks by the hydraulic process, and later it was got by improved machinery from the quartz rock. When the gold began to diminish, it was followed by the great silver discoveries, the "Bonanza" mines of Nevada. Consolidated Virginia alone produced in seven years $65,000,000 in gold and silver.

What fabulous sums besides—to leave our speculations on the shore, and go back to town—the individual managers made by the ingenious process of "milking the market," I do not undertake to compute. The prices of this celebrated stock at successive dates, not very far apart, were $17 a share, then $1, then $110, then $42, then $700, and then, in the final collapse in 1875, little or nothing at all. I have been shown a poor saloon called the "Auction Lunch," on Washington Street, near the Post-office, which is said to have been kept by the firm of barkeepers, Flood and O'Brien, who later attained to such a splendid prosperity. There is no historic tablet over the door, but one naturally looks with none the less admiration and awe at the place where the beginnings of such things could be. The proprietors of the Auction Lunch, it appears, were in the habit of receiving gold-dust occasionally in a friendly way from miners, and locking it up for safe-keeping while the owners were enjoying themselves about town. It was from these persons that they obtained the "points" which resulted in their getting possession first of "Hale and Norcross," and then of the greater properties on the Comstock lode.

I have seen, too, a friend of theirs of those early times, whose fortunes have not mended at the same pace. He descanted on the inequalities of fate, and on what he termed "bull-dog luck." He was prepared to prove that they were not even good business men, though "Jimmy" Flood does go about "with a wise air," and "Billy" O'Brien at his death left half a million dollars apiece to eight or ten nieces.

There is hardly a limit to the exceptional characters and exceptional doings to be heard of in San Francisco. Though the city affect—or has been driven into—a quiet air now, it has hardly ever done anything up to this time like any other place. It began with the wild life of the Argonauts of '49, which Bret Harte has so entertainingly portrayed. It had had six great fires, which destroyed property to the amount of $23,000,000, when yet less than three years of age. It was ruled for months in the year 1856 by a vigilance committee, which rid it of eight hundred evil-doers of one sort and another, the worst by summary execution, the rest by banishment.

The politics of the State before the war were Democratic, with a rather strong Southern bias. There was a long feud between the two great Senatorial paladins, Broderick and Gwin, which resulted in the death of Broderick by the duelling pistol of one of the partisans of the latter. There was the long fight against and final deliverance from the incubus of forged Spanish land titles, the manufacture of which, it was proven, "had become a business and a trade," and which covered the whole area of the city many times over. Then came the war, and the peculiarities growing out of the retention here of a solid currency, while the rest of the country was deluged with depreciated paper. The brilliant period later, when the

Bonanza mines were pouring out their floods of riches, and the favorite stocks were running delightfully up and down the gamut from $1 to $700 a share, was followed, when the excitement was over, by a depression of the blackest sort. In the unbearable disappointment of their losses, and the stagnation of trade, a considerable part of the community snatched at a theory held out to them by demagogues, that it was the political institutions which were somehow to blame. Upon this basis a singular new party, wild and half communistic in character, arose, and met with a brief success. The truckman Denis Kearney, its Caius Gracchus or Watt Tyler, set it in motion with blasphemous mouthings from his improvised tribune in the sand-lots. It elected a Mayor, who was at the same time Baptist preacher, and whose son, preacher too, rode up one day and assassinated at his door a newspaper editor who had passed strictures on their course. It voted a new constitution, which was thought to be but a prelude to universal confiscation, and before which capital fled in alarm. And finally, this remarkable city, having had the fortune to be the recipient of a Chinese immigration which has given a part of it the aspect of a settlement in the Flowery Kingdom, has allowed itself to be agitated by fears of a complete subversion by Orientalism, and has originated new problems in political economy and international law.

After but a tithe of such violent emotions and novel experiences it might seem that any city would be glad to rest awhile, and San Francisco seems entering upon a new period, and more likely to do things in a normal way henceforth than ever before. There has been a time of contemplation, and the lessons of the past have struck in. As affairs have slowly improved the violence of the reaction has disappeared, as well as the unhealthy inflation that gave it birth. The new political craze was of but short duration. I have never seen anywhere so quietly conducted an election as that of the last autumn, which dismissed the Kearney-Kalloch party from power. A special provision prevents the approach of any person but the voter immediately engaged in voting within one hundred feet of a polling-place. It is probable that our newspapers have exaggerated, as the way is to exaggerate doings at a distance, and many expected to see Chinamen dead and maimed at every

CHINESE FISHING-BOATS IN THE BAY.

corner, or fleeing before infuriated crowds. But though some San Franciscans have their own belief in the undesirability of a great Chinese immigration, during all my stay I neither saw nor heard of an attempt to molest any individual on account of it.

The new constitution itself proved a harmless bugaboo. It is a most gratifying tribute, in fact, to the power of native common-sense and Anglo-Saxon ideas upon communities trained up under their domination that this instrument, framed in a time of great excitement, and, as was charged, with the most subversive intentions, should contain not only so little that is dangerous, but so much that is in a high degree commendable. It does no harm to property. Frightened capital may return with entire safety. I will profess myself so far an anarchist and person of incendiary opinions as to hold that an honest directness of purpose in this new constitution, and its effort to lessen and simplify legislation, to sweep away embarrassments which one has often to think are maintained rather in the interest of legislators and lawyers than of the public good, are well worthy of imitation elsewhere.

The actual physical and commercial conditions also are changing. Life is no longer to depend upon spasmodic "finds" of treasure, but on the more humdrum and legitimate industries. Mining, though the supply of metals, through the introduction of improved machinery, holds out in a uniform way, takes a lesser rank, and agriculture and manufacturing come to the front. California produces a wheat crop of $50,000,000, a wool crop of $10,000,000, wines to the amount of $4,000,000, and fruits probably worth as much more, though these last two branches are but in their infancy. Of the greater part of these San Francisco is the *entrepôt*. And the smoke of the soft coals of Alaska, Oregon, and Australia thickens the air to some purpose, since it means the production in the city of manufactured articles to the amount of $75,000,000 per annum.

Kearney Street (sharing its distinction now with Market Street) has been in times past, in sunshiny weather, the favorite promenade of all the leisurely and well-dressed. It abounds in jewellers. These seem to combine very often the business of pawnbroking with the other, and to prefix "Uncle" to their names. Thus, Uncle Johnsons, Uncle Jacksons, and Uncle Thompsons await the visitor all along with a friendly air. There are naturally

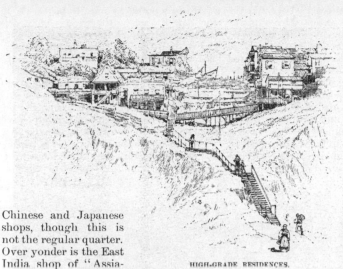

HIGH-GRADE RESIDENCES.

Chinese and Japanese shops, though this is not the regular quarter. Over yonder is the East India shop of "Assiamull and Wassiamull." Probably such distinguished foreigners as English lords, M.P.'s, and younger sons, German barons and Russian princes, on their way around the world, are not really more numerous here than in New York, but they seem more numerous in proportion. The books of the Palace Hotel are seldom free of them, and they are detected on the street at a glance, strolling, or gazing with interest at the large photographs of the Yosemite, the Big Trees, and other wonders, at the corners.

There is a certain genial feeling about Kearney Street. It arises partly, I think, from its being on a level exactly at the foot of the steep hills. The temptation is to linger there as long as possible. The instant you leave it to go to the residence portion of the town you begin a backbreaking climb. To ascend is like going upstairs, and nothing less.

The San Francisco householder, and the Crœsus particularly, has "a station like the herald Mercury new-lighted on a heaven-kissing hill." How in the world, I have asked, does he get up there? Well, then, by the cable roads. I should consider the cable road one of the very foremost in the list of curiosities, though I have been able to refrain till now from bringing it forward. It is a peculiar kind of tramway, quite as useful on a level, but invented expressly for the purpose of overcoming steep elevations. Two cars, coupled together, are seen moving, at a high rate of speed, without jar and in perfect safety, up and down all the extraordinary undulations of the ground. They have no horse, no steam, no vestiges of machinery, no ostensible means of locomotion. The astonished comment of the Chinaman observing this marvel for the first time, old as it is, may be worth repeating once more for its quaint force: "Melican man's wagon, no pushee, no pullee; all same go top-side hill like flashee." The solution of the mystery is in an endless wire cable hidden in a box in the roadbed, and turning over a great wheel in an engine-house at the top of the hill. The foremost of the two cars is provided with a grip or pincers, running underneath it, through a continuous crevice in the same box as the cable, and managed by a conductor. When he wishes to go on he clutches the always-moving cable, and goes with it; if he wishes to stop, he simply lets go and puts on a brake. Fortunately there is no snow and ice in this climate to clog the central crevice, which, by the necessities of the case, must be open. The system has been applied, however, with emendations, in Chicago, and no doubt could be in New York.

The great houses on the hill, like almost all the residences of the city, are found to be of wood. It seems a pity, to the outsider, considering the money spent, that they should be. The fact is attributed to the superior warmth and dryness of wood over brick or stone in a moist, cool climate, and also to its greater security against earthquakes. Whatever the reason, the San Francisco Crœsuses have reared for themselves palaces which might be swept off by a breath, and leave no trace of their existence. Their architecture has nothing to commend it to favor. They are large, rather over-ornate, and of no particular style. The Hopkins residence, which is a costly Gothic château, carried out, like the rest, in wood, may be excepted from this description. The basement stories, however, are of stone, and there is a deal of work in these and in foundations which would build many a first-class Eastern mansion alone. To prepare sites for habitations on these steep hills has been an enormous labor and expense. The part played by retaining-walls, terraces, and staircases of approach is extraordinary. The merest wooden cottage is prefaced by works of this kind, which outweigh its own importance a dozen to one.

When a peerage comes to be drawn up for San Francisco the grader of streets will probably follow the railroad and mining capitalist as the founder of a family. To hardly anybody else can such an amount of lucrative employment have been open. What cutting and filling! what gravelling and paving! Striking freaks of surface and arrangement result from the peculiar conditions. The city might have been terraced up with an aspect like Genoa, or Naples above the Chiaja. It is picturesque still, in the thin American way, through the absolute force of circum-

CORNER OF JACKSON AND DUPONT STREETS,
SAN FRANCISCO.

BALCONY IN THE CHINESE QUARTER.

stances. You enter the retaining-walls of stone or plank through doorways or grated archways like the postern-gates of castles. You pass up stone steps in tunnels or vine-covered arbors within these; or else zigzag from landing to landing of long wooden stairways mounting without. Odd little terrace streets and "places," as Charles Place, with bits of gardens before the houses, are found sandwiched between the more regular formations. A wide thoroughfare called Second Street has been cut through Rincon Hill, the Nob Hill of a former day, in order to afford access to water for vehicles in that part of the town. Some old houses, with a few cypress-trees standing in front of them, have here been left isolated on the banks, and are only to be approached by wooden staircases almost interminable. Dark at sunset against the red of the sky, they present an effect to delight the heart of the etcher.

In this line, however, nothing is quite equal to Telegraph Hill, which bristles now with the make-shift contrivances of a much humbler population. Bret Harte, who tells us that he lived there at one time, asserts that the Telegraph Hill goats were accustomed to browse on his pots of geranium in the second-story windows, and to prance about on the roof at night so that a new-comer thought it a hailstorm. Elsewhere, instead of precipices, you come to gloomy hollows, and looking down from the causeway, see some figure, a poor woman possibly sewing in a bay-window once filled with sunshine and air, but now commanding only a view of mildewed wall.

The views from the hills are of no common order, as may be imagined. As you rise on the cable road you seem to hang in the air above the body of the city, and above the harbor and its environment. The Clay Street road, one of the very steepest, passes through the Chinese quarter. Half-way up you have an ensign, consisting of a blue and crimson dragon upon an orange field, on the ordinary dwelling-house used as the Chinese consulate-general, flying as a bright bit of color in the foreground. The bay, so far below the eye, has a flat, opaque look. On some rare days it is very blue in color, but oftener it is slate or greenish gray, and the passing vessels criss-cross the white lines of their wakes upon it like pencil-marks on the slate. The prevailing atmosphere above it is rarely clear. Some wisp of fog is generally sneaking in at the Golden Gate, or lurking under the shore of dark Tamalpais, waiting its opportunity to rush over and seize upon the city. An obscurity compounded in part of fog and partly of coal smoke hovers in areas, now enveloping only the town, now the prospect, so that nothing can be seen from it, though the town itself be free. And now it lifts momentarily from the horizon, and shows glimpses of distant islands and cities, and of the peak of Mount Diablo thirty miles away, then shuts down upon them again as if they were but figments of the imagination. The bird's-eye view of the lights of the city at night is particularly striking. The street gas lamps, set in constellations, or radiating in formal lines, recall the bivouac of a mighty army. It is as if the hosts of Armageddon were encamped round about awaiting the final conflict. For several days, from California Street Hill, I was favored with the spectacle of a devastating fire in the woods on Mount Tamalpais. Its dark smoke rendered the sunsets lurid and ominous, and at night the burning mountain, reflected red in the bay, was like a dreadful Vesuvius or Hecla.

One is hardly yet supposed to travel much in an American town. One makes journeys in America for a definite object —because he has business. No doubt if we could bring ourselves to the same receptive frame of mind as in Europe, the same readiness to be amused by a travelling acquaintance, by all the odds and ends of experience that go to make up the sum of pleasure there—no doubt a great deal more could be got than is usually the case both out of American journeys and the places at which they terminate. San Francisco at least is not without a few of those details of exactly the kind which receive the attention of the leisurely traveller abroad. Their chief defect is their thin American setting. It must be admitted that this seems particularly thin on coming direct from the massive solidity of Mexico. The first thing at which I marvelled on coming ashore was the spider lines of the American buggy, the next at a frame house. It seems that we are getting ready to fly, while the Mexicans burrow in caves.

The fishermen are worth a visit. The Italians eat their macaroni, and drink their red wine, and wait upon the tides, about the vicinity of Broadway and Front streets. The Italian colony is numerous. The part of it which remains on shore is largely grocers, butchers, and restaurateurs. The Chinese shrimp-catchers are found in the cove at Potrero, behind the immense new manufacturing buildings of that quarter, and again at San Bruno Point, twelve miles down the bay. None of their boats or junks are on a large scale, but they display the usual peculiarities of their nautical architecture.

The French colony is also numerous, and their language heard upon the street continually. Taking advantage of the variety and excellence of supplies in the markets, French restaurants furnish repasts—including usually a half-bottle of wine of the country—of quite extraordinary cheapness. A considerable Mexican and Spanish contingent mingles with the Italians along Upper Dupont, Vallejo, and Green streets. Shops with such titles as *La Sorpresa* and the *Tienda Mexicana* adjoin there the *Unità d' Italia* and the *Roma* saloon. A Mexican military company, as at Los Angeles, marches with the red, white, and green tricolor on the anniversary of the national independence in September. During the Carnival a form of entertainment known as "Cascaron parties" prevails among the Spanish residents. The participants pelt one another with egg-shells which have been filled with gilt and colored papers. Sometimes a canvas fort is erected in the street, and attacked and defended with these missiles and with handfuls of flour. Such Spanish life as there is can hardly be said to have remained from the early days, since the Spanish settlement at best was so infinitesimal. It has been attracted here in the mean time like any other immigration. I recollect a dusky mother, in a palm-thatched hut on the far Acapulco trail, who told me that her son had gone away to San Francisco twenty years before and become a carpenter. He had forgotten now, she believed, to speak his native language.

The Latin race especially seems to have sought the place, originally of Latin traditions. But German and Scandinavian names upon the sign-boards, the Russian Ivanovich and Abramovich, and Hungarian Harasthy, show that no one blood or influence has exclusive sway. There appears an unusually free marrying and giving in marriage among all these components, one with the other. They are less clannish than with us. Lady Wortley Montagu remarking at Constantinople, some hundred years ago, a similar fusion of races—which is, after all, characteristic in the United States—believed that she found in it the reason for a debased and mongrel breed. But it must be borne in mind that it is a very different class of races which mingle here from the Orientals at Constantinople. At any rate, our own more cheerful theory is that we are to combine here the best qualities, the hardihood and good looks of all, while eliminating what is not desirable. Certainly the bright, intelligent aspect of the children of San Francisco does nothing to damage this view.

On the ground itself such vestiges of the days of '49 as remain do not fail to receive attention. They are extremely few, and I confess to surprise as well at the slightness of historic records at the Pioneer Society. I make little doubt that they could be easily paralleled in many other libraries of the country. "North Beach," however, under Telegraph Hill, may be visited both for the memories it recalls and its own picturesque aspect of ruin. It is the place where the first ships landed, where the ill-fated Ralston swam out into the bay, and it contains the ruins of "Harry Meigs's Wharf," built by a celebrated prototype of Ralston's in the Fifties. The blackened old pier is dumping-place for city refuse now, and swarms of chiffoniers gather around it to pick out such scraps of value as they may before they are washed away by the tide.

The leading streets of San Francisco commemorate in their names the pioneers of the State or the place. A newer series has adopted the names of the States of the Union, and numerical designations, carried already from First to Forty-fifth for "avenues," and from First to Thirtieth for simple "streets." The fast-growing, tough, fragrant, but scrawny eucalyptus is much in use along these streets as a shade tree. In the door-yards are seen sharp-pointed cypresses, the Spanish-bayonet, and ordinary—not exotic—flowers, which need a great deal of sprinkling to keep them in good order.

The San Francisco school of writers, developed in the successful days of the *Overland Monthly*, have made little use of the city itself in their literature. Bret Harte has confined his local range to the doings of certain small boys, and to some sketchy "Sidewalkings," and an account of the disagreeable features of the climate, in "Neighborhoods I Have Moved From." It was from Folsom Street, I recollect, that the adventurous Charles Summerton, aged five, set out on his great expedition to Van Dieman's Land, by way of the Second and Market Street cars. I had occasion to visit this street sometimes, and I confess that even this slight incident—such is the potency of the true literary touch—has given to Folsom Street a genial feeling which others, quite as good in appearance (and even the long stately Van Ness Avenue on the other side of town), do not have.

San Francisco has to offer among its other advantages that of saving a trip around the world; that is to say, whoever has seen Europe, and shirks further wanderings, may derive from the compact Chinese city of 30,000 souls, which makes a part of this, such an idea of the life and aspect of things in the Celestial Empire as will act as a considerable alleviation of curiosity. The Chinese immigrants, it is true, have rarely erected buildings of their own. They have fitted themselves into

what they found. But they have fitted themselves in with all their peculiar industries, their smells of tobacco and cooking-oil, their red and yellow signs, their opium pipes, high-soled slipper shoes, sticks of India ink, silver pens, and packets of face-powder in the windows, their fruits and fish, their curious groceries and more curious butcher's-meat—they have fitted all this into the Yankee buildings, and taken such absolute possession of them that it is no longer America, but Shanghai or Hong-Kong. The restaurants make the nearest approach to having a national façade, but this is brought about by adding highly decorated balconies, with lanterns and inscriptions, instead of building anew.

I had the curiosity to try the food at the best of these restaurants—quite a palatial place at the head of Commercial Street. It was both neatly served and palatable. There was a certain monotony in the bill of fare, it is true, which I thought might be ascribed to a desire to give us dishes as near to the American style as possible. We had a soup of chicken with a flour paste resembling macaroni; a very tender chicken, sliced through bones and all, served in a bowl; another bowl of duck; then, in a pewter chafing-dish, quail with spinach. All the food is set out in bowls, and each person helps himself from the common store with a pair of ebony chopsticks to such morsels as he may desire. The chopsticks, held in the fingers of the right hand somewhat after the manner of castanets, seem about as convenient to the beginner as a pair of lead-pencils might be for the same purpose. We drank *saki*, or rice-brandy, in infinitesimal cups, during the dinner, and at dessert a very fine tea.

The upper story in these places is reserved for the more prosperous class of guests. Those of slenderer purses are accommodated in a department below. To these latter is given the second drawing of the tea, still strong, after it has been sold above at twenty-five cents a cup, and such meats as remain in a tolerable state of preservation. The upper story is decorated as a rule with carved work, colored scarlet and heavily gilded, and with screens, lanterns, and teak-wood tables and stools.

Dropping in one evening for tea at the place above mentioned, I had the good fortune to witness a supper party which made a most novel *genre* picture, glowing

IN A CHINESE THEATRE.

with color. There were probably a dozen men, dignified-looking persons in handsome clothing of black, blue, and purple silks. With them were as many women, young, slender, and pretty in their way, though the women seen walking about the streets are very coarse and clumsy in type. These had carefully smoothed black hair, looped and sustained with silver pins, and their complexions were daintily made up with pink and white and vermilion. They realized precisely the heads we see painted on their silk fans. The most

interesting one had a decidedly Fellah or Hebrew aspect, and was probably not without an admixture of other blood in her veins. The men occupied the carved teak-wood stools about a large table, which was spread with a white cloth, and covered with charmingly painted china. The women stood by and served them. Now and then one rested momentarily on a corner of a stool, in a laughing way, and took a morsel too. The whole was a bit of bright Chinoiserie worth in itself a long journey to witness. The guests were merry. Among other amusements they played a game something like the Italian *mora*. One held up his fingers in rapid succession, and the others counted the number at the tops of their voices. What with this, their laughter, drumming on the table, and other hubbub of their gayety—besides an orchestra of their peculiar music, which added its din from behind a screen—the party was not so very unlike an assembly of Parisian *canotiers* and *grisettes* supping at Bougival.

The temple and theatre of the Chinese emigrant are always the same. I found here the same scenes I had already witnessed at Havana at the beginning of a long journey. The temple, economically set up in some rear upper room, abounds in gaudy dangling signs, and is little frequented. The theatre is vastly more popular. The dresses used are rich and of much interest. The performers are continually marching, fighting, spinning about, pretending to be dead, and jumping up again, or singing in a high cracked voice, like the whine of a bagpipe. A warrior of six feet high, though he may be Gengis Khan, and bear himself with the "haughty stride and withering pride" of a Major-General John in the *Bab Ballads*, will sing in this same voice, and no other. The slightness of the means by which illusion is attempted is one of the standing features of interest in the Chinese drama. As one of the naïve rustics in the *Midsummer Night's Dream* held up his arm to represent a wall, across which Pyramus and Thisbe might talk, so here, if it be designed to represent the march of an army through the woods, a small screen is put up at one side of the stage, bearing an inscription which no doubt says "woods," and around and around this the military betake themselves.

The cemetery seemed to me the most curious of all the sights connected with Chinadom in San Francisco. I came upon it in the course of a long stroll, and was, as it happened, almost the only outside spectator to peculiar ceremonial rites on the annual propitiation of the spirits of the dead. This burial-place is not grouped with the others in the general Golgotha at Lone Mountain, but adjoins that devoted to the city paupers, out among the melancholy sand-dunes by the ocean shore. It is parcelled off by white fences into inclosures for a large number of separate burial guilds, or *tongs*, as the Fook Yam Tong, the Tung Sen Tong, the Ye On Tong, etc. One has difficulty to persuade himself that he can be awake when witnessing the doings actually here taking place in broad sunlight and in Yankeeland.

It is the practice of this people to convey the bones of their dead to China, but preliminary funerals take place in regular form. One of the first class often enlists all the "hacks" in San Francisco. The bones are left in the ground a year or more before being in a fit condition for removal, and over these the rites of propitiation are performed. As I lingered in the vicinity toward three in the afternoon, first one, then another "express wagon" of the usual pattern drove up. They bore freights of Chinamen and Chinawomen, and curiously assorted provisions. The "hoodlum" drivers, though conducting themselves most peaceably, seemed to wear a certain sardonic air at having to draw their profits from such a class of patronage. The provisions were unloaded, and taken up and laid on small wooden altars, of which there is one in the front of each plot. Most conspicuous among them were numerous whole roast pigs decorated with ribbons and colored papers. There were, besides, roast fowls, rice, salads, sweetmeats, fruits, cigars, and rice brandy. The participants set to work at once to fire revolvers, bombs, and crackers, kindle fires of packages of colored paper, make profound genuflections before the graves, and scatter libations of the food and liquors. Only the larger articles were reserved to be taken home again. The din and smoke increased; the strangely garbed figures pranced about in the midst like sorcerers. The goblin-like roast pigs loomed out of the semi-obscurity with a portentous air. It might have been some Saturnalia at Eleusis, or a veritable witches' Sabbath.

Fruits and cigars were hospitably tendered me, had I wished to partake of them. I will say that I have not found parsimony a vice of the Chinaman, though he lives upon so little, and is content with such small returns. Coming back by the same way in the evening, I noted prowling figures, like those of tramps, gathering up among the graves for their own use the fragments cast out at the heathen ceremonial.

I am glad, on the whole, not to have to settle the mooted Chinese question in person. On the one hand, a great law of political economy—the natural right of man to seek happiness where he will; on the other, a view that the best good of a community does not necessarily consist in mere size and value of "improvements." The reflective mind will find it rather in the greatest average distribution of comfort. I should say that there have been no evils of consequence experienced from the presence of the Chinese population as yet. Without them the railroads could not have been built, nor the agricultural— and perhaps not even the mining—industries developed as they are. With all the complaint that has been heard, too, of competition from this source, the wages of labor are better here than at the East without it, and the cost of living is certainly not more.

A proper male costume for San Francisco is humorously said to be a linen duster with a fur collar. The variability of the climate within brief spaces of time—to devote a moment to a subject which on the ground itself will receive very much more —is thus indicated. The temperature varies considerably at different parts of the same day, though the mean for the year is remarkably even. The mean for January, the coldest month, is but fifty degrees, and for September, the warmest, but fifty-eight. It is a famous climate for work, but the average is rather chilly. People go away for warmth in the summer quite

as much as for coolness. The rainy season of the winter is really the pleasantest of the year. The air is clearer, at the same time that the prospects are verdant and best worthy to be seen. At other times fogs prevail, or bleak winds arise in the afternoons, and blow dust in a dreary way into the eyes of all whose misfortunes then call upon them to be on the streets.

Returning to town from our Chinese ceremonies, we pass along the wide Point Lobos Avenue, the favorite drive to the Cliff House. It is skirted at one side by a portion of the public pleasure-ground, the Golden Gate Park, an area of half a mile by three miles and a half, which is being redeemed from its original condition of drifting sand in quite a wonderful way. All this outer tract near the ocean is still a desert as yellow as Sahara. A few scattered dwellings begin to appear in the sands. Each has its water-tank and windmill, a yucca plant or two, and some knots of tough grass. On the edge of the steep hills eastward appears the city, as if it had climbed up and were looking over in surprise.

GOLDEN GATE FROM GOAT ISLAND.

BEAR-CHASING IN THE ROCKY MOUNTAINS

MR. MONTAGUE STEVENS is an Englishman who for the most part attends to the rounding up of his cattle, which are scattered over the northwestern quarter of New Mexico; but he does not let that interfere with the time which all Englishmen set duly apart to be devoted to sport. His door-yard is some hundreds of miles of mountain wilderness and desolate mesa—a more gorgeous preserve than any king ever dreamed of possessing for his pleasure—with its plains dotted with antelope, and its mountains filled with cougar, deer, bear, and wild turkeys. The white race has given up the contest with nature in those parts, and it has reverted to the bear, the Navajo, and Mr. Stevens, land grants, corrals, cabins, brands, and all else.

General Miles was conducting a military observation of the country, which is bound to be the scene of any war which the Apaches or Navajos may make, and after a very long day's march, during which we had found but one water, and that was a pool of rain-water, stirred into mud and full of alkali, where we had to let our horses into the muddy stuff at the ends of our lariats, we had at last found a little rivulet and some green grass. The coffee-pot bubbled and the frying-pan hissed, while I smoked, and listened to a big escort-wagon-driver who was repairing his lash, and saying, softly, "Been drivin' a bloody lot of burros for thirty years, and don't know enough to keep a whip out of a wheel; guess I'll go to jack-punchin', 'nen I kin use a dry club."

Far down the valley a little cloud of dust gleamed up against the gray of the mountains, and presently the tireless stride of a pony shone darkly in its luminous midst. Nearer and nearer it grew—the flying tail, the regular beating of the hoofs, the swaying figure of the rider, and the left sleeve of the horse-man's coat flapping purposelessly about. He crossed the brook with a splash, trotted, and, with a jerk, pulled up in our midst. Mr. Stevens is a tall, thin young man, very much bronzed, and with the set, serious face of an Englishman. He wore corduroy clothes, and let himself out of his saddle with one hand, which he also presented in greeting, the other having been sacrificed to his own shot-gun on some previous occasion. Mr. Stevens brought with him an enthusiasm for bear which speedily enveloped the senses of our party, and even crowded out from the mind of General Miles the nobler game which he had affected for thirty years.

At break of day the officers, cavalrymen, escort wagons, and pack-train toiled up the Cañon Largo to Mr. Stevens's camp, which was reached in good time, and consisted of a regular ranchman's grub-wagon, a great many more dogs of more varieties than I could possibly count, a big Texan, who was cook, and a professional bear-hunter by the name of Cooper, who had recently departed from his wonted game for a larger kind, with the result that after the final deal a companion had passed a .45 through Mr. Cooper's face and filled it with powder, and brought him nigh unto death, so that even now Mr. Cooper's head was swathed in bandages, and his mind piled with regrets that he had on at the time an overcoat, which prevented him from drawing his gun with his usual precision. Our introduction to the outfit was ushered in by a most magnificent free-for-all dog-fight; and when we had carefully torn the snarling, yelling, biting mass apart by the hind legs and staked them out to surrounding trees, we had time to watch Mr. Cooper draw diagrams of bear paws in the dust with a stick. These tracks he had just discovered up the Largo Cañon, and he averred that the bear was a grizzly, and weighed eighteen hundred pounds, and that he had been there two years, and that all the boys had hunted him, but that he was a sad old rascal.

After lunch we pulled on up the cañon and camped. The tents were pitched and

Mr. Cooper, whose only visible eye rolled ominously, and Dan, the S. U. foreman, with another puncher.

"He's usin' here," said Cooper. "That's his track, and there's his work," pointing up the hill-side, where lay the dead body

CROSSING A DANGEROUS PLACE.

the cooks busy, when I noticed three cow-boys down the stream and across the ca-ñon who were alternately leading their horses and stooping down in earnest con-sultation over some tracks on the ground. We walked over to them. There were

of a five-year-old cow. We drew near her, and there was the tale of a mighty struggle all written out more eloquently than pen can do. There were the deep furrows of the first grapple at the top; there was the broad trail down the steep

WATERING HORSES IN A 'DOBE HOLE.

hill for fifty yards, with the stones turned over, and the dust marked with horn and hoof and claw; and there was the stump which had broken the roll down hill. The cow had her neck broken and turned under her body; her shoulder was torn from the body, her leg broken, and her side eaten into; and there were Bruin's big telltale footprints, rivalling in size a Gladstone bag, as he had made his way down to the stream to quench his thirst and continue up the cañon. The cow was yet warm—not two hours dead.

"We must pull out of here; he will come back to-night," said Cooper. And we all turned to with a will and struck the tents, while the cooks threw their tins, bags, and boxes into the wagons, whereat we moved off down wind for three miles, up a spur of the cañon, where we again camped. We stood around the fires and allowed Mr. Cooper to fill our minds with hope. "He'll shore come back; he's usin' here; an' cow outfits—why, he don't consider a cow outfit nothin'; he's been right on top of cow outfits since he's been in these parts, and thet two years gone now when he begun to work this yer

range and do the work you see done yonder. In the mornin' we'll strike his trail, and if we can git to him you'll shore see a bar-fight."

We turned in, and during the night I was awakened twice, once by a most terrific baying of all the dogs, who would not be quieted, and later by a fine rain beating in my face. The night was dark, and we were very much afraid the rain would kill the scent. We were up long before daylight, and drank our coffee and ate our meat, and as soon as "we could see a dog a hundred yards," which is the bear-hunter's receipt, we moved off down the creek. We found that the cow had been turned over twice, but not eaten; evidently Bruin had his suspicions. The dogs cut his trail again and again. He had run within sight of our camp, had wandered across the valley hither and yon, but the faithful old hounds would not "go away." Dan sat on his pony and blew his old cow's horn, and yelled, "Hooick! hooick! get down on him, Rocks; hooick! hooick!" But Rocks could not get down on him, and then we knew that the rain had killed the scent,

We circled a half-mile out, but the dogs were still; and then we followed up the Cañon Largo for miles, and into the big mountain, through juniper thickets and over malpais, up and down the most terrible places, for we knew that the bear's bed-ground is always up in the most rugged peaks, where the rim-rock overhangs in serried battlements, tier on tier. But no bear.

Rocks, the forward hound, grew weary of hunting for things which were not, and retired to the rear for consultation with his mates; and Dan had to rope him, and with some irritation started the pony, and Rocks kept the pace by dint of legging it, and by the help of a tow from nine hundred pounds of horseflesh. Poor Rocks! He understood his business, but in consequence of not being able to explain to the men what fools they were, he suffered.

The hot mid-day sun of New Mexico soon kills the scent, and we were forced to give over for the day. A cavalry sergeant shot three deer, but we, in our superior purpose, had learned to despise deer. Later than this I made a good two-hundred-yard centre on an antelope, and though I had not been fortunate enough in years to get an antelope, the whole sensation was flat in view of this new ambition.

On the following morning we went again to our dead cow, but nothing except the jackals had been at the bear's prey, for the wily old fellow had evidently scented our camp, and concluded that we were not a cow outfit, whereat he had discreetly "pulled his freight."

We sat on our horses in a circle and raised our voices. In consideration of the short time at our disposal, we concluded that we could be satisfied with taking eighteen hundred pounds of bear on the instalment plan. The first instalment was a very big piece of meat, but was, I am going to confess, presented to us in the nature of a gift; but the whole thing was so curious I will go into it.

We hunted for two days without success, unless I include deer and antelope; but during the time I saw two things which interested me. The first was a revelation of the perfect understanding which a mountain cow-pony has of the manner in which to negotiate the difficulties of the country which is his home.

Dan, the foreman, was the huntsman.

He was a shrewd-eyed little square-built man, always very much preoccupied with the matter in hand. He wore a sombrero modelled into much character by weather and time, a corduroy coat, and those enormous New Mexican "chaps," and he sounded a cow-horn for his dogs, and alternately yelped in a most amusing way. So odd was this yelp that it caught the soldiers, and around their camp-fire at night you could hear the mimicking shouts of, "Oh Rocks! eh-h-h! hooick! get down on him, Rocks; tohoot! tohoot!" We were sitting about on our horses in a little *sienneca*, while Dan was walking about, leading his pony and looking after his dogs.

When very near me he found it necessary to cross an *arroyo* which was about five feet deep and with perfectly perpendicular banks. Without hesitating, he jumped down into it, and, with a light bound, his pony followed. At the opposite side Dan put up his arms on the bank and clawed his way up, and still paying no attention to his pony, he continued on. Without faltering in the least, the little horse put his fore feet on the bank, clawed at the bank, once, twice, jumped, scratched, clawed, and, for all the world like a cat getting into the fork of a tree, he was on the bank and following Dan.

Later in the day, when going to our camp, we followed one of Dan's short-cuts through the mountains, and the cowboys on their mountain ponies rode over a place which made the breath come short to the officers and men behind. Not that they could not cross themselves, being on foot, but that the cavalry horses could they had their solemn doubts, and no one but an evil brute desires to lead a game animal where he may lose his life. Not being a geologist, I will have to say it was a blue clay in process of rock formation, and in wet times held a mountain torrent. The slope was quite seventy degrees. The approach was loose dirt and malpais, which ran off down the gulch in small avalanches under our feet. While crossing, the horses literally stood on their toes to claw out a footing. A slip would have sent them, belly up, down the toboggan slide, with a drop into an unknown depth at the end. I had often heard the cavalry axiom "that a horse can go anywhere a man can if the man will not use his hands," and a little recruit murmured it to reassure himself.

TIMBER-TOPPING IN THE ROCKIES.

I passed with the loss of a quarter of the skin on my left hand, and later asked a quaint old veteran of four enlistments if he thought it was a bad place, and he said, "It's lizards, not harses, what ought te go thar."

Riding over the rough mountains all day sows poppy seeds in a man's head, and when the big medical officer opens your tent flaps in the morning, and fills the walls with his roars to "get up; it's four o'clock," it is with groans that you obey. You also forego washing, because you are nearly frozen stiff, and you go out and stand around the fire with your companions, who are all cheerfully miserable as they shiver and chaff each other. It

seems we do not live this life on a cold calculating plane of existence, but on different lines, the variation of which is the chief delight of the discriminating, and I must record a distinct pleasure in elbowing fellows around a camp-fire when it is dark and cold and wet, and when you know that they are oftener in bed than out of it at such hours. You drink your quart of coffee, eat your slice of venison, and then regard your horse with some trepidation, since he is all of a tremble, has a hump on his back, and is evidently of a mind to "pitch."

The eastern sky grows pale, and the irrepressible Dan begins to "honk" on his horn, and the cavalcade moves off through the grease-wood, which sticks up thickly from the ground like millions of Omaha war-bonnets.

The advance consists of six or eight big blood-hounds, which range out in front, with Dan and Mr. Cooper to blow the horn, look out for "bear sign," and to swear gently but firmly when the younger dogs take recent deer trails under consideration. Three hundred yards behind come Scotch stag-hounds, a big yellow mastiff, fox-terriers, and one or two dogs which would not classify in a bench show, and over these Mr. Stevens holds a guiding hand, while in a disordered band come General Miles, his son, three army officers, myself, and seven orderlies of the Second Cavalry. All this made a picture, but, like all Western canvases, too big for a frame. The sun broke in a golden flash over the hills, and streaked the plain with gold and gray-greens. The spirit of the thing is not hunting but the chase of the bear, taking one's mind back to the buffalo, or the nobles of the Middle Ages, who made their "image of war" with bigger game than red foxes.

Leaving the plain, we wound up a dry creek, and noted that the small oaks had been bitten and clawed down by bear to get at the acorns. The hounds gave tongue, but could not get away until we had come to a small glade in the forest, where they grew wildly excited. Mr. Cooper here showed us a very large bear track, and also a smaller one, with those of two cubs by its side. With a wild burst the dogs went away up a cañon, the blood went into our heads, and our heels into the horses, and a desperate scramble began. It is the sensation we have travelled so long to feel. Dan and Cooper

CONVERSATION AT 4 A.M.

"Do you think the pony is going to buck?"
"He does look a little hostile."

sailed off through the brush and over the stones like two old crows, with their coat tails flapping like wings. We follow at a gallop in single file up the narrow dry watercourse. The creek ends, and we take to the steep hill-sides, while the loose stones rattle from under the flying hoofs. The rains have cut deep furrows on their way to the bed of the cañon, and your horse scratches and scrambles for a foothold. A low gnarled branch bangs you across the face; and then your breath fairly stops as you see a horse go into the air and disappear over a big log

yelling dogs goes straight up, amid scraggly cedar and juniper, with loose malpais underfoot. We arrive at the top only to see Cooper and Dan disappear over a precipice after the dogs, but here we stop. Bears always seek the very highest peaks, and it is better to be there before them if possible. A grizzly can run down hill quicker than a horse, and all hunters try to get above them, since if they are big and fat they climb slowly; besides, the mountain-tops are more or less flat and devoid of underbrush, which makes good running for a horse.

THE FINALE.

fallen down a hill of seventy degrees' slope. The "take off and landing" is yielding dust, but the blood in your head puts the spur in your horse, and over you go. If you miss, it is a two-hundred-foot roll, with a twelve-hundred-pound horse on top of you. But the pace soon tells, and you see nothing but good honest climbing ahead of you. The trail of the

We scatter out along the cordon of the range. The bad going on the rim-rock of the mountain-tops, where the bear tries to throw off the dogs, makes it quite impossible to follow them at speed, so that you must separate, and take your chances of heading the chase.

I selected Captain Mickler — the immaculate — the polo-player — the epitome

DAN AND ROCKS.

of staff form—the trappiest trooper in the Dandy Fifth, and, together with two orderlies, we started. Mickler was mounted on a cow-pony which measured one chain three links from muzzle to coupling. Mickler had on English riding-togs — this is not saying that the pony could not run, or that Mickler was not humorous. But it was no new experience for him, this pulling a pony and coaxing him to attempt breakneck experiments, for he told me casually that he had led barefooted cavalrymen over these hills in pursuit of Apaches at a date in history when I was carefully conjugating Latin verbs.

We were making our way down a bad formation, when we heard the dogs, and presently three shots. A strayed cavalry orderly had, much to his disturbance of mind, beheld a big silver-tip bearing down on him, jaws skinned, ears back, and red-eyed, and he had promptly removed himself to a proper distance, where he dismounted. The bear and dogs were much exhausted, but the dogs swarmed around the bear, thus preventing a shot. But Bruin stopped at intervals to fight the dogs, and the soldier fired, but without effect. If men do not come up with the dogs in order to encourage them, many will draw off, since the work of

chasing and fighting a bear without water for hours is very trying. The one now running was an enormous silver-tip, and could not "tree." The shots of the trooper diverted the bear, which now took off down a deep cañon next to the one we were in, and presently we heard him no more. After an hour's weary travelling down the winding way we came out on the plain, and found a small cow outfit belonging to Mr. Stevens, and under a tree lay our dead silver-tip, while a half-dozen punchers squatted about it. It appeared that three of them had been working up in the foot-hills, when they heard the dogs, and shortly discovered the bear. Having no guns, and being on fairly good ground, they coiled their *riatas* and prepared to do battle.

The silver-tip was badly blown, and the three dogs which had staid with him were so tired that they sat up at a respectful distance and panted and lolled. The first rope went over Bruin's head and one paw. There lies the danger. But instantly number two flew straight to the mark, and the ponies surged, while Bruin stretched out with a roar. A third rope got his other hind leg, and the puncher dismounted and tied it to a tree. The roaring, biting, clawing mass of hair was practically helpless, but to kill him was an undertaking.

" Why didn't you brand him and turn him loose?" I asked of the cowboy.

" Well," said the puncher, in his Texan drawl, " we could have branded him all right, but we might have needed some help in turning him loose."

They pelted him with malpais, and finally stuck a knife into a vital part, and then, loading him on a pony, they brought him in. It was a daring performance, but was regarded by the " punchers " as a great joke.

Mickler and I rode into camp, thinking on the savagery of man. One never heard of a bear which travelled all the way from New Mexico to Chicago to kill a man, and yet a man will go three thousand miles to kill a bear—not for love, or fear, or hate, or meat; for what, then? But Mickler and I had not killed a bear, so we were easy.

One by one the tired hunters and dogs straggled into camp, all disappointed, except the dogs, which could not tell us what had befallen them since morning. The day following the dogs started a big black bear, which made a good run up a bad place in the hills, but with the hunters scrambling after in full cry. The bear treed for the dogs, but on sighting the horsemen he threw himself backward from the trunk, and fell fifteen feet among the dogs, which latter piled into him *en masse*, the little fox-terriers being particularly aggressive. It was a tremendous shake-up of black hair and pups of all colors, but the pace was too fast for Bruin, and he sought a new tree. One little foxie had been rolled over, and had quite a job getting his bellows mended. This time the bear sat on a limb very high up,

and General Miles put a .50-calibre ball through his brain, which brought him down with a tremendous thump, when the pups again flew into him, and " wooled him," as the cowboys put it, to their hearts' content.

While our bear-hunting is not the thing we are most proud of, yet the method is the most sportsmanlike, since nothing but the most desperate riding will bring one up with the bear in the awful country which they affect. The anticipation of having a big silver-tip assume the aggressive at any moment is inspiriting. When one thinks of the enormous strength of the " silver-tip," which can overpower the mightiest steer, and bend and break its neck or tear its shoulder from its body at a stroke, one is able to say, " Do not hunt a bear unless thy skin is not dear to thee." Then the dogs must be especially trained to run bear, since the country abounds in deer, and it is difficult to train dogs to ignore their sight and scent. The cowboys account for the number of the bear in their country from the fact that it is the old Apache and Navajo range, and the incoherent mind of the savage was impressed with the rugged mass of fur and the grinning jaws of the monster which crossed his path, and he was awed by the dangers of the encounter—arrow against claw. He came to respect the apparition, and he did not know that life is only sacred when in the image of the Creator. He did not discriminate as to the value of life, but, with his respect for death, there grew the speculation, which to him became a truth, that the fearsome beast was of the other world, and bore the lost souls of the tribe. He was a vampire; he was sacred. Oh Bear!

THE RAILROAD AND THE PEOPLE

WHEN the term "soulless corporation" was first coined, it was used to describe the nature of those largest of the then existing commercial organizations, the railroads. They were declared to be all that the dictionary of iniquity involves—dark, sinister, dishonest associations which robbed the people "right and left," as the old phrase put it, and gave nothing in return. They were, as the public press continually averred, bribe-givers, land-grabbers, political corruptionists, hard-fisted extortionists, thieves — in short, everything that an offended and an outraged opposition could invent or devise in the way of descriptive phraseology. To-day the application of the term has broadened considerably, but the railroads are not by any means exempt. By the masses of the people they are still viewed with suspicion, and everything which they undertake to do is thought to be the evidence of a scheme whereby the people are to be worsted, and the railroad strengthened in its position of opulent despotism.

That so much accusation and opposition has some basis in fact we may well believe, and yet not injure the subject of the present discussion. If we were to assume that all that has ever been said concerning railroads is absolutely true, the fact that a new policy had been adopted by some roads, looking to a cordial and sympathetic relationship with their public, would be all the more remarkable. For if the public has had nothing save greed and rapacity to expect of its railroads, the sight of the latter adopting a reasonable business policy, whereby they seek to educate and make prosperous the public in order that they in turn may be prosperous, is one which, if not inspiring, is at least optimistic. No corporation is soulless, whatever else may be thought of it, which helps all others in helping itself. The philosophy involved in this statement is the enlivening breath of the latest and most successful railroad policy, now being generally adopted.

Like many another good idea, this policy originated in the West, and it is there that it is to be found in its most advanced practical form. There the general freight agent of a road is an official of educational importance. He has associated with him as many as a hundred assistants, who carry out the work of instructing and educating the people in the knowledge that makes for prosperity. He has under him a horticultural agent, who in turn has assistants. There is a poultry agent, a superintendent of dairies, a land inspector, a travelling commercial agent, buyers, salesmen, and so forth, all with assistants, and all working under the direction of the general freight agent.

Through this department the railroads are doing a remarkably broad educational work—not only of inspecting the land, but of educating the farmers and merchants, and helping them to become wiser and more successful. They give lectures on soil-nutrition and vegetable-growing, explain conditions and trade shipments, teach poultry-raising and cattle-feeding, organize creameries for the manufacture of cheese and butter, and explain new business methods to merchants who are slow and ignorant in the matter of conducting their affairs. On two roads there is a poultry department, which buys for cash of all farmers along the route, running poultry-cars, which are scheduled for certain stations on certain days, with cash buyers in charge. On three other roads there are travelling agents who go over the line three times a year, stop at every station, and visit every merchant in the town and every farmer of merchant proclivities in the country. These men make plain the attitude of the railroad toward the citizen, inquire after the state of his business, ask him what his difficulties are, and what, if anything, can be done to strengthen and improve his situation. Lastly, there is a department of sales agents under the general freight agent, which, by individuals, represents the road in the great cities. These latter study the markets, look after incoming shipments, and work for the interests of the merchants and farmers along the line of the road by finding a market for their product. The reward for the road for all this is nothing more than an increased freight and passenger traffic, which flows from and to a successful community.

It has been seven years since the first of the roads to adopt the new policy began to reach out and study the social condition of its public, but since then the idea has spread rapidly, until to-day there is scarcely a road west of Chicago and St. Louis that is not doing more or less educational work among its public. The original movement was dictated by the fact that along great stretches of the line of one road were vacant tracts of land which were excellent for farming purposes, but which were somehow generally ignored. The road decided to make this region profitable to itself by calling attention to its merits and inducing farmers and merchants to settle there. The aid of the United States Department of Agriculture was called in. The ground was tested, and its specific qualities advertised. After that educational pamphlets were prepared, and agents of the road sent into various populous sections of the country to induce individuals to come and take up residence there. At the same time it was decided that it would be of little use to induce settlement and then leave the settlers to get along as best they could, so a policy of instruction and assistance was inaugurated. The road undertook to organize enterprises which should utilize the natural resources and production of the country and put ready money into the hands of the farmers. As a result, it found that it would need to discover markets for the goods manufactured, or it would lose much of the advantage of its labor, and thus came about the present policy, which is nothing if not broad. Its success has stimulated imitation to such an extent that nearly all roads have some one of the many features of the first road in operation, and several have all of them. So general has the feeling among railroad men become that the new policy is the

more natural and more profitable one, that a certain general manager felt called upon to apologize for the backwardness of his road by explaining that the general freight agent was of the old school of thought and not suited for the place.

Another understood the new policy so well that he readily formulated the attitude of his road toward its public, saying:

"To reach the man who is trying to do something is our object. The man with energy is our friend. I am not talking now about the man who has fifty or a hundred thousand dollars. He can take care of himself. I refer to the man who has little or nothing, but who wants to have something; the man who is ambitious and willing to work. Such men need encouragement, and they will get it if they are a part of our public. We have found that if we are to be prosperous our people must be prosperous, and so the welfare of every single individual in our territory becomes our welfare. That is business."

"But," I asked, "can a railroad deal with all of the individual members of its public?"

"Yes and no. It can deal with a great many individually. With more it deals collectively, but the result is the same. The individual is benefited. As, for instance, if a railroad gives a series of lectures on tomato-growing, it might be said to be dealing collectively with its public, and yet every farmer might have the benefit of personal counsel with the lecturer. Our aim is to reach the individuals, whether we do it collectively or not."

A railroad paying for lectures on tomato-growing! Shades of Mark Hopkins and Jay Gould!

"And why not?" said the general freight agent of another, a large Southwestern line which reaches Texas and New Mexico. "If the land is good for growing tomatoes, the farmers ought to be instructed. We have found that our road would be a great deal better if the farmers used their land for the purposes for which it is best fitted. If they do that, their crops are larger. It is our business to instruct them in the matter of soils and crops, and aid them in finding a market."

The instruction of farmers in the matter of soils and crops certainly has been anything but the function of a railroad in the past, and yet to-day we are told that it is good business. The agent for the inspection of land now makes it his business to discover just what the nature of the soil along the line of the railroad is, and what can be grown upon it. In this labor he has the co-operation not only of the national, but the State agricultural bureaus of the State through which his line travels. The government is only too anxious to spread information on this subject among the people, and gladly furnishes reports upon the nature of soils anywhere in the United States when requested. It also willingly analyzes specimens of soil and conducts agricultural experiments.

The knowledge thus gathered is used by the road in several ways. In the first place, in discovering what certain soils are good for, it picks out the thing which is least grown and is in greatest demand. The general freight agent will say to his horticultural agent:

"I see by this report here that the land around Denison, Texas, is good for tomato-raising. Tomatoes are in great demand now and bring good prices. Why couldn't we induce the farmers down there to go into the tomato business? It would be a great thing for that section."

The horticultural agent immediately takes the reports concerning the land about Denison and sends an agent into the country. Meetings of the farmers are called, and the nature of the land and the profit of tomato-growing explained.

"Now," says the horticultural agent, "you gentlemen are raising wheat on your land, and getting, say, sixty cents a bushel, if the market is fair. If not, you get less, or hold your wheat and wait for your money. Now this land about here has been tested, not only by the State, but by the United States Agricultural Department, and it is found that it is much better adapted to the growing of tomatoes. It will do a great deal better planted in tomatoes than it will in wheat. Besides, our agents in other places inform us that tomatoes, such as you can raise here early in the season, will command a dollar a crate. Allowing for the freightage and the cost of the packing-cases, which we will secure for you at the lowest possible rates, you still have forty cents on the crate. An acre of this ground will yield, say, a hundred and twenty crates at forty cents. Figure for yourselves, gen-

tlemen. Only remember the railroad guarantees you your market. You are not, as in the case of wheat, competing with a million other growers in your own country. You have something out of which you should make fifteen per cent. more on the acre easily."

The result of such lectures and conferences is that, with the aid and advice of the agent, the whole region is turned to tomato-growing. The general freight department keeps track of the progress of the crop. Through its representatives in the large and medium-sized cities it finds out where a number of car-loads of tomatoes will command a high market-rate. The local agent confers with the wholesale produce merchants, and contracts with them to deliver so many crates at a given time. The result is that the crop of the section is readily marketed and the region about Denison improved. The farmers, having slightly more ready money, indulge in farm or personal improvements, with the result that the whole district about Denison is enlivened and trade increased. The railroad profits in every way, not only by the new supplies that are shipped in to meet an aroused demand, but by the travel of the man who has a few cents more to expend on car fare in looking after his interests or visiting his friends.

The above is no hypothetical case, but an actual recorded occurrence. The region affected was that which lies sixty miles east and west of Trinity, Texas. The general freight agent who engineered this successful local enterprise said:

"We study the market question before we go into any region with any such proposition. We want our farmers to succeed, not fail. They will avoid an uncertainty as quickly as you will. Those tomatoes are shipped to all the Northern markets. We move them in car-loads only. We have people in the cities who are practical commission men, who have not only knowledge of the commission business, but also have knowledge of the trade. After we have secured the information as to where the tomatoes will be available, our horticultural agent, on the ground with the farmers, helps them decide where they will ship."

Such a tale may not only be recorded of tomatoes. The same general freight agent remarked:

"In addition to that success, our horticultural department is encouraging some sections, where the soil is adapted to it, to plant early cabbage. We want the farmers to make the best use of their land. Half the time they don't know; the other half they can't do anything because they have no way of reaching a market. With our knowledge of markets we can easily encourage them. Why, just the other day one of my men was in here, and I said to him, 'I want you to stop at every single station in Missouri; go out and see the farmers, and see what you can do with the development of the potato business.' We find that the soil along the Missouri River is particularly adapted to raising potatoes. Now I warrant you that our farmers along the Missouri will make more money out of potatoes in a year or two than they ever have made out of their other crops. We will show them how."

In looking over the Missouri Labor Commissioners' map, one finds that in 1898 there were 70,081,267 surplus pounds of poultry shipped out of the State, an increase of 18,267,743 over 1897. In the same year 4,081,833 pounds of butter were exported, an increase of 162,866 pounds over 1897; and in the matter of eggs, 33,-935,325 dozen were shipped, showing a substantial increase over previous years. Those figures tell an interesting story of the new railroad policy now in force, and the growth can be directly traced to the policy in question.

The dairy or creamery business, which involves the production of butter and eggs, has been energetically promoted by two great roads leading out of St. Louis, and encouraged in a moderate way by several others. This fact is attested by the presence in the State of twoscore or more of flourishing creameries, scattered throughout the counties, which were organized and built by the railroads, though the latter do not hold a single share of stock in any of them. The original idea was suggested, the meetings called, the money raised, and the buildings erected under the supervision of one or the other agent of the several general freight departments of the roads. Even the machinery was purchased in every case for the farmers by the railroad agent, and the method of conducting a dairy taught by another representative of the road free of charge, and all to make the county prosperous, in order that the railroad might be prosperous.

In this connection, the following letter, which was the beginning of one railroad's work of establishing creameries, explains itself. It was sent out some two years ago, since which time the work has broadened considerably:

St. Louis, Missouri, *November 7, 1899.*

Dear Sir,—With the view of developing the milk and dairy business along our line, and with the idea of determining whether or not such a business could be developed if the proper train service was established, I wish you would canvass the situation contiguous to your station, and let me know how many people you can interest in this business, and the number of cows each of them would be willing to keep and supply milk for shipping or creamery purposes.

The stations on the St. Louis Division are close enough to this market, if the people along the line will furnish volume to justify our putting forth every possible effort to develop this traffic. It would mean the bringing of a great deal more money into the community than can possibly be obtained by ordinary farming, and if we can lend assistance to the encouragement and development of this class of traffic, the results will be not only beneficial to the people along our line, but also to the railroad.

This is a matter that we desire you give your personal attention to, in the way of making a thorough and complete canvass; and when this is made, give us a full and complete report of the situation, at the earliest practicable date, with names of those who will supply milk, and the number of cows they will keep.

The good effect of the initiative action of the railroad in this matter is difficult to understand fully unless the territory is visited in person. These prosperous creamery plants would scarcely have been started by the farmers themselves. It takes thorough knowledge of dairy control to make butter and cheese, and after the same is made, only a broad understanding of the market conditions throughout the country will make it profitable. Very few farmers possess this knowledge, and yet the stockholders in these enterprises are all farmers. The railroads have been instruments in getting them together, of instructing them in the matter of manufacture and markets, and of developing that confidence which would cause them to invest their money. This last has been no easy matter in a region where suspicion of a railroad's motives and opposition to corporations are exceedingly common.

The officer in charge of the department

of dairy promotion and control is invariably a gentleman who has had practical as well as scientific training in the matter which he promotes. He is a man who is in thorough sympathy with the movement which the government has inaugurated, of educating the farmer, and avails himself of every document and paper relating to wiser and more economical farm methods. When he takes the field, it is with the set purpose of instructing the farmer concerning things of which he knows little or nothing, and a better understanding of which will make him more successful.

One such agent will enter a backward county, accompanied, as a rule, by some representative of the State Dairy Association, and will begin a campaign of practical education. He will visit the leading farmers, explain to them the advantage of some manufacturing plant of this sort which would use up the surplus dairy products of the farm and bring money into the community. He will then ask their co-operation, post notices of a meeting, and by his individual efforts get out as many as fifty farmers at least. Before these collectively he will again lay the proposition, with a clear statement of the railroad's interest in the matter, and its willingness to aid, to the end that the plant may be most economically established, a proper market assured, and a reasonable degree of profit guaranteed. When this is done, a proof of good faith is not wanting in the way of the free services of an employé of the company, who shall stay on the ground, supervise the erection of the building and the instalment of machinery. He is also left to run the plant until a representative selected by the stockholders is sufficiently instructed to conduct the plant alone.

These dairies consume from 3000 to 5000 pounds of milk a day, and yield fifty stockholders from fifteen to forty dollars, according to the number of cows maintained. The best markets for the product are readily indicated by the road which offers facilities for shipment which are, to say the least, encouraging.

"Why do you interest yourself in this phase of industry?" was asked of the general freight agent of one of the foremost roads of the West.

"Because," he returned, "it is a business which is close to the welfare of the farmer. The creamery business gives the farmer ready money, and it gives it to him regularly once a month. They have a system in these co-operative creameries which looks to the collection of the money monthly for the product, and disburses it as regularly through the man in charge. In some cases, however, they have a manager who is a butter-maker, sometimes a combination butter and cheese maker. We find that these creameries are splendid things for some counties where no high-priced vegetable can be grown abundantly. Some of our poor territory has been exceedingly improved by the introduction of these creameries. A ready market for milk, such as a creamery is, induces a farmer to keep cows. The latter are valuable in another way, as fertilizers, and so the crops of the district increase in value. By a roundabout process we profit more than you would imagine."

"Do you get all the freight business of these creameries?"

"Not always. As a matter of fact, the business we get from these small creameries does not amount to anything. In some cases we do not get anything directly. The entire business may go by express. But the community prospers, and we prosper with it. The farmer, with ready money, buys more goods, with the result suggested."

"How many dairies has your road been instrumental in organizing?"

"Some fifteen, in all. We organized the dairies at Leeton, Montrose, Rockville, St. Paul (Missouri), Parsons, Americus, Dunlap, Burlington, and so on; but I do not remember all the names."

"Do they ship dairy products only to the big cities which you reach?"

"Oh no. To the best market they can find. We undertake to advise them in this matter upon request. We have agents in all of the large cities, who study the markets. Some of the business goes to Texas, some to St. Louis, some to Kansas City. It depends largely on the demand at the various points."

The same methods hold in regard to the poultry business, which has been similarly developed. The railroads have been exceedingly successful in this work, and have spread considerable information concerning it among their public. Not only have they advised, but their agents have taken hold of several small enterprises of this kind and personally conducted them, in order to show the owners new ways and better markets. One road, traversing the West out of St. Louis, in order to stimulate interest in this field and to bring ready money into the territory, has undertaken the collection and sale of poultry on its own account, running poultry-cars over the road, buying for cash at the various stations, and finding its own market in the large cities of the country. The method in this case is for the agent to go over the road every week or ten days and paste up notices on the depot bulletin-board, announcing that on such a day the poultry-car of the Great National will be at this station, and will buy all poultry brought forward, at eight or ten cents per pound, cash. This affords a market which is a most excellent thing for many farmers, and aids wonderfully in building up a prosperous community.

This policy is one which reaches every enterprise and every individual in its territory, where possible. The man who has a small flour-mill, doing a business of, say, four hundred barrels a year, is some morning confronted by a representative of the railroad, who makes inquiry after his welfare.

"You have a plant here of how large a capacity?"

"Eight hundred barrels."

"And you do a business of how much?"

"Four hundred barrels."

"Could you buy wheat about here for four hundred extra barrels at a reasonable figure?"

The probabilities are that he could.

"Will you send us an itemized statement of the best you can do on four hundred barrels, to be delivered within six months? Send us a sample of the flour, and we will see what we can do."

The company has a telegraph arrangement whereby the transmission of ten words cost but a cent, or less. It communicates with its agents at the large cities throughout the country:

"What can you do with four hundred barrels of flour, or any fraction thereof, XX grade, $3 80 per barrel, delivered at the lowest figure?"

The local agent in New York uses his telephone to consult with the local commission merchants. He finds a place for sixty barrels delivered on a certain date. Another agent, in Chicago, wires that he

can use a hundred barrels. The Pittsburg representative can accommodate seventy-five barrels at a price which leaves a fair margin for freightages.

"Start your mill," advises the railroad company, "and deliver us four hundred barrels in the order of time specified below."

The man who has a farm or a small business is made to feel that he can call on the local agent and get advice and aid which will be valuable to him. If he is a farmer, he may sometimes have something for which there is no local market— a surplus of vegetables or fruit, which will rot on his hands. Such a man can call on the local agent, lay the matter before him, and receive all the aid that the road can give him. For instance, a farmer in Crawford County, at the close of the last fruit season, had a lot of fifty barrels of apples, which were worth nothing locally, and which were about to spoil. He visited the local agent and explained the case. The latter informed the general office by telegraph. From there the representatives of the road in the several cities were called up:

"What can you do with a lot of fifty barrels of apples for immediate delivery?"

One city quoted fifty cents a barrel; another, sixty-five; another, eighty. In this particular instance the New York agent wired that he could get ninety-five cents per barrel, and the apples were at once shipped to that city, bringing the farmer an agreeable sum of money for something which would otherwise have been a dead loss.

The old idea that railroads could concern themselves solely with their own advancement and draw upon the energy of every one else without making any adequate return still holds in many quarters, but the tide is turning. There are railroads and railroads, but the majority of the more successful ones have inaugurated this policy.

"If we can make it clear to our public why we do as we do," said one railroad official, "without overdrawing the results to them or underestimating the benefits to ourselves, we are never in doubt of the effect. Suspicion of the motives, especially when honest, is one of the most injurious elements a railroad has to contend with."

THE SECRET OF BIG TREES

IN the days of the Prophet Elijah sore famine afflicted the land of Palestine. No rain fell; the brooks ran dry; and dire distress prevailed. "Go through the land," said King Ahab to the Prophet Obadiah, "unto all the fountains of water, and unto all the brooks; peradventure we may find grass and save the horses and mules alive, that we may lose not all the beasts." When Obadiah went forth in search of forage he fell in with his chief, Elijah, and brought him to Ahab, who greeted him as the troubler of Israel. Then Elijah prayed for rain, according to the Bible story, and the famine was stayed.

From this famine in Palestine some eight hundred and seventy years before Christ, to the forests of the Sierra Nevadas in the year of grace 1911, is a far cry. The idea of investigating an episode of ancient Asiatic history in the mountains of California seems at first sight quixotic. Yet for the purpose of facilitating such an investigation the Carnegie Institution of Washington furnished funds, and Yale University gave the author leave of absence from college duties. The men in charge of both institutions realize that the possibilities of any line of research bear no relation whatever to its immediate practical results, or even to its apparent reasonableness in the minds of the unthinking. The final outcome of any piece of scientific work may not be apparent for generations, but that does not make the first steps less important. Already, however, our results possess a positive value. They demonstrate anew that this world of ours, with all its manifold activities, is so small, and so bound part to part, that nearly three thousand years of time and thrice three thousand miles of space cannot conceal its unity.

The connecting link between the past and the present, between the ancient East and the modern West, is found in the Big Trees of California, the huge species known as *Sequoia gigantea*. Every one has heard of this tree's vast size and great age. The trunk of a well-grown specimen has a diameter of twenty-five or thirty feet, which is equal to the width of an ordinary house. Such a tree often towers three hundred feet, or six times as high as a large elm, and within twenty-five feet of the top the trunk is still ten or twelve feet in thickness. Three thousand fence-posts, sufficient to support a wire fence around eight or nine thousand acres, have been made from one of these giants, and that was only the first step toward using its huge carcass. Six hundred and fifty thousand shingles, enough to cover the roofs of seventy or eighty houses, formed the second item of its product. Finally there still remained hundreds of cords of firewood which no one could use because of the prohibitive expense of hauling the wood out of the mountains. The upper third of the trunk and all the branches lie on the ground where they fell, not visibly rotting, for the wood is wonderfully enduring, but simply waiting till some foolish camper shall light a devastating fire.

Huge as the sequoias are, their size is scarcely so wonderful as their age. A tree that has lived five hundred years is still in its early youth; one that has rounded out a thousand summers and winters is only in full maturity; and old age, the threescore years and ten of the sequoias, does not come for seventeen or eighteen centuries. How old the oldest trees may be is not yet certain, but I have counted the rings of forty that were over two thousand years of age, of three that were over three thousand, and of one that was three thousand one hundred and fifty. In the days of the Trojan War and of the exodus of the Hebrews from Egypt, this oldest tree was a sturdy sapling, with stiff, prickly foliage like that of a cedar, but far more compressed.

It was doubtless a graceful, sharply conical tree, twenty or thirty feet high, with dense, horizontal branches, the lower ones of which swept the ground. Like the young trees of to-day, the ancient sequoia and the clump of trees of similar age which grew close to it must have been a charming adornment of the landscape. By the time of Marathon the trees had lost the hard, sharp lines of youth, and were thoroughly mature. The lower branches had disappeared, up to a height of a hundred feet or more; the giant trunks were disclosed as bare, reddish columns covered with soft bark six inches or a foot in thickness; the upper branches had acquired a slightly drooping aspect; and the spiny foliage, far removed from the ground, had assumed a graceful, rounded appearance. Then for centuries, through the days of Rome, the Dark Ages, and all the period of the growth of European civilization, the ancient giants preserved the same appearance, strong and solid, but with a strangely attractive, approachable quality.

After one has lived for weeks at the foot of such trees, he comes to feel that they are friends in a sense more intimate than is the case with most trees. They seem to have the mellow, kindly quality of old age, and its rich knowledge of the past stored carefully away for any who know how to use it. Often in remote parts of the world I have come to primitive villages and have inquired whether there were not some old men of long ex-perience who could tell me all that I desired to know. So it is with trees; like old men, they cherish the memory of hundreds of interesting events, and all that is needed is an interpreter.

During the summer of 1911 a theory as to the relation of climatic changes to some of the great events of history led me to attempt to get from the Big Trees at least a part of their story. I have discussed this theory in previous issues of this magazine and elsewhere, and hence will dismiss it briefly. During the three or four thousand years covered by history, the climate of western and central Asia and of the countries around the Mediterranean Sea appears to have

ONE OF THE LARGEST SEQUOIAS
Inside the hole at the foot of the tree a ladder and a man standing beside it are faintly discernible

changed. On the whole the climate seems to have grown drier, so that regions which once were fertile have now become desert. Farther north, however, or in regions which are cold and damp because of high altitude, an opposite result has apparently been produced. The relatively dry and warm conditions of the present have changed lands which once were too cold for the practise of agriculture into places where large numbers of people can live in comfort by means of that pursuit. Thus there appears to have been a change in the location of the regions best suited to human occupation. The change has not proceeded regularly, however, but in a pulsatory fashion. It seems to have been interrupted by centuries of exceptional aridity on the one hand and of exceptional moisture on the other hand. When these pulsations of climate are compared with the course of history a remarkable agreement is noticed. Among a mass of minor details this apparent relationship may be concealed, but the broad movements of races, the rise and fall of civilization, seem to show a degree of agreement with climatic changes so great that it scarcely seems possible to avoid the conclusion that the two are intimately related. Unfavorable conditions of climate, such as a change toward aridity in regions already none too well supplied with water, have apparently led to famines, epidemics, economic distress, the decline of trade, misgovernment, migrations, wars, and stagnation; while favorable changes have fostered exactly opposite conditions.

This theory strikes so profoundly at the roots of all historical interpretation, and is of such fundamental importance in its bearing on the future of nations and of the human race as a whole, that it demands most careful testing. The first step in carrying on the necessary tests is obviously to determine the exact degree of accuracy of our conclusions as to the dates and nature of climatic changes. Only when that has been done are we prepared to proceed to a fuller investigation of the relation of the changes to historic events.

After I had spent some years in a study of this great problem from various standpoints in Asia, the logical thing seemed to be to take up the same lines of work in some other conti-

A NATURAL BRIDGE

THE "WORLD'S FAIR" STUMP

nent and see how far the two agreed. Fortunately I was invited by Dr. D. T. MacDougal to co-operate with the Botanical Department of the Carnegie Institution of Washington in a study of the climate of the southwestern part of the United States. Some of the results of this work during the years 1910 and 1911 have already been published in this magazine. In general the phenomena of ancient ruins, old strands of inclosed salt lakes, the gravel terraces of rivers, the distribution of the prehistoric population and their agriculture seemed to indicate that the climatic history of America has been the same as that of Asia. The results, however, were unsatisfactory in two respects. In the first place, previous to the time of Columbus we know nothing about the dates of events in America, and hence it is absolutely impossible to know whether the apparent climatic fluctuations of America agree in time with those of Asia. In the second place, a theory is a dangerous thing. Strive as he will, its author is apt to be partial to it, and to interpret all that he sees in such a way as to fit his preconceived ideas. During all

the time of my work in Arizona, New Mexico, and old Mexico, I knew that when I announced my results critics would say, "That is all very interesting, but not convincing. You went out West expecting to find evidences of pulsatory changes of climate during historic times, and, of course, you found them. We will wait awhile before we believe you."

Manifestly it was necessary to devise some new line of research which should not only furnish dates, but should prove positively the existence or non-existence of changes of climate, and should do it in such a way that the investigator's private opinions, his personal equation, so to speak, should not be able to affect his results. The necessary method was most opportunely suggested by an article published in the *Monthly Weather Review* for 1909 by Professor A. E. Douglass, of the University of Arizona. In regions having a strongly marked difference between summer and winter it is well known that trees habitually lay on a ring of wood each year. The wood that grows in the earlier part of the season is formed rapidly and is soft in texture, while that which grows later is formed

MEN AT WORK UPON A DECAYING LOG

slowly and is correspondingly hard. Hence each annual ring consists of a layer of soft, pulpy wood surrounded by a thinner layer of harder wood which is generally of a darker color. Except under rare conditions only one ring is formed each year, and where there are two rings by reason of a double period of growth, due to a drought in May or June followed by wet weather, it is usually easy to detect the fact. In the drier parts of the temperate zone, especially in regions like Arizona and California, by far the most important factor in determining the amount of growth is the rainfall. Professor Douglass measured some twenty trees averaging about three hundred years old. He found that their rate of growth during the period since records of rainfall have been kept varies in harmony with the amount of precipitation. Other investigators have since done similar work elsewhere, and it is now established that the thickness of the annual layers of growth in trees, especially in regions with cold winters and dry summers, gives an approximate measure of the amount of rain and snow. Obviously the best trees upon which to test the theory of climatic changes are the Big Trees of California. They grow at an altitude of six or seven thousand feet on the western slope of the Sierra Nevada Mountains. Abundant snow

falls in winter, and there is a fair amount of rain up to about the first of June, but the rest of the warm season until the end of September is dry. Hence the conditions are highly favorable to the formation of distinct, easily measured rings. The size of the trees makes the rings fairly thick, and hence easy to see. The only difficulty is that the number of trees which have been cut is small. The region where they grow is relatively inaccessible, the huge trunks are very difficult to handle, and the wood is so soft that its uses are limited to a few purposes for which great durability is required. Hence several years may pass without the cutting of more than a few scattering trees. The resistance of the wood to decay is so extraordinary, however, that stumps thirty years old are almost as fresh as when cut, and their rings can easily be counted. They are just as useful as trees that were cut the present year, if only one can ascertain the date when they were felled.

Toward the end of May, 1911, I left the train at Sanger, near Fresno, in the great inner valley of California, and with two assistants drove up into the mountains through the General Grant National Park to a tract belonging to the Hume-Bennett Lumber Company. There we camped for two weeks, and then went to a similar region some sixty miles farther south on the Tulare River east of Portersvil'e. Few parts of the world are more delightful than the Sierras in the early summer. In the course of our work we often tramped through valleys filled with the straight, graceful cones of young sequoias overtopped by the great columns of their sires. Little brooks or rushing streams full of waterfalls flowed in every depression, and a drink could be had whenever one wished. On the sides of the valleys, where the soil is thin and dry, no young sequoias could be seen, although there were frequent old ones, a fact which indicates that conditions are now drier than in the past. Other trees, less exacting in their demands for water, abound in both their young and old stages, and one climbs upward through an array of feathery pines, broad-leaved cedars with red bark, and gentle firs so slender that they seem like veritable needles when compared with the stout sequoias.

We tramped each day to our chosen stumps, sometimes following old chutes made by the lumbermen to guide the logs down to the valleys, and sometimes struggling through the bushes or wandering among uncut portions of the primeval forests. Often there

was frost on the ground during the first week or two, and the last rains of the spring made the ground oozy, while the flat tops of the stumps smoked in the summer sun as soon as the clouds disappeared. Our method of work was simple. As soon as we reached a place where sequoias had been cut we began prospecting for large stumps. The method of cutting the trees facilitated our work by furnishing a smooth sawed surface. Before the lumbermen attack one of the giants, they build a platform about it six feet or more above the ground and high enough to be clear of the flaring base of the trunk. On this two men stand and chop out huge chips sometimes a foot and a half long. As the cutting proceeds, a great notch is

MEASURING A STUMP TWO THOUSAND YEARS OLD

formed, flat on the bottom and high enough so that the men actually stand within it. In this way they chop ten feet more or less into the tree, until they approach the center. Then they take a band-saw, twenty or thirty feet long, and go around to the other side. For the next few days they pull the great saw back and forth, soaking it liberally in grease to make it slip easily, and driving wedges in behind it in order to prevent the weight of the tree from resting on the saw. Finally, when the tree is almost cut through, more wedging is done, and the helpless trunk topp'es over with a thud and a stupendous cracking of branches that can be heard a mile. The sawn surface exposes the rings of growth so that all one has to do is to measure them, provided the cutting has taken place recently. In the case of older stumps we sometimes were obliged to scrape the surface to get rid of the pitchy sap which had accumulated on it. In other cases, especially where the stumps had been burned, we had to chisel grooves or to take a whisk-broom and sweep off an accumulation of needles and dirt.

When all was ready two of us lay down on our stomachs on the top of the stump, or it might be on two stumps standing close together, while the third sought the shade, or the sun, or a shelter from the rain as the weather might dictate. The two who were on the stump were equipped with penknife, ruler, and hand lens. The ruler was placed on the flat surface of the stump with its zero at the edge of the outer ring. Then we counted off the rings in groups of ten, read the ruler and called off the number to the one who sat under shelter with note-book and pencil. Had the lumbermen seen us we should have appeared like crazy creatures as we lay by the hour in the sun and rain calling out "forty-two," and being answered by the recorder, "forty-two"; "sixty-four," "sixty-four"; "seventy-eight," "seventy-eight," and so on, interminably. It was not inspiring work merely to measure, and it was distinctly uncomfortable to lie on one's stomach for hours after a hearty meal. Often it was hard to see the rings without a lens, and in some cases even the lens scarcely showed them all, for the smallest were only two-hundredths of an inch thick, very different from some of the big ones, half an inch thick. Nevertheless, the work was decidedly interesting. If we were busy on different radii of the same tree there was always a rivalry as to who would finish first, but undue haste was tempered by the danger that the results of our two measurements might not agree. The chief interest therefore lay in seeing how nearly the same number of rings would be counted on different radii. If we were at work on different trees the rivalry was as to whose tree would turn out oldest; for, like the rest of mankind, we had a feeling of personal merit if the thing with which we by pure chance were concerned happened to turn out better than that of our neighbor.

One of our chief difficulties lay in the fact that in bad seasons one side of a tree often fails to lay on any wood, especially in cases where a clump of trees grow together in the sequoias' usual habit, and the inner portions do not have a fair chance. Often we found a difference of twenty or thirty years in radii at right angles to one another; and in one extreme case, one side of a tree three thousand years old was five hundred years older than the other, according to our count. All these things necessitated constant care in order that our results might be correct. Another trial lay in the fact that in spite of the extraordinary durability of the wood, a certain number of decayed places are found, especially at the centers of the older trees, exactly the places which one most desires to see preserved. Even these decayed places, however, added their own small quota of interest. Looking down into the damp, decayed holes, we frequently saw the heads of greenish frogs, which slowly retreated if we became inquisitive and poked them. At other times, in drier places, lizards of a smooth, unpleasant complexion of brownish gray wriggled hastily into cavities in the rotten wood. Once I pulled off a large decayed slab from the side of a stump, and started back in surprise when two creatures with yellowish-brown bodies and black wings flew out. I was about to look for a bird's nest when one of my companions called out "Bats."

The frogs, lizards, and bats did not trouble us, and, fortunately, we were free from mosquitoes. There was one creature, however, which sometimes seriously interfered with our work. As we lay on our stomachs, our left fists resting on the black surface of a stump to prop our unshaven chins, and our right hands rapidly touching ring after ring with a penknife as we counted our decades—as we lay thus, with eyes closely focused at a distance of about eight inches, frightful forms came rushing into the field of vision. They were black and horny, with powerful nippers on their heads, and with white hairs on their abdomens, giving them a moldy look. They seemed nearly as large as mice, and their speed of movement was positively alarming. With open nippers they rushed at our rulers and knives and tried them to see if they were edible. Sometimes they even nipped our hands, and more than once one of us uttered a sharp exclamation and jumped so as to throw knife and ruler to the winds and cause the waste of ten or fifteen minutes in finding the place again. When we brushed the creatures away and looked at them from the normal distance they proved to be nothing but large black ants about half an inch long. More pertinacious insects I never saw. Again and again I brushed an ant away to a distance of six or eight feet, and watched that same ant turn the moment it alighted and rush back to the attack, and it did this not once but five or six times.

During the five weeks that we were in the mountains we succeeded in measuring nearly two hundred trees, forty of which, as has been said, were two thousand or more years of age. The others were of various ages down to two hundred and fifty years, for we measured a considerable number of relatively young trees for purposes of comparison. The process of constructing the climatic curve from the data thus obtained is less simple than might at first appear. The obvious method is to ascertain the average growth of all the trees for each decade from the earliest times to the present, and then to draw a curve showing how the rate has varied. The high places on such a curve will indicate times of comparative moisture, while the low places will indicate aridity. This method is too simple, however, for it takes no account of the fact that all trees grow faster in youth than in old age. Each species has its own characteristic curve of growth, as it is called. For example, during the first ten years of its life the average *Sequoia gigantea* grows about an inch in radius, that is, it reaches a diameter of two inches; at the age of two hundred years the average tree adds about nine-tenths of an inch to its radius each decade; at the age of five hundred years about six-tenths of an inch; and at the age of seventeen hundred, only three-tenths. These figures have nothing to do with the rainfall, but indicate how fast the trees might be expected to grow if they were subject at all times to the average climatic conditions without any variations from year to year.

Evidently if we desire to institute a fair comparison between the growth of a tree two hundred years old and of one seventeen hundred years old, we must either multiply or divide by three. By applying such corrections to each measurement among the forty thousand which made up our summer's work, we are able to eliminate the effect of differences in the ages of the trees. The process is purely mathematical and depends in no respect upon the individual ideas of the computer. In addition to the correction for age, there is another which I have called the correction for longevity. What sort of tree is likely to have a long life? Is it a vigorous, well-grown tree, the kind that one would pick out as especially flourishing in its youth? Not at all. The tree which is likely to live to a ripe old age of two or three thousand years grows slowly in its early days. Its actual rate of growth may be only half or two-thirds as great as that of the trees which attain an age of five hundred or a thousand years. Hence, in order to institute a fair comparison between the rate of growth in the days of Darius and now it is necessary to make still further corrections. This process, like the other, is purely mathematical. The only difficulty is that in order to secure high accuracy a large number of trees of all ages are necessary. It is easy to obtain plenty of young trees under two thousand years of age, but older ones are so scarce that we have not obtained enough to render the corrections fully exact. In the completed curve the fluctuations for minor periods and also for centuries show no appreciable errors except such as are due to special accidents. There is some doubt, however, as to whether the curve as a whole should slope more or less from early times down to the present.

The accompanying diagram sums up the results of our work on the Big Trees as compared with the results of work of an entirely different kind upon the climatic fluctuations of Asia. Horizontal distance indicates time; the diagram begins at the left-hand end with 1300 B.C., and ends on the right with 1900 A.D. Vertical distance indicates a greater or less amount of rainfall or more or less favorable conditions of plant growth. The solid line is the curve of the sequoias. During the periods where it is high, abundant moisture stimulated rapid growth; where it is low, periods of aridity lasting often for cen-

turies checked the growth of the trees. The other curve, the dotted line, is reproduced unchanged from the author's volume on Palestine. It represents the state of our knowledge of the changes of climate of western and central Asia at the time when that volume was written in 1910. The evidence upon which it is based is of very diverse types, and varies greatly in accuracy and abundance at different periods. For example, the low portion of the curve about 1200 B.C. is based on records of ancient famines, and upon the fact that at that time great movements of desert peoples took place in such a way as to suggest that the deserts had become much less habitable than formerly. A few hundred years later the curve is high, because at this time not only did great prosperity prevail in regions which are now poverty-stricken for lack of rainfall, but the kings of Assyria and the other countries lying near the Arabian Desert appear to have been able to take their armies in comparative comfort across regions where small cara-

CROSS-SECTION OF A SEQUOIA SHOWING THE GROWTH RINGS

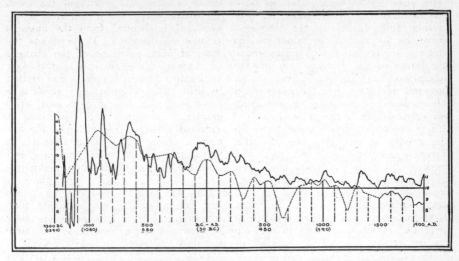

Diagram illustrating Asiatic changes of climate (dotted line) and the corresponding rate of growth of sequoias in California (solid line) from 1300 B.C. to the present day

vans cannot now pass, and which even the hardy Arab raiders avoid. At a later time, 300 A.D., the curve drops low, because at this period a great number of towns were abandoned in central Asia and in all the drier parts of the continent; trade routes which had formerly been much frequented were now absolutely given up in favor of those where water and forage were more easily obtained; and in countries like Syria stagnation seems to have prevailed, as is indicated by the scarcity of building operations during these years. The curve dips low at this point simply because evidences of aridity began to be conspicuous; but probably it dips too low, for there is as yet no means of obtaining exact data. In the seventh century A.D. evidence of the same kind as in the third causes the curve to drop still lower, but here we have additional proof of aridity in the form of traditions of prolonged famines in Arabia. Moreover, at about this same time the waters of the Caspian Sea and of other lakes without outlets were not replenished by rain, and hence fell to a level so low that buildings were built upon what is now the bottom of the lake. Then, at a later date, about 1000 A.D., the ruins in the desert were partially reoccupied, the old trade routes began to revive, the lakes rose higher than their

present level, and prosperity was the rule in many regions which had formerly suffered from aridity. These bits of evidence gathered here and there have enabled the curves to be drawn, but accuracy is as yet out of the question. At most the curves are a mere approximation, showing some of the main climatic pulsations, but likely to be greatly modified as further investigation is made. On the whole there are strong indications that further knowledge of the Asiatic curve will prove that it is much more like the California curve than now appears. Yet in the main the two curves even now show a high degree of agreement, and in that agreement lies the strongest evidence that both are correct in principle, although they may be wrong in detail.

Let us begin at the left-hand end, far back at the time of the Trojan War. There, about 1200 B.C., both curves drop very low, indicating an epoch of sudden and severe desiccation. That particular period, historians tell us, was one of the most chaotic in all history. The warlike progenitors of the Greeks swarmed into the country where they were later to grow great, the Mittani or Hittites came down out of the mountains into northern Mesopotamia, tribes from Arabia and the Libyan desert swarmed into Egypt and brought civilization down to the lowest possible ebb, famines such as that in the days of Joseph appear in the Egyptian chronicles, the lands surrounding Arabia on the north and northwest were swamped by the great Aramean invasion, and, in general, war, migrations, and disaster prevailed. If America was then inhabited we can scarcely doubt that similar disasters took place there; for, if the trees are to be trusted, vast areas in dry regions such as Mexico and the southwestern part of the United States, the only places where dense agricultural populations could have dwelt, must have fallen off tremendously in productivity.

Some fluctuations of the California curve, such as the upward bend between 1000 and 1100 B.C., are missing in that for Asia, not necessarily because they did not exist, but more probably because no facts yet happen to have been lighted upon which furnish evidence of them. The famine in the days of Elijah appears in both curves. Apparently at that time the climate did not become extremely dry, nothing like so bad as it had been a few hundred years earlier during the twelfth century, but there was a rather sudden falling off in the amount of rainfall after half a century of uncommonly good conditions. Six or seven hundred years before Christ both curves stand high in the day when the Greeks were laying the foundations of their future greatness and the empires of Mesopotamia were at their height. Then comes a slow falling off, with a recovery about 300 B.C., and another rather low place in the second century. The time of Christ and of the great era of universal peace under the sway of Rome was again an epoch of favorable climate, a time of abundant rain and consequent good crops in all the countries around the Mediterranean Sea and eastward in Asia, as well as in California. Next comes a long period of decline culminating six or seven centuries after the time of Christ. The sudden drop of the Asiatic curve about 300 A.D. is probably exaggerated, as are those from 550 to 650 A.D. and in 1200. Nevertheless, there

can be little question as to the general agreement of the two curves in showing that an epoch of extraordinary aridity reached its climax in the seventh or eighth century of our era, and that another period of aridity occurred in the thirteenth century. Previous to the seventh century the Roman world had been in the direst straits because of the invasions of barbarians, driven from their homes, it would seem, by increasing aridity and the consequent difficulty of obtaining a living. Then, toward the end of the long period of drought, there occurred the tremendous outpouring of the Arabs, unified by Mohammedanism, as is universally agreed, and also spurred by hunger, as we infer from a study of climate. Thus the Dark Ages reached their climax. No period in all history, save that which centers 1200 B.C., was more chaotic; and that early period also appears to have been a time of greatly diminished rainfall.

It is impossible here to trace further the correspondence of the two curves and their relation to history. The essential point is this: we have applied a rigid mathematical test to our theory of changes of climate, and the theory stands firm. By two methods absolutely dissimilar we have constructed curves showing climatic fluctuations in two parts of the world ten thousand miles apart. In essentials the two agree in spite of differences in detail. It now seems practically certain not only that climatic pulsations have taken place on a large scale during historic times, but that on the whole the more important changes have occurred at the same time all around the world, at least in the portion of the north temperate zone lying from 30′ to 40′ north of the equator. This, in itself, does not prove that great historic changes have occurred in response to climatic pulsations, but it goes far in that direction. It establishes the first part of the theory — that is, the reality of changes of climate, and thus clears the way for the solution of one of the most profound and far-reaching of the problems of history.

CATTLE-RAISING ON THE PLAINS.

ALL the region lying between the Sierra Nevada Mountains and the 101st meridian I rightly designate as the arid zone. The tract of land lying between the 97th and 101st meridians I properly designate as semi-arid. The western portion of the semi-arid belt is much drier than the eastern. West of the 101st meridian the land is, as a whole, unfit for agriculture, owing to insufficiency of rainfall. Westward from the 95th meridian the rainfall steadily diminishes, and the altitude of the land increases. Along the 95th meridian there is an annual rainfall of about 37 inches, 15 of which fall during the autumn and winter; along the 97th meridian, about 32 inches, 10 of which fall during the autumn and winter; along the 99th meridian, about 27 inches, 10 of which fall during the autumn and winter; along the 101st meridian, about 17 inches, 5 of which fall during the autumn and winter; at Denver, about 13 inches. In the basin lying between the Rocky Mountains and the Sierra Nevada Mountains little rain falls. The peculiarities of the climate west of the 101st meridian are determined by the direction of the wind and the physical configuration of the country. The prevailing winds on the Pacific coast are westerly. Sweeping over the warm Japan stream,

they strike the coast heavily laden with vapor. During the summer, when the land is warmer than the water, the moisture these winds carry is not precipitated in crossing the Sierra Nevada Mountains or the Rocky Mountains, nor is it precipitated in the arid basins, or on the parched plains, where the air is heated as if by a furnace. In the winter the land is colder than the water. The air is chilled as it sweeps over the Coast Range of mountains. Precipitation sets in. Then crossing the Sierra Nevada Mountains, the westerly winds sweep across the arid basin lying east of that mountain system, and strike the Rocky Mountains, consisting generally of three lofty and parallel ranges. The excessive cold encountered on these snowy heights, where the mercury stands far below zero for months, wrings the last particle of precipitable moisture from the clouds, and they disappear, leaving a cloudless sky over the great plains. The truth of this theory is shown by the snowfall in the mountains. From fifteen to twenty feet of packed snow falls in the Cascade Mountains in Washington Territory. The snowfall in the Sierra Nevadas is almost as great. In the third range of the Rockies I have seen sixteen feet of snow in the timber; in the second range, seldom more than six feet;

in the front range, not more than three or four feet falls. The rain-storms that occasionally rage over the arid plains during the summer are probably bred among the mountains, where the snow lies. The peculiarities of the climate of the cattle or range country are probably unchangeable, and if it is to remain a grazing country, it is essential that it remain arid.

By the middle of July the grass on nearly all the cattle ranges is dry. It has ripened. It is dead. Nature has not saved the cattle-growers the labor of providing winter's food for their animals, as they would have the ignorant believe; but she has, in conformity with her laws governing plant life in an arid land, hastened the growth of the grass, and brought it to early maturity. After the grass is thoroughly dry, every rain that falls injures it by washing out some of its nutriment. This being so, it is easy to see why the rains that fall in late summer and autumn are dreaded by the cattle-raisers. If but little rain falls after the grass is dead, the stronger cattle can live through almost any winter, it matters not how severe it may be, provided the range is not overstocked. But if a large portion of the nutriment has been washed out of the grass by unseasonable rains, and this disaster is followed by a hard winter, many thousands of range and pilgrim cattle die. It is not possible for an animal to eat sufficient quantities of dead, water-soaked grass to supply the fire of life with fuel.

During the winter of 1871 and 1872 I engaged in the handling of Texas cattle in the semi-arid belt of Kansas. I had provided no food for my stock. I knew that cattle could and did winter on the plains far north and west of where I was; but I did not know that there was a difference in the nutritious qualities of the different prairie grasses. I did not understand the peculiarities of the climate of the semi-arid belt, nor the effects of rain falling on dead grass. Stupid of me, of course, but I had plenty of company. My neighbors were bright Germans, intelligent Englishmen, and keen Americans from almost every State in the Union. We were a hopeful band, young, strong, and eager. When we gathered into our wretched hovels o' nights, and the pipes were glowing, our talk was of cattle, cattle, cattle. The sales of steers off the range at six cents per pound, live weight, made the previous spring, were strongly dwelt upon. I was

repeatedly assured that the Kansas winters were so mild that I would not need a coat. The height the new prairie grass would surely be on the 1st of March was measured on table legs by outstretched and dirty index fingers for my instruction and encouragement. There was not one of all the band of eager men who rode the Kansas plains in those days who did not firmly believe that our fortunes were made. The country was full of cattle. November came in with a blizzard, and, with slight interruptions, kindly allowed by Nature for the purpose of affording us opportunities to skin dead cattle, the blizzard lasted until March, and the cold, stormy weather for two months longer. There was no new grass until the middle of May. In all the Texas herds held in Kansas the losses were heavy. Hardly a herd lost less than 50 per cent., and 60, 70, and 80 per cent. losses were common. By spring we learned that great herds of heavy beef cattle, held on the Smoky, Cottonwood, and Arkansas rivers, had been frozen on the range, and that the Texans had saddled their horses and gone home. The creeks were dammed with the decaying carcasses of cattle. The air was heavy with the stench of decaying animals. The cruelties of the business of starving cattle to death were vividly impressed on me. Every wagon sent from the cattle ranges to the railroad towns was loaded with hides. The next summer, bankruptcy stalked over the Kansas plains and struck men down. Our trouble was that none of us knew that the tall blue-joint grass was worthless for winter feed unless it were made into hay, none of us knew that the fall rains had washed the nutriment out of it, and none of us knew that about once in ten years there is a hard winter in the far West, during which the mercury modestly retires into the bulb of the thermometer, and blizzard chases blizzard over the plains in quick succession. Some of us learned the lesson at once; others, who claimed that the cattle needed protection, not food, erected sheds, which proved to be death-traps, the cattle "stacking" under them during cold weather, and tried it again, and went into bankruptcy promptly after the second venture. As it was in Kansas, so it is, in a less degree, in the so-called "cattle country." A wet autumn, followed by a hard winter, kills the cattle held on Northern ranges by the thousand.

Where are the cattle? The cattle-growers who graze their herds on the northern ranges have kept the fact of their being engaged in that business so constantly before the public that they have created the impression that the larger portion of the cattle in the country graze on the arid plains or in the Rocky Mountain valleys and parks. This is a mistake.

Given a country where corn thrives, there will be found cattle and hogs in large numbers. All intelligent agriculturists know that the Mississippi Valley is divided into great belts of land, each distinguished by some marked peculiarity of soil and climate that determines the use to which it is devoted. The upper Mississippi Valley is wheat land; the lower upper, corn land; the upper lower, cotton land; and the lower, so-called sugar land. It is true that corn can be raised in the wheat and in the cotton belt, and even in the sugar belt; but it is not corn as the Western corn-growers use the word. The corn belt proper includes Illinois, Iowa, Missouri, and Eastern Kansas and Nebraska. Portions of Ohio, Indiana, Kentucky, and Tennessee properly belong in this belt. But I use the first division for convenience of illustration. Where corn grows to perfection there is always plenty of feed for cattle. Millet will grow and yield bountiful crops throughout the region. The same is true of oats; and wheat, though not a sure crop in the corn belt, is extensively sown.

In 1870 there were 22,501,337 domestic horned cattle in the United States. In 1880 the census shows that there were 31,931,670 cattle in the country—an increase of 12,430,333 during the decade. Of this increase 5,022,968 were in the five corn States of Illinois, Iowa, Missouri, Kansas, and Nebraska. When the last census was taken, more than one-fourth of the cattle in the country were in those States. In 1880 our production of corn was 1,754,591,676 bushels. The five corn States produced 1,071,505,344 bushels — more than half the crop. It is plainly seen that where the land yields large crops of corn, there the cattle naturally gravitate.

In 1880 there were, in all that extensive area composed of Montana, Wyoming, Colorado, New Mexico, Arizona, Utah, Idaho, Nevada, Oregon, and Washington, 1,786,262 cattle, or 594,714 less than there were in Illinois, and but 351,974 more than there were in the young State of Kansas. New York, which is never spoken of as a cattle-growing State, contained in 1880 2,300,088 cattle—613,826 more than then grazed on the whole of the arid belt, the much vaunted grazing grounds of the West. In my opinion the census of 1890 will show that there will be more cattle in the three corn-growing States of Illinois, Iowa, and Missouri than in the entire plain region, excepting Texas, of course. And there will not be as much acute suffering, nor as many miserable deaths from starvation and cold, in the three States as there will be among the cattle existing through the winter in a single county in the so-called cattle country.

In 1880 there were 3,994,102 cattle in Texas. The Texas cattle men so thoroughly understand their business, and the State is so well adapted to raising cattle, that nothing need be said of them or their lands. All Texas cattle-growers realize that they must not overstock their range, now fully stocked. Those at all familiar with Texas know that as long as grass grows and water runs that State can be relied upon to supply from 750,000 to 1,000,000 cattle annually; cows can raise calves on the Texas ranges and live, and the same is true of New Mexico and Arizona and portions of the Indian Territory.

The map of the United States shows that the unoccupied western portion, where the arid grazing lands lie, is about equal in area to the eastern or agricultural portion. It has been the fashion of Americans to boast of these uninhabited lands, and to assert, with intense self-satisfaction, that we have room for all the oppressed of all nations. The truth is that the agricultural lands of the United States are practically exhausted. The land that figures so brightly on the maps is but an arid tract scantily covered with herbage. A large portion of it lies so remote from water that it has no value at all, even to cattle-growers; other portions are sandy deserts; still others, alkaline plains. How large an area of the uninhabited West is available for cattle-raising? An accurate answer can not be given to that question, but I will state some facts that are vital factors in all estimates of the value of the grazing ground.

On the trail, when the cattle crowded off the Texas ranges are travelling north, they are driven an average of fifteen miles per day—some days a little more, some a little less. They are the best travellers of all domestic cattle : they travel free; they do not fret; they are easily guided. Many years' experience has taught the Texas cattle men that fifteen miles per day is the utmost distance these cattle can travel without serious loss of flesh. Driven that distance, they about hold their own. It is true that the yearlings and calves do not thrive when on the trail, but they live, and, if not driven over alkaline plains, are not seriously injured. The distance these cattle can travel being known, it is easy to compute the value of high-lying and waterless land. If the range is more than ten miles from water (and there are many extensive areas within the arid zone that are twenty miles from water), it is worthless, it matters not how plentiful the feed. It is true that cattle ranging at will, and free from the control of man, which they resent, will travel farther and hold their flesh better than if driven. Say they can thus travel twenty miles per day. Then, if their grazing ground is not more than ten miles from water, they can live, and maybe thrive. So far as the range lying beyond the ten-mile line is concerned, it might as well be a grassless desert. The cattle can not use it. The cattle like to loiter along the streams, to graze on the low lands, to make the valley their home. They journey long distances for food only when compelled. The effects of the cattle loitering in the valley can be plainly seen in the upper Arkansas Valley, in Colorado, where they have tramped the grass out. What has occurred in the Arkansas Valley will inevitably occur in other valleys if the range is overstocked. Once the destruction of the grass in the valley begins, the lines of destruction will annually recede farther and farther from the water, until all the grass within grazing distance of the stream is destroyed, and the range rendered valueless. In 1873 the Arkansas Valley in Colorado was carpeted with nutritious grass; in 1881 it was a desert where dust clouds coursed. The destruction of the grass in this valley was the direct outcome of overstocking the ranges. Fifteen miles from the river, on the uplands, the grass is as good as ever it was.

The native grasses of the arid belt do not stand close grazing, as the pastures of the Eastern States do. During the summer of 1871 I was in northern Montana, in the region between the Rocky Mountains and the Belt range, and northward to the Belly River in the northwest territory. At that time the Dearborn Valley range was virgin. On it was the best bunch-grass I saw in the Territory, excepting on the upper Milk River. The Sun River Valley was a famous cattle-feeding ground in those days. To-day the whole region, that was in 1871 covered with tall bunch-grass, has been practically abandoned by the cattle men. The grass is eaten out. The range was overstocked. Its value has been destroyed. The per cent. of loss among the cattle unwisely held there during the two winters last past was very large.

In 1883 the grass in northern Colorado was very badly injured by overstocking— so much so that many cattle men believed that it had been permanently injured.

The number of acres of arid land necessary to carry an animal without injury to the grass varies widely. The species of the grass, whether bunch, buffalo, or gamma, and the quantity standing on an acre, as well as the character of the soil, whether it is sandy or gravelly, must be taken into consideration. Intelligent cattle-growers assert that on a new range, such as the Yellowstone Valley was a few years ago, fifteen acres per head of cattle is sufficient to insure the permanency of the range. Others, more conservative, or maybe more greedy for range, assert that twenty-five acres is not too much if the range is to be a permanent one. This in the arid belt, of course.

In the semi-arid belt the grass forms a thick sod, and when the region is virgin there are but few weeds among the grass. But let this prairie be closely pastured for two years, and weeds, rank, unwholesome, and worthless, make their appearance. If the cattle are held on the ground, the grass will almost disappear in four or five years, and what looked to be an indestructible pasture will be only a field of weeds.

Westward from the 96th meridian all prairie grass lacks vitality. Close feeding injures it. Mowing seriously affects it. When the natural meadows lying within the arid belt were first mown, they yielded large crops of the most nutritious hay in the world. The first cutting was heavy; the successive crops were lighter and lighter, until now all these meadows must be carefully irrigated, or the grass crop will be so light as not to be worth cutting. So to a great extent is it in the semi-arid belt. But there, owing to the slight fall in the streams, irrigation can not be practiced. In the semi-arid belt land that has once been good hay land is always good corn land, and many meadows that no longer yield sufficient hay to pay for cutting will be ploughed and devoted to corn.

I have said that the annual drive from Texas will probably be from 750,000 to 1,000,000 cattle. A large proportion of these will be stock cattle—cows, heifers, and young steers. Where are these cattle to be held until fit for market? At the Cattle Growers' Convention, held in St. Louis, November, 1884, the Texas cattle-growers were unanimous in advocating the creation of a national cattle trail, six miles wide, and extending from Texas to our northern boundary. The Northern grazers opposed the proposed trail on the ground that the Texas cattle were infected with a disease known in the business as the Spanish fever. They asserted—and truthfully, too—that the driving of through Texas cattle along the trail would infect their herds. The Spanish fever does not injure Texas cattle; but all native cattle—that is, all Northern stock, no matter what their blood—catch the disease by grazing on the ground over which through Texas cattle have passed, and they generally die. Here were two parties disputing about a fact that both knew to be a fact, both cunningly endeavoring to conceal their real hopes and fears. There are Territorial and State laws in force in the West that forbid the driving of through Texas cattle on to many ranges. A national law enacted for the purpose of providing a cattle trail would override these local laws, which many lawyers pronounce unconstitutional, and open the Northern grazing ground to the Texas cattle. The Southern stock-growers want the trail created so that they can drive young steers that are strong enough to endure the severe winters of the Northwest through to the bunch and buffalo grass pastures of Wyoming and Montana in one season, and so avert overstocking their home range, which is secure from invasion of Northern herds, as no native cattle can be driven on to the grazing ground of Texas and live. The Spanish fever stalks abroad there. The Northern men assert and re-assert that the opening

of the trail would endanger their herds. They ignore the fact that the first heavy frost kills the Spanish fever, and ends all danger. They endeavor to conceal their real reason for opposing the opening of the trail, which is the danger of overstocking the Northern grazing ground if the Texas men are allowed to drive their surplus young steers there. They dread having from 200,000 to 300,000 young steers annually driven North to feed on a range that they all realize will, under the present land laws, be speedily overstocked, and eventually destroyed, and destroyed by the greed of the cattle men.

Underlying all talk of renting the public lands, or of buying them, and of any and all schemes concerning the disposition to be made of the public domain that emanate from the cattle-growers, is the determined purpose to secure the land, and to place it under the control of the cattle growing associations, and then limit the number of cattle that shall be allowed to graze on it. The spectre that is ever present to the Northern cattle-growers is overstocking. All talk of their desire to conserve the public domain is false. They desire to secure absolute possession of the range; and if they succeed, they will as surely stop agricultural settlers from entering the arid belt to acquire low-lying farms along the streams as if they owned the land in fee-simple.

During the few years last past cattle ranches have changed hands freely, at very extravagant prices. The price of beef has been high, and the profits of cattle growing or grazing exceedingly large. During this same time the tendency has been to the consolidation of individual cattle owners into corporate associations, for the more economical administration of the business. Corporations can manage the business of growing cattle cheaper and better than individuals, provided the active officers of the company hold its stock, for which they have paid either money or cattle. But if the stock is held by Eastern men or by foreigners, and their agents on the plains do not own stock for which they have paid, the stock of that cattle-growing association would be about as valuable as that issued by some of the silver-mining companies of Colorado.

The reason for the high price of cattle during the past four years has never been fairly stated so that Eastern investors could understand it. For three years previous to 1884 the West did not make a full corn crop. The failure of the corn crop forbade the breeding of swine on a sufficiently extensive scale to keep pace with our increase in population, and at the same time supply the foreign demand. With corn worth forty-five and fifty cents per bushel, the farmers could not afford to assume the risks incident to breeding swine in large numbers. They bred, to be sure, but they did not stock their breeding pens. The small supply of pork increased the demand for beef, and the price of the latter rose. But since 1884 large corn crops have reversed the situation, and we have entered upon an era of low prices.

The grazing grounds of great altitude are the grave-yards of cows. For years the trails leading from Texas to the Northern ranges have been crowded with stock cattle that were driven North to be used in establishing ranches. The number of cattle in Texas is so great, and so near the capacity of the land to carry, that during the decade ending in 1880 from 500,000 to 700,000 cattle, old and young, male and female, were driven from the State annually. It is fair to assume that in the past at least one-fourth of the Texas drive were females, and young females generally. Where are the cows that have been driven from the mesquite and gamma ranges of Texas during the past decade ? The business of raising cattle on the Northern plains is not old. It is safe to assert that at least 1,000,000 female cattle have left Texas for the Northern grazing ground during the ten years last past. In a suitable climate these cattle would have been alive to-day. Where are they? The bones of thousands of them lie bleaching on the wind-swept flanks of the foot-hills of mountain ranges; they pave the bottoms of miry pools; they are scattered among the pines standing below the eternal snow-drifts of the Rocky Mountains; they lie in disjointed, wolf-gnawed fragments on the arid, bunch-grass ranges; they are scattered over the short buffalo-grass, low-lying monuments of man's inhumanity to the dumb animals he has arrogantly assumed charge of; they have died of hunger; they have perished of thirst, when the icy breath of winter closed the streams; they have died of starvation by the tens of thousands during the season when cold storms sweep out of the North and course over the plains, burying the grass under snow. Other thousands have been frozen into solid blocks during blood-chilling blizzards.

There has been a movement of young cattle, steers generally, from the corn States to the plains, for several years. Many of the men who own or control Wyoming, Dakota, and Montana ranges have practically abandoned the business of breeding cattle, driven out of it by the severe losses of female cattle during the winters, and now confine their attention to grazing young steers, known as "pilgrims," which they bring upon the range from Eastern States. These animals are generally high-grade steers from the corn States, or long-horned cattle from Texas. If the latter are bought, those that have been held over one winter in Kansas or Nebraska or Indian Territory are preferred. In the past, this business has proved to be fairly remunerative, because, since it has been started, the price of beef has been high, and there has been no exceedingly severe winter on the plains. The country these cattle are held in has been in the white man's possession for but a few years. The men who have accurate knowledge of its climate can be counted on the fingers of one hand. The Northern cattle-growers assert that the climate is mild and the winters balmy. There are a few men in the Northwest who have traded in the Yellowstone Valley in the winter and early spring when the Sioux occupied the land. Some of these men have told me that during some winters the snow was deep on the ground for weeks, and the cold was most intense. They said that occasionally the winters were so severe that large numbers of hardy Indian ponies died. It is a well-known fact that Indian ponies can endure a greater degree of cold than American horses, and that American horses can endure a greater degree of cold than cattle, it matters not where the latter are raised.

It is estimated that 220,000 cattle were driven or carried into Montana and Dakota during 1884. The larger portion of this stock was brought on to the range to be fattened. They were young steers. It is also estimated by competent authorities that 100,000 of the 220,000 cattle that entered the far Northern range during 1884 were young native cattle from the corn States. The number of "through" cattle that were included in the great herd of Texans no man can tell. The Texas drover is famous throughout the arid belt for never telling the truth as to where his cattle come from. He is always willing to swear that they passed the previous winter in Kansas or Nebraska, and as cold weather kills the Spanish fever, his cattle are sound, and he is not responsible for damages if the disease makes its appearance in Northern herds. The truth is that a large proportion of the Texas cattle driven into Montana and Dakota during the season of 1884 were fresh from the Southern range. The young cattle that are brought on to the Northern grazing grounds from the agricultural States come from a land of plenty. They have been well fed and attentively watered from the day of their birth until they are sent West. They have been protected from severe winter storms. They have had intelligent and anxious care. Their instincts have been blunted by the protective care of man. These immature animals have been taken West and turned on the range to shift for themselves. They can do so in a mild winter. Last year, up to September 8, the Northern Pacific Railroad carried 68,860 young cattle from the East into Montana and western Dakota. Many thousands have been driven in, and other thousands carried in by other railroad companies. But let a hard winter come, following a wet autumn, and the grazing ground be covered with snow, and blizzard after blizzard sweep out of the frozen North in quick succession. Then how will these cattle fare? and how will the through Texans fare? I answer, just as they did in Kansas in the winter of 1871–2. They would disappear from the range. And if the winter should be as severe as some of the Indian traders told me they had seen in the Yellowstone Valley, so severe that the Indians were forced to cut cottonwood-trees so that their ponies could feed on the buds and tenderer limbs, the toughened range cattle will be decimated before spring.

It has frequently been asserted by interested parties that cattle keep fat on the range all winter. If this were true, the cities situated in the heart of the cattle country would be supplied with beef from the adjoining ranges. A stranger walking through the streets of Denver would, knowing himself to be in the cattle country, suppose that the prime quarters of beef he saw hanging in the butchers' shops were the carcasses of range cattle.

But if he will go to the railroad depots he will see those choice quarters, or others just like them, unloaded from cars that came from the corn belt. If a Denver butcher is remonstrated with for charging exorbitant prices for his beef, he defends himself by saying that he has to bring his meat from Kansas City, and that transportation charges are high on the Union Pacific Railroad.

Recently a new method of handling beef cattle on the range has sprung into existence, and one that has made one branch of the cattle business on the plains safe, reasonably profitable, and humane. The hay cut on the irrigated meadows lying within the strictly arid belt is the most nutritious in the world. The rule seems to be that the greater the altitude of the meadow, the finer and more nutritious the hay it yields. A few years ago it was discovered that steers that were full fed on this hay would gain flesh during the winter. I have seen as fat beeves killed in Wyoming in March as are killed in the smaller towns in the corn belt.

There are many small meadows lying along the streams that flow through the grazing country that, with irrigation, would annually yield from 100 to 150 tons of hay. Each of these spots would afford a young man of modest means a home, where he could live in comfort and save money for his old age. He could keep a hundred head of stock cattle, or he could feed from fifty to seventy-five steers, every winter. That the industry of feeding steers hay during the winters will rapidly increase is inevitable, and many men of small means, or who are conscientiously opposed to freezing and starving cattle to death, will engage in it, providing that the cattle-growing associations do not seize all the water rights and all the meadows, which they will surely do if they can. It is the aim of all cattle growing or breeding associations which operate in the arid belt to secure the water rights in the plain country, and the natural meadows of the grazing land of high altitude. On the plains the water determines the value of the land. In the highlands there is plenty of water; but hay is an article of prime necessity to the man of small means who seeks a home. So when an unoccupied meadow is found in the range used by a cattle-growing association, one of the employés of the association is instructed to homestead or enter it, which he promptly does. When he procures a patent from the government, he deeds the land to the association employing him. Another poor man has been deprived of a home, but the association has been benefited.

Where is the best cattle country? Where can cattle be handled or raised with small loss and sure profit and no cruelty? Unhesitatingly I answer in the semi-arid belt. Here are the requirements of a perfect cattle country. Grass to usually start early in the spring, say by the middle of April. The summers should be warm. The winters dry, so that the cattle will not tramp their feed into the ground, where the hogs that follow them can not find it. Corn should grow to perfection. The land should be comparatively free from hog and cattle diseases. Such a land is the semi-arid belt, lying between the 97th and 99th meridians, and extending from Dakota to Texas. Within that area hog cholera is almost unknown. The cattle are free from disease. There is plenty of cheap corn. Large crops of millet can be grown on all the land. Wheat is almost a sure crop. The corn stalks, wheat straw, and millet supply the cattle with an abundance of roughness during the winter. All points of the belt are convenient to market. The creeks seldom freeze over solidly, and the cattle have free access to water. The ground seldom becomes miry, and the cattle's feet are always sound. The business of raising cattle, or of feeding them, in the semi-arid belt is profitable. There are plenty of well-bred and intelligent people in the country. The country is healthful. There are good schools in every town. Land may be purchased on reasonable terms,

but only the bottom land in the western portion of the semi-arid belt is corn land. The best of corn land, say twenty miles from a thriving town, can be bought for from $20 to $30 per acre. Near the towns good bottom land can be bought for from $50 to $75 per acre. The upland of the western portion of the belt is dear at any price.

The increase in the number of cattle in the semi-arid belt during the five years last past has been most remarkable. As long as wheat sold at remunerative prices the farmers did not pay much attention to cattle-growing. But when the price of wheat began to fall, and the value of cattle to increase rapidly, they realized that it was no longer wise to burn their straw, or to devote corn land to wheat culture. To show how closely intelligent men who are engaged in the same business employ the same methods of thought and arrive at the same conclusions, I instance the farmers of Kansas. Up to the autumn of 1881 calves were freely sold by these men. After the crop of calves of 1882 was born, it was rare to see veal hanging in a butcher's shop. Almost all the calves born in the semi-arid belt of Kansas since 1882 have been raised. Last spring, when travelling in Kansas, in a region where but few cattle were held three years ago, I saw small herds of cattle in every barn-yard. The statistics of Kansas for 1883 show that there were 1,801,348 in the State in the spring of that year. There are about 2,500,000 in the State now. There has been a similar increase in Nebraska; and there has been an astonishing increase since 1880 in the number of cattle in the five corn States— amounting now to 13,000,000.

SALT LAKE CITY

LIKE "all Gaul," the United States is divisible into three parts—the Atlantic slope, the Pacific coast, and the Great Basin. All of the waters resulting from rain-fall or the melting of the snows on the mountains in the Great Basin can find no outlet to the ocean, but must either disappear in desert sands or drain into the Great Salt Lake.

The fame of this large body of "noxious and extremely salt" water penetrated southward to the early Spanish explorers, and the French from the Northwest got near enough to it a century ago to hear of its magnitude and peculiarities. It is put down, therefore, in maps made toward the end of the last century as much by guess as maps of twenty years ago contained the lakes of Central Africa in problematic positions. When the trappers of the fur companies began to overrun the Rocky Mountains, Utah was invaded, and the beautiful valleys of the northern Wahsatch became favorite wintering places. From any of these peaks the lake would be visible, but it is not known that before 1825 any white man had reached its shore. It was not until Captain Bonneville had come back from oblivion to the eyes of a surprised world, and Washington Irving had written his travels, in 1837, that we knew anything definitely about this inland salt sea, and could place it on a map correctly. It is a great pity that the good and proper name Lake Bonneville has been lost in the prosaic name it now bears, and will probably forever retain; but a just attempt to restore it has been made by Major Powell's survey. The present lake is only a remnant of a more ancient and larger body of water, whose bounds can now be easily traced in the horizontal benches along the base of the mountains.

Stimulated by Irving's book, emigration immediately began overland to Oregon. In 1842 and 1843, General Fremont piloted his celebrated expedition through the mountains and made a boat trip on the lake, although at that time it was not the property of the United States, but belonged to Mexico.

Utah and its lake were well known to geographers when the Mormon Church, expelled from Illinois, driven out of Missouri, and persecuted to the point of death in Iowa, decided to abandon their beautiful Nauvoo, and betake themselves not only to the far West, but outside of the lines of a country whose people and government they hated.

Days counted themselves into weeks, and weeks made months, and months followed one another from early spring into midsummer, and still the emigrants, likening themselves to Israel in the wilderness, kept their faces westward. On the 24th of July, 1847, the head of the advance train, winding its way down through the last tortuous little ravine in the western foot-hills of the Wahsatch, looked out on that great basin—miles of sage-green velvety slopes sweeping down on every side from the bristling mountain rim to the azure surface of the tossing salt sea.

But the camp was not made on the borders of the Great Salt Lake, nor is the present city in proximity to it. It is almost twenty miles away in a straight line, and just at the base of the range. Indeed, it is only from the "bench" that the lake can be seen at all from within the city limits, and then it appears only as a line of distinct color between the dusty olive of the hither plain and the vague blue of the further hills.

Among the first things that Brigham Young ordered done after his pioneers had come into the valley was to survey a site for the future city. This was done on a generous scale. The streets are a hundred and thirty feet wide, run true to the points of the compass, and cross one another at right angles. Each square contains ten acres, so that when of an evening you walk "around the block," just to smoke a post-prandial cigarette, you will tramp exactly half a mile. A square of nine blocks was made to constitute a "ward," of which the city now has twenty-four, each ward being presided over by a bishop of the Church, who, however, was more a temporal than a spiritual head in those first days, deciding all small cases in dispute, when there was no appeal, nor desire for one, from ecclesiastical decisions to civil judgment. This ward classification is one that even yet enters largely into the social constitution of the city, which is thus a sort of federation of bishops' wards, each inclined to be clannish.

The pioneers divided each ten-acre square into eight household lots, giving every man an acre and a quarter, and half the people corner lots. The result has followed that these have been divided and subdivided, to suit individual wants and notions, until many of the houses stand right in the heart of the block, behind those fronting on the street, and are approached by alleys, many of which are bordered by a double row of thrifty Lombardy poplars. Regularity and perhaps convenience are sacrificed by this, but picturesqueness is gained.

The next necessity was a regular water supply, for rain can not be expected here between May and October. Down out of Emigration Cañon, through which the trail passed from the East, comes a creek to empty itself into the Jordan, which latter stream connects Lake Utah and Great Salt Lake, just as its namesake of the Holy Land links together Gennesaret and the Dead Sea. It was simply a matter of ditching from a high level, and making subsidiary canals, to bring the snow-fed water of this city creek in never-failing plenty wherever it was desired. The combined labor of the pioneers, who all worked pretty much in common at first, accomplished this primitive irrigation very speedily, so that within a few days a great many seeds had been put in the ground.

The emigrants, however, did not stop with the planting of vegetables and a little grain. They at once began a nursery of fruit trees, while shade and ornament were not forgotten. Making it the duty of every citizen to plant seeds of Eastern shade trees, or set out saplings brought from the hills, on both sides of every thoroughfare, the public looked to their preservation by making broad, deep gutters along each curbing. Now those saplings of acacia, poplar, cottonwood, mulberry, box-elder, honey-locust, and maple have grown into wide-spreading and lofty trees that canopy with grateful foliage every avenue outside the business centre; and down those gutters flow rippling, sparkling streams of water, clear as their snowy fountains, and dashing over their beds of mossy pebbles with all the glee of native brooks.

Formerly this water alone was available for domestic purposes and drinking as well as for irrigation, and even yet the poorer part of the population dip it up for daily service. But the introduction of pipes has superseded this old way. The hydrant water, however, comes from the same sources as the ditches, and is really no better, since it is unfiltered. For table use, therefore, the water that has been drawn from very deep wells is preferred by every one.

But in spite of the copious water supply arranged for by the founders, and recently largely increased by a canal leading from Lake Utah, Salt Lake City is in summer the dustiest town I ever saw or heard of. This blinding, all-pervading dust forms the only serious objection I can bring against the town as a pleasant place to live in.

The houses built by the first settlers were mainly log cabins. Some few of these are yet to be found hidden away in orchards. The Spanish adobe house of dried mud was also a favorite, and has continued so to the present, though instead of almost shapeless chunks of mud, plastered in Mexican fashion, regular unburned bricks are made by machinery. These adobes are twice the size of ordinary bricks, and the wall into which they are formed is made twice as thick as one of burned bricks would be. Of course this material lends itself readily to any style of architecture, and many of the elaborate buildings as well as cheap cottages are made of it, the soft gray tint of the adobe reminding one of the cream-colored walls of Milwaukee. Generally, however, the adobe is overlaid by a stucco, which is tinted. Low houses with abundant piazzas are the most common type in the older part of the town, and over these so many vines will be trained and so much foliage cluster that one can hardly say of what material the structure itself is formed. The residences more recently built have a more Eastern and conventional aspect, and some are very imposing; but big or little, old or new, it is rare to find a home not ensconced—almost buried—in trees and shrubs and climbing plants, while smooth, rich lawns greet the eye everywhere in town, in brilliant contrast to the bleak, bare hills towering overhead just without the city. As for flowers, no town East or West cultivates them more universally and assiduously.

Salt Lake City, then, is beautiful — a paradise in comparison with the buffalo plains or the stony gulches in which the great majority of Rocky Mountain towns must needs be set.

The suburbs, except toward the rocky uplands northward, grade off into farms quite imperceptibly, the streets continuing straight out into country roads between dense jungles of sunflowers—glorious walls of gold edged with green and touched with innumerable dots of maroon. And in these suburbs you may find some of the quaintest, most idyllic homes. One such, for example, stands down in the third ward. The house is hardly bigger than a good-sized room, and is entered through a queer narrow cowled doorway. The second story is hardly half as large as the lower one, leaving a slanting roof between, and a picturesque hedge and fence inclose the whole. This would be striking enough alone for its shape; but every two weeks the whole adobe and stucco affair is whitewashed from rooftree to foundation, until it gleams like a fresh snow-bank against the grape-vines that creep around its angles, and the poplars and maples that photograph their boughs in shadow upon its spotless sides. But to set it off the better, the owner paints his small window-sashes bright yellow, his casings the reddest of red, and his sills and shutters and door panels vivid green. If the whole affair had just been handed out of a Dutch toy shop, it could not be more fantastic and childishly pretty.

One would think that with its dry and clear air, with an elevation of 4600 feet, with breezes sweeping down from a range of mountains where the snow is always to be seen, or across a broad and purifying lake, and with so much dry earth at hand to be used as a ready antiseptic, this locality ought to be as healthy as any on the face of the earth. So, with any care, it would be; but such care seems not to be taken, and there are few cities showing a larger death-rate among children. The bleak and desolate cemetery upon the wind-swept bench is a perfect Golgotha of infants' graves—a pitiful army of victims to diphtheria.

For this condition of things, and for much ill health among adults, there is no excuse. Even chills and fever are gaining a foot-hold where they should most easily be kept at a distance; but, strangely, all the malarial diseases seem more malignant and prevalent upon the bench than down in the lower part of the city, probably owing to the fact that the nightly draught of air down out of the cañons strikes the lower end of the city with more briskness, sweeping away what noxious gases may arise.

The climate of Salt Lake Valley is about what one might expect: in winter, much snow, and steady, intense, but dry cold; in summer, prolonged but dry heat. The sun blazes down day after day through a cloudless atmosphere, and burns like fire when its direct rays strike. The hot breath of the valley pours up when there is any wind from the southward, and one nearly suffocates. Yet perspiration does not flow copiously even under exertion, and the heat is not debilitating, for the moment you get into the shade you are comfortable. All day the earth sends upward volumes of heated air, but at night, striking the snow-banks on the neighboring peaks, the air rapidly chills and drops down to revive us, making sleep a luxury.

For their summer vacation, when they take any, the citizens can choose between the mountains and the Great Salt Lake, and generally end by going to both. The lake, indeed, is constantly visited. A narrow-gauge railway, aimed at Nevada, has got as far as the lake shore, and trains run out and back morning and evening, stopping long enough to give passengers time for a bath. The fare for the round trip (twenty miles each way) is only fifty cents. At the landings, in addition to bathing arrangements, there are dancing pavilions, and excursions often go out in the evening, returning by a special train in the morning.

On special occasions, such as Pioneer-day (July 24), when the Mormons celebrate their first entrance to the valley, great crowds of Saints, with all the wives and innumerable little ones, pack the open Coney-Island-like excursion cars, throng at the water-side, and spread their luncheons on the long tables under the bough-covered booths which give the only protection against the sun. Unfortunately it is impossible to make trees grow on the borders of the lake—the water and soil are too bitterly salt; moreover, there is no fresh-water in the rocky hills that tower straight up from the beach, and any irrigation is thus denied the would-be forest-

EAST SIDE OF SALT LAKE CITY.

er. Lack of shade seems to make little difference with the bathers, however. They go in under the noonday blaze, and say their bare heads suffer no discomfort, and children and horses rush about apparently as energetic as in October. While the danger of sun-stroke somehow seems very small, the lake is a treacherous water for swimmers. The great density of its waters sustains you so that you float easily, but swimming ahead is very hard work. Moreover, fatal consequences are likely to ensue if any of the brine is swallowed; it not only chokes, but is described as fairly burning the tissues of the throat and lungs, producing death almost as surely as the breathing of flame. Of course this occurs only in exceptional cases, but some lives are thus destroyed each summer, and many persons suffer extremely from a single accidental swallow.

The powerful effect of this water is not surprising when one remembers that the proportion of saline matter in it is six times as great as the percentage of the ocean, and almost equal to that of the Dead Sea, though Lake Urumiyah, in Persia, is reputed to contain water of a third

greater density yet. This density is due mainly to common salt held in solution; but there are various other ingredients. In Great Salt Lake, for example, only 0.52 per cent. of magnesia exists, the Dead Sea having 7.82 per cent.; and of lime Salt Lake holds 1.80 per cent., while the Dead Sea contains only a third as much. The waters seem utterly lifeless, yet the innumerable gulls and pelicans there must find something to live upon. Walking on the shore in midsummer, you are surrounded by clouds of little sand-fleas (*Artemia salina*), which quickly drive you away, and wherever the muddy shores are exposed to the sun a sulphurous stench arises which is nauseating. Salt is made in great quantities in summer by the simple process of damming small bays and letting the inclosed water evaporate, leaving a crust of crystallized salt behind. Several thousands of tons are exported annually, and great quantities used at home in chlorodizing ores.

I think few persons realize how wonderfully, strangely beautiful this inland saline sea is. Under the sunlight its wide surface gives the eye such a mass of brilliant color as is rarely seen in the temperate zone. Over against the horizon it is almost black, then ultramarine, then glowing Prussian blue, or here and there, close by, variegated with patches of green and the soft skyey tone of the turquoise. Gaz-

lights are blotted out in the uniform immaculate indigo which slowly solidifies heights and depths into a single grand silhouette of the whole Wahsatch.

Watching these changing and lovely exhibitions of lavish color, feeling the

BATHING RESORT ON THE LAKE.

ing straight down off the end of the pier, or from the rough little steamboat, which is now degraded to do duty at its moorings as a restaurant, you learn that the water is transparent as glass, and the ripple marks on the bluish-white sand are visible at a great depth.

If the lake were in a plain (remembering the total absence of forest or greensward), doubtless this richness of color would not suffice to produce the effect of beauty, but on every side stand lofty mountains. They seem to rise from the very margin to their riven, bare, and pinnacle-studded crests, where the snow lies in shaded patches. Some of these ranges are a score of miles beyond the further beach, others close by, a few completely surrounded by the water—mere islands; but every group has its own color, from the snuff-brown earthen hue of the nearer slopes to the blue and misty ranges far away. In the noonday blaze of the vertical sun, or when at dawn its rays glint upon them, their prominences stand out distinctly, and streaks of shadow mark each of the great cañons separating neighboring peaks; but at night, or when the sun loses its angle of advantage, these high

freshening and medicinal breeze, hearkening to the gentle lapping of the wavelets, one can choose many a poetic name and foreign latitude to fit the scene, and easily forget that he is in Utah, until his eye catches the sage-brush.

The mountain trip is of quite different character, and can be made by choosing any one of half a dozen cañons, into which miners long ago led the way. The favorite is the beautiful American Fork Cañon, in reaching which you have the advantage of a railway for the greater part of the distance. A fortnight's camping and trout-fishing in the mountains once a year is considered indispensable to health and happiness by most families.

At the very first, one square of the city was set apart, as the "Temple Block," for holy use. This was intended to be not only the spiritual but the geographical centre of the city (for in spite of their present claims the founders certainly had no idea that so great a town as this would ever arise here), and all the streets are named from this point out—First South, First West, and so on, oddly reversing the ordinary style of designation.

On this ten-acre lot the Mormons held

their first worship; here was built the small building now known as the Endowment House; here, later on, the combined voluntary labor of the members of the Church erected the first Tabernacle; and here were laid the foundations of the Temple, wherein (it is promised) Jesus Christ shall appear bodily to the faithful as soon as it is completed.

This Temple is to be a tall, many-turreted building of white granite, brought from Little Cottonwood Cañon — famous as the locality of the Emma Mine —where it is split from enormous detached fragments that have fallen from the cliffs. It is almost as white and crystalline as marble, and unexcelled as material for an imposing structure. Until the very recent extension of the Denver and Rio Grande Railway into the cañon, all this stone was brought to the city by bullock teams, but now the railway tracks run from the quarries into the Temple yard.

The Temple was contrived and sketched out by Brigham Young. The style is one unknown to architectural schools, I think, but more nearly resembles the Gothic than any other. The structure is of Cyclopean strength; its base, far below the surface, is sixteen feet in thickness, decreasing to nine feet in thickness at the surface. One course of the basement stones stands in the shape of a series of solid reversed arches. Above, the walls rise nearly seven feet in thickness to the present height of eighty feet, which is nearly to where the roof begins.

A BALCONY.

There is no hollowness, or "filling," or brick-work—nothing but solid chiselled granite through and through, not only the outer walls, but in the partitions, the ceilings, and the stairways. The window openings are like the embrasures of a fort, and the heavily walled compartments of the basement suggest the direst dungeons.

RESIDENCE OF BRIGHAM YOUNG.

JOHN TAYLOR.

All the externals of the building have a religious significance. For instance, near the ground are a series of great bosses, upon which are to be carved maps of various regions of the world—and there will be room for a full atlas. Between the windows of the first and second stories similar bosses express eight phases of the moon, while a row of great stone suns is placed between the windows of the second and third tiers, and a star is chiselled upon the key-stone of every arch. When by-and-by the New-Zealander visits the ruins of Salt Lake City, he will be justified, I should say, in concluding the Mormons to have been sun-worshippers or astrologers, or both. President Taylor told me Brigham Young's intention was that the building should last a thousand years.

This enormous Temple is not intended as a place of worship, but as a sacred edifice within which various ceremonies of consecration, marriage, etc., shall be performed that are now celebrated in the Endowment House. For this purpose the whole building is cut up into little cloister-like rooms. The houses for public worship are the Tabernacle, and a handsome granite building, more civic than ecclesiastical in appearance, which occupies one corner of the Temple Square. In the interior this building is arranged with galleries, tiers of pulpits, and organs just like the Tabernacle, but in a much finer style, and it is used for Quorum meetings, evening sessions, and winter services.

What has been the cost of the Temple, which during thirty years has been rearing before the eyes of the towns-people, is a subject of natural curiosity, and one hears many rumors of how many millions supposed to have been expended upon it have really gone into the pockets of a few dignitaries of the Church. These rumors arise, no doubt, from the difficulty of understanding how men formerly poor are now rich, although they have been engaged in none of the ordinary methods of acquiring even a competence. I have the word of President Taylor, however, that the total cost has been, in round numbers, two millions of dollars, nine-tenths of which is accounted for as cash. It is supposed that three years more time and another million dollars will complete it. It is doubtful whether there is in the United States another public building so massive and genuine.

Across the street, just east of the Temple block, Brigham Young took possession of another whole square for himself, erecting at the end nearest the Temple a series

A SUBURBAN COTTAGE.

of store-houses for the reception of tithing levied upon all members of the Church. At the other end were his residences—the "Lion" and "Bee-hive" houses, where he guarded his wives terrestrial and celestial; and behind them the vast stables and corrals where he kept his hundreds of horses and mules, and the sires of his flocks and manded the building of a general fortification around the whole young city—a "Spanish" wall of mud, which has now disappeared, saving a few remnants. Similarly the high walls have been replaced by fences, except that one which still protects the Temple and Young's house. The first Tabernacle was built by contributions of

THE TABERNACLE AND TEMPLE.

herds. Here too were the Church offices—the *sanctum sanctorum* of the Prophet of the Church on Earth of Jesus Christ of Latter-day Saints, the head-quarters of the military and civil ruler of the community, the Court of the High Judge of Zion, beyond whom there was no appeal, and the counting-house of the divinely appointed leader.

Mud and cobble-stones were cheaper than fence timber; the Canaanitish tribes, viz., Pah-Utes, Shoshones, Uintahs, etc., were thievish and belligerent, and, worst of all, unrighteous dwellers in Babylon were beginning to approach and inquire curiously into the ways and means of Mormondom. So walls sprang up in every direction. Not low picturesque stone fences with angular shadows and many-colored slabs and an embroidery of vines and lichens trailing pleasantly across them, but hideous forts of mud around every lot —walls ten to twenty feet high, supported by round bulging bastions at the corners, and guarded by prison-like gates at the entrances. Brigham Young's property in particular looked like a Moorish fortress. Not content with this, the President com-

manual labor for the most part, and was early completed. It had a general resemblance to the present structure, and was of great size. Interiorly it is said to have been exceedingly plain, but to have held a very fine organ. Only a few years elapsed, however, before the construction of the present larger edifice was begun.

The form of the Tabernacle is elliptical, and its roof an elliptical dome, arching everywhere from the eaves to the ridge, and supported upon a series of heavy stone piers, the shortest span between which is 172 feet. As their height is only about twenty feet, and the height of the arched roof much less than a hundred feet, the Tabernacle from without gives you the impression of an enormous building more than half buried. From the general level of the city it is almost impossible to obtain the smallest glimpse of it, either because of the trees or of the great wall behind which it is hid, and in order to get any notion of its size, you must climb to some eminence like the northern bench, where you can look down upon its huge fungus-like form. Elevate it sixty feet, or set it on a hill, and, perfectly fitting Utah scenery in its severe-

OLD MILL, AMERICAN FORK CAÑON.

days at two o'clock in the afternoon. The Saints assemble not only from the city, but from all the country round, and many vehicles of all sorts are left standing in the neighborhood. The centre of the church fills rapidly with women, while men predominate in the side rows of seats. There are seats for thirteen thousand persons in the amphitheatre and gallery, and many more crowd in at

ly simple outlines, it would be as grand in its place as the Parthenon at Athens.

Service in the Tabernacle is held on Sun-some of the great conferences. A broad gallery closes around at the front, where the choir sit in two wings, facing each other, the men on one side and the women opposite. The space between is filled by three long crimson-cushioned pulpit desks, in each of which twenty speakers or so can sit at once, each rank overlooking the heads of the one beneath. The highest was designed for the president and his two counsellors; the second one for the twelve apostles, and the lowest for the bishops, but I believe the order is not very rigidly observed.

The acoustic properties of the house are almost perfect. A former deficiency of light has been overcome by the use of electricity; and the chilling bareness of the huge whitewashed vault is relieved by hangings of evergreen and flowers made of tissue-paper, the effect of which is very good indeed.

Every Sunday the sacrament is administered, the table loaded with the baskets of bread and tankards of water occupying a dais at the foot of the pulpits. Gradually a number of bishops take their places behind this table, and watch the congregation gather, people coming in through the dozen or more side doors as though the Tabernacle was a huge sponge absorbing the population of the Territory. Mingling with the rest come many strangers, bringing the latest tailoring and millinery, and these strangers are always conducted to seats down in front, where they can be addressed effectively in a body. At one door stands a huge cask of cold water, with several tin cups handy, and nearly all stop to drink as they come in. Later you will see tin pails holding a quart or more, and having handles on both sides, circulating through the audience, and refilled from time to time by small Ganymedes running about in chip hats and well-starched pinafores. Precisely at two o'clock the great organ sends forth its melodious summons, and the noise of busy voices — the hum of the veritable honey-bees of Deseret in their home hive — is hushed. A hymn is announced (by some brother in a business coat whom you will meet in trade to-morrow, perhaps), and sung by the choir, for though the tune may be one of the old familiar ones, the audience does not join in the singing.

The music of the Tabernacle has a great reputation in the West, and it would hardly be fair to decry it because it does not come up to a New York performance. It is conspicuously good for the material at hand and the locality. The organ, a handsome instrument, nearly as large as the great organ in the Boston Music Hall, is not so readily discounted, however, and is played with much skill, to the constant delight of the people.

After the singing comes a long prayer by some layman-priest, and a hymn, during the singing of which eight bishops break the slices of bread into morsels. Then, while the bread is being passed through the audience to the communicants — everybody, old and young, partaking — President Taylor or some other dignitary reads a chapter from the Bible, usually from Revelation, and makes extempore remarks upon it. Sometimes the Hon. George Q. Cannon, the most eminent of the Mormon leaders, occupies the pulpit.

It is three o'clock before the bread and water have been partaken of by all, and fully four by the time the preacher has ceased, the bishop pronounced the benediction, and the congregation is dismissed. As the people scatter about the great dusty yard, picking their way among the blocks of stone awaiting their place in the Temple, one sees how largely foreigners they are, the predominant nationalities being British and Scandinavian. Their peasantry, too, is unmistakably stamped upon their faces, though they have exchanged their foreign characteristics for a rusticity of the American type. Among the most prominent of the Mormon apostles are Orson Pratt, the most distinguished scholar and writer in the sect, and Joseph F. Smith, a nephew of the original Prophet and founder of Mormonism.

In Salt Lake City there are four separate sections of society which react upon one another. First, the adherents of the Mormon Church — the Saints; second, those who never have been nor will be Mormons — the Gentiles; third, the seceders from the Mormon Church; and fourth, the renegades and irresponsible of all parties, for whom has been adopted the Californian word hoodlum. This classification makes queer bedfellows: the Jew finds himself a Gentile, and the Roman Catholic becomes a Protestant, making common cause with Calvinism against the hierarchy of the Tabernacle. The result, of course, is that each section keeps pretty well to itself, and is likely to despise the others.

A few women of Salt Lake, years ago, formed a mutual-improvement club, having for its object a uniform course of reading. Now there are two flourishing ladies' literary societies, which are of far more significance here as centres of a healthy intellectual and social existence and progress than they would be in any other com-

GEORGE Q. CANNON.

munity. Most of their members are also members of the Anti-polygamy Society, which publishes a monthly journal, *The Standard*, under the editorship of Mrs. Jennie A. Froiscth.

The McKenzie Reform Club, established under Gentile auspices for the suppression of intemperance, has prospered so that it has erected the handsome building known as the Walker Opera-house, which cost nearly $75,000. The corner-stone was laid with much ceremony early in August of 1881.

Mormons are publicly very sociable, and remarkably peaceable. In their various ward meeting-houses—for each bishop's ward has an assembly-room—are held at frequent intervals during the colder half of the year assemblies where dancing is the main object, and where it is indulged without stint. Gentiles are occasionally invited. These dances (and all other Mormon festivities) are opened and closed by prayer.

The Salt-Lakers are also diligent musicians. From the great organ in the Taber-

nacle down to a jew's-harp, everybody handles some sort of musical instrument, or sings, and the music shops of the city seem about as brisk as any places on the street. You will hear singing all the time, and in all localities. This has been encouraged by the Church, as has also been the dramatic taste of the people, who very early organized a company of actors, and long ago built the great theatre which is a prominent feature of the city. For a long time only "home talent" graced its boards, but since the railway gave easy access, every company of actors that crosses the continent stops here, and some great names have been among those who have played in this temple of histrionics. Among the local celebrities in the theatrical line were several members of the family of Brigham Young, and one of his daughters is yet "on the boards," in San Francisco.

The annals of this theatre, perhaps, afford quite as good a gauge of the change which has taken place in Salt Lake City during the last twenty years as any other one thing in town. At first, as I have said, it was wholly supported by the local company of amateurs, and patronized in a most unconventional way by the simple Mormons in their sun-bonnets, who came with their whole families. The floor of the theatre in those days was reserved to the Saints; Jews, Gentiles, and other "dwellers in Babylon" sat in the first gallery. The audience now does not noticeably differ from that of any Eastern theatre, and the new opera-house is one of the handsomest in the Union.

Concerning the sociability among Mormon families in a private way, an outsider can only know by report. It is said to be small. The interchanges of calls and the forms of neighborly etiquette prevailing in ordinary society are little practiced. Even in the case of the wealthy, social visiting is said to be infrequent.

The private home routine of a polygamous family is a matter upon which so much curiosity is constantly expressed by my acquaintances that I venture to say here what little I know; but the reader must remember that less than ten per cent. of the voting Mormon population of Utah are polygamists.

The polygamist, as a rule, has accumulated some property and owns a house

PULPITS AND ORGAN IN THE TABERNACLE.

before he takes a second and successive wives, though sometimes he begins by marrying two or three at once. All of these marriages, however, except the first, are made secretly by the Church, and no record of them is accessible.

In the city, at least, it is seldom that the different wives share the same quarters. In the country this is not so uncommon, but the natural unpleasantness follows in most cases. The general method is to have a large house, the main part of which, perhaps, is occupied by the first wife, and wings or additions by the successive candidates for marital honors. These large, straggling, hotel-like houses are common in Salt Lake City, and mark a difference between it and a town of small houses like Cheyenne and most other Western villages. In many cases, however, the husband sets up his wives in separate homes, either side by side or in different parts of the city. In any case each has her own kitchen-garden, etc. I have in mind a wealthy dignitary of the Church whom you might easily have mistaken for the late Peter Cooper, and who is possessed of seven wives. Each of these women has some farming and garden ground of her own, and all are greatly devoted to rearing bees. With the help of their grown children they each raise a large amount of produce and honey annually. The husband acts as their agent. He hives their swarms of bees, and charges them for it; he renders special aid when called upon, and is paid for it; he sells their crops and honey when it is ready,

and credits each wife with her due share. Most of them live in suites of apartments under the roof of his great house in town, but the first wife has a beautiful farm of her own a little out of the city, to which she and her children have retired, to end their days in peaceful independence.

The way in which this old gentleman has always arranged his domestic life is reported to be thus: He had certain rooms in his house where he kept his bed, his wardrobe, his books, and saw any visitors who called upon him. Here he was a bachelor, and here he staid every other day and night. On alternate days and nights he was the guest of one or another of his wives in regular rotation, devoting the one day (in this case fortnightly) which was hers diligently to her society. Of course this routine was not invariable, but for the most part it was regularly followed.

In respect to the general morals of the community, it may be said that they are simply those of any old and well-regulated town East or West. If as a Western city it differs from an Eastern town of similar size, it is merely in classification, not degree. Anything like open violence is extremely rare ; ladies walk the streets at night unmolested; and burglary is almost

JOSEPH F. SMITH.

sorts are never so crowded as on Sundays. To be sure, it is the plebeian element which goes, for the most part; but the patricians stay at home more as a matter of taste than righteousness, for you will see them playing croquet in the orchard, and hear them singing decidedly secular songs around the household piano in the evening. Undoubtedly there are many conscientious to "keep the Sabbath holy"; but what I mean to say is that the City of the Saints is little better than its neighbors in this particular form of religious observance.

So far as my own observation went, the condition of Salt Lake City did not seem at all superior to other well-settled towns of its size either East or West as regards that special kind of immorality which Mormonism professes to eradicate.

Of the arrests made annually in Salt Lake City, by far the larger number belong to the non-Mormon minority. Many of the culprits, however, are not residents of the city, but are a part of the floating crowd of miserable and dissolute men that infest every Western city.

The Gentiles of the city probably enjoy themselves more than they would if they could run off to a great town in an hour,

unknown. Thievery, however, is common enough, and a large police force is needed. Gambling is wholly "on the sly." In the matter of liquor-drinking, a great change has recently come about. For many years after the foundation of the city Brigham Young rigidly excluded all liquors, and even as late as a dozen years ago only two or three bars met the patronage of ten or fifteen thousand people. Whatever else they might be, the President evidently intended his people should not become drunkards. Now, however, local breweries turn out great quantities of lager-beer; every hotel and nearly every restaurant has its bar, while dozens of liquor saloons exist, some managed by Mormons.

Observance of Sunday used to be very rigid and sanctimonious, and even now it is far more strict than in most cities west of the Missouri; for in California, as in New Orleans, Sunday is mainly devoted to recreation, the theatres are opened, and pleasure excursions of all sorts are encouraged. Denver is dropping into this way somewhat also, while as for Santa Fe, Cheyenne, and Helena, they never had any principle at all so far as the Sabbath was concerned. With the growth of Salt Lake City this worldly influence is more and more apparent, and the trains to the bathing re-

ORSON PRATT.

and were not necessarily so self-centred as the isolation of the locality compels them to be. It is a society made up of the families of successful merchants and mining men, of clergymen and teachers, of the officers of the army stationed at Camp Doug-

long produced pretty well up to their several capacities. There must, then, be an increased area of plantation if there is to be a greater supply; but examination proves that it is probably impossible to bring under cultivation a hundred thousand acres

A TYPICAL MORMON FAMILY.

las, and the representatives of the government in the judicial and other Territorial offices. This composition, it will be seen, presupposes considerable intelligence and culture, the effect of which is plainly to be seen in their homes.

Utah has always been pre-eminently an agricultural district. Out of her 150,000 people probably 120,000 are now farming or stock-raising in some capacity or other. When you look down the valley from the city your eye takes in a wide view of fields and orchards and meadows, green with the most luxuriant growth, and marked off by rows of stately trees or patches of young woodland. All these farms are small holdings, and though cultivated by no means scientifically, have

more of land in the whole Territory. Leaving out the cactus plains of the south, the bleak plateaus east of the Wahsatch, the saline deserts on the western border, and the volcanic sands which run down from Idaho, nearly all the rest of the Territory where water is accessible has already been taken up. It must be remembered that all the agriculture of Utah is by artificial irrigation. Every mountain cañon discharges a stream fed by the melting snows of the heights. This stream is dammed, its waters led along the "benches" beneath the foot-hills in great ditches, and thence distributed through slender conduits to each man's land. The sources of the water are held to be public property, and many questions of law are more and more becoming involved in the consideration of the rights and responsibilities of the public in relation to its water supply.

The important fact in this connection is that the limit of otherwise arable land is not so soon to be reached as that of irrigation. The Mormon leaders recognize this, and are continually sending colonies of new-comers away into neighboring Territories to establish themselves. The present waste of water may be largely saved, and more economical methods of farming introduced, but Utah can hardly expect to do more than double her present agricultural population. This class, however, will be able to produce far more than would be needed for their own consumption. That is done now, and the export of all sorts of grain, fruit, and produce is large, and is constantly increasing.

To something more than agriculture, then, which in the opinion of the first settlers was their stronghold, must Utah and her metropolis look for future growth. The Mormon leaders, and particularly Brigham Young, always opposed any attempt at a development of the mineral resources of the Territory, though 'it is said that he informed himself as thoroughly as he could upon their character and value. He forbade all mining to his devotees, and would have closed the mountains to Gentile prospectors if he had been able. So far as a desire existed to avoid the evils of a placer-working excitement, drawing hither a horde of ruffianly gold-seekers, this course was commendable. But as years went on it was seen by the shrewder heads among the Mormons themselves that this abstinence from mining was harmful. There was no cash in the Territory, and none to be got. If a surplus of grain was raised, or more of any sort of goods manufactured than could be used at home, there was no sale for it, since at that time the market was so far away, and transportation was so deficient and expensive, that no profits could possibly be made. Business was almost wholly by barter, and payments for everything had to be by exchange. A man who took his family to the theatre wheeled his admission fee with him in the shape of a barrel or two of potatoes, and a young man would go to a dance with his girl on one arm, and a bunch of turnips on the other with which to buy his ticket. The Gentiles soon began to bring in coin, but the relief was gradual and inadequate.

Finally, about fifteen years ago, it was publicly argued by some bold minds, in the face of the Church, and to their own discomfort, that the only things Utah had which she could send out against competition were gold and silver. When from preaching they began to practice, and such men as the Walker brothers encouraged outside capital to join them in developing silver ledges in the Wahsatch, then Salt Lake City began to rouse herself. Potatoes and carrots and adobes disappeared as currency, and coin and greenbacks enlivened trade, which conformed more and more to the ordinary methods of American commerce.

One perfectly legitimate means taken for monopoly of trade was the establishment, twenty-five years ago, of Zion's Co-operative Mercantile Institution. In the early days it was exceedingly difficult for country shop-keepers to maintain supplies, when everything had to be hauled by teams from the Missouri River, and extortionate prices would be demanded for staples when, as frequently happened, some petty dealer would get a "corner" in them. The design of this establishment was to furnish goods of every sort known to merchants out of one central depot in Salt Lake City, under control of the Church, and partly owned by it. This was a joint-stock "co-operative" affair, however, and the capital was nearly a million dollars. The people were commanded from the pulpit to trade there, but they would have done so anyhow, for the "co-op," as it is called, was able to reduce and equalize prices very greatly. Branches were established in Ogden, Logan, and Soda Springs, and a warehouse built in Provo. These and other additions were rapid. The central sales-rooms in this city now occupy a four-story brick building three hundred and eighteen feet long by ninety-seven feet wide, where every species of merchandise is to be found. In other quarters are a drug-store, a shoe factory (supplied by its own tanneries, and running one hundred and twenty-five machines propelled by steam), and a manufactory for canvas "overall" clothing. Altogether about two hundred and fifty persons are employed, working at reasonable hours and reasonable pay. The stock, which originally was widely scattered in small lots, has been concentrated for the most part in the hands of a few astute men, who are credited with large

CAMP DOUGLAS.

profits. There is an air of great prosperity about the institution, whose business is stated to reach five millions of dollars annually, derived almost wholly from Utah and Southern Idaho.

Though this concern had a practical monopoly at first, as soon as the railways came to Salt Lake individual merchants could sell goods about as cheap, and opposition arose. Then the power of the Church was brought directly to bear to crush competition.

For example, the four Walker brothers, sons of a Mormon father, were engaged in trade, and were getting rich, having surmounted obstacles fatal to lesser strength. Brigham Young, in the height of his pride and power, chose to insist that their tithe offerings were not large enough, and to demand a large amount of cash additional—$30,000, it is reported, at one fell swoop. Instead of a check he received a refusal. Instantly relays of Saints were established to stand in front of the Walkers' shop, and report for condemnation every Mormon who traded there. Nevertheless the Walker brothers survived, and are to-day probably the most powerful mercantile firm in Utah.

Brigham Young's attitude led to a schism in the Church, and a small but far-reaching rebellion among some of his most trusted followers.

The leaders of this movement were W. S. Godbe, H. W. Lawrence, and E. L. T. Harrison, and they had plenty of encouragement. Through the pages of the *Utah Magazine* they declared that Young was not a dictator over their temporal as well as spiritual life, that commerce should be left to its own laws, that Utah's prosperity lay in the development of her mines, that

the United States was above the Church in civil matters, and that the priesthood should confine itself to its proper function —that of spiritual guidance. They were expelled from the Church, which did all it could to ruin their business. All they asked was independence and religious liberty to worship God in the same forms that Brigham Young professed to enjoy and to enjoin; but that autocrat would brook no opposition to his infallibility. Nevertheless, the Godbe movement was of lasting strength, and through it Salt Lake City took an important step toward the freedom and prosperity of the present.

The policy, or at any rate the action, of the Church has changed greatly since Young's death. Everybody now buys in the best market, modern manners in all the walks of life are cultivated, better schools are being established among both Mormons and Gentiles, and the best newspapers are patronized no matter what their creed.

The Church is as ambitious as ever, and taking advantage of the general indifference to its movements, is steadily aggressive through all its missionary channels. If it has grown weaker among its earliest adherents and in its first stronghold, it is growing stronger through new accessions, and in other Territories is quietly laying the foundations of future political power.

Salt Lake City is one of the points in the United States that all tourists think should not be missed. It is one of the certain stopping points in the programme of the globe-trotter. Consequently the city is always full of strangers, and various excursion facilities have grown up and flourished almost wholly by patronage of sight-seers. Hotels are well supported, too, and consequently are unusually good. A few days after the arrival at San Francisco of each steamer from the other side of the Pacific there is a special flux of visitors. Then it is highly entertaining to sit in the long, Southern-like, acacia-shaded veranda of the Continental and watch the omnibuses unload their foreign travellers, with heaps of queer-looking luggage bearing marks affixed in Yokohama or Melbourne, and concealing a stratification of labels that would read right around the world. This tourist business is of value to the city, and is becoming more noticeable than ever now that a second line of railway, the Denver and Rio Grande, has been opened between this city and the East. Heretofore the only railway communication had been by the Union Pacific at Ogden, the Utah Central connecting Salt Lake City with that town. The famous narrow-gauge railway of Colorado, however, pushed its line through the southern passes of the Rockies, and made a rival connection with the Central Pacific at Ogden. This diverted at once so large a body of travellers who were anxious to avail themselves of the opportunity to see the marvellous scenery of the interior Rocky Mountains that the old line was obliged to bestir itself.

The competition in the transportation of farm products, ores, and merchandise also caused a very considerable diminution in rates of freight, and has been a stimulus to all business in eastern Utah. Grain and potatoes, hitherto fed to the hogs or not harvested, found a quick market at advanced rates. The new road made accessible new coal mines also, and cheapened fuel and coke, while important concessions were made to those who wished to send their ores to Denver, Pueblo, or eastward, or to bring Colorado ores, for the advantage of the smelters, here. The building of the western end of the Denver and Rio Grande was done almost wholly by Mormons, and great sums of money have been expended here, so that cash has been abundant, trade and building brisk, and the increase of population in and about the city very rapid. The census of 1880 gave the city only a little over 20,000; she now has close upon 25,000. At the same time the rise of large towns in Montana, the opening of railway outlets in the north, and eastern demands have made unlooked-for drafts upon the cattle herds and the farms of the whole region. The result has followed in Salt Lake that the cost of living has advanced nearly fifty per cent. in two or three years.

GRAVE OF BRIGHAM YOUNG.

DOWN THE WEST COAST

A BIT OF SEA-WALL AT PANAMA.

AN "ocean-voyage" which is all ocean hardly earns the appellative; for it denies the kinship of *voyage* and *way*. Neither is it fit to be called a journey, which, by essence as by etymology, is made of days and not of miles; each day of its own, and between each pair of days something different. For that which makes travel is the way-side, and there needs a less word to fit such goings as the five days' jump of the Atlantic, that road without a side. There remains at least one American voyage that is truly a voyage; an ocean-journey with a way-side of changing nights and days, and from day to day of world past world—a neutral strip where even steam and happiness can lock arms. It has even the better of its brother coast-voyage on the other side—that charming journey through the sea of islands—for it has more way-side, and a more variegated one. The west coast is the right-hand side of the continent, as any one can see who will look at a geography right side up; and we shall yet recognize in this long-neglected dexter the full force of its anatomical location

—though unto this day the self-sufficient left hand outscriptures the text, and cares as little as it little knows what the right hand doeth.

The voyage from San Francisco to an equivalent point on the Pacific coast of South America is no six-day matter. On comfortable steamers of ten and twelve knots it takes twenty-seven days. One can come left-handed to Peru in several days less. From New York, Panama is about 1800 miles; from San Francisco nearly twice as far, and more than twice as interesting.

If ever there be extenuating circumstances for a premeditated departure from California, it is for this voyage. On no other side can one step off from the New Hesperides to alight with so little jar. California's dream ends at the State line; but down the west coast the awakening is gradual. It is only from the honey-moon to the after-years—a finding that there are other sides to the tropics than sun and orange blossoms; but for all the realities below, the same sky still.

In October the passenger list of the

Pacific Mail is well filled. The coffee season begins, and the wealthy dons of Central America go now to their crops, *aguantando como puedan* until such time as they may come back to life, otherwise California. Three months of the year suffice to pursue their money; the rest of the time it must better its gait to keep up with them. Here, too, is the blond clerk who has, in the march of German destiny, acquired the daughter of the don, and by her a family and a plantation. A predestined "drummer," carrying brass whither the gold of courtesy is current; a polite gentleman, who has bought the faro monopoly of Guatemala, and is going to till this condensed-coffee plantation; and half a dozen wise "Americans," who have learned the pleasantest way to New York at $120 for 5200 miles, with board for four weeks—fill the ultimate state-rooms.

The coast of California from the Golden Gate southward gives little hint of the interior. It is largely a barricade of abrupt brown ridges, springing almost from the surf to hide the real California from inquisitive eyes and winds. Nature has spent too much on the garden to have capital left for painting the fence, and it stands the primal pattern which humanity has unconsciously followed in all such lands—Eden hidden behind an adobe wall. Here and there through a crack in the weathered fence a green tendril of a valley creeps. Yonder is a bit of shore with its dark citrus patch; a barren candlestick of a headland, with the white shaft of its light-house; a roadstead flecked with fishers' sails; clouds of sea-birds that snow upon a smelt-ruffled reach of sea.

With dawn of the third day we are at the beginning of the way-side—tying up, at San Diego, to the last wharf with which our steamer will venture upon such familiarities in five weeks, with time to visit that *Arabian Nights* hotel whose site I knew first as sandspit dear at ten dollars the mile; then as sandspit plus auctioneer and buyers of lots to a million dollars; and now as sandspit turned garden, whose chief fruit is one of the finest hotels in America.

San Diego is the last of the United States, but not the least. It is already characteristic as New England—more so, for the New-Englander rules here as not at home. Spain has gone to the wall; and the Yankee, with new wings and

room for them, pervades all. One may half guess the patron saint of Spain set down now in the lap of his namesake daughter, to rub his eyes at the changed face of her, and at her sons, who know not a saddle from a *santo*, and whose only saints ring their own mass. It is the last anachronism. The Spanish spirit is as far to-day from the twenty-five-foot-front idea as in the golden age of Cortes. To its benighted understanding still, money is good for what it will buy, and the object of life is to live.

Face and form are new, but the old names are cherished—with the distortion which is the peculiar Saxon privilege and joy. Four-fifths of all the place names in California are Spanish, and four-fifths of them a Spaniard would not recognize in the mouth of the intruder.

A few hours' stay, and then the city, etched on its tilted sheet of sand, the peninsula and its great hotel, the blue islets of Coronado, fall behind, and our land is the first profile of Baja California—gray-brown arid peaks, featured like those northward, but more careworn and more inhospitable. Presently the Pacific blue overflows them, and we are quite at sea. Two days thus; and on the sixth the mountainous desert wades out again to greet us, and with the last ray of red, the striking front of Cape St. Lucas, southernmost tip of the great peninsula, and outpost sentinel of the Vermilion Sea.

With sunrise of the seventh morning we waken ungrateful to the blankets of bedtime. The step across the gulf's mouth is from the temperate to the tropics—a change of worlds overnight. We are anchoring off Mazatlan. Its turquoise semilune of a bay, symmetrically set between three tall abrupt islands to the north, and three to the south, cuts the very edge of the town, whose adobe turns marble with distance and the sun. On its northern outer island—once stronghold of countless runaway slaves—perches the light-house, 300 feet aloft.

This outpost of the tropics—six leagues south of the tropic of Cancer, and already in sight of the Southern Cross—is the commercially first port of the Pacific coast of Mexico, and the second of the whole republic. It is key to the Gulf of California—or Gulf of Cortes, for its discoverer; or *Mar Bermejo*, for the tinging of its waters by ferruginous rivers—and to an extensive interior of vast potentiality. It was port not only for Sinaloa, but for Sonora, Chihuahua, Durango, and even to Zacatecas, until the opening of ports at San Blas and Manzanillo cut it down at home, and San Francisco put a knee in its direct China trade.

For a town founded in 1822 with a few huts, Mazatlan has had its taste of his-

ish-American wheel scores revolutions. Time was that we were spunky too, when our nose was pulled, and Spanish America is boyish as we began. As bad politicians as ours get into office there, and as frequently, but they do not stay as long. There the mugwump votes with a bullet, if the ballot fails to bring down reform;

CIGÁRETTE-MAKERS, MAZATLAN.

tory. Thrice it has changed its name. It has been several times capital of Sinaloa, and all times a nest of revolution. With seven other sieges, it was stormed by us in 1847, and twice bombarded by Maximilian's fleet. It was his for two years to a day—the only foothold in Sinaloa of the meddlers. The list of governors of Sinaloa since the state was formed (1830) is of more length than breadth, with its incumbents "for ten days," "for two days," "for seven days." Nor shall we gird too flippantly at the "ball-bearing" ease wherewith the Span-

and such misrule as is in any one of our great cities is enough to set him afoot.

Mazatlan is our preface to the new volume, and characteristically ear-marked. Flat-topped, low, compact; cleaned to the ultimate crumb by its dual health department—the vultures of heaven and the donkey carts of the municipality; with fresh light walls, sharp in the *rilievo* of their shade-trap angles (there are no other shadows like those of the adobe) and the darker plumes of palm and plantain; with narrow streets, painfully but eternally *empedradas* with cobbles, deserted on the side to the sun, alive, but leisurely, on the side to the shade; with picturesque folk of five different bloods, and over all and around all the indescribable atmosphere of New Spain, with all its courtesy and its rest.

The few chief streets of this town of 10,000 are endeared with stringent neatness and with glimpses by cool doorways to wide *patios*. The Spanish-American idea of a dwelling is not met by a box of whatsoever size or sumptuousness. It must be home not only for the family, but for a bit of out-doors as well. Instead of losing that he may dazzle the passer, the transplanted Iberian still takes his lawn into the sitting-room. He builds not behind it, but around it; and every room opens into it, and every inmate can lounge in its freshness secure from unentitled eyes. Its fountain, its foliage, its blessed verandas, are part of the household and not of the street.

Back of these homelike homes, in little tilted alleys, are the *chozas* of the poor; rude apologies to a complacent sky, with careless cane and rushes, and naked babes and laughter, and all the trade-marks of the tropics, where to be poor is not to want.

A prudent New England relative, prone to the warning "money does not grow on every bush," had never been below the United States. Had she known the west coast, the Puritan conscience would have forced her to seek some other saw to lop boyish prodigalities. For here it *does*. Here we begin to realize the common—but at home empty—dream of something for nothing. Bargains in Dollars! Coin Selling out Below Cost! Help yourself to what you Want, and the Cashier will Give you your Money back, and Dollars to Boot! One may dream what our advertisers would do with such a text.

After a cup of heaven's next-last, next-best gift to man—it is worth while to make the voyage to Under-America to find out what coffee really is—I entered a store on the plaza and bought twenty-five excellent cigars for seventy-five cents. The merchant rang my five-dollar gold piece on the counter, and without emotion handed me six silver dollars and seventy-five cents in small silver. Fortunately the Western habit of "always coming down stairs that way" stood by me. He had counted too exhaustively to make any mistake. There was contagion

in this. I went to an opposite store and purchased a box of twenty-five such *excepcionales* as are seldom smoked with us, for two dollars, handing out another half-eagle. The vender counted out and gave me five dollars and fifty cents silver with a pleasant smile. It was hard to leave a spot where one can make a handsome salary simply by spending money. There was but one hard reality. I tempted the national drink for a dime, and got back but ninety cents from my silver dollar. That, however, is easily overcome. All one has to do is to take gold along. Plenty of gold. Then one can revel in swapping dollars for dollars and a half, if one have the mind to withstand prosperity. Some would require a strait-jacket after a few miles on this royal road to fortune.

At San Blas, twelve hours from Mazatlan and 1474 miles from San Francisco, we are boarded in the open roadstead by swart benefactors, each staggering under an Atlas-load of cigars. It is also worth while to get out of the United States now and then for a smoke. Here we buy far better than a ten-cent cigar at two Mexican dollars the hundred; and for *three* "'dobes"—or $2 10 gold—a Reina Victoria in every way preferable to a twenty-five-cent cigar in New York. San Blas is outlet of the famous Tepic tobacco belt, and its poorest smoker enjoys a weed such as not all of us can afford at home. The town, of 2000 people, is undiluted tropics, beset with palm and plantain, parrots and mocking-birds, built of adobe for the rich, and of cane for the rest.

Seven hours of San Blas, and our ocean stage-coach rolls on to new scenes. At morn of the ninth day we are entering the beautiful toy harbor of Manzanillo, with one exception the prettiest *poblacion* of the west coast. This little jewel of the tropics has not over 600 people, but beauty to an independent fortune per capita. Snuggling into the hollows of abrupt and matted hills behind, its front is bent to the perfect curve of the white beach. Its snowy adobes peaked with the ever-adorable red tiles, its ways neat as after the besom of a New England housewife, and "enstoned" (by the Spanish of it) in wonderful patterns of cobble, its massy little church, its sobersides of a custom-house, its blossom of a plaza, its soft air a very distillation of flowers and birds and butterflies, its Italian blueness of a bay—altogether it is an exquisite thing.

At noon on the tenth day our prow suddenly splits the precipitous cliffs. Steering into a blue channel, we leave on the left the isle of La Roqueta—captured in the war of Mexican Independence by the meteoric Galeana—and head straight upon the inland ridges. But timely before them another unforeseen channel opens sharply to the left, and in ten minutes we are at anchor in the second-best harbor on the globe. Sydney is first, but Acapulco is undisputed second. It is the very foot of a stocking—the ankle to sea, the instep to shore, our anchorage in the toe. The peninsula and islands deny whatever wind from seaward, and back of town the abrupt mountains wall off the interior.

The tender green of the unruffled bay is cut in sharp profile by the sombre green of beachless hills, which mock the impotent word "wooded." They are *woolled*, in a dark mat which seems rather carved than grown, so dense and unyielding is it. On a long narrow strand of the north shore, backed by the dark peaks, ended on the west by low hills, and on the east by the gray old fort, are strung the irregular white beads of the town.

It is five o'clock before the deliberate *visita* is done and the launches dare approach to peddle fruits and infinite shells. We tumble into the first, and are speedily ashore, hurrying through the quaint plaza, with the gray bulk of the church behind, and at one side the picturesque tatters of the market-place. The town is of 5000 souls, compact and bright; a short measure for the legs, but so full of fascinations that the mind has to run to keep up.

From the western ridge, and with the sun's last benediction upon the town below, the view is precious to remember:

GROUP OF NATIVES, ACAPULCO.

and the lens saves all that could be hoped of a picture whose soul is the elusive air. Then, with silver spur to my *portador*—a ten-year-old Cortes, who carries the fifty-pound camera-box on uncomplaining head—back to the foot of the hill in bare time for two characteristic photographs of types. A pool in a rivulet is wash-tub, whereat a score of sturdy supple women in a recreant skirt and *camisa* apiece are correcting their linen; and on a level bench of the slope a horde of children—some in scant raiment and some in naked truth—run their races and fly their kites. The sun has already set, but eagerness for a photograph keeps my groups quiet for the minute-long exposure.

The fort lies just past the eastern tip of the town, and the ramble to and around it on such a tropic night is the crown of all. Away from the more pretentious centre, with its two stories and its *portales*, up a sloping street of ancient cobbles, half tunnel-like under the spread of

THE STREET TO THE FORT.

the gigantic *amates*, whose ten-foot trunks stand in clumsy tiptoe of high-arching roots, with furtive loop-holes between these and the high-peaked cabins to a moon-lit bay, and under the shadowy bastions which laughed at Morelos but opened to the first knock of Maximilian—it all is a memory which comes half to be distrusted. It seems too perfect to have been true—such more than moonlight, such angles of shade, such salients of whiteness, such hush and peace and beauty.

The fort crowns a rocky headland, beetling nearly 200 feet above the bay. It is of a style no more valuable than our own "coast defences"; but with its massive masonry, its superannuated draw-bridge and moat, the lay eye may dare be impressed, though the warrior deride. Upon a western re-entrant still gapes the knuckle-mark of French intervention—the one cannon-ball which gave Maximilian the key to the state of Guerrero and the best port in the western hemisphere. The fame of the harbor goes back to Cortes. He was here in 1531, and from here sent the expedition which discovered Sinaloa, and perished there.

Acapulco is the last port of Mexico. The eleventh day shows but a faint blue rim of Oaxaca; and in the evening we begin the Gulf of Tehuantepec. On the twelfth we have crossed the gulf, and ride day long upon a mill-pond. With dark we come to Ocos, the northernmost portlet of Guatemala, and deposit a few of our coffee-planters, and three hours later reach Champerico for a night's anchorage. We are at this chief coffee-shipping port of the Pacific till five of the next afternoon. The town is petty, the port an open roadstead, with the heavy ground-swell of all this coast; the fine iron pier unapproachable except by the launches, from which passengers and freight dangle up twenty uncertain feet in a big cage. For leagues inland the coast is marsh and miasma; but with higher levels begins the great coffee belt of Guatemala. Coffee-planting is now fairly a "boom" on the west coast, and already overdone. Here, too, is the home of the most magnificent of all birds, the beloved quetzal (*Trogon resplendens*), the national bird of the Coffee Republic. For it is named the important town of Quet-zaltenango — *tenango*, "place"—being a favorite ending of town names which retain the Guatemaltecan form, as Ma-zatenango, Deer-place; Chimaltenango, Shield-place; Huehuetenango, Drum-place, and the like.

Twenty leagues inland from Champerico stands the symmetrical cone of Santa Maria, 12,467 feet above us. There are also Atitlan, with its 11,633 feet; Santa Clara, with 9098; Pacaya, with 8400. Far southeast are seen the twin peaks so tragically associated with the beginnings of Guatemala.

Six hours' sail from Champerico brings us to a night's anchorage in the roadstead of San José de Guatemala, and to an unforgettable sight. Forty miles east the Volcan de Agua and the Volcan de Fuego front us, so far up the sky, so sublimated in the moonlight, as to seem the very

Agua, at an elevation of 4855 feet, and Acatenango and Fuego almost overhang it from the north. Fuego has an altitude of 12,603 feet, and is still alive. Agua is 12,334 feet tall, and Acatenango, 12,890. In figures, this is not overpowering; but our taller Pike and Sierra Blanca seem babies by contrast. Either is hardly more than 8000 feet above any point from which it can be seen. Even great Popocatepetl has but 11,000 feet the better of the high plateau which bears and commands it. But the nearly 13,000 feet of the giant trinity now before us is *net*—from the first foot to the last of those not easily

THE DRAWBRIDGE OF THE FORT AT ACAPULCO.

ghosts of peaks. Better than by day their wraiths recall the fate of Pedro de Alvarado's little capital three centuries and a half ago—how the Volcano of Fire boiled over, and the split Volcano of Water gave up the lake of its dead crater, and wiped from off the slate of humanity the city and its people. Beatriz de la Cueva, Alvarado's young bride, was among the victims, and the conqueror of Central America never recovered from the blow. Relic-seekers still spade up the grave of his city, Antigua. Guatemala, the capital, is on the eastward slope of

realized digits—and the figure they cut in the sky is unaccustomed and awesome. Of the far greater peaks of the upper Andes, not one is seen from the sea at anything like so short range—if ever from the sea at all—and the traveller may safely reckon that between Alaska and Ecuador he will enter no other presence so overtopping as that of the titan triad of Guatemala.

From our eighth way-side halt we move on at sunset of the fourteenth day. At midnight, despite the storm, an uncommonly powerful glass makes out the faint, high candle of Isalco, the most active volcano of the northern continent, and the only one of Central America in constant eruption, though Fuego and San Miguel are still alive, and Santa Ana scored an outbreak in 1876. Isalco was upheaved in the latter part of the last century. For a long period, ending in 1877, it slept, but since then has been steadily active. It serves as a light-house for this stretch of coast. At one of the morning, as we sailed by, there was a sudden flare as of wet powder on the horizon, and then a fiery lace wrapped the black peak from head to foot, tracing in each ravine its golden thread—like nothing so much as a skeleton grape leaf laid on charcoal and smitten with sudden flame from an invisible blow-pipe.

Isalco is forty miles inland from Acajutla, whence its eruptions every seven minutes are fascinating. Between that port and La Libertad stretches the most beautiful coast of Central America, the famous "Balsam Coast" of Salvador. The so-called "Peru balsam" (*Toluifera balsamica*) is found nowhere else, and takes its popular name from the fact that in old times the Spanish crown—anxious to hide the real source of this precious gum—had it covertly shipped to Peru, and thence exported to Europe as a Peruvian product.

Twelve hours from San José puts us off La Libertad—the best its tiny republic boasts in the way of a seaport. It is the front door of San Salvador, and forty muleback miles from the capital. Over the hills, behind its two pinched streets, rosy cumuli puff up momently through the rain-washed morning air, like the smoke rings of an inconceivable locomotive. Each rises far aloft in a knotted club of vapor, breaks off, and floats away eastward, still upright, to be followed directly by another. It is the smoke of Isalco's torments.

San Salvador, though by far the smallest of the five Central American republics—having less than half the area of even Costa Rica, and not one-sixth that of Nicaragua—is the most prosperous and the most thickly populated. It has 780,000 inhabitants—three times as many as Costa Rica, nearly as many as Nicaragua and Honduras put together, and more than half as many as Guatemala, which has almost five times the area. Besides balsam, sugar, cotton, coffee, cocoa, rice, and precious woods, it is a chief producer of indigo. Its crop goes to Germany, France, and England; hardly any to the United States.

This is our last stop before Panama, 850 miles ahead, while we have covered 2628. We pass the ports of Nicaragua and Costa Rica at a distance; the coasting steamers will attend to them. The sixteenth and seventeenth days pass the Wet Coast. Here it would sooner rain than not, and for ten months of the year follows its head. Sharks and porpoises, and orange-and-black snakes, and sober turtles, are our constant companions.

At noon of the eighteenth day we are well up the Gulf of Panama, and off the Isle of Taboga, home of the most perfect pineapple—and an addendum grave outside the neighboring cemetery of French millions. Here stands the vast

PLAZA AND CATHEDRAL, ACAPULCO.

hospital of the Panama
Canal Company, stricken
with the death it so mul-
titudinously ministered
unto. The soul of enter-
prise has gone out from
it—as from all that giant
body—and the shell falls
to the swift decay of the
tropics. As for the canal,
so few workless seasons
have sufficed to undo the
millions; and if the en-
terprise ever be resumed
(which is more than
doubtful), it will have to
begin again at the a b c
of its infinite alphabet.

Of Panama it is not
useful to write at length.
Since the tide of De Les-
seps went out, there is not
much more than stagna-
tion. The population is
now 12,000. There are
many picturesquenesses,
already enough described,
and associations of his-
tory and its true romance
not quite so finally dis-
posed of. The ruins of
the old town, six miles
from the new, recall the
supreme heroism and the
ultimate infamy of the
New World—the gulf be-
tween Pizarro in 1533
and Morgan in 1668. By
what sentimental jug-
glery have we kept the
buccaneers aloft? There
is not, in the history of
all the Americas, another page so dam-
ning black and vile. Yet one may still
find pretentious volumes which gravely
compare these pirates, who wallowed in
the blood of women, babes, and priests
of God, whose only law was license, and
whose only after-thought debauchery,
with those Spanish world-openers who
laid in the very trenches of conquest
the sure corner-stone of law and order,
morality, education, and religion. At
this day and date one wearies of the insular singsong of "Spanish barbarities
in America." History is old enough to
know better, and we to put off the in-
nocence of shouting "stop thief!" in
unison with the most interested party.

A STREET IN PANAMA.

Thus far with our kindly stage-coach
of the Pacific Mail, which has given us
taste, since California, of one territory
and six states of Mexico, and the five
Central American republics. From San
Francisco to New York by the Isthmus—
5200 miles, and nearly four weeks' accommodations—is the cheapest travel open to
North America, as it is certainly the most
interesting.

From Panama south there are two
lines, non-competing, and an excellent
through steamer leaves weekly. The first
two days are out of sight of land. Forty-
four hours from Panama we slip over the
equator, and on the morning of the third
day spy the coast which gave Pizarro his

A BALSA IN THE RIVER, GUAYAQUIL.

first ray of hope after the incomparable sufferings of the Colombian swamps. This is in northern Ecuador, between Esmeraldas and Manta. The ancient gem beds are lost, and the region where Alvarado found so many hundreds of great emeralds on his march to Quito now yields gold and silver extensively, but no precious stones. It is still crude, and absolutely primitive tribes remain in the jungles of the coast.

Guayaquil, chief port and second city of Ecuador, is 840 miles from Panama, forty miles up the Guayas River, but still on tide-water. From mid-stream it is a pretty sight, the long slight curve of its walled water-front enlivened below by a huddle of tropical small craft, and above by the white ranks of its characteristic architecture. Here the Spanish Idea bows its lowest to the earthquake, with "After you, sir." The lower stories are of adobe, the upper of scantling frame lathed with split bamboo and plastered. In front the whole upper story projects generously, thereby gaining to itself a jalousie full of windows, and giving to its inferior a deep shaded sidewalk *portal*. Thus one may quarter the whole city, always shaded from that tropic sky except at street cross-

ings. Two-story mule-cars drawl along the principal streets. Square rods of the chocolate nut, drying in the sun, usurp the pavement, and wheeled travel goes around without a protest, while the front sidewalks are drifted deep with picturesque venders and their wares.

This city of 40,000 souls fully merits its ill repute for heat, pestilence, and earthquakes. The seismic "belt," which begins with the end of the United States, has its buckle in Ecuador, and thence southward tapers again, though not rapidly, for Peru is no stranger to *temblores* of the first magnitude. Guayaquil, on the edge of the greatest of volcanic centres, has suffered sorely. But even thus far from the sea the great peaks are almost never seen. Personal inspection of the Pacific coast of South America gives one to understand how much more visible are the Andes through the atmosphere of a reference library in New York than through their own. For the closet traveller the giant peaks politely march coastward twenty to fifty leagues to colonize his paper voyage with sights never seen by the veteran of twenty years' coasting. In truth, the backbone of the southern continent is hardly more distinguished by the enormous height of its scattered vertebræ than by the infallible vapors which curtain them from the passer on the Pacific. Now and then some finger of the wind pokes through the veil, and lets see the fleeting hint of a blue Presence behind; but the rent is repaired as quickly as made. Until Chile, where the chain edges toward the coast, the great mountains are so far inland that the sight would not be impressive even if the horizon were ever clear enough to expose them to the sea. For a view of the Andes one must go inland—back of the fog curtain. Were it not for this obstacle great Chimborazo should be magnificently visible from Guayaquil, being but eighty miles away and four perpendicular miles higher; but sometimes for years at a stretch the vision is balked. I had come to doubt, but at last, on the 17th of July, 1893, we had a wholly unspeakable view of Chimborazo from Guayaquil for nearly two hours—with glasses. The commodore of the P. S. N., after twenty years' coasting, has never seen the peak yet.

The most picturesque bit of Guayaquil is along the narrow winding way at the foot of the Peñas, a ledgy hill which ends the city on the north. Here are some really charming residences, and much the handsomest view of the city is from the bluff above them.

Characteristic as the city itself is the motley throng afloat at the mole—the country delegation. Given a few logs of the buoyant *balsa* wood, lashed with *lianas;* a few bamboos planted upright in the cracks to support a *toldo* of banana fronds; still easier of achievement, a family garnished with monkeys and paroquets; and for ballast and larder a few

tons of plantains, oranges, mangoes, pineapples, and the like, and the current will furnish the only factor lacking for a successful junket to the city.

Tropic fruit is here at its cheapest and best, and we take on a deck-load for the less-favored south. Another process of lading is even more interesting than the *hormiguillo* of the fruit-launches. An attenuated canoe, thirty feet long and

SHIPPING STEERS AT GUAYAQUIL.

three feet beam, hollowed from one log, with stout outriggers, comes sweeping down the fall of the twenty-foot tide with a mystery — solved only when it belays alongside. This crank craft is swimming six steers, lashed by horns and tails to the outriggers, and with no more abovewater than their noses and a strip of spine. The donkey-engine drops its hooked chain down the side; the two agile boatmen unlash a bullock, throw a

CATHEDRAL AT GUAYAQUIL.

loop around its horns, and hook in the chain. "*Jale!*" shouts the craning mate; and with a snort of steam and clank of chain the astonished brute comes dangling up to the hatch, swung by its horns. This method of hoisting, which prevails all down the coast, is safer than the more familiar sling, and for the racers of the pampas is quite as comfortable.

With the cattle we acquire a full steerage of *paisanos*. No class travels more liberally handicapped. Each lounges upon or by a very mound of fruit, pottery, and crates of paroquets. Each has also the alforja—that amiable and all-admitting saddle-bag valise of Spanish America. Each has the portable bed of a rush mat, and other mitigations of the night.

A few hours out of the Gulf of Guayaquil we pass Tumbez, the northernmost port of Peru. Here Pizarro found his first "city" of adobe, and was greatly impressed by it; but the place has fallen away, and now only coasters stop there. It is the beginning of the wonderful ruins of Peru. All the way down from here every valley has its aboriginal remains.

Five days and 1040 miles from Panama we reach Paita, fit introduction to the inhospitable coast of Peru, and a very fair sample of that vast reach of desert whose rare and hidden oases deluge us with coffee, sugar, rice, and alcohol here, at Eten, Pacasmayo, and Salavery. On the ninth day we are at last in the still harbor of Callao, 1550 miles from Panama, and knocking at the front door of Peru.

WYOMING – ANOTHER PENNSYLVANIA

YOUNG AMERICA builds bigger than his forefathers. Wyoming is not an exceptionally large State, yet it is as big as the six States of New England and Indiana combined. Indiana itself is the size of Portugal, and is larger than Ireland. It is with more than ordinary curiosity that one approaches Wyoming during a course of study of the new Western States. From the palace-cars of the Union Pacific Railroad, that carries a tide of transcontinental travel across its full length, there is little to see but brown bunch-grass, and yet we know that on its surface of 365 miles of length and 275 miles of width are many mountain ranges and noble river-threaded valleys of such beauty that a great block of the land is to be forever preserved in its present condition as the Yellowstone National Park. We know that for years this had been a stockman's paradise, the greatest seat of the cattle industry north of Texas — the stamping-ground of the picturesque cowboys who had taken the place of the hunters who came from the most distant points in Europe to kill big game there. We know that in the mysterious depths of this huge State the decline of its first great activity was, last year, marked by a peculiar disorder that necessitated the calling out of troops; but that was a flash in a pan, much exaggerated at a distance and easily quieted at the time. For the rest, most well-informed citizens outside the State know nothing more than the misnaming of the State implies, for the pretty Indian word Wyoming, copying the name of a historic locality in the East, is said to mean "plains land."

Excepting Idaho, it is the newest of the States in point of development. It waits upon the railroads to open it up. The Union Pacific Company has done this for the southern part, but until three years ago no other railway entered the State. Even now the other roads merely tap its eastern and northern edges. The Burlington and Missouri Railroad, of the Chicago, Burlington, and Quincy system, is pushing its rails into the northeastern part, having come up from Nebraska. It is finished to the Powder River in Sheridan County, and is graded to Sheridan, which is in a region of rich agricultural promise. This railroad must soon, one would think, push on to the Big Horn country, as we shall see. The Fremont, Elkhorn, and Missouri Valley Railroad, of the Chicago and Northwestern system, is also building into the eastern part of the State, and so a beginning is made. But the old-fashioned stage lines are far more numerous than the railroads, and are the sole links between the railways and many interior communities. The State has a population of only about 65,000, and only one town that is well known all over the country. That, of course, is Cheyenne, long the headquarters of the stockmen of the West, and once a very wild and "wide-open" city. It is not easy now to see where it stowed its wickedness as one walks its tree-lined streets bordered by pretty homes and trod by a sober and self-respecting population. Cheyenne has 12,000 population, strong banks, good schools, notable churches, some large and enterprising mercantile establishments, a fine park, and a great State capital. The town languishes. Not that the people regret the loss of the dance-houses and gambling lay-outs, but because the vim has gone out of business. The range cattle industry is failing, and the railroads have opened up other centres where mining and agriculture are the chief interests. But Cheyenne is like Wyoming itself, in a transition state, and its future is far more glorious than the noisy, profligate, and unnatural past.

The people call their State a second and Western Pennsylvania, because it contains such great stores of coal and iron among many another sort of natural wealth. They are right in asserting that coal and iron such as theirs have been the bases of great wealth for many powerful commonwealths and nations, but we shall see, in making a hasty tour of the State, that a still surer and greater asset is Wyoming's soil. Agriculture and stock-raising combined will surely give birth and impetus to a degree of development that will produce many a thickly settled, prosperous district, where now there is little else than the magic soil itself.

It must not be thought that its conditions are more primitive than they are, merely because I have called it next to the newest State. There are twenty banks in the State, and nine or ten are national banks; there are five daily and two dozen weekly newspapers; there are several scores of settlements, and seven of these are of the grade of cities, and provided with water-works and lighted by electricity. The school system is a thorough one, capped by a free university, and representing a million dollars' worth of school property. Free public libraries are also maintained there. But it is the future of such a State that is most interesting, and it is the future that we have looked toward throughout this series.

The best maps of Wyoming, issued by the Department of the Interior at Washington, are almost as useless as no maps at all. Because what is called "mountain work" in surveying pays better than mapping the plains, this map was heaped with mountains, like the surface of a potful of boiling water, and where there should be a few well-defined chains and parallel valleys, there are more mountains, scattered higgledy-piggledy all over the map, than there are in British Columbia or in Switzerland. To make a tour of the State and see it as it is, let us begin with the northeastern part, that corner which is bounded by South Dakota and Montana. The mountains that are here form the Bear Lodge Range—broken spurs and isolated mountains not higher than timber grows, and not sufficient in number, extent, or height to produce much water. This is now a great range cattle country, of course. Around the bases of the mountains, where there is an appearance of more moisture than elsewhere, there are great reaches of fine grass land, on the benches and elevated plateaus where the soil seems formed of decomposed gypsum. Big beds of gypsum are exposed in this region. Here, on these inviting benches, farming to a considerable extent has crept in, pushed by a population that is thought to be an overflow from Nebraska. There is no market, so the farmers farm only for food for themselves and cattle. Note, however, that they fence in their cultivated land and keep cattle of their own to be fed in the winter. Thus the character of Wyoming and of the stock business both change—quietly, steadily, surely. The agriculture centres around Sundance

just now. The stockmen do not consider it a serious invasion of the ranges yet. Cow companies as large as any in the State headquarter to the west of this farming country on the head-waters of the Belle Fourche. The historian of the next decade will, almost surely, write the reverse of this—that agriculture is the mainstay, and cattle deserve a passing notice.

Passing along to the middle of the northern part of the State, in Sheridan and Johnson counties—famed as the seat of last year's "war" between the rustlers and the cowmen—we find the Big Horn Mountains dominating the region. The east slope of these mountains almost duplicates the rich plains country around Denver or Cheyenne. It is more broken, and the ridges between the mountain streams are higher, yet the narrower benches and smaller mesas are of the same fruitful character, well watered by just such sparkling, crystal-like streams as one sees leaping from the sides of the Rockies in Colorado. The Big Horn is a noble range of the Rocky Mountain system. From its tallest point at Cloud Peak, 13,400 feet in air, in the heart of Johnson County, it sinks, in one distinct chain, into nothingness in Montana. Its bold granite knobs and points tower far above timber-line, maintaining a direct northwesterly course with few spurs and side ranges, and with the eastern foothills taking the form of an inclined reach of plains land. Already on this slope, in both counties, agriculture is the principal reliance. This is most true of Sheridan, the border county, because there are still immense herds of cattle on the Johnson County ranges. There is a larger percentage of farmers among the people in these counties than anywhere else in Wyoming. It is not that the land is the best. It is very good, indeed, but it owes its advancement in value to the fact that whereas in other parts of the State the big cow companies pre-empted the water, here it was the farmers who took the first claims of land, and water with it. The Burlington and Missouri Railroad, now being pushed to the heart of this region from the Nebraska border, will, before this is printed, connect these farms with Christendom, but up to this time the farming has been only sufficient to satisfy the home demands of an army post, a few villages, and an Indian res-

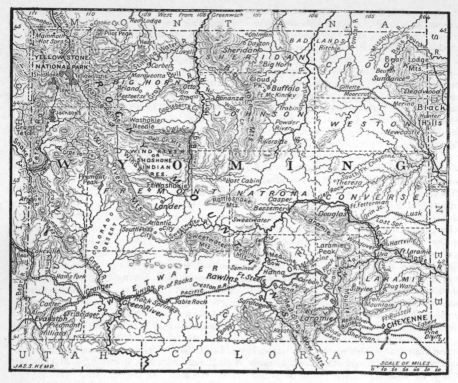

MAP OF WYOMING.

ervation in Montana. Yet it has been enough to prove that the land is sure of a great future. Barley that is said to be as rich as any grown in Canada; very good wheat, oats, and rye; luscious big strawberries, fine cherries and apples, and, in short, all the common fruits of that zone, except peaches, grow well there. The farm land is between 3800 and 5500 feet above sea-level, and but a small portion of the best of it has been taken up.

Westward again, across the Big Horn Mountains, we find a superb country between those mountains and the Yellowstone Park. It is a great basin, walled in on the east by the Big Horns, on the south by the Wind River Mountains, and on the west by the Snake or Shoshone range of the national park. The Big Horn River, a splendid stream, runs northward through this region, on its way to pour its waters into the Yellowstone in Montana. Two large streams—the Gray Bull and the Stinking Water—enter it from the west, and the No Wood, a large stream, runs into it from the east; all these have their own smaller tributaries. The Big Horn, at its best, is $12\frac{1}{2}$ feet deep and 300 feet wide. The arable lands here are at elevations between 3600 and 5500 feet above sea-level, and they constitute the largest mass of unoccupied arable land in the State. Much of it is comparatively low, and it is all sheltered by great mountain ranges. It is not a corn country, of course, yet good corn matured there last summer, proving an unlooked-for length of the warm season. Surveys have resulted in determining that there are 172,000 acres of irrigable land on Gray Bull River, that south of this strip is a piece comprising 100,000 acres on the Big Horn, and that on the Stinking Water there are at least 100,000 acres that can be watered. In addition, there are a dozen large and small streams, on all of which are valley lands capable of irrigation. They are in tracts of varying sizes, but they are bottom lands and good. This Big Horn basin has an apparent measurement on the maps of 7800 square miles, which, considered as a field for the combined industries of farming and cattle-raising, is one of the largest in the mountainous States of the West. The biggest bit of irrigable land along the Gray Bull is a great and uncommon prize for future comers. Not above 500 persons now live in this entire basin. There is a little town, called Otto, near the junction of the Gray Bull and the Big Horn, and there are solitary settlers here and there along the river, as well as a few tiny settlements ("bunches of houses" they would say out there) on the foot-hills in the shadow of the mountains. The basin is, therefore, practically unoccupied. The land is government land, obtainable by homesteaders. One man, who grew forty acres of oats there, succeeded in obtaining sixty-five bushels to the acre, it is said. But there is no market, there is no railroad, and there are no wagonways. The good land of which I have spoken is that near the streams; the rest of the region is a wilderness of deep gulches, high broken plateaus, sage-brush country, and "bad lands."

I have dwelt thus at length upon this brand-new bit of America so desolate now, so inviting to speculation, because it is plain that its future must be grand. How strange a thing it is to be able, after reading the signs of development everywhere in the far West, to point to a vast bowl, unpeopled except by half-wild cattle, and to say, with more confidence than one may prophecy of his own life to-morrow: "Here will come thousands upon thousands of men and women. Here will soon be seen vast areas of land fenced in, set with tidy farm-houses and out-buildings, gay with green and yellow grain, dotted with orchards, lively with teams upon a tangle of wagon roads. Railroads will thread the scene, and somewhere" (ah! that would be great prophesying to say just where) "in this same basin there is certain to arise a city of wealth, size, and importance, with factories and wholesale and retail shops, high-schools, stone churches, parks, and mansions." Yet it must be so, and the days that are near at hand will see this basin so peopled that the force of this prediction will even then be lost, for its force lies in the fact that there is nothing of all this in the region to-day.

Wyoming is so very new a State that there are many regions very similar to the Big Horn basin in present status and future likelihood. Look on the map. Below this basin is the great Wind River Indian Reservation. This great reserve is practically the same sort of country. Below it, where the Big Horn River is new and slender, is another fine farming country, and one that is already beginning to be settled. The army post—Fort Washakie—on the reservation is a market that has developed a comparatively settled region. The town of Lander is the capital of this small but thrifty section, which is made valuable by reason of the rich but narrow little valleys of the tributaries of the main river—there called the Wind River, though it is the Big Horn none the less. The farms support two flour-mills. There is some land for new-comers, but not much.

West of the Indian reservation and south of the Yellowstone Park is what is called the Snake River Country—a very mountainous territory, but with several fine valleys and an abundance of water. Its defect is that the arable land is very elevated. The value of the land has not been determined, but it is superior to its present limited task of growing hay for small holders of cattle who are feeding their stock in corrals in the winter.

South of this is the Salt River Valley, at one time an ancient lake-bed, but now a level plain at the bottom of a bowl—a little isolated world among the mountains, and a place of exceeding great beauty. The Mormons, 1500 strong, have pre-empted it all. Originally they began taking quarter sections of 160 acres under the Homestead Law, but later they filed claims for 640 acres at a time under the Desert Land Act. Many of the holders of large tracts are the sons of rich men, but they will find, what every one else has discovered, that the greatest profit is not in large holdings, but in tracts that a man can grasp, so to speak—twenty to forty acres—on which the owner works, and every inch of which he studies. These thrifty saints have a vast amount of stock in this valley, and produce cheese, butter, and meat, which they ship into the outer world. They raise grain and make flour. Theirs is fine and very productive land, and yet it is more than 6000 feet above sea-level.

All of this great belt that I have been describing, south of the Yellowstone Park, is called Uintah County, and at the bottom of it is the Bear River Country, which is largely taken up by great cattle corporations. One man in this region owns the river-side land for twenty miles on either side of the Bear River. The main use he makes of this is to grow hay for live-stock, the whole region being principally taken up by great stock-men's corporations. The Desert Land Act offered a very convenient instrument for wholesale land-grabbing. Altogether one person could take up 1120 acres, and it was easy for cow-men to employ their cow-boys to file claims upon great tracts. The employers provide the nominal land-office fees and the government price of a dollar and a quarter an acre. This act when it was in force operated in the arid belt, and affected any land that had to be irrigated. The amount upon which a claim can be filed has been reduced to 320 acres, but the principle is very mischievous, because the only hope for a land where soil is plenty and water is scarce is to limit the individual settlers to small holdings, that there may be as many of each as the land will support. Of course these large holdings will in time be broken up, and the region will be thrown open to the multitude. This will happen when the grabbers can make more money by selling the land than by holding it for stock-raising. This is fine farm land in a narrow valley fifty or sixty miles long. Behind this land, on either side of the valley, is broken land that is of no use for farming, but which with the farm land forms the happy combination so frequent in Colorado, Montana, Wyoming, and Idaho, by means of which agriculture and stock-raising can be easily and profitably coupled. In the southwestern part of the State is the Green River, a large stream that drains a wide country. This is yet a great stock country, and the farming along the tributary valleys is for hay for the cattle.

But times and conditions are changing. The Mormons, for instance, are pouring into the land around Fort Bridger, where there are at least 50,000 acres of irrigable land on half a dozen little streams. The Mormons are single-minded. They want land only to till it. Along the entire southern end of the State there had been but one flour-mill, and that (at Laramie City) had failed. As I write, three mills are building: one at Evanston; one at Douglas, in Converse County; and one at Saratoga, on the North Platte River.

There were four flour-mills in Wyoming in 1890, but when this is published there will be nine. Moreover, the new mills are of a character and capacity far superior to the first ones.

The story of the transformation of Saratoga from a cow outfit to a farming settlement is, in great measure, the same as the story of the transformation of the entire State from a stock-man's paradise to a nineteenth-century commonwealth. And one such story is worth ten pages of argument and explanation. In the valley of the North Platte River, seven or eight years ago, there were twenty-five herds of cattle, large and small, owned by men or corporations. Fifteen bore the brands of large companies. Then the valley and the country around it were open and unfenced. The soil was uncultivated. The people who lived there bought even the potatoes—indeed, they bought everything—that they used. Hay, however, was wild, natural, plentiful. They did not know that they could raise anything; in all probability they never gave the matter a thought. It was an axiom that Wyoming was only fit for grazing; even to-day there are plenty of stock-owners and store-clerks who say that potatoes and hay are the only forms of vegetation that can be cultivated in the State. The first man in the valley who planted a garden was ridiculed by all the others; but ridicule will not affect the laws of nature, and as the soil was excellent, his garden was a success. Then others followed suit, all in an experimental, groping way, beginning with potatoes, following with turnips and beets, and so going on through all the grades of general garden truck. At last came experiments with grain, until to-day single fields of wheat and oats comprise 200 or 300 acres, and, as I have said, a thirty-barrel flour-mill is now going up there. So rich is the soil that oats have been grown there to weigh forty-five pounds to the bushel, though the number of bushels to the acre has not been exceptional. The people have learned to cultivate alfalfa (lucern), the rich and beautiful plant that serves for grass and hay in the arid region, and already it yields two crops in a summer.

The agricultural development is closely associated with the changing of the stock-men's methods. The Eastern men who had gone into the valley to grow cattle on the open range had supposed the conditions would for an indefinite period remain as they were, based upon plenty of pasture and water. During the first four years they came gradually to admit that the range business was not profitable. They saw that the first prices they got for their stock were "boom" prices. These depreciated rapidly. Then came a reduction in the range area. Men began to fence for pasture for horses and for winter hay. Each man as he fenced in land also fenced in water, and made it difficult for cattle in the open to get to water. Then settlers began to arrive in numbers, always to locate on water, to fence it in, and to cut off more of the open range. The stock no longer wintered as it had done; wanting water and food, the animals died to an extent that piled up losses to the owners. At last it was necessary for each cow-man to maintain an outfit of riders through the winters to look after the stock. That was expensive, but it was still more expensive to feed the animals in winter, putting ten-dollar hay into fifteen-dollar beasts, for the hay could be sold for ten dollars a ton. It gradually dawned on the stock-men that they had better have one hundred head of cattle, and care for them well, than keep a thousand, with the risks and cost attendant upon large herds. The big herds were gradually driven out and sold off, and the places of most of the early range operators were taken by men who took up land and staid there with smaller herds, farming as well as beef-raising. The result is peculiar and unexpected. There are as many cattle in the valley as there ever were, but they are owned by a great number of persons, and these persons are cultivating the soil. Against fifteen herds, say, of 2000 heads each, under the range system, there are still 30,000 cattle, but they are in 150 herds of 200 heads.

There is only one large cow company left in the valley. It has to keep six or seven riders out in the winter looking after the she-stock. It has to take the precaution, early in each autumn, to make a cow and calf round-up, in order to gather the cows in one pasture and the calves in another, so as to wean the calves. The winter shelter that the cattle get is generally in the natural brush, but it is sometimes necessary to drive them into a long shed, which has had to be put up

against the severest storms—the cruelty of which is in the winds that rage there. This valley, or rather the range which goes beyond the valley, is sixty by sixty miles in area. The cow company herds 3500 to 4000 head. It has to hire a ranch for growing its hay, and this it piles around the cow and calf pastures in the winter. Thus is the business now managed by what is spoken of as "the only company that has withstood the revolution" in that valley. It will look to the reader, if he knows about the range stock industry, as if the company has its business yet, but the profits of old have vanished. Thus is told the story of the range cattle business in one valley, but it will answer for all Wyoming, since in every other part of the State the same things have happened, are happening, or must happen.

The middle southern part of Wyoming is just what it seems from the cars of the Union Pacific Company—of problematical value except for grazing and for its mineral resources. We shall see, farther along, that the mineral resources of most parts of the State are extraordinary.

We have now gone over the State in all its parts except the eastern end. A study of the progress of the work of irrigation will lead to a more complete acquaintance with it. Over all the State timber is heavily distributed in large areas, which altogether form about 16,-000,000 acres. The State comprises about 63,000,000 of acres, and, though more than two-thirds of the area has been surveyed, only 5,000,000 of acres are owned by individuals and corporations, the rest being public land. With so small an amount yielding a revenue, the State has no money with which to develop irrigation; it is as much as it can do to support a government. The State is very forward in progressive legislation affecting irrigation. Its Constitution declares that the waters within its boundaries are the property of the State. If this principle were acted upon, and the State constructed its own ditches and reservoirs, with a single eye to the distribution of the water among the greatest number of landholders, then all that I have urged in other papers upon the other States in the arid belt would here find its consummation. But, having announced the prime fact that it owns the water, it proceeds to give it away. This is not done in the reckless manner we noted in other States, but it gives it away, and to men who want to make money out of it, saying through its officers, "We are only too glad to give it away in order to invite settlers." Still Wyoming is in advance of its neighbors in even this respect, and too much praise cannot be given to its State Engineer, Professor Elwood Mead, whose views are large and practical, who does all that the laws permit toward the conservation of the water supply, and who would make Wyoming's the best system in the country if he had his way, and if it were not for the mischief that was done before Wyoming became a State.

The State has been at the mercy of water-grabbers nearly twenty-one years, but has only enjoyed its own government two years. Under the Territorial system there were no restrictions, and there was no supervision in respect of the distribution of water. Any one who wanted it took it, not as the Mormons have always done, for the greatest good of the greatest number, but like ordinary white men, solely for individual gain. The grabber filed a claim and stated what he had done and for what purpose he did it, but that was a mere formality. The claims were mainly taken by stockmen who wished to get water on land so that they might utilize great tracts taken under the Desert Land Act. There was a tremendous building of ditches; and some of it was crazy work, as where one company built a $70,000 ditch and only watered 340 acres. Around Lander and a few other places farmers took water for the legitimate uses of farming. Three thousand and eighty-six ditches were run out of 631 streams, and were applicable to 2,172,781 acres under the territorial system. And that is about how the case stands to-day.

Now, Wyoming is divided into four grand water districts, to meet as many natural systems of surface drainage. In charge of each district is a superintendent, and these superintendents, with the State Engineer as president ex officio, constitute a Board of Control, which meets twice a year to try and determine causes growing out of the distribution and use of the water. Wyoming alone among all the States in the arid region aims to limit the supply each water-owner may have. This is the next but one most important step

that the States in that region must yet take. In the territorial days men built ditches as they pleased, and then thought that they owned all the water such ditches could take. They were obliged to go before the district courts to get decrees validating their claims, and the courts were supposed to see that each claimant took only what water he needed. As a matter of fact, the courts did as they do elsewhere: took an affidavit by the owners as to the capacity of the ditches, without regard to whether such quantities of water had been, were, or could be utilized, and then issued the decrees. Though the machinery of law courts was not calculated to settle those questions the decrees stand, governing 200 of the 3000 ditches of the State, or, to put it in another way, forever disposing of the water of six of the streams in the State.

The new Board of Control has decided that the mere diversion of water from its natural channels shall not constitute appropriation thereof. The water must be applied to some beneficial use, and if that use is irrigation, the water must be actually applied to the land. The new decrees restrict allotments to actual acreage reclaimed — already watered and growing crops. If a ditch is built to reclaim 10,000 acres, and yet is only watering 1000 acres that are cultivated, the board allots the water for that 1000 acres, crediting the owners with water for the other 9000 acres only when such land is cultivated. Where new ditches are built an extension of time for development is made; in the cases of old ditches, no attention is paid to their future possibilities. In Wyoming, then, the land is reclaimed before the water is parted with by the State. The reader will understand how important and wise this course is when he comprehends the evils that result from the absence of such a rule. In Colorado, for instance, A taps a stream, and runs his ditches as far as he pleases. Then B taps the stream above A, and runs his ditches in the same or another valley or locality. Farming is carried on along both sets of ditches, but when there exists a scarcity of water, A appeals for his priority rights, and gets all the water his ditches will carry. B has his ditches closed, and the orchards and gardens and grain fields along his ditches must die of drought, even though A's territory may not be all under cultivation, or though he may have twice the water he needs. Under the Wyoming system priority rights prevail, but only water that is actually benefiting land is at any man's disposal.

It has been determined in Wyoming that a stream of a cubic foot per second shall serve to irrigate seventy acres, but this estimate is considered non-essential there, because every acre which has water can keep it, there being plenty for all who now use it. The law declares that the first comer must have all that he needs, and the second and third comers must follow in their order, but it is said that priority rights have occasioned little trouble so far, owing to the quantity of water, and the fact that the distribution keeps pace with the actual improvement of the soil. The old haphazard water-grabbing freedom of the Territorial days has left its evils, nevertheless. I saw on a map of part of "the Little Laramie Country" a place where 150 ditches paralleled and duplicated one another in land which two ditches would have served thoroughly well. Eventually, when water is not so plentiful, there will be great trouble and expense in watching the head-gates in such localities, to make sure of fair play with the water on hand, and in the mean time there will be great loss from the heating and evaporation of the fluid in so many ditches, nine in ten of which must eventually be abandoned.

The surest way to prevent this would be for the State to survey all its districts, and prescribe the route of all ditches; but there is no law for such a course in any State. Nevertheless, in Wyoming, whenever proposed ditches are palpably unnecessary, permits are refused; that is to say, if two applications describe one set of lands, the second one is refused until the time set for the completion of the first one has expired.

It is estimated that between six millions and seven millions of acres of land in Wyoming are irrigable from the streams. Of the five millions of acres now held in the State only a little above two millions are under ditches. The great majority of the ditches are small ones, and most of these are owned by stock-men, although a few farming communities operate their own. The stock-men's ditches will eventually be applied to agriculture. In all, in this baby State, ten millions of dollars or more have been invested in these artificial waterways. When the Board of

Control came, with its new rulings, the stock-men as well as the farmers saw that the only way to hold their water rights was to make use of their water, and so they have been ploughing their land and seeding it (for hay at first), and thus in the last two years have caused the State to take an extraordinary stride forward in agricultural development. Thus have come the four flouring-mills where there had been none before. Between January, 1891, and November, 1892, there were 352 applications for the right to build new ditches, and the State Engineer has been notified that at least one-third of the number have been completed and are in use. Nothing could speak more eloquently of the new forces of civilization and improvement that are at work in the State.

These new ditch companies have not been large ones. The experience of the people of the State has been that such corporations should control the settlement of the land, or—as I believe, and the State Engineer adds as an alternative—the State should own both the land and the water. The rule is seen to be that when great ditches are built squatters pre-empt the land to be benefited in order to bother and blackmail the ditch-owners into buying them out. If the State owned the public lands and surveyed them, and encouraged the building of ditches, it could sell the land for its value as improved land, and could reimburse the local ditch company by buying the shares and joining them with the land thus sold until the water and the shares were at an end. Thus even a State with a low and new treasury could prevent the creation of water-barons and avoid the troubles that must come under the grab system of to-day.

A bill has been introduced in Congress for the surrender of the public lands to the State; but before we can consider this proposition clearly it is necessary to glance at the past and present of the cattle business in this one of its former strongholds. The range cattle business is in a bad way there. One of the shrewdest capitalists in the State, himself a former range cattle owner, told me that not a cow company there made a dollar of profit in 1892. He afterward corrected himself by saying that he believed a little money had been gained from a new form of the business by men in the northern part of the State who had gone out of the breeding business and were grazing steers exclusively. This safer method, which discounts the risk to cows and calves, has been widely adopted in Montana and the western end of the Dakotas.

The rapid decline of the range business began six years ago. Before that it had been of a character to tempt even the rich. At one time men paid two per cent. a month for money, and made 100 per cent. profits a year. That was when cows came up from Texas at a cost of $7 each, sold in two years for $22, and in three years for $40 and more, when the ranges were not overstocked, the pasturage was good, and all the conditions, including "boom" prices at the stock-yards, were favorable. The men who did the best pushed into new territory as fast as the Indians were crowded off, and kept finding new grass and plenty of it. But the risks soon came, and multiplied. If one man was careful not to overstock a range, he could not be sure that another cow outfit would not do so precisely where he had put his cattle. Prices fell, fences cut up the ranges and shut off the water, winter losses became heavier and heavier, and the "good old days" of this inhuman, devil-may-care, primitive, and clumsy business came to an end. The cowboys of picture and story existed in the brilliant days. At first they had come from Texas, but in the zenith of their romantic glory they came from everywhere and from every class. They included young Englishmen, college graduates from the East, well-born Americans —all sorts who did not "strike luck" at anything else, and who were full of vim and love of adventure. They got $40 a month and good keep during the greater part of each year. They rode good horses, that had as much of the devil in them as the "boys" themselves. They bought hand-stamped Cheyenne saddles and California bits that were as ornate as jewelry, and stuck their feet in grand *tapaderos*, or hooded stirrups, richly ornamented, padded with lamb's wool, and each as big as a fire-hat. Their spurs were fit for grandees, their "ropes," or lariats, were selected with more care than a circus tight-rope, and their big broad felt sombreros cost more than the Prince of Wales ever paid for a pot-hat.

And then, alas! the cow-men began to economize in men, food, wages—everything. The best of the old kind of cowboys, who had not become owners or fore-men, saloon-keepers or gamblers, or had not been shot, drifted away. Some of the smartest among them became "rustlers" —those cattle-thieves whose depredations resulted in what almost came to be a war in Wyoming last year. They insisted that they had to do it to live.

From the cowboy stand-point it was time for the business to languish. Towns were springing up every here and there, each with its ordinance that cowboys must take off their side-arms before they entered the villages; wages were low down; men had to cart hay and dump it around for winter food; settlers fenced in the streams, and others stood guard over them with guns: it was time such a business languished. From the stand-point of nineteenth-century civilization the same conclusion was reached—the range business was an obstruction to civilization, a bar to the development of the State, a thing only to be tolerated in a new and wild country. And now I am assured that there is not an intelligent cow-man who does not know that the business is doomed in Wyoming, and that the last free-roving herds must move on. There is not one who does not know that small bunches of cattle, held in connection with agriculture, must take the places of the range cattle, because better grades of cattle can be bred, better meat can be produced, all risks will nearly disappear, and the expenses of the care of the cattle will not be a tithe of those of the old plan.

And so we come to the much-discussed plan for having Wyoming intrusted with the public domain within her borders. This plan takes account of the fact that she will ever be a great cattle-raising State. The plan is to sell the agricultural or arable land in connection with the water and with the upper or range land, always combining the irrigable bottoms or mesas and benches with the higher unirrigable territory. Then farmers may grow hay with one hand, so to speak (along with whatever else they choose to plant), while with the other they look after their cattle. With thoroughbred bulls, sheltered winter pasture and feed, and an income from farming, the farmers will be rich and the beef will be the finest that it is possible to produce. There is an unexpected opposition to this project, and by the men most certain to be benefited were it carried out. They are ignorant and suspicious, and fear that the plan cloaks some effort toward a land-grabbing monopoly or steal of some sort. Nevertheless, the plan is peculiarly well suited to the natural conditions in Wyoming, and, for that matter, in Colorado and other States in the arid belt. It turns to good account land of a sort that is all too plentiful there that it is not easy to employ otherwise, and that is not attractive or profitable as pasture-land for cattle-owners other than such as own farms in the neighborhood. For such it should be held against wild cattle, and against the devouring bands of sheep that otherwise might and often would pass over the hills and leave them as bare as the back of one's hand.

The number of cattle in the State in 1892 was estimated to be 428,823, and the value of the stock was considered to be $4,654,379, but I was told that the State never gets reports of more than six-tenths of the number actually within her borders. However, in 1886 the number reported was 898,121 head, or more than twice as many as now, and then cows were considered worth $16 31 apiece as against $10 50 now. But this falling off argues no such ill to the State as it would have been to have the range cattle industry thrive. The auditor's figures show that while there has been a decrease of ten millions of dollars in the valuation of the cattle in the State within seven years, the total assessable value of properties in Wyoming has increased $1,236,713 during that period.

The reports of horses indicate that there are 78,286 of them on the ranges, and these are computed to be worth $2,681,000; but this is also an untrustworthy item. In truth, there are no less than 100,000 head of horses, and many of them are of excellent stock. Sheep exceed all other animals in numbers. The auditor reports 639,205, and there are really close to 900,-000 of these animals on the ranges. They are worth, at graded values, $1,750,000.

Wherever the cow business is carried on there exists the most fanatical prejudice against sheep and sheep-herders. The English language fails every cow-man who tries to express his opinion about this sister industry. This is worth recording here, because it is true in all the States where cattle are fattened, from British Columbia to Texas, and because it is a prejudice without warrant or base; and it is bound to die out. We shall see why, after telling what a cow-man said of it when I brought up the topic in Wyoming:

"The sheep-herder is the worst blot on the State," said he. "He is no good, and much harm. He may have his office in New York, Chicago, or London. He fits out a wagon, with a Mexican and a dog and several thousand sheep, and away they go, like an Egyptian scourge, eating the grass down to the ground, and, in sandy soils, trampling it down so that there are great regions where once the bunch-grass grew knee-high, but where the country is now bare as a desert. You might search acres in such a place with a microscope and not discover an ounce of grass. These people pay no rent, don't own an acre, send their profits abroad, and are bitterly opposed to the settlement and development of the State."

But new men are constantly drifting into the sheep business, and mutton, which always hung back in the meat markets of America, is coming to be a favorite meat, as it is in England. There is no more remarkable change in our country than this general turning toward mutton after it had been so long and generally disliked. Men who harbored the same ill will toward the business of sheep-herding, are now rushing into it because of the money there is in it. He who was always spoken of on the ranges as "that —— sheep-man," is now on top, the subject of the envy of his neighbors. It is not true that the sheep are largely owned by foreigners or outsiders. The three largest sheep-herders in Wyoming are residents of the State. In Carbon County, the largest sheep county in the State, 138,438 sheep are ranging, and they are owned at home. The manner of conducting the business, and the figures of the cost and profit in it, are very interesting.

Five thousand sheep are considered a good holding, because that number divides into two herds convenient to handle. The owner of such a bunch will employ three men—two herders and a foreman, who is also the "camp-mover." Each herd will have a wagon, a man, and a dog, or usually two dogs. The wagon in use on the ranges is the typical "schooner" of olden time—a heavy box on wheels, covered with a canvas top, and appointed with a bed in the back, a locker, and a stove. The camp-mover divides his time between the two herds. He has a team of horses, and after he has moved one wagon and herd to new pasture, he leaves that outfit and goes off, perhaps fifteen or twenty miles, to the other herd, to find new pasture for that, and to leave it till the grass is nipped close. The sheep are not exclusively grass-eaters. They like to browse on brush and the bark of willows, and they do well on what is called "browse," which is the short white sage-brush of that region. It is estimated that it costs seventy cents a head to maintain a herd, but the wool greatly more than meets this expense. The herders sell the old ewes to feeders in Nebraska and elsewhere to fatten for market, getting $3 50 to $4 a head for such stock. Occasionally, if they think the herds are increasing in numbers too fast, they sell off a bunch of young lambs, and yearlings fetch as high as $2 75 a head. The profits lie in the increase of the animals by multiplication. This amounts to almost a doubling of the herds in a year, the percentage being between 75 and 100 per cent. At an average cost of $3 50 for stock sheep, and a doubling of the animals, with sales at $2 75 to $4, and with an additional margin from the wool, after expenses are met, it is plain that the business is not a bad one. Wool has fetched from eleven to sixteen cents during the last few years, and good sheep yield about nine pounds as an average clip.

The coal and iron of Wyoming form a wonderful treasure. Unlike nearly all the other far Western States, Wyoming's settlement was not connected with mining. The first actual settlements were around forts Laramie and Bridger. Gold was discovered on the route of the old trail in 1867, and there have been many mining flurries in the State since then, but these were as nothing to those which built up the neighboring States, or to what must yet draw millions from this one. It was the extension of the cattle business that lifted Wyoming into prominence, and yet it will not do to say that this led to the State's settlement, since that was an industry which rather obstructed than fostered the development of the territory. Yet the rocks and the earth bear treasures comparable with those of any State in our West. Coal is found in every county. From the northern centre to the eastern end of the State it is a lignite of low grade, which crumbles when exposed to the air. It outcrops frequently and generally. It is in use in the towns of Sheridan and Buffalo, and is found to burn very well. Near Buffalo there is a vein that is said to be seventy feet thick. The nearer this deposit approaches the mountains, where it has been subjected to more pressure, the more commercial value it has. The coal burned in the settlements around Bonanza, in the western part of Johnson County, is so free from sulphur and phosphorus that it can be used by blacksmiths. Close to the Montana border the same good bituminous coal that is found in that State extends its field into Wyoming. In the eastern part of the State, where the Black Hills enter from South Dakota, is Newcastle, a busy coal-mining town, whose neighborhood is richly veined with a bituminous coal that makes high-grade coke. Coking ovens supply that material for the Black Hills smelters. This is the only coal of the kind in the State. It is of such quality that the Burlington and Missouri Railroad Company uses it for locomotive fuel, mining 800 tons a day for that use and for sale along the line in other localities.

The next best deposit yet mined is at Rock Springs, in Sweetwater County, in the southwestern part of the State, and on the Union Pacific Railroad. More than a million tons were shipped from this immense field last year. It is the best soft coal in the Wyoming markets, and as good as any in the West. The Union Pacific Railroad is heavily interested here, but there are some small private mines. In order that the people of the State may have no rose without its thorn, and may not grow too proud of their good fortune, this coal is sold in Cheyenne at $6 a ton. From Rawlins, to the eastward, comes a good coal, and eastward again is the Carbon coal field, where the railroad also owns producing mines. This coal is not so good as that from Rock Springs, and sells at thirty-five cents less per ton. Away down in the southwestern corner of the State are other great coal beds, from one of which the Southern Pacific Railroad Company gets its supply. It is a lower grade than the Rock Springs coal. The Fremont, Elkhorn, and Missouri Valley Railroad (Chicago and Northwestern system) came into Wyoming for coal, among other reasons, and has a large mine in the Platte River field, near Fort Fetterman. This is not a good locomotive or steam coal, but finds a ready market in Nebraska and elsewhere along this gigantic system. There are at least half a dozen large coal fields in the central belt of counties of whose merits I find no mention in my notes. Their development doubtless awaits that of the country around them.

Iron is as plentiful. First in importance is the great district around Hartville, north of Fort Laramie. It is theoretically pure hematite—as nearly so as hematite is found, and it has been developed or mined sufficiently for the owners of the present mines to be confident of its value. Duluth and Eastern capital has been invested here, and active operations only await the building of a railway connection with the Skull Creek (Newcastle) coal mines. Next in promise are the Seminoe, Carbon County, mines to the northwestward of the Carbon coal fields. Here is plenty of fine hematite, with fuel and fluxes close by, and only transportation facilities needed. There is a large soft deposit of mineral paint (oxide of iron), which is being ground and readily marketed. It has been found to be excellent for painting freight cars, iron and tin roofs, and buildings, is a valuable wood-preservative, and retains its color longer than most paints. The Chugwater River runs through an immense field of iron ore, but it is impregnated with what is called titanium. Iron carbonate ore is found in the Big Horn Basin, and in the basin east of the South Powder River. This will be mined, in time, for use in Bessemer steel making.

The tin of the Black Hills extends into Wyoming. The State has some extraordinary soda deposits, some of these being actual lake-beds of soda. Copper is found all along the North Platte River. Lead appears at least twice in large quantities in a survey of the State, and kaolin, fire-clay, mica, graphite, magnesia, plumbago, and sulphur are more or less abundant. Gypsum is found in almost every county, and plaster of Paris is being made of it at Red Buttes, on the Union Pacific Railroad. Marbles—some of them very fine and beautiful—are being gathered in every county for exhibition at the World's Fair in Chicago. They are of all colors; but the only white marble is found in the Sibylee region, where, by-the-way, is another undeveloped agricultural section of great promise. The granites of the State are very fine, and the sandstones, which are of unlimited quantity, include beautiful varieties for building purposes and for interior decorative work.

Petroleum appears in several places in the State. There are wells at Salt Creek in Johnson County. The Omaha Company have flowing wells at Bonanza, in another part of the county, and this oil, whose flow is stopped by the company, is a splendid illuminant. A mile away is a spring carrying oil on its surface. Near Lander, south of the Indian reservation, are more than two dozen borings. All have flowed, and all are now cased, but there is a three-acre lake of leakage from them. There are signs of oil elsewhere in the State. The oil production and supply of this county are controlled by one company. If any other company offers to compete with this giant concern, it would be possible for the master company to give oil away until the opposition was starved out. The money of the great company is in its by-products, and it would not suffer greatly by making a free gift of all the oil that is consumed in Wyoming. It is generally believed that the controllers of the oil supply look to the wells of Colorado to piece out the supply if the Pennsylvania wells fail. After that, or at that time, perhaps, humanity will be interested in the oil of Wyoming; but it is noticeable now that this oil excites little human interest, and interests still less capital.

Gold is still being mined where it was first found, below the Indian reservation in the South Pass district. Here is both lode and placer mining, but the principal placer-owner is working the quartz. Within the past year many new mines have been opened there, and one shipper claims to be getting from $200 to $400 a ton out of his ore. Another gold district is east of this on the Seminoe Mountains. Others are on both sides of the Medicine Bow range, southwest of Laramie city, and near the Colorado line; in the Black Hills, in the Little Laramie Valley, in the Silver Crown district, and in the Big Horn country. The gold-mining in the State is sufficiently promising to interest a great many miners and considerable capital; but the best friends and best judges of the new State see the richest future for her in the development of her splendid agricultural lands first, and next in her coal and iron fields.

In certain of the newer States the citizens are especially proud of the constitutions they have adopted as the bases of their governments. In Montana, for instance, the Constitutional Convention comprised an assemblage of men who, it is said, would win distinction anywhere. Wyoming's convention may not have been so notable in its make-up, but its product, the Constitution, is very remarkable. It is *fin de siècle*, if I may apply French to anything so extremely American; it is thoroughly "up to date."

Wyoming had progressed under Territorial government for twenty years, when, in January, 1888, her Legislature memorialized Congress for an enabling act, in the belief that Territorial government retarded the progress and development of the region. The Congress committee to which the matter was referred reported it favorably, as it also did a bill preparing for the admission of the other Territories which were so soon to become full-fledged members of the Union. In June, 1889, the Governor, Chief Justice, and Secretary districted the Territory, and apportioned the number of delegates for the convention upon a just basis. Then the Governor directed that an election be held in July to choose delegates to a constitutional convention in September. Fifty-five delegates composed the convention, and drafted the Constitution, which was afterwards ratified by a vote of five-sixths of the citizens. Wyoming was admitted as a State in 1891.

In its declaration of rights the Constitution perpetuates the right of the women to vote as they had been doing when Wyoming was a Territory. "Since equality in the enjoyment of natural and civil rights," it declares, "is made sure only through political equality, the laws of this State affecting the political rights and privileges of its citizens shall be without distinction of race, color, sex, or any circumstance or condition whatsoever, other than individual incompetency or unworthiness duly ascertained by a court of competent jurisdiction. Article VI., entitled "Suffrage," farther declares that "the right of citizens to vote and hold office shall not be denied or abridged on account of sex. Male and female citizens of this State shall equally enjoy all civil, political, and religious rights and privileges." The age when a citizen may vote is fixed at twenty-one equally without regard to sex, but "no person shall have the right to vote who shall not be

able to read the Constitution of the State" (physical disability in this respect being no bar). The method of voting is what is generally called "the Australian system."

The situation in Wyoming is especially interesting, because women cut a small figure in a new State, and what they have got there the men must have given them. Do they vote—now that they may? How many vote? Do they vote as their husbands do or tell them to? Is the voting of women mainly done by the respectable, the intelligent, the ignorant, or the disorderly classes? To what extent, if any, do the women study politics and statecraft in order to vote intelligently? I am drifting to one side of a study of Wyoming's Constitution, but these are interesting questions, and the Constitution is responsible for them.

In the first place, when I put these queries, here and there, I said "women" whenever I spoke of that sex, for which I have the highest respect—the most sentimental, if you please. But I never heard any other man in the State apply any other word to the better sex except the much-abused and demoralized term "ladies." That is a marked peculiarity of the language in the West. It does not contain the noble word "woman." It sickens the ear with the overuse of the word "lady." For my part, I know a woman when I see one, but I find it difficult to determine ladyhood except upon hearsay or acquaintance. When I do find it I compliment it with the dignified word "woman"; a statement which I hope will free me from even a suspicion of rudeness or lack of gallantry here and in what follows.

I found that the great majority of the women in Wyoming are in the habit of voting. Not all of them vote as their husbands do, and, as one official expressed himself, "good men pride themselves upon not influencing their wives." Yet it is true, I am told, that very many women, of their own volition and unconsciously, copy the politics of their husbands. Occasionally the men of the State hear of women who refuse to embrace the privilege, who do not believe that women should meddle in affairs which concern the homes, the prosperity, and the self-respect and credit of the communities of which they are a part; but such women are, of course, few.

On the other hand, other women are very active in politics. There is a Ladies' Republican League among the political clubs of Cheyenne. It is seen that the right to vote acts as an incentive to study the principles and records of the opposing parties, and if there are women who blindly vote as their husbands do, there are yet others who fail to agree with the views of their life companions upon public matters.

Among the women who show an intelligent interest and take an active part in politics, a few resort to the stump, and speak for whichever cause they have adopted. But there are many who serve side by side with the men as delegates to conventions and voters in the party primaries. In the last State convention of the Republicans there were three women delegates; in that party's last county convention, in Laramie County, the secretary was a woman, and three delegates were of her sex. Women literally flock to the primaries — in the cities, at all events. At the primary meeting in the Third Ward of Cheyenne last autumn, out of 183 who were present at least 80 were women. In the other wards the proportion of women was as one is to three. On election days the women go a-voting precisely as they go a-shopping elsewhere. On foot or in their carriages they go to the polls, where, under the law, there are no crowds, and where all is quiet and orderly. There is no doubt that female suffrage has an improving effect upon politicians and their manners. All sorts and every sort of women vote; but it is to be remarked that this affords no criterion for larger and Eastern States, since the proportion of women of evil lives is very small in Wyoming, even in the cities, and, so far as other women are concerned, our new States are nearer like democracies than our old ones. The lines of caste are more apt to be noticed by their absence than by their enforcement.

To return to the Constitution, so remarkable if only because of this recognition of woman's equality to man: it forbids imprisonment for debt except in cases of fraud; it guarantees liberty of conscience, but declares that such liberty "shall not be so construed as to excuse acts of licentiousness or justify practices inconsistent with the peace or safety of the State." (A notice to the Mormons, who are already forming colonies there.) It provides that "no money of the State shall ever be given or appropriated to any sectarian or religious society or institution." The old maxim, "the greater the truth the greater the libel," receives its quietus, so far as Wyoming is concerned, in this clause: "Every person may freely speak, write, and publish on all subjects, being responsible for the abuse of that right; and in all trials for libel, both civil and criminal, the truth, when published with good intent and for justifiable ends, shall be a sufficient defence, the jury having the right to determine the facts and the law under direction of the court." And here is a truly modern clause: "The rights of labor shall have just protection through laws calculated to secure to the laborer proper *rewards for his service* and to promote the industrial welfare of the State." (The *italics* are mine.)

"No power, civil or military, shall at any time interfere to prevent an untrammelled exercise of the right of suffrage.

"No distinction shall ever be made by law between resident aliens and citizens as to the possession, taxation, enjoyment, and descent of property.

"Perpetuities and monopolies are contrary to the genius of a free State, and shall not be allowed. Corporations being creatures of the State, endowed for the public good with a portion of its sovereign powers, must be subject to its control.

"Water being essential to industrial prosperity, of limited amount, and easy of diversion from its natural channels, its control must be in the State, which, in providing for its use, shall equally guard all the various interests involved.

"The State of Wyoming is an inseparable part of the Federal Union, and the Constitution of the United States is the supreme law of the land.

"No session of the Legislature after the first, which may be sixty days, shall exceed forty days.... No Legislature shall fix its own compensation." (The sessions are biennial.)

"No bill [before the Legislature], except general appropriation bills, and bills for the codification and general revision of the laws, shall be passed containing more than one subject, which shall be clearly expressed in its title; but if any subject is embraced in any act which is not expressed in the title, such act shall be void only as to so much thereof as shall not be so expressed.

"No appropriation shall be made for charitable, industrial, educational, or benevolent purposes to any person, corporation, or community not under the absolute control of the

State " (nor to any sectarian or denominational institution, as we have seen).

The provisions to prevent bribery and
corruption in the Legislature are intended
to be especially finely drawn. No legislator may give his vote or influence for
or against any measure in consideration
of the promise of another legislator's influence in favor of or against any other
measure before, or to be brought before
the Legislature. To make such a proposition is declared to be "solicitation of
bribery"; to carry out such a bargain is
to be guilty of bribery. Witnesses may
be compelled to testify in trials of such
causes, and shall not-withhold testimony
on the ground that it may criminate them
or subject them to disgrace, but such testimony may not afterward be used against
such witnesses, except upon a charge of
perjury in giving such testimony. "A
member who has a personal or private
interest in any measure or bill proposed
or pending before the Legislature shall
disclose the fact to the House of which he
is a member, and shall not vote thereon."
"All fines and penalties under general
laws of the State shall belong to the public-school fund of the respective counties."
This is in addition to the usual two sections in each township, to all lands given
to the State for purposes not otherwise
specified, the proceeds of all property that
may come to the State by escheat or for-
feiture, and in addition to all funds from
unclaimed dividends or distributive shares
of the estates of deceased persons.

"In none of the public schools shall distinction or discrimination be made on account of
sex, race, or color.

"No sectarian instruction, qualifications, or
tests shall be imparted, exacted, applied, or in
any manner tolerated in the schools, ... nor
shall attendance be required at any religious
service therein, nor shall any sectarian tenets
or doctrines be taught or favored in any public school or institution that may be established under this Constitution.

"Railroad and telegraph lines heretofore
constructed, or that may hereafter be constructed in this State, are hereby declared
public highways and common carriers, and as
such must be made by law to extend the same
equality and impartiality to all who use them,
excepting employés and their families and
ministers of the Gospel.

"Exercise of the power and right of eminent domain shall never be so construed or
abridged as to prevent the taking by the Legislature of property and franchises of incor-
porated companies, and subjecting them to
public use the same as property of individuals.

"No street passenger railway, telegraph,
telephone, or electric-light line, shall be constructed within the limits of any municipal
organization without the consent of its local
authorities.

"Eight hours' actual work shall constitute
a lawful day's work in all mines and on all
State and municipal works.

"It shall be unlawful for any person, company, or corporation to require of its employés
any contract or agreement whereby such employer shall be released from liability or responsibility for personal injuries to such employés while in the service of such employer,
by reason of the negligence of the employer,
or the agents or employés thereof." (Condensed
to give the mere substance of the clause.)

"No armed police force or detective agency,
or armed body or unarmed body of men, shall
ever be brought into this State for the suppression of domestic violence, except upon the
application of the Legislature, or Executive,
when the Legislature cannot be convened."

The laws governing taxation and revenue are equally notable. Except for the
support of educational and charitable institutions, and the payment of the State
debt and interest thereon, the annual levy
may not exceed four mills on the dollar
of the assessed valuation of the property
in the State. Twelve mills on the dollar
is the maximum levy in the counties for
all purposes, exclusive of the State tax and
county debt. An annual and additional
tax of two dollars for each person in each
county is imposed for school purposes.
No city or town may levy a tax greater
than eight mills on the dollar, except to
meet its public debt and the interest
thereon.

It will be seen that in preparing this
great establishment for the reception of
future millions, the furniture is as complete as the variety of attractions in the
soil, and the future millions will find, already settled for them beforehand, many
of the problems which we in older States
are sorely troubled to decide—such as the
female suffrage question, the eight-hour
law, the Pinkerton problem, the question
of religion or no religion in the schools,
the mischief of discrimination in freight
rates, and the evil of free passes on railways, with fifty other greater or lesser
matters that foment doubt and contention
far to the eastward of this forward and
vigorous commonwealth, which thus has
everything it needs, except the trifle called
population.

THE WAHLAMET VALLEY OF OREGON

THE old emigrant trail to Oregon, getting well away from the route to California and across the Idaho deserts, followed down the northern bank of the Boise River to the Snake, crossing which, it made its way northwestward to The Dalles of the Columbia. The "Oregon" those first settlers sought was only a small area out of the half a million square miles then included in the boundaries of the new Territory, and lay south of the Columbia, between the Coast Range and the Cascade Mountains, where now are the oldest settlements in the State. The present interest of this region to us is derived from this fact, and from its natural beauty, agricultural wealth, and prosperous population.

The coast of Northern California and Oregon is defined by a bulwark of basaltic hills, with peaks three or four thousand feet high, resisting further encroachments of the ocean. Parallel with this Coast Range, but about one hundred and fifty miles inland, runs the magnificent continuation of the Sierra Nevada here called the Cascade Mountains. The everlasting snows of the central crest of this range are guarded by rank upon rank of foothills, but there remains space between the outermost of the three and the slopes of the Coast Range for a wide area of level and cultivable land, and in this area is comprised the two valleys, Wahlamet and Umpqua, that form the subject of the present article, together with the low cross spur of hills dividing them.

The greatest river of the Northwest, every one knows, is the Columbia—a river

equalled by only two or three on the continent. Of tributaries, nevertheless, it has very few below where the Snake comes in, and it does not receive its greatest auxiliary until within a hundred miles of its ocean bar. This is the Wahlámet, or Willámette, as it is often spelled, as though it were a French diminutive instead of an Indian word. About the Wahlamet, indeed, there is nothing diminutive. At the city of Portland, twelve miles above its junction with the Columbia, it is nearly half a mile in width. Ocean steamers of the heaviest draught — steamers going round the Horn and traversing the Pacific in the China trade—come there to discharge and to be loaded, while river boats steam a hundred miles further up.

Receiving many deep tributaries, such as the Santíam, Tual'atin, Yamhill, Molálla, Cláckamas, Long Tom, and Luckiámute, finally itself forking into a cluster of sources whose fountains never fail, because fed by Sierra snows, it is apparent at a glance that the wide valley of this river is well drained. Lack of water, indeed, is far removed from the Oregon farmer's fears in respect to his crops; if anything, he suffers from too much rain, especially in winter and spring, when inundations are likely to occur, though they rarely amount to wreck-making floods. The average annual rain-fall in the upper part of the valley is nearly the same as around Lake Erie, but in the lower Columbia Valley it is twice as great.

For several years the Oregon and California Railway Company has been run-

ning trains up the Wahlamet and on beyond, aiming to meet an approaching line
from California, and so make an all-rail
route from San Francisco to Portland—
cities now connected only by steamers.
This railway now runs to Roseburg, two
hundred miles south of Portland, and
throws off several branches, so that the
whole agricultural region of Western Oregon possesses ready means of shipment
for its produce. A trip over the main

however, the valley is forest-grown—
woods made up almost wholly of evergreens, and, so far as timber is concerned,
of a single tree, the Douglass fir (*Pseu-
dostuta douglassii*). It is this species
that furnishes all the lumber of the district; but the forests easily accessible have
been despoiled of all likely trees, and only
one saw-mill is to be seen along the railway, breaking the monotone of forest
green with its stacks of fresh planking

line at least of this railway ought not to
be missed by the visitor to Oregon, not
more as a matter of instruction than as a
pleasure, for few regions are fairer, and
the domestic scenes that intermingle with
nature's unchanged grandeur are doubly
interesting to eyes weary with the utter
wilderness encountered in coming from
the East.

The vicinity of Portland being rough
and wooded, the cultivable area of the
Wahlamet Valley begins only about twenty miles above, where the receding hills
leave wide spaces of level ground. Here,

and its great heaps of bright yellow sawdust. Abandoned by the choppers, these
tangled woods, rapidly choking with second growth, become the resort of an abundance of game, and the tumbling streams
that traverse them are full of trout. The
land covered is good enough soil, but as
yet there is not the demand which makes
its clearance profitable, in view of cheaper holdings farther away. The little district about Oregon City makes a break beyond which the old woodland covers another score of miles, more entertaining to
the seeker of things picturesque than to the

"practical" man. Then begins the open prairie region which is the pride of Western Oregon, and where there is so dense a farming population as to support several branch lines of railway penetrating to remote settlements. This open area is about a hundred miles long, and averages perhaps fifty miles in width, with side valleys penetrating far into the foot-hills of the Cascade range. Much of it is prairie, but in general it is diversified by lines of woodland following the courses of streams, by copses of detached fir woods, and by low hills covered with an open, park-like growth of two sorts of oak. The immediate vicinity of the Wahlamet (up which steamboats go regularly to Salem, and occasionally as far as Eugene City) is liable to overflow, and the railway crosses its swift flood at Harrisburg upon a bridge approached by long trestle-work; but these wide bottoms support a magnificent growth of deciduous trees—ash, maple, alder, cottonwood, and innumerable of lesser size which closely reproduce the appearance of the Upper Mississippi lowlands.

To these fertile districts attention was attracted almost half a century ago. "Oregon" then comprised everything north of California, indefinitely, and was claimed by both England and the United States. In 1846 a treaty designated the parallel 49° the boundary between British Columbia and the United States, at which time Oregon contained about 10,000 people. By 1850 the Territory had been organized under the United States, and 3000 more immigrants had arrived. In order to make good titles to land taken up when the sovereignty of the region was doubtful, and also to encourage further immigration, Congress passed what is called the "Donation Law." This perfected titles originating under the previous provisional government, and gave to every actual new settler 320 acres of public land; or, if he were married, it gave him and his wife 640 acres. This law during its brief existence aided the settlement of the country so rapidly that the census of only a decade later showed over 50,000 inhabitants. It must be remembered, however, that the Oregon of that day included the present Territories of Washington, Idaho, and Montana. So far as the present limits of the State of Oregon are concerned, there was little habitancy outside of these very valleys we are discussing, and it was here that the Dona-tion Law operated both for good and evil. Its good lay in the impetus it gave to immigration; its evil, in the fact that, in a region where the really choice land was in small areas, it placed too much in single hands.

This, perhaps, would not have been an evil under some circumstances; but the unfortunate fact in the present instance was that the people who came, took up land, and settled, were, as a rule, an extremely poor class of vagabond farmers from the border States, the Pike County region of Missouri and the lowlands of the Ohio River and Arkansas furnishing the majority. They were poor, also, in the sense of having little money, and this helplessness, added to their thriftless habits, made their possession of the best land in the valleys a misfortune to the State, since they shut out those coming later from fields they would have cultivated to far greater advantage.

This unenterprising class of farmers, locally spoken of as "the old Oregonians," has declined in influence, however, and is represented by the loungers of the community. Their children have lost their drawl of speech and action, or their property has been bought by their betters, so that now, for the most part, an active and well-to-do race of farmers till the acres and control the destinies of the western slope of the State.

That this is true is plainly seen in the landscape. The farms will average more than a hundred acres in area, and follow one another uninterruptedly from the river back into the wooded foot-hills, the two valleys of Wahlamet and Umpqua containing now about one hundred thousand people outside of the metropolis. The houses are almost invariably of frame, and of good size and appearance, with far more attention paid to comfort and attractive surroundings than it is customary to see even in the Eastern States. The general air of thrift and neatness in the little villages scattered here and there is very noticeable also, and the school-houses and churches are as thickly planted as in Ohio or New York. The many scattered groves of splendid oaks, in which, perhaps, grew one or two yellow pines or a few stately firs, gave an opportunity not lost sight of to place one's house where the effect would be that of an ancient homestead, around whose sacred altars trees planted in grandfather's youth had

had time to become of great size and dignity. This pleasant deception is seen everywhere; and it *is* deceptive in spite of your knowledge, giving an impression of a country occupied for centuries, and full of traditions.

To this appearance of domestic felicity —"happy homes of a free people," as the land agents are fond of shouting—is added at the bright season of early summer the utmost charm of great natural beauty. The whole wide basin lies open to the eye, robed in green, but green of what infinite variety of tint and shading, between the emerald squares of the new wheat and the opaque mass of the far-away hill forests sharply serrate against the sky, or melting into a farther and farther indistinctness of hill and haze. The foreground, too, is always pleasantly sketchy; or, if you think my picture lacks bright color, look at that great golden swath of ranunculus laid athwart the meadow; at that brown patch of freshly ploughed ground; at this brilliant red barn and white farm-house half hidden in its blossoming orchard!

All the cereals are raised here, but you will see little of anything except wheat, which for half a century has made Oregon famous. In 1831, it is related, the first wheat was sowed at French Prairie, in Marion County; and that same field yielded thirty-five bushels to the acre in 1879. Rich land that, but equalled in many parts of the western valleys, where the soil is a dark loam, underlaid by clay. The richest acres of course lie along the wooded river-bottoms, in many of which can be traced extensive beaver dams. The beavers have long ago departed, but their occupation, by making broad reaches of still water, overflowing the lowlands, and permitting wide deposits of alluvium, has produced a soil of extraordinary fertility.

Of wheat, the yield to the acre runs from twenty to thirty-five or more bushels, full and heavy grain often exceeding by five to nine pounds the standard weight of sixty pounds to the bushel. "Land summer-fallowed and fall-sowed is certain to produce twenty-five bushels as a minimum yield. In some parts of this valley [the Wahlamet] where the fields have been cropped continuously for a quarter of a century, they still produce enormously, thus demonstrating the great strength and permanent qualities of the soil. The wheat of this region is a plump,

full berry, from which flour of uncommon whiteness is made. Its excellence in this respect is so fully recognized that in the English markets it commands a premium of from three to five cents over the best produced in California. Many varieties of wheat are cultivated. The old white winter wheat, originally introduced by the Hudson Bay Company, is excellent in quality, and retains its hold on popular favor. White velvet wheat is certainly as good, and perhaps more productive. Spring varieties of white wheat, as Chili Club, Little Club, Australian, and others, are well liked and give good crops. The peculiarities of the soil in the various counties mainly determine, however, the kind of wheat which is used for seed in different localities."[*]

The surplus yield of wheat at present is about 150,000 tons annually in Western Oregon—more than two-thirds of the crop of the whole State. This amount represents about 5,000,000 bushels, much of which was converted into flour here. This year the acreage and crop will be a little larger. There is at every little railway station a great warehouse, to which the farmer brings his wheat for sale as fast as it is threshed. This obviates the need of barns; and you will see very few of these structures in Oregon, except stables used for live stock. All the wheat thus gathered in the country warehouses finds its way before the winter is over to the wharves at Portland, the railway charging a uniform freight rate from all points. At Portland vessels are loaded, and the grain or flour starts on its long voyage around the Horn. "Neither mildew nor rust has appeared to any great extent, and no failure of the wheat crop has been known since the settlement of the country..... Owing to the dry summers, the wheat is not affected by the long sea-voyage to Great Britain, whither most of it is exported, and by the double passage through the tropics incidental to its transportation."

Next to wheat, oats are the most important crop, there being raised yearly a surplus of the finest quality for export. Rye and barley are also planted extensively. On the river-bottom lands hops are grown to a large extent, the Wahlamet Valley being famous for the excellence of this product and the extraordinary yield. The picking is done by Indians, for the most

---

[*] From *The Pacific Northwest*, p. 42.

part, and an exciting picture it makes. Flax also is a plant widely cultivated, as well as magnificent clover and all the vegetables, the potatoes being of superior quality; but nowhere in Western Oregon will you see "the silken sweep of the corn billows rushing through yellow fields" of maize. For this plant the nights are too cold. That refreshing coolness following quickly upon the retreat of the sun, hastening down from the mountains to close our eyes in well-blanketed and undisturbed sleep, is fatal to Indian corn, which glories in the blaze of the midsummer heat, and waxes fat and succulent through damp and sultry midnights.

Farmers in Western Oregon, however, by no means restrict their energies and capital to raising grain, or growing the varied fruits that flourish so well in the Wahlamet orchards. Vale and open hilltop are clothed in a turf of rich grasses and weeds, blossoming into loveliness for the farmer's eye, while storing up juices relished by his grateful beasts. Unadapted to the raising of herds of beef cattle, as a dairy country the region is most admirable, and everywhere one sees hosts of sleek kine pasturing in full content. Milk, butter, and cheese are staple products, therefore, and on the Wahlamet much attention has been paid to the improvement of the milch stock, short-horns finding the most favor. For these cattle very little fodder is provided, the custom being to let them run out-of-doors all winter; but this results in deterioration, and often in loss, so that it would be far better to shelter and feed them during the midwinter, when cold sleety rains follow one another in doleful succession. As for snow or hard ice, neither is often seen.

The same remarks apply to the sheep, which are annually increasing in numbers and growing in excellence through higher admixture of Merino and Cotswold blood. Sheep-raising, indeed, especially in the southern counties, is one of the most profitable and extensive of all industries, great flocks being driven every year for sale into California and Nevada, the surplus of those preserved for shearing.

The Wahlamet Valley is separated from the valley of the Umpqua by the Calapooia Hills, connecting the Coast Range with the mountains of the interior, Calapooia being the tribal name of the aborigines here. It is a low divide, and offers no great difficulties to the railway, which winds through Pass Creek Cañon, affording an hour of steady delight to the passenger, and scenery for a whole summer of painting to the artist who takes his sketching kit on his back, and threads its old wood roads and cattle trails afoot.

During the past ten years a considerable agricultural settlement has followed the lumbermen into this range. All the prairie and open bottom-lands having long ago been taken, settlers who are unable or unwilling to purchase improved farms are compelled to go into the brush on the foot-hills, where land is to be bought of the railways at about $2 50. This certainly is cheap; for when it has been cleared—devastating fires are greatly aiding this process—a soil only slightly, if at all, inferior to that of the lowlands (albeit of different character) lies ready for long tillage. This fact, nevertheless, was slow in becoming apprehended. For example, there is a range of highlands near Salem, called the Waldo Hills, the soil of which is red and easily worked. A few years ago this soil was believed sterile and almost worthless, but some adventurous spirits experimented with it, and now those hills are said to produce the best grain in the State, 350,000 bushels having been garnered there in 1880. For cleared farms there you must pay from $30 to $50 an acre, exclusive of improvements.

Volcanic, like all these ridges, the Calapooia Hills are rough, with broken ledges, and the streams pour saucily through narrow gorges or tumble headlong down many a black and white cascade. Mighty firs, clean-shafted and straight, stand as thickly upon the highlands as the crowding triangles of their bushy tops will let them, their outer edges, where the prairie reaches up or the axe has cleared a space, guarded by a thick hedge of youngsters as shapely and ornamental as the pets of a gentleman's park. Thus the hill-tops. Over the streams which knit the hills together in silver seams arch the verdant boughs of ash and maple, the stiff-jointed limbs of oaks, whose bark is hidden in soft swathings of olive-brown moss, the wide-reaching alders, every twig traced vividly white through the green, and many another bright-foliaged tree or bush. The rocks are black and hard, to be sure, but how exquisitely does nature apologize for them! The grasses lean over the very brink of the precipice; thick mosses rest upon every ledge and projection; vines bearing pink garlands or red-stemmed briers starred with snowy blossoms climb its rugged walls; minute lichens, crowding closely, lay a silver tissue over smooth cleavage faces; and in every cleft nod tiny bright flowers, poised delicately as jewellers display gems upon flexible pins that their facets may sparkle fitfully in tremulous light. The cool shadow baths under these huge firs, the sun-lit canopies of hazel and oak (if you like that better), the sorrel-reddened banks of the brooks, and those brilliant rocks, make summer pictures beyond belief beautiful.

The Umpqua region is prominent in agriculture like that of the Wahlamet, the latter, indeed, having nothing to show equal to the beautiful Yoncalla Valley. But in the Umpqua region there is to be had also much mineral wealth, including gold and iron. Coal, however, is the mineral of greatest importance, immense beds of semi-bituminous and lignite coal underlying portions of the country west of the Cascade Mountains, especially in Douglas and Coos counties. One of the Coos Bay mines alone is said to be capable of an output of a thousand tons a day, and two small steam-colliers, with several sailing vessels, are kept busy taking the coal to San Francisco. The iron region of Oregon lies in the neighborhood of Portland, extending from Kalama almost to Oregon City, and furnishing ore of great value.

It will readily be understood from the description in the foregoing pages that this is a population that lives scattered on farms, so that many towns are not to be expected. There are only half a dozen worth mention in Western Oregon. Jacksonville and Ashland are busy centres of an agricultural and great fruit-growing and wine-making region at the southern edge of the State, beyond our scope. Roseburg, the present railway terminus, is a prettily placed village on the south fork of the Umpqua, settled largely by Germans. Here died the famous Senator Joe Lane, in a little cottage beside the river. At Eugene City is located the State University, the town having given it a fifty-thousand-dollar building—far more useful, I hope, than it is attractive to the eye.

This university is the highest institution of learning in the State, and has about one hundred and fifty students (not counting the preparatory department), about one-third of which are young women, and it is old enough to have graduated three classes. These students come from all parts of the State, and are admitted upon the strength of a local competitive examination, entitling the winner to a scholarship, of which there are as many as there are members of the Legislature. Such scholarships are free, and it is considered that an expenditure of four dollars a week ought to supply a pupil at the university with all the privileges and comforts he could ask. The equipment of the school, except in the matter of a library, is very fair, and Professor Condon has placed there a local paleontological collection which is unique and of great value.

Further down the Wahlamet, Albany on the eastern and Corvallis on the western bank are farmers' villages, having flouring and woollen mills, together with factories run by water-power for various small wares. From Corvallis a railway is building to the coast, finding a harbor at Yaquina Bay. This railway has a large land grant, is supported by New York men, asserts its harbor a better one than the Columbia can afford, and proposes to build straight eastward through Lebanon Pass to a junction with the Union Pacific Railway in Idaho. Corvallis boasts an academy, dignified by the title of State Agricultural College, and aided by the State.

The capital of the State, Salem, is the largest village in the valley, having about six thousand people. There is a curious coincidence in the name, which means a place of peace, for, strangely enough, the Indians dwelling there were the Cheméketas, or *peace-makers*. It is only recently that civilization has obliterated the old circular embankment, like a circus ring, where the councils of all the valley Indians used to be held, the pipe passing from hand to hand around the grave circle, while the orator of the moment spoke in the centre. What a pity the town was not named Cheméketa, and that the metropolis was not called Multonomah, Salem and Portland having about as much real significance in their situation as if they were simply lettered A and B.

Salem is chiefly of consequence as a flour-making place, possessing the largest mills in the State now, and looking forward to another great mill just begun. These establishments contain improved machinery, and all their flour is intended for export, being sent to Liverpool in ships of their own chartering, and sold in England by one of the owners, who lives there.

Salem stands at the head of navigation on the Wahlamet, except at very high water. Several miles below, a volcanic ledge crops up square across the river's course, making a heavy cataract. The ledge has broken in the middle, so that the main body of the stream rushes into a big notch, making far more noise and turmoil by its leap of forty feet in this ragged crevice than a sheer, smooth fall would occasion. The banks of the river here are cliff-like and forest-hidden, and the scene is almost grand, reminding one somewhat of the Falls of St. Anthony.

A practical view of its water-power advantages led to the placing of the first settlement in the State here—Oregon City. The narrow river-bank is now given up to woollen and flouring mills and other factories chiefly, most of the dwelling-houses standing upon a high cliff, which is scaled by picturesquely contrived stairways. For many years a portage was necessary about these falls, the steamboats all transferring their cargoes; but lately, and at great expense, a canal with locks has been opened on the western side of the river, through which steamers pass and repass.

The lower part of the Wahlamet Valley, especially on the western side, is solidly timbered, many firs there reaching 250 feet in height. Prairies and oak-openings occur here and there nevertheless, such districts showing settlements of long standing, and now threaded together upon the west side branch of the Oregon and California Railway.

One of these villages, the little town of Forest Grove, where you can scarcely see how pretty the white houses are for the crowding of bountiful orchards, and the wide-reaching shade of oaks and evergreens, is the seat of one of the government's Indian training schools, in charge of Captain William C. Wilkinson, of the Third Infantry, U.S.A. Captain Wilkinson has been on staff duty in this department for several years, and has added to a wide knowledge of the Indians a deep interest in their regeneration. It is only by untiring exertions that he has been able, within the last three years, to begin this school for Indian youth; but his enthusiasm is sufficient to brush away obstacles that would stagger another man.

Not the least of these obstacles is that miserable spirit of intolerance so constantly met with on this coast, and particularly from the old settlers and their sons. When this spirit is unrestrained, it manifests itself in a ruffianly bullying of everything not within the pale it chooses to erect, and a very narrow pale that is.

To that sort of man (and unfortunately he is in tremendous force among the people still influential in Oregon) the Indian is merely something to be kicked out of the way. He is never spoken of save as a "damned Injun," and never conceded to be "good" until he is dead. The man who asserts the red man's humanity and immortal worth in the eyes of his and our Creator goes flatly against the theory and practice of this class, and must expect much the same treatment as martyrs to other unpalatable truths have received.

Fighting his way through opposition from this and other circumstances, Captain Wilkinson secured two years ago an appropriation of $5000, out of which he was to establish a school to embrace not less than twenty-five Indian children. This put him up a wooden building on land loaned by the Pacific University (a struggling academical school at Forest Grove), and gathered his children. The next year he was given $15,000, while this year the appropriation is increased to $30,000, but he is required to teach 150 pupils. This gives $200 a year apiece, out of which the superintendent must house, feed, clothe, and teach his wild young household, and pay the travelling expenses to and fro of all recruits or graduates. The government paid a single bill of $80,000 for a steamer to carry troops and munitions of war to the front at Lewiston, Idado, during the Nez-Percé war of 1879!

What has been the success so far? At Forest Grove you will see where the first building was set right in the unhewed woodland, a large, well-fenced clearing, from which all the stumps have been grubbed, and every inequality levelled and turfed or ploughed. This the boys did unaided, their strong young arms bending eagerly to the task—but never was such playing heard of as they make the oaks ring with when work is done! You will see also, instead of one building, two. The second, used as a school-house for nearly one hundred youngsters, and as a domitory for the boys, and which is two and a half stories in height, was built wholly by the boys; not a white workman did a day's job upon it, except in the way of a few preliminary directions. Then furniture was needed—desks for the school-room, tables and drawers and shelves for the office, bedsteads for the dormitory. The lumber was bought, the tools provided, and the boys did the rest; it is not ornamental and costly, but it is strong, neat, and answers every purpose. The young carpenters learned something of the use of tools, saved wages for the general fund, and have the satisfaction of sleeping and eating on their own handiwork. These necessities provided for, the girls' quarters are beginning to be enriched by little cupboards, small bureaus, and a variety of such conveniences, which there is no money to buy, and which it pleases both giver and recipient to get in this way. It was gratifying to find in a governmental institution a carpetless, paintless frugality that Puritans and ascetics might have admired, until I recalled that this was not the creditable economy of newly conscientious politicians, but an enforced simplicity in order to make a pittance about the size of a campaign committee's stationary bill do all the philanthropic service possible to be squeezed out of it.

To get the children together, Captain Wilkinson visits the different tribes in Oregon and Washington Territory, and receives recruits, which are selected by the principal men of their tribe, and are usually their own sons and daughters. The first doubts the Indians had in respect to the school were dispelled by coming to see it; now they are anxious to send more than can be accommodated. From Alaska, even, has come a large squad, whose home is on the Stickeen River. Some have been in the school two years, others only a few weeks; some are approaching eighteen years of age, others are under ten; all are thorough Indians,

save a few half-bloods, who might as well be, so far as manner of life is concerned. They are wigwam babies in a Christian nursery.

The details of school life are uninteresting. The children are set at once to learn English, and if you should hear the school recite in concert, or sing, you would not suspect that in nearly every case the language had been learned within a year or two, so fluently and distinctly is it uttered, or read and written. Apt to learn, they have advanced rapidly in their books, and are equally quick at their trades, every one being set at blacksmithing, carpentering, wheelwrighting, or at making shoes, as soon as he has strength or capacity. All work more or less at farming, but arrangements for this branch of education and profit are sadly inadequate as yet. Shoemaking has been carried so far that money is earned every day by the boy-cobblers in pay for outside job-work. The girls make straw hats, and sew in various ways.

It is not this sort of thing, however, that tells so well as their social, domestic education. Here rare wisdom is required to get proper results. The discipline and home life of a hundred young Indians fresh from the squalor and unrestraint of the wigwam were problems requiring careful handling. The effect must be not merely to teach civilized methods, but to make these methods so appeal to the good judgment and affection of the children that, when they return to be lights to their race, they shall not be tempted to relinquish them for their old savagery.

Captain Wilkinson thinks that the Indian must be wholly separated from his people and their influences in order to reconstruct and educate him. Accordingly, every child receives an English name, and its own, or its home tongue, is never heard.

THE DEAD SEA OF THE WEST

PEARLY gulls, old and wise in the lore of their fathers, circle up from the banks of the Jordan. In the east they can descry a great city shimmering white against the purple foot-hills of the snow-clad Wasatch; in the west, the sunlight upon the ever-changing emerald and turquoise hues of a lake that laps the base of the gigantic Oquirrh range. Poplars, branching box-elders, cottonwoods, and an occasional rose-of-Sharon tree fringe the outskirts of the distant Mormon capital, proclaiming it an oasis of comfort as well as of splendor. Here and there the tremendous valley in which it lies is dotted with prosperous green farms, but in the main the fifteen-mile tract of alkaline monotony between the city and the lake is relieved by nothing save withered-looking sagebrush. The gulls rise a thousand feet in the air, and only then are they as high as were the waters of the ancient lake that once stretched three hundred and fifty miles through this huge basin. Marks of the water-line still show far up on the mountain-sides, and gull legends bear witness that it was nearly three thousand miles around this prehistoric lake with its interesting crustacea and its outlet to the sea.

Now three comparatively small bodies of water are all that remain of the overgrown pond of the past. Of these Utah Lake alone, which empties into Great Salt Lake through the Jordan River, is filled with fresh water; Sevier Lake, scarcely a mud-puddle in dry weather, and Great Salt Lake, are unbelievably salt. What became of the more extensive lake, known by geologists as Lake Bonneville in honor of the man who discovered its shore-line in 1831, no one can say with certainty, but it is supposed that climatic changes finally brought about its shrinkage by evaporation until the waters were too low to connect with the stream that joined the Snake River through Red Rock Pass. At any rate, the lake was left without the outlet which had carried away the modicum of salt borne down by the inflowing rivers. Evaporation went on, the rivers did not desist from bringing salt, and at last this inland body of water became a solution of brine. Some authorities claim that Lake Bonneville dried away completely, leaving only ripple marks in a desert of gleaming sand, but it seems more reasonable to suppose that before it vanished entirely there were other climatic changes which caused more rainfall, increased the size of the streams, and so preserved the present lake. However it came to exist, Great Salt Lake to-day, as in the centuries past, continues to reflect the mountains in its opalescent depths, and will probably never cease to do so in spite of the dire prophecies resulting from its curious habit of receding and coming back.

Because of the queer phenomenon of its occasional withdrawal, the area of this surfless lake is variable. Sometimes it is ninety miles long, sometimes only sixty. The mystery of its movements is not known, but for many years it has been the subject of wild conjectures and much serious investigation. At one period, not long ago, the lake was shrinking in such an alarming manner that those who regarded it as an old friend were filled with apprehension. Among other ingenious theories was the one that a hole had been made in the bottom of the lake by driving piles, and all the water was pouring down into a subterranean cavern. Another claimed that the rivers had been diverted for irrigating purposes, and that, besides, there was less rainfall. The old settlers meanwhile placidly chewed their gum and gathered crops. Their composure was not unfounded. When the scientists were in the midst of demonstrating that the lake was disappearing for all time, it suddenly rose again higher than it had been in a decade. Discomfited, the geologists then stated and tried to prove that there had been a volcanic disturbance of the lake bottom which

apparently caused the water to overflow, though its volume was in reality the same; but the unbelievers in the climatic-change theory scoffed at such a statement and pointed out that the unchecked denudation of the hills was increasing the amount of water transported to the lake by the streams. No really adequate explanation of the lake's vagaries has ever been furnished, but there is a popular superstition that the water recedes every seven years, and then comes rushing back at the end of three. The numbers three and seven in themselves savor of witchcraft. While scholars study the ripple marks and work out their formulas, the lake lies year after year in the sun and rain, now golden-brown like the algæ on the rocks, now filled with every tint of a painter's pallet—a wonderful foreground for the mountains looming out of the lavender haze upon its edge, a refreshing contrast to the dingy sagebrush and the glare of the snow-white shore.

Poets, as a rule, do not sing of matters commercial, and yet there is an epic quality about all the industries connected with the lake. Especially is this true of the salt-works, which are represented to the ordinary traveler by great, smooth mounds of crude salt ready for the dun-colored freight-car or the weather-beaten refinery. They resemble truncated pyramids more than anything else, and the imaginative mind straightway repictures the blazing Egyptian sun and mirroring Nile.

On April 1st the brine from the lake is pumped into the salt-beds, or

A CHAIN OF BATHERS

evaporating - ponds, which cover several hundred acres about a mile and a half from the lake. The brine remains in the beds until the "harvest," which takes place during the latter part of August or the first days in September. Throughout the summer the heat of the sun is drawing out the moisture and effecting the deposit of salt. It is noticeable that when the water begins to evaporate, it has the peculiar, iridescent hue of s u n l i t ice, and the salt showing through presents the appearance of great patches of snow. Indeed, when the superfluous brine is returned to the lake and the sixty harvesters pitch their tents preparatory to gathering the harvest, the salt - beds resemble a vast plain of speckless snow, now white, now blue under the shadows.

The beds do not lie long undisturbed. First, they are plowed to a depth of from two to four inches; then hand - cars are run out over temporary rails for the salt that is carried to the ever-growing pyramids. The laborers working in the dry, blistering heat, miles from any tree and forced to drink the brackish water sent from a distance, are objects to excite compassion, and yet they seem more like a comic-opera chorus than toilers with shovel and pick. Their overalls glitter with salt crystals, their eyes are protected by smoked glasses, their faces look as if they had been daubed with vermilion. Occasionally one of the big Swedes wears an eye-shade instead of the spectacles, and as he peers up at a flight of gulls overhead or at the ragged mountains on the horizon, his

FLOATERS

eyes are startlingly blue in his poor, raw face.

For three months the laborers draw their dollar and a half and two dollars a day for digging the coarse salt. This is sold at the works for a dollar a ton to any who care to purchase it there. Refined salt is run through a drying - cylinder, separated from the undesirable elements by fanning, and then ground into the different grades to be found on the market. F o r t y thousand tons a season is the usual harvest, but twenty - five times that amount could be furnished if there should ever be a demand for it. For a number of years the salt-manufacturers had no adequate refining process, a n d though the present product is ninety per cent. pure, it has taken s o m e time to counteract the unfavorable impression that the first s h i p m e n t s caused.

In spite of the early ban, many salt-packed cars have rumbled after the great, black Moguls in their journey south through the dusty valley of Zion, or west over the Lucin cut-off, that marvelous engineering feat which cannot but stir the imagination, goad ambition, and compel applause. Its story is so miraculous that it reads like a fairy-tale. When the Southern Pacific was built in 1868, the engineers shook their fists at Great Salt Lake for lying in their path, and then meekly built the road around, over rocky Promontory Mountain, across creek and gaping gully. For about fifty years the long, olive-drab trains wheezed up the grades and stalled on the turns, and at last the officials decided to save curves and the extra forty-three miles around the lake. Accordingly, rails, piling, and extra steam-shovels were peremptorily ordered, and in June, 1902, train-loads of these things came to a stop at the lakeside.

The car crews stared out at the vast expanse of water before them. Little, white-capped waves licked the shore, covering with sparkling crystals a bottle and an old shoe that some child had tied to a peg — to be made into playthings as fair as the jewels in the crowns of kings, as beautiful as the dome of fairy-land. Gulls fought where the Bear and Jordan rivers met this inland sea, for as soon as the fish reached the brine they died, and their glistening bodies became easy prey. The trainmen saw it all, and signaled and threw switches with little speech. A railroad track across this Nile-green ocean! A cut-off through this dead, dead sea! Then one word suggested itself from the bigness of it all, and some man was seen to cross himself and heard to murmur a low, "God!"

Meantime the public was clamorous and incredulous. "A cut-off from Ogden, Utah, to Lucin, Utah!" it cried.

"Why, don't you know it's twenty-seven and a half miles across Great Salt Lake at that point, and that the water's from fifteen to thirty feet deep all the way?"

"Yes, we know it," returned the sun-browned engineers, with some defiance, "but sixteen miles of that distance is to be a solid earth track, sixteen feet wide at the top and seventeen feet above water."

"Do you mean that you can make a ridge of dirt from thirty-two to forty-seven feet high for sixteen miles in spite of the water?" gasped the public.

The engineers nodded. "Of the twenty-three miles of trestle, eleven will be filled with earth, leaving only twelve miles of trestle proper and four and a half miles of firm earth pathway at the beginning. We shall make over a thousand feet of trestle a day," they added.

The public smiled.

The engineers did not smile. They knew that they had a stupendous undertaking before them. To begin with, they discovered that the lake bottom was quite unlike any other lake bottom. A layer of loose sand first confronted the shovels; then a foot or two of hard sand; underneath this a seven-foot crust of soda and

HARVESTING THE SALT CROP

GARFIELD PAVILION WAS THE PRIDE
OF THE COUNTRY-SIDE IN ITS DAY

salt which it was almost impossible to penetrate; and last of all, unending depths of ooze. The difficulty of driving piles into the seven-foot crust was surmounted by dissolving through steam-pressure the substance which they could not otherwise affect, and a mile of trestle went up each week. Three thousand men worked day and night, through heat and cold, for the sake of this great enterprise; the rattle and creak of steam-shovels raising seven tons of gravel at a scoop was heard at Promontory Mountain, at Little Mountain, and in the Hogup Mountains, as four hundred cars a day were filled and hurried off; steamboats and tugs, built for the occasion, wrestled with escaped piles and carried tons of water and food to the panting laborers. The work progressed swiftly and surely, and just as the engineers were congratulating themselves on their conquest of the lake a terrible storm came up one night, and the inky waters lashed at both sides of the "fill," until morning showed a skeleton of ties and rails across the lake, with nothing underneath. Un-

daunted, the engineers filled in again and made the pathway wider; and finally, on November 13, 1903, the track from the west and the one from the east were joined in the center of the lake. That was a day of rejoicing for the brain-fagged engineers and the swollen-handed laborers, but the public remained skeptical.. "It won't stand," was the verdict; but it did stand, and has stood for nearly ten years, supporting from six to twelve trains a day, and valiantly resisting the action of wave and wind.

Level as a floor, straight as a ruler's edge, this splendid cut-off stretches across the beryl-green lake like a colossal brown centipede — a unique monument to the men who have made it. Indeed, it will probably have the enduring qualities of a monument, for piles after hardening in the crust of soda and salt cannot be moved and are preserved like so much stone. Also, the continuous wave-motion against the embankment coats it with a cement of salt crystals as hard and unyielding as flint. The passengers, then, who sail across Great Salt Lake — for it is virtually that, as the trestle is not discernible unless one leans far out of the window—can revel in the taste and smell of salt air without experiencing the unpleasant sensations of a boat-ride.

One can never fully know the lake until one has bought a ticket in the isolated little brown station on South Temple Street, and climbed into a width-long seat of one of the queer open cars making up the antiquated train that hourly carries the bathers to the resorts. Of the pavilions in the neighborhood of the lake, Saltair is by far the largest, the most popular, and the most beautiful. Like a white mosque in a houseless Venice, it towers above the three thousand piles which support it. The railway running on piles for nearly a mile over the water to its entrance seems almost a sacrilege, but this insignificant little narrow-gage track is the means of carrying some two hundred thousand happy, beribboned pleasure-seekers each season to the popcorn booth at the gates, and is, therefore, not to be despised.

The incoming crowd is of many ages, many costumes, and of such varying tastes that it scatters immediately, going in different directions. Some members of each party, however, are usually seen to hurry under the great central arch of the pavilion to lay claim to a long, brown dining-table, where the luncheon-hampers are left as a token of ownership; others make their way toward one of the semicircular wings that flank the main building, and, secure in some of the seven hundred bath-rooms, array themselves quickly in rented suits of blue or red or indigo. Perhaps that portion of the party so aptly designated by the old butler as "the trundle-bed trash" prefers the attractions of the scenic railway and the sauce bicycle-track in an adjoining amphitheater to the fun of bathing; and the strains of the orchestra on the second floor send a few scurrying up to the enormous ball-room under the steel-ribbed dome.

The dancers are followed by the grandmothers who witness the gaiety and sit silent, swinging partners in the Virginia reels of memory. They draw their chairs up to the south railing and look out at the now-deserted Garfield pavilion, crowded into the water by the imposing Oquirrh Mountains rising abruptly from the shore-line. Garfield was the pride of the country-side in its day! They smile as they recall Old Folks' Day, when the aged came from all parts of Utah as guests of the state. There were red badges for those between sixty

LIKE A MONSTER SHIP, SALTAIR SHINES FAR OUT INTO THE NIGHT

Barrall.

OLD FOLKS' DAY

and seventy years of age, blue badges for those between seventy and eighty, and for those reaching eighty a white one. They had longed to wear a white badge once, for it was rather distinguished-looking, and many, many persons patted the gnarled hands of the wearer. Now the day for the white badge is approaching all too swiftly; life after the toilsome march across the plains and the completion of the more arduous home-building seems very easy and very sweet.

Slowly the grandmothers rise and walk to the north side of the pavilion. Below them scores of bathers, arms extended, heads slightly raised, are supported cork-like on the foam-flecked water. Sometimes a human chain of eight or more floats by, toes under arm-pits, arms outstretched, and the other bathers cheer and splash sticky water at them, hoping that it will not reach their faces; for carbolic acid taken internally is far more soothing than lake brine, which strangles its victim and continues to smart and burn for many days as a reminder of the experience. Interested boys hunt for the only forms of life to be found in the lake. One is a shrimp about a quarter of an inch long, which is said to be quite palatable. The other is the larva of a small, black fly. The shrimp is supposed to live upon the latter and also upon the algæ brought down by the streams. This algæ at times streaks the lake like patches of green-and-brown sawdust. Though it is not unpleasing in a panorama of the lake, the bather finds it sufficiently slimy and unpleasant to be avoided.

The shouts of the bathers finally fall on deaf ears, for the grandmothers are gazing at the west, where Antelope Island stands out like an uncut amethyst. Its setting of lapis-lazuli has changed to jade, and the sky is a bed of coral. This peak of the past seems too perfect to be aught but picturesque, yet it, too, has been turned to account. A wild herd of seventy-five buffaloes and five hundred cattle graze within the well-defined range of its sage-brush shores. When the lake has been low, the cattle have been driven across from the mainland; in other seasons they are ferried across in proper style. There are fascinating tales of this island—tales of its treasure and the hardships of the dwellers in its early ranch-house; but tales of suffering are best forgotten in these more prosperous days.

In the lake are eight other islands,

HALF-FLEDGED PELICANS CROWD THE ROCKY SHORE

which are known as Frémont, Carrington, Stansbury, Gunnison, Mud, Dolphin, Strong's Knob, and Hat. Hat, or Egg Island, as it is more often called, is by far the most interesting, for here it is that the gulls, pelicans, and heron come from no one knows where to breed. There is no water, no green thing upon this former mountain-tip, and yet in the proper season one cannot step upon the rocky shore without treading on half-fledged pelicans eagerly waiting for the return of parents from a journey to the verdure-flanked inlets. When the grown birds are at home, the visit of a man sends them up in such numbers that the sky is darkened, and their shadows upon the water below turn the green to gray. It is as if a whole alphabet of V's had been sprinkled

in the heavens, and the intruder, half aghast at what he has done, hurries back to his salt-jeweled boat and sets out for Saltair.

As he glides over the ripples, his companion discourses knowingly on the subject of these boats. They have to be made, he says, especially for Salt Lake, as ordinary craft would ride so high as to capsize easily; but the oarsman hears no statistics, so drunk is he with the color of the lake and clouds. The lavender haze changes to blue, and then rises higher and higher until the islands melt into it and the mountains and placid lake are also engulfed. There is no sound but the gentle lapping of the water and occasionally a few rich, sweet notes from the distant violins. The pavilion is lighted now. Like a monster ship or a giant's palace, Saltair shines far out into the night, sending its lure to the poor sentry trudging out his watch on the Fort Douglas mesa, and to the slag-foreman wiping his smutty brow near Black Rock. The wicked red smelter fires glow from the base of the sable mountains like the flame-drenched teeth of a slumbering dragon, and their reflection turns the water into ruby pools of liquid glass. Sounds of revelry and merrymaking grow louder. The oncoming boat scrapes against a pile, and a rope, stiff with salt, makes it fast.

To his amazement the oarsman finds the older members of his party still sitting where he left them, staring out at the peacock shades in the illuminated water. As he stands by his grandmother's chair, inhaling deep breaths of the fresh, clean air, she smiles up at him wistfully, and her frail hand points over the railing while she quotes:

"The water, like a witch's oils,
 Burns green and blue and white."

"It's pretty, isn't it, grandmother?" says the young man, sympathetically, helping her to rise in order that they may round up the children and catch the train.

She pauses a moment without responding, and gazes once more at the tranquil lake. "They say she's going out again," she at last states, regretfully, and then adds with assurance, "but she'll come back; aye, she'll come back."

Thus has the personality of this desert lake taken hold of those who know it, and thus would it take hold of you, could you, after the last train has left for the city, see the moon rising above those austere peaks and covering the waves with fleece of gold while the now darkened pavilion towers like a palace of carved ivory against the starlit sky. The scene is so solemn, so vast, so full of the infinite, that it would make a little ache steal into your heart and a gray mist fill your eyes; but you, too, would turn away from it, murmuring confidently, "She'll come back; aye, she'll come back."

CHINESE IN SAN FRANCISCO

WHILE gratifying my curiosity, and experiencing the pleasure of studying the habits and customs of a strange people during the recent Chinese civil and religious festival of the new year, it occurred to me that a short article giving the result of these observations might be of interest to readers, many of whom never have had, and possibly never will have, the opportunity to examine for themselves any of the peculiarities of this alien Asiatic race at present sojourning on the shores of the Pacific, apparently unaffected by contact with our Anglo-Saxon civilization, and which, while submitting respectfully to our laws when they touch its interests, or where its outward life comes in contact with our ordinances, still retains in the land of its present residence unswerving allegiance to the customs and traditions of its fathers, and recognizes with loyal and orderly obedience the fiats of tribunals of its own organization.

Within the confines of the Chinese quarter in San Francisco is presented probably the most curious phase of life to be seen on this broad continent. Within a circle whose radius is half a mile, in the heart of an intensely Western American city, itself the growth of little more than a quarter of a century, is found what we might call an Asiatic colony, and a colony bringing with it and retaining in its new home all the characteristics of its Chinese parentage. Traverse but a few feet, and the dividing line between a Mongolian and a Caucasian civilization, usually measured by an ocean, is crossed. Features, language, costume, merchandise, the exterior individuality of houses, and the hurried glimpses of interiors revealed by the passing glance, all proclaim what might be a quarter in some Chinese city. Strangers and visitors to San Francisco in many cases see more of the life of this curious people than residents of the city. The strong local prejudice against our Asiatic immigrants, and the proverbial procrastination of those who can avail of an interesting experience at their convenience, unite to keep "Chinatown" practically a sealed book to the better-class denizens of the "Queen City of the Pacific."

Availing ourselves of the invitation of a Chinese friend to visit him on New-Year's Day—February 9 of our calendar—through his kind attentions we were able to receive on the camera of our mental experience impressions which, in spite of their meagreness of outline, are herewith offered for the benefit of those interested in the festival customs of all divisions and types of the great human family.

Forty-five centuries ago this Oriental people had constructed astronomical instruments analogous to the quadrant and armillary sphere, which enabled them to make observations remarkable for their accuracy, and making possible, even at that remote period, the formation of a useful calendar.

Their present system is a very complicated one, but, like every arrangement of this ingenious people, works with absolute accuracy, once the principle of its procedure is understood.

Like that of the Hindoos, the Chinese civil year is regulated by the moon, and from the time of the Han dynasty, two centuries before Christ, has begun with the first day of that moon during the course of which the sun enters their sign of the zodiac corresponding to our sign Pisces. They have also an astronomical year which is solar, and for the adjustment of these solar and lunar years employ a system similar to our leap-year plan, except that instead of an intercalary day every fourth year, as in the Gregorian calendar, they insert an intercalary month, occurring alternately every third and second year in periods of nineteen. For instance, last year had an intercalary month; the next one will come in 1882, again in 1884, then in 1887, etc.—two intercalary months in five years, or seven in nineteen years. The year, therefore, contains thirteen or twelve months according as it has or has not an intercalary one. A month has either twenty-nine or thirty days, the number of days being intended to correspond to the number of days which the moon takes to make the revolution around the earth. A *month*, indeed, means one *moon*, the same Chinese character being used to indicate both. So, too, the number used to indicate the age of the moon at any time denotes also the day of the month: thus there is always a full moon on the 15th, no moon on the 1st, etc. Consequently the moon always presents the same appearance on the same day in any month from year to year. This plan is particularly convenient for farmers and sailors, whose memory is thus materially assisted in remembering the changes of moon and tides. The spots on the moon which we call the "man in the moon" suggest to the Chinese mind the idea of a small animal shelling rice, their chief staple of food; and a common saying in China is, "There is a little white rabbit in the moon pounding out rice." The era used by the Chinese in their histories is, next to that of the Jews, the oldest employed by any nation, as for over four thousand years they have for chronological purposes made use of a series of daily, monthly, and yearly cycles of 60. Each day, month, and year has its own name in its cycle, and by compounding these names a single one is made to express the date employed. A new cycle began in 1864, so that the present year is the 17th year of the 75th cycle. But the common events of every-day life amongst the Chi-

DAWN OF NEW-YEAR.

nese have during these last twenty centuries been dated from the year of the accession of the reigning emperor. Some particular name, usually that of the new sovereign, is given by official proclamation to each reign, the years being number-

ed 1, 2, 3, 4, etc. The present emperor, Qwong See, came to the throne in 1875, consequently we are now living in the 6th year of Qwong See. A record of these eras is kept, called a Catalogue of the Nienh-hao, by reference to which the chronological date of any event is determined. Some hundreds of years hence an inquisitive Chinese student, wishing to place the historical date of some occurrence in this year, such as some barbarous acts of legislation against his countrymen in California, would turn to the Nienhhao, and so ascertain the historical bearings.

On the last evening of the old year—February 8 in the Gregorian calendar—"Chinatown" presented a busy, bustling, weird air, which plainly betokened an impending feast of importance. The signboards, with their curious hieroglyphics—well adapted for decorative effects—had generally been repainted and regilded, most of them being draped with bright scarlet cotton cloth—a favorite material for festooning. Red is the Chinese festal color, and is believed to be efficacious in keeping away evil spirits, and it is not unusual to see strands of red silk braided in children's queues to prevent them from being cut off by malicious spirits. Many of the shops displayed within and without sprigs of *kinhwa*, or "golden flowers," which are merely bunches of brass tinsel wire and foil twined and cut into floriated forms; these are principally used as offerings before the ancestral tablet and in the temples. The lintels of the doors, the windows, and blank spaces on the walls were already covered with new colored papers, principally red and orange, of various sizes, on which sentences appropriate to the season are printed. White paper denotes that the inmates have lost a parent during the past year; blue or yellow signifies a second year's mourning for father or mother; the death of a grandparent is indicated by dark carnation; but the joyous red predominated, and mingled with them were many red and orange papers stippled with gold. The advertisement boards were freshly covered with clean notices printed in the same style — black characters on red ground. The writing on the papers pasted

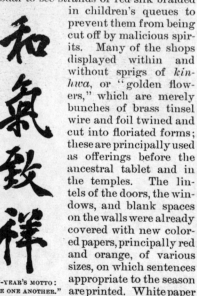

above and beside the doors mainly expressed the hope that the five blessings in which are summed up all the elements of human felicity—health, riches, longevity, love of virtue, and a natural death—might be the portion of the indwellers. The larger ones contained such sentences as these: "May Heaven give happiness!" "May I never be without rich customers!" "Good hope." "Good will come to us." "Love one another." "Peace be to those who come out and go in." "May we never be without wisdom!"

Devout Chinese avail themselves of this season to settle their accounts with the gods, and the walls of the hall and staircase of the principal Joss-house were covered with colored slips of paper, about twelve inches long by four wide, containing the names of the donors to the idols. Besides these records of generous fidelity to a national creed, were scrolls on which were written antithetical sentences referring to the attributes of some favorite god. Ornamental tablets of wood are also presented by admiring votaries, and hang from the ceilings or against the walls of the temples.

Gorgeous lanterns were suspended in front of doors or hung in rows from the numerous balconies. The flags of the Consulate, of the Six Companies, of the several temples, etc., fluttered in the breeze, and the occasional crackle, crackle, of firecrackers gave warning of the coming bedlam at midnight, when gongs, tom-toms (drums), bombs, and unlimited quantities of fire-crackers were to unite in driving away all evil spirits from the birth of the new year—the 6th of Qwong See. At nearly every window was to be seen a dish of the favorite Chinese lily, the narcissus, in full bloom. The shops displayed tables covered with them to tempt tardy purchasers, and the streets were crowded with "Celestials," some carrying a New-Year's offering to friend or master, others hastening to make final household investments before the shops closed—not to reopen until the first three days of the holiday season were passed.

Glimpses into interiors and down basements revealed strange sights. The whole population appeared to have submitted its head to the razor, and an unprejudiced observer, noting the conformation of the various Chinese foreheads, could not but be impressed by the phrenological indications, suggesting at least an average intelligence. New clothes were being extensively donned: those who can not afford to purchase a suit at this season borrow for the occasion. Clean white stocking-leggings caught the eye below each blue blouse, and silk and satin had replaced the ordinary cloth or cotton attire of many a worthy merchant. A favorite New-Year's present amongst the lower classes is a pair of shoes. But the most momentous business of the hour was the settling of accounts. All debts must be cancelled before the new year, and this universal obligatory *custom*—not law—has manifest advantages. The *swan-pwan*, or counting-board, and brush pencils, were not at rest for an instant, and it was far into the small hours of the night before many merchants left their desks. Before midnight a feast took place in each household, when food was eaten with certain ceremonies, variously apportioned to the sacrifice to Heaven and Earth, the worship of the favorite family gods, and the offering to deceased ancestors. Before the ancestral tablets, or household idol, incense was consumed, punk or joss-sticks, mock money, and pieces of red paper covered with printed prayers, were burned. Many parties of Chinese whose ordinary homes are with their American employers clubbed together for this festal season, and rented rooms, where conjointly they held their midnight feasts. As the bells announced the mystic hour of twelve, the dawn of a new period was welcomed by musical strains peculiar to the inhabitants of "the Middle Kingdom," by crackers, bombs, and "flowers" (rockets, etc.). A procession of priests curiously costumed, walking in single file, with lanterns, made a tour of the different temples, where they were received by the resident priests. Food, incense, tea, printed prayers, and mock money were offered to the gods, and appropriate fare partaken of by their earthly ministers. Generous hospitality is the feature of the New-Year season, and there is a Chinese saying "that during the first part of the first moon no one has an empty stomach." And here permit the remark that there is a decorousness amongst all classes of Chinese in their manner of partaking of food which is not always seen amongst "the people" of more civilized nations. We laugh at the chopsticks of these barbarians, but a polite mandarin once remarked to an English-

BARBER-SHOP IN CHINATOWN.

man, "In remote ages, before we became civilized, we used knives and forks as you do, and had no chopsticks. We still carry a knife in our chopstick case, but it is a mere remnant of barbarism. We never use it. We sit down to table to eat, not to cut up carcasses."

At an early hour on New-Year's Day the streets of "Chinatown" were full of well-dressed men, many of whom were really gorgeously apparelled, blue, olive-green, and gray being the prevailing colors. They were hastening to pay congratulatory visits, although, according to "Celestial" etiquette, it is permissible to settle some social debts simply by cards. Friends, as they pass, salute each other with exclamations and greetings which answer very much to our Anglo-Saxon formula of "A happy New-Year!"

No shops were opened. In front of some the heavy wooden doors were in place, barred and bolted, excluding most

MARKETING FOR NEW-YEAR'S DAY.

ors; and the official almanac for the new year, conspicuously framed — transformed trading shops into Chinese reception-rooms. The characters for happiness and longevity are frequently placed on the same scroll, and hung over the inside doors, as we would use the motto "A merry Christmas," or "A happy New-Year"; and another usual combination is made of four characters—for happiness, longevity, joy, and official rewards. In each of these rooms a table prominently placed displayed the usual festal bill of fare, such as tea, sam-shu (Chinese wine), oranges, lemonade, cakes—the recipes for some having evidently been secured in America—and a great variety of Chinese candied fruits and candies, these last being much less sweet than civilized bon-bons, and some by no means distasteful to a Caucasian palate. One special delicacy is candied pork fat, from which all grease

effectually all inquisitive inspection, but, as a rule, only the glass doors were closed, some of them being made to serve as screens by having strung half way across them scarlet cotton curtains. A complete metamorphosis had taken place within the counting-houses, which for so many days in the year appear but as trading-places, with small regard for decoration or æsthetics. Every one had been swept and garnished most successfully. Carved tables and chairs, in many cases covered with scarlet cloth and satin embroideries; colored scrolls, with sentences and mottoes; pictures of gods or ancestral warri-

appears to have been extracted. Oranges are particularly popular, as the colloquial name for them—*kĕk*—is the same used to express "fortunate" or "lucky." Water-melon seeds are also "fashionable." Cigars, opium, and the appliances for "high play" were not forgotten. Gambling is indulged in during the New-Year festivities to a vicious extent, and even during a visit to a Christian Chinese boarding-house it was very evident to observant ears that some of the inmates were enjoying themselves at play up stairs. The Grand Theatre, on Clay Street, with its new green and gold sign, but otherwise most civilized exterior, advertised startling attractions for the holidays; and as Chinese plays apparently have neither beginning nor end (and at this time are kept up day and night), crowds of men, and some women and children of the lower classes, were constantly streaming in and out. Indeed, children, dressed in clothes cut after those of their elders, but of a New-Year's visit amongst the better classes, I shall conclude with a description of this visit, paid by request on the second day of the new year, the first having been reserved by the consul exclusively for receiving his own countrymen. The Chinese greet each other with low and ceremonious bows, shaking their own hands, each congratulating the other; but

NEW-YEAR'S CALLS AMONG THE MERCHANTS.

with much more brilliant and fantastically combined colors, seemed suddenly to have swarmed from all quarters, and formed by no means the least interesting phase of this alien life. The temples were very thinly attended, except by curious Caucasians, as the special services for the New-Year had been held the night before.

As our call on the Consul-General, Mr. Chun Suw Ton, and his wife, can probably be considered a fairly typical experience as a courtesy to their American guests, both Mr. Chun and his wife complied with our Yankee prejudices, and shook hands in the orthodox manner, although in the lady's case it evidently was done with a real effort, and as she wore no gloves, I am confident that when the ceremonies of the day were over she confided to her liege lord her disapprobation of this one amongst some other "barbarian" American customs.

A bright, scrupulously neat servant, in Chinese livery, opened the door, and ushered us into General Bee's office. (General Bee is Chinese consul in San Francisco, his vice-consul is a Chinese, and Mr. Chun is the Consul-General for the United States.) We were asked to deposit our cards in a civilized bric-à-brac card-receiver, a pile of red paper beside it showing how many of Mr. Chun's countrymen had been before us. The New-Year's visiting-card is a sheet of red paper averaging nine inches by four inches, its dimensions and the size and position of the characters printed on it differing with the rank and importance of the visitor ; generally it merely contains the name, but sometimes a complimentary sentence or wish is added.

In a few moments General Bee appeared, and my Chinese friend introduced me. He greeted those present *en masse*, amongst them some half-dozen ladies, and told us to follow him into the next room, a double apartment, one half an anteroom, the other a large, comfortable office, where we were each in turn presented to the commercial representative of his sacred Majesty the Emperor of China —a fine-looking man of the Tartar type of feature, in full Chinese consular uniform, who spoke English fairly well, and most graciously. Having fortunately gone in with a feminine party, we were included in the invitation almost immediately extended, "Will you walk up stairs and see the ladies?" Following General Bee down some steps, and along a short corridor into what was evidently an adjoining house, we passed by the council-chamber, where some guests were being entertained by the vice-consul, and so on up stairs into a decidedly American-looking double parlor, furnished with Pacific coast made sofas and chairs, where we found the sweet-faced, gentle-mannered lady who, in obedience to her husband's commands, had put aside her native customs and bravely taken up a rôle not only strange, but, owing to her entire ignorance of English, embarrassing and fatiguing. Receiving with Mrs. Chun, and acting as interpreter, was a friend, the wife of a prominent Chinese merchant, equally attractive in appearance, perfectly self-possessed, with the charm of simplicity, and speaking English with a very agreeable soft voice and remarkably good accent. In the adjoining room a little child some three or four years old was playing ; her curiosity— that of her sex—soon brought her to make friends with us, although finally she returned to her companion, a young Chinese student on "sick-leave" from Harvard. A nurse, dressed in perfectly plain dark blue trousers and skirts, was seated at the far end of the room, evidently quite as much to enjoy the treat of seeing so unusual a ceremony as to watch her young charge, who had small need for her services.

A small embroidered screen and some scrolls on the wall were, the hostesses excepted, all that reminded us that we stood on the foreign soil of a Chinese consulate. As for these hostesses, they were certainly two very womanly, well-bred, unaffected creatures, whose handsome, bright-colored, but well-toned, fashionable Pekin-cut garments formed a most striking and curious contrast to the serviceable (it was a rainy day) close-fitting Ulster rigs of the American ladies who formed the majority of the party, and who used their eyes to examine with feminine capacity the superimposed layers of various silks and satins and embroideries which disguised the figures, and alas! even the feet, of the Oriental ladies. Their hair was stiffened into side wings, behind which were two bunches of artificial pink and gold asters, flanking a central bow of hair. Their cheeks had been artistically beautified with cosmetics—a universal Chinese custom.

We remained standing, after our presentation, until, Mrs. Chun resuming her seat, we, under General Bee's direction, followed her example. The next move was to hand to Mrs. Chun, according to suggestion, our visiting-cards, which apparently gave her as much gratification as we Americans had earlier in the day experienced in the possession of some hieroglyphically marked red papers. In exchanging a few sentences with the merchant's wife, I asked her if it was customary in China for ladies to receive. "Oh yes; we always do on New-Year's Day. We receive our friends, but not gentlemen." General Bee, overhearing the remarks, said we owed the privilege we were then enjoying to his influence with Mr. Chun, and that in the future this innovation would probably be kept up.

Conversation, in spite of the efforts of the gentle interpreters, having flagged to an appalling extent, we bowed, and shook hands indiscriminately in adieu. We were accompanied to the head of the stairs by a Chinese Harvard student, and taken down to the council-chamber, where refreshments, of too civilized a description to be interesting, were offered and declined. But little time was allowed for examining the decorations of this room, which were brilliant, almost the whole wall space being covered with scarlet scrolls hung perpendicularly. Back of a raised platform or table at the end of the room—on which was a pyramid of sugar-peaches, emblems of longevity—was a sacred picture, and here evidently the family feast had taken place two nights before.

Returned to the Consul-General's room, we were again greeted by him, asked how we enjoyed our visit, introduced to the vice-consul, Mr. Hwang Tak Kneu, understood to be a graduate of Amherst Col-

lege. Then having relieved ourselves of some few cordial speeches, and been the recipients of most polite and complimentary ones in return, we made our bow to our Chinese host, and separated as a party, each to go his or her way, and ruminate on the strange fate which had brought face to face on the soil of the American Union two such diverse civilizations as the Anglo-Saxon and Mongolian.

By the third day of the new year, social dues having been discharged, the denizens of "Chinatown" were principally occupied in domestic, theatrical, or gambling pleasures; comparatively few were to be seen abroad; most house servants had returned to their American homes, and the streets were mainly given up to Chinese scavengers, who were busy collecting and carrying away the débris of the feasts, and the remnants of exploded bombs and effete fire-crackers.

NEW-YEAR CALLS OF CHILDREN.

THE AMERICAN NILE

"WHEN you have drunk of the red waters of the Colorado you will be filled with an infinite longing to linger within sound of its voice. You may wander afar, but never again will you cease to hear the river calling. Some day you will obey and we will see you again," the Indians who dwell along its banks will tell you, and many a white man who has felt the indescribable charm of this mighty American Nile repeats the Indian legend in explanation.

Like the Nile, the Colorado owes its being to the melting snows of mountains thousands of miles from its mouth, flows through arid lands, and terminates in an immense delta as large as the State of Massachusetts. Unlike the Nile delta, renowned for the many generations to whom it has given homes and sustenance, the great delta of the Colorado, equally if not more fertile, has lain almost idle for ages.

It is the home of the Cocopa Indians, and they alone have raised scant crops in the generous land these many years past. They build their houses of arrow-weed, *Pluchea sericea,* with supports of willow or poplar, and conduct their crude husbandry according to the river's moods.

Each recurring spring the released waters rush from their mountain fastnesses and swell the river to resistless volume and current. Then follows a period of awaiting the river's pleasure to all who dwell or roam within the sphere of its influence. To casual observers there is naught of good, but much of seeming wanton destruction, in the annual bursting of the river's bonds and bounds, for the floods carry enough wreckage and sediment down to the sea each year to make a goodly State. Its quantity can only be estimated in thousands of tons, and its bulk is yearly crowding the ocean

waters farther south by slowly but surely filling in the Gulf of California. As the sea recedes, the characteristic flora of the region as constantly advances. As with most impetuous rivers, the Colorado floods subside as suddenly as they appear, and the river recedes to its usual channels, or such new ones as it frequently develops, while the ever-thirsty earth absorbs all lingering traces of the overflow with surprising rapidity.

Dr. D. T. MacDougal abandoned his duties as assistant director of the New York Botanical Garden for a trip down the Colorado early in March, and we made a hurried run across the continent. It was midnight when we were cast adrift at Mellen, a solitary station which the railroad people insist upon calling Topock. Kindly the brilliant Western moon arose to light us to welcome rest on a near-by hilltop. A hundred feet below, the Colorado was speeding on its ever-restless way, and beyond it the strangely worn and eroded Needles presented a singular medley of dignified and fantastic forms, silhouetted against the western sky. Daylight broke upon us seemingly before we had time to settle down cozily in our sleeping-bags, and the Needles appeared to have moved close upon us during the night from across the river in California.

In these lands of constant change one almost feels that he must be witnessing the birth of a new world. He finds the actual processes of moulding the earth going on all about him, and the mountains are affected only in less degree than the shifting sands which break into ripples and ridges at the behest of every idle wind.

At one point in the great desert is a chain of sand-hills averaging a hundred feet in height, which are slowly but steadily moving across the plain in the

DELTA WHERE THE COLORADO BURSTS ITS BOUNDS

direction of the prevailing winds. The wagon road which skirts them has been shifted many times, else it would have been covered. Ahead of them is the typical desert vegetation of the plain. The hills carry with them plants peculiar to themselves, and behind them, on the plain bared by the march of the hills, a flora distinctly different from either has appeared.

Erosion and weathering have honeycombed the Needles with pits and hollows and carved their summits into numberless domes, turrets, and pinnacles. Many of the more needlelike of the pinnacles are completely perforated. The sinking sun gleams through the openings with strange effect, and these sunlighted eyes suggested the mountain's name.

This year the river reached its maximum height, which only occurs at intervals of ten to twenty years. Nothing approaching its power of destructiveness

had been noted since 1891, when it did not reach the height of this year's record by several feet. Not for a decade will the conditions be likely to prove so favorable for study of the river's action and effects. To those dependent upon it for transportation or supplies the discomfort was proportionately great.

The explorers were joined at daybreak by Stanley Sykes, of Flagstaff, Arizona, who was to guide them down the river to Yuma, some three hundred miles distant. A folding canvas boat, twelve feet long, but broad of beam, and a skiff about as long, but much narrower, were depended upon for safe and speedy voyage. Volunteer advisers shook their heads ominously when they saw the little crafts loaded to their full capacity with camp-outfit supplies and apparatus, and all along the route we heard of danger-points just ahead which the tiny boats surely could not pass; but if those who would know the river at its best, learn its

THE MOVING SAND-HILLS OF THE DESERT

ever-interesting moods, and realize what it is accomplishing in the development of a new and exceedingly interesting land will trust the river, even in its wildest moods, in the very fulness of its strength, it will not betray their confidence. With ordinary precaution and the watchful observation that alone can make such a trip of any value, the journey can be and was made in a boat that two men could carry anywhere if portages were necessary. Camping alternately on the California and Arizona shores, delayed a day in camp near the mouth of Bill Williams Fork by a rain-storm, and a second day at Ehrenberg by a sand-storm, we reached Yuma on March 22, having accomplished the trip in eight days.

The upper valley of the river had received a maximum of rainfall, and numberless small annual plants, which in years of minimum moisture might not develop at all, had clothed the generally bare rocks and levels in green. The river was still rising in irregular stages and cutting into banks and shoals. It was carrying enormous quantities of driftwood, and the shifting current, destroying alternate banks at every turn, added hundreds of living trees and tons of soil to the débris it was sweeping to the sea. One day we rode the crest of a rise of two feet; it passed us while we slept that night, but quickly swept us onward to its head when we resumed our oars the next morning. That day the current carried us eighty miles in about seven hours with but little work at the oars.

The giant cactus, *Cereus giganteus*, was found to grow as far north as Bill Williams Fork and to cross the river there into California — interesting discoveries to the botanist as extending the known area of distribution of these remarkable plants. It has hitherto been supposed that the eastern bank of the Colorado marked the western limit of the plants.

Sand-storms are of frequent occurrence

on the extensive gravel mesa at Ehrenberg. The sand-laden wind obscures the view like a fog, and in the teeth of the gale the driving sand stings like needlepoints. It pervades everything; camp cooking becomes a task of magnitude, and eating an affliction, for at best a due proportion of sand must be swallowed.

The larger plants, especially the giant cactuses, suffer severely from these natural sand-blasts, and bear the scars of the encounter for many days. They are weird plants in their way, showing best perhaps standing, as they did in California, high up on rocky shelves on the mountainside, like giant sentinels ready to warn comrades on the plain below of any impending danger. Most people have been made familiar with the general appearance of the plant by numerous illustrations of it, but no photograph can convey the effects of its singular beauty amid its natural surroundings, nor tell the tale of the quaint music awakened by every breeze at play among its many spines.

The Gila River enters the Colorado just west of Yuma, and we crossed its angry waters through a maze of eddies and whirlpools through which immense quantities of driftwood were whirling in mad race. Escaping the worst of the turmoil, we reached the town at racing speed and made triumphant landing, with half our journey accomplished.

For eight days we had been cutting through the desert, but had found no barren land. Cottonwoods and willows lined the shores on either hand, to the exclusion of all view of the sandy wastes; in many places only a few feet behind the leafy screens. Tall canes diversified the scene at numerous points, and where the mud-flats prevailed the green blades of the cattail gave a familiar aspect to the scene. Most of the poplars—or cottonwoods, as the Western man invariably calls them—are a white-trunked variety: the white remarkably pure and the tree exceedingly handsome. They and the willows grow rapidly at the slightest opportunity. Thus it occurs that a mud-

GRAVELLY MESA BELOW SPUR OF COCOPA MOUNTAINS

flat escaping a single season's flood becomes a veritable nursery of young trees the following year.

In our rapid run down the river we had witnessed the destruction of dozens of such nurseries. At most places alongshore the river had reached the line of older growths and was levelling the larger trees by hundreds wherever a bend of the river directed the force of the current against the far shore. Trees ten inches in diameter and twenty to thirty feet high were constantly toppling into the insatiable river.

The fall of these larger trees was always graceful. The first intimation of it was a distinct shiver that ran through the entire tree, but was most marked in the upper branches; a moment later the tree would bend gracefully forward as if bowing to its enemy. An instant's pause and it would sink slowly into the rushing waters that had reached to and loosened the inshore roots.

Tree after tree of this larger growth would start down the river broadside to the current. Slowly at first, it would roll over and over, tangling its branches into a great skeleton wheel, rolling faster and faster as the branches became more impacted and presented fewer projecting points to catch and hold a moment in the shallower reaches. Eventually the branches would be worn off in such progress, leaving only the tougher roots to retard it. Then the denuded tree would give up the struggle, and whirling into the line of least resistance, would float head on down-stream until caught by the spreading roots in some shallow. Such snags anchored in favorable situations quickly gather and hold a tangled mass of drift, rising ten feet or more above the water. Others lie well submerged, with only a ripple above them to warn the navigator of their presence.

Mud banks, too recent to have developed vegetation, are absorbed by the river with even greater facility. Undercut by the current, such a bank will slough off in great masses, the size governed by the height of the bank and the tenacity of its composition.

Visible bars are not the only ones absorbed by the rapacious river. Floating over a surface level as a board, a ripple breaks under the bow of the boat and is rapidly followed by others of greater and greater height, and before the little craft can be fairly turned aside it is pitching and plunging over waves of sometimes dangerous dimensions. At other times the turmoil is heralded by a sudden boiling upheaval of the waters that almost irresistibly swings the boat aside, generally into the puzzling swirl of a like upheaval. Quicker even than in the first instance, the boat is tossing on a more dangerous sea, choppy in character and usually foam-crested. In both instances the river has attacked submerged bars, and in the former is cutting it away in long slices, and in the latter in great cubes. The ultimate destination of all this sand and silt and vegetable débris is the delta, lying idle under a tropic sun, awaiting a conqueror.

At Yuma we found Godfrey Sykes awaiting us; and E. H. Goldman, of the United States Biological Survey, also decided to join the expedition to make collections of small mammals, birds, and reptiles. A larger boat was needed, and the Sykes brothers built one with a carrying capacity of a ton. We left Yuma with the new boat and the small skiff loaded to their fullest extent.

At three points the river cuts directly into the Sonora mesa. At these points the absolutely dry sand and gravel rise forty feet above the water, and every gale aids the river in cutting away the bank. The result is three of the most graceful sweeping curves in all the river's winding course.

A light gale was blowing as we passed the upper mesa. Light as it was, it had started hundreds of streams of sand flowing from the top of the bank as freely as water. One of these streams was fully eighteen inches in diameter. As we ran rapidly past the lower end of the exposure a ton or more of sand fell from the top of the bank.

We made a short stop on one of these exposures, and again were confronted with evidence of the persistence of desert vegetation and the fertility that no one would expect to find on the vast expanse of sand.

The plain was liberally dotted with white lilies blooming luxuriantly. Yet more plenty was a diminutive plant quite like the moisture-loving forget-me-not, in

BOILING SPRING WHERE THE ALGERIAN ALGA WAS FOUND

full bloom. Shrubs were plentiful enough to appear to form quite close thickets in the near distance, but all strictly desert plants are of individual habit, and none are ever crowded. Collectively they are a multitude, and in variety and in beauty of form and blossom compare well with plants of more favored climes.

Four families of Cocopa Indians were found at Colonia Lerdo. They had laid out melon-patches along the river front, and each group of seedlings occupied the centre of a depression six feet in diameter and a foot deep, excavated to retain moisture.

We engaged Cocopa Mike, the head of the colony, to help us row the big boat against the current of the Hardy—or Hardy's Colorado, as it is generally known. A short run took us to this river's mouth, and three days later we reached a point where the main channel runs for several hundred yards along the base of a spur of the Cocopa Mountains. Here we camped for ten days.

Back of this spur lies an extensive gravel mesa, and we found the desert expanse gay with flowers. The tall, thorny, rugged ocotillo uplifted its gaudy crest of crimson flowers. At frequent intervals throughout the plain the yellow blossoms of a plant quite like the coreopsis nodded and bowed to every passing breeze. The lycium, or matrimony-bush, was ablaze with its brilliant red fruits, and the crested quail feasted upon them to repletion without being able to reduce the quantity appreciably. Farther northward, evening-primroses, some of most delicate pink, others a lemon yellow, bloomed abundantly; while on the stonier mounds and levels to the southward varieties of cacti displayed their beautiful blooms. The river banks were guarded by heavy thickets of mesquite and willow, affording shelter to innumerable birds.

Across the narrow river, as far as the eye could reach, stretched the flooded delta that some day will be brought under subjection and bent to the will of man. Climb

MUD-VOLCANOES STILL ACTIVELY AT WORK

high on the spur or mountain as one might, and the view of the flooded plain was merely extended. Laughingly we called our camps our happy homes, but this one was the brightest and most interesting of all.

Many living plants and a large variety of specimens of small mammals, reptiles, and birds were collected. Extensive observations were made, from which Mr. Godfrey Sykes is preparing a sketch map as a contribution to the geography of the country. The mysterious Cocopas, long so called because of their inaccessibility and the little there was known about them, had been fairly well conquered.

In the closing days of the expedition we followed the Hardy to its head at Volcano Lake, and spent a day in examining the many active mud-volcanoes, which cover an extent of some two square miles overlooking the lake. The land all about is strongly impregnated with salts and sulphur, but even here sesuvium sessile was abundant in places, and in a hot spring near the volcanoes was found an alga hitherto only reported from Algeria.

The expedition disbanded at Calexico, a town too young to yet be indicated on any map. It is located on New River, and the boundary-line between the United States and Baja California is all that separates it from its Mexican neighbor, Mexicala. It is an object-lesson in what a slight control of the abundant waters will accomplish in the delta of the Colorado. Only some three years old, it is the prosperous centre of an area devoted mainly to fruit and grain, and its people talk enthusiastically of four to six crops of some farm products in a single season.

Expert gardeners who desire to develop the finest of fruits and flowers seek the woodlands and swamps, and there laboriously gather leaf-mould, the wreckage of forest and stream. Carefully they combine this with sand, lest the plants become cloyed with the overrich food or sodden from improper drainage, and not a plant ever fails to repay them their intelligent care. And this is precisely the work that the Colorado is performing, and the product is stored in the great delta of the American Nile.

ARCADIAN BEE-RANCHING

THE month of May is the carnival of bee life in California, and at no other time of the year is the half work, half play of "bee-ranching" so wholly fascinating and delightful. After spring showers are over, a delicious warmth and fragrance steam up from the circling foot-hills, where every notch and byway is choked with flowering wildwood. The long blooming slopes stretch sunnily to fruitful valleys, and the whole riotous floral zone is voiced by honey-hunting bees. Their lilliputian cities are seen just without the open arms of cañons, the white hives arranged with the precision of dwellings along the streets. Sometimes these mimic thoroughfares are shaded by scattering oaks and sumac, or the green umbrellas of elderberry bushes, now fringed with freighted, creamy clusters. Where there are no indigenous trees it is not unusual for the thrifty apiarist to plant grape-vines and orchard rows between the hives, which serve the double purpose of shade and forage. A neighboring bee ranch is often four to five miles distant, and again this Palestine of the New World shows leagues on leagues of ideal pasturage, left solely to the harvesting of wild bees and various species of wasp and humming-bird, or to that interesting lover of sweets the Mexican honey-ant.

A typical Western apiary belongs to the foot-hill region of southern California. Here the atmosphere has that degree of heat and dryness essential to an abundant saccharine flow, and the high gravelly soil grows a luxuriance of nectar-bearing plants, the chief of which are the numerous varieties of sage. During the blossoming of these aromatic spikes the amount of honey stored by strong colonies is almost incredible. A summer's product will often average seventy-five to two hundred pounds a hive, and instances are not uncommon where a single Italian swarm has produced one thousand pounds of extracted honey in one year. This sage honey has rare virtues, and is said to be more delectable than the famed nectar of Hymettus or Chamouni, and whiter and finer flavored than the celebrated honeycombs of Atacama. To set one's teeth through an exquisitely frail comb brimming with the delicate nectar of the white sage—Audibertia—is a gustatory relish not to be otherwise equalled. More especially is this true if one has all the concomitants—a warm clean stone under a singing sycamore, mountain air spiced with countless odors, the monotone of bees at their voluptuous toil, a landscape billowing up to gigantic summits, and a stream hard by to keep the shout up in the heart.

To experience all this, and more, one need not go far from the partly cultivated district of Ventura. A few miles' drive mountainward from the nearest station, and the bee-man's province is entered upon. The country thereabout is sure to be stupendously wild and picturesque, a sublime uprising of massive heads above range upon range of tufted lower hills. A jagged gash through the granite precipices lets down a torrent of swirling, flashing foam. This furious stream appears bent upon carrying out the diabolical significance of its Indian name of Sespe (Devil). During the winter it is utterly impassable, but after the rains subside the horseman gathers up his feet and goads his mustang across, and the hardy occupant of cart or wagon risks the wetting of his load as the wheels wrench and jerk over the polished stones of its bed.

Where the great hushed peaks stand reverently apart at the sharp - toothed jaws of the gorge a strip of bench-land follows narrowly up the Sespe, its surface covered with an enchanting tangle of purple and lavender sage, yellow mustard blooms, the blue of larkspur and phacelia, mimuluses swinging their golden censers, and a bewildering galaxy of other flowers nodding upon their slender scapes. And how the bees revel, each eager worker greedily cramming with yellow meal the baskets strapped to his sturdy thighs, or gorging his pocket with the colorless nectar of chalice and tube! Many of their numbers dive recklessly into cavernous cups, and emerge therefrom with their natty spring jackets absurdly dusted with pollen. Nevertheless, they cease not to hum ecstatically, being assured of flour for the home kneading of their bread and ambrosia for its spreading.

A half-mile up the cañon the slope widens to make room for five hundred colonies of bees, set uniformly under the beautiful tents of orange and lemon trees, or between grape-vines garmenting their uncouth stumps with a profusion of gray-green leaves. The bee-master's welcome is full of cordial fellowship and hospitable service. Like every one long habituated to the care of bees, the culture of retrospect is in his speech, and there is naught fictitious in the courtesy of his manners. Though masked like a highwayman, and going serenely about the wholesale robbery of his little charges, you perceive in him no hint of cruelty. On the contrary, there is admirable thoughtfulness, and an accuracy of judgment as to their nature and requirements which is positively scientific. Indeed, between the almost infallible intuition of the master and the marvellous instinct of the bees, my interest is boundless.

"How do you prevent your new swarms from taking to the hills?" I asked, having read of the impossibility of domesticating bees.

"If you will put on this veil, I can readily show you how I manage it," he replied, his stalwart figure preceding me to the apiary.

Stopping in front of a hive where the swarm hung listlessly on the outside, my companion cautiously drew out from the black moving mass a small wire cage, and held it toward me. No fear but I should recognize imprisoned royalty behind those tiny bars! When once beheld, the queen-bee can never be mistaken for either of her plebeian subjects, the drone or the worker. Not only is she far more elegant in shape, but she has the distinctive habit of crossing the tips of her wings after the helpless manner of genteel femineity in disposing of their hands. Truth, however, compels me to state that in this instance the dainty sovereign lacked the repose under indignity which imagination is wont to relegate to royalty. Her fretful racing to and fro savored of the impetuosity of the *canaille*, and ill comported with the aristocratic taper of her sashed and jewelled body, and the silvered lace of her lady wings. Fortunately her subjects proved less hypercritical, for instantly upon discovering the whereabout of the cage, they heaped themselves upon it, their frenzied buzz and motion eloquently testifying the genuineness of their anxiety for the safety of their mother and queen.

"You see how it is done." And the bee - master carefully slipped the cage back into place. "I have only to secure the queen to control the swarm, and so manage to avoid no end of loss and bother. I know the age of all my queens, and have only to refer to the letter and number of a hive to learn if she is old enough to be superseded. Kill her? Yes, that's the only way; but she's so pretty I have to shut my eyes to do it."

While obliging me by a sight of royal cells, the stiletto of an exasperated worker pierced his hand.

"'Whom the gods wish to destroy, they first make mad,'" quoted my companion, gently brushing aside the perishing insect.

To give one's life in exchange for a moment's indulgence in bad temper seems hardly worth while, even from the stand-point of bee intelligence; but then, who knows but the little fellow felt a hero, nobly sacrificing himself in defence of the rights of property!

Out in the dazzling sun, for twenty or thirty feet up from the teeming hives, the air was thronged with bees on the wing, crossing and recrossing each other in an intricate maze of fine steely lines. There was summer music in their sustained murmur, and they carried about with them the delicious perfume of honey. The master looked on with eyes beaming behind the black folds of bobbinet.

"It's a good day for work. The thermometer is ninety-four in the shade, and there's lots of moisture still in the ground. By sundown that hive on the scales will show an increase of ten to twelve pounds."

Every twenty minutes a cart packed with two hundred pounds of snowy comb intact was wheeled into the honey-house, where the eight baskets of the extractor were turned by a water-motor, with a connecting pipe to the reservoir high up on the bench. The extracted honey is run into enormous iron tanks, the largest with a capacity of 8000 pounds. Afterwards it is drawn off into sixty-pound cans to be put on the market. In 1884, an exceptionally good year for bees, the honey export from California aggregated 9,000,000 pounds.

There is something amazing in such wholesale collecting of a product so choice, and we no longer question the possibilities of this industry in a land so palpably favored by that amiable Grecian goddess Melissa. In one place on the Sespe there is a mighty drawing together of the walls of the cañon, forming a narrow neck dividing the upper and lower defiles. Late in sunshiny afternoons there is seen here a remarkable exhibition of bees in these parts. They stream through the rocky cleft like smoke from a funnel, their "business hum" drowned in the rush of the stream.

A man should have a good deal of the hermit in him to get the best there is in Arca-

dian bee-ranching. He must think himself good company, and his bees better than neighbors, for the isolation of his territory precludes all social advantages. In the long festival of honey-gathering the apiarist is rarely met with in the settlements, for a true lover of bees accounts it a hardship to miss the swarming of a single one of his hives. If he has wife and children willing to share his exile, no man is more envied of the gods. The most careless eye mistakes not the seal of his divine prerogative. The primitive shanty standing on the outskirts of

AN APIARY IN SOUTHERN CALIFORNIA.

the apiary bourgeons with lean-to and porch, and takes on a respectable coat of whitewash. Fruit trees grow up like magic, roses and geraniums riot about the door, and you hear the homely clatter of barn-yard fowls. At this Sespe apiary the bee-master's wife is his most efficient co-worker—a fact the big lovable fellow admits with an honest glow:

"Why, in '86 there was no one on the ranch but her and me, and together we took out two thousand pounds of honey."

His four little daughters threaded their way through the colonies with the intrepidity of veteran bee-hands. The mother looked after their bobbing curls with the beautiful eyes of maternity.

"It *is* strange they don't get stung," she said, at our surprised comment. "But they soon learn to dodge the bees. Even baby has a trick of slipping to the other side of a tree if one is after her."

There is every advantage in establishing the right sort of understanding between one's self and bees. Being natural conservatives, they are intolerant of interference, and will brook no alteration in their plans. A swarm becomes accustomed to the presence of certain individuals, and one is tempted to think the subtle little critics are contemptuously aware of a "prentice hand," for a bungler working among them is sure to get more than his share of stings.

The next day after visiting the Sespe apiary my landlady in the modest country inn where I was stopping introduced to me a mild, stoop-shouldered man in worn coat and overalls.

"I was telling Mr. Martin you wanted to know all about California bees. He's the oldest bee-hunter in Ventura, and is going to Lake Glen this afternoon, and will be glad o' your company."

This was unexpected good fortune, and I thanked them both warmly. Mr. Martin took a chair, and carefully placing his hat on the floor beside him, pulled out a coarse cotton handkerchief and wiped his sunbrowned face and neck. His kind blue eyes had the manly straightforwardness of one not ashamed of his thoughts, and when he spoke it was directly to the purpose:

"You're more'n welcome to the ride, ma'am, though you won't see so many bees up to the Glen as on the Sespe ranch. But you'll find the place sightly; jes the kind women folks like—a lot o' posies an'

ferns, an' trees bigger'n the valley oaks, with a lake in the middle pretty enough to make po'try 'bout. The folks there is friends o' mine, an' would make you to home overnight, an' next mornin' you could ride horseback 'cross the mountains to 'Happy Camp.' That's Richardson's place. He keeps two three hunderd stands there, and the same 'mount on Las Posas. There ain't no better bee-pasture anywhere than you'll see in them Tapo an' Simi mountains. It's a reg'lar Canaan: not ezzactly 'flowin' with milk,' fur most the cows is beef critturs, but the 'brooks o' honey' is there all the same."

This scriptural quotation was made with a gravity so opposed to the humor of his interpolation that I checked my inclination to smile, while hastily packing into a basket-valise a few necessaries for the trip. When all was in readiness I was helped to a seat in the two-wheeled cart, the bee-hunter taking his place by my side, and zealously intent upon my comfort and entertainment. Our road led south down a poppy-hedged farm lane, terminating in the wide bed of the Rio de Santa Clara, a joyous stream ploughing its way seaward through dense thickets of *guate mote* and willow. We forded the crystal current, and tugged through levels of deep sand studded with rank patches of ill-smelling wild tobacco and swampy growths of "Indian arrow timber," its silver foliage in blithe contrast to the rusty green of *yerba santa*, already putting forth its heliotrope clusters. Bees find precious storage in the microscopic nectaries of this "blessed herb," and Spanish matrons enthusiastically extol the medicinal properties of the rough, bitter leaves.

For nearly a mile we forced a passage through the sultry vistas of river vegetation, hard pressed by a cloud of stinging gnats, and inhaling scant breaths for the pungent odors and dust. Meanwhile I listened to a graphic description of the tremendous floods that sweep down here when rains are incessant:

"Sometimes it's like the ocean, all roll an' tumble, an' no one can git 'cross. Then, you'd hardly b'lieve it, but late in the fall there's weeks you won't see a speck o' water till you git lower down the valley. I rec'lect once, nigh on to twenty years ago, when I wa'n't much used to Californy rivers, me'n sister Hettie started to go up to Lake Glen afoot.

EXTRACTING HONEY.

Hettie didn't weigh more'n a hunderd pounds, 'cause she was kind o' sickly, an' 'fore we come to the river I kep' sayin', 'Now it won't do for you to git yer feet wet, so I'm goin' to carry you 'cross.' But, like mos' women, she was spunky, an' said she'd wade, the same as me. Well, we kep' on arguin' an' arguin' while we tramped ahead, expectin' ever' minute to strike the river, an' I'm boun' if we wa'n't climbin' the op'site bank 'fore either of us guessed we'd crossed 'thout seein' a drop o' water."

As we emerged from the willows he touched the horse smartly with the whip to encourage him up the steep rise. The road now wound into the deeper privacy of the Tapo heights, the rounded foot-hills breaking abruptly into colossal peaks, padded far up their fronts with the pale verdure of scented mints. Along the bristling chaparral margining their base the bleached trunks of sycamores marked the course of unseen streams. My companion pointed with his whip to these venerable trees:

"Many's the tree or rock in these mountains whose holler is chuck full o' honey. It beats all how short a time it took fur bees to git so plentiful. Up to '53 there wa'n't one o' the little fellers this side o' the Rockies. I knew the man who fetched the first swarms 'cross the Isthmus. They was the German black bees, an' he sold his young swarms fur a hunderd dollars a stand, an' honey fur four dollars a pound. Now most the reg'lar bee-keepers have I-talian bees, fur they ain't so cross, but at first we all depended on catchin' wild swarms. It took me an' my pardner a long while to learn that night wa'n't the bes' time to cut a bee tree. Mebby they do sting less then, but there's a hunderd times more of 'em to git in their work, fur when the sun shines they's mostly off after honey. The grizzlies used to give us lots o' trouble, fur there's nothin' they like so well as honey. Once we cut down a sycamore over on the Simi that was so big we got right in the holler to chop it. After we'd chipped open the trunk we saw all o' three four hunderd pounds o' nice comb layin' up an' down inside. Well, if them pesky bees didn't lick us out, an' we had to go back to camp after thicker clothin'! We come back bright an' early next mornin', an' first thing we see was a big grizzly helpin' himself out o' our trough. We kep' fur 'nough away, so he didn't know we's 'bout, but we could see the bees make it warm fur him. While he'd scoop up the drippin' comb with his huge paw, they'd settle on his muzzle, an' he'd whine like a dog, but kep' right on eatin'. He'd stuff in a slab o' comb, an' then wipe off the bees with his sticky paw. It made me mad to see the old feller manglin' all that good honey we'd counted on fillin' our tubs with, but we hadn't the right sort o' tools to tackle him, an' knew better'n to try it."

Seeing my absorbed attention, he gave a preparatory cough, and continued:

"Another time we'd commenced takin' honey out a rock as big's a meetin'-house, when we noticed the horses gettin' scared an' pullin' at their halters. They was tied to a tree a rod or two away, but 'fore we got to 'em we made out to see through the dusk somethin's big as an ox circlin' jes outside the bushes. We wa'n't long concludin' it was a grizzly, by the way the snorts come rattlin' up through his lungs. I ain't 'shamed to say my hair riz up straight, an' Jack's would have too if he'd had any. We stood the crittur off by keepin' the fire goin', fur we didn't have but one ole musket between us, an' only one load fur that. Well, that bear hung roun' smelling the honey till plumb sunup, an' when we heard him goin' 'bout his business we got out o' there lively."

Here a frightened ejaculation from me caused a brief cessation of bee reminiscences; the cart appeared to be settling upon the back of the horse, and the animal coolly gathering his legs under him for a precipitous slide into a bottomless pit.

"Don't be oneasy, ma'am; it's ruther steep, but Nick's used to the road."

I braced my feet, and nervously clutched the seat with both hands. A moment of breathless suspense, and the cart struck bottom, only to be suddenly jerked backward in the first mad plunge up the bank, my glazed eyes fixed upon the taut bow made by Nick's spinal column, as the faithful beast fairly hooked his hoofs into the successive steps of the hill. Never had mountain pass more perilous ups and downs.

"How far is it to the Glen?" I asked, beginning to feel hysterical.

The clear eyes that met mine had a twinkle of merriment.

"Why, as to that, ma'am, folks don't agree. Comin' up, they're apt to think it's three four miles from the river; but goin' down, the same ones declare 'tain't half that fur. Now I say it's a long mile, comin' or goin'."

So pleased was he at my enjoyment of his little witticism that he took his own way to further keep up my spirits:

"I've seen worse roads than this in my time. I don't rec'lect any accident hap-'nin' here worth speakin' 'bout, leastways nothin' ser'ous. Once Mrs. Wiley was pitched off that p'int we're jes comin' to. She had the baby in her arms, but neither on 'em got more'n a scratchin'. As fur her husband, he says he don't mind tippin' over now 'n' then if he has Toby in the harness. That horse really knows more'n a preacher. Once he was driv'n' down this very place, when Toby shied at somethin', an' next thing Wiley knew he was hangin' head first down that bank, with both feet catched in one o' the wheels. He said he sung out 'Whoa!' when he was goin' over, an' Toby stopped short, an' never moved a muscle till he'd righted himself, which wa'n't no quick job, I reckon. So, you see, there ain't no cause fur worry, though I won't say," with a painful exactness as to truth, "that my Nick's altogether as 'liable as ole Toby."

Another stout pull up the crumbling rim of an abyss, and poor Nick, drenched and quivering, was allowed to rest in the shade of a chalky cliff. Behind us a regnant concourse of ranges lifted sunset crowns in the great azure bowl of the sky. A host of shadows crept into the ragged gaps of the hills, and the golden distances of the valley began to take on violet dyes. The heart of a mountain solitude is primordial in its solemn tranquillity and stillness. Only the sylvan plaintiveness of the moaning dove came up from the stirless woods, and the resonant tapping of the yellow-hammer.

A piping "Halloa!" broke the rapt exaltation of the moment. With a startled glance aloft I beheld two magnificent silhouettes of horses sharply outlined on the brow of the cliff, each bestrode by a diminutive pantaletted mite in peaked cap.

"Two brownies!" I cried, enthusiastically.

"Oh no, ma'am. Brown's ranch is ten miles t'other side. Them's Wiley's little shavers. They ride bareback all over the range, and ain't but four an' six year old. The house is jes behind the cliff."

There was nothing in this primitive wilderness to suggest human habitation except those baby equestrians gingerly picking their way up against the crimsoning heavens. Nevertheless, upon rounding the butte, we found ourselves almost within the enclosure of a corral, and close at hand a weather-worn dwelling, with low roof, embowered in jessamine and roses. Before us nestled a cuplike glen, all smoothed to velvety softness by slanting fields of grain. In its deepest dimplement an alpine lakelet flashed like a jewel among the oaks and sycamores standing statelily up from the reedy rim. The place had the unspeakable sequestration belonging to all remote heights, and was inconceivably wild and picturesque.

The inmates of the cottage turned out to be intelligent, refined people, possessed of a cordiality so inviting that it was with no sense of strangeness or restraint that I found myself domiciled with them for the night. In noting the comforts of this cheerful home I remembered that each article in it had been brought piece by piece up the formidable grade we had come. Formerly everything had been packed upon horses, but improvements in the road made it now possible to use a cart, or even a light wagon, for the larger commodities. A flourishing garden and orchard surrounded the house, with apple, peach, plum, nectarine, and apricot trees, and branching figs, whose gray trunks upheld spacious canopies of soft, flapping leaves.

The Lake Glen bees make the most of the orchard, especially in later months, when summer heats have subdued the passionate efflorescence of these sun-nurtured mountains, and they are confined to the darker nectar of hoarhound, buckwheat, golden-rod, and fall-growing species of mint. They are particularly fond of grapes, figs, and apricots, their greedy partiality for the last often resulting in

their death. Some fermented quality in this "golden apple" of Solomon's acts as an intoxicant, and the unwary triflers become hopelessly confused and fall by the way-side.

There is rarely a season so dry in this climate that bees cannot keep the hive going with an inferior quality of honey, but the indefatigable workers have frequently to travel a wearisome tour for the priceless modicum of sweet. At such times the little creatures are noticeably faded and irritable, and the tattered web of their fragile wings bears mournful evidence of superhuman exertion. Unless urged by famine, a bee does not go over two miles for forage, and the radius of this distance cannot well support more than two or three hundred colonies. When more than this number of swarms are crowded into this space, the amount of the honey product is apt to be sacrificed to the greater convenience of the bee-master.

The immediate range about Lake Glen gives pasture to a hundred head of horses and two hundred swarms of Italian bees. The apiary occupies a romantic dip at the head of the cañon, where the sycamores are of superb girth and height, and the cool sweet water of a gurgling stream sucks at the long grass and ferns on its banks. The nearest bee ranch, "Happy Camp," is four miles westward over the mountains, where a fairly good country road leads outward across the Las Posas Valley to Saticoy and Hueneme. An hour after a semi-tropic dawn, we gayly ascended a zigzag trail on our way to the "Camp," our sacks of luncheon dangling from the saddle-bows, with coils of twisted rawhide for the noonday tethering of our horses.

The glory of awakened day rested upon the peaks, the cañons sent up floods of bird melody, and brambly brake and bush were alive with chirrup and hum. Such a morn in the mountains is a transport to the soul, and every pulse throbbed to the ineffable harmonies of the hills. On the topmost eminence I drew up for a farewell look at the idyllic spot which had sheltered me for the night. The lake lay dark and unrippled in the hollow of the glade, not a glint of the bright spring sunshine filtering through the screen of the trees. I turned my gaze from its peaceful loveliness to the sublime freedom of the landscape beyond. Hun-

SMOKING DOWN THE BEES.

dreds of feet below stretched a magnificent sweep of the Santa Clara Valley, a thin mist lifting from its innumerable squares of farms, and revealing the blue, silent reaches of the river. Far across, fronting us in grim, awful majesty, the Sespe summits unflinchingly pierced the morning sky with their dominant, storm-battered domes. No eyes of mortal ever looked out upon a nobler or fairer picture.

A quarter of an hour's heedful treading of a downward gutter, a tingling scramble up a briery scarp, and our horses struck into an old wood road, curving under green arcades of branches. Thence on the cañon views were perfect. Through loops in the curtains of the leaves we had ravishing glimpses of gentle divisions in the hills, and slopes all asparkle with sungold and dew. A shallow stream braided sheeny rivulets through the clean sand of its bed, and walnut, laurel, and willow waved virgin wreaths of beautiful wild clematis. At times the rude prominence

of a rocky ledge crowded us into a shadowed pool, and again we advanced single file in the creek through a tunnel of interlaced boughs.

Long before noon, despite our loiterings in the lovely defile, but we sighted "Happy Camp," but not before we were almost in the midst of its little city of hives gleaming whitely through the oaks. The place had all the requisites for ideal bee-ranching — a high, warm altitude, perennial springs in the ravine, a lavish allurement of honey plants, and distance from the orchardist who has reason to complain that his sun-dried fruit finds its way to his neighbor's hives. A black-veiled figure moved among the colonies, busily engaged in the swarming of the bees. With a May sun deluging the cañon and a fleckless sky overhead, it was just the kind of day to cause a fever of ferment in overcrowded hives.

We held up our horses at a safe distance from the boiling stands, but were yet near enough to see a vortex of agitated bees rising in the air, thousands upon thousands of them, all flying in a circular net-work of lines, involving the queen as a nucleus. Not sure of their destination, but with never a break in their anarchic hum, they sway up and down, now gathering their ranks about an attractive bush, then as quickly disbanding, and again whirling and massing themselves in dizzy evolutions, until finally the dark moving cloud settles into obstinate compactness on the limb of a tree. Here they continue to hang motionless in an elongated pendulous cluster until captured for the hive.

Nothing in nature furnishes so felicitous an illustration of cheerful work as bees at this season. They appear to be conscious that only Omniscient Love could have created the necessity to labor. Every hive has its multitude of ardent workers, all busy in a zestful fashion inspiriting to witness. Ecstasy is the law of their being, and it bubbles outward in the sweetness of their humming and a tireless exuberance of energy. When not too heavily swathed in pollen, bees will travel with a speed exceeding that of the fleetest horse. The astute little chemists are invariably discriminating in their taste, often heedless alike of the showiest and most fragrant flowers, and settling with a passion of acquisitiveness on the hispid florescence of sordid weeds. Where a poisonous sweet is suspected, they will delay the capping of their cells until the dangerous essence has had time to evaporate.

From time immemorial the intelligence of the bee, *Apis mellifica*, has been the marvel of naturalists and a fascinating study to the apiarist. Its chastity likewise is well understood, there being only one departure from this rule, and that for the high motive of perpetuating the swarm. Unlike many worthy dames, the queen-bee is never known to take a second wedding journey, though the object of her fatal preference dies upon that fateful occasion, without even being aware that he has fathered her prospective ten thousand progeny. These charming insects seem not to be troubled by the grosser instincts of human animals, and it would be interesting to trace this fact to the exquisite refinement of their food. As a slight foundation to begin with, we find everywhere in ancient bee classics a widespread belief in the high degree of

spiritual and mental vigor following the persistent use of honey as a diet. Nor can we overlook the poetic, if apocryphal, evidence of the prophet Esdras, who lived upon flowers in the field of Ardath, and was not only wonderfully enlightened thereby, but also, according to his comfortable assurance, "was satisfied with the meat of the same"—results plausibly attributable to the globule of nectar secreted in the minute floral laboratories.

After a brief stay at "Happy Camp," we entered upon the great Simi Rancho, an extensive tract of agricultural and grazing lands, sparsely inhabited, and as yet gloriously given over to untrammelled nature. The original grant of this noble rancho is the only one in California that came direct from the crown of Spain. It once belonged to the famous De la Guerras, who lived for generations here in half-civilized luxury, supported by the princely revenue of their countless herds and flocks. The interests of the horticulturist have compelled the flocks far back into the territories, and limited the herds to a few thousand head, confined to breezy upland pastures in the mountains. A notable number of bee ranches have sprung up in the foot-hills here, and bear the musical Spanish names which yet cling to the localities: "Las Chupa-Rosas" (Humming-Birds' Nest), "Las Posas" (The Wells), "Mesa de Queso" (Table of Cheese), and "Cañada Verde" are all found in this paradise of the pastoral bee.

For a refreshing distance we kept to the bed of the stream, our horses straining at the bridles to sip of the babbling current or seize a mouthful of succulent herbage. A cooling ocean breeze stole up the dreaming aisle of the cañon, tumbling the blossoming tree-tops and setting afloat a myriad faint perfumes. There were nestling murmurs in the secret places of the branches, a restful hum of insects, the rich soprano of a white-barred mocking-bird, quail chattering sociably in the underbrush, and afar, on a pinnacled height, the raucous summons of a buzzard to a grewsome meal. One could hardly imagine these tranquil hills reechoing to less soothing sounds, yet we were destined to a startling interruption. Once out of the creek and galloping around a jutting flank of the ridge, a strange rumbling struck upon our ears. The mountains reverberated to some appalling and continuous shock, the ground trembled, and visions of earthquakes and cyclones darted through my brain.

" A *rodeo!* See! the cattle—the cattle!" shrieked my companions, laughing, shouting, and pointing in the wildest enthusiasm at some spectacle still hid from my view.

The next moment I was at their side, and beheld a whole mountain tumultuous with thundering herds racing and circling to the hoarse yells of swarthy vaqueros, each swinging the loose end of a lasso, and spurring his horse recklessly, now up, now down, to head off the maddened beasts. All the cattle in these thousand hills were being driven to a "round-up" on the Little Simi, where the annual separating and branding would take place on the following day.

It was a sight for a lifetime—that mottled phalanx of glancing horns and hoofs held in check and swept upward by the trained mustangs of the Spaniards. They made brave, barbarous music, those goaded hundreds, with harsh chords distinguishable to the deafened ear—the ponderous basso mutterings of the bulls, a universal maternal bellow filling in the middle register, the tremolo of calves hustled underfoot, steers sounding the trump of doom, horns clashing like cymbals, hoofs drumming, and shrill and defiant above all the clangor the fifelike notes of rawboned Mexican cattle. It was deeply exciting to man and beast, and when a couple of stray yearlings crashed through alders next our trail, my horse made a splendid dash after, under low-hanging boughs which liked to have forced me from the saddle. The sagacious animal was but following out his training on a stock ranch, and it was some minutes before he could be induced to let the frightened steers seek covert in a copse.

By this time the speeding herds on the crest of the hill looked a jumbled mass of hides and horns, disappearing with terrific rapidity over the other side. Almost immediately the last rumble died away, the landscape resumed its wonted aspect of unbroken solitude, and only the broad trampled swaths of wild-oats marked the devastating of that hurricane of hoofs.

It was not so easy to rehabilitate one's mood with serenity. The summer languor had slipped from us, and an exaggerated stimulus quickened every sense to some new surprise. This jubilance of spirits communicated itself to our horses, and they sharpened their pace through vast blooming gardens, where the fountains of plenty were unsealed to humming throngs of wild bees. Many of the flowers were rare even to the botanist, but the loveliest of all these mountain beauties were the *Romneya coulteri*, a royal bush-poppy rooted in the stony flange of an arroyo, and those pale Parsees of Southern heights the *Calochortus nuttalii*. Whole hill-sides were lighted by the tall gray shafts of sage; and here and there, a king among floral subjects, the yucca waved its imperial white plume.

Where we stood on the summit the wide uplying pastures of oat and foxtail grasses rippled in the wind like a great lake. A world of mountains surrounded us, and afar, in the dazzling mists of high noon, we made out the shadowy outlines of the Channel Islands. From this imposing outlook our eyes turned wonderingly down the dizzy declivity at our feet, where nestled the hermit home of a bee-rancher.

THE SPIRIT OF THE WEST

      . . . . now promises
Upon this land a thousand thousand
    blessings,
Which time shall bring to ripeness.

WHY do the mockers call it the
"Woolly West"? This is a
question that must go unan-
swered, for no answer is to be found
in any mind. A woolly man is not unknown in any of the haunts of men, and
some professors have met him in the
class-room.

"Explain the pessimism of Ecclesiastes," said the professor of a not far-
distant university.

"I do not understand the question,"
answered the football giant.

"What is the difficulty?"

"I don't know what the question
means."

"You know what Ecclesiastes means?"

"Oh yes," said the captain of elevens;
"it is a book in the Bible."

"Then it must be pessimism that
troubles you," suggested the amazed (he
was young) professor.

"That's it; that's it," bubbled the
catapult.

"Why, you must know that; you cannot be ignorant of that. You know the
words pessimism and optimism, do you
not? Pessimism and optimism, optimism
and pessimism; you certainly know what
they mean?"

"Oh yes," replied he of the well-
greaved shins; "I know what they mean,
but I can't tell them apart."

Now here was intellectual wool; but
you will not find its like in the far-
reaching West,—or if you do, its victim
will be on his way back East with pessi-
mistic views of the possibilities of the
new country. The prevailing element of
the intellectual atmosphere of the West
is ozone.

It is in this far region that we
find the adventurous colonists of the
country. Individual and social traits in
this land of at least outward equality are
atmospheric and geographical. They
may be realizations of our Western
visions, accentuations of proclivities not
wholly unfamiliar to us, but with us
they are not traits, as they are in the
West. Perhaps attention has been arrested
by an apparent misuse of the word Western, but it was deliberate, for we of the
Atlantic fringe especially are of the
Western habit of nearest Europe, while
they of the plains and mountains are, to
some extent, our Orientals. When we
go among them we visit our dreamers of
dreams, differing, from the nature of
their blood, from the star-gazers of the
real East because the best among them
dream things that they can do.

When we turn our backs upon the
"twin cities" or upon Duluth, we leave
the meeting of the sections. Emigration
within our boundaries, as they say in the
newer part of the country, has moved by
jumps. First went the New-Englander
and the western New-Yorker into that
Northwestern territory which is ours—
and this cannot be too frequently emphasized—by the gracious desire of Lord
Shelburne to do his best for reconcilia-
tion with the conquering colonies, and
against the strong opposition of Ver-
gennes. This is well to think of when we
are erecting statues to our allies in war:
but for our English friends in peace,
we would now be contemplating the possibility of the adoption of Chamber-
lain's hostile tariff policy by the people
dwelling on what would have been, if
France had prevailed, Canadian lands,
but which now constitute the States of
Ohio, Illinois, Indiana, Michigan, and
Wisconsin. These broad, rich States
were settled from the farthest East, and
are the better for it, as the East is better for the projection of its stock into the
middle of the land. When the time came,
the movement westward made a new leap,
and this time the children of the Middle

West took the step forward. It is interesting, however, that in the midway of our national life, when the seething of adventure was in the young blood of the East, the youth of New England and of its neighbors sailed round the Horn, or toiled in prairie-schooners over the mountains, to the gold-fields of the Pacific, so that these and their descendants coming inward toward the Rocky Mountains met on the slopes the sons of their New England kin settled on the plains and ranges which had been skipped by the eager hunters for the gold of California.

Nowhere better than in Duluth is illustrated this meeting of the sections. In one end of the town, which, years ago, began the race so joyously, fell heavily, gathered itself up and went forward so bravely and so successfully,—in one end of this young community are the houses and shops of the East, the temples to the so-called Anne, the shop-windows shining with the colonial mahogany of Grand Rapids, Michigan, or behind which are displayed the most recent additions to the joys and comforts of life; where also, as in the older parts of the country, you may find the most talked-about novel of the minute, "just in" or "just out." In the other end of the same town are the beginnings of settlements. The first part being grandiloquized as "residential," after the manner prevailing in Woolet and elsewhere, it may be appropriate to describe the second part as extemporential. Many of the houses in this part are home-made, constructed out of flotsam and jetsam, while the aspect of the spot as a whole is that of new countries generally, suggestive of such haste to get to work that there has been no time for building homes, the earnest "developers of the country" being content with shelters.

There are other indications of the mixing, for meeting thus always comes in the end to mixing; this, however, is the indication afforded by the look of the town. These two parts constitute its features. The dividing-line is very distinct, but the seed of culture is germinating in the shop-windows. Here we catch, among the people who are laying out the territory of the great Northwest, a glimpse of a social phenomenon that is sure to grow on us as we wander farther on toward Asia. The leaders and lieutenants of industry in the smaller towns have not only great conceptions of enterprise and Oriental dreams of future magnificence, but they are possessed of a larger metropolitan manner than one can find in like settlements—like in size—of the more thickly settled, the more finished parts of the country. Indeed, it is just because the smaller town in the East is rounded out and complete, as it were, and has got through with the disfiguring process of growth, that people there begin to fit their minds and habits to their simple environments. It is the impatient custom to call these people of the rural town of the elder land human vegetables, perhaps because it is pleasant to resort to them after a too rich dish of the red blood of the money-market or of the ranches. At any rate, throughout this Northwest country we find the city man in evidence, usually managing the bank, "making the advances," and, in a large, general way, keeping up the connection of farms and mines, of railroads and of "bunches" of cattle, with the investors of capital. Usually he is the kind of man whom we expect to see back in New York, and as a permanence, in the near future—the kind of man who will suddenly appear as the owner of a box at the Metropolitan Opera House, having plunged into the society which is stretching out its hands in welcome to all the millions that are willing to come its way.

It seems to be much easier to a man at, say, Butte to grab a "grip" and to board a train for Chicago or New York than would be even the contemplation of such a journey to a man at Keokuk, or at Dayton, or even at Elmira. If the Butte man wants a million dollars for an enterprise, he takes a train for the most likely lending centre. He carries his dreams with him as security; usually the dreams take, and often they materialize. Let it not be understood that dreams as security are always to be classified with the visions of Colonel Sellers. These dreams make our West our Orient, and investment in them has enormously increased the wealth of the whole country. Besides, there is calculation behind many of them, a considerable experience to add substance to them;

moreover, there are the character and credit which have been gained by the dreamers whose dreams have come true. If the man from Keokuk or Royalton wants to borrow $100,000, his desire alone is quite likely to give him pause, and he is noticed by his neighbors for many days at a time figuring on the backs of envelopes. Then he does a deal of letter-writing, some cautious telegraph-sending, breaking out at last with a telephone message. When he goes to the bank for the loan, he takes good, substantial securities with him, printed on bond-paper, and on his return he very likely tries to make on his borrowed capital one or two per cent. in excess of the rate which he must pay, while the Far - Western brother is hoping for something more than a paltry doubling of his borrowed capital.

The air is full of the stimulus and the mystery of chance. It cannot be escaped. One is not inclined to fly from it, because the prizes are too many and too rich. Along the side of the dusty road between St. Paul and Minneapolis is the wagon of the fortune-teller—the selfsame gypsy who used to add to the mystery of our childhood's Eastern woods, but now he is near cities; and in the railroad yard in Duluth we find the rich blue private car with its silvered letters announcing that it is the palmist's car, and that the palmist will tell his visitor where to strike for fortune, "between the hours of 10 A.M. and 3 P.M." Still, these plungers into the dark mysterious things, these snappers-up of every offered opportunity for wealth, are but the restless and often the unsuccessful. The dreams that go back East as security are not likely to be as unsubstantial as the fortune-teller's prediction. They are the visions of men who know what is—who have imaginations which not only tell them what they may expect, but they also convince the man back in the Atlantic seaport who wishes his idle dollars to be doing something.

There is nothing more interesting in the world of modern effort than the solid achievements of the men who are building up the West, and who are really making the empire west of the Mississippi. We have heard of the "pioneers who go out into the wilderness, and whose brawny arms have transformed dark forests into sunny and smiling farms." Poetry has been written about these pioneers, imaginative pictures have been painted of them, speeches have been made to them, and votes have been coaxed from them; but the pioneer of our time is not the pioneer of the seventeenth century who sought religious and civil liberty on the shores of Massachusetts Bay. There is a vast difference between a migration and a raid. There is a distinction, which is to be observed, between the man who moves with his family to a new home and the man who goes out alone in the excitement of a new discovery of gold or silver to get his share and to bring it back, or the man and the woman who go out with the hunters after gold to hunt them in turn for whatever gold they may find. The day of the "pioneer" has gone by in most of the Far-Western country, although some of his habits remain.

The men who do the American country good are the same kind in the Far West and in the Middle West. In the Middle West the pioneers were the seekers after new homes, but in the farther country most of the Americans who first travelled out were not of the settling or of the settled class. They who went to build homes stopped on the plains of Dakota, and many of them were foreigners. They who went to the mines carried in their company the attendant vices. They who went to herd cattle had the stir of adventure, often of thriftlessness, in their blood. The vices went with them also, for they fasten on the nomadic, and the vicious pitched their tents for faro and bad whiskey and other temptations where they might be within easy reach. As the railroads moved their tracks out, the dens faced the railroad track; and once, out of the car window, at a place which hoped to thrive in a sage-brush country, I saw, at the side of the train, on the board walk which ran between the station and the saloon, a faro-table which was presided over by a lady with golden curls, red cheeks, and a pink Mother Hubbard. These things have changed in older and better days, and though a red shade now and then flutters in the wind of the main street, the second lot of Americans have been received, and these are the real builders of the empire. These decent Americans do not care to dwell and to bring up their children in the midst of an immorality which is so prevailing as to make the social atmosphere of the community, and therefore the tough and his companions are moved off quickly by a vigilance committee, or else they slink back into slums, thereby increasing the slumminess. The process of human betterment has not been entirely completed. Time is required to bring about all that civilization demands, without counting the luxuries which it may bestow in return. Not long ago an indignant railroad president, moved to wrath by the obstreperous viciousness of a town that is a division headquarters, sent word to it that unless it mended its morals he would take his shops away from it—which in reality meant that he would move away most of the population.

It is impossible, apparently, that there shall be a frontier, or anything like it, without the youth who have wildness in the blood. It is the fashion to call the life of the ranches and of the mining towns free and unconventional. The idea that is hoped to be conveyed by this overtaxed word unconventionality is, as the mundane says, fetching, for it means relief from restraining artificialities; but experience teaches us that there is no decent community without its conventions, only these conventions differ in different places. There are, indeed, artificial restraints which are irksome, and apparently arbitrary and meaningless, but it is a great deal better, for the community and for the individual, that they be observed. Unrestrained freedom is bad all round, and socially bad, whether it is that of the beer-cellar in Bohemia or of a dance-hall in the Far West. The young man who seeks in the Northwest liberty from all the sedate checks of civilized public opinion, including those which deserve the disdain of the intellectual, has before him varied opportunities. How he is to come out is the problem of his own nature. He may become a cattle-thief or a steady "puncher"; he may take to liquor and gambling or he may become a "leading citizen"; he may become a politician or a maker of politicians; he may graduate as a typical cowboy nuisance, wear queer clothes, shoot off pistols and strange oaths to frighten tenderfeet, or he may become a real ranchman—a "builder-up of empire," to use one of our newest phrases, —with a strong hankering after churches, schools, broadcloth, and other conventions from which in his youth he fled. The tendency of good Americans and of good American communities is in this direction; it is toward respectability, which means the ability to inspire respect in others by respecting one's self. It is the Americans, the sons of Americans, who impress themselves upon the far-out lands, as the same people have put their stamp upon the institutions of the Middle West. The foreigners who come to anything in the one as in the other part of the country reach their climacteric of citizenship by becoming Americanized.

Politics is perhaps queer, to say the least, in the newer parts of the country; but while, by reason of the hammer of the reformers, who love their country with a much stronger and more unselfish passion than do the self-dubbed optimists, the public is making up its mind to improve politics, still we cannot say that political vagaries, in municipal affairs, for example, are peculiar to the Far West. We continue to possess our "halls" and our "organizations" in the fringe along the Atlantic, even if it is true that in some respects, where there has been exposure and where penalties have been suffered, politics is a less flagrant vice than it used to be. Perhaps it may be said that the East is gradually waking up to the fact that party politics may afford virtuous occupation and be beneficial to the state, while a perceptible part of the men of the Northwest, or the Far West, are still regarding government, with its resources and its powers, as a quarry—and this virtuously, it may be. A quarry it is in sooth, to all parts of the country. There are three ways of looking at politics in our dear victimized land. In the East the tendency of the class is to take an office for "the money in it," although there are some men, who have arrived or who have inherited, who like to do the work of real statesmanship, or of something nearly akin to it. There are also those most dangerous enemies of the public weal, mere opportunists. It is true that all, or nearly all, democratic progress is made through compromises, but there are compromises for the advancement of the good cause, and there are compromises looking toward securing a reelection at the cost of the good cause; the latter are made by the mere opportunists. In the Middle West, men who have made firm their place in the community and who want greater advancement in the esteem of their fellows, having played the game of business to a successful end, strive for the honors of public office, spurred by their lifelong desire to win. It is true that the spirit of winning is essentially an American spirit, and that its excesses blemish other activities than those of intercollegiate athletics; but in endeavoring to draw between the sections a distinction as to motives for the avocation of politics one cannot intend a sharp distinction, but can only hope to catch the prevailing instinct. In the Middle West there seems to be a trifle more of the personal element in the political rage; the man who is at its head is the party. In the East it is likely to be the man who is the most adroit captain of the machine who is at the head; in the Far West the leader is usually the man who can get the most out of the nation for the good of his neighbors, or of his own town, or of his State, or of his section. These, more or less, are sectional idiosyncrasies.

Out in the Far West men go into political life for the advantage of their own community. They live in that part of the country which, more than any other, is possessed of the colonial spirit; they are the children of the nation—and the favored children. When the adventurous, good and bad, had filled the land behind them with the glory of the great territory beyond the Mississippi, then the real builders went out, and with these came real exploitation and real business. For twenty years the great Northwest has been growing in such a way that its endeavors, covering this brief distance in the pathway of the nation, have added so many new States to the Union that in a few years more the dominant power in the Senate will be that of the States west of the centre of population. This is a prosaic fact, but full of significance to the States whose capital is seeking pecuniary progeny on these plains and under these mountains. The vision of these people is very far; their dreams have the right to soar higher than the dreams of other people; their own achievements, discoveries, "strikes," justify their belief that under the soil and in the soil is wealth the like of which no land has yet produced. They tell the nation that the welfare of the whole country depends upon their welfare, and that it is the duty of the nation to pour its money into railroads, into irrigation, into a thousand and one works which will aid their commerce. The commercial spirit is set on fire by the bigness of the plains and of their seeming opportunities. It appears to the makers of this empire as though it "would pay" the whole world to turn its saved-up millions into canals for the conveyance of fruitful streams from the mountains to the brown, waste places on which rain rarely falls. Trade and commerce and "output" become rhythmic, melodious, harmonious, sounding in great and inspiriting measures. Alfalfa's three annual crops grow to the sound of six-footed verses, and the stream from the irrigation ditch babbles a golden tune to the fruit-trees that stagger under their rich and luscious burdens, growing out of land which but for those nourishing streams would still be blown sand held together by the roots of sage-brush.

What could not the great government do if its people in the East would but tax themselves more heavily for this land of miracle and prodigy! The individual, however, has worked these wonders. The railroad that has justified its building with profits from the beginning of its existence is the railroad which has never received a dollar of given money or an acre of public land from the government. Other railroads have become income-breeders since they ceased to regard the beneficence of the great father at Washington as sufficient for their day and generation. "It is too big for private citizens and for private enterprise," is the cry of the thoughtless, and the consequent adoption of enterprise by the paternal government has invariably brought injury to the enterprise itself.

The politics of the Northwest is for the Northwest, because the people out there believe in their land, and the politicians are of the people as well as the servants of the people; but the Northwest itself is, as it stands—to use the vernacular — the work of the earnest, eager, sound reasoning, sane American citizen. To none other, not even to his government, is the glory due. He has made it, and the fact that the government anticipated him in the matter of fostering a railroad may be a pure accident. His life-giving enterprise found the capabilities of the land, and its development, its fruitage, is his and his alone. Its great railroads tell the tale as they run their courses. They leave the waters of the Mississippi and the lands whose crumbling iron ore helps to make us the richest country in the world. What wonder is it that the palmist in the blue and silver car reads the hands, and the gypsy tells fortunes midway between the twin cities, to the wondering and helpless multitude who dwell near the most magical of nature's storehouses, where the forest is cut into millions of dollars only to leave behind a far greater number of millions under the tangled roots of its stumps! Leaving this abode of wealth behind it, the road runs through the wheat-lands of the Red River, the cattle plains, the copper and silver, the varied agriculture west of the mountains, on to the great timber of Puget Sound. And in running thus through these varied gifts of nature, the railroads have nourished industry, have stimulated the arts of production, have taught the unready and have aided the ready, in obedience to the great and universal law that one who would serve profitably to himself must serve profitably to others.

In twenty years, since Mr. Villard's company of distinguished guests crossed the continent to see and participate in the completion of the first of the great northern roads, well-built towns have succeeded the wooden shelters of the first day, while the face of nature itself has been changed. The once brown plains, whose many unfenced acres were seized perhaps in obedience to the law of seeming necessity—for necessity is oftenest seeming,—but contrary to the law of legislatures, are greening under the influence of irrigation, and the husbandman once more, as in all times past, is moving on the herdsman and is driving the cattle into smaller and richer fields, to the betterment of all. All this that we see,

the growing splendor of the land, is the work of the individual man, either alone or in voluntary association with others. Together men have led the mountain streams to the arid sage-brush plains, and alone man has made green and fruitful squares from forbidding bits of territory. These green oases in the Great American Desert are the fine achievements of the Western men who are, let us remember, Eastern men and sons or grandsons of Eastern men, working with their own and with the capital of other Eastern men who have faith in them and in their land, —all these achievements are tributes to the individual and a great sustainer of the old-fashioned faith in individualism.

It ought not to be possible to look upon the wonderful gains of this wonderful region without the reflection that the individual has ventured millions and succeeded, where government has granted thousands and partly failed. This is not the place for the discussion of the fundamental difference between those who want the government to try to do more than they have done and those who think that the private citizen will continue to do better and more wisely than the political power can ever do, but there is room for such discussion, which, however, as in almost all human problems, will doubtless be settled in the end by hard experience; but this is now the truth, that, whatever may be done in the time to come, men unaided by government, or despite the efforts of government to aid, have created a rich empire out of lands once ridiculed as the " Banana Tract," and that men uncherished by the politicians who manage the government have built a pathway from the manufactories of the East, the corn and wheat prairies of the Middle West, the cotton-plantations of the South, across the plains to the Pacific coast, gold and timber bearing, and that, farther still, the pathway is going on across the Pacific, so that this marvellous Western empire of ours is looking onward with wise prescience into mysterious and still undeveloped Asia.

Can government, with its little war-fleets and its pampering laws, which, like all pampering, weakens character, expect to do as much for the welfare of the world of men as the men of the world have done for themselves and their fellows—the men whose fleets of peaceful commerce far outnumber destructive and protective squadrons; the men whose wealth is greater, whose intelligence is keener and is better instructed, and whose wisdom in these affairs is larger than the wisdom which government has manifested in the management of its own?

Very little of what the Far West has grown to be is due to Congress, or to Presidents, or to the various departments of government which are charged with the administration of public business peculiarly interesting to that big and reaching part of the land. The government has, indeed, accomplished something through its scientific men of the Geological Survey; it has, however, wasted its public lands, although some of them have gone cheaply to worthy citizens whose enterprise has stirred the pulses of life in seemingly dead lands, and who have thereby added to the country's wealth. The government has been preyed upon by the seekers of fortunes, and much of its land has been stolen. It has set a bad example to those pioneers who should be thrifty but who hope only to be lucky. It has not conducted its affairs in a businesslike manner, but has invited people to cozen it. Politics has been mixed up with the land business and with the cattle business. This, however, is to say as slightly as possible the word which must be said by one writing of the Far West. Bad men and women always go in the early trains to a new country; but when the country is worth while, the men of character and of achievement go after them and send the others to their holes. This is what is happening in the West. The good and conservative citizen who acts with wisdom as well as with energy is on the plains and in the mountains and forests. He has developed the riches of the empire and he has improved its character; but it should always be borne in mind that the empire looks watchfully to Washington as to its parent. The nation built these States, while in the East the States built the nation; therefore much of the paternalistic sentiment entertained by men who have nevertheless worked wonders without aid, and who will work all the greater wonders in the future

if they are left to their own wisdom and their own courage. Besides, paternal aid is invariably accompanied by paternal restraint.

This great West has its difficulties, as have other sections. Cities grow so rapidly that they are compelled, for their grown-up necessities, to run in debt so largely that their interest charges consume their income, and streets must go for more years than they ought unwatered and unpaved. Moreover, the good men are so busy attending to the great affairs which increase the wealth of the nation and of the community, as well as reward the adventurous with fortunes, that they have no time for public improvements or for local politics. Therefore we have the dusty streets and the rude sidewalks; therefore we have the distinguished and eccentric criminals. Still, these small evils adjust themselves in the end. The troubles are what one sees on the surface of life, but when one rubs the dust of the unpaved streets out of one's eyes, and looks about him at the dwellings in which men and women live, and when one enters there, the virtue and force of the individual's effort and of his character are evident once more, as they have been in the work which he has accomplished in the material world. Collectively, the people of Seattle, for example, may leave their streets unpaved and unwatered, but individually they build beautiful houses, fill them with domestic and social delights, force green lawns with abundant water, and plant along the borders of the street the planes, the elms, the maples, and the red-berried mountain-ash. These leaders of great hosts of activity in business, in industry, in mining, in transportation, in the thousand walks out-of-doors, may not yet have had time to study and to act upon municipal and police problems, but they have had time not only carefully and surely to work out the gigantic problems of their imaginations, but to make a within-doors most attractive and most stimulating. In time this American individual who has built the empire and has made himself a home will be comprehended in his just proportions.

There is no wool in the Western mind, and there is no decadence in the Western conscience.

NATHANIEL J. WYETH, AND THE STRUGGLE FOR OREGON

IN 1540 the eyes of civilized man first rested upon Oregon, when Cabrillo and Ferrer, sailing under the Spanish flag, coasted along until they reached as high as Cape Blanco, 43° north latitude, which Cape Blanco, in the year of our Lord 1892, is in Curry County, Oregon, and only a few miles north of the California line.

If Captains Cabrillo and Ferrer thrilled with enthusiasm in contemplating the possibilities of this portion of the rim of the North American continent, they successfully concealed it in their report to

* For many data in this article the author is indebted to the following sources : *History of the Expedition under the Command of Captains Lewis and Clarke;* Washington Irving's *Astoria;* the same author's *Bonneville; Oregon,* by William Barrows, in the "American Commonwealth Series"; *Oregon: a Short History of a Long Journey,* by John B. Wyeth; the Reports from the Census Bureau in Washington City.

that king of theirs, Charles V., under whose reign Cortez pillaged Mexico, Pizarro robbed Peru, and Almagro carried back to Spain all that was portable of Chili, for nearly two hundred years elapsed before another white man gazed upon it! Or perhaps Charles was too busy to settle Oregon then, since he had settlements of a bloody kind with Francis I. of France, with Germany, the Netherlands, Tunis, Algiers, and a single round with his Holiness, Pope Clement VII., spending more money in these European pastimes than his able lieutenants could steal from the murdered natives of the Western World.

Again a Spaniard, one Juan Perez, in 1774, sailed as high along the coast as the 54th degree of north latitude, discovered Nootka Sound, and theoretically planted the flag of Castile and Arragon over this

NATHANIEL J. WYETH.

quarter of the earth and sea, while his colleague, Bodega, a year later, took in the 58th degree of north latitude, together with the remaining earth and sea, including Mount St. Elias, which was in sight.

Up to this point everything was Spain's, but north of this a greedy Russian, who had long been engaged in building a town on the Gulf of Finland, had put in a prior claim, having hired a Dane, by name Vitus Behring, to go cruising along the northeast coast of Siberia. This Dane discovered a sea which was named for him, and which the United States bought, or was supposed to have bought, October 18, 1867. Anyhow, they do not allow any other nation to go fishing in it. Behring also found out that it was only a few miles across from Siberia to America, and on July 18, 1741, he " discovered " the coast of Alaska as far down as Mount St. Elias, and claimed everything for his master, Peter the Great, or rather for Elizabeth, the daughter, for Peter had been a saint since 1725. Honors were about even as between Spain and Russia, but in 1778, Captain James Cook, a famous English navigator, who was afterward fatally run through the middle with a javelin by a Sandwich-Islander, and then devoured in true cannibal style, came coasting along these shores, saw that the country was good, and evidently told it, for in 1785 a school of British trading vessels swarmed in these seas, and they have swarmed there ever since.

In 1790 the French navigators got up courage enough to get that far from home, and entered into competition for trade on the northwest coast. It was, however, not until 1800 that France put in her claim for Oregon, by virtue of her acquisition of the Spanish title to that vaguely bounded territory, "Louisiana."

In 1791 seven American vessels found their way to this quarter of the globe, and one of these on May 11, 1792 (George Washington had been three years President), commanded by a Massachusetts Yankee, Captain Gray, who distinguished himself by discovering and sailing into a broad and swift stream, "the waters of which were so perfectly fresh that the casks of the ship were filled within ten miles of the Pacific." He named it Columbia River, after his vessel of that name. Of course he landed and claimed the country all around, including the rivers and a fair share of the Pacific Ocean.

Meanwhile the Anglo-Saxons of the British Isles and from the United States were pushing into the Western wilderness from the rapidly filling Eastern country. As far back as 1778 one Frobisher, an agent of the Hudson Bay Company, had established a trading-station on Athabasca Lake, 59° north latitude, which in 1778 was transferred to the extreme western end of this lake and named Fort Chippewayan. About this time there came hither Sir Alexander Mackenzie, who, in 1789, footed it to Great Slave Lake, built some canoes, and finding a good-sized stream flowing out of this lake, floated down and on until he found himself on the shores of the Arctic Ocean, near the northwest corner of the American continent. Not wishing to be caught there in winter, he hurried back as he came, and reached Chippewayan on the one hundred and second day after leaving it. Like Keats, he "wrote his name in water," and as long as water runs down Mackenzie River, both will be remembered of men. Three years thereafter this danger-loving Scot left this same fort, canoed it up Peace River, got "snowed in" in the Rocky Mountains, camped there all winter; in May of the next year crossed the "Great Divide," and reached the Pacific Ocean, 52° north latitude, July, 1793, *the first white man to cross the North American continent.* On a rocky eminence he engraved : "Alexander Mackenzie, from Canada by land, the twenty-second of July, Seventeen hundred and ninety-three."

In 1804 Lewis and Clarke started on their famous expedition, reaching the Columbia River November, 1805, and returning to St. Louis September, 1806.

In 1806 Simon Frazer, a Canadian, settled on Frazer River, and is claimed to have been the first white settler west of the Rocky Mountains. In 1808 Mr. Henry, of the American Fur Company, established Post Henry on Lewis River. Two years later Mr. Wilson Price Hunt, with about sixty persons, left St. Louis, and travelling overland, fifteen months later reached the mouth of the Columbia, and built Astoria. He was driven out by the British in 1813, and Astoria was rechristened Fort George. In 1818 it again fell into the hands of the United States, and the name of Astoria was restored. In 1820 a resolution was introduced in Congress to establish a chain of trading-posts on the Missouri and Columbia, and to secure immigration to Oregon from the United States and China. In 1824 President Monroe advised the military occupation of this territory, and President Adams, a year later, repeated this advice in his message. The gallant pioneer and trader Ashley had, however, paved the way for military occupation, for in 1823 he reached the head-waters of the Platte; in 1824 established a fort near Salt Lake, to which, for purposes of defence, in 1826, he conveyed a 6-pounder cannon. In 1827 Pilcher, bent on a trading expedition, left Council Bluffs with 45 men and 100 horses, struck the upper waters of the Columbia at Fort Colville (now in Washington), went northeast by the Columbia, recrossed the Rocky Mountains, and in 1829 descended the Missouri.

At this date, 1827, there was not in the possession of an American citizen a single settlement or trading-post in all this vast region. The ownership of the country was in warm dispute. It had been claimed in turn by Spain, Russia, Great Britain, France, and the United States. In the struggle for possession prior to 1827 Spain had sold out to France; the latter, for a consideration paid Napoleon Bonaparte, had disposed of her interests to the United States, while Russia had retired within the icy circle of Alaska. The battle was now between the British Empire and the United States. The Anglo-Saxons were holding on. Time and time again it seemed that war could not be averted. That blood was not shed was probably due to the statesmanship of Webster, and that eloquent champion of peace, Rufus Choate. Although the Columbia River was discovered by Captain Gray in 1792, the treaty which settled upon the 49th parallel as the boundary line between British Columbia and the United States was not signed until July 17, 1846, nor were all the details closed until left to the arbitration of Emperor William of Germany, who gave the final decision October 21, 1871.

In 1830 the excitement over the occupation of Oregon was running high. Newspapers were teeming with articles descriptive of its vast resources, and the inducements it offered for settlement. Congress had been asked for the authority to establish there a territorial government, or an independent State governed by Americans. Others decried the effort to try to colonize and hold this remote region, and the question was asked, "Was Oregon worth winning?" Oregon, with its 251,000 square miles of territory, its hundreds of miles of sea-coast, its fertile valleys, wide ranges of pasture-lands, rich deposits of minerals, its magnificent rivers sweeping from mountains of perpetual snow with impetuous haste to pay their tribute to the great Pacific! The verdict of three-quarters of a million inhabitants to-day is that it was worth the struggle.

I have before me the private correspondence and diary of a man who in 1831 was far-sighted enough to see the value of acquiring a territory so vast and important, and that to acquire it, it was necessary to colonize it with Americans.

Though but twenty-nine years of age, with a courage, skill, and energy which challenge admiration and deserved success, he organized a movement for the colonization of Oregon, and between 1831 and 1836 led two expeditions across the American continent in the effort to found a State in the great Northwest.

With what enthusiasm he was filled to give up a prosperous business, a happy home commanding the comforts of life in the centre of American civilization, to part from a loving wife, family, and friends, and tempt fate in a perilous journey of thousands of miles through trackless forests, across seemingly boundless prairies, over rugged and unknown mountains, at every turn exposed to dangers from hostile savages as brave as they were cunning and merciless! No one can read this old and musty diary, stained with frequent wettings from overturned bull-boats or drenching rains, in many places illegible by actual wearing out of the leaves by friction upon each other, without paying the tribute of profound respect and admiration for the man.

Of him Washington Irving wrote:* "His enterprise was prosecuted with a spirit, intelligence, and perseverance that merited success. All the details that we have met with prove him to be no ordinary man. He appears to have the mind to conceive and the energy to execute extensive and striking plans. He had once more reared the American flag in the lost domains of Astoria; and had he been enabled to maintain the footing he had so gallantly effected, he might have regained for his country the opulent trade of the Columbia, of which our statesmen have negligently suffered us to be dispossessed."

This extract from his diary, written January 11, 1835, when "snowed in" in the mountains, at last convinced that after all he had done or could do Oregon must be given up, speaks with a pathos deeper than I can command:

"The crackling of the falling trees and the howling of the blast are more grand than comfortable. It makes two individuals feel their insignificance in the creation to be seated under a blanket with three and one-half feet of snow about them and more coming, and no telling when it will stop. The thoughts that have run through my brain while I have been here in the snow would fill a volume; my infancy, my youth, my manhood's troubled stream, its vagaries, its plans, mixed with the gall of bitterness, and its results, viz.: under a blanket, hundreds, perhaps thousands, of miles from a friend, the blast howling about, smothered in snow, poor, in debt, nearly naked, and considered a visionary."

Nathaniel Wyeth lived to see Oregon a Territory of the United States, and although he died before it was admitted as a State in 1859, his last years must have been happier in the knowledge that he had done much to make the occupation of this territory possible to his fellow-countrymen.

Barrows, in his *Oregon*, pays a tribute to his genius and skill in the selection

* *Bonneville.*

of a site for Fort Hall (Idaho), which he built in 1834.

In a letter he says: "I have built a fort on Lewis or Snake River, in latitude 43° 14' N. and longitude 113° 30', which I named Fort Hall. We manufactured a magnificent flag from some unbleached sheeting, a little red flannel, and a few blue patches, saluted it with damaged powder, and wet it in villanous alcohol, and after all it makes a very respectable appearance."

Nine years later, in 1843, when, in the race for the occupation of Oregon, Dr. Marcus Whitman led his great caravan of about two hundred wagons and eight hundred souls, he selected the route by Fort Hall, which even at that date was in the hands of the Hudson Bay Company. Barrows writes: "As this expedition turned the balance for Oregon, so Fort Hall was the pivotal point. This Fort Hall, on Lewis or Snake River, about one hundred miles north of Salt Lake City, was originally an American trading-post, built by N. J. Wyeth, but the Hudson Bay Company crowded him out by the many monopolizing and outraging means which a wilderness life made possible. Many of his traders and trappers were scattered wide; some of them were killed, and his business generally was ruined. At this point many immigrant companies had been intimidated and broken up, and so Fort Hall served as a cover for Oregon, just as a battery at the mouth of a river protects the inland city on its banks.

In later days, when the spirit was aroused for "the whole of Oregon or war," the question was raised whether it was to be taken under the walls of Quebec or on the Columbia. Neither was the place. Oregon was taken at Fort Hall.

The first indication of the proposed expedition I find is in a letter dated Cambridge, Massachusetts, October 5, 1831, written to his brother, Mr. Charles Wyeth, of Baltimore: "My plan is to go out there and carry with me what property I can spare after leaving a support for my wife," etc. On November 11th he wrote to a brother in the South for explicit instructions in regard to the cultivation of tobacco, which he hoped might be introduced and cultivated successfully in the new colony.

On December 19, 1831, he wrote from Cambridge to the Secretary of State: "Hon. Edward S. Everett: Sir,—Enclosed you have a letter from Mr. Nuttall, containing in part my views in regard to this application to the Executive. I have to repeat that no view of emolument induces it, but only a desire to serve the views of the government in regard to that country. It occurred to me that the government might avail itself of my services to obtain information concerning that country, which in time would be useful. I would willingly devote a portion of my time to their service without other compensation than the respectability allotted to all those who serve their country."

To the same gentleman, on January 6, 1832: "I believe it is not lawful for armed bodies of men to pass through the country. I would beg leave to inquire of you whether any permission is required, and to obtain the same, and also permission for trading with the Indians beyond the Rocky Mountains." He also in this letter expresses the hope that the attention of Congress may be called to the subject in such manner as to induce them to act in "aiding good men to *form a settlement in that region, and assume the government of the colony.*"

On March 11, 1832, with a company of twenty-one men, fully armed and equipped, Mr. Wyeth sailed out of Boston Harbor, and landed fifteen days later in Baltimore. From Baltimore they journeyed by rail for sixty miles to the terminus of the Baltimore and Ohio Railroad at the foot of the Alleghanies, and thence on foot to the nearest point on the Monongahela River, where they took a steamboat for Pittsburg. At a tavern on the mountains the proprietor refused to entertain the members of the expedition because they were *Yankees.* "The disagreement ran so high that the tavern-keeper and the Yankee captain each seized his rifle. The latter demanded lodging and refreshment, and the dispute ended in our captain sleeping in the house with three of his party, well armed, determined to defend their persons, and to insist on their rights as peaceable and inoffending travellers."* From Pittsburg the voyage was continued to St. Louis by steamboat, reaching this latter city April 18, 1832; thence by steamer to Independence, the last white settlement on the Missouri River, near the present Kansas City. Here two of the company deserted and returned to the States. From Independence, in the latter part of May, the expe-

* J. B. Wyeth, *Short Account of a Long Journey.*

dition started out across the plains, struck the Platte River (near Grand Island, Kearney County, Nebraska), followed along its bank, crossed the South Fork (Lincoln County), marched along the south bank of the North Fork of the Platte; on June 9, 1832, passed "the Chimneys" (Chimney Rock, Banner County, Nebraska); reached the Black Hills (present State of Wyoming) June 15th, and Rock Independence, on Sweetwater River (Wyoming), on the 21st. "From this time to July 2, frost each night, and snow." July 2d: "This night, at about twelve o'clock, we were attacked by Indians, probably the Blackfeet. They fired about forty shots and some arrows into the camp."

On July 8, 1832, the expedition arrived at Pierre's Hole, and remained there to July 17th, "during which time all my men but eleven left me." July 18th, "when near starting we observed two parties of Blackfeet Indians coming, about two hundred in number. A skirmish ensued, and one of the Blackfeet was killed, and his blanket and robe brought into camp. The women and children were seen flying into the mountains. The Indians made for the timber, and fortified themselves in a masterly manner. We attacked them, and continued the attack all day. There were about twenty of them killed, and thirty-two horses were found dead. They decamped during the night, leaving their lodges and many of their dead. We lost three whites killed; eight badly wounded. Ten of the Nez Percés and Flatheads (fighting on the side of the whites) were killed or mortally wounded. One of our men who was killed inside of their fort was mutilated in a shocking manner. This affair will detain us some days."*

On July 25th the remnant of the expedition, eleven in number, with a small party of Nez Percé Indians, continued their march for the valley of the Columbia.

On the 21st of August they encountered a village of Snake Indians who were friendly. Ten days later, following the bed of a creek, "the rocks on each side closed over the top and formed a natural bridge, elevated about fifty feet."

From Pierre's Hole the route of the

expedition was west and a little north until the Snake or Lewis River was reached, then along this stream, arriving at Fort Walla Walla, a trading station of the Hudson Bay Company, October 13, 1832, having on the way been forced to kill their horses for food. On the 19th they left Walla Walla, and travelled down the Columbia in canoes to Fort Vancouver, another station of the Hudson Bay Company, arriving there October 29, 1832. "Here I was received with the utmost kindness and hospitality by the acting Governor of the place. Our people were supplied with food and shelter from the rain, which is constant."

Scarcely without exception throughout the entire experience of Mr. Wyeth within the area controlled by the Hudson Bay Company, its officers were personally kind and courteous. It was in matters of business they were harsh, exacting, and ultimately ruinous to competition.

Later in a report to Congress he wrote, "Experience has satisfied me the entire might of this Company will be made to bear on any trader who shall attempt to prosecute his business within its reach."*

He was impressed with the productiveness of the country around Fort Vancouver on the Columbia: "They raise 4000 bushels of wheat; barley, 3000; Indian corn, 3000; potatoes, 1500; pease, 3000; and a large quantity of pumpkins. There are about eight settlers on the Multonomah (Williamette), old 'engagés' of the Company. The soil is good, timber is heavy and thick, and almost impenetrable from underbrush and fallen trees."

November 4th, one of the remaining seven men of the twenty-one which left Boston eight months before died, and the others, becoming discouraged, asked to be released from their contract, which was to remain for five years in the attempt to settle Oregon. November 15, 1832, "I have now no men, and am afloat without stay or support, but in good hands, i.e., myself and Providence."

With the loss of his entire force Mr. Wyeth immediately set about to acquaint himself with the topography and resources of the country, determined to return to the States and enlist a larger and better-equipped expedition, and again seek a home and fortune in the valley of the Columbia. His will was indomitable, he

---

* In Irving's *Bonneville* there is a thrilling description of this bloody encounter with the Blackfeet, in which Nathaniel Wyeth is spoken of in the highest terms of praise for the active part he took in the fight.

* House of Representatives, No. 101, February 16, 1839. Barrows's *Oregon*.

believed in himself, and if success was possible he would achieve it.

By November 30th, with two men and a canoe, "I started up the Wallamet or Multonomah River" on a voyage of discovery. The diary is rich in notes concerning the topography of this region, the forests of heavy pines; "on the bottoms there is considerable oak of a kind not found in the States, of excellent quality for ship-building." "I have never seen a country of equal beauty except the Kansas country, and I doubt not it will one day sustain a large population. If this country is ever colonized, this is the point to commence." This prophecy is fulfilled, for Portland, Oregon, is built on this location. In January, 1833, having finished his expedition in the Willamette country, he volunteered to accompany a party starting to the Northeast, but the Governor would not consent, "which I interpreted into a jealousy of my motives."

Under date of January 16, 1833, from Fort Vancouver, is a letter to his parents: "After much delay and some difficulties in the shape of long marches on foot, I am at last here. You can have but little idea how much men improve in some points of character in situations like these, and if polite carriage and shrewd intellect are best acquired in the more populous parts of the earth, generous feelings are fostered in the wilds, and among savages the civilized man seems to uphold his character better than among his fellows."

To Messrs. Tucker and Williams on same date: "My men have all left me, and I am about returning across the mountains with two men that I have hired for this purpose." He left for Walla Walla February 3, 1833, arrived there on the 13th, and by April 23d was "fairly in the dangerous country. Near here two hundred Flatheads, Couterays, Ponderays, and others were killed by the Blackfeet Indians."

On the 29th he encountered a village of friendly Indians of "one hundred and sixteen lodges, containing upwards of one thousand souls." Here he remained for some days, studying the customs and character of these Indians.

April 30, 1833: "Every morning some important Indian addresses either heaven or his countrymen, exhorting them to good conduct to each other and to the strangers among them. On Sunday there is more prayer, and nothing is done in the way of trade or games, and they seldom fish, kill game, or raise camp. Theft is a thing almost unknown among them, and is punished by flogging. The least thing, even to a bead or pin, is brought you if found, and even things we throw away are brought again to us. I think you would find among twenty whites as many scoundrels as among one thousand of these Indians. They have a mild, playful, laughing disposition, and their qualities are strongly portrayed in their countenances; they are polite and unobtrusive, and, however poor, do not beg except as pay for services. They are very brave, and fight the Blackfeet, who continually steal their horses. They wear as little clothing as the weather will permit. The women are closely covered and chaste, and the young women are good-looking."

These friendly tribes were chiefly Nez Percés and Flatheads, and evidently they had been influenced by association with missionaries, and chiefly those of the Catholic Church.

On May 5th there was some excitement among the Indians. "There is a new 'great man' here getting up in the camp, and like the rest of the world he covers his designs under the great cloak of religion. His followers are now dancing to their own vocal music, and perhaps one-fifth of the camp follow him. He is getting up some new form of religion among the Indians more simple than himself. Like others of his class, he works with the fools, women, and children first. While he is doing this the men of sense stand by and laugh; but they will soon find out that fools, women, and children form so large a majority that with a bad grace they will have to yield. These things make me think of the new lights and revivals in New England."

The Messiah craze and the ghost dances of 1890 created a little more disturbance than in 1833!

May 21st: "Snow as usual." 24th: "Rain, hail, snow, and thunder;" and then follows the only effort at being jocular in the diary. "We are so near where they make weather that they send it to us as if it cost nothing!" This jocularity is, however, short-lived, for the next entry is: "Twenty lodges of Blackfeet are now camped at our last camp;

moved seven miles." June 5th: "The 'Three Buttes' came in sight one by one, and then the *Trois Tetons*." On the 7th, "moved fifteen miles, without water the whole route; enough dust to suffocate one." 10th: An Indian was mortally gored by a buffalo; "he very composedly made his will by word of mouth, the Indians responding in concord at the end of each sentence; he appeared not in the least intimidated at the approach of death. I think the Indians die better than the whites. Perhaps they have less superstition in regard to the future, and argue that as the Deity makes them happy here, he will also hereafter, if there is existence for them."

June 15th: "Last night some Blackfeet fired into our camp." For one of the crippled Indians a novel stretcher or litter was made. "He has a good bed made on poles, the points of which, like shafts, were carried by a horse led by his wife; the hinder part, by six men and women, on their shoulders."

On July 9th he was again at Pierre's Hole, where the big battle was fought a year previous. Six days later there were new alarms that the terrible Blackfeet were upon them, but still no enemy in sight. "On this day killed thirty buffalo."

On July 18, 1833, Mr. Wyeth wrote Mr. Ermatinger: "I arrived here nine days ago, saw no Indians, but saw the bones of Mr. Moore, killed by the Blackfeet last year, and buried them. He was one of my men who left me in Pierre's Hole. A Mr. Nudd was also killed. I have letters from the States .... Cholera has killed five thousand people in New York.... General Jackson, President.... Insurrection in Southern States on account of the tariff."

July 26th: "Country covered with buffalo. Shot a cow with a very young calf, which followed our mule for a long way before it discovered its mistake." 28th: "I found a grizzly in a thicket, and after firing pistol and throwing stones, he came out as though he meant fight. I gave him the shot of my rifle through the body. He then rushed on us, and I ran as fast as I could. Mr. Sublette also ran."

August 1, 1833: "Mr. Bredger sent four men to look for us, Smith, Thompson, Evans, and a half-breed. Fifteen Snake Indians came up to them, and after smoking departed. After they had gone, Thompson, having been out hunting and fatigued from loss of sleep, was dozing. He was awakened by a noise among the horses, and, opening his eyes, the first thing that presented itself to his sight was the muzzle of a gun in the hands of an Indian. It was immediately discharged, and so near his head that the front piece of his cap alone saved his eyes from being put out by the powder. The ball entered the head outside of the eye, and breaking through the cheek-bone, lodged in the neck. While insensible an arrow was shot into him from the top of the shoulder downwards."

August 7th: "Camped on Gray Ball River. Here I found a piece of about five pounds of bituminous coal, which burned freely. Its fracture was too perfect to have come far." August 11th: "Saw four grizzlies. 12th: Arrived at Big Horn River, and went out to get bull hides to make boat."

This boat was eighteen feet long, and was made in this way: Slender willow poles or branches were cut and the butts forced a short distance into the ground in an elliptical shape, corresponding to the rim of the boat. These were about one foot apart. The ends of opposite poles were now bent towards each other until the proper curve for the bottom of the boat was secured, and then tied together with leather thongs. Other poles and branches were interwoven in an antero-posterior direction until a strong wicker frame was completed. The skins of three buffaloes were sewed together with thongs, and these were laid raw side out upon the frame, to which they were securely stitched. A slow (not blazing) fire was then started underneath the shell, and in this way the skins were dried and made to contract tight upon the frame.

In this boat, on August 15, 1833, accompanied by Mr. Milton Sublette, two Indian lads and two half-breeds, Mr. Wyeth undertook one of those perilous voyages occasionally recorded in the annals of frontier life. The starting-point was near the fatal ground where, in 1876, the gallant Custer and his entire command perished at the hands of Sitting Bull and his merciless braves, and not very remote from the place where this unprincipled savage met a bloody end, December, 1890. A thrilling description of this voyage is given by Mr. Irving in *Bonneville*. Down the Big Horn they floated into the

Yellowstone, and thence into the Missouri, and on to St. Louis, traversing Wyoming, Montana, Dakota, Iowa, Nebraska, Kansas, and Missouri, thousands of miles of perilous windings, over rapids, bars, drift-wood, snags, and rocks, requiring as much vigilance to keep their frail bark from being sunk as to keep out of rifle or arrow shot of the cunning savages who prowled along the banks. With all their precautions of crawling into the willows and dragging their boat after them at break of day, and travelling only at night to prevent their being seen by the Indians, they were taken in by a large band of Crows. Fortunately they met with this mishap so near to Fort Cass, a trading-post at the junction of the Big Horn and Yellowstone, that the Indians, fearing to kill, only robbed them, and allowed them to depart.

On August 21st: "Passed the mouth of Powder River, and on the 24th struck the Missouri. Here the bull-boat was abandoned for a canoe, or a 'pirogue.'"

September 3d, they came in sight of twenty-one lodges of Indians. "I immediately had the boat put into a thicket and fortified as well as I could. As soon as it was dark we proceeded forward with a high wind and cloudy sky. All went well until we were just opposite the village, when we unluckily went aground on a sand bar. Here we worked hard for some time to get off, and had the Indians seen or heard us we could have made little resistance; but they did not, and after some time we got off. These were the Aricaros, and would have scalped us."

With all these dangers the trip was not without its fascinations. On September 4th, after tipping the boat, getting wet, and then going ashore to dry, they "floated through the night eleven hours, a beautiful still night, the stillness interrupted only by the neighing of the elk, the low of the buffalo, the hooting of the large owl and the screeching of the small ones, and occasionally the splashing of a beaver in the water,"—a picture of wildness and solitude now only possible in retrospection.

September 6, 1833: "Seeing an elk on the sand, killed him. Very acceptable, as we had had nothing to eat since yesterday noon; saved his horns for my best friend, Mr. F. Tudor, of Boston. 16th: "Run on a sand bar and was unable to extricate the boat in the dark; the mosquitoes almost murdered us!" September 21st: "Passed Council Bluffs;" and on September 27th the voyagers reached Fort Leavenworth (Kansas). On the 28th this long and exciting boat voyage ended at Liberty, Missouri, where Mr. Wyeth took a steamboat for St. Louis and the East.

The indomitable energy and undaunted pluck of this man is evinced in the immediate execution of his purpose to again go over this terrible journey to the Oregon country. He would not give up his dream of civilizing this valuable territory. His clear mind saw in the near future a vast commonwealth, dotted with farms, villages, and cities, on the Pacific slope of the Rocky Mountains, and this a part of the Union! Scarcely half a century has elapsed, and lo! in this wilderness, out of which he was forced to go, dwell to-day nearly three-fourths of a million citizens of the United States.* He was a visionary then; a prophet now!

I have a proposition written to Mr. E. M. Samuel, dated Liberty, Missouri, September 29, 1833, asking for an estimate for an equipment of a second expedition, as "it is my intention to return across the mountains to the Columbia next spring."

October 17th, Mr. Wyeth arrived at Cincinnati, and I find a note to General Harrison ("Tippecanoe"): "Sir,—The enclosed I received from your son on the Big Horn. I met him on Green River, or the Colorado of the West; was with him some twenty days. He was in good health, and told me he should remain in the Indian country through the winter. He has taken an outfit from Fitzpatrick and Co. of some horses and men for the trapping business. It would have afforded me much pleasure to have delivered the letter to you in person, but haste prevents."

October 26th, he arrived in Baltimore, and was in Cambridge, Massachusetts, November 8, 1833, one year and seven months having elapsed since his departure for the Pacific coast.

He was already busy arranging for the return trip, for on this date, November 8, 1833, he wrote to Henry Hall and Messrs. Tucker and Williams a long letter setting forth his plans. A vessel was chartered on November 20th, and was soon loaded

* Census of 1890. Oregon, 317,767; Washington, 349,390; Idaho, 84,385. Total, 751,542.

and ready to sail for the Columbia River *via* Cape Horn.

There is also a letter dated at Cambridge, Massachusetts, December 9, 1833, directed to Hon. Lewis Cass, Secretary of War, the subject of which is to enquire if trappers and employés of the Hudson Bay Company would be unmolested in their possessions should they settle and open up lands on "the Wallamet or Multonomah, a river coming from the south into the Columbia."

From New York, December 20, 1833, he wrote to Messrs. Samuel and More, Liberty, Missouri, to proceed to the purchase of animals for an early start, May 1st, for the mountains. "Thirty-five Spanish riding saddles without finery, for the men, and six of a superior sort for '*us gentlemen*'; not expensive, but good and plain."

On same date he wrote to his old friend and companion in the bull-boat trip from the Big Horn, Milton Sublette, to hasten his expected visit, as "I am desirous of a spree with an old *mountaineer;* these folks here won't do."

Mr. Wyeth left Boston early in February on his second expedition, by way of New York, Philadelphia, and Baltimore, and was in Pittsburg February 26th, Cincinnati February 28th, Louisville March 5th, St. Louis March 11th.

The following letter was written from this last place, and dated March 5, 1834:

"DEAR WIFE,—... It is true that Mr. Fitzpatrick was robbed by the Crow Indians, but I was in hopes you would not hear of it. I knew of it before I left Cambridge, but did not wish to alarm you. I do not think there is much danger with so large a party as I shall have. Mr. Nuttall, and Mr. Townsend, another naturalist, passed through this place to the rendezvous last week.... Baptiste* continues a pretty good boy. I shall not forget my promise to send for you if there is any chance of doing so with propriety, but you must not be too sanguine; a thousand circumstances may prevent, although I desire it much. I feel as much as you can the lonesomeness of my way of life, *but you know the success of what I have undertaken is life itself to me,* and if I do fail in it they shall never say it was for want of perseverance. I am yet sanguine that I shall succeed. I will take good care of myself, and perhaps the life which began in turmoil may yet end in quiet and peace, and our sun go down from a clear sky. I cannot but reproach myself that I have made you in some measure

* The Indian boy who accompanied Mr. Wyeth on his first return trip from the Pacific coast.

a widow, and I fear you will brood over hopes that have been blasted by me. These things make me melancholy, and I believe I have got the *blues.* Good-bye, my dear wife, and may God bless you.   N. J. WYETH."

On May 5, 1834, our explorer was again on his way across the continent, with sixty men and a sufficient number of horses and mules, starting from Liberty, Missouri, crossing the Kansas near its confluence with the Missouri, day after day pushing on in a direction slightly north of west through Kansas (of our present map) into Nebraska, striking the Platte about 41° north latitude and 99° west longitude, following the north fork of this stream into Wyoming, passing the Black Hills, and on June 9, 1834, the expedition arrived at Rock Independence, on the Sweetwater, 42° 30' north latitude and 107° west longitude.

Beyond an occasional bout with Indians, nothing occurred worthy of note, although the diary faithfully details the march of each day.

June 1, 1834: "Crossed Laramie Fork." 8th: "This day killed two grizzlies." 16th: "The grass is miserable, and my horses are starving." Several hunters had also not returned to camp, and the diary reads, "Fearful they have been scalped." July 8th: "Made northwest to a place where there is a soda spring, or, I may say, fifty of them. There is also here a warm spring which throws out water with a jet." This location is now within the National or Yellowstone Park. They were now on Bear River, and it was well named, for on July 10th they "killed three grizzlies."

From July 14th to August 6th they were busy in building Fort Hall, on Lewis River. The strategic importance of this fort has already been referred to in the introduction to this article.

The expedition now bound for the Pacific coast numbered "in all twenty-nine." They were now entering the section of country in which Mr. Hunt's party in 1811 suffered so severely for food, being forced finally to scatter in small detachments to seek subsistence. Some of these perished in the mountains.

August 15th the expedition struck Snake River. Food was getting scarce. "Killed some dusky grouse, and dug some kamas root, which assisted in living a little. Saw one Indian at a distance on horseback." 19th: "This day found a colt left by the Indians, on which we will break-fast, as provisions are running short." Rations were still shorter two days later, for the entry on the 21st, with a grim suggestion of a joke, says, "No breakfast; feel very much purified in the flesh." 24th : "Scorpions are quite common. Two nights since, just as I was about lying down, I saw something move on my blanket, and found it to be a good-sized scorpion." "Our party now numbers seventeen — Indians, *literati*, and all." The *literati* referred to were Mr. Nuttall, the botanist, and Mr. Townsend, the ornithologist. September 1st: "Camped at ten o'clock, having found no water, and the whole country as bare as my hand, affording a bad prospect for our poor horses." On the next day, pretty well worn out, the remnants of the expedition reached Walla Walla.

September 4th: Mr. Wyeth left Walla Walla in a canoe for Fort Vancouver. 9th, had reached "The Dalles" (or Narrows) of the Columbia. "Party arrived with news that they had drowned one of the horses and the jackass. I valued him more than ten horses as a breeder." Down the Columbia was not smooth sailing, for September 10th "the gale swamped one of our canoes, which frightened the Indians back." 13th: "Made the portage of the Cascades; and next day, September 14, 1834, arrived at Fort Vancouver, nineteen months after leaving this place for the East, *having in this time twice traversed the American Continent.*"

September 15th: "Early in the morning, having hired another canoe, put ahead down the Columbia, and at twelve o'clock met the brig *May Dean.* Boarded her, and found all well." This ship Mr. Wyeth had loaded with supplies and despatched from Boston. "She had been struck by lightning and much damaged, having put into Valparaiso for repairs. Captain Lambert brought me twenty Sandwich-Islanders, two coopers, two smiths, and a clerk." September 22d Mr. Wyeth settled upon a large prairie near the Wallamette River, about fifty miles from its mouth. "It is about fifteen miles long, seven wide, surrounded with fine timber, and a good wide stream on it." On the 25th he was back at Fort Vancouver, making preparations to send out parties on exploring and trading expeditions. 27th: "Sent Stout up the Wallamet with two men and implements to commence farm."

From this date to October 13, 1834, he was busy "making preparations for an expedition into the Snake country, and in building a fort on the Columbia River, forty miles from its mouth (Fort William).

October 6, 1834, he wrote to his old friend Mr. Frederick Tudor, of Boston, "I am now making an establishment on the Multonomah [Wallamet, now called Willamette], about fifty miles above its mouth, and one on the Columbia forty miles from its mouth. This winter I go up Lewis River to make one more fort on its waters, and one on the south side of Great Salt Lake."

On November 23d, Mr. Wyeth with four men descended the Walla Walla and Columbia to the mouth of the River Des Chutes, along which he ascended directly south into the heart of Oregon. By December 10th they were well into the unknown country, across "an extensive plain, beyond which, white and high, rose a range of mountains, disheartening to look at; *but ahead is the word*, and the spirit seems to rise to the occasion."

By December 25th they were reduced to such straits that one of the horses was killed for food. "Snow and rain all day, and a miserable Christmas."

January 2, 1835: "Made snow-shoes, but they were too small. I frequently sunk into the snow, and it bothered me much to get out again." 5th: "Killed two swans so fat we could not eat all the grease. Seems good to live well after poor horse-meat," which suggests an adage, Scotch in origin, I believe, that a mighty little does a poor body good. "One swan furnished two of us only two meals; they do not eat so in the States." On the 16th the thermometer was below zero. One of the men had his feet badly frozen. The snow was four feet deep now, so that further advance was impossible. Fearful of perishing, and as delay was dangerous, "we abandoned everything but our blankets, books, and ammunition, axe and kettles, and took it on foot with about sixty pounds each on our backs. Made six miles, killed one deer, and camped. Am tired and hungry, but the deer will cure all." January 22, 1835: "Snowed all night; breakfasted on two beaver tails." 25th: "We heard a gun, and fired in return, and a Snake Indian came to us and led us to his camp; he brought a lean dog on which we supped, and had enough left for breakfast."

January 29th: "This is my birthday, but I have forgotten how old I am." Mr. Wyeth was on this day thirty-three years old. February 3d: "At this camp there is a hot spring, too hot to bear the hand in, and smoking like a coal-pit, 134°; took a good bath by going down stream until I found a suitable temperature." By February 10, 1835, Mr. Wyeth was again on the Columbia, *en route*, "in a very leaky canoe, which kept us bailing all the time," for Fort Vancouver, where he arrived two days later. This tour of exploration occupied nearly three months, in the dead of winter, and in the more elevated and coldest part of Oregon. I cannot, in the limits of a magazine article, give the details as I have them in the daily record of his wanderings. Enough is given to show that this man possessed untiring energy, guided by superior intelligence and tact. He realized that in order to induce immigration the country must be fully explored and described, and this was his great aim in life, to succeed in the colonization of Oregon.

By February 27th he was again on the Wallamet, and established a post at Wappatoo Island, near the mouth of this river. He immediately put his force to work, getting out a cargo of hoop-poles and lumber for the Sandwich Islands, and making a large canoe to "lighter" over the shallows into deep water near the mouth of the Wallamette. "The whole tree was two hundred and forty-two feet long, and this by no means the largest tree on Wappatoo Island." This island is near Portland. This "canoe was sixty feet long, deep enough to chamber twenty-five barrels, clear of knots, shakes, and almost of sap."

The diary of Mr. Nathaniel J. Wyeth ends with this date. If any further record of his labors was kept it is lost. From a study of his character I think it is more than likely that the journal was continued, for he not only was industrious and exact in keeping his diary up to this period, but even kept copies of his correspondence, which copies, covering this interesting chapter of his career, are now in my possession. From these letters I gather that he established a settlement, which he hoped would be permanent, on Wappatoo Island, about four miles from the mouth of the Wallamette.

From Fort William, in the winter of 1834, the brig *Ida*, loaded with lumber, coopers' material, etc., had sailed for the Sandwich Islands, returning on April 3, 1835. He had, in addition to building Fort Hall on Lewis River (now in Idaho), built Fort William on the Columbia, about forty miles above its mouth, opened a large farm fifty miles up the Wallamette, and made an establishment on Wappatoo Island. About this time he was prostrated by an illness, brought on by overwork and reckless exposure, which long threatened to terminate his career. In the mean time his men became discouraged and demoralized in the absence of their leader, upon whom their hopes rested. The Indians, fearing that they were about to be supplanted by the settlement of their lands by enterprising whites, took advantage of the demoralization; and, as Barrows, in his *History of Oregon*, suggests, it is probable that the Hudson Bay Company, seeing in Mr. Wyeth's persistent energy and pluck a formidable competitor for the trade and possession of this country, were silent abettors of the persecution and ultimate destruction of this expedition. Governor Pelly, of this company, writes in 1838, "We have compelled the American adventurers to withdraw from the contest."

This was doubtless their policy, for they avowedly built Fort Boisé, near Fort Hall, for the purpose of killing off the trade and influence this establishment rapidly acquired. Mr. Wyeth, however, always acknowledged the personal courtesies and kindnesses he received from the officers of this company, and did this publicly in one of the Boston newspapers after his return. After a terrible struggle, well deserving a better fate, and more than this, deserving a recognition of his services for Oregon, which his countrymen in that section of the country have not yet accorded him, broken in health and bankrupt in purse, and deserted by those of his followers who survived, he gave up the fight.

Here is his last letter written from Oregon:

"COLUMBIA RIVER, *Sept.* 22d, 1835.

"DEAR WIFE,—I have been very sick, but have got well, and shall be on my way to the mountains, to winter at Fort Hall, in about six days. I expect to be home about the first of November, 1836. Mr. Nuttall is here, and well. I have sent you a half-barrel of salmon, which I hope will be in good order. I cannot attend to putting them up myself, therefore they may not be so good. The season has been very sickly. We have lost by drowning, disease, and warfare seventeen persons up to this date, and fourteen now sick."

The people of Oregon, Washington, and Idaho will no doubt do honor to his memory, now that his services are a matter of record. General Fremont was styled the Pathfinder in 1846, yet Whitman had gone over this route in 1843, and Nathaniel Wyeth had four times made the trail between 1832–6. During his life, which ended in 1856, he shrank from publicity to a degree that was almost morbid. In one of his letters from Oregon to a friend in the East he closes by saying: "Now I do not wish this letter published. I hate anything in print." He never would consent to have a portrait or photograph of himself, and the only one in existence was taken after his death. He was only twenty-nine years old when he led his first expedition over the "Rockies," and but thirty-four when, after five years of perilous labor, having four times traversed the American Continent from ocean to ocean, he reached the fireside of his home in Cambridge, "a visionary and a failure."

Will Oregon, Washington, and Idaho, with their three-quarters of a million inhabitants within fifty-five years of the time he left it, when there was not a single American settler in that country, their busy cities, fertile farms, their transcontinental railroads, their ocean steamers, clearing for China, Japan, and the Orient, and their glorious future, of which this is but the dawn, deem Nathaniel Jarvis Wyeth a failure?

THE OUTLOOK IN SOUTHERN CALIFORNIA

FROM the northern limit of California to the southern is about the same distance as from Portsmouth, New Hampshire, to Charleston, South Carolina. Of these two coast lines, covering nearly ten degrees of latitude, or over seven hundred miles, the Atlantic has greater extremes of climate and greater monthly variations, and the Pacific greater variety of productions. The State of California is, however, so mountainous, cut by longitudinal and transverse ranges, that any reasonable person can find in it a temperature to suit him the year through. But it does not need to be explained that it would be difficult to hit upon any general characteristic that would apply to the stretch of the Atlantic coast named, as a guide to a settler looking for a home: the description of Massachusetts would be wholly misleading for South Carolina. It is almost as difficult to make any comprehensive statement about the long line of the California coast.

It is possible, however, limiting the inquiry to the southern third of the State—an area of about fifty - eight thousand square miles, as large as Maine, New Hampshire, Massachusetts, Connecticut, and Rhode Island—to answer fairly some of the questions oftenest asked about it. These relate to the price of land, its productiveness, the kind of products most profitable, the sort of labor required, and its desirability as a place of residence for the laborer, for the farmer or horticulturist of small means, and for the man with considerable capital. Questions on these subjects cannot be answered categorically, but I hope to be able, by setting down my own observations and using trustworthy reports, to give others the material on which to exercise their judgment. In the first place, I think it demonstrable that a person would profitably exchange one hundred and sixty acres of farming land east of the one-hundredth parallel for ten acres, with a water right, in southern California.

In making this estimate I do not consider the question of health or merely the agreeability of the climate, but the conditions of labor, the ease with which one could support a family, and the profits over and above a fair living. It has been customary in reckoning the value of land there to look merely to the profit of it beyond its support of a family, forgetting that agriculture and horticulture the world over, like almost all other kinds of business, usually do little more than procure a comfortable living, with incidental education, to those who engage in them. That the majority of the inhabitants of southern California will become rich by the culture of the orange and the vine is an illusion; but it is not an illusion that twenty times its present population can live there in comfort, in what might be called luxury elsewhere, by the cultivation of the soil, all far removed from poverty and much above the condition of the majority of the inhabitants of the foreign wine and fruit producing countries. This result is assured by the extraordinary productiveness of the land, uninterrupted the year through, and by the amazing extension of the market in the United States for products that can be nowhere else produced with such certainty and profusion as in California. That State is only just learning how to supply a demand which is daily increasing, but it already begins to command the market in certain fruits. This command of the market in the future will depend upon itself, that is, wheth-

YUCCA-PALM AND DATE-PALM.

fruit-raising and fruit-curing, but it already knows that to compete with the rest of the world in our markets it must beat the rest of the world in quality. It will take some time yet to remove the unfavorable opinion of California wines produced in the East by the first products of the vineyards sent here.

The difficulty for the settler is that he cannot "take up" ten acres with water in California as he can one hundred and sixty acres elsewhere. There is left little available government land. There is plenty of government land not taken up and which may never be occupied, that is, inaccessible mountain and irreclaimable desert. There are also little nooks and fertile spots here and there to be discovered which may be preempted, and which will some day have value. But practically all the arable land, or that is likely to become so, is owned now in large tracts, under grants or by wholesale purchase. The circumstances of the case compelled associate effort. Such a desert as that now blooming region known as Pasadena, Pomona, Riverside, and so on, could not be sub-

er it will send east and north only sound wine, instead of crude, ill-cured juice of the grape, only the best and most carefully canned apricots, nectarines, peaches, and plums, only the raisins and prunes perfectly prepared, only such oranges, lemons, and grapes and pears as the Californians are willing to eat themselves. California has yet much to learn about

dued by individual exertion. Consequently land and water companies were organized. They bought large tracts of unimproved land, built dams in the mountain cañons, sunk wells, drew water from the rivers, made reservoirs, laid pipes, carried ditches and conduits across the country, and then sold the land with the inseparable water right in small parcels. Thus the region became subdivided among small holders, each independent, but all mutually dependent as to water, which is the *sine qua non* of existence. It is only a few years since there was a forlorn and struggling colony a few miles east of Los Angeles known as the Indiana settlement. It had scant water, no railway communication, and everything to learn about horticulture. That spot is now the famous Pasadena.

What has been done in the Santa Ana and San Gabriel valleys will be done elsewhere in the State. There are places in Kern County, north of the Sierra Madre, where the land produces grain and alfalfa without irrigation, where farms can be bought at from five to ten dollars an acre—land that will undoubtedly increase in value with settlement and also by irrigation. The great county of San Diego is practically undeveloped, and contains an immense area, in scattered mesas and valleys, of land which will produce apples, grain, and grass without irrigation, and which the settler can get at moderate prices. Nay, more, any one with a little ready money, who goes to southern California expecting to establish himself and willing to work, will be welcomed and aided, and be pretty certain to find some place where he can steadily improve his condition. But the regions about which one hears most, which are already fruit gardens and well sprinkled with rose-clad homes, command prices per acre which seem extravagant. Land, however, like a mine, gets its value from what it will produce; and it is to be noted that while the subsidence of the "boom" knocked the value out of twenty-feet city lots staked out in the wilderness, and out of insanely inflated city property, the land upon which crops are raised has steadily appreciated in value.

So many conditions enter into the price of land that it is impossible to name an average price for the arable land of the southern counties, but I have heard good judges place it at $100 an

acre. The lands with water are very much alike in their producing power, but some, for climatic reasons, are better adapted to citrus fruits, others to the raisin grape, and others to deciduous fruits. The value is also affected by railway facilities, contiguity to the local commercial centre, and also by the character of the settlement, that is, by its morality, public spirit, and facilities for education. Every town and settlement thinks it has special advantages as to improved irrigation, equability of temperature, adaptation to this or that product, attractions for invalids, tempered ocean breezes, protection from "northers," schools, and varied industries. These things are so much matter of personal choice that each settler will do well to examine widely for himself, and not buy until he is suited.

Some figures, which may be depended on, of actual sales and of annual yields, may be of service. They are of the district east of Pasadena and Pomona, but fairly represent the whole region down to Los Angeles. The selling price of raisin grape land unimproved but with water at Riverside is $250 to $300 per acre; at South Riverside, $150 to $200; in the highland district of San Bernardino, and at Redlands (which is a new settlement east of the city of San Bernardino), $200 to $250 per acre. At Banning and at Hesperia, which lie north of the San Bernardino range, $125 to $150 per acre are the prices asked. Distance from the commercial centre accounts for the difference in price in the towns named. The crop varies with the care and skill of the cultivator, but a fair average from the vines at two years is two tons per acre; three years, three tons; four years, five tons; five years, seven tons. The price varies with the season, and also whether its sale is upon the vines, or after picking, drying, and sweating, or the packed product. On the vines $20 per ton is a fair average price. In exceptional cases vineyards at Riverside have produced four tons per acre in twenty months from the setting of the cuttings, and six-year-old vines have produced thirteen and a half tons per acre. If the grower has a crop of, say, 2000 packed boxes of raisins of twenty pounds each box, it will pay him to pack his own crop and establish a "brand" for it. In 1889 three adjoining vineyards in Riverside, producing about the same average crops, were sold as follows: the first vineyard, at $17 50 per ton on the vines, yielded $150 per acre; the second, at six cents a pound in the sweat boxes, yielded $276 per acre; the third, at $1 80 per box packed, yielded $414 per acre.

Land adapted to the deciduous fruits, such as apricots and peaches, is worth as much as raisin land, and some years pays better. The pear and the apple need greater elevation, and are of better quality when grown on high ground than in the valleys. I have reason to believe that the mountain regions of San Diego County are specially adapted to the apple.

Good orange land unimproved but with water is worth from $300 to $500 an acre. If we add to this price the cost of budded trees, the care of them for four years, and interest at eight per cent. per annum for four years, the cost of a good grove will be about $1000 an acre. It must be understood that the profit of an orange grove depends upon care, skill, and business ability. The kind of orange grown with reference to the demand, the judgment about more or less irrigation as affecting the quality, the cultivation of the soil, and the arrangements for marketing are all elements in the problem. There are young groves at Riverside, five years old, that are paying ten per cent. net upon from $3000 to $5000 an acre; while there are older groves which, at the prices for fruit in the spring of 1890—$1 60 per box for seedlings and $3 per box for navels delivered at the packing-houses—paid at the rate of ten per cent. net on $7500 per acre.

In all these estimates water must be reckoned as a prime factor. What, then, is water worth per inch, generally, in all this fruit region from Redlands to Los Angeles? It is worth just the amount it will add to the commercial value of land irrigated by it, and that may be roughly estimated at from $500 to $1000 an inch of continuous flow. Take an illustration. A piece of land at Riverside below the flow of water was worth $300 an acre. Contiguous to it was another piece not irrigated which would not sell for $50 an acre. By bringing water to it, it would quickly sell for $300, thus adding $250 to its value. As the estimate at Riverside is that one inch of water will irrigate five acres of fruit land, five times $250 would be $1250 per inch, at which price water for irrigation has actually been sold at Riverside.

The standard of measurement of water in southern California is the miner's inch under four inches pressure, or the amount that will flow through an inch-square opening under a pressure of four inches measured from the surface of the water in the conduit to the centre of the opening through which it flows. This is nine gallons a minute, or, as it is figured, 1728 cubic feet or 12,960 gallons in twenty-four hours, and $\frac{1}{50}$ of a cubic foot a second. This flow would cover ten acres about eighteen inches deep in a year; that is, it would give the land the equivalent of eighteen inches of rain, distributed exactly when and where it was needed, none being wasted, and more serviceable than fifty inches of rainfall as it generally comes. This, with the natural rainfall, is sufficient for citrus fruits and for corn and alfalfa, in soil not too sandy, and it is too much for grapes and all deciduous fruits.

It is necessary to understand this problem of irrigation in order to comprehend southern California, the exceptional value of its arable land, the certainty and great variety of its products, and the part it is to play in our markets. There are three factors in the expectation of a crop, soil, sunshine, and water. In a region where we can assume the first two to be constant, the only uncertainty is water. Southern California is practically without rain from May to December. Upon this fact rests the immense value of its soil, and the certainty that it can supply the rest of the Union with a great variety of products. This certainty must be purchased by a previous investment of money. Water is everywhere to be had for money, in some localities by surface wells, in others by artesian wells, in others from such streams as the Los Angeles and the Santa Ana, and from reservoirs secured by dams in the heart of the high mountains. It is possible to compute the cost of any one of the systems of irrigation, to determine whether it will pay by calculating the amount of land it will irrigate. The cost of procuring water varies greatly with the situation, and it is conceivable that money can be lost in such an investment, but I have yet to hear of any irrigation that has not been more or less successful.

Farming and fruit-raising are usually games of hazard. Good crops and poor crops depend upon enough rain and not

RAISIN-CURING.

too much at just the right times. A wheat field which has a good start with moderate rain may later wither in a drought, or be ruined by too much water at the time of maturity. And, avoiding all serious reverses from either dryness or wet, every farmer knows that the quality and quantity of the product would be immensely improved if the growing stalks and roots could have water when and only when they need it. The difference would be between say twenty and forty bushels of grain or roots to the acre, and that means the difference between profit and loss. There is probably not a crop of any kind grown in the great West that would not be immensely benefited if it could be irrigated once or twice a year; and probably anywhere that water is attainable the cost of irrigation would be abundantly paid in the yield from year to year. Farming in the West with even a little irrigation would not be the game of hazard that it is. And it may further be assumed that there is not a vegetable patch or a fruit orchard East or West that would not yield better quality and more abundantly with irrigation.

But this is not all. Any farmer who attempts to raise grass and potatoes and strawberries on contiguous fields, subject to the same chance of drought or rainfall,

has a vivid sense of his difficulties. The potatoes are spoiled by the water that helps the grass, and the coquettish strawberry will not thrive on the regimen that suits the grosser crops. In California, which by its climate and soil gives a greater variety of products than any other region in the Union, the supply of water is adjusted to the needs of each crop, even on contiguous fields. No two products need the same amount of water, or need it at the same time. The orange needs more than the grape, the alfalfa more than the orange, the peach and apricot less than the orange; the olive, the fig, the almond, the English walnut, demand each a different supply. Depending entirely on irrigation six months of the year, the farmer in southern California is practically certain of his crop year after year; and if all his plants and trees are in a healthful condition, as they will be if he is not too idle to cultivate as well as irrigate, his yield will be about double what it would be without systematic irrigation. It is this practical control of the water the year round, in a climate where sunshine is the rule, that makes the productiveness of California so large as to be incomprehensible to Eastern people. Even the trees are not dormant more than three or four months in the year.

But irrigation, in order to be successful, must be intelligently applied. In unskilful hands it may work more damage than benefit. Mr. Theodore S. Van Dyke, who may always be quoted with confidence, says that the ground should never be flooded; that water must not touch the plant or tree, or come near enough to make the soil bake around it; and that it should be let in in small streams for two or three days, and not in large streams for a few hours. It is of the first importance that the ground shall be stirred as soon as dry enough, the cultivation to be continued, and water never to be substituted for the cultivator to prevent baking. The methods of irrigation in use may be reduced to three. First, the old Mexican way, running a small ditch from tree to tree without any basin round the tree. Second, the basin system, where a large basin is made round the tree, and filled several times. This should only be used where water is scarce, for it trains the roots like a brush instead of sending them out laterally into the soil. Third, the Riverside method, which is the best in the world, and produces the largest results with the least water and the least work. It is the closest imitation of the natural process of wetting by gentle rain. "A small flume eight or ten inches square of common redwood is laid along the upper side of a ten-acre tract. At intervals of one to three feet, according to the nature of the ground and the stuff to be irrigated, are bored one-inch holes, with a small wooden button over them to regulate the flow. This flume costs a trifle, is left in position, lasts for years, and is always ready. Into this flume is turned from the ditch an irrigating head of 20, 25, or 30 inches of water, generally about 20 inches. This is divided by the holes and the buttons into streams of from one-sixth to one-tenth of an inch each, making from 120 to 200 small streams. From five to seven furrows are made between two rows of trees, two between rows of grapes, one furrow between rows of corn, potatoes, etc. It may take from fifteen to twenty hours for one of the streams to get across the tract. They are allowed to run from forty-eight to seventy-two hours. The ground is then thoroughly wet in all directions and three or four feet deep. As soon as the ground is dry enough, cultivation is begun, and kept up from six to eight weeks

before water is used again." Only when the ground is very sandy is the basin system necessary. Long experiment has taught that this system is by far the best, and, says Mr. Van Dyke, "those whose ideas are taken from the wasteful systems of flooding or soaking from big ditches have something to learn in southern California."

As to the quantity of water needed in the kind of soil most common in southern California, I will again quote Mr. Van Dyke: "They will tell you at Riverside that they use an inch of water to five acres, and some say an inch to three acres. But this is because they charge to the land all the waste on the main ditch, and because they use thirty per cent. of the water in July and August, when it is the lowest. But this is no test of the duty of water; the amount actually delivered on the land should be taken. What they actually use for ten acres at Riverside, Redlands, etc., is a twenty-inch stream of three days run five times a year, equal to 300 inches for one day, or one inch steady run for 300 days. As an inch is the equivalent of 365 inches for one day, or one inch for 365 days, 300 inches for one day equals an inch to twelve acres. Many use even less than this, running the water only two or two and a half days at a time. Others use more head; but it rarely exceeds 24 inches for three days and five times a year, which would be 72 multiplied by five, or 360 inches, a little less than a full inch for a year for ten acres."

I have given room to these details because the Riverside experiment, which results in such large returns of excellent fruit, is worthy of the attention of cultivators everywhere. The constant stirring of the soil, to keep it loose as well as to keep down useless growths, is second in importance only to irrigation. Some years ago, when it was ascertained that tracts of land which had been regarded as only fit for herding cattle and sheep would by good ploughing and constant cultivation produce fair crops without any artificial watering, there spread abroad a notion that irrigation could be dispensed with. There are large areas, dry and cracked on the surface, where the soil is moist three and four feet below the surface in the dry season. By keeping the surface broken and well pulverized the moisture rises sufficiently to insure a crop.

Many Western farmers have found out this secret of cultivation, and more will learn in time the good sense of not spreading themselves over too large an area; that 40 acres planted and cultivated will give a better return than 80 acres planted and neglected. Crops of various sorts are raised in southern California by careful cultivation with little or no irrigation, but the idea that cultivation alone will bring sufficiently good production is now practically abandoned, and the al-

there is no exception to the rule that continual labor, thrift, and foresight are essential to the getting of a good living or the gaining of a competence. No doubt speculation will spring up again. It is inevitable with the present enormous and yearly increasing yield of fruits,

IRRIGATION BY ARTESIAN
WELL SYSTEM.

IRRIGATION BY PIPE SYSTEM.

the better intelligence in vine culture, wine-making, and raisin-curing, the growth of marketable oranges, lemons, etc., and the consequent rise in the value of land. Doubtless fortunes will be made

most universal experience is that judicious irrigation always improves the crop in quality and in quantity, and that irrigation and cultivation are both essential to profitable farming or fruit-raising.

It would seem, then, that capital is necessary for successful agriculture or horticulture in southern California. But where is it not needed? In New England? In Kansas, where land which was given to actual settlers is covered with mortgages for money absolutely necessary to develop it? But passing this by, what is the chance in southern California for laborers and for mechanics? Let us understand the situation. In California

by enterprising companies who secure large areas of unimproved land at low prices, bring water on them, and then sell in small lots. But this will come to an end. The tendency is to subdivide the land into small holdings—into farms and gardens of ten and twenty acres. The great ranches are sure to be broken up. With the resulting settlement by industrious people, the cities will again experience "booms"; but these are not peculiar to California. In my mind I see the time when this region (because it will pay better proportionally to cultivate a small area) will be one of small farms, of neat cottages, of industrious homes. The

owner is pretty certain to prosper—that
is, to get a good living (which is independence) and lay aside a little yearly—if the
work is done by himself and his family.
And the peculiarity of the situation is that
the farm or garden, whichever it is called,
will give agreeable and most healthful occupation to all the boys and girls in the
family all the days in the year that can
be spared from the school. Aside from
the ploughing, the labor is light. Pruning, grafting, budding, the picking of the
grapes, the gathering of the fruit from
trees, the sorting, packing, and canning,
are labor for light and deft hands, and
labor distributed through the year. The
harvest, of one sort and another, is almost
continuous, so that young girls and boys
can have, in well-settled districts, pretty
steady employment—a long season in establishments packing oranges; at another
time, in canning fruits; at another, in
packing raisins.

It goes without saying that in the industries now developed, and in others as
important which are in their infancy (for
instance, the culture of the olive for oil
and as an article of food, the growth and
curing of figs, the gathering of almonds,
English walnuts, etc.), the labor of the
owners of the land and their families will
not suffice. There must be as large a
proportion of day-laborers as there is in
other regions where such products are
grown. Chinese labor at certain seasons
has been a necessity. Under the present
policy of California this must diminish,
and its place be taken by some other.
The pay for this labor has always been
good. It is certain to be more and more
in demand. Whether the pay will ever
approach near to the European standard
is a question, but it is a fair presumption
that the exceptional profit of the land,
owing to its productiveness, will for a
long time keep wages up.

During the "boom" period all wages
were high, those of skilled mechanics especially, owing to the great amount of
building on speculation. The ordinary
laborer on a ranch had $30 a month and
board and lodging; laborers of a higher
grade, $2 to $2 50 a day; skilled masons,
$6; carpenters, from $3 50 to $5; plaster-
ers, $4 to $5; house-servants, from $25 to
$35 a month. Since the "boom," wages
of skilled mechanics have declined at least
25 per cent., and there has been less demand for labor generally, except in con-

nection with fruit raising and harvesting. It would be unwise for laborers to
go to California on an uncertainty, but it
can be said of that country with more
confidence than of any other section that
its peculiar industries, now daily increasing, will absorb an increasing amount of
day-labor, and later on it will remunerate
skilled artisan labor.

In deciding whether southern California would be an agreeable place of residence there are other things to be considered besides the productiveness of the soil,
the variety of products, the ease of out-
door labor distributed through the year,
the certainty of returns for intelligent
investment with labor, the equability of
summer and winter, and the adaptation
to personal health. There are always disadvantages attending the development of
a new country and the evolution of a new
society. It is not a small thing, and may
be one of daily discontent, the change
from a landscape clad with verdure, the
riotous and irrepressible growth of a rainy
region, to a land that the greater part of
the year is green only where it is artificially watered, where all the hills and unwatered plains are brown and sere, where
the foliage is coated with dust, and where
driving anywhere outside the sprinkled
avenues of a town is to be enveloped in a
cloud of powdered earth. This discomfort must be weighed against the commercial advantages of a land of irrigation.

What are the chances for a family of
very moderate means to obtain a foothold and thrive by farming in southern
California? I cannot answer this better
than by giving substantially the experience of one family, and by saying that
this has been paralleled, with change of
details, by many others. Of course, in a
highly developed settlement, where the
land is mostly cultivated, and its actual
yearly produce makes its price very high,
it is not easy to get a foothold. But there
are many regions—say in Orange County,
and certainly in San Diego—where land
can be had at a moderate price and on
easy terms of payment. Indeed, there are
few places, as I have said, where an industrious family would not find welcome
and cordial help in establishing itself.
And it must be remembered that there are
many communities where life is very simple, and the great expense of keeping up
an appearance attending life elsewhere
need not be reckoned.

GARDEN SCENE, SANTA ANA.

A few years ago a professional man in a New England city, who was in delicate health, with his wife, and five boys all under sixteen, and one too young to be of any service, moved to San Diego. He had in money a small sum, less than a thousand dollars. He had no experience in farming or horticulture, and his health would not have permitted him to do much field work in our climate. Fortunately he found in the fertile El Cajon Valley, fifteen miles from San Diego, a farmer and fruit-grower who had upon his place a small unoccupied house. Into that house he moved, furnishing it very simply with furniture bought in San Diego, and hired his services to the landlord. The work required was comparatively easy, in the orchard and vineyards, and consisted largely in superintending other laborers. The pay was about enough to support his family without encroaching on his little capital. Very soon, however, he made an arrangement to buy the small house and tract of some twenty

acres, on which he lived, on time, perhaps making a partial payment. He began at once to put out an orange orchard and plant a vineyard; this he accomplished with the assistance of his boys, who did practically most of the work after the first planting, leaving him a chance to give most of his days to his employer. The orchard and vineyard work is so light that a smart intelligent boy is almost as valuable a worker in the field as a man. The wife, meantime, kept the house and did its work. House-keeping was comparatively easy; little fuel was required except for cooking; the question of clothes was a minor one. In that climate wants for a fairly comfortable existence are fewer than with us. From the first, almost, vegetables, raised upon the ground while the vines and oranges were growing, contributed largely to the support of the family. The out-door life and freedom from worry insured better health, and the diet of fruit and vegetables, suitable to the climate, reduced the cost of living to a minimum. As soon as the orchard and the vineyard began to produce fruit, the owner was enabled to quit working for his neighbor, and give all his time to the development of his own place. He increased his planting; he added to his house; he bought a piece of land adjoining which had a grove of eucalyptus, which would supply him with fuel. At first the society circle was small, and there was no school. But the incoming of families had increased the number of children, so that an excellent public school was established. When I saw him he was living in conditions of comfortable industry; his land had trebled in value; the pair of horses which he drove he had bought cheap, for they were Eastern horses; but the climate had brought them up, so that the team was a serviceable one in good condition. The story is not one of brilliant success, but to me it is much more hopeful for the country than the other tales I heard of sudden wealth or lucky speculation. It is the founding in an unambitious way of a comfortable home. The boys of the family will branch out, get fields, orchards, vineyards of their own, and add to the solid producing industry of the country. This orderly, contented industry, increasing its gains day by day, little by little, is the life and hope of any state.

It is not the purpose of this paper to describe southern California. That has been thoroughly done; and details, with figures and pictures in regard to every town and settlement, will be forthcoming on application, which will be helpful guides to persons who can see for themselves, or make sufficient allowance for local enthusiasm. But before speaking further of certain industries south of the great mountain ranges, the region north of the Sierra Madre, which is allied to southern California by its productions, should be mentioned. The beautiful Antelope Plains and the Kern Valley (where land is still cheap and very productive) should not be overlooked. The splendid San Joaquin Valley is already speaking loudly and clearly for itself. The region north of the mountains of Kern County, shut in by the Sierra Nevada range on the east and the Coast Range on the west, substantially one valley, fifty to sixty miles in breadth, watered by the King and the San Joaquin, and gently sloping to the north, say for two hundred miles,

is a land of marvellous capacity, capable of sustaining a dense population. It is cooler in winter than southern California, and the summers average much warmer. Owing to the greater heat, the fruits mature sooner. It is just now becoming celebrated for its raisins, which in quality are unexcelled; and its area, which can be well irrigated from the rivers and from the mountains on either side, seems capable of producing raisins enough to supply the world. It is a wonderfully rich valley in a great variety of products. Fresno County, which occupies the centre of this valley, has 1,200,000 acres of agricultural and 4,400,000 of mountain and pasture land. The city of Fresno, which occupies land that in 1870 was a sheep ranch, is the commercial centre of a beautiful agricultural and fruit region, and has a population estimated at 12,000. From this centre were shipped, in the season of 1890, 1500 car loads of raisins. In 1865 the only exports of Fresno County were a few bales of wool. The report of 1889 gave a shipment of 700,000 boxes of raisins, and the whole export of 1890, of all products, was estimated at $10,000,000. Whether these figures are exact or not, there is no doubt of the extraordinary success of the raisin industry, nor that this is a region of great activity and promise.

The traveller has constantly to remind himself that this is a new country, and to be judged as a new country. It is out of his experience that trees can grow so fast, and plantations in so short a time put on an appearance of maturity. When he sees a roomy, pretty cottage overrun with vines and flowering plants, set in the midst of trees and lawns and gardens of tropical appearance and luxuriance, he can hardly believe that three years before this spot was desert land. When he looks over miles of vineyards, of groves of oranges, olives, walnuts, prunes, the trees all in vigorous bearing, he cannot believe that five or ten years before the whole region was a waste. When he enters a handsome village, with substantial buildings of brick, and perhaps of stone, with fine school-houses, banks, hotels, an opera-house, large packing-houses, and warehouses, and shops of all sorts, with tasteful dwellings and lovely ornamented lawns, it is hard to understand that all this is the creation of two or three years. Yet these surprises meet the traveller at

GRAPE-VINES ON THE GROUNDS OF MR. MAGEE, MONTECITO VALLEY, SANTA BARBARA.

every turn, and the wonder is that there is not visible more crudeness, eccentric taste, and evidence of hasty beginnings.

San Bernardino is comparatively an old town. It was settled in 1853 by a colony of Mormons from Salt Lake. The remains of this colony, less than a hundred, still live here, and have a church like the other sects, but they call themselves Josephites, and do not practise polygamy. There is probably not a sect or schism in the United States that has not its representative in California. Until 1865 San Bernardino was merely a straggling settlement, and a point of distribution for Arizona. The discovery that a large part of the county was adapted to the orange and the vine, and the advent of the Santa Fe Railway, changed all that. Land that then might have been bought for $4 an acre is now sold at from $200 to $300, and the city has become the busy commercial centre of a large number of growing villages, and of one of the most remarkable orange

and vine districts in the world. It has many fine buildings, a population of about 6000, and a decided air of vigorous business. The great plain about it is mainly devoted to agricultural products, which are grown without irrigation, while in the near foot-hills the orange and the vine flourish by the aid of irrigation. Artesian wells abound in the San Bernardino plain, but the mountains are the great and unfailing source of water supply. The Bear Valley Dam is a most daring and gigantic construction. A solid wall of masonry 300 feet long and 60 feet high, curving toward the reservoir, creates an inland lake in the mountains holding water enough to irrigate 20,000 acres of land. This is conveyed to distributing reservoirs in the east end of the valley. On a terrace in the foot-hills a few miles to the north, 2000 feet above the sea, are the Arrow-head Hot Springs (named from the figure of a gigantic "arrow-head" on the mountain above), already a favorite resort for health and pleasure. The views from the plain of the picturesque foot-hills and the snow peaks of the San Bernardino range are exceedingly fine. The marvellous beauty of the purple and deep violet of the giant hills at sunset, with spotless snow, lingers in the memory.

Perhaps the settlement of Redlands, ten miles by rail east of San Bernardino, is as good an illustration as any of rapid development and great promise. It is devoted to the orange and the grape. As late as 1875 much of it was government land, considered valueless. It had a few settlers, but the town, which counts now about 2000 people, was only begun in 1887. It has many solid brick edifices and many pretty cottages on its gentle slopes and rounded hills, overlooked by the great mountains. The view from any point of vantage of orchards and vine-yards and semi-tropical gardens, with the wide sky-line of noble and snow-clad hills, is exceedingly attractive. The region is watered by the Santa Ana River and Mill Creek, but the main irrigating streams, which make every hill-top to bloom with vegetation, come from the Bear Valley Reservoir. On a hill to the south of the town, the Smiley Brothers, of Catskill fame, are building fine residences, and planting their 125 acres with fruit trees and vines, evergreens, flowers, and semi-tropic shrubbery in a style of landscape-gardening that in three years at the far-thest will make this spot one of the few great show-places of the country. Be-hind their ridge is the San Mateo Cañon, through which the Southern Pacific Rail-way runs, while in front are the splen-did sloping plains, valleys, and orange groves, and the great sweep of mountains from San Jacinto round to the Sierra Madre range. It is almost a matchless prospect. The climate is most agreeable, the plantations increase month by month, and thus far the orange-trees have not been visited by the scale, nor the vines by any sickness. Although the groves are still young, there were shipped from Redlands in the season of 1889–90 80 car loads of oranges, of 286 boxes to the car, at a price averaging nearly $1000 a car. That season's planting of oranges was over 1200 acres. It had over 5000 acres in fruits, of which nearly 3000 were in peaches, apricots, grapes, and other sorts called deciduous.

Riverside may without prejudice be re-garded as the centre of the orange growth and trade. The railway shipments of or-anges from southern California in the season of 1890 aggregated about 2400 car loads, or about 800,000 boxes, of oranges (in which estimate the lemons are in-cluded), valued at about $1,500,000. Of this shipment more than half was from Riverside. This has been, of course, greatly stimulated by the improved rail-road facilities, among them the shorten-ing of the time to Chicago by the Santa Fe route, and the running of special fruit trains. Southern California responds like magic to this chance to send her fruits to the East, and the area planted month by month is something enormous. It is esti-mated that the crop of oranges alone in 1891 will be over 4500 car loads. We are accustomed to discount all California es-timates, but I think that no one yet has comprehended the amount to which the shipments to Eastern markets of vegeta-bles and fresh and canned fruits will reach within five years. I base my prediction upon some observation of the Eastern de-mand and the reports of fruit dealers, upon what I saw of the new planting all over the State in 1890, and upon the statistics of increase. Take Riverside as an exam-ple. In 1872 it was a poor sheep ranch. In 1880–1 it shipped 15 car loads, or 4290 boxes, of oranges; the amount yearly in-creased, until in 1888-9 it was 925 car loads, or 263,879 boxes. In 1890 it rose to 1253 car loads, or 358,341 boxes; and an important fact is that the largest ship-ment was in April (455 car loads, or 130,226 boxes), at the time when the supply from other orange regions for the markets east had nearly ceased.

It should be said also that the quality of the oranges has vastly improved. This is owing to better cultivation, knowledge of proper irrigation, and the adoption of the best varieties for the soil. As differ-ent sorts of oranges mature at different seasons, a variety is needed to give edible fruit in each month from December to May inclusive. In February, 1887, I could not find an orange of the first class com-pared with the best fruit in other regions. It may have been too early for the varie-ties I tried; but I believe there has been a marked improvement in quality. In May, 1890, we found delicious oranges al-most everywhere. The seedless Washing-ton and Australian navels are favorites, especially for the market, on account of their great size and fine color. When in perfection they are very fine, but the skin is thick and the texture coarser than that of some others. The best orange I happened to taste was a Tahiti seedling at Montecito (Santa Barbara). It is a small orange, with a thin skin and a compact sweet pulp that leaves little fibre. It resembles the famous orange of Malta. But there are many excellent varieties—the Mediterranean sweet, the paper rind St. Michael, the Maltese blood, etc. The experiments with seedlings are profitable, and will give ever new varieties. I noted that the "grape fruit," which is becoming so much liked in the East, is not appreciated in California.

The city of Riverside occupies an area of some five miles by three, and claims to have 6000 inhabitants; the centre is a substantial town with fine school and other public buildings, but the region is one succession of orange groves and vineyards, of comfortable houses and broad avenues. One avenue through which we drove is 125 feet wide and 12 miles long, planted in three rows with palms, magnolias, the *Grevillea robusta* (Australian fern), the pepper, and the eucalyptus, and lined all the way by splendid orange groves, in the midst of which are houses and grounds with semi-tropical attractions. Nothing could be lovelier than such a scene of fruits and flowers, with the background of purple hills and snowy peaks. The mountain views are superb. Frost is a rare visitor. Not in fifteen years has there been enough to affect the orange. There is little rain after March, but there are fogs and dew-falls, and the ocean breeze is felt daily. The grape grown for raisins is the muscat, and this has had no "sickness." Vigilance and a quarantine have also kept from the orange the scale which has been so annoying in some other localities. The orange, when cared for, is a generous bearer; some trees produce twenty boxes each, and there are areas of twenty acres in good bearing which have brought to the owner as much as $10,000 a year.

The whole region of the Santa Ana and San Gabriel valleys, from the desert on the east to Los Angeles, the city of gardens, is a surprise, and year by year an increasing wonder. In production it exhausts the catalogue of fruits and flowers; its scenery is varied by ever-new combinations of the picturesque and the luxuriant; every town boasts some special ad-

vantage in climate, soil, water, or society; but these differences, many of them visible to the eye, cannot appear in any written description. The traveller may prefer the scenery of Pasadena, or that of Pomona, or of Riverside, but the same words in regard to color, fertility, combinations of orchards, avenues, hills, must appear in the description of each. Ontario, Pomona, Puente, Alhambra—wherever one goes there is the same wonder of color and production.

Pomona is a pleasant city in the midst of fine orange groves, watered abundantly by artesian wells and irrigating ditches from a mountain reservoir. A specimen of the ancient adobe residence is on the Meserve plantation, a lovely old place, with its gardens of cherries, strawberries, olives, and oranges. From the top of San José hill we had a view of a plain twenty-five miles by fifty in extent, dotted with cultivation, surrounded by mountains—a wonderful prospect. Pomona, like its sister cities in this region, has a regard for the intellectual side of life, exhibited in good school-houses and public libraries. In the library of Pomona is what may be regarded as the tutelary deity of the place, the goddess Pomona, a good copy in marble of the famous statue in the Uffizi Gallery, presented to the city by the Rev. C. F. Loop. This enterprising citizen is making valuable experiments in olive culture, raising a dozen varieties in order to ascertain which is best adapted to this soil, and which will make the best return in oil and in a marketable product of cured fruit for the table.

The growth of the olive is to be, it seems to me, one of the leading and most permanent industries of southern California. It will give us, what it is nearly impossible to buy now, pure olive oil, in place of the cotton-seed and lard mixture in general use. It is a most wholesome and palatable article of food. Those whose chief experience of the olive is the large, coarse, and not agreeable Spanish variety, used only as an appetizer, know little of the value of the best varieties as food, nutritious as meat, and always delicious. Good bread and a dish of pickled olives make an excellent meal. The sort known as the Mission olive, planted by the Franciscans a century ago, is generally grown now, and the best fruit is from the older trees. The most suc-

IN A FIELD OF GOLDEN
PUMPKINS.

cessful attempts in cultivating the olive and putting it on the market have been made by Mr. F. A. Kimball, of National City, and Mr. Ellwood Cooper, of Santa Barbara. The experiments have gone far enough to show that the industry is very remunerative. The best olive oil I have ever tasted anywhere is that produced from the Cooper and the Kimball orchards; but not enough is produced to supply the local demand. Mr. Cooper has written a careful treatise on olive culture, which will be of great service to all growers. The art of pickling is not yet mastered, and perhaps some other variety will be preferred to the Old Mission for the table. A mature olive grove in good bearing is a fortune. I feel sure that within twenty-five years this will be one of the most profitable industries of California, and that the demand for pure oil and edible fruit in the United States will drive out the adulterated and inferior present commercial products. But California can easily ruin its reputation by adopting the European systems of adulteration.

We drove one day from Arcadia Station through the region occupied by the Baldwin plantations, an area of over fifty thousand acres—a happy illustration of what industry and capital can do in the way of variety of productions, especially in what are called the Santa Anita vineyards and orchards, extending southward from the foot-hills. About the home place and in many sections where the irrigating streams flow one might fancy he was in the tropics, so abundant and brilliant are the flowers and exotic plants. There are splendid orchards of oranges, almonds, English walnuts, lemons, peaches, apricots, figs, apples, and olives, with grain and corn—in short, everything that grows in garden or field. The ranch is famous for its brandies and wines as well as fruits. We lunched at the East San Gabriel Hotel, a charming place with a peaceful view from the wide veranda of live-oaks, orchards, vineyards, and the noble Sierra Madre range. The Californians may be excused for using the term paradisiacal about such scenes. Flowers, flowers everywhere, color on color, and the song of the mocking-bird!

In this region and elsewhere I saw evidence of the perils that attend the culture of the vine and the fruit tree in all other countries, and from which California in the early days thought it was exempt.

Within the past three or four years there has prevailed a sickness of the vine, the cause of which is unknown, and for which no remedy has been discovered. No blight was apparent, but the vine sickened and failed. The disease was called consumption of the vine. I saw many vineyards subject to it, and hundreds of acres of old vines had been rooted up as useless. I was told by a fruit buyer in Los Angeles that he thought the raisin industry below Fresno was ended unless new planting recovered the vines, and that the great wine fields were about "played out." The truth I believe to be that the disease is confined to the vineyards of Old Mission grapes. Whether these had attained the limit of their active life, and sickened, I do not know. The trouble for a time was alarming; but new plantings of other varieties of grapes have been successful, the vineyards look healthful, and the growers expect no further difficulty. The planting, which was for a time suspended, has been more vigorously renewed.

The insect pests attacking the orange were even more serious, and in 1887–8, though little was published about it, there was something like a panic, in the fear that the orange and lemon culture in southern California would be a failure. The enemies were the black, the red, and the white scale. The last, the *Icerya purchasi*, or cottony cushion scale, was especially loathsome and destructive; whole orchards were enfeebled, and no way was discovered of staying its progress, which threatened also the olive and every other tree, shrub, and flower. Science was called on to discover its parasite. This was found to be the Australian lady-bug (*Vedolia cardinalis*), and in 1888–9 quantities of this insect were imported and spread throughout Los Angeles County, and sent to Santa Barbara and other afflicted districts. The effect was magical. The vedolia attacked the cottony scale with intense vigor, and everywhere killed it. The orchards revived as if they had been recreated, and the danger was over. The enemies of the black and the red scale have not yet been discovered, but they probably will be. Meantime the growers have recovered courage, and are fertilizing and fumigating. In Santa Ana I found that the red scale was fought successfully by fumigating the trees. The operation is performed at night under a movable tent, which covers the tree. The cost is about twenty cents a tree. One lesson of all this is that trees must be fed in order to be kept vigorous to resist such attacks, and that fruit-raising, considering the number of enemies that all fruits have in all climates, is not an idle occupation. The clean handsome English walnut is about the only tree in the State that thus far has no enemy.

One cannot take anywhere else a more exhilarating, delightful drive than about the rolling, highly cultivated, many-villaed Pasadena, and out to the foot-hills and the Sierra Madre Villa. He is constantly exclaiming at the varied loveliness of the scene—oranges, palms, formal gardens, hedges of Monterey cypress. It is very Italy-like. The Sierra Madre furnishes abundant water for all the valley, and the swift irrigating stream from Eaton Cañon waters the Sierra Madre Villa. Among the peaks above it rises Mount Wilson, a thousand feet above the plain, the site selected for the Harvard Observatory with its 40-inch glass. The clearness of the air at this elevation, and the absence of clouds night and day the greater portion of the year, make this a most advantageous position, it is said, to use the glass in dissolving nebulæ. The Sierra Madre Villa, once the most favorite resort in this region, was closed. In its sheltered situation, its luxuriant and half-neglected gardens, its wide plantations and irrigating streams, it reminds one of some secularized monastery on the promontory of Sorrento. It only needs good management to make the hotel very attractive, and especially agreeable in the months of winter.

Pasadena, which exhibits everywhere evidences of wealth and culture, and claims a permanent population of 12,000, has the air of a winter resort; the great Hotel Raymond is closed in May, the boarding-houses want occupants, the shops and livery-stables customers, and the streets lack movement. This is easily explained. It is not because Pasadena is not an agreeable summer residence, but because the visitors are drawn there in the winter principally to escape the inclement climate of the North and East, and because special efforts have been made for their entertainment in the winter. We found the atmosphere delightful in the middle of May. The mean summer heat is 67°, and the nights are always cool. The hills near by may be resorted to with the certainty of finding as decided a change as one desires in the summer season. I must repeat that the southern California summer is not at all understood in the East. The statement of the general equability of the temperature the year through must be insisted on. We lunched one day in a typical California house, in the midst of a garden of fruits, flowers, and tropical shrubs; in a house that might be described as half roses and half tent, for added to the wooden structure were rooms of canvas, which are used as sleeping apartments winter and summer.

This attractive region, so lovely in its cultivation, with so many charming drives, offering good shooting on the plains and in the hills, and centrally placed for excursions, is only eight miles from the busy city of Los Angeles. An excellent point of view of the country is from the graded hill on which stands the Raymond Hotel, a hill isolated but easy of access, which is in itself a mountain of bloom, color, and fragrance. From all the broad verandas and from every window the prospect is charming, whether the eye rests upon cultivated orchards and gardens and pretty villas, or upon the purple foot-hills and the snowy ranges. It enjoys a daily ocean breeze, and the air is always exhilarating. This noble hill is a study in landscape-gardening. It is a mass of brilliant color, and the hospitality of the region generally to foreign growths may be estimated by the trees acclimated on these slopes. They are the pepper, eucalyptus, pine, cypress, sycamore, redwood, olive, date and fan palms, banana, pomegranate, guava, Japanese persimmon, umbrella, maple, elm, locust, English walnut, birch, ailantus, poplar, willow, and more ornamental shrubs than one can well name.

I can indulge in few locality details except those which are illustrative of the general character of the country. In passing into Orange County, which was recently set off from Los Angeles, we come into a region of less "fashion," but one that for many reasons is attractive to people of moderate means who are content with independent simplicity. The country about the thriving village of Santa Ana is very rich, being abundantly watered by the Santa Ana River and by artesian wells. The town is nine miles from the ocean. On the ocean side the land is mainly agricultural; on the inland side it is specially adapted to fruit. We drove about it, and in Tustin City, which has many pleasant residences and a vacant "boom" hotel, through endless plantations of oranges. On the road toward Los Angeles we passed large herds of cattle and sheep, and fine groves of the English walnut, which thrives especially well in this soil and the neighborhood of the sea. There is comparatively little waste land in this valley district, as one may see by driving through the country about Santa Ana, Orange, Anaheim, Tustin City, etc. Anaheim is a prosperous German colony. It was here that Madame Modjeska and her husband, Count Bozenta, first settled in California. They own and occupy now a picturesque ranch in the Santiago Cañon of the Santa Ana range, twenty-two miles from Santa Ana. This is one of the richest regions in the State, and with its fair quota of working population it will be one of the most productive.

From Newport, on the coast, or from San Pedro, one may visit the island of Santa Catalina. Want of time prevented our going there. Sportsmen enjoy there the exciting pastime of hunting the wild goat. From the photographs I saw, and from all I heard of it, it must be as picturesque a resort in natural beauty as the British Channel Islands.

Los Angeles is the metropolitan centre of all this region. A handsome, solid, thriving city, environed by gardens, gay everywhere with flowers, it is too well known to require any description from me. To the traveller from the East it will always be a surprise. Its growth has been phenomenal, and although it may not equal the expectations of the crazy excitement of 1886-7, 50,000 people is a great assemblage for a new city which numbered only about 11,000 in 1880. It of course felt the subsidence of the "boom," but while I missed the feverish crowds of 1887, I was struck with its substantial progress in fine, solid buildings, pavements, sewerage, railways, educational facilities, and ornamental grounds. It has a secure hold on the commerce of the region. The assessment roll of the city increased from $7,627,632 in 1881 to $44,871,073 in 1889. Its bank business, public buildings, school-houses, and street improvements are in accord with this increase, and show solid, vigor-

OLIVE-TREES SIX YEARS OLD.

ous growth. It is altogether an attractive city, whether seen on a drive through its well-planted and bright avenues, or looked down on from the hills which are climbed by the cable roads. A curious social note was the effect of the "boom" excitement upon the birth rate. The report of children under the age of one year was in 1887, 271 boy babies and 264 girl babies; from 1887 to 1888 there were only 176 boy babies and 162 girl babies. The return at the end of 1889 was 465 boy babies and 500 girl babies.

Although Los Angeles County still produces a considerable quantity of wine and brandy, I have an impression that the raising of raisins will supplant wine-making largely in southern California, and that the principal wine-producing will be in the northern portions of the State. It is certain that the best quality is grown in the foot-hills. The reputation of "California wines" has been much injured by placing upon the market crude juice that was in no sense wine. Great improvement has been made in the past three to five years, not only in the vine and knowledge of the soil adapted to it, but in the handling and the curing of the wine. One can now find without much difficulty excellent table wines—sound claret, good white Reisling, and sauterne. None of these wines are exactly like the foreign wines, and it may be some time before the taste accustomed to foreign wines is educated to like them. But in Eastern markets some of the best brands are already much called for, and I think it only a question of time and a little more experience when the best California wines will be popular. I found in the San Francisco market excellent red wines at $3 50 the case, and, what was still more remarkable, at some of the best hotels sound, agreeable claret at from fifteen to twenty cents the pint bottle.

It is quite unnecessary to emphasize the attractions of Santa Barbara, or the productiveness of the valleys in the counties of Santa Barbara and Ventura. There is no more poetic region on the continent than the bay south of Point Conception, and the pen and the camera have made the world tolerably familiar with it. There is a graciousness, a softness, a color in the sea, the cañons, the mountains there that dwells in the memory. It is capable of inspiring the same love that the Greek colonists felt for the region between the bays of Salerno and Naples. It is as fruitful as the Italian shores, and can support as dense a population. The figures that have been given as to productiveness and variety of productions apply to it. Having more winter rainfall than the counties south of it, agriculture is profitable in most years. Since the railway was made down the valley of the Santa Clara River and along the coast to Santa Barbara, a great impulse has been given to farming. Orange and other fruit orchards have increased. Near Buenaventura I saw hundreds of acres of Lima beans. The yield is about one ton to the acre. With good farming the valleys yield crops of corn, barley, and wheat much above the average. Still it is a fruit region, and no variety has yet been tried that does not produce very well there. The rapid growth of all trees has enabled the region to demonstrate in a short time that there is scarcely any that it cannot naturalize. The curious growths of tropical lands, the trees of aromatic and medicinal gums, the trees of exquisite foliage and wealth of fragrant blossoms, the sturdy forest natives, and the bearers of edible nuts, are all to be found in the gardens and by the road-side—from New England, from the Southern States, from Europe, from North and South Africa, southern Asia, China, Japan, from Australia and New Zealand and South America. The region is an arboreal and botanical garden on an immense scale, and full of surprises. The floriculture is even more astonishing. Every land is represented. The profusion and vigor are as wonderful as the variety. At a flower show in Santa Barbara were exhibited 160 varieties of roses all cut from one garden the same morning. The open garden rivals the Eastern conservatory. The country is new, and many of the conditions of life may be primitive and rude, but it is impossible that any region shall not be beautiful, clothed with such a profusion of bloom and color.

I have spoken of the rapid growth. The practical advantage of this as to fruit trees is that one begins to have an income from them here sooner than in the East. No one need be under the delusion that he can live in California without work, or thrive without incessant and intelligent industry, but the distinction of the country for the fruit-grower is the rapidity with which trees and vines mature

to the extent of being profitable. But nothing thrives without care, and kindly as the climate is to the weak, it cannot be too much insisted on that this is no place for confirmed invalids who have not money enough to live without work.

The immense county of San Diego is on the threshold of its development. It has comparatively only spots of cultivation here and there, in an area on the western slope of the county only, that Mr. Van Dyke estimates to contain about one million acres of good arable land for farming and fruit-raising. This mountainous region is full of charming valleys, and hidden among the hills are fruitful nooks capable of sustaining thriving communities. There is no doubt about the salubrity of the climate, and one can literally suit himself as to temperature by choosing his elevation. The traveller by rail down the wild Temecula Cañon will have some idea of the picturesqueness of the country, and, as he descends in the broadening valley, of the beautiful mountain parks of live-oak and clear running water, and of the richness both for grazing and grain of the ranches of the Santa Margarita, Las Flores, and Santa Rosa. Or if he will see what a few years of vigorous cultivation will do, he may visit Escondido, on the river of that name, which is at an elevation of less than a thousand feet, and fourteen miles from the ocean. This is only one of many settlements that have great natural beauty and thrifty industrial life. In that region are numerous attractive villages. I have a report from a little cañon, a few miles north of Escondido, where a woman with an invalid husband settled in 1883. The ground was thickly covered with brush, and its only product was rabbits and quails. In 1888 they had 100 acres cleared and fenced, mostly devoted to orchard fruits and berries. They had in good bearing over 1200 fruit trees, among them 200 oranges, and 283 figs, which yielded one and a half tons of figs a week during the bearing season, from August to November. The sprouts of the peach-trees grew twelve feet in 1889. Of course such a little fruit farm as this is the result of self-denial and hard work, but I am sure that the experiment in this region need not be exceptional.

San Diego will be to the southern part of the State what San Francisco is to the northern. Nature seems to have arranged for this, by providing a magnificent har-

SEXTON NURSERIES, NEAR SANTA BARBARA.

bor, when it shut off the southern part by a mountain range. During the town-lot lunacy it was said that San Diego could not grow because it had no back country, and the retort was that it needed no back country, its harbor would command commerce. The fallacy of this assumption lay in the forgetfulness of the fact that the profitable and peculiar exports of southern California must go East by rail, and reach a market in the shortest possible time, and that the inhabitants look to the Pacific for comparatively little of the imports they need. If the isthmus route were opened by a ship-canal, San Diego would doubtless have a great share of the Pacific trade, and when the population of that part of the State is large enough to demand great importations from the islands and lands of the Pacific, this har-

bor will not go begging. But in its present development the entire Pacific trade of Japan, China, and the islands gives only a small dividend each to the competing ports. For these developments this fine harbor must wait, but meantime the wealth and prosperity of San Diego lie at its doors. A country as large as the three richest New England States, with enormous wealth of mineral and stone in its mountains, with one of the finest climates in the world, with a million acres of arable land, is certainly capable of building up one great seaport town. These million of acres on the western slope of the mountain ranges of the country are geographically tributary to San Diego, and almost every acre by its products is certain to attain a high value.

The end of the ridiculous speculation in lots of 1887–8 was not so disastrous in the loss of money invested, or even in the ruin of great expectations by the collapse of fictitious values, as in the stoppage of immigration. The country has been ever since adjusting itself to a normal growth, and the recovery is just in proportion to the arrival of settlers who come to work and not to speculate. I had heard that the "boom" had left San Diego and· vicinity the "deadest" region to be found anywhere. A speculator would probably so regard it. But the people have had a great accession of common-sense. The expectation of attracting settlers by a fictitious show has subsided, and attention is directed to the development of the natural riches of the country. Since the boom San Diego has perfected a splendid system of drainage, paved its streets, extended its railways, built up the business part of the town solidly and handsomely, and greatly improved the mesa above the town. In all essentials of permanent growth it is much better in appearance than in 1887. Business is better organized, and, best of all, there is an intelligent appreciation of the agricultural resources of the county. It is discovered that San Diego has a " back country" capable of producing great wealth. The Chamber of Commerce has organized a permanent exhibition of products. It is assisted in this work of stimulation by competition by a " Ladies' Annex," a society numbering some five hundred ladies, who devote themselves not to æsthetic pursuits, but to the quickening of all the industries of the farm and the garden, and all public improvements. To the mere traveller who devotes only a couple of weeks to an examination of this region it is evident that the spirit of industry is in the ascendant, and the result is a most gratifying increase in orchards and vineyards, and the storage and distribution of water for irrigation. The region is unsurpassed for the production of the orange, the lemon, the raisin grape, the fig, and the olive. The great reservoir in the Cuyamaca, which supplies San Diego, sends its flume around the fertile valley of El Cajon (which has already a great reputation for its raisins), and this has become a garden, the land rising in value every year. The region of National City and Chula Vista is supplied by the reservoir made by the great Sweetwater dam — a marvel of engineering skill—and is not only most productive in fruit, but is attractive by pretty villas and most sightly and agreeable homes. It is an unanswerable reply to the inquiry if this region was not killed by the boom that all the arable land, except that staked out for fancy city prices, has steadily risen in value. This is true of all the bay region down through Otay (where a promising watch factory is es-

tablished) to the border at Tia Juana. The rate of settlement in the county outside of the cities and towns has been greater since the boom than before—a most healthful indication for the future. According to the school census of 1889, Mr. Van Dyke estimates a permanent growth of nearly 50,000 people in the county in four years. Half of these are well distributed in small settlements which have the advantages of roads, mails, and school-houses, and which offer to settlers who wish to work adjacent unimproved land at prices which experience shows are still moderate.

In this imperfect conspectus of a vast territory I should be sorry to say anything that can raise false expectations. The country is very big, and though scarcely any part of it has not some advantages, and notwithstanding the census figures of our population, it will be a long time before our vast territory will fill up. California must wait with the rest. But it seems to me to have a great future. Its position in the Union with regard to its peculiar productions is unique. It can and will supply us with much that we now import, and labor and capital sooner or later will find their profit in meeting the growing demand for California products.

There are many people in the United States who could prolong life by moving to southern California; there are many who would find life easier there by reason of the climate, and because out-door labor is more agreeable there the year through; many who have to fight the weather and a niggardly soil for existence could there have pretty little homes with less expense of money and labor. It is well that people for whom this is true should know it. It need not influence those who are already well placed to try the fortune of a distant country and new associations.

I need not emphasize the disadvantage in regard to beauty of a land that can for half the year only keep a vernal appearance by irrigation. But to eyes accustomed to it there is something pleasing in the contrast of the green valleys with the brown and gold and red of the hills. The picture in my mind for the future of the land of the sun, of the mountains, of the sea—which is only an enlargement of the picture of the present—is one of great beauty. The rapid growth of fruit and ornamental trees and the profusion of flowers render easy the making of a love-

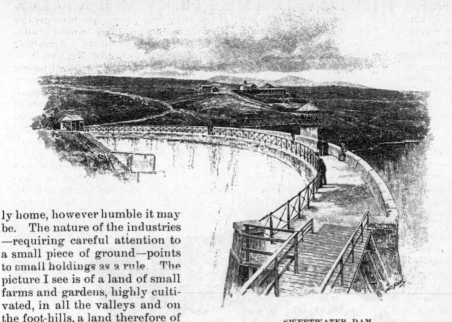

SWEETWATER DAM.

ly home, however humble it may be. The nature of the industries —requiring careful attention to a small piece of ground—points to small holdings as a rule. The picture I see is of a land of small farms and gardens, highly cultivated, in all the valleys and on the foot-hills, a land therefore of luxuriance and great productiveness and agreeable homes. I see everywhere the gardens, the vineyards, the orchards, with the various greens of the olive, the fig, and the orange. It is always picturesque, because the country is broken and even rugged; it is always interesting, because of the contrast with the mountains and the desert; it has the color that makes southern Italy so poetic. It is the fairest field for the experiment of a contented community without any poverty and without excessive wealth.

ELK HUNTING IN THE ROCKY MOUNTAINS

OF all the large game on the American continent, the elk (*Cervus canadensis*) is the noblest, the grandest, the stateliest. I would detract nothing from the noble game qualities of the moose, caribou, deer, or mountain-sheep. Each has its peculiar points of excellence which endear it to the heart of the sportsman, but the elk possesses more than any of the others. In size he towers far above all except the moose. In sagacity, caution, cunning, and wariness he is the peer, if not the superior, of them all. He is always on the alert, his keen scent, his piercing eye, his acute sense of hearing, combining to render him a vigilant sentinel of his own safety.

His great size and powerful muscular construction give him almost unbounded endurance. When alarmed or pursued he will travel for twenty or thirty hours, at a rapid swinging trot, without stopping for food or rest. He is a proud, fearless ranger, and even when simply migrating from one range of mountains to another, will travel from seventy-five to a hundred miles without lying down. He is a marvellous mountaineer, and considering his immense size and weight, often ascends to heights that seem incredible. He may of-

FOLLOWING AN ELK TRAIL.

ten be found away up to timber line, and will traverse narrow passes and defiles, climbing over walls of rock and through fissures where it would seem impossible for so large an animal, with such massive antlers as he carries, to go. He chooses his route, however, with rare good judgment, and all mountaineers know that an elk trail is the best that can possibly be selected over any given section of mountainous country. His faculty of traversing dense jungles and windfalls is equally astonishing. If given his own time, he will move quietly and easily through the worst of these, leaping over logs higher than his back as gracefully and almost as lightly as the deer; yet let a herd of elk be alarmed and start on a run through one of these labyrinthine masses, and they will make a noise like a regiment of cavalry on a precipitous charge.

I have stood on the margin of a quaking-asp thicket and heard a large band of elk coming toward me that had been

"jumped" and fired upon by my friend at the other side, and the frightful noise of their horns pounding the trees, their hoofs striking each other and the numerous rocks, the crashing of dead branches, with the snorting of the affrighted beasts, might well have struck terror to the heart of any one unused to such sights and sounds, and have caused him to seek safety in flight. But by standing my ground I was enabled to get in a couple of shots at short range, and to bring down two of the finest animals in the herd.

The whistle of the elk is a sound which many have tried to describe, yet I doubt if any one who may have read all the descriptions of it ever written would recognize it on a first hearing. It is a most strange, weird, peculiar sound, baffling all efforts of the most skilful word-painter. It is only uttered by the male, and there is the same variety in the sound made by different stags as in different human voices. Usually the cry begins and ends with a sort of grunt, somewhat like the bellow of a domestic cow cut short, but the interlude is a long-drawn, melodious, flute-like sound that rises and falls with a rhythmical cadence, floating on the still evening air, by which it is often wafted with singular distinctness to great distances. By other individuals, or even by the same individual at various times, either the first or last of these abrupt sounds is omitted, and only the other, in connection with the long-drawn, silver-toned strain, is given.

The stag utters this call only in the love-making season, and for the purpose of ascertaining the whereabouts of his dusky mate, who responds by a short and utterly unmusical sound, similar to that with which the male begins or ends his call.

On one occasion, when hunting in the Rocky Mountains, in northern Wyoming, I had a most exciting hunt after a large bull elk. We had killed a cow and calf in the evening about four miles from our camp, high up on the mountain-side. Our photographer was not with us at the time, and before we could go to camp and get him it would be too late to have pictures of them made that night, and the chances were that if left there alone till morning, they would be destroyed by bears, which were very numerous in that vicinity. So I decided to camp by and stand guard over them.

I built a fire near the carcasses, stretch-

EXTERMINATORS.

ed up a rubber poncho for a shelter, cut down a large bed of hemlock boughs, provided a liberal supply of wood, and by keeping up a bright fire was able to save our game from the ravages of Bruin.

Rain fell heavily nearly all night, but toward morning it grew colder. The rain turned to snow, which fell to the depth of about an inch. Then the clouds broke, the temperature continued to fall, and day dawned upon a most beautiful spectacle. Pines, cedars, hemlocks, and in fact every variety of tree and shrub that grew there, were tinged with fleecy white, the snow having frozen on the most delicate twigs and branches as it fell.

Just at daylight I heard the whistle of an elk. It came from the mountain-side above me, and in a moment I was moving toward the locality whence came the thrilling sound, rifle in hand, and peering eagerly forward in search of the game. Arriving at the point whence the sound came, I found the tracks, large as those of a three-year-old steer, but the author of them was not there. While pondering over them the bull winded his horn from the top of another ridge half a mile away. He had not heard or scented me, but was roving wildly in search of a mate, for it was the love-making season. I pushed forward across deep gulches, over high peaks and "hog-backs," and arrived at the scene of his second amorous call, to find only his tracks again. It was extremely difficult to move through the thickets of underbrush and over the rocks and beds of frozen leaves fast enough to overtake him without making a noise that would alarm him, and the utmost caution was necessary. Consequently a long chase was the result. Presently, however, I heard a rustling in the leaves, and saw the snow fall from a cedar-tree. Then all was quiet again, and peering cautiously through every opening in the net-work of twigs, I was finally able to see a small patch of reddish-brown hair, which, from its peculiar shade, I took to be well back on his side. As it did not cover a vital part, it was not a desirable place to plant a ball, but I was not in a position to choose, nor could I get into such a position without danger of losing my chance of a shot entirely. So, adjusting the shining front sight of my rifle in the centre of that little brown spot, I fired. There was a great rushing, stumbling, crashing in the brush, and in an

instant I saw the huge beast dash across an opening in the thicket. Another cartridge had found its way into the chamber of the rifle, the heel-plate was already pressing my shoulder, and simultaneously with the appearance of the game there was another sharp report, and again the elk stumbled. This ball had gone close to his heart, and he could not travel far. I followed, and soon saw him standing with his head thrown forward. He was bleeding rapidly, but desiring to end his suffering as soon as possible, I fired several more shots in rapid succession. Finally he fell, and then, as I walked up and stood over his prostrate form, my soul was filled with remorse and regret at having caused the death of this majestic monarch of the forest.

His head now graces my library, the proudest and grandest of all my many trophies of the chase. Yet I never look at it without feeling a pang of sorrow for the part I played in that great tragedy. His antlers measured as follows: length of main beam, 4 feet 8 inches; length of brow tine, 1 foot 6½ inches; length of bes tine, 1 foot 8½ inches; length of royal tine, 1 foot 7 inches; length of surroyal, 1 foot 8¼ inches; circumference around burr, 1 foot 3¼ inches; circumference around beam above, 12 inches; circumference of brow tine at base, 7½ inches; spread of main beams at tips, 4 feet 9 inches. They are one of the largest and finest pairs of antlers of which I have any knowledge. The animal would have weighed nearly a thousand pounds.

The elk is strictly gregarious, and in winter-time especially the animals gather into large bands, and a few years ago herds of from five hundred to a thousand were not uncommon. Now, however, their numbers have been so far reduced by the ravages of "skin hunters" and others that one will rarely find more than twenty-five or thirty in a band.

In the fall of 1879 a party of three men were sight-seeing and hunting in the Yellowstone National Park, and having prolonged their stay until late in October, were overtaken by a terrible snow-storm, which completely blockaded and obliterated all the trails, and filled the gulches, cañons, and coulees to such a depth that their horses could not travel over them at all. They had lain in camp three days waiting for the storm to abate; but as it continued to grow in severity, and as the snow became deeper and deeper, their situation grew daily and hourly more alarming. Their stock of provisions was low, they had no shelter sufficient to withstand the rigors of a winter at that high altitude, and it was fast becoming a question whether they should ever be able to escape beyond the snow-clad peaks and snow-filled cañons with which they were hemmed in. Their only hope of escape was by abandoning their horses, and constructing snow-shoes which might keep them above the snow; but in this case they could not carry bedding and food enough to last them throughout the several days that the journey would occupy to the nearest ranch, and the chances of killing game *en route* after the severe weather had set in were extremely precarious. They had already set about making snow-shoes from the skin of an elk which they had saved. One pair had been completed,

A SKIN HUNTER.

and the storm having abated, one of the party set out to look over the surrounding country for the most feasible route by which to get out, and also to try if possible to find game of some kind. He had gone about a mile toward the northeast when he came upon the fresh trail of a large band of elk that were moving

toward the east. He followed, and in a short time came up with them. They were travelling in single file, led by a powerful old bull, who wallowed through snow, in which only his head and neck were visible, with all the patience and perseverance of a faithful old ox. The others followed him—the stronger ones in front and the weaker ones bringing up the rear. There were thirty-seven in the band, and by the time they had all walked in the same line they left it an open, well-beaten trail. The hunter approached within a few yards of them. They were greatly alarmed when they saw him, and made a few bounds in various directions; but seeing their struggles were in vain, they meekly submitted to what seemed their impending fate, and fell back in rear of their file-leader. This would have been the golden opportunity of a skin hunter, who could and would have shot them all down in their tracks from a single stand. But such was not the mission of our friend. He saw in this noble, struggling band a means of deliverance from what had threatened to be a wintry grave for him and his companions. He did not fire a shot, and did not in any way create unnecessary alarm amongst the elk, but hurried back to camp and reported to his friends what he had seen.

In a moment the camp was a scene of activity and excitement. Tent, bedding, provisions, everything that was absolutely necessary to their journey, were hurriedly packed upon their pack animals; saddles were placed, rifles were slung to the saddles, and leaving all surplus baggage, such as trophies of their hunt, mineral specimens, and curios of various kinds, for future comers, they started for the elk trail. They had a slow, tedious, and laborious task breaking a way through the deep snow to reach it, but by walking and leading their saddle animals ahead, the pack animals were enabled to follow slowly. Finally they reached the trail of the elk herd, and following this, after nine days of tedious and painful travelling, the party arrived at a ranch between the upper falls of the Yellowstone River and Yellowstone Lake, on the Stinking River, which was kept by a "squaw man" and his wife, where they were enabled to lodge and recruit themselves and their stock, and whence they finally reached their homes in safety. The band of elk passed on down the river, and our tourists never saw them again; but they have doubtless long ere this all fallen a prey to the ruthless war that is constantly being waged against them by hunters white and red.

It is sad to think that such a noble creature as the American elk is doomed to early and absolute extinction, but such is nevertheless the fact. Year by year his mountain *habitat* is being surrounded and encroached upon by the advancing line of settlements, as the fisherman encircles the struggling mass of fishes in the clear pond with his long and closely meshed net. The lines are drawn closer and closer every year. These lines are the ranches of cattle and sheep raisers, the cabins and towns of miners, the stations and residences of employés of the railroads. All these places are made the shelters and temporary abiding-places of Eastern and foreign sportsmen who go out to the mountains to hunt. Worse than this, they are made the permanent abiding-places and constitute the active and convenient markets of the nefarious and unconscionable skin hunter and meat hunter. Here he can find a ready market for the meats and skins he brings in, and an opportunity to spend the proceeds of such outrageous traffic in ranch whiskey and revelry. The ranchmen themselves hunt and lay in their stock of meat for the year

when the game comes down into the valleys. The Indians, when they have eaten up their government rations, lie in wait for the elk in the same manner. So that when the first great snows of the autumn or winter fall in the high ranges, when the elk band together and seek refuge in the valleys, as did the herd that our fortunate tourists followed out, they find a mixed and hungry horde waiting for them at the mouth of every cañon. Before they have reached the valley where the snowfall is light enough to allow them to live through the winter their skins are drying in the neighboring "shacks."

This unequal, one-sided warfare, this ruthless slaughter of inoffensive creatures, cannot last always. Indeed it can last but little longer. In ranges where only a few years ago herds of four or five hundred elk could be found, the hunter of to-day considers himself in rare luck when he finds a band of ten or twelve, and even small bands of any number are so rare that a good hunter may often hunt a week in the best elk country to be found anywhere without getting a single shot. All the Territories have good, wholesome game-laws which forbid the killing of game animals except during two or three months in the fall; but these laws are not enforced. They are a dead letter on the statute-books, and the illegal and illegitimate slaughter goes on unchecked.

THE GREAT AMERICAN DESERT

IN the maps of the United States contained in the school geographies of thirty years ago, that strip of territory lying east of the Rocky Mountains and west of the Missouri River, extending on the south to the Mexican border, and to British America at the north, was verily a *terra incognita*. A considerable portion of these United States was designated as "The Great American Desert" on our maps. This feature of our old United States maps has been dropped only within the last twenty years. Even where a better intelligence has latterly completely expunged it from the maps, it still remains obstinately fixed in the minds of thousands of otherwise intelligent people, who have not kept pace with the developments of the past quarter of a century.

A very interesting book could be written on the history of the cattle trade, which has grown to enormous proportions on the vast plains of the West. It is not our purpose, however, to dwell on this feature of the history of our desert, because, owing to the tinge of romance which is connected with the ranch, the vaquero, the broncho, and the lasso, the subject has already received attention from many pens. The development of this region presents even more curious and interesting features than the cow-boy and his mustang.

It may surprise the younger readers of this Magazine to learn that a great part of our desert is designated on the maps of to-day as Dakota, Kansas, and Nebraska. There is enough of it left for a kingdom, after it has been robbed of these two large States and a Territory of dimensions geographically appalling, which is knocking very hard at the door of the sisterhood of States for admission—already surpassing some of them in wealth and population.

It is impossible to compute how much damage has resulted to the interests of the State of Nebraska from the fact that the Union Pacific, long its only trunk line, crosses it through the Platte Valley, the dreariest portion of the entire State. It is unfair to judge of any country from such superficial observations as are made of Kansas and Nebraska from the cars; and as these, together with Dakota, show the most remarkable and rapid progress toward civilization, let us limit our discussion to that portion of the desert which they occupy. The conditions of pioneer life in each of them are substantially the same, and speaking for one of them is generally speaking for all.

Shortly after the financial disasters of 1873, precipitated by the failure of Jay Cooke, and when the stock of his pet road, the Northern Pacific, was selling at nine dollars a share, a number of shrewd investors, seeing the opportunity of buying this stock on the market, selecting railroad grant lands along the line of the Northern Pacific in Dakota—which the road had then just penetrated—and paying for them in this almost worthless stock at par, bought large tracts of these lands, and began as an experiment to till them. Soon marvellous stories were heard repeated among Eastern farmers about the fertility of the soil and the remarkable quality of the grain grown on it. About the same period the surplus population of Iowa and Missouri drifted into middle Nebraska and Kansas. There was only a sprinkling of them, but when the locust scourge came in 1874 and 1875 they found they had no use for the broad acres at their disposal in that country, and the first wave of civilization was driven back. The few who staid through two years of the pestilence suffered another raid from the destroyers in

THE DAWN OF CIVILIZATION.

1876, and then they too succumbed to the inevitable. Fortunately for Dakota, there were not enough people within her borders during these years to afford any comfort to the grasshoppers, and thus it happened that the sufferers, returning penniless ·to their Eastern homes, with woful tales of their sufferings, had nothing to say of Dakota. Kansas and Nebraska, however, received a very thorough advertising from the evil, and the result was that when, with returning financial prosperity in 1877 and 1878, the tide of surplus population again rolled westward, Dakota was the promised land; nor was it until Dakota was well filled by this influx that western Kansas and Nebraska received any benefit from it, several years later. This was a tidal wave, though it came never to recede; for now this territory is a part and parcel of the resistless sea of population which is steadily rolling toward the Pacific slope.

But at what a cost has this final success been achieved! How many reverses and failures before a permanent foothold has been established in the desert by the sturdy pioneers! Sturdy? God save the mark! I wonder if it is not true of all pioneers, as it is of these, that as a rule they were the poor devils of the community, who were forced by stern necessity to go to a new country to strive again to make a stand in the battle of life? There are old stagers here who "pioneered it" first in Illinois, next in Iowa, then in eastern Nebraska, western Nebraska, and who now have Colorado in view for their next stand. One wonders where they will stop. Experience proves that it takes three sets of pioneers to make a permanent population. The first settler, with rare exceptions, ekes out a half-starved existence until he can make proof on his land; by this time he is ready and eager to sell out to one of the second crop of pioneers—men who bring a little money with them to fight the battle with; as a rule, though, the necessity of incurring debts to keep things going beats this second class, and they in turn give way to the thrifty farmers who come prepared and able to stay. For it must not be supposed that the original homesteader is necessarily a farmer. You will find all sorts and conditions of men among them, from ministers to cow-boys, from bankrupt business men to the latest exile from Russia. All of these, together with professional men and tradesmen in the villages, and a fair sprinkling of *bona fide* farmers, appear in the ranks of the homesteaders.

And the oddities of their life!—what

A SOD HOUSE, DAKOTA.

chapters of queer tales could be written of them! To begin with, the habitation of the homesteader is either a dugout or a house built of squares of sod taken from the prairie—Nebraska or Kansas brick, as they are facetiously termed. The dugout consists of a hole dug in the side of a cañon or any sort of depression on the prairie which will serve as a wind-break. This hole is roofed across, about on a level with the prairie, with inch boards, and these are covered with sod. A foot or so of stove-pipe protruding from the roof is the sole indication of a human habitation. One room generally serves all the purposes of the homesteader and his family. If he prospers for a season, he adds to the front of his abode by erecting walls of sod on the sides and putting in a new front, the old one serving as a partition between the two rooms. This is considered a commodious dwelling. After riding over the quarter section looking for an owner, espying such an abode, and guiding your team carefully down a break-neck descent to the front door, would it surprise you, upon entering this hole in the ground, to find, for instance, a very modern organ with an imposing cathedral back towering high in one corner of the room? But this is no cause for astonishment—

very frequently organs and ornate designs in furniture are to be found in the dugouts. Or, if the lady of the house should invite you to remain for the meeting of the literary club there in the evening, would you stare at that? Not at all. Literary clubs, which the members ride all the way from five to twenty miles to attend, and where they discuss with great earnestness everything from the latest political problem to the most abstruse point in metaphysics, are quite the regular thing with our homesteaders. But to behold this life so full of paradoxes in the height of its incongruousness you should be a spectator in the dugout when a neighborhood dance is in full blast. The earthen walls have been skilfully tapestried for the occasion with calico, and when the fun begins, the clay floor speedily responds to the capering of the many twinkling feet, and there arises a cloud of dust that would stifle an Indian. But, bless you! they don't mind a bit of dust. A polished floor and the most perfect system of ventilation attainable could add nothing to their enjoyment.

The homesteaders are very honest. You can leave a house unlocked at all times and your stores are perfectly safe—with the exception of what liquor you may have on hand for medicinal purposes. In other words, the homesteader will steal whiskey every time. As a class they are neighborly, kind to one in distress, and exceedingly hospitable.

But it must not be supposed that all homesteaders live in dugouts or sleep six or seven in a room; such experiences attach to the first year or two of frontier life more than to any later period. Many sightly, commodious, and comfortable sod houses have been built, of which our illustrations will afford examples. The walls are usually two feet in thickness, the roof shingled, doors and windows set into the walls, and the house plastered inside, sometimes outside, altogether making a very neat and desirable residence. These structures, too, are free from the annoyances of dugouts, in which are found all manner of insects and rodents. Occasionally a rattlesnake will burrow through the earthen sides, and coil himself snugly in the bedclothes, where you will find him on a cold morning. Such intruders are rare, but there are some people who strenuously object to even rare visits of this sort; such are usually energetic enough to get out of the old house and into a new one before spending many months in an abode so uncomfortably near to nature's heart.

It is very common to find a lone and unprotected female "holding down a claim," as the Western phrase runs. The women of the East would look aghast at the prospect of living alone in a sod house for six months, miles from the nearest neighbor. Yet experience proves that the "unprotected" is much safer out on the lonely prairie than she would be in New York city. I never heard or read of a woman on a homestead receiving an insult at the hands of anybody. To be sure, they are always armed, and know how to handle a pistol, but they rarely have a more deadly use for it than the killing of a jack-rabbit or a prairie-dog. Such women complain more of loneliness than of fear. For whatever charms solitude may have for the sage, it certainly has none for the fair sex, not even for our hardy Western representatives of it. Here is one of their ingenious ways of avoiding it. Two of them will locate on adjoining "quarters," and build their houses on the dividing line; so that while each house is on its occupant's claim, the two structures are practically one, affording frequent oppor-

tunities for the ladies to call on each other and discuss social topics. They are all provided with ponies, and think nothing of a horseback ride of fifteen or twenty miles, either for business or pleasure.

The land laws of the United States are such that a citizen of this country, or one who has declared his intention to become a citizen, can, under certain restrictions, file his homestead or pre-emption papers at a nominal cost on a quarter section—one hundred and sixty acres—of any agricultural land belonging to the government. If he makes an actual residence on his homestead for five years, he can make proof of the fact before the register of the United States land-office of the district in which his land lies, and take what is termed a Final Receiver's Receipt for his quarter section. When the Circumlocution Office at Washington—Department of the Interior—gets around to making out a patent from the government for him, he exchanges the receipt for the patent. This takes from two to five years after making proof; and meantime the receiver's receipt answers for all practical purposes, such as buying, selling, or mortgaging, for a warrantee deed from the United States. Another section of the law provides that in case the homesteader wishes to make proof after having resided for the space of six months on his land, he may do so, and be entitled to the receiver's receipt upon the payment of one dollar and a quarter per acre for the land. This is termed a commuted entry, and nine-tenths of the rights are used in this way, for very good and sufficient reasons. It is very seldom that the party holding the claim can sustain life on it for five years without borrowing money. To do this he is obliged to "prove up," that is, get title from the government. Accordingly he borrows money from one of the numerous companies that negotiate farm mortgage loans—perhaps six or eight hundred dollars, according to the location of his land. The company pays out for him at the land-office the required sum for a commuted entry—one dollar and a quarter per acre—and gives him the balance of the loan, taking a mortgage on his farm for security. Under the pre-emption laws precisely the same commuted entry can be made, though under these laws the settler is obliged to pay the government two hundred dollars for his claim, whether he proves up after a six months' residence,

A PRAIRIE TOWN.

or waits the full limit of his time for making proof—thirty-three months. One man is entitled to both of these rights, and also to a third quarter section under the timber culture act. So it may be seen that our liberal government allows a man—or woman either, if she be single or the head of a family—to acquire four hundred and eighty acres of as valuable farming land as can be found in America, and at a total expense, if the full benefits of each law are taken, of less than five hundred dollars.

But the worst vice of the average pioneer is his improvidence. It is true that there are many things against him, such as poverty, to begin with, exorbitant railway charges, high rates of interest, and finally, and fatally in most cases, a total lack of thrift and management. His first step is to make his commuted entry at a cost of two hundred dollars. This means a mortgage on his farm. Then it is not a question of how little money he can get along with, but how much money he can borrow on his "quarter." They talk the matter over with great interest among themselves, and will travel fifty miles half a dozen times if they hear of an opportunity to make a deal with a loan agent whose company will lend a hundred dollars more on a quarter section than the others.

With few exceptions the only people among the first comers who retain their farms are the foreigners, principally Germans and Scandinavians. These men, drilled into the most rigid habits of economy by the experience of hundreds of years in a hard struggle for existence, will start with the Americans under precisely similar circumstances, and while the latter give way under the severe conditions imposed upon them, the foreigners will surmount the same obstacles, and make a success of life; if indeed they do not go to the other extreme, and work or starve themselves to death—instances not so rare as one might imagine.

The farms of nearly all of the unfortunate representatives of old-time Yankee industry and economy are provided with the most expensive kind of modern agricultural machinery, for all of which they are in debt, and which is left exposed to the elements when not in use.

Yet these people are the pioneers of a true civilization; upon the wrecks of their fortunes abler hands will build anew; and if the second attempt fails, success crowns a third effort. Here the law of the survival of the fittest is seen in full play.

Let us glance further at the financial aspect of the situation in the desert. Money, of course, is the prime factor in all problems of civilization. Without the wealth which begets leisure, and the leisure which begets thought, there would be no progress in human affairs. But out here we must begin a step back of Buckle's proposition: we must first acquire the wealth. From what has been said it will be readily inferred that the homesteader did not bring it with him; rather he came because he lacked it; and it takes many a long and hard year of labor to accumulate it by farming, even under the most favorable conditions. Thus it follows of necessity that the new West is heavily in debt. The western frontier always has been, but as the border line steadily advances toward the Sierra Nevada, the mortgages are lifted from the older States, the rates of interest lessen, and the indebtedness is gradually extinguished.

Twenty years ago, money was worth ten per cent. in Michigan; to-day it is worth six to seven per cent.; fifteen years ago it was still worth ten per cent. in Iowa; to-day it loans at seven to eight per cent. Fifteen years ago it was considered an oversight if a business block in Chicago was not covered with a Boston mortgage. To-day not a little of the money which helps to develop the desert comes from Chicago—no longer a borrower, but a lender, in the world of finance.

It required millions upon millions of dollars of borrowed money every year to make possible the extraordinary progress of Dakota, Kansas, and Nebraska during the past ten years. One of the first things to excite surprise in the mind of a stranger is the great number of banks in these new Western towns; they are everywhere numerous. But their combined capital would not suffice to supply a respectable fraction of the demand for money in their territory. The great bulk of it comes from the East, New England particularly, in the way of farm loans. These are negotiated by loan and trust companies, whose name is legion—there are hundreds of them in the business. Their method of procedure is well understood here, but perhaps a *résumé* of it may be of interest to Eastern readers. They have loan agents in every small town, who take an application from the party wanting a loan, and forward it to the Western office of the company. Omaha, Kansas City,

Minneapolis, St. Paul, Lincoln, and Sioux City are the principal centres. The application, if accepted, is filed, and the necessary papers being made out, they are forwarded with the money to the front. The farmer signs a mortgage, running, say, five years, for one thousand dollars. The rate of interest he pays is ten per cent., but it is divided in this way: the principal mortgage draws seven per cent., and the semiannual interest coupons on this are for thirty-five dollars each. He then signs a second mortgage on his farm for an amount equal to three per cent. per annum for five years on the loan of one thousand dollars; this is divided into semiannual payments of fifteen dollars each—not bearing interest, as these are really interest notes—payable on the same dates as the interest coupons of the principal mortgage are. The loan company then sells the first mortgage drawing seven per cent. to the Eastern investor, keeping the second mortgage—or what is really the balance of the ten per cent. interest which the farmer pays—for its profit. It will be observed that there is a handsome thing in

REMNANT OF AN OLDER RACE.

this business for the companies, and the result is that the competition caused by numberless new companies entering the field to secure the profits is exceedingly fierce, and cuts the margin for them finer every year.

Many ingenious variations are based on this business. Some companies sell a guaranteed loan—principal and interest guaranteed by them—at six per cent.; a loan without their guarantee at eight per cent. Others deposit their mortgages with trust companies, and issue debenture bonds against them, drawing six per cent. interest, and running from ten to fifteen years.

These Western farm mortgages find their way to all parts of the East, and many are sold in London. They afford a good investment for the small capitalist, and are also held largely by savings-banks and insurance and trust companies. The competition referred to, or, to put it more clearly, the eagerness of the companies to lend, the eagerness of their agents to make their commissions as large as possible by lending all the company will permit, and the exceeding great eagerness of the homesteader to borrow every nickel he can, give rise to the evil which must be naturally apprehended under such conditions, namely, over-loaning: But this does not exist to an extent to cause any alarm to the investor, since nineteen-twentieths of the loans are guaranteed by the negotiators, and if they loan more than a farm is worth, the loss is theirs. Latterly, too, they are much more thorough in their investigations, and now make very few mistakes.

There are a few wiseacres in the East who shake their heads impressively, declaring that three-fourths of the farms of Nebraska, Kansas, and Dakota are mortgaged, and predict ultimate disaster to both borrower and lender. But this does not by any means follow. We are heavily in debt, and there is no reason for denying it. Every State west of the Alleghanies has borne the same burden in its pioneer days, and developed its resources under precisely the same conditions. Go to a new country that is not in debt, and you will find the inhabitants as near a state of nature as they can get, and content to remain there. They will live like the crackers of Georgia or the moonshiners of Tennessee, who are never in debt—except, perhaps, to the Internal Rev-

enue Department. They are happy: perhaps theirs is the wiser plan—to rust out instead of wearing out. But the restless, hustling, struggling Westerner is not cast in that mould. If he succumbs in the struggle against high interest, an exorbitant tariff, and the practical confiscation of his farm products by the freight rates of the railroads, another man stands ready to take his place.

Of almost equal importance with money as a civilizing factor is the railroad. It is no longer the fashion for the community to develop and await its advent. The railroad now precedes the population everywhere, and makes its own towns. So true is this in some parts of the desert that the roads own all of the principal town sites on their new branches. To mention all of the roads which have penetrated the region we are discussing would be to name a majority of the best managed, best paying, and largest railway corporations in the United States; but those which have pre-empted the best part of the disputed territory are the Santa Fe, the Rock Island, the Burlington, the Northwestern, and the St. Paul roads. That giant of other days, the Union Pacific, though wide-awake enough now, has slumbered for years, while such tireless Lilliputians as the Burlington, the Northwestern, and the Rock Island have invaded every mile of its territory, and bound it hand and foot with a net-work of branch lines running in every direction, making resistance on its part at this late day wellnigh useless. Already the Burlington, which has literally gridironed Nebraska, is in the coal-fields of Wyoming. It has obtained control of lines west of Denver, and is headed for the Pacific coast. The Northwestern, besides its large holdings in Dakota, stretches one long arm into the Black Hills *viâ* northern Nebraska, and another has passed Fort Fetterman in Wyoming. Not content with these vast undertakings, a third great branch of this corporation has penetrated southern Nebraska, and is now half-way across the State on its way to Denver. It will be a race between it and the Rock Island, for this is the objective point of both at present; and who shall have the hardihood to predict that they will stop there?

The St. Paul system, lying furthest north of all the lines competing for the possession of the new West, prompted by

WAUNETA FALLS, NEBRASKA.

the advice of one of the quietest, but, all round, one of the brainiest merchants and financiers in the United States, Philip D. Armour, has just finished perhaps the greatest *coup* in its history. At one step it has planted its iron heel in Kansas City—a point never dreamed of by its original projectors. And this is but a starting-point for its southwestern extensions—a city of which another great railway magnate has but lately prophesied—and with good reason—that half a century hence it will surpass the Chicago and St. Louis, not of this day, but of that, in population and commercial importance. The Santa Fe road—a child of the desert—most powerful of the Southwestern lines, simply as a matter of convenience in Eastern connections, has quietly completed an extension from Kansas to Chicago, where its terminal facilities alone will cost from five to ten millions of dollars. To realize fully what has been done since 1880 in

the line of railway building in the Great American Desert, take a copy of Poor's Railway Manual for 1887, and note how suggestively near the head of the list of States Nebraska, Kansas, and Dakota are in miles of railroads built each year. The lines constructed in Nebraska alone during the past two years would make a single-track road from New York city to Salt Lake.

To touch upon the climate of this greatly abused country is to develop one of its strongest points. The main basis for its excellence lies in the altitude of the region, which ranges from fifteen to eighteen hundred feet above the sea-level, on the Missouri River, and gradually ascends as you travel westward until the foot of the mountains is reached, where you attain an altitude of five to six thousand feet. The atmosphere is dry and invigorating. Nebraska is noted for the great number of its sunshiny days, though Dakota and

take a medium latitude, such as southern Nebraska, and there you can find as near perfect a climate as the United States affords. As between wintering there or in Florida, there is much in favor of the former.

The prairie country, it is true, is subject in winter to blizzards of the utmost severity, but these last for two or three days only, and twenty-five days in the month, every month in the year, are to be relied upon as certain to be lovely. The crisp frosty air and clear sunshine in winter put a life and mettle into one which the soft and balmy atmosphere of Florida cannot supply.

It follows that such a climate is remarkably healthy. There is but one disease which is at all climatic; that is a species of typhoid fever, which appears generally in the fall. This may be occasioned by undue exposure to the sun in summer,

Hastings College—McCormick Hall.

Second Street.

Hastings, 1873.

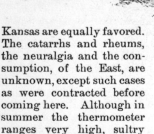

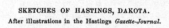

A Desert Home

SKETCHES OF HASTINGS, DAKOTA.
After illustrations in the Hastings *Gazette-Journal.*

Kansas are equally favored. The catarrhs and rheums, the neuralgia and the consumption, of the East, are unknown, except such cases as were contracted before coming here. Although in summer the thermometer ranges very high, sultry heat is, of course, an impossibility at such an altitude. To be perfectly comfortable in the hottest weather it is necessary only to keep out of the direct rays of the sun; the nights are always cool. It must be noted that as regards heat and cold there is great difference between Dakota and Kansas, for instance; this is merely a question of latitude; but

by the water, or by what is the most plausible reason, the upturning of the prairie sod.

Newly ploughed land is not anywhere considered health-giving. At all events, whatever the cause may be, new-comers generally have a siege with this fever—almost invariably in the fall.

The idea is prevalent in the East that a location anywhere on the plains means living in a flat and featureless country, where the horizon presents in every direction a monotonous stretch of prairie, devoid of any objects of interest or natural beauty, and impressing upon one feelings of dreary loneliness. This is a mistake.

Certainly the most enthusiastic resident of the desert would not deny that the lovely groves of the East would be a great addition to our landscapes; but we are by no means in the poverty-stricken state in which our Eastern cousins have pictured us in respect to the beauties of nature. The vicinity of Wauneta Falls, in the Frenchman Valley, on the western edge of Nebraska, would not be esteemed commonplace even in Minnesota or Wisconsin, the homes of dainty cataracts. In the view of them which we present their picturesqueness may be marred for some eyes by the rude but useful imitation of the Brooklyn Bridge which appears in the foreground. But to others this will exhibit the ingenuity of the homesteader applied to the scanty materials at his command. The valley of the Republican Riv-

away. The bluffs of the Missouri River have frequently been seen in towns forty miles east of them by means of this curious and beautiful phenomenon.

The soil of these prairies possesses such marvellous qualities in the way of productiveness that the stories told of it seem incredible; nor will I inflict upon the reader any tales of the enormous yield of grain, and of the vegetables and fruits of wondrous size which we yearly send east to astonish the farmers of the Middle States. Occasionally something occurs which astounds even the natives regarding the fertility of the soil, as when some immigrant, unable to find anything better to pre-empt, and lacking

Public School Building in Mitchell, Dakota.

A Street in Mitchell, Dakota.

er affords any number of beautiful landscape effects. The pure clear air and the great expanse of sky in every part of our country afford the loveliest cloud effects and the most magnificent sunsets to be found east of the mountains. Dakota is favored with the mirage which lifts into photographic clearness towns thirty miles

the means to go further or to go back, in desperation enters a quarter section in what we call the sand-hills, such as are found in portions of western Kansas and Nebraska. In the fall he will emerge from his barren one hundred and sixty acres of desert land with melons, potatoes, pumpkins, and squashes of simply pro-

GLIMPSE OF McCOOK, NEBRASKA.

digious size, capturing the premiums at the local fairs, to the intense chagrin of the farmers who have been laughing all summer at his lunacy in locating on sand. The fact simply is, there is no known limit to the richness and depth of this desert soil. Earth thrown out of a well from a depth of one hundred feet, if sown with wheat or oats, will grow as fine grain as ever headed. I excavated a cellar to a depth of eight feet last year, and graded a lawn with the earth thrown out. After seeding it in the spring, one summer was enough to make a lovely grass-plot of it. Such stories sound like exaggerations to those who are familiar with the worthless clay subsoils of the East, but they are nevertheless strictly true.

The one thing needful to develop the agricultural and pastoral possibilities of this region—in a word, the key to its destinies—is an adequate rainfall; and this suggests a topic regarding which has arisen nearly all of the controversies connected with the success of the new West. Experts who knew absolutely nothing whatever about the actual facts in the case have written many a weighty article to prove that we do not have, never have had, and never can have any rainfall worth mentioning. On the other hand, the people out here who know from their actual experience that we do have a liberal and *bona fide* rainfall in every portion of our immense desert are not content with stating the facts, or making affidavits to them, but rack their brains to find ingenious reasons for the beneficence of Providence. One asserts that every yard of steel rail laid in the desert will draw from the heavens a gallon of water per annum; another claims that there has always been a good rainfall here, and points in evidence to the numberless cañons and creek beds twisting and turning in every direction, but all ultimately converging to the rivers which empty into the Missouri. A third contends that rain follows the upturning of the sod, and that every acre of land ploughed makes a draft on the clouds for a definite quantity of water. It is certain that the buffalo-grass sod which has covered these plains for centuries has become as impervious to water as a cow-boy's slicker. Hence the rain never penetrates it, but rushes off the "divides" in a fury to reach the rivers. Any one who has seen it rain on the plains can understand something of the deluge which covers the entire prairie to the depth of twelve to twenty-four inches during summer showers. It is easy to comprehend then how the numerous cañons in Kansas and Nebraska are cut by the eagerness of the flood to roll eastward. But when the prairie sod has once been ploughed, the soil absorbs water like a sponge. After a day's heavy rain there is no mud visible in a ploughed field: the moisture soaks downward to great depths, and the soil retains it through weeks of dry weather afterward, sustaining its crops without additional rain for a wonderful length of time. It is at least reasonable to suppose that under this changed condition of large portions of the soil, which now absorbs rain instead of shedding it like a rubber coat, the climate retains its atmospheric moisture better, and the rainfall becomes more regular, less falling at a time, but falling oftener. This change may account, too, for the heavy dews which of late years have been remarked in this country—a thing absolutely unknown ten years ago. The upturned soil parting with but a little of its moisture every day, it returns to it at night, wellnigh as refreshing as a shower.

General Morrow, in a very interesting and valuable address delivered at the Cheyenne County, Nebraska, fair last fall, notes the advent of these dews, and he records a rainfall of fourteen inches for the first nine months of 1887 at Sidney, Nebraska, which, it should be observed, lies on the extreme western frontier of the State. An editorial in a late number of the New York *Nation*, calling attention to General Morrow's observations, and the way in which the actual facts have upset the theories of the wondrous wise prophets of former days, quotes the *North American Review* in 1858 as saying that our people at that date, when there was scarcely a hamlet forty miles west of the Missouri River, had "already reached their inland western frontier," and describing the Missouri bluffs as "a shore at the termination of a vast ocean desert nearly one thousand miles in breadth," which it was proposed to traverse, if at all, "with caravans of camels, and which interposed a final barrier to the establishment of large communities—agricultural, commercial, or even pastoral." The closing comment of the editor of the *Nation* upon this is, "Yet before the close of 1880 Nebraska numbered half a million inhabitants," and he might have added, with equal truth and additional force, that to-day Nebraska numbers twice that many.

General Morrow instances 83,000 acres of land entered by homesteaders in a single county in Nebraska during three months of 1887. All the land officers of the West tell the same story; their statistics sound like fables. The United States land office for the extreme southwestern part of Nebraska, embracing but a few counties, remitted last year to Washington five hundred thousand dollars to pay for homesteads and pre-emptions.

In view of these facts—this phenomenal increase in population in all parts of the new West—we naturally look for the new centres of population which supply this people, and to these, in the words of the political platform, "we point with pride." If the facts herein set forth have been carefully considered, how easy to understand the *raison d'être* of the Omaha, Kansas City, Lincoln, and Wichita of to-day! These towns are simply a reflection of the farms of Kansas and Nebraska, and are dependent entirely on the desert for their business.

Of greater interest, I take it, and reflecting more perfectly the substantial development of the new West than the great centres mentioned, are the well-built, bright, and attractive inland towns of Ne-

braska, Dakota, and Kansas, cities of the second and third class, ranging from 3000 to 15,000 inhabitants. There are so many of these in the desert that it is almost a pity to single out a few for mention; but out of many of perhaps equal merit let us glance at Hastings, Nebraska, a town fifteen years old, with a population of 15,000 intelligent, enterprising, and prosperous people, possessed of all of the conveniences of city life, such as gas and electric light, water-works, street-cars, and a free mail delivery; its streets lined with blocks of handsome brick structures; a centre of heavy financial and industrial interests; its homes representing all that is modern and progressive in architecture. How surprised one would be, who has not seen this country for five years, at the towns numbered by the score in Dakota, Kansas, and Nebraska which rival in every respect the most prosperous towns in New York and New England! Among the younger cities there is Mitchell, Dakota, less than seven years old (four thousand inhabitants), containing several churches, fine schools, refined society, substantial banks, large packing interests —enough, in a word, to make life pleasant socially and prosperous financially. Or look at McCook, Nebraska, one of the newest and farthest west of all desert towns—an infant of five years, for there was nothing but a sod house five years ago where the town of 3000 people is now; nearly five hundred miles west of the Missouri River, in the midst of a fertile farming country, possessing everything necessary in the line of churches, schools, and social advantages to make any one content with a habitation in the desert, and whose founders had confidence enough in its future to supply it with a system of waterworks equal in extent to that of Lincoln.

These are merely types; there are dozens of such towns, not of the mushroom order of mining towns or centres of speculative activity. They are the legitimate product of a rich agricultural region, and are in no sense ephemeral. They are here to stay; and in looking at them, and considering what they represent, the conviction forces itself irresistibly on one that the best advice ever offered to a young American was contained in the words—which have been bandied about in many a joke, but are as full of wisdom to-day as when Horace Greeley uttered them—"Go West, young man—go West."

IN THE SIERRA MADRE WITH THE PUNCHERS

ON a chill black morning the cabins of Los Ojos gave up their inmates at an early hour. The ponies, mules, and *burros* were herded up, and stood shivering in an angle, while about them walked the men, carefully coiling their hair lariats, and watching for an opportunity to jerk them over the heads of the selected ones. The *patron's* black pet walked up to him, but the mounts of my companion and self sneaked about with an evident desire not to participate in the present service. Old *Cokomorachie* and Jim were finally led forth, protesting after the manner of their kind. I carefully adjusted my Whitman's officer-tree over a wealth of saddle blanketing, and slung my Winchester 45–70 and my field-glasses to it. The "punchers," both white and brown,

and two or three women, regarded my new-fangled saddle with amused glances; indeed, Mr. Bell's Mexican wife laughed at it outright, and Tom Bailey called it "a d—— rim-fire." Another humorist thought that "it would give the chickens the pip if they got onto it"; all of which I took good-humoredly, since this was not the first time "your Uncle Samuel" had been away from home; and after some days, when a lot of men were carefully leading sore-backed horses over the mountains, I had cause to remark further on the subject. A Mexican cow-saddle is a double-barrelled affair; it will eat a hole into a horse's spine and a pair of leather breeches at the same time. If one could ask "Old Jim" about that saddle of mine, I think he would give it an autograph recommend, for he finished the trip with the hide of his back all there.

Leaving the "burro men" to haul and pull at their patient beasts as they bound on their loads, our outfit "pulled out" on what promised to be plenty of travelling. We were to do the rounds of the ranch, explore the mountains, penetrate to the old Apache strongholds, shoot game, find cliff-dwellers' villages, and I expect the dark minds of the punchers hoped for a sight at the ever-burning fire which should discover the lost mine of Tiopa. We were also promised a fight with the "Kid" if we "cut his trail"; and if he "cuts ours," we may never live to regret it. Some tame Indians, just in from a hunt in the Rio Chico, had seen three fires, but they had "rolled their tails "* for Bavicora so promptly that they had not ascertained whether they were Apache or not. The same men we were in the company of had run the "Kid's" band in to the States only two months before, but on our trip that very elusive and very "bad Injun" was not encountered. Much as I should like to see him, I have no regrets, since it is extremely likely that he would have seen me first.

Our little band was composed of the patron, Don Gilberto; my travelling companion from New York city, who had never before been west of the Elysian Fields of New Jersey; Bailey and Bell, ranch foremen, and as dauntless spirits as ever the Texas border nurtured; the ranch bookkeeper, a young man "short" on experiences and "long" on hope; Epitacio, an Indian hunter, since outlawed; William, the colored cook; four buckskin Mexican "punchers"; an old man who was useless for practical purposes, but who was said to be "funny" in Spanish; and two "burro men." We were that day to go to the farthest outlying ranch, called the Casa Camadra, and then to stop for a short hunt and to give the punchers time to "gentle" some steers for work-cattle. The puncher method of doing this is beautifully simple, for any animal undergoing this is gentle or dead after it. After scouring the plain for antelope until late, we followed up a creek toward the cabin where we expected to find the punchers and the burro men with their loads of creature comforts, and as we rode in, it was raining a cold sleet. The little log cabin was low,

* Cowboy for travelling rapidly.

MY COMRADE.

small, and wonderfully picturesque. It was a typical "shack," such as one used to see in the Northwest when the hunters were there. Out in the rain sat two punchers, enveloped in their serapes, engaged in watching a half-dozen big steers eat grass. Inside of the cabin was William by a good fire in a most original fireplace, glowing with heat and pride over his corn cakes and "marrow-gut." Between various cigarettes, the last drink of *tequela*, and the drying of our clothes,

PORPHYRY ROCK.

we passed the time until William had put the "grub" on a pack-saddle blanket and said, "Now, gemmen, fly in."

"Fly in" is vulgar, but it is also literal, for we did that: we did not dine—we flew in. The expression and the food were both good. Outside, the cold rain had turned into a wet snow, and we all crowded into the little place and squatted or lay about on the floor. With fingers and hunting-knives we carved and tore at the mountain of beef. The punchers consume enormous quantities of meat, and when satiated they bring forth their cornhusks and tobacco-pouches and roll their long thin cigarettes, which burn until they draw their serapes about their heads and sink back in dreamless sleep. It is all beautifully primitive, and as I rise on my elbow to look across the blanketed forms packed like mackerel in a cask, to hear their heavy breathing, and see the fire glow, and hear the wind howl outside, I think how little it takes to make men happy. Tom Bailey and Johnnie Bell, the ranch foremen, had faces which would have been in character under a steel headpiece at Cressy, while the wildest blood of Spain, Morocco, and the American Indian ran in the veins of the punchers; and all these men were untainted by the enfeebling influences of luxury and modern life. A chunk of beef, a cigarette, an enveloping serape, with the Sierras for a bedroom, were the utmost of their needs.

The sunlight streamed down the big chimney, and William's "Goodmo'nin', sah," brought back my senses. Beyond his silhouette, as he crouched before the fireplace, I could hear the sputtering of the broiling steak. I repaired to the brook and smashed the ice for a rub-down. It was still drizzling, and the landscape lay under a heavy fog. Outside the cabin lay the dead body of a skinned wolf, and about a small fire crouched the punchers.

Breakfast over, the men rode off by twos into the fog, and as Tom Bailey and I jogged along together we reasoned that if we were to strike the point of the mountains and then keep well in the timber we might catch a bunch of antelope which we had "jumped" the day before on the plain below. So all day long we rode over the wet rocks, under the drip and drizzle of the mountain pines, up hill and down dale, and never "cut a sign." It was our luck; for on riding up to the "shack" we saw the bodies of deer, antelope, a

SHOOTING IN THE SIERRA MADRE.

big gray wolf, and the skin of a mountain-lion. We were requested to view the game, and encouraged to comment on it; but Tom and I sought a dark corner of the cabin to consume our coffee and cigarettes in silence.

At the Casa Camadra are two other log houses, and in them live some squalid, yellow-hided humans who are to farm a little stretch of bottom-land this year. They require work-steers to do their ploughing, and Mr. Bell has brought up half a dozen vicious old "stags," which are both truculent and swift of foot. The Mexicans insist that they are not able to handle them; and Mr. Bell orders his punchers into action. I strolled out to the corrals to see the bulls "gentled." After a lot of riding and yelling they were herded and dragged into the enclosure, where they huddled while seven punchers sat on their ponies at the gate. I was standing at one corner of the corral, near the men, when out from the midst of the steers walked a big black bull, which raised its head and gazed directly at me. The bull had never before in his stupid life observed a man on foot, and I comprehended immediately what he would

do next, so I "led out" for the casa at a rate of speed which the boys afterwards never grew weary of commending. No spangled *torero* of the bull-ring ever put more heart and soul into his running than did I in my great-coat and long hunting-spurs. The bull made a "fo'-lorn hope" for the gate, and the gallant punchers melted away before the charge.

The diversion of the punchers made the retreat of the infantry possible, and from an intrenched position I saw the bulls tear over the hill, with the punchers "rolling their tails" behind. After an hour of swearing and hauling and bellowing, the six cattle were lugged back to the pen, and the bars put up. The punchers came around to congratulate me on my rapid recovery from a sprained ankle, when they happened to observe the cattle again scouring off for the open country. Then there was a grunting of ponies as the spurs went in, some hoarse oaths, and for a third time they tore away after the "gentle work-oxen." The steers had taken the bars in their stride. Another hour's chase, and this time the animals were thrown down, trussed up like turkeys for the baking, and tied to posts, where they lay to kick and bellow the night through in impotent rage. The punchers coiled their ropes, lit their cigarettes, and rode off in the gathering gloom. The morning following the steers were let up, and though wet and chilled, they still roared defiance. For agricultural purposes a Mexican "stag" would be as valuable as a rhinoceros or a Bengal tiger, and I await with interest the report of the death rate at the Casa Camadra during spring ploughing.

In the handling of these savage animals the punchers are brave to recklessness, but this is partly because it seems so. In reality they have a thorough knowledge of bull nature, and can tell when and where he is going to strike as quickly as a boxer who knows by the "skim on the eye" of his opponent. But still they go boldly into the corral with the maddened brutes, seeming to pay no heed to the imminent possibilities of a trip to the moon. They toss their ropes and catch the bull's feet, they skilfully avoid his rush, and in a spirit of bravado they touch the horns, pat him on the back, or twist his tail.

After hunting for another day, with more success, we packed up and "pulled out" up the Varras Creek toward the mountains, leaving the last house behind us. Beyond was the unknown country. For many miles it had been ridden by some of the punchers, but the country is large, covered with vast mountain ranges, with wastes of stony foot-hills at the bases, while *barrancas* yawn at your feet, and for a great many years the policy of the Apaches has been not to encourage immigration. In 1860 a heavy band of

Mexican prospectors undertook to penetrate this part in the quest of Tiopa, but they were driven out. It is now possible for strong outfits to travel its wilds with only a small chance of encountering Apache renegades, but very few have attempted it as yet. It is so remote that prospectors for silver or gold could hardly work a mine if they found one, and for other purposes it has little value. The most magnificent pine timber covers its slopes, but it would take a syndicate to deliver one log at the railroad. As we wound

ON THE MOUNTAINS.

our way up the Varras Creek we passed beetling crags and huge pillars of porphyry rock cut into fantastic shapes by water and frost, resplendent in color, and admirably adapted for the pot-hunting of humans as affected by gentry temporarily stopping at San Carlos.

In a dell in the forest we espied some "mavericks," or unbranded stock. The punchers are ever alert for a beef without half its ears gone and a big HF burned in its flank, and immediately they perceive one they tighten their *cincha*, slip the rope from the pommel, put their hats on the back of their heads, and "light out." A cow was soon caught, after desperate riding over rocks and fallen timber, thrown down, and "hog-tied," which means all four feet together. A little fire is built, and one side of a *cincha* ring is heated red-hot, with which a rawhide artist paints HF in the sizzling flesh, while the cow kicks and bawls. She is then unbound, and when she gets back on her feet the vaqueros stand about, serape in hand, after the bull-fighter method, and provoke her to charge. She charges, while they avoid her by agile springs and a flaunting of their rags. They laugh, and cry "Bravo toro!" until she, having overcome her indignation at their rudeness, sets off down the cañon with her tail in the air.

Thus we journeyed day by day over the hills and up the cañons, camping by night under the pines in mountain glades or deep ravines, where the sun sets at four o'clock, while it is light above. The moon was in the full and the nights were frosty, and many times we awoke to think it morning when only our heads had become uncovered by the blankets and the big white moon shone fair upon us. Getting up in the night to poke the fire and thaw the stiffening out of one's legs is called by the boys "playing freeze-out," and we all participate in the game. A cigarette at two o'clock in the morning, with one's back to the fire, while the moon looks down on you, your comrades breathing about you, a wolf howling mournfully from a neighboring hill, the mountains towering on every side, and the tall pines painting inky shadows across the ghostly grass, is a mild sensation and rather pleasant. Some of the men are on foot, from soring their horses' backs, and their buckskin boots are wearing out, so they sit about the fire and stitch. We are all very dirty, and I no longer take comfort in watching the cook who makes the bread, for fear I may be tempted to ask him if he will not wash his hands, whereat the boys may indicate that I am a "dude," and will look down on me. The flour is nearly gone, and shortly it will not matter whether the cook's hands are rusty or not. The coffee and sugar promise to hold out. When William can no longer serve "bull gravy" with his fried meat I shall have many regrets, but they are swamped by the probabilities of a tobacco famine, which is imminent. We get deer every day, but to one not used to a strictly meat diet it begins to pall. The Indian hunter takes the stomach of a deer, fills it with meat, and deposits it under the coals. We roast it in slices and chunks, but I like it better when "jerked" brown, as it then affords somewhat more mystery to a taste already jaded with venison. In travelling with pack animals it is the custom to make a day's march before halting, and a day's march ends about four o'clock, or when water is found. Ten hours' march will loosen one's cartridge-belt five or six holes, for venison and coffee is not a strong food. By 12 M. we acquire a wolfish yearning for the "flesh-pots," but that shortly is relieved by the contraction of the stomach, or three or four quarts of mountain water will afford some relief. By nightfall one can "fly into" a venison steak, while cigarettes, coffee, and a desire to lie down restore one's equanimity.

We have passed some small ranges and worm our way down bottomless pits, but at last there rises ahead the main range of the Sierra Madre. From the depths of a great *barranca* we begin the climb. Never have I seen hills as sideling as these. It is terrible work for one not used to mountain-climbing and the short allowance of air one finds to subsist on. The feeling of exhaustion is almost impossible to overcome. The horses are thin, and Old Jim is developing more ribs than good condition calls for, so I walk to ease the old fellow. There are snow fields to cross, which intensifies the action. The journey is enlivened at times by shots at deer, and the rifles echo around the mountains, but being long shots they are misses. We passed the *cordon* of the mountains, and stopped

THE CLIFF-DWELLINGS.

on a knifelike ridge where the melting snows under one's foot ran east and west to the two great oceans. The climb from here over the main range was a bellows-bursting affair, but as we pulled on to the high *mesa* our drooping nerves were stiffened by shots, and presently deer came bounding down the ravine to our left. Jack made a bully flying shot, and the stricken deer rolled many yards, until caught by a fallen log. My companion, who was in advance, had fired into some deer, and had shot a buck which was lying down, and he was much puffed up with pride over this achievement in still-hunting. From there on we passed through the most wonderful natural deer park. The animals did not fear man, and stood to be fired at, though the open timber and absence of underbrush made the shots long-range ones. After killing all we could carry, we sat down to wait for the burro train.

That night we camped on a jutting crag, with the water running in the *barranca* 200 feet below us. For a hundred miles the mountain and plain lay at our feet—a place more for an eagle's eyry than a camp for a caravan. The night set very cold, and from out in space the moon threw its mellow light down upon us. Before the camp-fire our Indian hunter told the story of the killing of Victoria's band, where he had been among the victors, and as he threw his serape down, and standing forth with the firelight playing on his harsh features, he swayed his body and waved his hands, while with hoarse voice and in a strange language he gave the movement of the fight. The legend of the lost mine of Tiopa was narrated by a vaquero in the quiet manner of one whose memory goes far back, and to whom it is all real— about the Jesuits, the iron door over the mouth of the mine, its richness, the secrecy enjoined by the fathers on the people when they fled before the Apache devils, and how there is always a light to be kept burning at its entrance to guide them back. It was a grand theatre and an eerie scene.

On the other side of the mountain we found the trail most difficult. I would never have believed that a horse could traverse it. To say that it was steep is commonplace, and yet I cannot be believed if I say that it was perpendicular; but a man could toss his hat a mile at any moment if he pleased. Then, underfoot, it was all loose lava rock, and the little ponies had to jump and dance over the bowlders. When we had finally arrived on a grassy *mesa* I concluded that if ever again I did the like of that, it would most certainly be the result of a tremendous error in my calculations. The pack-train was here detached and sent to water, but we followed Jack to see his "discovery." After miles of travel through the dry yellow grass we came out on a high bluff, with a *barranca* at its foot the bottom of which we could

not see. On the overhanging wall opposite were Jack's cliff-dwellings, perched like dove-cots against the precipice. It was only a quarter of a mile to them, but it took two days to get there, so we did not go. There are also holes in the cliffs, and underground passages. The paths up to them are washed away, but Jack and some of his men have invaded the silent village. They climbed up with lariats, and he was let down over the cliff, but they found nothing left but dust and cobwebs.

We could not get down to water, and as our horses were thirsty and foot-sore, we "mogged along." On our ride we "cut the trail" of a big band of mustangs, or wild horses, but did not see them, and by late afternoon we found the camp, and William busy above his fire. After hunting down the valley for a few days for "burro deer" and wild turkey, we found that the tobacco was promptly giving out, according to calculations, and being all inveterate smokers, we "made trail fast" for the Neuearachie ranch. Our ponies were jaded and sore; but having "roped" a stray pony two days before, which was now fresh, the lightest vaquero was put on his back, and sent hot-foot in the night to the ranch for tobacco. He made the long ride and returned at noon the next day on a fresh mount, having been thirty-six hours in the saddle. This fellow was a rather remarkable man, as it was he who, on the beginning of the trip, had brought some important mail to us one hundred and seventy miles, and after riding down two ponies he followed our trail on foot through the mountains, and overtook us as we sat resting on a log in the woods.

How we at last pulled into the ranch at Neuearachie, with its log buildings and irrigated fields, and how we "swooped down" on Mr. John Bailey, and ate up all his eggs and bread and butter at the first onset, I will not weary you with, but I believe that a man should for one month of the year live on the roots of the grass, in order to understand for the eleven following that so-called necessities are luxuries in reality. Not that I would indiscriminately recommend such a dietary abasement as ours, yet will I insist that it has killed less men than gluttony, and should you ever make the Sierra trails with the punchers, you will get rather less than more.

AMERICA'S ANCIENT LAKE REGION

FOR seven hundred miles the narrow thoroughfare of civilization traverses the desolate plains of Utah and Nevada, and winds among sterile mountain ranges which seem to have been waiting since the dawn of creation for refreshing showers that have never come. Yet it is comparatively but a little while since that thirsty region, covering an area equal to that of our Eastern and Middle States combined, was flooded with sweet water and lush with vegetation; while all around it, in place of the present barren mountains and alkali plains, lay fair expanses of fresh-water seas or fertile savannas, thronged, it may be, with a population denser and more varied than that of any part of the world of to-day.

The story of the transformation is not hard to read. The depth of water in the saline lakes and marshes of the Great Basin is far from constant. Latterly it has been slowly increasing; but the frequent occurrence of salt-pans, or areas thickly covered with salt deposited from evaporated water, is enough to prove that the general level of the waters must have been considerably higher at a period not far distant. Both Fremont, the first to explore the basin, and Stansbury, who followed him, make frequent mention of such salt-encrusted areas, the latter describing one field in the valley of Great Salt Lake seven miles across and more than ten miles long, the deposit lying so thick that his mule train crossed it as upon a sheet of solid ice. At the northern end of the valley Captain Stansbury counted thirteen successive terraces, each marking a former level of the water, the highest fully two hundred feet above the present surface of the lake. Corresponding terraces around all the minor depressions of the Great Basin show that the ancient lake must have spread over the entire area, converting its mountain ranges into chains of islands; while high above these diminutive banks of later times are benches of uniform elevation, three, six, eight hundred feet above the plain, the shore lines of a majestic inland sea, which at its higher levels must have filled the uplifted cup of the continent almost to the brim. It was a period when water was as abundant in the high lands of the far West as it is now deficient.

To the north of the present deserts of Utah, filling the oval basin traversed but scarcely watered by the deep-flowing Snake River and its tributaries, a broad expanse of fresh water then stretched across Idaho and southeastern Oregon, filling all the valley between the Rocky and the Blue mountains—a distance of four hundred miles.

Westward, between the Blue Mountains and the Cascade Range, lay several smaller sheets of sweet water, each a giant lake according to modern standards, covering the greater part of central Oregon and Washington.

The trough between the Cascade Range and the newly risen Coast Range was similarly flooded.

Southward, filling the great valley of California, now drained by the Sacramento and the San Joaquin, lay another lake, five hundred miles long by fifty wide, its outlet flowing over the yet unopened Golden Gate.

Eastward, across the Sierras from its southern end, lay the broad lake whose deserted shores, "outliving the memory of a cooler past—a period when the stony mountain chains were green islands among basins of wide watery expanse"— are so graphically sketched by Clarence King from the summit of Mount Tyndall.

South of the arid basin of Owen's Lake, the Gulf of California at that time thrust a broad arm northward several hundred miles beyond its present limit, receiving at its side the independent floods of the Gila and the Colorado as they plunged over their terminal slopes from the elevated plains above.

Watering the surface of its lofty plateau, instead of burrowing a mile beneath it as at present, the Colorado enriched and vivified an immense territory—the garden spot of primeval America, the Egypt of American civilization.

Between the Wasatch border of the great interior sea and the broad belt of the Rocky Mountain ranges, filling the valleys now drained by the Green River and its tributaries, two or more vast sheets of fresh water were slowly depositing those layers of sediment which the geologist of to-day finds so richly stored with the remains of the life forms of that ancient period; while the unbroken walls of the many-looped Rocky Mountains— that "nation of mountain ranges," as Fitz Hugh Ludlow styled them—enclosed hundreds of oval lakes, whose level beds, since emptied through the deeply eroded cañons of their outflowing streams, now form the sheltered parks so attractive to the pioneer herdsman.

Thus the great interior sea was the centre of a lake region for which the earth of to-day can show no counterpart. Its fauna and flora were on a scale of corresponding magnitude and variety.

The best-studied record of the period is that deposited by the waters of a broad fresh-water sea which lay on the eastern flank of the Rocky Mountains, covering an area four or five times that of our boasted Lake Superior. In the successive layers of its marly sediments we may read the history of its rise and decline, as the Assyrian scholar reads the chronicles of ancient empires in the layers of imprinted tiles dug from the long-buried libraries of Babylon or Nineveh.

The record begins in the Middle Tertiary or Miocene period, with a broad marsh, the wallowing-place of gigantic beasts, hog-like in character, elephantine in size. Every year's exploration adds to our list of these strange creatures, still a sufficient number have been made out to enable us to form a tolerable notion of the population of the time.

As the water deepened, multitudes of turtles took possession of the lake, leaving thousands of their shells, from an inch to three feet across, to attest their presence. As time passed on, and the tributary streams increased in number and magnitude, the lake deposits enclosed more numerous representatives of the fauna of that ancient world. The surrounding country appears to have swarmed with animals which have passed away, the most of them leaving no known descendants. Especially numerous were many varieties of deer-like ruminating hogs, which roamed the plains in vast troops, and were frequently driven by their enemies into the watercourses, to be drowned and drifted into the lake.

The marks of carnivorous teeth on the skulls of these antique swine show that the tigers of that early age had as keen an appetite for pork as their descendants of to-day.

During the next or Pliocene period a distinct yet closely allied fauna occupied the shores of our great lake. Semi-aquatic pachyderms, vast in size and countless in number, wallowed in the marshes—one as large as the African hippopotamus. Sharing the same mud beds were five species of rhinoceroses, the largest rivalling the existing unicorn of India.

In most respects the country at this

time resembled the marshy regions of central Africa, as described by Livingstone and other explorers; but it lacked one creature common enough in Africa, for whose sustenance and comfort it would seem to have been admirably adapted —there were no crocodiles. They had swarmed in the earlier Tertiary lakes farther west, but had disappeared. "Where were they," asks Dr. Leidy, "when the shores of the ancient Dakotan and Nebraskan waters teemed with such an abundant provision of savory ruminating hogs?"

To this question no satisfactory answer has been given.

But hogs were not the only occupants of those shores. Great herds of mammoths and elephants, specifically distinct from any elsewhere known, trampled the banks of the watercourses and browsed on the trees which bordered them; while troops of deer, horses, camels, and other herbivorous animals cropped the fresh pasturage of the adjacent plains.

Singularly, though both the horse and the camel were unknown in North America on the first arrival of the European explorers, the continent was no stranger to them. In prehistoric times the continent seems to have been the especial home of horses, something like thirty fossil species having been already discovered.

In that remote age the continents were not divided, as now, nor was the arctic circle an icy barrier to human migration. A bridge of dry land joined America with Europe and Asia, and gave free passage to the plants and animals of the three continents, which had not yet begun to show the marked divergence they have since developed. Alaska and Greenland enjoyed a climate as mild as ours, and were clad with forests whose lineal descendants now flourish in China, in California, and on both shores of the Atlantic. Fan-palms with leaves fifteen feet broad grew as far north as the Yellowstone River, and a tropical or sub-tropical climate prevailed in the region of the great lakes now passed away.

This state of things continued, with little variation, through the Pliocene period, and up to the time when the climate of the northern hemisphere began to chill before the coming reign of snow and ice. Gradually the polar cold crept down to the latitude of New York, and the northern

half of the continent slept under its arctic mantle. The mountains around our once luxuriant lake region were heaped with snow. Glaciers slid through the valleys, carving Yosemites, and strewing the plains with continental débris.

The stages of their gigantic work do not concern us here, nor can we stay to trace the history of the gradual return of milder days, the slow retreat of unbroken winter northward, the repossessing of the land by the plants and animals which had survived the terrible ordeal of glacial cold and forced migration. Millenniums passed, the ice melted from the mountains, the lakes were swollen with accumulated water, and the final transformation of the scenery began.

The last act was the drainage and destruction of the great lakes. By degrees the rocky barrier of the Coast Range had been cut through at the Golden Gate. The ceaseless rush of outflowing water deepened the channel of the discharging stream, steadily sinking the level of the lake which filled the great valley of California, until its fertile plains were ready for human occupation. A similar process was going on in the north, where the lakes of western Oregon and Washington were discharged through the deepening gorge of the Columbia. Meanwhile the Klamath River and the Pitt were cutting their tremendous cañons through the Sierras, for the drainage of the region made memorable by Modoc treachery. Then the second barrier of the Columbia was cloven at the Cascades, and the eventful history of its upper lakes was slowly brought to an end.

The life of these great fresh-water seas had been largely coincident with that of the lakes we have studied farther east. The history of both covers the same geologic ages, and their deposits tell pretty much the same story of animal and vegetable life. Still there are striking differences in the two records. The lakes of California, Oregon, and Idaho witnessed stormier times than those of the eastern slope of the Rocky Mountains, being more severely scourged by volcanic disturbances. From time to time terrific storms of ashes were blown out from numerous volcanic centres, destroying life and covering the lake beds with ash deposits many feet in thickness. Again, floods of lava overflowed the country, burying hundreds of square miles under continuous sheets of molten matter, and paving the lake beds with thick layers of solid basalt.

Then there would come ages of peace and quiet. Forests would repossess the land; troops of animals—mammoths, elephants, camels, horses, bisons—would return to the reviving pastures; fish would repeople the waters; and fine sediment, full of organic forms, would gather in thick layers above the sheets of lava. During these alternations of peace and paroxysm nearly every portion of the country, particularly in the great region drained by the Columbia, was deluged by lava torrents. The lakes were filled up, while their outlets wore deeper and deeper into the rocky barriers which kept back their waters.

The ceaseless attrition of flowing water is irresistible. In process of time the hardest rock is cut away, and the best-defended lake is drained to the dregs. So thoroughly have the Columbia and its branches done their allotted task that they have not merely emptied the great lakes through whose ancient beds they flow, but in many cases they have cut their channels two thousand vertical feet into the deposits accumulated beneath the once wide-spreading waters. This unkindly drainage, together with the devastating lava flows, has converted vast expanses of fair water and fertile land into a "monotonous blank desert," as Clarence King describes the Snake Basin, "leaving only here and there near the snowy mountain-tops a bit of cool green to contrast with the sterile uniformity of the plain."

While the desiccation of the northern third of the great interior table-land was going on, the deepening channel of the Colorado was slowly depriving the southern third of its former greenness and fertility. At our first view of this great river—a river without parallel on the globe—we saw it flowing as a majestic stream across its lofty plateau, bathing and fertilizing a region great even in the great West, then plunging down its precipitous slope into the Gulf of California, a hundred miles or more above its present mouth. Gradually its stupendous falls wore backward into the plateau, carving out the marvellous cañons through which it now burrows. For hundreds of miles it has cut its channel from three to six thousand feet deep

through all the orders of sedimentary rocks, from the Tertiary down, and from six to eight hundred feet into the primordial granite below! As the channel sank, age after age, the surrounding country—more and more thoroughly drained of its surface water, and less and less frequently revived by mists and showers drawn from the river's surface—was slowly converted into a region of sterility and desolation, a process evidently hastened by the erosion which began it. The Colorado could not excavate its enormous cañons without discharging somewhere an equal volume of triturated rock. This vast body of mud and sand and gravel necessarily accumulated in the quiet waters of the gulf, steadily raising its bed until a broad sea arm stretching two hundred miles into southern California was cut off from the sea. The scanty rainfall over this heated basin failed to make good the loss by evaporation, and the imprisoned water wasted away, leaving in its place the Colorado Desert, a wide reach of sterile country, more than four thousand square miles of whose area is said to lie below the ocean level.

The transformation of this broad region from an evaporating surface into a thirsty plain must have greatly diminished the rainfall over the Colorado plateau, and hastened the increasing desiccation, which century by century made it less and less able to sustain the populous nations which had developed a semi-civilization on its once fertile plains.

The story of the great central lake of the Utah Basin can be told in few words. It had no outlet, consequently there is no record of erosion and drainage to read, as in the case of the fresh-water seas which encompassed it. It was wasted by sun and wind. As the surrounding regions were drained and dried, thirsty plains and sterile mountains took the place of the former expanses of lake and forest, which had tempered its climate and kept up its supply of moisture. In the mean time the Sierras had thrust higher their snow-compelling summits, depriving the sea-winds of their stores of rain. Age by age the rainfall lessened within the basin, the dwindling streams which drained the inner slopes of the surrounding mountains grew less and less able to make good the increasing loss by evaporation, and the end, as we behold it, was but a question of time.

OUR SEABOARD ISLANDS ON THE PACIFIC

THERE are upon the southwest extremity of the United States, and distributed along the coast for three hundred miles, from the latitude of San Francisco to that of San Diego, certain islands, nine in number and of various areas, about which neither geography nor history has much to say. These are the only seaboard islands on the Pacific belonging to the United States, if we do not consider those of Alaska, and those numerous tiny aits or eyots in the waters of the Sound country, nor the Hawaiian group. There are from the Golden Gate to the British line a few rock reefs or single cones sitting like black stacks here and there in the sea, and at greater or less distances from the bluffy shores; but these have no claim to be spoken of as islands; that dignity belongs alone to those insular elevations in the ocean lying south of the thirty-eighth parallel, and ending, for us, at the Mexican boundary.

Nature, however, taking no note of political division-lines, has not stopped at this point the southern trend of her island deposition, but she has carried them on across the line, along the mountainous coast of Lower California, where they are found under the names of San Marten, San Geronimo, Cerros, Los Lobos, and so on, to the equator.

None of these are large, and the entire aggregate area of the nine belonging to us does not exceed three hundred and fifty-one square miles, or less than two hundred and twenty-five thousand acres. Separately they grade in size from one hundred and seventy-six square miles, which is the area of Santa Catalina, to less than two square miles, which is that of both Santa Barbara and the largest of the Farallones. The others, measured in square miles, are Santa Cruz, 115; Santa Rosa, 112; San Miguel, 183; San Clemente, 72; San Nicolas, 36; and Anacapa, 12. They lie in the arid region, at an average distance of thirty miles from the mainland, and they are uniform in their aspect of desolation. For the most part their surfaces present the characteristics of table-lands; some are rounded hummocks; but Santa Catalina is formed of two mountains, which pinch into sharp peaks three thousand feet high, and spread below them a jumble of ridges and ravines, the broken surface occasionally interrupted by small plateaus.

The Farallones group is a granitic dike, but the others are mostly lava. It is a heavy black basalt that lies massed in its hardened meltings, and shows a surface often of smooth rounded lumps or semi-spheroids, revealing the contracting effects of the extrusion of heat.

Sometimes along with the basalt there is country rock such as is found on the mainland. This rock has, by the action of the weather, become degraded, and often at the mouth of a canyon on the lee side of the island there is spread a pleasant level of land. It has been formed by the detritus borne down from the higher areas by the canyon's stream. This has been deposited here, and it has built up the ocean floor beside the roots of the island. As it arose, the sea was pushed back, until a little flat was made, and it stands there now covered with its scrub oak, its juniper, or its wild gray grass, and meets the water with a crescent shore, upon which the little wavelets softly lap as they rock in from the stilly bay.

But upon the

opposite side of the island, where the southwest winds, sweeping over the broad field of the Pacific, throw the blue waters against the black gaunt rocks, the wild elements war and play havoc. The white-frothed breakers roll and boom and burst, and the feathery spray is flung high against the scowling cliffs, until their face is varnished with a bath of spume.

And all along the cliffy coasts of these sea-girt islands there have been hewn by the waves' resistless action great caverns, with high arches above the entrances, and burrowed deeply by successive chambers into the bowels of the islands. Santa Cruz abounds with these wonders of marine erosion, the largest of which is Painted Cave. It is a succession of arches, the outermost the highest, the others grading down as depth in penetration is attained. Branching from either side of this range of compartments are other openings, so that a labyrinth of recesses appears. For fifteen hundred feet into the interior of the Painted Cave the light will enter, and there can be seen upon the walls and ceilings the infinite brilliant frescoes, red, green, yellow, and their blends, deposited by the oozing mineral waters from above.

On the lee side of the islands these grottos are floored with the stillest, softest, serenest waters. The sea about the

ON THE NORTH COAST OF SANTA CRUZ ISLAND.

THE TWO CAVES AT VAL DEZ HARBOR, SANTA CRUZ.

The larger opening affords the only landing-place from the harbor, and the smaller one the only way to the beach.

The patient artists of nature have worked upon a surface scarified into strange devices by the contraction of the heated mass, and the wild scheme of embellishment has been accentuated and elaborated in remarkable details. What primarily were depressed lines have become deep gashes; smooth rounded bulges have been worn into jagged protuberances, sharp points, and keen hatchetlike blades of enormous size.

Much of this fantastic sculpturing strikingly resembles the effects of architecture. The castellated style predominates, and you are impressed with the profusion of spires, turrets, and towers, and parapets edging the outline of the tops with merlons and crenelles. And then there are Byzantium domes and Grecian columns, the entire filigreed with the tracery of the arabesque.

And not alone have wave erosion and that of water from the clouds in their processes of island degradation wrought marvels in nature-carving, but the wearing action of the wind has been scarcely less effective. On San Nicolas, more perhaps than upon any other of the islands, is this phenomenon observable. Upon this island there is a singular subsidence, forming a canyon some hundreds of feet deep and half a mile across. It contains many little peaks of cerulean slate draped with vari-colored foliage and sitting upon a ground of white sand which has been blown thither by the winds. These winds at some seasons strike strongly over the islands, and effects of their exertions are everywhere presented. Now such is seen in a broad pebbly surface swept clean, the mosaics smoothly polished; again the feathery files have rasped the hard dark rocks, gouged them with emaciated hollows, ofttimes threatening the very security of their posture. The sharp fine particles give teeth to the blasts, and these gnaw at the structure of whatever interposes.

sheltered coasts is intensely blue and, when under the shade of a bluff or beneath the roof of a cave, where the calms allay the waters into glassy sheets, your boat will appear to be sitting upon the top of a nether world, which spreads with its innumerable population of fish and other life. Far down gardens of maidenhair, algæ, and sea-ferns are seen, curved or laced by paths of white sand, against which goldfish, the mackerel, sheep's-head and the yellowtail show their floating bodies in repose, or moving slowly with rhythmic motion of gills and tail. And over all that scene there is an atmosphere pellucid, balmy, soft as the cloudless azure which overhangs it, and the sea is a shimmering breast of sunshine. The breeze brushes your cheek like silken velvet, fans you into dreamy moods, or suffuses you with gentlest slumbers.

But on the weather side of the islands the water is rough, and this agitation of the surface impairs your vision into the abyss below; a tapestry of froth edges the line of shore, and the surging, ebullient billows drive in from the sea, plunge into the caves, explode, roar, and fill them with their fury.

But the results of the erosion of the sea at the base of these island rocks are not more curious than those of the rain and sun upon the cliffy faces of the lava.

At the Farallones the erosive agents have worked with queer caprice. This rock being granite, has been acted upon by the sea at all levels, and throughout the long period when it has been rising out of the watery depths. Through a long narrow hole, slanting, and communicating with the ocean, there comes at intervals a terrific stream of air, forced by the spasmodic heaving of the waves against the lower orifice. The government, which uses this island for light-house purposes, enclosed the upper end with the nozzle of a fog-horn, and every few seconds there was blown an ear-splitting brawl, which was heard far out at sea and above the din of the breaking rollers. It was allowed to roar only in foggy weather, but it was eccentric in that it would only sound at high tide. When the tide was low, although the weather might be very thick, the thing was silent. For lack of its warning a ship went ashore upon the island rocks, and then it was that the government abandoned its location on the wind hole and erected a steam-siren, or mechanical

LOOKING INTO VAL DEZ HARBOR.

fog-horn, which has since very faithfully performed the necessary service.

Another singular perforation in this island rock is a passageway about two hundred feet long, intersected by several globose enlargements. One enters it on hands and knees, proceeds eighty feet, when it suddenly widens into a chamber about thirty feet in breadth and six or seven feet high. On the farther side the channel again contracts, proceeds, branches, becomes labyrinthine, and finally emerges to the surface in small unexplored holes. As though a ghastly circumstance was needed to make this boring grimly interesting, it is related that the first white person who entered this globular apartment found in it the skeleton of a woman. Her bones were delicate, and her teeth were freshly white. Who she was, how she came there, and for what reason, all this was sealed to the discoverer of her remains.

ON THE NORTH FARALLONES.

THE INTERIOR OF SANTA CATALINA ISLAND.

These were withdrawn into the open and interred beneath a cairn of stones.

There is but little vegetation upon the islands, and that much of the same character as is found upon the mainland. Santa Catalina, however, differing from the others in the numerous springs of fresh water—a circumstance which has been availed of to make it a resort—has considerable verdure and many groves of trees. Among these is the *Lyono thamnus*, a tree not found elsewhere than upon the islands. It has a stout branched trunk, and bears white blossoms in June. This island is also decorated with various charming and refreshing flowers —white lilacs, tree-poppies, and lavender, with ferns and lichens draping gloomy walls or weaving a carpet over the broken surface. Santa Cruz also has a good stream of water, which allows the growth of considerable vegetation.

But upon the other islands there is little else than a bleak desert, a waste of sand and cacti, the latter interspersed with blackthorn, the glistening fleshy ice-plant covering terraces and terraces of bluffs, which rise step by step to the plateaus above. A sparse growth of grass brought up by the winter rains heightens the tawny aspect to a light faint green, but the immense herds of sheep with which all these places are populated soon eat this off back to the bare brown earth; or if it is not devoured while green, it dries into an ashy herbage—scant fodder for the hungry mouths.

These winter rains also supply the chief water sources of the islands. They are caught in holes in the rock surface called water-pots; in these the fluid collects, and for several months after the lapse of the humid season it may remain sufficiently fresh to be palatable; but after it stagnates or evaporates there is little of potable moisture accessible, and vegetation would soon perish were it not for the heavy fogs, which during three months of spring are so dense upon the islands and deposit such heavy dews as to amount almost to showers. On San Clemente there is a well from which a brackish liquid is pumped, and on the Farallones there is a mineral spring— pure water agreeably impregnated with iron and sulphur. But beyond this the water-supply is not material, and frequently, in periods of long drouths, with feed all consumed and water scarce, great sacrifices are made in sheep life by the owners of these animals. There are in all perhaps sixty thousand sheep maintained upon the islands, and the number has a constant tendency to increase in excess of the possible food-supply. When such a condition is conceived to have been reached, a fiat of wholesale execution goes out, and then it is that *matanzas*, or great abattoirs, are erected, in which thousands of sheep are killed merely for their pelts, tallow, and glue. In 1875, on Santa Cruz Island, twelve thousand were thus slaughtered, and in 1887 twenty-five thousand were in like summary manner taken off.

The few persons who herd these sheep comprise the populations of the islands. An exception to this is presented by Santa Catalina, which, being a resort, has several thousand inhabitants, gathered principally into its village, Avalon. The owners of the islands are the proprietors of the sheep. In the early fifties, when these lands were taken possession of, in some instances by the parties who now own them, they were stocked with about two hundred sheep apiece. Fenced in by their fluid barrier, there was no possibility of the animals' escaping, and small danger of the preserves ever being invaded by thieves. The stock was left to their own shift, and their owners concerned themselves with other affairs in divers parts of California, But soon the sheep had so multiplied that the island principalities came to be veritable El Dorados. Thousands of dollars of annual income were derived from them, and are to-day, though when first seized upon the islands were covered with heavy growths of rich grasses, which had accumulated upon them through successive years

of unmolestation, and which it took even a large number of animals a long time to eat off, and the areas would then support larger flocks than now. In those days, too, which were the early period of California's settlement, the prices of wool and mutton were much in excess of present quotations; so that a very few years of the earlier returns which these gentlemen acquired through their island estates made them comfortably rich.

Of animals *feræ naturæ* upon these islands there are several species — wild hogs on Santa Cruz and Santa Rosa, wild goats on Santa Catalina and San Clemente. Both of these were placed there by whites, though the year of their introduction is not known. Originally domestic, they have returned to a state of nature through neglect. Rats and mice are also upon the islands, having been cast thither by vessels wrecked upon their rocks; there are also a small red fox and a skunk, which are indigenous mammals; but there are neither serpents, frogs, nor poisonous insects, these noxious things never having been transported thither.

The tourist exploring the interior of the island caves will experience an unpleasant shock when, after proceeding far into the grotto, he discovers that the

SANTA CRUZ ISLAND—THE MAIN RANCH.

place has inhabitants; and the splash, panic, and roar which follow tell him that the occupants are sea-lions. Quickly he must needs speed out, for they will plunge straight toward him, dive under him, and he must be wary, else they will upset his boat, and once he is in the water they will attack him, with possibly fatal results.

Sea-lions are abundant about all of the islands. At Anacapa there is an enormous kelp-bed, where they breed and have their metropolis. These carnivora are not fur-bearing, but are covered with hair which grows upon a thick, unelastic hide. The hide has few uses, and the flesh is not palatable, though Indians find many services for the former, and the latter has furnished innumerable meals to both whites and natives. About Anacapa, too, there is a variety of shell-fish, the most notable of which is the haliotis, or abalone. It is a univalve, which seizes hold of a rock with its strong, muscular foot, and floats idly upward upon the surface, its broad scooped shell shielding its body like a dark umbrella. When disturbed it will suddenly contract, collapse, and its shell will be drawn over the body tightly against the rock. These abalone are much sought, and their fisheries sustain a numerous population of Italians and Chinese. The shell is iridescent, the nacre being variegated blue and green or pink and white; they are exported to London, where they are worked up into mother-of-pearl of commerce, and so employed in the manufacture of buttons and ornaments. The flesh of the animal is dried, and becomes a hard, soap-colored ball as large as a woman's fist. It is sent to China, where it is used as food. The shells bring $30 per ton, while $90 is paid for a like quantity of the desiccated meat.

Upon San Nicolas, the farthest seaward of the islands, lying about sixty miles off shore, there are innumerable remnants of an aboriginal population. Evidences appear upon all the islands of their having been the abode of a race of people who have passed; but at San Nicolas appear all the specimens that are found elsewhere, and many that have not been duplicated by any other spot. Immense mounds of abalone shells, some half an acre in extent, are among these curiosities, revealing the sites of periodic feasts of the islanders upon this fish. Among these piles are scattered the shells of the limpet, mya, mussel, and other mollusks, while stone mortars and pestles, implements of bone and ornaments of teeth, are both numerous and curious.

On a knoll two miles from the island beach is an Indian burial-ground. A dozen or more grim skeletons with their whitened skulls lie upon the shore, denuded of the sand in which they were once interred. The wild winds have swept it away, and the rains and fogs and the bleaching suns have been striving to dissolve and eradicate them, but they still remain. Some of the skulls show evidences of the tragic manner in which their owners met their deaths. The Innuits, it is said, coming down from the Alaskan archipelagoes, fell upon these harmless children of the south, massacred the men, and after a little while abandoned the women and the young, and carried off all they could steal. This was long after 1542, when Ca-

ONE DAY'S CATCH.
Jew-fish, a shark and small fry.

SHEEP-SHEARING.

brillo, the Spanish navigator, visited the islands, and found them tenanted by a mild and vigorous people, who, revelling in the soft ether of their climate, found their sustenance in the plenitudinous spontaneity of nature.

After the invasion of the Innuits and their departure, those who remained managed to maintain themselves until 1835, when the Franciscan friars went to the islands, and gathering them all into boats, took them to the mainland, where they were mingled with the neophytes of the missions. It is related that after the last boat had pushed off from San Nicolas a woman screamed for her child, which, in the excitement of the movement aboard the transports, she had forgotten. She jumped out of the vessel and sped away to seek it. The boat continued its passage, and the woman was left to her fate. The baby died, but the lone and miserable creature remained the solitary inhabitant of the place for many years. In her old age she was rescued and brought to Santa Barbara, where she died soon after her arrival.

Of all the several islands the Faral-

lones are the most remarkable, for the fact that they comprise the rookeries of vast numbers of sea-fowl, which assemble there and breed. These lie opposite the bay of San Francisco, and they are used by the government for a light-house station. The maintenance of this requires the residence upon the island of a small colony of persons who in the service of the government consent thus to banish themselves from society. The light-house steamer visits them every three months, then restocks their larder. Aside from this their only communication with civilization is by an occasional tug which may stop there to allow its captain to spy abroad from the light-house tower for incoming craft. Sometimes such a landing is not possible, owing to the height of the sea, and weeks may pass before the waters will subside so such can be effected.

At nearly all times a strong cool wind prevails, and often in the afternoon it is sifted through with fog. A high board fence has been erected to protect the vegetation in the tiny patch of the light-house-tender's garden from being uprooted by

THE GREAT MURRE ROOKERY, SOUTH FARALLONES.

the wind. But even with that, plant life does not thrive—or rather it thrives excessively, so that foliage becomes rank, and the fruit is a failure through growing too fast. Cabbages spring up, rush quickly into an abundance of green heavy leaves, but will not head. Onions and potatoes become immense in stalk and foliage, but will not "bulb" or "tuber." The cause of this is the strong guano soil in which the plants are grown; and the guano is deposited by the wild sea-fowl, which infest all the Farallones, three in number, making of them, in the opinion of ornithologists, the greatest bird islands in the world.

There are eight varieties of these birds. They are the guillemot, commonly called the murre, the gull, the auk or auklet, the sea-pigeon, the shag or cormorant, the ashy petrel, the tufted puffin or sea-parrot, and the rock-wren. The first of these, the murre, dominates in number and importance upon the island. It is a kind of duck, with a black head, white breast, and bluish back, and sits upright like a penguin. Its food is vegetable, dissection never having revealed the presence of fish. Its eggs are valuable for food, and until recently and for many years they were extensively gathered and sold in the San Francisco market, about fifteen thousand dozen yearly being disposed of there, purchased mainly by restaurants and boarding-houses, at an average price of twenty-five cents per dozen. The egg is about twice the size of that of a hen, is white or bluish-green, and flecked with brown. When fresh it is indistinguishable from the hen product, but it soon develops a fishy taste. The murre lays one egg upon a nest of roots or grass, and proceeds to incubate the next generation. At night, when she is off duty, the male succeeds her. If unmolested, the nest will thus be covered until the young is hatched, when it will be guarded for a few weeks, then escorted off into the indefinite distance of the sea.

But if the murre is disturbed by an egg-hunter and its single egg taken, it will return and replace its successively stolen ovum until eight have been laid. It is loath to leave its nest even when the despoiler approaches, and when he comes up she leans away from him and moves over to the far side of the nest. But presently, yielding to the alarm within her breast, she emits a sudden squawk and flies off, flushing the entire rookery as she moves toward the sea, leaving the pickers to fill their pouched shirts with the booty. They must hurry the work, for as soon as the eggs are uncovered the gulls hover close and become thick upon the scene. These the men must fight off, for they brazenly interpose themselves and battle with the humans for the possession of the eggs.

AN EGG-PICKER'S CABIN.

The opportunity being open, the gull sweeps down upon the murre egg, seizes it in its mouth and goes sailing aloft; cracks it in its bill and gobbles what of its contents it can, the residue falling on the rocks below; then it takes another swoop away and balances itself to spy out a new egg.

The gull's egg also is palatable. It is slightly smaller than that of the murre, whitish and speckled, three eggs being a litter. The eggs of the other birds are worthless for human uses, but their nests are raided by gulls and by each other. The albuminous fluid of the cormorant egg will not coagulate, and the puffin's egg has a repulsive fishy flavor. This bird has black plumage, with red beak and feet, while the cormorant is a large light blue bird, and flies in pairs. The sea-pigeon is dark slate with some white in its wings; it has red feet, and lays a light blue egg. The auk is as large as a pigeon, and is nocturnal in its habits. The petrel has a musky smell, by the odor of which its nest is easily traceable.

The murres make their nests high up, and often in the open, but the others hide theirs in the crevices of the rocks. Their note is loud, shrill, not pleasing to the ear; all except the cheery little rock-wren, whose liquid warble is a sweet, harmonious solo in the concert of shrieks and screams which ascend from the thousands of feathered throats.

That these islands were a great repository of edible eggs became known in the early fifties. At the time of the discovery of this fact provisions were scarce and gold was plentiful in San Francisco, and the rookery eggs offered in the markets of that city brought one dollar a dozen. The opening of this new and free opportunity to acquire wealth precipitated numbers of people upon the islands and in the business of egg-gathering. Quarrels ensued

A GULL'S NEST.

between the competitors as to their respective "rights" in the premises, with the result that a company was formed among a number of the pickers, which bought out the claims of the others. This company managed to hold on to its advantages for some years, not, however, without experiencing contests and encroachments, until the bickerings ultimately grew so fierce as to attract the attention of the United States district attorney at San Francisco. He sent a detachment of government soldiers there and deported every egg-picker.

Following this the murres and gulls were permitted for a season to lay and hatch in safety; but later, the government revealing no desire for revenue from the eggs, those on the island allowed them to be picked on shares. This introduced a company of about eighteen Greek and Italian egg-pickers into the nidus-robbing enterprise; but disputes soon again arose, and ultimately to re-establish peace upon the islands it became necessary to forbid permanently any traffic in the eggs. This has accordingly been done by a recent order from Washington.

A Handful of the Flock, Santa Cruz Island.

IN WESTERN CAMPS

AS Bishop of Wyoming and Idaho my Sundays, during the summer months, were usually passed in the mining-camps of Idaho. At Challis, Bay Horse, Clayton, Silver City, Idaho City, Placerville, Murray, Wallace, Wardner, and many others, services were held annually, and in some of these places churches were erected and clergymen maintained. In those days the visit of a bishop was an occasion of unusual interest. The camps, as a rule, were far from a railroad, and the annual visit of the bishop brought into the life of the place a new interest, which, for the time being, was all-absorbing. Especially was this the case where, as often happened, the bishop was the only minister of any religious body who visited the settlement from year to year. If any of the young people were looking forward to being married, the important question was, "When is the Bishop coming?" He could not be expected to make so long a journey simply to perform the ceremony, but it was often possible to so time the event as to have it coincide with his visit, and hence it was desirable that the date of his coming should be widely published in the local papers some months in advance. Then there were the children to be baptized, when a feast was generally given and the neighbors invited to be present.

I recall very vividly my first visit to a certain mining-camp. It involved a stage ride of seventy-five miles over a rough mountain road. I reached the place about sundown on Friday evening. As I alighted from the stage-coach in front of the hotel, a little man demurely presented himself. He extended his hand and asked, "Is this the Bishop?" "Yes," I replied. "Well, Bishop, I am Brother May, the new minister. I arrived only yesterday. I am so glad to see you, Bishop; for this is the most God-forsaken hole I ever struck." "Oh, well, do not be discouraged, my good brother," I answered, "for if it is such a place as you describe, you and I are much needed here, and we shall find plenty of work to do. I shall see you a little later, and we shall have a good talk." So I passed on into the hotel.

As I registered my name, I noticed, behind the counter, all the attractive paraphernalia of a first-class saloon. I was dusty and tired and hungry. After having made myself somewhat presentable, I was soon eagerly paying my respects to the various dishes set before me in the dining-room. Hunger is, indeed, the best sauce, and how I did relish the food in the mining-camps after those stage rides over the mountains! Dinner over, I returned to the hotel office. There I found Brother May awaiting me. I offered him a cigar, but he declined, with a look of some surprise that a bishop should be addicted to such a vice. I proposed a stroll up the canyon, for, after sitting on the stage-coach all day, I felt the need of a walk. Brother May was very communicative. He proceeded to tell me the story of his life. He said he had been living in San Francisco; that as a boy he had been apprenticed to a printer, and had learned to set type, and might have done well, but had fallen into bad company and acquired the habit of drink; that he had also been addicted to gambling; that he had gone from bad to worse, until finally he had lost his position and his friends and was an outcast. About that time there was a great revival in the city. He dropped in one night and became

* Bishop Talbot (now of the diocese of Central Pennsylvania) was the first Bishop of the missionary district of Wyoming and Idaho, which was established in 1886. For eleven years he carried on his work in the far West, journeying constantly over wide and wild territory, meeting at every turn unusual adventure.—EDITOR.

BISHOP TALBOT ON A MISSIONARY JOURNEY

interested. He was gradually led to see the evil of his way, and determined, with God's help, to lead a new life. His conversion was so unmistakably the work of the Spirit of God that he felt he must consecrate the remainder of his days to the preaching of the gospel. He was over thirty years of age. He had no time to lose. The authorities of his church advised him to go to some theological seminary and prepare himself; but he told them that he knew the story of the cross and the love of God, and felt eager to proclaim the message to men. He asked for no large place, no important church. Indeed, he begged them to send him to the most neglected and sinful place to be found. "And so, Bishop," he said, "they sent me here. I came only yesterday. This is my first charge, and my church has certainly sent me to the most God-forsaken hole it could find." I again tried to reassure him, and suggested that while, as he said, there were many saloons in the camp, it was not strange that such a situation should obtain, as there was no church and no minister before he came. I also expressed the hope that he would find the people kindly and warm-hearted and ready to cooperate with him in his efforts to do them good. But he evidently considered the prospect almost hopeless. We arranged that I should preach in the dance-hall on the morning and evening of the approaching Sunday, and that he should hold forth at four o'clock

in the afternoon. I told him that at my eleven-o'clock service I should take pleasure in announcing his appointment, and also formally introduce him to his flock and ask him to say a word to them. This conversation took place Friday evening.

After enjoying a good, refreshing night's sleep I found myself ready on Saturday morning to prepare for my Sunday duties. First of all, it was important to make sure of my congregation. I had come so far that I did not like the idea of a mere handful of women and children. I longed to get hold of the men. The main street seemed full of miners. It was pay-day, and the place presented a sort of holiday appearance. It occurred to me that it was a good opportunity to become acquainted. As I walked down the street, I saw advancing toward me an elegantly dressed gentleman, with large diamonds shining upon his spotless linen. There were seven saloons in a row. As I drew near my handsome young friend and was about to extend my hand, he surveyed me, concluded I was a parson and might wish to interview him on some subject with which he was not familiar, and suddenly disappeared into one of the saloons.

The experience was a little discomfiting, but I summoned up courage and determined to try again. The next man was in his shirt-sleeves, but had an open, frank countenance. I assumed as gracious and friendly an aspect as I could command and was about to greet him, when he too darted into a saloon. Twice defeated, I went back to the hotel, and asked Colonel Burns, the proprietor, to let me have some large writing-paper. In bold hand I wrote out a few notices. I announced that, as Bishop of Idaho, I had come to the camp, and would preach the next morning, Sunday, at eleven o'clock and in the evening at eight; that both services would be in the dance-hall. All were cordially invited to attend. Then the Colonel let me have some tacks. I put up a notice at the hotel, at the post-office, at the large store, and at the blacksmith's shop. I then stood off and looked to see if any one would read my notices. But, alas! there were already so many notices ahead of mine! One announced an exciting horse-race Sunday afternoon, a second a mine to be sold, a third a ranch to be rented, etc., etc. I soon discovered that my method of advertising was not likely to be successful. What more could I do? As I walked by the saloons, I observed that they were full of men. If only I were not a bishop, I reflected, the problem would be easy of solution; for then I could go into the saloons where the men are and deliver my invitation in person; but how would it look for a bishop to

BISHOP TALBOT

A photograph taken while on a hunting-trip

visit such places, even with the best of motives? At last I became desperate. I selected the first saloon in the row. I went in. I introduced myself to the proprietor. I told him I was the Bishop of Idaho, and had come in to pay my respects to him. He met me very cordially. "Why, Bishop, I am proud to know you. What will you have?"

I thanked him and told him I should be greatly indebted to him if he would kindly introduce me to those gentlemen, pointing to a large room back of the saloon, where the men were gathered. "Do you mean the boys in the pool-room?" he asked. "Yes, I presume I do." Thereupon he came out from behind the counter, put his arm in mine in a familiar way, as though we had been boon companions all our lives, and escorted me to the open doorway of the pool-room. "Boys," he cried out, "hold up the game. Put up the chips just a minute. This is the Bishop right among us, and he wants to be introduced." With a politeness and courtesy which would have done credit to any drawing-room in New York or Boston or Philadelphia, the men rose from their seats and welcomed me. I said briefly: "Excuse me, gentlemen; I do not wish to interfere with your pleasure or your amusement. I have just come in to pay my respects to you. I am the bishop, and am going to hold services in the dance-hall to-morrow morning at eleven and in the evening at eight, and I shall be very glad to see you there." I remember that one of them, evidently speaking in a representative capacity, thanked me for letting them know, and asked me again the hour, and assured me they would all be present. In this way I visited all the seven saloons in the row. Everywhere I was treated with the most respectful consideration, and I did not hear one word that could have offended the most delicate conscience. When I had completed the round, I felt that I was reasonably sure of a goodly number of men as my hearers.

Coming out of one of the saloons, I suddenly encountered on the street my little friend Brother May, the new minister. He gave me a look of commingled surprise and pity, and with it a slight touch of scorn; but no words were exchanged between us. When, after my visitation of the saloons, I returned to my hotel, I found Brother May with his face buried in a newspaper. He hardly deigned to speak to me. He had been greatly shocked at seeing me emerge from a saloon. His ideals of the episcopal office had received a terrible blow. I asked him some question. He hardly vouchsafed a reply. I tried him again. At last he put down his paper, and looking at me with a much-aggrieved expression, said, " Look here, Bishop; didn't I see you coming out of a saloon ?"

" Yes, Brother May, you did, and if you had watched me, you would have seen me coming out of seven." " Well," he continued, " all I have to say is I am sadly disappointed in you. My heart had gone out to you, and I was thanking God for sending you to this awful place, and now to think of a bishop going into one of those hells !" I tried to explain to my reverend little brother that I had visited more saloons that day than in all of the days of my life before; that I was not a drinking man, and regretted the evils of strong drink as much as he or any man could, but that I had come to get hold of those men; that I only visited the camp one Sunday a year, while he would have an opportunity every week to talk

to them. Gradually it dawned upon him that my act was, after all, susceptible of a charitable interpretation, though he could not justify it; nor could he agree with me in thinking that my efforts to secure the presence of the men would prove successful, but felt sure they would not come out, no matter what they promised,—in short, that I had hopelessly impaired my influence with them. I could only ask him to wait and see. It was clearly evident that Brother May's faith in me had been subjected to a severe test, and had almost reached the breaking-point.

That evening we gathered together a few good people and practised some familiar hymns. A young woman was found who played the little organ. The morrow came—a bright and beautiful Sunday. As the hour of service approached, I could see that a great crowd was gathering. I had already put on my robes, and was seated on the platform of the dance-hall, where also the organ and the choir were placed. As the men filed in, they occupied every available space. I invited some to sit on the edge of the high platform. Others took advantage of the fact that the windows were opened and stationed themselves there. A large number had to stand near the doorway; but from the beginning to the close of the service a hushed and entirely reverential demeanor characterized the assembly. They listened most patiently to all I had to say. There was something peculiarly solemnizing and inspiring in those manly and earnest faces as they seemed to respond to the appeal I was making. After I had finished the sermon, I introduced Brother May. I told the men that while the church I had the honor to represent had not yet seen its way to send them a minister, yet I rejoiced that Brother May, representing another religious body, had come; that he was present in the congregation, and I was glad to introduce him; that he was to preach that afternoon at four.

Then Brother May arose. He was extremely short of stature, and had a long black mustache, curled up at the ends. He wore a bright-green cutaway coat, a blue waistcoat, and red necktie. His boots had high heels, tapered after the cowboy fashion. All eyes were instantly fastened upon him. A stillness that was painful fell upon the scene. Brother May stood near the platform. Instead of turning around and facing the people, he stood sidewise, looking at them over his shoulder. "Yes, brethren, as the Bishop has said, I am here, and I am here to stay. I have come to preach the gospel, and my first sermon will be at four o'clock here in this place. I want you all to be on hand, for God knows you need the gospel. Just think of it; you have seven saloons here in this camp. Seven dens of hell! The fact is, this is the most God-forsaken hole I ever struck." He sat down. There was no audible expression of dissent, but I could feel that my little brother had forfeited his opportunity to commend himself to the people. I was sorry.

Another hymn was given out, and I was about to dismiss the congregation with my blessing, when Colonel Burns, my landlord, stepped forward, and in a low but distinct voice said, "Bishop, haven't you forgot somethin'?" "What do you mean?" said I. "Why, the hat," replied the Colonel. "Excuse me," I answered; "you are right. I had quite forgotten the collection." "I thought so," said the Colonel. "It won't do to forget the hat, for yesterday was payday, and these boys have a lot of money, and if you don't get it the saloons will, and it is much better for you to have it. Now, Bishop, if you will allow me, I will run that part of the business myself."

"Very good," I said. "Have you any suggestions, Colonel?"

"Only this, Bishop: I wish you would give us about five hymns."

"Five!" I exclaimed. "You surely do not mean five hymns."

"Yes, Bishop," he replied. "I want plenty of time. I do not want to be crowded. The boys are a little slow on collections."

I stepped over to the organ and arranged with the young woman who was playing for us to give us five familiar hymns. We started in. The Colonel presented the hat to the man immediately on my left. He was sitting on the edge of the platform. He brought out a silver dollar, called a "wheel" in the language of the camp. The second and third men to whom the hat was passed followed the example of the first, each giving a dollar; but the fourth man seemed nervous, and hesitated while he fumbled in his pocket. After considerable delay he brought out a quarter.

"Oh, put that back. Come now, Bill," said the Colonel, "the Bishop is not after small game to-day. White chips don't go here. He wants a wheel out of you. Hurry up."

"But, Colonel," said the man, "I hain't got no wheel; I'm busted."

"Oh, what you givin' us?" said the Colonel. "Borrow one from Jack. Jack will loan you one."

I was not supposed to hear this dialogue, but the Colonel evidently took no pains to conceal what was going on. After some little parleying, Jack loaned his neighbor a "wheel," and the hat passed on. I can remember the Colonel, when he reached the crowd standing at the door, held out the hat with one hand, while with the other he expostulated with the men. The hymns were being rapidly used up, and at last the Colonel returned to the platform with the hat. His face beamed with satisfaction. After the service I asked him why it took him so long. "Oh," he replied, "Bishop, you see, I 'sized' up every feller accordin' to his pile. I know these boys. Most on 'em grub with me. I made one feller cough up a ten-dollar gold piece, and you will find a good many fives in the hat. Let's count it." I need not say that the collection was a generous one.

At four o'clock I went to the hall to help and hear Brother May. As yet no one had come. At length a few women and children and one old man straggled in. Brother May preached on the "Rose of Sharon." It was his maiden effort. The afternoon was very warm, and the perspiration poured forth as my little friend labored with the text. He was thoroughly discouraged, and could not understand why the hall was not full. I ventured to suggest that I feared he had not been very tactful in the morning when he told them that their town was the most "God-forsaken hole" he had ever seen. I learned afterward that Brother May remained at the camp only about three weeks. At the end of that time a committee waited on him. The spokesman said, "Brother May, we un-

INDIAN TEPEES NEAR AN IDAHO MINING-CAMP

derstand you don't like our camp." "No," said Brother May; "it is the worst I ever struck." "Well, Brother May, would you like to shake off the dust of our camp and leave us for better diggin's?" "You bet I would," was the reply. "Well, will you leave if we give you seventy-five dollars?" "Sure I will." "Will you leave by to-morrow's stage?" "I certainly will." "Then here's your money." And Brother May departed for parts unknown.

To return to our Sunday's work. That evening there was another service and another great crowd. I begged the men to do something toward securing a minister and building a church. I reminded them that they had had no one to bury their dead, minister to their sick and wounded, baptize their children, administer the holy communion and preach the gospel. I told them I would be glad to cooperate with them in any effort they might make. When Monday morning came, a committee waited on me with a petition signed by more than a hundred miners, begging me to stay over and give them another talk that night. I consented, and the dance-hall was again com-

pletely filled. Tuesday morning, just before I took the stage, a committee came to me from a neighboring saloon with a subscription paper. One of the committee said:

"Now, Bishop, you have been going for us about not having a preacher. Here is a proposition. If you will stay here, and rustle up this preachin' business, and be our parson, we will stand by you to the tune of $2000 a year. Here it is down in black and white. This is all gilt edge."

Of course I was surprised and gratified. I replied that while I felt much complimented by their offer, it was evident they did not understand the nature of my office; that I was a bishop, and had to go from place to place, and could tarry nowhere long; that I was on my way to the next camp; but I added, "With this liberal offer of $2000 a year, I can send you a first-class man." They hesitated and seemed a little embarrassed. After some consultation one of them said:

"Bishop, that was not the deal. The boys subscribed this for you. If you can't come, we will have to make a new deal." With that they again disappeared into the saloon. Returning in a few moments, the spokesman said:

"Bishop, here is a new list. If you will send us a first-rate man, a good talker and a good mixer, we will guarantee him at least $1000 a year. Tell him, Bishop, there will be no trouble about money. He sha'n't be allowed to suffer. We boys will treat him white. Only, please remember," he added, with a twinkle in his eye, "don't send us no stick."

They had not forgotten Brother May's rebuke, and were not willing to take any chances. The term "good mixer" was new to me then, but I learned it meant the qualities of good-fellowship and sympathy and fraternity. The successful man of God in the mining-camp need not lose his dignity or self-respect, but it is of vital importance that he be a man among men, and, above all, possess the capacity of loving men, and with the aid of that gift know how to reach their hearts.

The palmy days of the stage-coach in the Rockies have now passed away. The advent of the railroad has left comparatively small distances to be compassed by this primitive mode of locomotion. The day when six horses were the regulation number gradually gave place to that of the four-horse team; and now two horses sleepily plod along, and carry the mail and such occasional passengers as may be compelled to travel in this way. In my early days in Wyoming and Idaho there were some superb outfits and many interesting and enjoyable features. Runaways, breakdowns—narrow escapes of various kinds—often occurred, recalling the epitaph once found on an old gravestone:

Weep stranger for a father spilled
From a stage-coach, and thereby killed.
His name, Jay Sykes, a maker of sassengers,
Slain with three other outside passengers.

The long distances through a country almost entirely uninhabited exposed the passengers to hold-ups by the "road-agents," as the highway robbers are called out West. Especially was this the case when large sums of money had to be sent through Wells-Fargo's Express Company, or bars of gold and silver had to be carried from the mines. The robbers were wonderfully astute, and generally managed to know just when the consignments were made. At such times it was the custom of the stage company to have one or more fearless men, well armed, ride with the driver; but men who embark in the hazardous calling of the road-agent are very desperate, and take fearful risks when a rich haul is in sight. In these encounters it is simply a question as to which party shall get "the drop" on the other; for, however brave a guard may be, it would be sheer foolhardiness to refuse to throw up his hands when he found himself and companions suddenly covered by three or four deadly Winchesters. Again and again one desperate road-agent has been known to rob a stage-coach full of passengers and compel the driver to throw out the bullion and express-box, while those within the stage, though armed, have meekly looked on in amazement. I usually found it convenient, through the advice of my friends, to make my journeys when the stage did not carry such tempting booty; so it was never my fate to be held up, though frequently the stage which just preceded or followed mine was robbed. Therefore I never had Bishop Kemper's experience in the early days of Kansas. The bishop was the victim of a hold-up one night when he was the only passenger. The driver told the road-agent, who had covered him with a six-shooter, that his only passenger was a bishop. "Well," said the robber, "wake up the old man. I want to go through his pockets." When the bishop was aroused from a sound slumber and realized the situation, he gently remonstrated with the man behind the gun. He said: "Surely you would not rob a poor bishop. I have no money worth your while, and I am engaged in the discharge of my sacred duties." "Did you say you were a bishop?" asked the road-agent. "Yes, just a poor bishop." "What church?" "The Episcopal Church." "The hell you are! Why, that's the church I belong to. Driver, you may pass on."

When spring approached and the heavy snows in the mountains began to melt, there was more or less danger in fording the rivers. The Platte River in Wyoming was particularly treacherous in this respect. When I reached this river at one time on my way to Douglas, I was riding a bronco. The stream looked angry and swollen, and I was debating in my mind whether or not I should plunge in and swim my horse across. Just then a kindly ranchman came upon the scene. He remonstrated with me; he said my bronco was rather small for a man of my size; that the current was swift, and that he thought it would be unsafe to try it. But I said, "I must get to Douglas to - night." "Well," he replied, "I have a boat here, and will row you over, and we will lead the bronco." Accordingly we secured a rope, which we tied around the bronco's neck, placing the saddle and bridle in the boat. We then pulled out, but the bronco would not budge; and all the purchase we could get on him from the boat was unavailing. The ranchman suggested that we should row down the edge of the river and lead him until the bank should get so steep there would be no standing-ground for him. "Then," he added, "we can yank him in." That change of tactics was entirely successful, for we both took hold, and by a united pull brought him into the swift current. My companion was a good oarsman, and he struck out bravely, but it was soon evident that the bronco was making straight for the canoe. The ranchman became somewhat excited lest the pony should capsize us. "Beat him back, beat him back with the other end of the rope! There ain't no room in here for three." I landed several blows on the head of the determined little beast, but they did not seem to discourage him; and it required our combined effort to pilot that frail little craft to the other shore without being upset.

Those of my readers who have ever been at Lewiston, Idaho, will remember that just across the river Clearwater, which flows by the town, is an enormous and most dangerous mountain. If one can keep the road and has a good team, it is safe enough; but there are several places, called "hogbacks," where the road is barely wide enough to allow another team to pass; while on either side of this narrow driveway the mountain

so suddenly recedes that a misstep must precipitate driver and team to imminent destruction. With this inviting prospect on the other side of the river, I found it necessary one dark night to cross the Clearwater and set out for the railway station some miles beyond. The clergyman at Lewiston had a fine pair of horses, which, while full of life, were gentle and trustworthy. On reaching the river, which the clergyman had forded a few days before, we found it unexpectedly swollen. A rope ferry regularly plied across the river, the boat usually landing at the far side of a little island, which teams could reach by fording when the stream was normal. My companion's eyesight was somewhat defective at night, and he did not observe that the river had risen so high as to entirely submerge the island. After hailing the boatman and giving him the signal to come over for us, we waited until we could see the light on the boat, which was approaching the spot where the island was supposed to be. We then drove in. We had not advanced far before I heard frantic screams from the boatman. "Go back; for God's sake go back or you'll drown." Meanwhile the buggy seemed to be fairly throbbing under the power of the current, and our horses had almost lost their footing. I begged my brother to turn round; but he would not. I then snatched the reins from him and got the horses round just as the boat came upon us. The captain said: "Well, parson, one more step and you and the Bishop would have been swept in. Were you trying to drown him?" The experience was one that I did not soon forget.

It was rather curious, and interesting to those who believe in thought transference or mental telepathy, that both my wife and daughter—the former being at that time in Missouri and the latter at school in Pennsylvania—were suddenly awakened that night out of sound sleep by the vivid and painful impression that I was drowning. They agree that the sensation was not in the least like an ordinary dream.

After we had been ferried safely over, we came to the mountain. The wind was howling, and almost blew the buggy off the hogback. Our lantern, suspended from the dashboard, had been blown out. It was pitch dark. Suddenly I felt the buggy sliding down-hill and the horses gradually following. I jumped out, caught the horses by their bridles, and feeling my way back to the road, recovered the trail. When with great difficulty we had relighted our lantern, we found that we had been slipping over the edge of a precipice, and that a few more steps would have hurled us down hundreds of feet.

These are some of the perils by the way which added zest to one's travels, but which it is more pleasant to describe than to experience.

I must be allowed here to pay my grateful tribute to the respectful kindness and consideration always shown me by the stage-drivers. I cannot say that I never heard an oath; but again and again when one slipped out, most gracious apologies have followed. Bishop Clarkson's experience was never mine, but I can fully sympathize with his dilemma.

It seems that on one occasion the bishop was due to preach at a certain town on the prairies of Nebraska. It was in the spring, and the mud was up to the hubs in places. Already it was growing dark, and the lights of the village which the bishop was trying to reach seemed still a long way off. He became

a little nervous lest he should be late for his appointment. Just then they encountered a mud-hole, and the stage-coach stuck fast. The driver laid on the lash, but in vain; the horses would not move. The bishop was on the box with the driver, who was getting desperate. Unable to stand it longer, he turned to the bishop and said, " Do you see those wheelers looking back at me?" " Yes, Harry; what does that mean?" " Bishop, you know I have always tried to treat you right, and I respect your cloth; but do you say you want to preach in that there town to-night?" " Of course I do, Harry. Why don't you whip your horses?" " Whip 'em, Bishop! Ain't I been a-whippin' of 'em my level best? Do you say that you must preach there to-night?" " Of course I must." " Well, Bishop, I ask it just once. You see, these horses are used to my style of talkin' to 'em. I know it's a bad habit, and I know it's wrong, but will you please give me a dispensation just this one time? If you will, I'll get you there or bust. What do you say, Bishop?" The bishop felt the case to be extreme. " Well, Harry, I suppose I'll have to. Fire away this one time." Harry ripped out an oath, and the horses got down on their haunches, cleared the mud-hole, and just in time landed the bishop in town.

THE VIGILANTES OF CALIFORNIA, IDAHO AND MONTANA

IN the month of November, 1850, there were eight primitive houses situated on the extreme point of a little peninsula far projecting into the Bay of San Francisco. It was separated from the surrounding country by a rocky mountain range. The eight houses were occupied by an American hunter and seven French fishermen, deserters from a French man-of-war. On the opposite side was another French settlement of five fishermen. All of the cattle owned by the two settlements was a single goat, the loss of which would have proved a public calamity. Its master had brought it from France, around Cape Horn. Besides the hunting and fishing people, there was, beyond these settlements also, a regular farmer called the Irish Captain, although he was neither Irish nor a captain. He was a Dane by birth,

and a farmer all his life by occupation. He possessed a valuable stock of imported cattle—a rare thing at that time. Farther into the interior, on the other side of the mountain range, was the Cornelia Rancho, a California manor-house, constructed of rough beams, and surrounded by mud and cattle instead of gardens, parks, green grass, and flowers. Cornelia was a native grandee, and claimed the right to four hundred square miles of territory. Although the invasion of her country by the gold-hunters had swept away the greater part of her herds, yet there still remained over a thousand head. In full dress, adorned with gold chains, pearls, and jewels, she looked very magnificent, seated in a large wagon drawn by two oxen and sixteen mules, roughing it over a country without roads. This, however, was upon state occasions, and of rare occurrence. Her home dress was an old broad-brimmed straw hat, leather boots, a loose white shirt, and a short petticoat of coarse red flannel. She ruled over thirty Indian servants besides her son—twenty-four years of age—and a homeless Portuguese adventurer, who, seeking a support, had drifted to that Eden before the rude gold-hunters dispersed the charm of silence, simplicity, and ignorance that reigned complete everywhere. The Irish Captain was not slow to perceive his advantage over the señora. He therefore proposed to her to take charge of her cattle and sell to the best advantage, on condition that he should have one-half of the sum realized, which proposition was reluctantly accepted by the señora. The Irish Captain now organized for the common defence by calling a general meeting, and binding each by a covenant to take care of his neighbors' property by armed force when necessary. But a short time thereafter a boat laden with stolen beef from the señora's herds was captured, and the cattle-thieves taken prisoners by the Frenchmen of Low Point. The thieves were tied, put under a boat turned upside down, and closely watched. The Irish Captain himself escorted the prisoners to San Francisco the following morning, and delivered them into the hands of the civil authorities. Instead of being punished for their lawless crimes, they were set at liberty by the civil authorities, and retaliated upon the Irish Captain by butchering and carrying off all his milch-cows. These thieves and this system of robbery received the countenance of rich and influential butchers of San Francisco, who furnished the means for these predatory incursions, and the money to retain influential counsel to defend and acquit, through technicalities of the law, such of the thieves as should fall into the hands of the Irish Captain and his cohorts. Convinced that no redress could be obtained from the civil authorities at San Francisco, a second general meeting was held, and it was unanimously resolved that the residents of the peninsula should form themselves into a permanent committee, and assume all the duties of police and courts martial. No suspected party should be permitted to land. Thieves and other criminals should be tried before the committee, and, if found guilty, executed on the spot. Thus was formed the first Vigilance Committee that ever existed within the limits of California. Within a week three men, who confessed themselves to be Australian convicts, were tried, convicted, and executed by hanging to a tree. Cattle-thieves abounded, and retribution swift and sure was meted out whenever the crime could be fixed by the logic of circumstances. Justice and injustice met on a common level. Small bodies of people took the law into their own hands with the same degree of conscious right as emboldened the acts of two or ten thousand. Sometimes a single individual became at once judge, jury, and executioner. On the highway from San Francisco to San José was found a corpse shot through the body, and to the lower button-hole was tied a placard upon which was written, in very legible characters, these significant words:

> I SHOT HIM BECAUSE HE STOLE MY MULE
> JOHN ANDREW ANDERSON
> ANDERSON RANCHO SANTA CLARA VALLEY.

He was not a murderer, but an executor of the law, the *lex non scripta* against all cattle-thieves. If ten men could capture and slay him for the crime, the same right belonged to but one of the party, provided he alone could accomplish it.

Pressed by these vigorous methods, the thieves and robbers in the country retired to the larger towns and settlements to ply their vocation. Popular justice there was neither so swift nor so sure. Public opinion, however, opposed any infringement of the rights and methods of the civil authorities. What five men could do in the country, five hundred could not accomplish in San Francisco or Sacramento.

Sacramento was the first of the large towns to organize a committee of its citizens for the protection of social order, and its executions became celebrated for the interest displayed in them by the people of the surrounding country. The first of these was at night on the Plaza, in the light of a great fire and in the presence of a great multitude. The office of hangman was conceded as a post of honor to the most reputable and wealthy citizen of the town. Two days after, he paid the penalty of this honor by being himself shot by the desperadoes.

San Francisco seemed loath to begin

the exercise of this inherent power of the people; but the great fire of May already alluded to, and the appeals of the *Alta California* and *California Herald*, which declared that nothing could disturb the culprits' equanimity but the extreme measure of hanging by the neck, caused a revulsion of feeling, and early in the month of June following two hundred of its most influential citizens formed an association, which they named a Committee of Vigilance, for the maintenance of the peace and good order of society and the preservation of the lives and property of the citizens of San Francisco.

Large placards affixed to the walls in public places of the city and private houses of the citizens, containing the rules and regulations adopted for maintaining the public peace of the city, and the manner in which public justice should be administered, gave notice of their organization. The tolling of the bell of the Monumental Fire-Engine house on the Plaza was the signal for the members to instantly assemble fully armed.

Thousands of citizens secretly joined the organization, and their services were soon called into requisition. On the evening of the 10th of June the shipping office of a Mr. Virgin, on the wharf, was robbed of a small safe containing a considerable sum of money. The thief was captured and placed in the custody of members of the Vigilance Committee at their rooms. The property was identified, and the prisoner convicted on the testimony of the boatman who had pulled out with the prisoner and his booty into the bay, where he was subsequently arrested. The Chief of Police now appeared at the rooms of the committee and demanded admittance and the custody of the prisoner. His request was refused.

After carefully deliberating upon the character of the punishment, it was finally determined that though not a capital offence, the necessity existed for the execution of the criminal, and that it should take place at once to prevent a rescue by the friends of the culprit, or an armed interference on the part of the civil authorities. He was accordingly notified of his doom, and given one hour to prepare for death. Shortly after midnight the condemned man was taken under a strong guard to Portsmouth Square, and hanged to the cross-beams of the gable end of an adobe building which had been used in former times as a post-office, but was then unoccupied. A coroner's jury of inquest on the day following returned this verdict: "John Jenkins, *alias* Simpkins, came to his death by being suspended by the neck with a rope attached to the end of the adobe building on the Plaza at the hands of an association of citizens styling themselves a Committee of Vigilance, of whom the following members are implicated." Then followed the names of the citizens who had been most conspicuous on the occasion.

When this verdict and the names were published on the day following, the Vigilance Committee ordered the names of all its members published likewise. The committee, however, was strongly opposed by the civil authorities and the legal fraternity generally, and Judge Campbell, of the Court of Sessions, holding his assizes on the days appointed, charged his Grand Jury that "all those concerned in the illegal execution had been guilty of murder, *participes criminis.*" The Governor of the State, MacDougal, afterward United States Senator, issued a proclamation addressed to the people at large, in which he referred to the action of the people as the "despotic control of a self-constituted association unknown to and acting in defiance of the laws in the place of the regularly organized government of the country."

In the month of August the committee tried two men named Samuel Whittaker and Robert McKenzie. They were proven guilty of very serious offences—burglary, robbery, and incendiarism. It was understood that they were to be executed on the 21st of that month. A writ was issued by Judge Norton, of the Supreme Court, commanding the sheriff to bring the prisoners before his court at a certain hour to be dealt with according to law. That night the sheriff and one deputy gained admission in some way to the rooms of the committee, where the prisoners were confined, led them down stairs, and placed them in charge of police-officers awaiting them below. No immediate steps were taken by the committee to remedy this interference with their purposes, but on the following Sunday, shortly after two o'clock in the afternoon, a carriage turned into Broadway from Du Pont Street, and halted a short distance from the jail. It was at this hour that the prisoners were brought from their cells to hear divine service from the chaplain of the prison. A preconcerted rush was made from the outside, the prisoners captured, and carried off to the rooms of the committee. The fire-bell tolled the signal for the assembly of the members of the committee, and along with them poured a stream of fifteen thousand people before their rooms, wild with excitement, and yelling their approbation of the recapture of the prisoners. Brought face to face with the civil authorities, they would stand or fall by that act. The prisoners were sentenced to immediate execution, and hanged at once from the windows of the rooms of the committee, in the presence of and with the approbation of the assembled multitude. Only seventeen minutes elapsed between the reception of the prisoners and their execution by order of the committee. Public opinion and the press declared that the Vigilance Committee had redeemed its honor.

Having thus established their authority and vindicated their cause, they arose to the full height of their power, and struck terror among criminals of every degree. Henceforth there was no need of their services. Crime fled before their power of suppression, and they now left the execution of the laws in the hands of the civil authorities, retaining, however, their unaltered organization, and imparting to the officer as well as the criminal within his hands the knowledge that at any moment when necessary the committee would again ring the alarm upon its fire-bell, and protect and preserve that social order which by their vigilant acts they had rescued from a chaos of crime and placed in the hands of the civil authorities.

As far as known, but one woman died at the hands of the Vigilantes of California. She was a Spanish woman, of remarkable beauty, who dealt the game of monte in the early days of Downieville. Clothed in her gay attire, her dark lustrous eyes flashing with the excitement of the game, and a profusion of dark locks falling upon her shoulders, together with a voluptuous form and superb carriage, she was the object of much attention from the rough miners and others who gathered around the table, and sat beneath her spell at the fascinating game of monte.

Among the miners was a young man who had come from Kentucky to the distant El Dorado to seek his fortune among its gold hills. He was of fine physical appearance, genial disposition, warm and generous nature, and ever ready to do a good turn for his neighbor, or perform some deed of charity or kindness to the suffering, and withal as hard a toiler as the rest. He became a general favorite among all the rough miners.

Of course the sole places of amusement in those early days of Downieville were within the garish lights of the saloon and by the side of the monte tables, over one of which the Spanish beauty presided. Like all his sex, the Kentuckian was charmed by her fascination. One night, with some companions, on his way to his tent after the game had closed and the señorita Dolores had retired, he passed the tent of the fair Spaniard, and while peeping for an instant through the canvas lapel of her abode was suddenly, in a playful freak, pushed by his companions through the door into the darkness of her tent, and fell prostrate upon its floor. Without a moment's hesitation or an inquiry as to the intruder's identity, she sprang upon him like a tigress in its lair, and plunged her dagger repeatedly in his prostrate form, until he lay a bleeding corpse at her feet. Information of the bloody deed soon reached every miner in the camp, and one and all hurried to the spot where lay the victim of her mad fury. The sight of his fair young face, and sunny hair clotted with his life-blood, and the innumerable ghastly wounds upon his body as it lay uncovered in the hands of the doctor, who hoped to find some spark of life remaining, so worked upon the sympathies of the miners that some cheeks long unused to tears were wet with weeping. The young life had gone out forever, and the bright sunny eyes of the boy favorite of the camp were closed in the unawakening slumber of death. The rage of his rough friends knew no bounds. The woman was instantly seized and placed in the custody of guards while the Vigilance Committee of Downieville should determine her fate. That decree was death by hanging, and the murderess, with her hand yet reeking with the blood of her victim, was taken to the upper bridge of the Yuba, and there hanged until life was extinct. Such was the swift punishment meted out by the rude populace in the excitement of the hour.

It was, indeed, an ungloved iron hand that, in the homes of these early pioneers, first upheld the pillars of society and put to death the disturbers of the public peace in the absence of an organized form of government. They reasoned, however, that the institution of government for a people is that the governed may obtain security of life and property; that without such safeguard social order could not exist; society would be anarchy, and the law of right would be that of might.

The ignominious death of these outlaws at the hands of Vigilance Committees was the result of crimes for the most part cowardly and barbarous. Yet within the veins of some given over to deeds of violence that blacken the pages of criminal history flowed blood from which heroes are made. It has been known that in moments of extreme peril, when humanity, overwhelmed by surrounding dangers, halted and surrendered, and in despair lay down to die, a lawless but master spirit from life's royal blood rose up like a giant to lead the way to hope and success.

When the news reached California that gold had been found in great abundance in the water-shed of the Columbia River, without waiting for a confirmation of the rumor, great numbers of miners poured over the mountain walls of California and Nevada in search of their fortunes in the new gold field. It was, however, but another of those "stampedes" which wreck the hopes and lives of the adventurous and roving miner, and one by one they struggled back to the more prosperous fields they had abandoned for this *ignis fatuus*. One of these parties, nearly starved, attempted to reach Shoshone Falls through the thickly timbered mountains from Elk City. While searching for game one day they chanced to strike a little stream that ran down from the mountain on the edge of a prairie lying near the centre of a large snow-covered horseshoe opening to the south, about thirty miles in diameter. A fallen tamarack had thrown up the earth, and, moved by the instincts of his nature, one of the gold-hunters took up a pan of the earth and carelessly washed it in the stream. What was his astonishment to reap as his reward a handful of rough little specimens of gold-dust of the size of wheat grains! It was of poor quality, but it proved to be the original discovery of the great gold belt embracing Salmon, Warren, Boisé, Owyhee, and Blackfoot, that afterward formed the political division of Idaho Territory, now in its Statehood—the star of Idaho in the Federal flag.

On the 3d day of December, 1862, a fierce storm swept over the whole gold belt, and the thousands of homeless and unprotected miners, who had been sleeping on the ground in their blankets while working their claims, began to pour over the horseshoe in the direction of Lewiston, taking with them the proceeds of their labor on the bar and in the gulch. A party of nine, of whom Joaquin Miller was one, were making their way through Walla Walla *via* Lewiston with a large amount of gold-dust belonging to the individual members of the party. They had been followed from the mines by Dave English and Nelson Scott, two of the most noted desperadoes, accompanied by four others of like character, but not so well known. As there was not a shadow of civil law to protect the honest toiler, nor any other form of protection as yet, at these mines, these men, black with crime, moved about the various tents with the same freedom as men of good character. English was a thick-set, powerful man, with a black beard and commanding manners. One of his gray eyes appeared to be askew, otherwise he was a fine-looking man, usually good-natured, but terrible when aroused. Scott was tall, slim, brown-haired, with features as fair and delicate as those of a woman. All of the band of six were young men well known in California, one of them having been connected with a circus. The party of miners, after six days' travel, reached Lewiston in safety, and English and his companions arrived the following day. The river was frozen over, the steamboats all tied up for the winter, and the ferry almost impassable. The miners and robbers watched each other's motions, and the latter knew that their motives had been divined. The miners had scarcely crossed the ferry when the robbers followed. The large amount of gold-dust of the miners was the object of their pursuit. They were splendidly mounted and well armed, and prepared for any deed to accomplish their end. It was twenty-four miles to Petalia, the nearest station. The days were short and the snow deep. With the best of fortune, the miners did not expect to make it until night. At noon they left the Alpowa, and rode to a vast plateau without stone, stake, or sign to point the way to Petalia, twelve miles away. The snow became deeper and more difficult, and a furious wind set in that blinded and discouraged their horses. The cold was intense. They had not been an hour on this high plain before each man's face was a mass of ice and their horses white with frost. The sun faded in the storm like a star of morning drowned in a flood of dawn. Grave fears now beset them. English and his robber party were now in advance. Once they stopped, consulted, looked back, and then in a little while moved on. The storm was so terrific that the trail behind them was obliterated the instant they passed on; return was therefore impossible, had it been possible for them to recross the river should they reach it. Again the robbers halted, huddled together, looked back, and again struggled on, English, the man of iron, for the most part keeping the lead. The miners now knew they were in deadly peril, not from the robbers, but from the storm. Again the robber band halted, grouped together, gesticulating wildly, as if in violent argumentative altercation, and again moved slowly on. The party of miners followed, the horses floundering in the deep snow, while the trail closed like a grave behind them. About three o'clock in the afternoon, standing up to his waist in snow, English shouted to them to approach. Pushing on through the storm, with their heads bowed and necks bent, like cattle, shielding themselves in the fierce blast, they reached the robber party.

"I tell you h—l's to pay, boys," said English. "If we don't keep our heads level, we'll go up the flume like a spring salmon. Which way do you think is the station?"

No one could tell. To add to the consternation, they now found that three of their party were missing. They shouted through the storm, but no answer came back. They never saw them again. In the spring some Indians found and brought in a note-book, in which was recorded this writing: "Lost in the snow December 19th, 1862, James A. Keel of Macoupin Co., Illinois; Wesley Dean of St. Louis; Ed Parker of Boston." At the same time they brought in a pair of boots containing bones of human feet. A party of citizens went out and found the remains of the three men, together with a large amount of gold-dust.

English stopped, studied a moment, and then, resolving to take all in his own hands, said: "We must stick together; stick together and follow me. I will shoot the first man who refuses to obey, and send him to hell a-fluking."

Again the robber chief, now in supreme command in the hour of danger and death, led on. The band struggled on in silence, benumbed, helpless, and half dead. Scott seemed like a child beside his chieftain. The remainder of both parties were as feeble and as spiritless as he. English was the only one whose spirit rose above the storm. His whole ferocious nature seemed aroused. At times he swore like a madman. The storm increased in fury, darkness came suddenly on, and they could not see each other's faces.

English shouted aloud, above the blast, "Come up to me." They obeyed, and huddled around him like children. "There is but one chance," said he; "cut your saddles off your horses." He got the horses as close together as possible and shot them down, throwing away his pistols as he emptied them. Placing the saddles on top of the pile of horses, he made each man wrap his blankets around him and huddle together on the mass. "No nodding now," said English. "I'll shoot the first man that fails to answer when I call him."

To sleep a moment meant death by freezing, and this robber chief, this king of men, in the hour of dire peril and death knew it. Every man seemed to surrender all hope, save this fierce man of iron. He moved as if in his element. He made a track in the snow around the party on the heap, and kept constantly moving and shouting. Within an hour they saw the effect of his rude action. The animal heat from the horses warmed their benumbed and stiffened limbs as it rose from their prostrate bodies, while darkness and the storm reigned over them. Thus they remained during the stormy hours of the night. English, shouting and swearing through and above the blasts, tramped in the circular track he made about them, pistol in hand, to keep them awake and alive, while he battered his own body to keep it from freezing. Thus the terrible night wore on until toward morning, when suddenly English stopped shouting, and uttered a terrible oath of surprise. The storm had suddenly lifted like a curtain, and far above in the heavens moved the round moon on its stately course. It was to that band of half-dead and wellnigh frozen men as a pillar of flame to the children of Israel. They were saved. With the dawn of the morning the iron man bade the others follow him. It was almost impossible for them to rise. They fell, rose again, fell, and finally stood on their feet; all save one, a small German named Ross. He was dead—frozen to death.

At eleven o'clock in the morning English, who still resolutely led the way, gave a shout of joy as he stood on the edge of a basaltic cliff and looked down on the *parterre*. A long straight pillar of white smoke rose from the station, like a column of marble supporting the overhanging dome. Again it was the pillar of cloud that led the children of Israel now leading these lost children of the mountains amid the snow wastes of the dreary plain. Warmed back to life again, they returned and brought in the body of their companion, with his bag of gold-dust, and in a few days the trail was broken. The company of miners voluntarily gave to some of English's band a portion of their wealth. English, however, resolutely refused to accept a present. They parted at the station, and the miners pursued their way in safety to Walla Walla.

Some months later English, Scott, and another of his band, named Peoples, were arrested for highway robbery, and were placed, securely bound, under guard in a log house on the stage road. That night was organized the first Vigilance Committee in Idaho, and, in fact, in the Northwest Territories. It consisted of six men belonging to the Idaho Express Company. At midnight they condemned the robbers to death, and acquainted them of their fate. Scott asked for time to pray, English swore furiously, and Peoples was silent.

One of the Vigilantes approached Scott while in the attitude of prayer, and began to adjust the noose about his neck. English cried out, "Hang me first, and let him pray!"

The wonderful courage of the man appealed to the sympathies and admiration of these rough men of the mountains, and they would have spared him, but having proceeded thus far, they felt they could not falter now. They had but one rope, and executed them one at a time. When the rope was adjusted about the neck of English, he was quietly asked by his executioners to invoke the mercy of his God. He held his head down a moment, muttered something, and then straightening up, turned toward Scott and said, "Nelse, pray for me a little, can't you, while I hang?"

Peoples died without a motion or a struggle. When Scott's turn came he was still praying devoutly. He offered large sums of money, which he had secreted in the mountains, for his life; but they told him he must die too. Seeing there was no escape, he removed his watch and rings, kissed them tenderly, and handed them to one of the Vigilantes, saying, "Send these to my poor Armina," and quietly submitted to his fate. At dawn the three men lay dead and rigid upon the cabin floor. The blood that dried in the veins of one was of the kind that runs through heroes' veins, and had he in his early days been guided in the nobler channels of life, he might have been a Cæsar or a Marlborough. With a courage as sublime as that of the bride of Collatinus, and the fortitude of an Alexander, he saved the lives of eleven human beings, and within four months after this sublime act of heroism died an ignominious death by the halter for robbing a stage-coach.

Far to the northwest, among the cañons and gorges of the Rocky Mountains, and near the head-waters of the Missouri, running up to the British line, and forming a part of the territorial boundary of the United States, is the young State of Montana. At the time of which I am now writing it was a young Territory, or rather a part of Idaho Territory, with no settlements or signs of civilization save the mining camps scattered through its southern division. But its growth was rapid. Thriving, prosperous communities and cities of wealth and refinement have taken the places of rude mining camps. Traversed by railroads, it is now filled with farms and gardens, workshops and factories, mills and mines, and is inhabited by a brave, intelligent, self-reliant race, embracing all trades and professions of life, and now forms one of the brightest stars shining in the blue field of the imperial banner of the mighty "sisterhood of States."

But, as I have stated, it was not always thus. It was once but "the first low wash of the waves where now rolls a human sea"—mountain walls, rude civilization, tented homes, wild debauchery, robbery, rapine, and mid-day murders.

Early in the spring of 1862 the rumor of rich discoveries on the Salmon River flew through Salt Lake City, Colorado, and many other places in the far West. A wild rush to the "new diggings" was the result, and a stream of human beings set in for the new El Dorado by the toilsome way of Fort Hall and the Snake River. As their trains drew nearer the long-sought spot they found further conveyance by wagons impossible, as the rocky, mountainous roads were impassable for wagons. They were likewise informed that the mines were already overrun by a vast army of gold-hunters from California, Oregon, and all places on the Pacific slope. They also learned that many of those who had been driven by adverse circumstances from Salmon River had spread far over the adjacent country, and that new discoveries had been made at Deer Lodge.

The streams of immigration now diverged toward that point, crossed the mountains between Fort Lemhi and Horse Prairie Creek, and taking a cut-off to the left, sought to strike the old trail from Salt Lake City to Deer Lodge and Bitter Root valleys. A mining camp was also established with success on Grasshopper Creek, afterward called Beaver Head Diggings. It was the first to work the gulches east of the Rocky Mountains.

From these incipient labors flowed the great mining industries which in an incredibly short space of time gave to Montana her well-deserved reputation as the richest gold-mining field discovered since that of California. A tide of immigration now poured in from all directions, and with it came the bad as well as the good; and among the former were the desperadoes Henry Plummer, Charles Reeves, Moore, and Skinner, all of whom suffered death at the hands of the honest men of the Territory, who, when they found they could not apply the forms of law in a community where the written law was a dead letter, or had never existed, maintained the right with their own strong hands to subdue the brute force of violence and murder. The wonderful discoveries at Alder Gulch of the almost fabulous placer diggings attracted a vast tide of rapid immigration—that which is known

among gold-seekers as a stampede. It likewise attracted a large number of the dangerous class, who saw a broad and rich field for their lawless operations.

They quickly organized themselves into a secret compact body, with signs, grips, and with a captain, lieutenants, secretary, road-agents, and outriders, who became the terror of the whole country. A correspondence was inaugurated between Bannock and Virginia City, and a surveillance placed on all travel between those points. To such a fine point was their system carried that horses, men, and coaches were in some intelligible manner marked to designate them as objects of plunder. In this manner were the members of the gang notified by their spies, ofttimes employed by the very object of their plunder, in time to prevent the escape of their victims. They were all armed with a pair of revolvers, a double-barrelled shot-gun with a large bore, the barrels cut short off, and a dagger or bowie-knife. Thus armed, and mounted on swift and trained horses, and disguised with masks and blankets, they awaited their victims in ambush, from which, on approach of a conveyance, they would spring forth, and covering the inmates with their guns, command them to alight and throw up their hands. If this order was not instantly obeyed, the result would be sudden death. Otherwise they would be disarmed, and made to throw their wealth upon the ground. Concluding their operations with a search for concealed property, they would permit the despoiled passengers to proceed on their way while they themselves rode rapidly in an opposite direction.

Wherever a new settlement was effected, or new discoveries of the precious metals made, there followed the bandits, until their operations spread in all directions. They became the scourge of the mountains, and no men or class of men were safe from their attacks.

To illustrate the class of desperadoes engaged in this nefarious work, we will take the case of Henry Plummer, a man of such smooth manners and insinuating address that he was termed a "perfect gentleman," although known to be both thief and assassin, and had once filled the office of marshal of Nevada City, whence, after having been twice imprisoned for murder, he had fled to Oregon, and thence to Montana. In Montana he was elected sheriff of Beaver County. He first made his way, in company with his companion, Jack Cleveland, to Bannock City, whose fame, in the winter of 1862 and 1863, had widely spread. It was the first mining camp of importance established east of the Rocky Mountains, and a large immigration ensued, with the customary number of the ruffian class. Among them all, Plummer was chief, noted for his desperation and his skill in the rapid handling of his pistol. He shot and killed his friend and old acquaintance and companion Jack Cleveland, who was disposed to dispute his title as chief, and frequently boasted of his own murderous exploits.

Shortly after that occurrence another of the gang, named George Ives, was conversing on the street with his friend George Carhart, and not liking the style of his speech, laid him low with a shot from his revolver.

Another eminent road-agent, named Haze Lyon, owed a citizen of Bannock four hundred dollars for board and lodging, and one morning, having won a large sum of money the night previous at the gaming-table, was asked by his landlord to settle his account. He answered the modest request by drawing his revolver and ordering the citizen "to dust out," with which gentle command he immediately complied.

Plummer was tried for the murder of Cleveland, and acquitted on the ground that his opponent's language was irritating. Charles Reeves and a man named Williams, who had fired into a camp of friendly Indians just to see how many they could kill at one shot, were also tried and acquitted. Others who had likewise been guilty of heinous offences were also acquitted, and the baser elements of society felt themselves secure in the performance of their lawless deeds, and murder and robbery went on unmolested.

Plummer, who had been chosen chief of the road-agents, had likewise, as previously stated, succeeded in having himself elected sheriff of the county, and appointed two of his band as deputies. In the mean time an honest man had been elected sheriff at Virginia, and was informed by Plummer that he "would live much longer if he would resign his office in his favor." Fear of assassination compelled him to do as bidden, and Plummer became sheriff at both places. With his robber deputies to execute his orders, the people of Montana were at the mercy of thieves and bandits. One of his deputies was an honest man, and becoming too well versed in the doings of Plummer and associates, was sentenced to death by the road-agents and publicly shot by three of the band. There was no longer any security of life and property.

A Dutchman sold some mules, and receiving the money therefor in advance, was driving the animals on a public road to deliver them to the purchaser, when he was met by Ives, murdered, and robbed of both money and mules. The sight of this man's body brought into town in a cart stirred the blood of the honest men of the community, and they determined to capture and hang his murderer. A party of citizens thoroughly armed scoured the country, surprised accomplices of the murderer, and wrung from them the confession that George Ives was the murderer. By the following evening he was captured, and taken a prisoner to Nevada City. He was given a trial. The bench was a wagon; the jury, twenty-four honest men; the aroused citizens stood guard with guns in hand while the trial proceeded, with their eyes fixed upon the desperadoes, who had gathered in force to aid, support, and, if possible, to rescue their comrade in crime. Counsel was heard on both sides; reliable witnesses proved the prisoner guilty of numerous murders and robberies. Condemned to death, his captors repressed every attempt at rescue, and held the prisoner with cocked and levelled guns. It was a moonlight night, and the camp fire shed its gleam on all around. Amid the shouts and yells and murderous threats of the assembled ruffians, the condemned assassin and cowardly murderer was led to the gallows, upon which he expiated his manifold crimes. The next day the far-famed Vigilantes of Montana were organized. Five brave men in Nevada City and one in Virginia City, the towns lying adjacent, formed the secret league who opposed, on the side of law and order, force to force and dread to dread against the road-agents' organization. This league became as terrible to the outlaws as they themselves had been to the honest, order-loving, and industrious part of the community.

Plummer, the sheriff, was seized, and before he could escape, was executed, on a Sunday morning, together with two of his robber deputies, on a gallows which he himself had erected.

The Vigilantes, to put an end to the long reign of terror, assumed the duties of captors, judges, jurors, and executioners. But they were not guilty of excesses. They struck terror to those who had defied the weaker arm of the law by sure, swift, and secret punishment of crime. In no case was a criminal executed without evidence establishing his guilt. How closely they hewed to the line in this respect is attested by the dying remarks of one of the last men hanged by their order: "You have done right. Not an innocent man hanged yet!" But it was understood that the work they had undertaken to perform should be faithfully and thoroughly performed; that there should be no half-way measures, no reprieves, the verdict having once been rendered.

An instance of the severe labor, exposure, and real hardship encountered by these guardians of peace and order is furnished in the pursuit and capture of William Hunter.

At the time of the execution of Boone Helm and his five confederates, Hunter managed to elude his pursuers by hiding by day among the rocks and brush, seeking food by night among the scattered settlements along the Gallatin River. Four of the Vigilantes, determined and resolute men, volunteered to arrest him. They crossed the divide, and forded the Madison when huge cakes of floating ice swirled down on the flanks of the horses, threatening to carry them down. Their camping-ground was the frozen earth, the weather intensely cold, and they slept at night under their blankets, by the side of a fire which they had built. Next day their way led through a tremendous snow-storm, which they welcomed as an ally. About two o'clock in the afternoon they reached Milk Ranch, twenty miles from their destination, obtained their supper, and again proceeded, after dark, with a guide well acquainted with the country. At midnight they reached the cabin where they learned Hunter had been driven to seek refuge from the severe storm and cold. They halted, unsaddled, and rapped loudly at the door. On being admitted, they found two persons in the cabin —two visible, and one covered up in bed.

The Vigilantes made themselves as comfortable as possible before a blazing fire on the hearth. They talked of mining, prospecting, panning-out, and terms of that character, as if they were travelling miners. Before going to sleep, however, they carefully examined the premises as to its exits, and placed themselves in such manner as to command the only entrance and exit. They refrained from saying anything concerning their real business until early the following morning, when their horses were saddled and they appeared ready to proceed on their journey. Then they asked who the sleeper was, who had never spoken or uncovered his head. The reply was that he was unknown; had been there two days, driven in by the storm. Asked to describe him, the description was that of Hunter.

The Vigilantes then went to the bed, and laying a firm hand on the sleeper, gripped the revolvers held by him in his hand beneath the bedclothes. "Bill Hunter" was called upon to arise and behold grim men with guns levelled at his head. He asked to be taken to Virginia City, but he soon found a shorter road lay before him. Two miles from the cabin they halted beneath a tree with a branch over which a rope could be thrown, and a spur to which the end could be fastened. Scraping away a foot of snow, they built a fire and cooked their breakfast. After breakfast they consulted and took a vote as to the disposition of the prisoner. That vote determined upon instant execution. The perils of the long tramp over the mountain divide, the crossing of the icy stream, the small force involved in his capture, and the certainty of an attempt at rescue when his capture became known to his accomplices, all rendered this necessary. The long catalogue of crimes he had committed was read to him, and he was asked to plead any extenuating circumstances in his own behalf. There were none, and he remained silent. He had once been an honest, hard-working man, and was believed to be an upright citizen. In an evil hour he joined his fortunes with the wicked band who had likewise perished on the scaffold. His sole request was that his friends in the States should not be informed of the manner of his death.

Thus died the last of Plummer's famous band of outlaws, executing in his last moments the pantomime of grasping an imaginary pistol, cocking it, and discharging in rapid succession its six ghostly barrels.

POLITICAL ASPECTS OF MORMONISM

IN a singularly interesting depression of that basin or trough which lies between the Sierras of the Pacific and the great chain of the Rocky Mountains lies the much-discussed Territory of Utah.

As the great seat and centre of Mormonism it has been celebrated for more than thirty years, and it still presents the unsolved problem in political government of the eradication of polygamous institutions consolidated into one community, consistently with republican theories of government and with Anglo-Saxon notions concerning the trial of persons accused of crime. It is quite unnecessary to discuss at this day the Mormon theories of polygamy as a part of a religious institution, and as being therefore entitled to immunity. Public opinion, acts of Congress, and decisions of the Supreme Court of the United States have put this question in the category of things finally decided. Assuming polygamy, then, to be a crime against the political institutions of our country, the serious question of how to get rid of it remains to be settled. Measures of violence by neighboring communities acting under a sense of outrage at the practices of the Latter-day Saints have not been found adequate to the destruction of the institution, to say nothing of the evil character and consequences of that method of rectifying wrong. When assailed and broken up in one State, they migrated to another, and when their tem-

ples were destroyed there, they sought refuge a thousand miles westward in the then uninhabited heart of the continent, and established once more, and more firmly than ever, their institutions. Isolation, indeed, has appeared to be the most favorable condition for the development and increase of Mormon institutions, and if such isolation and development were not to end in placing the Mormons in the centre of a great family of civilized States, it might be open to question how far measures of repression or destruction of any kind could be resorted to consistently with modern ideas of the rights of separate and independent communities. But such is not the case. The Mormon Church, as a concentrated, coherent, and growing force, is now found, not in the almost inaccessible valley of Great Salt Lake, as it was thirty years ago, but in the centre of the greatest thoroughfare across the continent. The institutions of modern civilization, morality, and progress have travelled across the great plains, and enveloped the distant oasis where in 1847 the Mormons finally established themselves. The problem must now or in the near future be solved, and the irrepressible conflict between polygamous Mormonism and the social and political systems of the people of the rest of the United States must have a decisive issue. It is the object of the Mormons, as shown by repeated and persistent efforts, to set up for themselves and maintain an exclusive political domination in the Territory of Utah, and to so frame and administer laws as to encourage rather than repress polygamy. Since their final settlement in the valley of Great Salt Lake, their policy has been consistent and steady, always looking to the establishment of a State controlled by a hierarchy, and resting in all its parts on the special ideas of Mormonism, and these people have plainly seen that once established as a State in the Union, their domestic concerns, including polygamy and every revolting practice which they might choose to set up, would be absolutely beyond the legal reach of the people of the other States.

Within two years after the first settlement a memorial was sent to Congress asking for a State government, and all the preliminary steps to its establishment were taken. On the 9th March, 1849, Brigham Young was elected Governor; Richards, Secretary of State; Whitney, Treasurer; Kimball, Chief Justice; Wells, Attorney-General, etc. Congress did not accede to the demand for a State government, but on the 9th September, 1850, passed an act organizing Utah Territory, and in October Brigham Young was appointed Governor. The organic act itself was all that the Mormons could have wished. It left everything to their own management, and in effect allowed them to authorize or even require polygamy if they chose. The administration of the affairs of the Territory was so conducted as to discourage Gentile immigration, and to cause nearly all development to be that of the Mormon Church.

In March, 1856, another attempt was made to establish a State. A constitution was adopted, and a memorial sent to Congress asking for the creation of a State. Young continued Governor until July, 1857, when a Gentile Governor was sent out, and so strong was the opposition of the Mormons to this step that it was thought necessary to send a heavy military force to support the new Governor. He found, as all his successors have, that he possessed very small means for overcoming the exclusive policy of the Mormon leaders; and it was not until July 1, 1862, that Congress took any positive step for the punishment of polygamy, or for the rectification of various laws and ordinances of the Legislature of the Territo-ry which had been passed in aid of the polygamous policy of the Church. In the same year the Mormons made another effort for the admission of Utah as a State. The Congressional prohibition of polygamy, the building of the Pacific Railroad, and the discovery of rich and extensive mines had by 1870 produced a large increase of the Gentile population of the Territory, and there came to be considerable danger that the Mormons would be outvoted, and the Territorial Legislature and the minor officers might be anti-Mormon. Accordingly the Mormon Legislature passed a woman suffrage bill, which, of course, added enormously to the voting force of the Mormons. Again in 1872 a fresh effort was made to establish a Mormon State, but without success. In the last ten years efforts have been made at nearly every session of Congress to provide such regulations for the administration of law in that Territory as to enable effective steps to be taken for the punishment of polygamy, and particularly with a view to the prevention or discouragement of further polygamous marriages. But very little success has attended such efforts. For one cause or another, acts that would have gone far toward the accomplishment of this end have been repeatedly defeated, and the difficulty in procuring convictions for polygamy under existing laws has been found almost insuperable. This difficulty lies mainly in two points of legal procedure. The first is in the nature of the constitution of juries. On the theory prevalent in the United States, a jury must be unanimous in order to convict. If, therefore, a single Mormon be a member of a jury in a given case, it is impossible to obtain a verdict, for he believes, or professes to believe, that polygamy is a divine institution, and that they who practice it are rendering obedience to God, and so he thinks, or professes to think, that prosecutions for that offense are the most wicked tyranny, and he will not find a verdict of guilty under any circumstances. And it has been found, too, naturally enough, that the process of challenging for bias is generally ineffectual in such cases. But if in some rare instances it has been found possible to obtain an impartial jury in the only correct sense—that is, a jury who, as responsible members of the community, believe in the necessity of the execution of its laws, and who are willing to find verdicts accordingly upon fair proof—a second difficulty has at once presented itself in the inability of the prosecution to prove the fact of polygamous practice, although every Mormon privately and publicly out of court admits its existence and defends it. This difficulty of proof grows out of the rule of the law of procedure, which it has been insisted required record or other direct evidence of the two or more marriages. The Supreme Court has lately held, however, that proof of the admissions, etc., of the accused can be given in evidence, which may make convictions possible. These marriages, it seems, are made by the Mormons, latterly at least, in secret, and however august may be the ceremonial, and however numerous the witnesses, the event takes place with closed doors and under the most stringent obligations of secrecy, so that when a Mormon witness is called to prove the fact, he has no scruple usually in denying any knowledge of it.

Under such circumstances the institution continues to flourish, and the proportion of polygamous marriages is probably now considerably greater than it was fifteen years since. The Mormon population of Utah in 1866 is estimated to have been about 60,000. In that population the proportion of "plural marriages" is believed, from certain testimony taken in that year by a committee of Congress, to have been not less than one-third of the whole number of married males.

From the evidence taken by this committee, and from the whole course of events in that Territory since the passage of the act of 1862 denouncing polygamy as a crime, there is strong reason to believe that the institution has been more and more promoted by the Mormon leaders, and has become almost a cardinal test of Mormon faith. The present population of Utah purports, by the census returns of 1880, to be 143,963, more than 73,000 of which are under eighteen years of age. The official statistics do not show the number of polygamous marriages, or the number of persons practicing polygamy, or the number of children of such marriages, but carefully collected unofficial information furnishes good reason to believe that the number of polygamists and their children in the Territory greatly exceeds the whole anti-Mormon population. The reader will, it is thought, soon be able to correct this estimate by data of substantial precision.

Down to the decision of the Supreme Court of the United States in the case of Reynolds, in the winter of 1878-9, the Mormons professed to vindicate their opposition to the law against polygamy and their refusal to obey it on the ground of its unconstitutionality, as prohibiting the free exercise of religious faith. That case having finally exploded this pretension, it might have been expected that the institution of polygamous marriages would be abandoned, but such does not appear to have been the case. Delegations of Mormons visited Washington for the purpose of appealing to Congress for such legislation as might annul or mitigate the effect of the law as declared by that decision, and some committees of Congress were disposed, for the protection of innocent women and children, to take such measures as would legitimize the children of such marriages born within a year after the promulgation of this decision, and to ameliorate the condition of the unfortunate females who had been the victims of these practices, but accompanied by provisions adequate, so far as legislation could go, for the absolute suppression or punishment of future polygamous marriages. But these measures were not at all satisfactory to the Mormon interest, which seemed to demand not only "indemnity for the past," but "security for the future"; and, for reasons not easy to explain, Congress failed to make any provision upon the subject.

There is no reason to suppose that the final settlement of the rightful power of Congress to provide for punishing polygamy, notwithstanding it may be exercised under a claim of religious duty, has had any effect to deter Mormons from a continuation or even increase of the practice.

Notwithstanding the difficulties attending prosecutions for this crime growing out of the laws regarding the formation of juries, technical rules of evidence, and the falsehood of witnesses, there is fair reason to suppose that if Congress should choose to enact suitable legislation to meet the case, and the Executive department should endeavor to enforce such legislation with the same vigor that it exercises in punishing illicit distilling, the practice of polygamy might in a very few years be entirely broken up. But judging from a dozen years of effort and failure to pass laws in this direction, the hope of immediate legislation can not be considered as very well grounded. Even with the law as it now stands, a sincere and persistent Executive policy, and with judicial courts in the Territory that will hold it to be the same duty to administer the law against polygamy as against other crimes, it is probable that a decided check to the growth of the institution could be established. If the people of the United States are really in earnest in desiring to prevent the establishment of a powerful polygamous State in the heart of the continent, whose chief institution is so in opposition to the social institutions and moral ideas of all the other States, and which (Utah once becoming a State with it) can never be lawfully broken up by the national power, it will be easy to accomplish the extinction of polygamy by lawful and by just means.

The encouragement of non-Mormon immigration, and the discouragement of the appropriation—which has been extensively practiced—of large tracts of the most valuable lands to or for the benefit of the Mormon Church, would have a valuable effect in the right direction. Another effectual disposition of the subject might be made in the annexation of different parts of the Territory to the contiguous States and Territories, by which the concentrated strength of the voting power of the hierarchy would be broken, and political Mormonism would find itself in a minority in the making and administration of local laws. If no measures of legislation are to be resorted to, and if the administration of existing laws continues to be feeble, lax, and intermittent, Mormonism in Utah, with its cardinal doctrine polygamy, may no doubt count on a pretty long career. Is it not quite time that in one direction or the other a definite and living policy be adopted and put in practice? If the polygamy of Mormonism is to be considered as within the category of crimes that every well-ordered government is bound to prevent and punish, then the sooner the real strength of public opinion and the law is exerted, the better for all concerned. The intrinsic evils of crime are sufficiently great always, but the evils of crime against which laws denounce penalties that are never or but rarely enforced are infinitely greater, for there is brought into play the constant lesson of disregard for law which people everywhere are but too ready to learn. If, on the other hand, polygamous Mormonism is to be considered by public opinion, and by those intrusted with the making and execution of the laws, either as a local institution the regulation of which ought to belong to the community itself, or as a mere venial and sentimental offense that is only to be condemned because it is out of the fashion of the rest of civilized mankind, and so ought not to be punished by the persistent power of the law, and only discouraged through the sermons of clergyman, debates in Congress resulting in no legislation, and messages of the Executives followed by no vigor of administration, would it not be far better, on the whole, for the government of the United States to renounce its dominion of the subject, and remit its treatment to the Mormon hierarchy itself?

Either course is unquestionably open to practical accomplishment by the people and the government of the United States. If we really mean to exterminate polygamy in Utah, it can easily be done by lawful and just means, and without doing an injury even (but rather a good) to all morally innocent persons involved in the practice, and their children.

FOG POSSIBILITIES

THE city by the Golden Gate has been pictured by one of its poetic children as a Franciscan friar wrapped in robes of gray. But in truth the city resembles more the face of a fresh young girl masking in Quaker garb. For while the frequent fogs roll in from the Pacific and lie heavily upon the bay of San Francisco, one can see from any of the lofty hills of the city views surpassingly beautiful in themselves, and exquisitely set off by the fog robes and draperies. Our poet also sang of the island of Saint Thomas, and "the black-browed hurricane brooding down the Spanish Main," but probably never dreamed that the fogbank and the hurricane, though seldom found together, are closely related. Further on we hope to show how the cyclonic condition controls the movement of the fog.

A convenient though not strictly scientific classification of fog types is, sea or coast fog, valley or hill fog, and town or dust fog. The last-named has been given the euphonic designation *nebula pulverea*. It is an artificial rather than natural condition. The Rev. Clement Ley, who gave a large portion of his life to cloud study, says, in his book on "Cloudland," that in some parts of the globe nebula pulverea is occasionally so thick as to obscure almost totally the sunlight, and in Abyssinia has led to the tradition that the plague of darkness in Egypt was in reality an unusual "dust fog." The amount of moisture varies so much in different fogs that the terms "dry" and "wet" are used, the scientific name of the latter being *nebula stillans*. In wet fog the particles are apt to be larger than in dry fog. A still further division, due, we believe, to Mr. Robert H. Scott, is anti-cyclonic fog, or fog in which no rain falls, while the temperature, generally low in the morning, continues to rise during the day; and cyclonic fog, in which rain does occur, while the temperature remains about stationary. Before leaving these town fogs we may notice the part played by them in affecting the health of the community. Mr. Scott has given figures showing the mortality from diseases of the respiratory system for some of the more memorable fogs of London.

We have room for but one of the many periods he gives. From January 26 to February 6, 1880, London experienced eight days of fog. The average temperature at eight o'clock in the morning was 26° Fahrenheit. The total death rate was 48.1 per thousand, a rate unequalled since the last cholera epidemic, and there were no less than 1557 deaths from diseases of the respiratory organs. It is not always an easy matter to trace direct relationship even where the statistics are carefully gathered, but there can be little doubt that these town fogs are unwholesome. Indirectly they affect the health of the community in a way few would imagine. A town fog is an excellent trap for noxious gases, holding them close to the ground. Dr. R. Barnes, studying this question, found, by inspection of gas plants near London, that in foggy weather the escaping gas was held in concentrated form in and near the works. There are other sources of contamination in foul emanations from the ground, sewers, etc. On clear, bright days, even if no wind is blowing, the law of diffusion of gases acts more effectively, and helps disperse the gases.

A few years ago the question of the artificial production of rain excited public interest. The governing principle of the experiment, as commonly stated, was that an extensive and continued concussion of the air would result in rainfall. The experiments were neither countenanced nor accepted by meteorologists, and the results were exactly such as might have been forecasted by physicist and engineer. There was also a prime mistake in the reasoning which sought to precipitate the moisture of the air without a proper precedent condensation. Before we undertake to make rain artificially we must understand how to make and unmake clouds. When we can control absolutely the thermo-dynamic conditions and condense at pleasure a given amount of invisible vapor in the free air into visible cloud, and, conversely, change visible fog into invisible vapor, we shall be nearer artificial rain-making than we have yet been.

Fog may form in at least three different ways: first, where the air is cooled by rapid radiation; second, where the cooling results from a mixture of different air currents; and third, where a cooling has been caused by an uplifting of the air. The first is the most common cause of fog formation. Radiation fog is generally formed over surfaces nearly level, when warm air comes in contact with cold ground. Sea fogs occur when there temperature found with the anti-cyclonic conditions illustrate this excellently. At such times we find that at the foot of a large hill or mountain it is colder than at the top. The air is often twenty or thirty degrees warmer on the summits than in the valleys. Our great fog-banks and the fogs which remain for days are due to such temperature inversions. On

MOUNT HAMILTON—LICK OBSERVATORY.

is a marked difference between the temperatures of the water and air, or when two water currents of different temperatures are contiguous. Coast fogs are formed when inflowing moist air from the sea passes over a chilled land, but more generally are formed at sea during the prevalence of some great area of high pressure, or "anti-cyclone," as it is technically known, and then are carried inland, dissolving as they go. It must be remembered that the atmosphere is something like a great gaseous sponge. Compression and expansion are constantly going on, with resulting cloudy and clear skies and different temperatures for various layers. Some of the inversions of the Pacific coast it is easy to trace the relation between the movement of the "high" area and the fog. Professor Davis tells of somewhat similar conditions in December, 1879, when the lowlands of Europe were shrouded in fog for most of the month, while in the mountains it was clear and mild, and over twenty degrees warmer than below. The low countries were lost beneath the sea of fog, and the hills piercing through were like islands in their isolation. Fruit-growers are familiar with these temperature inversions and the fogs which sometimes accompany them. Fruit and vegetables in the valleys are frost-bitten, while on the hill-sides they escape.

FOG AT LICK OBSERVATORY.

Nature provides in the blanket of fog a means of preventing the extreme low temperatures which would otherwise result. More than a century ago Thomas Jefferson, who appears to have been the first to notice these peculiarities of frost, wrote: "I have known frosts so severe as to kill the hickory-trees around about Monticello, and yet not injure the tender fruit blossoms then in bloom on the top and higher parts of the mountain, and in the course of forty years during which it has been settled there have been but two instances of a general loss of fruit on it, while in the circumjacent country the fruit has escaped but twice in the last seven years."

In California, last year, a large amount of fruit was saved by following certain "fog-building" methods. Mr. W. H. Hammon, of the United States Weather Bureau, pointed out to the fruit-growers the five essential ways of preventing frost: First, by diminishing the radiation; second, by increasing the moisture in the air and raising the dew-point; third, by adding heat to the air; fourth, by removing the cold air — actually draining it off; and fifth, by mixing the air and removing the cold air from the ground. Smudge fires are based upon the first method, and are fairly effective; but the great improvement consists in the introduction of large amounts of moisture in the vaporous state. When this vapor condenses, or, in other words, when the fog forms, an enormous amount of heat is given off, generally at the very height at which it is most needed. Fog and frost both occur when the skies are clear and little or no air is stirring. A strong wind so thoroughly mixes the air that there is little chance for cold dry air to settle in the hollows and low places. Fog, then, as the natural preventive of frost, may be a blessing to the orchardist; but there are others, particularly travellers, to whom the fog can be but a source of annoyance and danger. For example, on December 17 and 18, 1895, an area of high pressure lay off the Middle Atlantic coast. At New York such a dense fog prevailed over the rivers and bay that the Sound steamers did not attempt to pass through Hell Gate, and the ocean steamships were all detained below Quarantine. Of course there were numerous accidents.

Can we at such times, by any means known to science, dispel the fog? We may say at the outset that it is a simpler problem than the artificial production of rain. John Aitken, of Edinburgh, about five years ago, devised a very sensitive dust-counter, and with it has measured the dust particles in the air at a number of places. These measurements and the experiments of Carl Barus have shown how close is the relationship between fog, cloud, or haze and the number of dust particles in the air. Whether the vapor shall condense as fine Scotch mist or coarse black London fog is largely determined by the dust. If we can remove the dust from the air, we have removed the nuclei of condensation. Dr. Lodge has pointed out five different methods of accomplishing this, viz., filtration, settling, recondensing, calcining, and electrification. There may be other ways, but of those mentioned the last is the one which seems to contain the greatest possibilities when applied to the problem of fog-dissipation. There can be no doubt that air is speedily cleansed of solid matter in suspension by continued electrification. One of Dr. Lodge's experiments may be quoted here:

"A bell-jar of illuminated magnesium smoke is connected with the pole of a Vose machine. A potential able to give quarter-inch or even tenth-inch sparks is ample. The smoke particles very quickly aggregate into long filaments, which drop by their own weight when the electrification is removed. A higher potential tears them asunder and drives them against the sides of the jar. . . . If the jar be filled with steam, electrification rapidly aggregates the particles or globules into Scotch mist and fine rain."

Lodge further shows how a small cellar may be cleared of thick turpentine smoke by a point discharge; also that there are many other applications of the principle, such as purifying the air of smoking-rooms, theatre galleries, disinfecting hospital wards, etc. To dissipate the fog we would either, by a gentle electrification, increase the size of the dust nuclei until they settled, or, under strong electrical discharges, scatter and precipitate them. Ten years have barely passed since Lodge made the suggestion of thus dissipating fog. Great changes have been made in electrical apparatus since then, and insulating materials then hardly known are now in common use. Potentials of fifty thousand volts are less rare to day than potentials of five thousand volts were five years ago. Within a reasonable distance fog can probably be dissipated and the air clarified. Of course the supply of fog may be such that there would be little appreciable diminution, but as a rule fog has well-marked limits and is localized. Fog-dispellers might be placed upon warships, ferry-boats, and at all terminal depots and crowded thoroughfares. We cart away from our busiest streets the snow or solidified vapor of the air. Is it not better economy to attempt the conquest of the water vapor in another form?

FOG SEEN FROM MOUNT HAMILTON.

PLANT LIFE IN THE DESERT

NATURE is the most perfect economist. She utilizes every atom of material, turns to advantage all elements and situations. The limits of present possibility seem to have been reached in the spread of life on this earth. It descends to the uttermost depths of the sea, rises in the air above the mountain-tops, is not daunted by polar cold or the heat of almost boiling springs. There appear to be no substances in the composition of the globe which have not been tested for nourishment for organisms, and few that are not compelled to yield it to further the insatiable impulse of life to spread and increase.

It is probable that long ago was reached the fullest capability of the earth to support its population of plants and animals under natural conditions —that is, although local changes are ever taking place as physical conditions (land areas, climate, etc.) alter, the sum of individual organisms remains substantially the same, and stands equal to the maximum that may find space and sustenance in which to flourish.

The economies of the desert are mainly directed to surmounting two physical obstacles—lack of water and excess of wind; and the adaptations to meet these and accompanying hardships are exceedingly curious and interesting. A man from Arizona showed me, the other day, a harsh, dry, almost leafless little bush, about as big as his two fists, all of whose branches curled in at the top, until the whole form was globular, with a small tuft of fibrous roots at one side. A few days later I saw it again and it was greenish, had expanded a little, and unfolded minute leaves; he had set its roots in the soil, and the long-dried plant had revived and begun to grow. This was one of a large class of plants (Amarantus, Erigonium, etc.) called "rolling weeds"

By courtesy of the Carnegie Institution

VEGETATION IN THE GRAND CANYON OF THE COLORADO, ARIZONA
The cactus is an Echinocereus, and the shrub behind it Ephedra Nevadensis

or "tumbleweeds," which are broken off or pulled up and then sent travelling by the gales. When they catch against some obstacle they drop their seeds there, or if roots remain and get covered by the blown soil, the bush is replanted; and by this means their race is dispersed. The desert plants must, indeed, depend mainly on the wind for the scattering of their seeds, and so they turn to account one of their enemies. Few of the seeds are light enough to be carried far in the air —there would be danger of their flying too far; but as fleshy, pulpy fruits are rare, owing to the paucity of moisture, the round hard seeds characteristic of this group may be rolled far across the comparatively open ground.

The globular form of the various tumbleweeds is characteristic of all the desert vegetation, and results from its sparseness. The supply of moisture is adequate only for a scanty and small-sized growth: the wonder is that any at all is possible, when the total rainfall may be only four or five inches (five times as much will not insure a crop of wheat to a farmer of excellent soil without irrigation); and this falls almost altogether in a short series of spring storms, followed by months of unbroken drought, with excessive heat and sunlight. Hence each shrub stands at such a distance from its neighbor that it is never shaded; and, equally exposed to light and air on all sides, becomes compact and rounded.

This scantiness of growth shows that in the desert the plants have returned to primitive conditions. Their competition is not with each other for light and space, as in a forest or meadow, but with a niggard Nature for the very necessaries of existence—a struggle against inorganic forces; first, to obtain enough moisture and dissolved food from the arid and often sterile soil, and, second, to prevent losing it to the thirsty, restless air and the blazing sun. In a semi-desert, like the South-African veldt, or the Mexican cactus plains, animals must also be guarded against, and hence there all the bushes and trees are intensely thorny; but in the real desert this danger is spared them, since large beasts are absent, and therefore little energy need be wasted upon providing armor.

The defences in such arid areas as the Death Valley and Mohave deserts, or those of the drearier parts of the Kalahari country, the Sahara, Arabia, and Tibet, must be against the loss of moisture.

The scarce and precious water is collected in various ways. In damp regions the roots of perennial plants sink deeply, and sustain a great growth above ground. In a moderately dry climate plants develop bulky roots, and store up supplies which outlast the summer drought; or the plants themselves, as in the case of the cactuses, become fleshy reservoirs of water and food. In the extreme desert, such as here considered, neither of these resources is available, and perennial herbs are consequently few. Only stunted shrubs and hardy annuals are able to exist at all, the former growing very slowly, with toughness of texture, the latter flourishing briefly during the spring rains, devoting little energy to making stem or leaves or flowers — mostly inconspicuous and wind - fertilized — and hastening (while sometimes still of very small size) to perfect the seeds by which alone the species will survive until the next year's short period of wetness gives a possibility of germination and growth. Frequently desert plants are overtaken by drought too soon, and must postpone blooming until autumn; and plants such as elsewhere exhibit large, showy blossoms will here bear nothing worthy of the name of flower.

The only source of moisture in the real desert is rain and dew, for there is no accessible store of underground water; but dew is totally absent in some regions, as in our Death Valley, although said by Volkens to occur frequently in Egypt and Arabia. This chance moisture is gathered by the leaves somewhat, but mainly must be absorbed by the roots. Hence the roots of arid-district plants keep close to the surface, extending themselves far out in slender threads (a mesquit examined by Dr. Coville had roots fifty feet long), in order to exploit the widest area of absorption; but while this

By courtesy of the Carnegie Institution

BELT OF PALMS (NEOWASHINGTONIA FILIFERA) IN THE COLORADO DESERT, CALIFORNIA

The whitish soil about the palms is encrusted with alkali   Mesquit bushes grow among the palms

practice gives a bush stability against the wind, it also renders its roots easily uncovered. Moreover, there is a limit to the extent of roots a plant may have, since it can spare only a certain amount of vitality to make them.

The ceaseless wind—to digress a moment—is a factor always to be reckoned with. Where the soil is loose enough it is heaped into hillocks, which change and travel, exhuming herbage and trees in some places and burying them in others. Yuccas were found by the investigators of the Desert Botanical Laboratory, established in Arizona in 1903 by the Carnegie Institution, that had grown up thirty feet through a slowly heightening dune of gypsum sand in the Tularosa (Sonora) "white desert." The steady gales over the sand wastes of the Colorado Desert, in southern California, constitute a veritable sand-blast. "The western faces of the wooden telegraph-poles," it is said, "are deeply cut within two feet of the ground by the sharp driving sand, and the railroad employees have found it necessary to pile stones about the bases of the poles in

some spots to keep them from being actually cut off. The creosote-bushes have been moulded into the most fantastic shapes. One of them standing in the lee of a small boulder ran its branches freely to the eastward, but the twigs that projected upward and outward beyond the protection of the boulder were killed by the sand-blast, so that the plant presented the appearance of a miniature box-hedge."

That any plants can withstand such conditions is amazing, yet some do, and even control them. Thus in the Tularosa Desert the most characteristic growth is a sumac, which forms low, dense, widely spreading bushes, whose trunks at or beneath the surface often reach three inches in diameter. "The binding and protecting effect of this bush is manifest whenever an old dune is cut down by the wind, for one or more columns of sand are likely to be left standing, protected from the rain by the close covering of the branches and leaves, while the sand in the column itself is bound together by the long, penetrating roots. One such column, observed by the laboratory workers above mentioned, was fifteen feet tall.

By courtesy of the Carnegie Institution

THE WHITE SANDS, TULAROSA DESERT, NEW MEXICO

The view toward the San Andreas Mountains. In the foreground are parallel dunes with characteristic vegetation

TREE OCOTILLO (FOUQUIERIA MACDOUGALII) NEAR TORRES, MEXICO
The tree is in full leaf and about twenty-five feet high

The obtaining of water, however,—to return to the previous theme,—is only a part, and perhaps a minor part, of the problem before the xerophyte. The water gathered by a plant is carried along the roots, bearing food in solution, up the stem and branches, and then given off by the leaves and all suitable surfaces. Such transpiration is a vital necessity, by which life - functions are carried on. Where water is plentiful in the soil, the supply absorbed by the roots keeps pace with the transpiration (exceeds it a little when making new growth), and all goes well; but in a drought plants shrink and wilt because the evaporation from the broad green surfaces is then in excess of what the roots can supply. In the desert, drought—killing drought—is the normal condition. The very climatic situation which makes the district arid presupposes a local atmosphere extremely dry. It does contain some moisture, which is hygroscopically absorbed by the soil and goes to feed the roots, but at best it is dry enough to suck moisture out of plant leaves with killing speed and persistence.

Hence for desert vegetation an even greater problem than the getting of moisture is the keeping and use of it; and to this end very serviceable modifications have been gained by the plants of the arid wastes. Such annual herbs as sprout, flourish, and die during the two or three rainy months which suffice to perfect their seeds, are not much different from ordinary types; but in the characteristic perennial herbs and shrubs, which must endure throughout the year, are seen many special adaptations for resisting evaporation. In general, the growth is very slow, the wood close-grained, hard, and resinous, and the bark, both under ground and above, thickened, corky, and relatively impermeable to water. In some cases the bark has layers of cells just beneath it, especially formed to retain water—an arrangement developed mostly in regions, like the Mediterranean borders, where water may be obtained in some abundance by the roots, yet not sufficiently to meet ordinary transpiration during a long dry season.

It is in the leaves, however, that the most striking modifications are seen. First, these are greatly reduced in size. A leaf more than half an inch square is a curiosity in such deserts as those of southeastern California. None is thin and bladelike, but rather all are thickened, elongate, often needlelike, and erect, thus reducing the evaporating surface to a minimum. Some species no longer put forth leaves at all, their functions being performed by the greenish stem.

One of these features is the habit of shedding all the leaves as soon as the annual rainy period and its stimulated growth cease, thus cutting off all the outlets of the plant, except a needful few on the stem, preparatory to the long hot rest-season. This adaptive habit has been acquired by many of the shrubs of the dryest deserts; and where leaves persist they lose entirely, or in great degree, their power of transpiration. The general olive or grayish hue of the foliage of steppes and deserts, so noticeable even on the "sage-brush plains" of our West, results from the efforts of the plants to conserve their moisture (and also to check the effect of too much light and heat) by clothing themselves, and especially their leaves, with a screen of hairs. All parts of the world furnish examples. In the dry elevated plains of Brazil, Quito, and Mexico there are large tracts covered with gregarious, spurgelike growths and gray-haired species of Croton, and observers say that when the wind blows undulations are set up over wide extents of country, like a billowy sea of gray foliage. Speaking of the prevalence of these botanical characteristics in the flora of the Mediterranean district, Kerner may be cited as follows:

"The trees have foliage with gray

By courtesy of the Carnegie Institution

SAND COLUMN, IN THE WHITE SANDS, NEW MEXICO

Caused by the protection afforded by the three-leaved sumac growing over it. Distance from base to summit of column about fifteen feet

hairs; the low undergrowth of sage and various other bushes and semishrubs (for which the name 'Phrygian undergrowth,' used by Theophrastus, may be retained), as well as the perennial shrubs and herbs growing on sunny hills and mountain slopes, are gray or white, and the preponderance of plants colored thus to restrict evaporation has a noticeable influence on the character of the landscape. . . . It is also very interesting to see that so many species which have a wide range of distribution, and which, from Scandinavia to the coasts of the Mediterranean, have bare foliage, can in the South protect themselves from drying up by developing hairs on their epidermis."

The protection referred to is gained in this way: the hairs as soon as formed become dead hollow tubes containing air; and a layer of dry unchanged air is entangled among them, acting as a curtain against the excessive light and heat from without, and an impediment against the escape of both moisture and warmth. The nights in the desert, as is well known, are cold, and the excessive radiation thereby induced would be highly injurious to plants were it not checked by some such non-conductor of heat as this layer of dry still air. Hence both plants and animals there have found it necessary to put on woollen clothing—the best material, as even humanity has discovered, for either shutting heat out or keeping it in. The edelweiss is a good example.

The superabundance of light and heat in such regions as those of the Rio Colorado plains would alone be fatal to plants unprepared for it by gradual adaptation. Excessive sunlight injures, and may destroy, the essential green coloring-matter (chlorophyl) of vegetation, which exists only within certain limits of light-intensity and temperature; and may harm the protoplasm generally by the action of the blue-violet rays; and as the intensity of the insolation on such deserts is much higher than in humid regions, it is evident that the protoplasm of desert plants must have acquired a superior chemical resistance in this direction. Similarly these plants (illustrating again their plasticity) have become inured to

a degree of heat which would quickly kill those transplanted from damp situations. It is a general rule that vegetable protoplasm will not survive a temperature of about 113 F., yet many observations in Arizona show that soil in which some plants thrive there, and the substance of the plants themselves, are much hotter than that each day for months together.

To the same end has arisen another beautiful series of adaptations, by acquiring which many plants have become successfully deserticolous, which otherwise could not hold their own against the fierceness of their physical surroundings. This is the varnish of waxy, or resinous, or saline excretions, with which their leaves and twigs become more or less completely coated. The well-known creosote-bush (Covillea tridentata) of the Southwest, for which no torrid and sandy waste seems too forbidding, is a prominent example of this method of defence. In spring, when the leaves are young and growing, the foliage is soft and clean, but as the rains cease and the drought advances, both leaves and twigs become coated with something resembling shellac, which gives the pungent smell and dense smoke familiar to campers, who must often resort to this bush for fuel. Both reason and experiments show that this balsamic coating restricts without wholly stopping evaporation—just how is not known. A similar coating prevails among the plants growing in like circumstances in the Old World, but on the Australian deserts the covering is usually waxy. It is secreted by glands at the roots of the hairs, or from pits in the leaves, and forms a delicate bloom.

The account of these and various other adaptations could be greatly extended. Enough has been presented, however, to illustrate how, by small size, diminished foliage, extensive root-spread, reduction of transpiration, thorny armament, bitter taste, and extraordinary vitality and resistance to desiccation, nature has economically enabled plants to occupy and thrive in the otherwise waste places of an overcrowded earth, and thus furnish their small quota of food and shelter to higher organisms, otherwise unprovided for.

FORESTS OF THE CALIFORNIA COAST RANGE

THE Coast Range of mountains running through California, and fringing the western shore of the continent, is a great natural arboretum—a paradise of forest trees and flowering shrubs. North of Shasta the forests awe with their grandeur; south, the scenery is park-like and sylvan, and the shrubs are at home.

Looked at from Shasta or the peaks of the Sierras, the tract of which we write is almost continually shrouded in an amethyst haze, that turns at times into garments of purple, and shreds out into all the hues of crimson and gold. Beneath the ever-hanging haze is a spine of miniature mountains, flanked by rounded hills and smooth-sided cañons, with thousands of little valleys dimpling the entire area, and nursing in their snug warm bosoms a luxuriance that is something more than semi-tropical. Here can be found the extremes of tree growth. The hardy species of the North are not only neighborly, but familiar, and even intimate, with the delicate representatives of the South. The resinous breath of the pine and hemlock, juniper and fir, mingles on the same hill-side with the spicy fragrance of the bay-tree and the perfume of the balm. The evergreen redwood rises, straight as an arrow, to a height of from two to three hundred feet. There are whole tribes of the coniferæ, dozens of species of cypress and cedar, a variety and relationship of the oaks that drives the botanist wild, ravines filled with the flowering dogwood, sweeps of glistening manzanita, spattered patches of the red-berried buckthorn, rifts of the pink-petaled rhododendron, sanguinary patches where stands the Judas-tree. In this favored country also bloom and bear the pomegranate, fig, olive, almond, apricot, lemon, orange, and the nectarine. The camellia is a tree, the heliotrope a stout shrub; geraniums are used for scarlet hedges; the calla-lily is a weed. And to round out this riot of luxuriance—this saturnalia of foliage, fruit, and flower—Nature sows every spring, in and through it all, a crop of wild oats such as was never even dreamed of by the original prodigal son.

East of the Coast Range lies one of the largest bodies of fertile land in the world. It is a valley about four hundred miles long by fifty to seventy wide, and contains over five millions of acres in its sixteen thousand or more square miles. Through it run two great rivers. The Sacramento, rising in an immense spring at the base of Mount Shasta, flows to the south. The San Joaquin, born in the Sierras and nursed in the foot-hills, winds its tortuous way north, till about the centre of the valley the two meet, and passing—a ribbon of silver—through the Strait of Carquinez, mingle in the Bay of San Francisco with the grass-green waters of the Pacific that crowd eastward through the Golden Gate. These great continuous valleys of the Sacramento and the San Joaquin have a climate of their own. Shut in by mountains, and covering about six degrees of latitude, there is at times a brewing here of the atmosphere that actually makes vegetation jump with life.

West of the Coast Range is an expanse of deep sea bewildering in its immensity. As long as the hemisphere, the Pacific has a clear breadth of seven thousand miles to the Asiatic shore. The Japanese Stream from the eastern Asiatic coast comes within thirty miles of the coast of California. The passage of this warm current through the cold waters of the Pacific generates immense clouds of vapor.

This incoming of the fog is one of the fascinations and peculiarities of the dry season in California. It is this and "the trades" which give to San Francisco an atmosphere that admits of furs on the Fourth of July, and that reaches for the human marrow on what elsewhere is a sultry summer afternoon. By mid-day, after a forenoon of absolute perfection, there are hints of the daily invasion. Thin streamers of fog creep slowly along the spines of the low-lying and westward-sloping hills, and cautiously feel their way into the interior. Until it reaches the high Sierras the mist is victorious. But the valleys of the Sacramento and the San Joaquin have never yet been conquered by the silent battalions of the sea; for they hold in storage and reserve

FOG IN THE REDWOODS, RUSSIAN RIVER.

the power of the sun—now quite down behind the western waters—and bending over the crowded and confused enemy the resistless wave of reflected and refracted heat, they start back the mighty host in full and disastrous retreat. Victorious almost to the end, the charging cohorts are thrashed back over the whole ground, till finally, aided perhaps by a breeze from the Sierras, they are swirled ingloriously into the ocean waste, while hills and valleys, and even the streets of a great city, drip with the moisture of annihilation and the perspiration of the great endeavor.

With this somewhat superficial description of the location and climatic peculiarities of the Coast Range, the marvellous variety and character of its vegetation can be better understood. Thoroughly soaked during the rainy season; supplied with surface moisture during the dry; blest during the day by the direct rays of the sun, and visited at night by wandering currents of warmth from the great valleys; free from ice and snow and frosts, but favored by the cool and bracing breezes of the ocean—the whole region teems with life and beauty, health and strength. There is not the tangle of the India jungle, the miasma of a Southern swamp, or the suffocation of the torrid zone; but

there is a listlessness and languor sufficient to the requirements thereof, and an atmosphere, especially in the early morning, that draws into the human system like draughts of extra dry champagne.

Here, then, is the home and habitat of one of Nature's masterpieces, the redwood-tree. A stranger almost to the botanist, this Apollo of the woods. Belonging to the tribe of the giant pines, which stand in groups of proud exclusiveness in the foot-hills of the Sierras, these stalwart children of virtually the same progenitors, in the years long gone by, came in seed form from the paternal location to root and grow where they could look out upon the heaving sea, and revel in the relish of its moist and salty exhalation. For the redwood loves the fog. Where the mist hangs dense and lingers the longest, there this giant stem stands the thickest and the straightest. They colonize in the upper parts of all the ravines sloping to the Pacific, occupy the valley of the Russian River and the narrow gulches of the smaller streams, and from the Clear Lake country or the region of San Francisco Bay the tall plumes of their handsome tops can be seen standing clear and straight above the vapor clouds that toss and tumble across the mountain outline for more

A LIVING TOMB—YOUNG REDWOODS FROM AN OLD STUMP.

library with beautifully polished shelves.

Valuable, beautiful, and majestic as is the redwood, it has been wastefully and shamefully raided upon by the ruthless woodmen of the West. Even Nature recognizes the shame, for about the trunks of her fallen favorites she has caused to grow in a closed and sacred circle a hedge of the same beautiful green-leaved species, not to attain greatness or any industrial worth, but simply to screen from the vulgar gaze the great scar within, and with the vines and the ferns, wet with the tears of the fog, to stand and mourn the first and best born in this its living tomb.

The redwood, while the bright particular star, is not, however, the all in all of the wonderful forest combination. There is the California white cedar, and its own cousin the giant arbor-vitæ, one hundred and fifty to two hundred feet tall—stalwarts both of them; the magnificent Lawson cypress, the great silver-fir, and the noble silver or red fir, growing in groves at the base of Shasta. Then comes the Douglas spruce, a coarse-grained fellow with three hundred feet of trunk, and by its side the graceful California hemlock, with its slender and drooping twigs and branches hanging from the same great height. As for pines, there are varieties at Monterey which grow to the water's edge: the beautiful twisted-branched, the prickly-coned, the hook-coned, the swamp, the scrub, the sugar, and the nut pine—the favorite food of the Indians. There are species of the soft and the sugar maples, one or two representatives of the ash, black and white and weeping willows, buckeyes like unto those of the Middle States, and the "chinquapin," or golden-leaved chestnut. Often in midday, in the close and sultry cross cañons, one will be driven almost insane by the heavy perfume of the mountain-laurel or spice-tree, and as frequently delighted by the aromatic odor of the native nutmeg. And as for oaks, a bewildered botanist summed up the situation when he ex-

than a hundred miles. Fairly in the presence of these trees, the human pigmy is conscious of his littleness. Like the great pines, the redwoods stand in family groups or groves, the trunk straight as the plummet's fall, with oftentimes a hundred and fifty feet to the light hemlock-green foliage of the first limb. "The tall pine of the Northern forest," over which the chief Red Jacket used so eloquently to rave, was a stripling beside this Hercules of an evergreen. Its height is from two to three hundred and fifty feet. It is as round as a cylinder, tapering from root to tip like a finely finished mast. Its girt is so great that ten men could not compass the circumference of many of them, clasping their outstretched hands. Its bark is brown and clean and beautifully seamed; its wood soft and straight-grained, the color more of a maroon than red. It is as fragrant as the cedar, its cone long and round, and the silver of its double under-leaf is a choice tint of the moonlight. Felled to the earth, one of the monsters will furnish the material to frame and board and shingle—in fact entirely build—a large country villa. It will do more: it will finish the interior, supply with furniture, and fit dining-room and

claimed, "I know not where the varieties end and the species begin." There are tall oaks from little acorns grown, and abnormally large acorns grown from little oaks. There are large and small, quicker than a recently acquired inheritance, "the sheep-herder's delight," the "real devil" of the hill-top, "the terror" of the ravine—the so-called poison-oak. Most of the open valleys of the Coast

BLACK OAK, SONOMA VALLEY.

squat and tall, thorough-bred and scrub. There is a live-oak, a very gnarled, rheumatic-looking, and nearly dead oak, a chestnut-oak, the evergreen white oak with pendent branches, a black and blue oak, a desert variety, and that insignificant-looking but potent member of the family that can swell the human head Range are filled with the beautiful evergreen or live oak, distributed as no landscape gardener could arrange for parklike effect. The valley of the Sacramento is thick spotted with the low and broadspreading mounds of green, the region about Clear Lake a marvel in the beauty of these trees. At Oakland and Alameda

SCRUB OAK AND CHAPARRAL.

and Menlo Park, and thence down the valleys of San José and Gilroy, there are a number and a beauty of veterans that Old England and all Europe cannot show, while the Ojai Valley, back of Santa Barbara, is the ideal of the great temple the Druid priestess saw in her dream. North of the Golden Gate, in the ravines of the Saucelito Hills, there is a square-topped variety known as the holly-leaved oak, bright and beautiful and very closely growing, so much so that when suddenly through a heavy layer of mist there bursts the glory blaze of the sun at high meridian, the dense-foliaged shrubs blend into a solid color, and the shallow ravines and favored places of the hills are upholstered in a plush such as was never thrown from weaver's loom. Other varieties of the oak join with the holly-leaved to give richness of color to Mount Tamalpais, and one of the beautiful sights about the bay is to sit at San Rafael and watch the evening shadows come and go, pick out on the steep slopes the exquisite shading of the seven or eight varieties of manzanita and kindred shrubs to contrast with the darker tints of the laurel and the oak, while the drapery of the fog folds itself about the mountain's throat, and the tinge of the great green waistcoat is lost in the summit fading of the sunset's golden glow.

To the south of San Francisco there is even a greater range of color and diversity of tree growth. The San Mateo hills are rich with evergreens; the country sweeping up from the pebble beach at Pescadero is made up of sunny ridges, and rifted with narrow and close-grown valleys, where thread-like brooks murmur their way through tunnels of foliage to the sea, while the mountains of Santa Cruz furnish another rendezvous for the mammoth redwood, the chestnut, and the oak. But distinguished from all the rest of these Southern nabobs, curious in shape and almost humanly beautiful, stands the giant madrona, or arbutus-tree. The genus really belongs to the Old World. Asia has its species, and Mexico claims one or two representatives, but the pride of the family and delight of arboriculturists is the strong, healthy, and handsome child of the west coast. It is often eighty to one hundred feet high, three feet in diameter, and a famous specimen in Marin County has a measured girt of twenty-three feet at the branching point of the tremendous stem, with many of the branches three feet through. The foliage is light and airy, the leaves oblong, pale beneath, bright green above. The bloom is in dense racemes of cream-white flowers; the fruit, a dry orange-colored berry, rough and uninteresting. But the charm of the madrona, outside of its general appearance, is in its bark—no, it is not a bark, it is a skin, delicate in texture, smooth, and as soft to the touch as the shoulders of an infant. In the strong brown lithe body of an Indian, and in the moonlight the graceful upsweep of its branches is like the careless lifting of a dusky maiden's arms. Every feature of the madrona is feminine. They grow in groves or neighborhoods, and seldom

CYPRESS POINT, MONTEREY.

sunlight of the summer these trees glisten with the rich color of polished cinnamon, and in the moist shadow of the springtime they are velvety in combination colors of old-gold and sage-green. There is a human pose to the trunk. Seen through the tangle of the thicket, it looks like the stand in isolation, courtesy to the winds, mock at the dignified evergreens and oaks, and with every favorable breeze and opportunity flirt desperately with the mountain lilacs that toss high their purple plumes on the head waters of Los Gatos Creek.

WILD GRAPE-VINES, SONOMA CREEK.

Out of the Santa Cruz Mountains, by way of the famous San Lorenzo cañon, across a sweep of bay as blue and beautiful as that of Naples, around a point of bright green pines, and the seaside hermitage of one of California's wonders is reached, the cypress of Monterey — a strange, picturesque, and peculiar tree. Botanists say it has not a near relative in all the world. Monterey and one other spot on the coast are its only home. It is far from being handsome. The trunk is large and fairly tall, and the branches wide-spreading; but the bark is wrinkled and rough, the limbs, partially dead and often distorted, are hung with beards of gray moss; and with its dark green leaves matted and bunched with the terminal twigs, the whole grove looks like a wan and weary survivor of some strange vendetta of the past. The tree still fights for life, disputes with the broad Pacific. For it grows on a bed of granite bowlders on the very edge of the sea, and in places its naked roots cling in desperation to the rocks, while its stiff neck is twisted, and it is assaulted and battered without mercy by the uncompromising storm. A thing of wonderful endurance—in fact, so is its kindred the world over. The fibre of the cypress is almost as tough as iron, its grain more enduring than stone.

From Monterey south the ocean shore is devoid of tree growth, but a few miles inland spread miles upon miles of foliage. The evergreens get smaller, the madronas are not so grand, the varieties of manzanita multiply, and the hard-wooded shrubs are bewildering in number. Back of San Buenaventura the valleys are parks of the evergreen oak. Santa Barbara is not only a sanatorium, but the entrance to a floral paradise; and the steep mountainsides of the San Fernando, just north of the bluffs at Santa Monica, are dense and dark with thickets of chaparral, shading down into the light green streak of bottom willows that follows up the valley to the orange groves and apricot orchards surrounding Los Angeles—the City of the Angels. North again through the San Francisquita Cañon, across the Mohave Desert, through the Tehichipa Pass, and following the west side of the great valley of the San Joaquin, the hills and shallow valleys of the eastern slope of the Coast Range, unknown to the fogs and sheltered from the ocean winds, smile serenely out upon the plain through a vegetation of tropical luxuriance. The Gilroy Valley is a garden, and wonderful in the spring-time is the passage of Pacheco Pass. San José and the beauty of its surroundings are known to every tourist. Here, in amazing growth by the road-sides, can be seen thousands of the imported strangers, the eucalyptus, or Australian blue-gum tree. In the same neighborhood is also the famous "Alameda," or avenue of willows planted by the old padres, and shading miles of carriageway to Santa Clara. But to the lover of the naturally beautiful there is little to admire in these innovations. There is nothing in the euca-

CYPRESS WOOD INTERIOR, CYPRESS POINT, MONTEREY.

lyptus, with its bilious blue-green foliage, but the rapidity of its miserable sprawling growth; and the straight lines of the be-headed willows only remind of the for-estry of the Old World, that amputates everything in the shape of a tree to the nakedness of the trunk and the loneli-ness of the terminal tuft, clips hedges into square-backed abominations, prunes vines into horrible deformity, and combs the hair of Nature even to the snow line of the bald mountain-top.

Out of the inhabited valleys, then, and into the abandon of the hills. There can be found "sermons in trees, books in the running brooks," health and happiness in hundreds of nooks of Arcadian beauty all along the coast. Places of rural peace and absolute rest are the Napa and Calis-toga valleys, where roses and the honey-suckle smother a cottage in a fortnight, and wind one a prisoner within the doors. On Sonoma Creek the wild grape-vine fairly runs riot. It climbs into the over-hanging oaks, droops to the pebble bed of the dry stream, and swept down and across by the rushing waters of the period of rains, mounts the trees of the opposite side, and thus from season to season weaves madly back and forth, till whole ravines are a labyrinth, and the tangle of green and brown is a net-work of won-der. At times the mountains about Clear Lake are thick with underbrush in bloom, and when the high Sierras are bound in snow, the flower-carpeted valleys here-about are white with what is known as "the blossom storm." The woods of

Mendocino are primeval and grand, and the explorer who has survived the wilderness of the Southland can be forever lost in the vast reaches of forest, never yet pressed by human footsteps, on the head waters of the Eel, Klamath, Sacramento, and McCloud.

And thus end our glimpses of the California Coast Range. They have been given for a purpose—to in a measure redeem a splendid State from the reputation of grossness, to silence the everlasting rattle of the tourist regarding the Yosemite, big trees, big cañons, big strawberries and pears, and to testify that with all the wonders of the great and the grand, there also exist the sylvan and the delicately beautiful.

WESTERN CLIFF-DWELLERS

PEOPLE rarely consider what an interesting experiment in the evolution of man was going on here in America when Columbus set out on his crazy adventure across the sea, nor how abruptly the experiment ended when the white race and the red race met. For most of us the history of America begins in 1492.

We, of course, all have some notion, framed partly from fact, largely from fiction, of the original possessors of our continent. But, after all, I fancy that most of us only dimly realize that back of the wars which made the country free, back of the struggle with forest and soil and forbidding wastes which made it rich, back of the bold adventures which made it known, stretch long ages, in which masses of dusky people, from one seaboard to the other, lived out their simple lives face to face with nature, won their way slowly through savagery to barba-

rism, and even here and there began to
press eagerly through the portals which
open toward civilization.

Then from countries in which mankind
started earlier, or had more quickly scaled
the heights of communal life, came the
white men. The native advance was
stayed, and soon the doors were closed
forever upon a genuine American barbarism just shaping itself into a crude civilization in favored corners of the land. The
Old World experiment in man-culture
was grafted on the New, or, more frequently, replaced it altogether.

But here and there in the Southwest
some small groups of red men, called
Pueblo or village Indians, the wreckage of
the abortive experiment in primitive man-
culture in America, still survive. These
Indians are mostly in Arizona and New
Mexico, living in quaint stone or adobe
houses in far-away fertile valleys, or
perched atop of great plateaus. Until
within a decade or two they lived and
thought and worshipped powers unseen
in just such fashion as they did, and in
the very places where they were, when
the Spaniards found them, more than
three centuries ago; and even in some
instances they still do so.

These Pueblo Indians are not to be con-
founded either with the savages upon the
Atlantic seaboard or in the eastern interior, with whom much of our early national history is concerned, nor with the
nomadic tribes elsewhere in the land.
Some of them present to-day a significant
transition phase in the advance of a people from savagery toward civilization,
whose study is of priceless value in the
understanding of the science of man.

But each year—nay, each month—
brings new ideas, new aims, new needs
into the barbarian simplicity of this native life. Old traditions, old customs, old
aspirations, are fading swiftly and surely
in the presence of the white man. It is
humiliating not only for an American,
but for any educated human being, to
realize that in this great, rich, powerful
United States, boasting ever of its general
enlightenment, there is neither the intelligent public spirit nor the sustained private devotion to the wider aspects of science to secure the myths and traditions
and lore of those wonderful people before
this page now open upon the Story of
Man shall be closed forever. For nowhere else upon this planet does this par-

ticular illumining phase of human life
exist, nor will it come again. There are
many fields of science in which it does
not make very much difference if the
work which is waiting to be done shall
wait a little longer. A decade more or
less is of little importance in the end.
But here delay is fatal.

The school-houses near the pueblos, the
new requirements in food and dress, the
new conceptions of the world, which begins for them to reach out beyond the
cliffs upon the far horizon—these may all
be very important to the material welfare
of these waifs from the past, with a higher
world culture pressing in upon them.
But it means the speedy extinction of old
customs in life and worship and ceremonial, which still are full of the spirit and
practice of a primitive culture. It means
that all natural things and happenings in
their out-of-door world will soon lose their
spiritual meanings, and that the quaint
myths out of forgotten centuries will fade
with the old folks who still may cherish
them. When such people get on cotton
shirts, need coffee and sugar, want rum,
and begin to name their sons after the
Presidents—for it has come to this save in
one or two far-away places—they will not
continue long to send messages to the
gods by rattlesnakes, nor propitiate the
elements with feathers and songs.

It is not an untrodden way which must
be followed if this treasure in the Man-
Science is to be secured. The Bureau of
Ethnology in Washington, under the direction of Major Powell, has done admirable work already. Cushing, Bandelier,
Lummis, Stephen, Fewkes, Mrs. Steven-
son, and others have rescued much. But
the work should be more extended, more
sustained, more amply supported, and
must withal be quickly under way.

In a recent issue of this Magazine the
writer indicated the importance of a practical knowledge of the modern Pueblo
Indians in forming a conception of the
elder people to whom they are closely
linked. For the later workers in American archæology have finally made it clear
that the Pueblo Indians are in all probability the descendants of the erstwhile
mysterious Cliff-Dwellers of America,
whose architecture and industries and
habits, and no doubt traditions and myths,
they inherit. Some of the largest and
most imposing of the old cliff dwellings
are situated in southwestern Colorado and

THE SAN JUAN COUNTRY—PLACER-MINERS FINDING A NUGGET.

in northern Arizona, along the tributaries of the San Juan River. But from the Rocky Mountains to the Colorado River, and from the northernmost tributaries of the San Juan southward to Mexico, smaller cliff-houses are abundantly scattered in the walls of the cañons. The ruins and burial-places of the Cliff-Dwellers in many parts of the country have been eagerly explored, and their ethnical position in the higher stages of barbarism has been established.

The purpose of this paper relates to some recent discoveries in the hot wonderland which lies along the San Juan River and its northern tributaries, mostly in southeastern Utah. It relates to people whom the Spaniards never saw—for the very good reason that they had long been buried safe under the sand before the Old World folks knew how "the other half lived," or even that there was another half. Buried, too, they were in a region into which those intrepid and heroic explorers were never lured by God's service or the color of gold.

But all these red folks, like their surviving types in the pueblos, lived no doubt in sympathetic touch with the spirit of the earth and air and sky; and so, before unveiling the secret which the parched earth has kept so long, I should like to give to the reader a passing glimpse of their deserted land.

As you go over the Rocky Mountains towards the west from Colorado Springs or Pueblo or Trinidad, you come into a region of jumbled ranges interspersed with mountain parks. The Colorado River, sweeping southwestward, has sculptured the wonderful valleys and sublime gorges known as the Grand Cañon. From the east the San Juan River, rising in the San Juan Mountains, and receiving from the north several tributaries, now mostly dry, joins the Colorado in southern Utah. North of the San Juan River, and between its namesake mountains on the east and the Colorado River on the west, lies a triangular region about as large as Massachusetts, Rhode Island, and Connecticut together, and called the Northern San Juan Plateau Country. A few small peaks rise here and there above the plateau, while everywhere great cañons, wild and forbidding, or broad valleys with terraced sides, and lofty buttes or mesas rising gigantic from the bottoms, relieve the general level. The plateau region south of the San Juan River is the home of the Navajos.

There are two or three small villages along the upper reaches of the San Juan River. But for the most part the broad valley, bordered by imposing bluffs, is in summer a hot, bare, stifling stretch of desert, with the sullen, muddy stream sweeping silently through it. Only toward the end the river enters a profound chasm, and roars its way to the Colorado. But one town, Bluff City by name, with some two or three hundred of the Chosen, a solitary outpost and oasis of Mormon-

dom, exists, and even thrives in a half-hearted way, as thrift goes in a desert, in the southeastern corner of Utah. This town, ninety miles from the railroad, is the metropolis of the San Juan Valley. A swiftly subsiding gold craze brought many adventurers to the valley a few years ago. But now only a few placer miners are left, struggling here and there against odds, far down the stream, picturesque and pathetic beside their rough sluices and quaint water-wheels.

It is from Bluff that you most conveniently enter the country of which I write, and you see no fixed human habitation, and probably no white man, until you get back, brown, tired, and dusty, to Bluff again. The nearest railroad is at Mancos, in Colorado, and here at the Wetherills' Alamo Ranch one can obtain an outfit and most competent guides, hardy, bright sons of the household, and wise in the lore of the hills, for the rough trip by way of Bluff to the plateau of the northern San Juan district. Access from Bluff to the plateau is mostly by dim and devious Indian trails, which meander along the rough bottoms of the cañons, or clamber toilsomely to the uplands, over whose bare or pine-clad surfaces they stretch tortuously away. Water is scanty at the best, its situations known only to a few, and in dry seasons long and trying marches must often be made to reach the hidden and meagre pools and springs.

The explorer must secure hardy ponies or mules, accustomed to forage for themselves on the scantiest of herbage, and capable, if need be, of sustaining life for a day or two on the willow-twigs and rank dried weeds of the bottoms. The pack is intrusted to mules. A canvas wagon-sheet and a blanket must serve in lieu of tent and bed. It is no hardship, however, in this dry and bracing air, to sleep under the stars. Water, no matter what color or consistency it may possess, is the only thing which the traveller longs and strives and prays for, and for lack of this many an unwise adventurer in these arid wastes has left his bones to bleach beside the way.

The great cañons and their tributary gorges, which have been carved out of the plateau in the past, thousands of feet deep in places, by wind and sand and rain and mighty rivers, are now almost wholly dry, save when a cloud-burst or a storm on the far mountains sends a mad torrent roaring down. But this soon passes, and in a few hours the horseman may be struggling along the parched bottom faint from thirst.

In the high country the great pines sing and moan in the wind at night and morning. The piñons and cedars on the lower levels murmur fitfully to the passing breeze. Small lizards rustle in the dried grass as they whisk from your presence. Prairie-dogs here and there chatter and whistle at you as you pass. As night comes on, the howls and barks of the coyotes circling far about the camp are weird and mournful. But the great country stretching away for hundreds of miles has scarce a human habitation, few wild animals and birds, and these largely of the still kind, and so is mostly silent. It is very hot in the daytime, with the sun straight at you from above and back at you from the rocks as you ride. It is sometimes rather trying to stop at mid-day, unpack, and get dinner. Perhaps there is no shade for twenty miles, except under your mules—and your mules kick. But the air is so dry and bracing that a temperature of from 108° to 112° in the sun is never disheartening, as is the ordinary summer weather of our Eastern cities, with that combination of heat and moisture which so remorselessly saps the energies. And ever above is the marvellous sky. The nights are always deliciously cool. Altogether, the wanderer who doesn't mind the wholesome sunburn upon the skin, and has a good supply of water, is about as free and comfortable and happy as good mortals deserve to be. How far away New York seems! And for the thousand unnecessary things which we gather about us in our winter thraldom and dote upon, how pitiful are they, if we deign to recall them! This is living. You get down to sheer manhood, face to face with the bare, relentless, fascinating old earth. And no memory of art rebukes your willing thraldom to the glorious pictures which momently rise and fade.

The tints of the cliffs in Monument Valley, south of the San Juan, shimmering through the hot haze of eighty miles; great sand columns which rise from the valleys, swaying pillars of pink and yellow and gray, now singly, now in groups, poising for hours, or gliding in stately fashion beyond the vision or melting away before you; the deep black shadows upon the broken faces of the cliffs; the dark moving acres of forest and bush and plain, saved for a moment by drifting clouds from the pitiless thraldom of the sun—these, and a nameless witchery of the air, which makes all far things strange and beautiful, and which more than all else lures back the wanderer to these hot wastes year after year, dwell in the memory when the trials are forgotten.

This great desolate plateau, so inaccessible and so far from the usual routes of travel, is rarely visited save by cattle-herders, and is inhabited only by a few renegade Utes, who in summer live in wickieups built of boughs, and cultivate the few moist bottoms in the valleys. Even the best government maps are very faulty, and practically useless for the location of water.

One of the great cañons, about fifty miles long, and in places two thousand feet deep, with sheer cliffs overhanging the narrow winding bottom, and unnamed upon the map, is known to the herders as Grand Gulch. It harbors scores of large and imposing cliff ruins. But for the most part the ruined houses of the Cliff-Dwellers in this region are small and widely scattered. Some are built in shallow caves far up the cliffs; some are under the overhanging rock near the bottom.

Explorations of these ruins and their adjacent graves show that these Cliff-Dwellers were the same sort of folk as those who once inhabited the Mesa Verde in southwestern Colorado, and the vast region stretching southward from the valley of the San Juan. The stone weapons, pottery, fabrics, etc., are similar, as are the skulls, which are short and flattened behind.

Richard Wetherill and his brothers, of Mancos, Colorado, have made many and fruitful explorations of the cliff dwellings in this region. Part of their collections are now at the American Museum of Natural History in New York, some are in Denver, some in Philadelphia, some are in their possession at Mancos, and some are in private hands elsewhere. Several persons from Bluff have gathered valuable material from these cliff ruins, part of which is in Salt Lake City, part dispersed without record.

But I must hasten to my purpose and speak of a remarkable discovery made by the Wetherills in their work among the cliff ruins, and in the caves of the cañon walls in the northern San Juan country, which has not, so far as I am aware, been yet recorded. In some of their excavations in this region the explorers were impelled, for what reason I do not know, to dig under the walls of the houses of the Cliff-Dwellers and beneath their graves. Here, much to their surprise, they came upon another set of graves of entirely different construction, and containing relics of what appear to be a different group of people.

These older graves are in the floors of shallow caves. They are egg-shaped holes, in the earth or sand, either stoned at the side, or lined with clay plastered directly upon the sand. The mummies of men, women, and children are found, often two bodies in one grave.

Sandals woven of yucca fibre upon the feet, a breech-cloth of woven cedar bark, strings of rough beads around the neck, about the body a rudely constructed blanket of rabbit fur, enveloped in a yucca cloth, over the head a small flat basket, and a great finely woven basket over all—such was their burial fashion.

The graves never contain pottery, as those of the Cliff-Dwellers are so apt to do, and the skulls of the people are narrow and long, and never flattened at the back. Bone implements, stone spearheads and arrow-heads, twisted cords of human hair, well-formed cylindrical stone pipes, and baskets filled with seeds and ornaments are found with the bodies.

Spear-points between the ribs, stone arrow-heads in the backbone, a great obsidian spear driven through the hips, crushed skulls and severed limbs—these secrets of the old graves show clearly enough that there were rough times in the cañons now and then, and that these old fellows were proficient in the barbaric art of killing men—the art towards which some of our wind-and-paper patriots would fain have us climb back.

Over these graves the rubbish heaps of the Cliff-Dwellers have in places accumulated to a depth of two feet, showing a long residence above the graveyards, of whose existence they may well have been unconscious. In many places great rocks have fallen upon the graves.

The Wetherills soon recognized the ethnological importance of their discovery, and have provisionally named the people who buried in these older graves the "Basket-Makers."

There is no evidence that the Basket-Makers ever built in these caves. While their graves are often found under the cliff dwellings, they also occur in caves in which the Cliff Men had no houses, and with the earth level and hard above them. The skull has great significance in the lore which anthropology gleans here and there the world over out of forgotten graves, and the difference in the form of the skull between the Cliff-Dwellers and the Basket-Makers would seem—I speak with the reserve which becomes a poacher upon anthropological preserves—to exclude their identity.

One need be a student only of the human nature of to-day to conclude that the newly found people were not mere intruders upon the domain of the Cliff-Dwellers, vanquished, and hurriedly buried; for the solicitous care with which the bodies are furnished for their journey into "the country which is out of sight" forbids the notion.

It seems to me to be not without possible significance in determining the ethnical status of this new aborigine that no pottery of any kind has been found in his graves. He certainly knew the value of clay, for he plastered his graves with it. Students in the crude art of pottery-making have been led to believe that the use of clay was preceded by the acquirement of considerable skill in basket-making, and that from the earliest application of clay coverings or clay linings to baskets, to make them impervious, or resistant to heat, the manufacture of pottery was gradually evolved.

Now if this old American did not know how to make pottery, he must, according to the widely accepted system of Morgan, be denied admission to the ranks of barbarism, and, in spite of the fact that he had discovered clay and just missed the achievement of a dish, be thrust sternly back among the savages. He might still be saved, however, by the creed of Tylor, if he knew how to till the soil; and though no agricultural implements were buried with him, as they often are with the Cliff-Dwellers, he was thoughtful enough to stow away in his excellent baskets some corn and seeds. So, as far as I can see, while he is damned to savagery by the American doctrine, he is saved to barbarism by that of the Englishman. May we not give him the benefit of the doubt?

People who know about these things

have told me that the stone hatchet fastened to a wooden handle by thongs is to be considered an implement of very high order, when you know, or guess wisely, about the genesis of inventions among people of the stone age. But I regret to say that while these Basket-Makers possessed most excellent stone arrow and spear heads, stone hatchets are not found among their belongings. Nothing of this nature better than a crude pounding-stone, bearing the form of a natural un-worked pebble, has been as yet unearthed. In the ruins and graves of the Cliff-Dwellers, on the other hand, stone hatchets with wooden handles, or with grooves for the attachment of these by thongs, are common. This fact might perhaps be wisely adduced with the rest as evidence of the lower status of the Basket-Makers.

The whole matter at present rests just here, until the various furnishings of their burial-places shall have received systematic study, and the country shall have been more widely explored. But one may hazard a guess that these Basket-Makers were nomadic Indians who used the sheltered caves as burial-places before the Cliff-Dwellers settled the country and utilized the rocky shelters for their homes. There must in the old days have been many a fierce encounter up and down the rugged faces of the rocks when the Cliff Men met their foes with stone-tipped arrow, axe, and spear — perhaps over the very spot where the elder folk, now still and crumbling in their unsuspected graves, had fought and lost.

To one who has travelled much in this southwest plateau country, and knows not only just how dry it is, but also just how dry it is not, the residence of these early peoples in small scattered communities along the now remote cañons and valleys is neither surprising nor mysterious. Here were warmth and shelter the year round, and for those who had learned to build were houses half made already by the cave walls of the cliffs.

It does not require very much food for bare subsistence, and a very small patch of corn suffices for a family. While springs and pools are rare, there are a good many places, in valleys apparently dry the summer through, in which the seepage from the back country comes down some sag in the hills and furnishes moisture enough for a crop of corn. The beds of dry streams also, where sand is plenty, are often moist beneath the surface.

In fact, here and there all over the Cliff-Dwellers' country to-day, in stream-beds, mostly dry, or in low places in the bottoms, with no water visible, one comes across groups of Navajos or Utes camped beside little green patches of corn which seems to be growing out of the driest of sand banks. It is easier for the corn roots than it is for the humans to get enough drinking-water, and the Indians are very clever to-day, as the older fellows doubtless were, in finding the few places here and there in which the deep moisture suffices for a modest crop of corn.

It has been the writer's good fortune, half on knowledge, half on pleasure bent, to journey over this desolate country under the skilful guidance of Al. Wetherill, to delve among the ruins of the cliff dwellings, to search through the opened graves of the Basket-Makers, and so to gain a conception at first hand of the land they lived in, the old folks, and their graves. And it is with Richard Wetherill's permission that I record this interesting discovery of the Basket-Makers which he and his brothers made some time ago. I am eager to do this because the enthusiasm, devotion, and practical knowledge which he has brought to his life work in the cause of American archæology should find more general appreciation, and in the hope that means may be forth-coming from some quarter for the pursuit, under Wetherill's direction, of this promising research.

Will none of our great universities realize before it is too late that the treasure-house of folk-lore among the Pueblo Indians is crumbling fast, and that these fields of American archæology in the Southwest are wide and fruitful?

If you have seen the living Indian from his better side, which too often is the side away from the white man, have learned to admire the qualities which so well fit him for his life in the open, and have come to realize—not mayhap without a tinge of wistfulness—how close he stands in every act and purpose and sentiment to the powers above and to the presences about him, you may come to have an esteem, and even a certain dreamy affection, for the silent Cliff-Dweller, so abounding that it shall include, bloody old warrior though he was, this new-found elder brother also.

A SANTA BARBARA HOLIDAY

IF Reginald Gray, young, lately married, and actively engaged in business at a little town in northern New York, had been told in October that he would pass the greater part of the coming winter in southern California, he would very likely have thought it impossible. And yet it was only early December when he decided to go to Santa Barbara for six months or a year.

His wife was not well. She was far from being an invalid, but had been having trouble with her throat ever since the end of July, when she had a violent cold. Instead of getting better, she grew rather worse, and old Doctor Kimball, who had known both the young people all their lives, told Reginald that he ought to take his wife to a warm climate for the winter. "It will cure her," he said; "and if she stays here, I won't answer for the consequences."

In deciding upon Santa Barbara, Reginald was influenced by William Good-now, his friend and classmate, who had only lately returned from California, and was now enthusiastic in his praise of its climate and natural attractions. Because of their many agreeable qualities, Reginald had asked two cousins of Anna, Edith and Kate Maynard, to join the party.

Strangers seeing Kate and Edith together never imagined them sisters. The former was a blonde, and had never known an ache or pain. An excellent lawn-tennis player, skilful with the oar, a perfect rider and good walker, tall, lithe, strong, and even-tempered, she was universally popular. Edith was more slender than her sister and more quiet. She was clever, played and sang well, sketched a little, and was always happy, no matter what her surroundings. Everybody liked Kate and loved Edith. She wore her hair brushed carelessly back from her forehead, and had a glorious pair of eyes—dark, large, and wonderfully expressive.

Goodnow had graduated at Harvard without class honors, but in the athletic records his name was left opposite the best time made in hundred-yard and half-mile dashes, and he pulled on the 'Varsity. After graduation he went to California to see what business opening he could find. At Reginald's wedding he met the Maynards, with whom he at once became good friends.

It was at the beginning of winter when the long journey across the continent was begun, and the cold was intense. On reaching Los Angeles, however, perfect summer weather was found. The grass was green on all the hill-sides, and the gardens were filled with flowers. The city is the largest in southern California, and is surrounded by a rich fruit country.

There are two ways of reaching Santa Barbara from Los Angeles. One may go by boat up the coast, or by train to Newhall, and from there overland by a stage which makes daily trips to and from Santa Barbara. By this route the ride is nearly ninety miles long, but the road is through a beautiful valley and along the edge of the sea. Had Reginald been alone, he would have gone overland, but for Anna's sake he went by boat. Los Angeles, like Athens, is some six miles inland, and its Piræus port is San Pedro. A railway connects the two places.

Leaving Los Angeles early in the morning, the little party rode past a succession of groves, and later out upon wide salt-marshes, at the edge of which is the bay and town of San Pedro. The harbor is an exceedingly good one for California, but is at best a poorly protected and shallow haven. The larger steamers cannot come to the dock, but anchor about two miles from shore. On reaching the end of the railway Reginald and Goodnow rechecked the luggage, and then all boarded a small tug-boat, on which were gathered nearly a hundred other passengers. The confusion equalled that which marks the departure of an Atlantic steamer. In time, however, the starting whistle was blown, and the little boat began ploughing its way down the harbor. The day was perfect; not a cloud was visible, and the hills guarding the bay were all a deep green from wave-washed base to very top.

"Imagine its being December!" said Edith. "You have been in California before, Mr. Goodnow: is this a typical winter's day?"

"Yes, I think it is. Of course it is not always so bright and warm. There are heavy rains, but the 'wet season' is little understood. It rains hard at times, and often for a week, but there are more clear than cloudy days."

"How good it seems, not having to be wrapped up!" said Anna. "I feel better already. Is there anything about Eastern weather in the paper to-day?"

"Yes; there's a flood in Boston, a blizzard at Chicago, and a terrible snow-storm in New York," replied Reginald.

On reaching the steamer the passengers were transferred from the tug, after which the two boats separated, one returning to the San Pedro wharf, and the other making up the coast. "Is it far to Santa Barbara?" asked Kate.

"No; only eighty miles from San Pedro," said Goodnow. "We'll get there by early evening. They're not fast ships on this line, and don't make over ten miles an hour. Do you notice the coast-line? Not much like that along the Atlantic, is it?"

"No. Is it rough and hilly like this all the way?"

"Yes. There are only three or four harbors along the entire nine hundred miles of California's shore. The best and largest is that of San Francisco, next is that of San Diego, and you have seen the third—San Pedro."

From where Kate sat she could see, toward the west, the vast expanse of the Pacific. The boat had but little motion. Scores of sea-gulls followed the ship, and in the distance were white-sailed boats. Beyond the line of hills following the coast were the higher peaks of the Sierras. Some of these were capped with snow, and about all the dark blue slopes hung a filmy haze. Here and there appeared a cottage or two, or a flock of sheep could be seen feeding on the steep hill-sides. Kate tried to read aloud, but no one paid attention, and so she abandoned her book.

"It's all too beautiful to be neglected," said Anna. "I never saw more glorious colorings nor breathed such delicious air. What is the name of the range we see ahead of us?"

"That's the Santa Ynez," replied Goodnow. "It runs nearly due east and west, and forms the northern boundary of the Santa Barbara Valley. Southern California is covered with a net-work of these minor ranges. They run in every con-

THE ARLINGTON VERANDA.

ceivable direction, and form an infinite variety of valleys. You will know the Santa Ynez Mountains thoroughly before leaving Santa Barbara. Everybody visits them, and they are one of the attractions of the place. Not every resort has the sea and mountains together."

It was well into the evening before the red light at the end of the Santa Barbara wharf was seen. The mountains made long dark marks against the starlit heavens, and the light was invisible until the steamer was within two miles of where it shone out over the waters of the harbor. Nearing the wharf, where there could now be seen the dim outlines of waiting hacks and a long storehouse, the wharf bell rang out a welcome to the new arrivals, and the cannon which was discharged from the bow of the boat sent thunder-like echoes rolling along the hill-sides. It was a novel landing. No other ships were at the wharf, and the town was still hidden from view, since the dock extends for nearly a mile out into deep water. In half an hour the tired travellers were safely domiciled at the Arlington, a large home-like hotel, in which every Santa Barbaran takes much pride. Wood fires were burning brightly in open fireplaces, and the

wide veranda surrounding the hotel was filled with promenaders, who eyed the strangers with that air of superior wisdom and experience always worn by those who happen to be one's predecessors in a new place by a fortnight or less. Supper was being served, and after it our friends sought their beds, Anna tired out, Reginald rejoiced that she could now rest, Edith quiet and satisfied, Kate anxious for daylight, and Goodnow happy to be once more in the American Mentone.

The morning sun flooding the valley sent a stray beam into Kate's room, and waked that heavy sleeper into the full consciousness that she had a new world to conquer. Drawing aside the curtain, she looked out upon the town. Beyond the few house-tops and trees which lined the long street leading to the wharf she could see the ocean, and in another direction the Santa Ynez range. Between the mountains and the sea, and occupying a long narrow valley, lay the town of Santa Barbara, a quiet, listless little village, its face turned southward, and its cottages surrounded by trees. The birds were holding a carnival of song that morning, and the air was filled with the perfume of flowers. High up the mountain-side the

ROWS OF EUCALYPTUS.

grass was green and velvety, and the low hills that separate a part of the town from the bay were covered with rank grass. Kate had seen many an Italian village, and knew Naples thoroughly, but as she looked down on Santa Barbara she thought it prettier than any place she had ever seen. "You can't describe it," she wrote home that first day. "It suggests other places, but has charms peculiar to itself. Here it is the last of December, and yet the weather is exactly like that of June at home. The town is full of people. I'm glad I have both summer and winter dresses. I need the light ones during the day, and the others at evening. Mr. Goodnow has made many plans for us. He is delighted to get back, and this morning half a dozen picturesque old Mexicans called to see him. He speaks Spanish, and so these men like him. Anna is so happy; and so is Reginald."

The first morning in Santa Barbara was passed in utter idleness by all excepting Reginald, who went down town to interview a real estate agent regarding a furnished cottage. After breakfast Anna and the two girls sat on the "Arlington" veranda reading the letters they had found waiting their arrival, while Goodnow went to call on some old friends. A strangely quiet and beautiful place was the "Arlington" veranda. It was wide and long, and extended along the entire northeast side of the hotel. A thick mass of vines had grown over the pillars and sides and formed high Gothic arches, through which was had a view of the lawn and deer park. The walk that led from it to the street was bordered with rose-bushes, and on the lawn were broad-leafed palms and ornamental trees. Everybody visits the veranda after breakfast —the old men to consult the thermometer, the young people to talk, and the ladies to sew or read.

Reginald had little trouble in finding a cottage. It stood near the head of the valley, and commanded a clear view of the bay, and of the mountains that stretch along the coast. The house was plainly but comfortably furnished, and the garden surrounding it contained a profusion of flowers, vines, and trees. To the right stood a gnarled old pine which had been brought across the Isthmus in '55, and was now nearly twice as high as the house. Just beyond its shadow was the garden, divided into different beds by a series of walks that radiated from a fountain. By the side of the latter, shading and half hiding it, grew a banana-tree; and at different corners of the beds were orange and lemon trees. North of the house there was an elm, brought from New England. As soon as they were fairly settled, Anna moved her easy-chair out upon a balcony overlooking the garden.

CASTLE ROCK.

"I like the air here," she said to Reginald, "and the view can never grow monotonous. I have been enjoying it all the morning. Did you ever see anything more perfect?"

And Reginald, looking in the direction she indicated, thought he never had. The balcony answered every purpose of a lookout tower. From it the town and valley were visible; and beyond was the ocean, with the islands of Santa Rosa and Santa Cruz rising above the placid waters like huge mountains. Skirting the edge of the bay ran a crescent beach of yellow sand, extending from Castle Rock, near the wharf, to Review Hill, twenty miles away. From the balcony, too, the waves could be seen rolling in upon the beach, while the mountains that overlook the valley were visible for many miles as they stood clearly outlined against the sky.

In a week the family were settled, and at once began to look about the place which they had selected as a winter home.

To Reginald, accustomed to an active business life, it seemed a very quiet little town; and indeed it is. The population is not above 5000, and there is not a manufacturing establishment anywhere to be found. Attempts have frequently been made to establish a fruit cannery, but no one has ever been successful in doing so, and to-day Santa Barbara has quietly accepted the alternative of being known as a health resort. Every year sees an increased number of visitors attracted by the climate, and the town is the American Nice. It occupies the centre of a narrow sheltered valley, guarded by the sea and mountains, and overlooks a bay that bears a striking resemblance to that of Naples. A long wide street extends through the village from the wharf to the Mission, and facing this are the shops, banks, and hotels, around which is whatever of activity there may chance to be. From this thoroughfare other streets run at right angles toward the mountains on the northwest, and to the range of low green hills that rise abruptly from the water's edge on the southeast. Bordering these streets, never without their long rows of eucalyptus or pepper trees growing by the road-side, are vine-clad cottages and houses half hid behind a dense mass of shrubbery. To walk past such homes on a midwinter morning, when the air is soft and clear and the birds are singing, instantly compels one to admire Santa Barbara. Reginald was delighted when he made his first tour of inspection. It is a New England village transplanted, he thought. As for quiet Edith, she was silent with admiration when she saw the flowers and breathed their rich perfume. Choice varieties of roses were hers for the asking. The bushes grew higher than her head, and were set out in hedges along the walks. Every shrub grows in Santa Barbara. Plants that require careful attention in the East—geraniums, fuchsias, and the more tender roses—grow vigorously and without care. Edith gathered great baskets of choice flowers every morning, and yet the garden seemed as full as ever after she had visited it, and the different beds were masses of beautiful colors. Juan Valento, the gardener, noticing her fondness for his roses, smoked fewer cigarettes than was his custom, and displayed an energy in taking care of the beds that was surprising. He was a walking encyclopædia of information. It was not only during the winter, he told Edith, that the roses were in bloom; it was the same in July as in December. He could not understand her love for the geraniums. They were a pest, he thought; they grew so high and rank. But the roses he liked, and was always trimming and pruning. In some of the beds Juan had hollyhocks twelve feet high, and marigolds that were masses of gold. In others were pinks and calla-lilies and mignonette.

Life at Santa Barbara is mostly an outdoor one. Up to the present time the decrees of fashion have not begun to restrict and restrain one, and as a result the resident is free to do as he pleases. In no other village in America is housekeeping reduced to such a minimum of care as at Santa Barbara. The open hospitality of the people is proverbial. Friends "drop in" to luncheon without invitation and as a matter of course. Conventional rules are observed, to be sure, but do not restrict one in his enjoyment. People live quietly. Nature compels placidity of temperament, and invites good-will and pleasure.

Before two weeks had passed both Anna's and Reginald's attention was diverted from all that was humdrum or prosaic. They had had one honey-moon, and were now having another, sitting beneath the pine or orange trees together, gathering flowers, taking long walks about the garden. It was delightful to see how rapidly Anna improved. Reginald noticed with wonder the sudden loss of her former weakness and pallor. She looked ten years younger than she did on her arrival, and said that she felt so. There was a stable connected with the house, and Reginald had bought a steady-going horse and a low phaeton, so that Anna might be driven about the town. As she grew stronger he took her down to the beach every pleasant day, and for an hour drove up and down the stretch

SANTA BARBARA HARBOR.

of sand which extends for miles along the bay. There were little boats always anchored near the end of the wharf, and curiously rigged Chinese junks were often seen cruising about. By eleven o'clock the beach was the scene of much animation. Horseback parties galloped over its hard yellow sands, and groups of idlers sat on the dunes, reading, or gazing seaward upon the blue expanse of waters.

To Kate the beach was a never-failing attraction. She and Goodnow had many a horse-race from Castle Rock to the wharf, a good half-mile, and often rode as far as Ortega Point, an extension of the hill dividing the valley of Carpenteria from that of El Montecito. It is only possible to take this ride at low tide, for when the water is high the various points extending into the bay are impassable. A mile beyond the wharf the beach is bordered by a series of low sand heaps, over which one looks far up the valley to the Mission. Beyond these, again, are high bluffs which rise abruptly from the water's edge to a height of fifty feet. Their face is scarred and yellow, but their tops are carpeted with grass, and in spring with patches of yellow mustard and wild flowers. Two people were never better fitted to enjoy this beach ride than were Kate and Goodnow. Both were appreciative and observant. The deep coloring of the bay, the dull yellow of the beach and bluffs, the green tufts of grass and the wild flowers creeping over their edges, the distant hazy islands, the long stretch of curved coast, mountain-guarded, were always noticed and admired. As they cantered over the shining sands the waves softly broke in snowy masses of foam, and the waters often bathed the horses' feet. It is possible to ride all the way to Carpenteria by way of the beach at low tide, a distance of eleven miles. There is a constant succession of coves and crescents, and at the western edge of Carpenteria begins a line of sand-dunes, low and rolling, and fringed with low-growing reeds and bushes.

There was still another beach ride that all liked. It began at the wharf and extended westward along the beach, past steep bluffs, to a foot-path that turned inland through a narrow opening among the coast hills. Half a mile beyond the wharf a rocky headland, known as Castle Rock, projects across the beach, and over this the road led. Kate always rested her

horse on reaching the top, and took a good long look at the prospect it commanded. The view across the valley to the mountains, and along-shore to Carpenteria, Ruicon, and Ventura points, was unobstructed. This headland is thirty miles from Santa Barbara, and forms a narrow neck of land that at first is only a few feet above the water's edge, but which soon merges into a mountain. Edith, who rarely rode, always liked to visit Castle Rock. Making a seat there, she would sit for hours looking out upon the wide, beautiful bay or upon the mountains, and watching the riders cantering over the smooth, shining beach. To where she sat there came no noise; only the murmur of the waves breaking upon the rocks at her feet disturbed the perfect quiet. It was the middle of January now, but the air was warm, the sky was a cloudless blue, and among the grasses growing along the edge of the cliffs were brightly colored wild flowers. Tiring of the sea, she had only to turn her head to see the valley, or could look on both at the same time. Old Juan came with her one day, and told what he knew of the neighborhood. The Point, he said, used to be called La Punta del Castillo, and when the Spaniards were the only people living in Santa Barbara there was a strong fort on the level ground back of the rock—a fort of earth mounted with four brass cannon. When a ship sailed into port, laden with goods from Spain, and bringing many a lover to his sweetheart, the soldiers fired the cannon and the ship returned the salute. On hearing the noise the people ran down to the beach, and waded into the surf to pull the boats ashore. Among those who one day went down to meet the ship was old Tomaso. He expected a certain señorita from Spain to be his bride. When all the boats had landed, and she did not appear, they told him the truth. She whom he sought had died on the voyage, and was buried at sea. Poor Tomaso! He fell on the sands, and was as one dead. From that time his mind was gone. After a long illness he came every day to the beach, watching for his beloved one. For many years he waited, running down to help haul in every boat, and looking long into each face, but never saying a word. He died watching, too, for one day they found him dead on the beach, his face turned toward the sea and his eyes wide open.

THE HIGH WALL OF THE MISSION.

Just to the left of Castle Rock, at the edge of the beach, is a low rounded hill called Burton's Mound. When the Spaniards first sailed into the Santa Barbara channel they found the coast and islands inhabited by a race of Indians living in large villages. On Burton's Mound was one of their largest towns. All traces of it have now disappeared, but the ground is still filled with the stone and earthen articles made by the forgotten people. On the crest of the mound is a low adobe house surrounded by a wide veranda overgrown with vines. Near it is a sulphur spring, the water from which is pumped into heated tanks, and used for bathing. Anna took regular baths, and was greatly benefited. The place is a favorite picnic resort, and will some time be a hotel site.

It makes little difference how one enters the Santa Barbara Valley, for the Mission which overlooks it is the first object that attracts attention. It occupies an elevated site at the head of the valley, and is clearly outlined against a background of hills. The church was begun in 1786, and finished in 1822. In 1812, and again in 1814, it was nearly destroyed by earthquakes. It was intended by Father Junipero Serra to build the Santa Barbara Mission long before it was really begun, but he died before doing more than select its location and consecrate the ground. From 1822 until 1833, when the act of secularization was passed, the building was the centre of great wealth and power. The fathers were temporal as well as spiritual rulers of the land, and their church was the best and largest in California. The walls were of stone six feet thick, and plastered with adobe; the roof was covered with bright red tiles, and in the towers was hung a trio of Spanish bells. In the rear of the Mission the fathers had their garden—a shrub-grown half-acre completely isolated from the outside world. From the west tower a long L extended at right angles to the body of the church, and facing this was an open corridor. The Indian converts lived in huts, and the fathers raised large quantities of grapes and olives. When war was made upon the Franciscans, the Santa Barbara brothers were the only ones who dared remain at their posts. That they did so is due the excellent preservation of the old building. Time has changed it

somewhat, to be sure, but has mellowed and softened rather than destroyed. The stone steps leading to the façade are cracked and moss-grown; only one of the original six fountains is left; the Indian cabins have disappeared. A few Franciscans, shaven, and dressed in long coarse robes girded at the waists, still inhabit the bare narrow cells, and loiter about the corridors and garden, and regular service continues to be held.

To Edith there was no road more attractive than that leading to the gray-walled church. The Mission fascinated her, as, indeed, it does all who see it. There was hardly a day that she did not visit it. Sometimes she sat on the rim of the fountain basin dreamily gazing past the town to where the blue waters were glistening in the strong sunlight, or wandered about the olive grove, and rested in the shade of the trees to read. One day, while absorbed in her book, and only stopping now and then to glance about her, she was aroused by the sound of some one coming. Looking up, she saw one of the fathers. He had thrown back his hood, and his clean-shaven face was suffused with a deep blush at thus coming

THE MISSION FOUNTAIN.

GARDEN OF THE MISSION.

unexpectedly upon so delightful a vision as that of a young girl seated on a grassy mound beneath an olive-tree.

"You are a daughter of our Church, child?" asked the padre.

"No, father, not a daughter, but a lover of it."

"Would there were more children belonging to our Mission!" the old gray-haired man said. "I fear Father Junipero would grieve to see the California missions now. It is little we can do to-day."

At Edith's request the old man seated himself at her side, and after telling of the life he and his brothers led, asked if she would like to go with him to the church. On her accepting, they both left the orchard, and passing the fountain, entered the dimly lighted interior. Directly above the entrance was the choir, and before it stretched a long nave, the walls of which were set with rows of small windows, and hung with paintings of saints and apostles. A few of the pictures were admirably executed. The largest and best was "Heaven and Hell."

"Many were painted in Spain," said the father, "and others were done by the Indians."

There was a decidedly musty smell to the church, and both the visitors spoke in whispers. Edith's guide showed her all the paintings, and gave the history of each—who this was done by and when, how it came to Santa Barbara, and other facts of interest. Just beyond the choir were two small chapels, each with its altar pictures and ornaments, and a few steps from that on the right of the nave the father stopped before a high double doorway, and began unlocking the heavy doors. When he had thrown them open he crossed himself, and leading the way, asked Edith to follow. Doing so, she found herself in a walled enclosure overgrown with rank grasses and rose-bushes. Above the doorway Edith saw three whitened skulls set in the wall, while under the eaves of the church, which projected upon thick buttresses, the swallows were flitting back and forth from their nests of sun-baked mud.

"This is our cemetery, señorita," said the father at last.

"Are the skulls real, father?" asked Edith.

"Yes, child."

"And are many people buried here?"

"Oh yes, very many.. We do not use it now. There is not room, to tell the truth. You need not dig deep to find skulls and bones in here."

It was not a pleasant thought to Edith to feel that she was walking over the last resting-place of she knew not how many pious fathers and Indians. It was very quiet. A high wall completely hid the road to Mission Cañon, and on the west was the church, above which rose the towers. There were several vaults, and each had its wooden cross and vines. Doves were cooing on the eaves, and the swallows chatted incessantly.

On leaving the cemetery the father and Edith returned to the church, and passed up the long nave to the altar, which was covered with a snowy cloth, and decorated with tall candlesticks and other ornaments. Behind it, filling the end of the room, was a wooden reredos, elaborately carved, and having fine life-sized colored statues before each panel. On either side of the altar, set on white pillars, were two other statues, and between them was a large cross, with the Christ upon it. To the right Edith noticed a curiously shaped hat hanging upon the wall, which was covered with dust.

"It belonged to Garcia San Diego, the first Bishop of California," said the father, when he saw Edith looking at it. "His body is entombed here, as the tablet says. He was a patient worker and a godly man. Would I could be buried here, in the very walls of the church I serve!"

To the left of the altar a narrow doorway leads into the sacristy. With her guide Edith entered the small room, and saw directly opposite her another doorway opening upon a garden, or what seemed to be that.

"Yes, it is our cloister—our garden," said the padre. "I wish you could step into it, child, but no woman is allowed there. When the Princess Louise was here an exception was made, and she was shown our quiet walks and flowers."

"Can I look in?" asked Edith.

"Oh yes, but do not step outside the door."

With this permission Edith crossed the sacristy, and stood for some time looking through the open doorway. It was almost as though she stood within the garden, for her position commanded a view of nearly the entire place. In speaking of it afterward she said she could not well describe it. "There was perfect quiet, and the sunlight made beautiful shadow patches on the walks. There is a deep corridor along the south side, made by a row of stone pillars supporting a tiled roof. Some of the fathers were seated in its shade. I wish I could have painted it, but fear I couldn't give the true coloring, it was so varied and deep. In one of the arches hung a queer old bell from Spain. From where I stood I could see down the path to the corridor, and to the old building that forms one side of the garden. An old padre came out and struck the bell three times. It had a beautiful, low, deep tone. On hearing it the old men all went to their rooms to pray, and my friend went back into the church and left me alone."

On returning from his devotions the father found Edith still looking upon the scene, and was greatly pleased at her enjoyment.

"Is it beautiful?" he asked at length.

"It is more than that, father; I never saw so lovely a place. How happy you must all be, having such a garden!"

"So we are, child. It is our home, and some of us could not live without it now."

There was not much to see in the sacristy. In a chest of drawers were the vestments used when high mass is said, and on the bare white walls were a few statues of saints and apostles. In a smaller room the father showed Edith some curious copper vessels fashioned by the Indians a century ago. He also showed

THE CORRIDOR OF THE MISSION.

her the brass candlesticks used on Corpus Christi and other fête-days, and a little forge at which the fathers repair anything that may become broken.

On leaving the Mission the father walked with Edith to the end of the olive grove, and there said good-by. Turning to look back toward the Mission, Edith saw him standing on the steps of the church, his tall, heavily robed figure clearly outlined against the white façade.

When Reginald and Goodnow visited the Mission for the first time, they made a much more thorough examination than Edith had been allowed to do. Their first exploit was to climb the belfry of one of the towers. From where the bells hung they could see far down the valley; in one direction to Gaviota Pass, forty-five miles westward, and in another down the coast to Ventura. As it nears Gaviota Pass, the Santa Barbara Valley loses its width, and becomes a mere neck of land crowded down between the sea and the mountains. From where they stood the two men could look far up the narrow vale to farms and orchards. In many of the fields grew dark green live-oaks, and in others nothing but waving grain. They watched the shadows grow fainter and the colorings begin to change as the sun sank low toward the sea, and at last was hid from sight behind the watery horizon. When the light was entirely gone, the bells in the towers rang for evening mass, and as Reginald and his companion returned to the body of the church, the fathers had already gathered at the altar, and were busy with their prayers.

The two men were free to go where they pleased. Both made friends with the padres, and were always welcome. Reginald liked the garden best, but Goodnow was more interested in seeing the cells where the fathers slept, and in visiting the corridor, with its view between the arches, of the town and bay. It extends the entire front of the Mission wing, and is fully a hundred feet long. Opening from it are the living apartments, and above are the bare and narrow cells in which the brothers sleep. To the left of the Mission are a small corral and stable, where the padres keep their few cattle and sheep. Reginald always went there, if he happened to be at the church late in the afternoon, to see Father G—— milk the cows. The old man was an adept, and handled his robes most gracefully. If a cow forgot to behave, he forgot his meekness in a moment, and pounded her with his stool. The young calves were his particular care. He led them tenderly about, but when refractory, pulled hard at the rope, reminding Goodnow of the picture of the refractory ass and the angry friar. Edith made several sketches of the church. It was her great delight to study it in all its details, and she found many of its features as picturesque as those of cathedrals in Spain. In fact, one is constantly impressed with the idea, while he is at the Mission, that he is in Spain. For at noonday the shadows are as dark and clearly defined as they are at the Alhambra; and at evening the gray-white walls are suffused with a softening light such as one expects to find only in the countries across the sea.

In their rides about the country Goodnow was never an idle wanderer. It had been his desire, ever since seeing Santa Barbara, to find a ranch that would return a fair per cent. on his investment. He and the girls always rode, while Reginald and his wife drove. Kate had at first worn a black habit and stiff hat, but had discarded these in time, and adopted a costume that made her figure a conspicuous object wherever she went. Her hat was light straw, like those worn by college oarsmen, and her jacket was a bright flannel Norfolk. Edith wore a broad-brimmed felt hat, and was always as fresh-looking after a long ride as when she started. Goodnow had bought a Mexican sombrero.

At first Goodnow was tempted to buy a place in El Montecito Valley, which lies near Santa Barbara, and is only separated from it by a low ridge of hill extending nearly to the beach, and between which is a view of Ruicon Peak and a bit of the bay. The valley faces the sea, and runs back to the mountains. It is in reality a suburb of Santa Barbara, and contains a score or more beautiful residences, erected by those who have been attracted to the region by its delightful climate and su-

perior natural attractions. The valley has a quick slope from the sea to the range, and is dotted with groves and live-oaks. The first time Goodnow piloted his friends there he took them to the base of the mountains, and bade them look upon the country at their feet. The view was like a picture. There lay the ocean, pressing upon yellow sands; westward rose the low hills, oaks growing on their sides, and behind which was Santa Barbara; eastward ran a higher ridge, tree-grown and covered with fields of grain; in the valley were red-roofed cottages surrounded by luxuriant groves of orange and lemon trees. Summer and winter the Montecito never loses its verdure or its freshness. It is literally the home of an eternal summer.

Goodnow would have bought one of the places offered him, but could not obtain land enough to make a profitable farm. His next hope was to find something at Carpenteria—a valley separated from El Montecito by the Ortega Hill. It is a productive region, and contains large ranches and small farms, on which oranges, walnuts, beans, and almonds are grown. It occupies a long, narrow neck of land lying between the mountains and the sea. At its extreme eastern end is Ruicon Peak, over and by the sea edge of which extends the stage road to Ventura and Newhall. The fields are all cultivated, and scattered over them are numerous cottages. Goodnow and his friends made several trips to the valley, as all do who wish to see everything of interest around Santa Barbara. But he could not decide what to purchase, and there was not much property offered for sale. They invariably took their lunch and were gone all day, resting for a few hours at some Carpenteria grove, and returning home late in the afternoon.

In the western part of the Santa Barbara Valley, however, Goodnow found what he wanted. When Kate saw the place she said at once it was just what they had long been seeking. The property comprised a tract of 160 acres, and was one-half level and one-half rolling land. But little of the land had been improved, and the house was not worth considering. From the higher parts of the ranch Goodnow could see across the valley to the sea; in another, had a glimpse of Santa Barbara; and in still another, looked far away to Gaviota Pass. Over the level fields were scattered live-oaks, and the rolling land

IN GAVIOTA PASS.

extended into the range through winding cañons choked with shrubs and sycamore-trees. There was not a prettier spot in the country than up these cañons. Good-now began immediately to plant his olive and nut trees, and rode out nearly every day to superintend affairs, and see that the men did good work on the cottage he was building. Later, he and the girls, leaving Reginald and his wife to rest beneath the trees, rode into the cañons for a mile or more. The trail followed a creek that ran over a rocky bed in the deep shadow of the leafy sycamores, and led to an elevated spur of the range, from which the country for miles around was seen. Very often Reginald and Anna followed the riders a short distance up the gorge, taking their luncheon on a bit of level ground by the stream.

A short distance beyond Goodnow's new ranch were those of Glen Anne and Ellwood. Both of these famous places are well known and very valuable. They are respectively twelve and sixteen miles west of Santa Barbara, and extend from the sea-shore far into the cañons. At Glen Anne, owned by Colonel W. W. Hollister, a California pioneer, who has done much to make Santa Barbara attractive, the chief business is orange-growing, stock-raising, and general farming. But on the ranch may be found trees and shrubs of almost every known variety. Leading to the house is an avenue of tall palms, and beyond there are olive, orange, lemon, banana, date, peach, apple, nectarine, and fig trees, with here and there acres of wal-nut, almond trees, and vineyards. The grounds are carefully kept, and the flow-ers were such as to fill the soul of Edith with a joy which she could not express.

"Here you see the sort of place I shall have," said Goodnow, as he conducted the party through the Glen Anne grounds.

"Yes, in the future," replied Kate.

"In the future, of course," answered Goodnow. "And yet it will not be very long before I can show some progress. There are no hard, long winters in Cali-fornia, remember. Next year I'll have wheat, flowers, and all my orange and olive cuttings out; in twelve months more, my vineyard growing. In six years my income from the place will be worth having, and in ten years I can live like a nabob on what my ranch produces."

"Provided nothing goes wrong," said Kate.

"Oh, well, I am not too sanguine; but you can see as well as I, of how much this soil is capable, and what the climate is. I wish I could give ten acres of land in this State to every man in New York who works in an office all day for a thousand a year. He only gets a bare living there, and here ten acres would give him that, and sunshine, good air, and independence besides. 'Get land,' is my motto. Our cities are over-full, and our professions crowded. We must begin to cultivate our country more carefully. California is equal in size to France, and yet has only a million inhabitants."

At Ellwood, Reginald found much to interest him. The land is planted with olives, English walnuts, almonds, and wheat. The nuts are superior to those imported. From the olives is made a finely flavored oil. It has a wide reputation in the East, and is in great demand. The various orchards are planted with great care, and the trees are set out in long rows that extend for a great distance over the gently rolling ground. The home at Ellwood is a small, vine-covered cottage standing in the shadow of some huge, wide-branching oaks. Near the grove are the packing-houses, drying-furnaces, and a garden filled with choice varieties of flowers gathered from nearly every part of the world.

Beyond Ellwood the country highway follows the beach past the Sturges ranch, occupying the upper end of an oak-grown cañon, and to Gaviota Pass, a wild, narrow passage crossing the Santa Ynez range. High ledges of rock rise on each side of the road, and from the mouth of the pass one may look far down the valley in the direction of Santa Barbara.

By the time Goodnow's house was completed the California spring had come. The rainy weather was over. Day after day the sun rose in a cloudless east and set in a cloudless west. Every shrub was in bloom, and the violet beds in Reginald's garden were blue with blossoms. Out in the country the almond, peach, and apricot trees were all a mass of delicate color, and with the oranges still weighing down the branches were pure white blossoms whose perfume filled the air with a delicious fragrance. Fields were a velvety green; the leaves of the oaks were washed bright and fresh; the sycamores had sent forth new leaves and branches, and birds were busy building their nests. By the side of country roads the wild mustard grew higher than one's head, golden and delicate, a rich contrast to the blue of sky and ocean; and in many of the meadows were long wide patches of blue-flax. Farmers were planting their corn and beans; gardeners were spading their flower beds for the last time. Old Juan and Edith were all day pruning, raking, and watering slips and seedlings. There was no dust and no mud. The air was soft, warm, and fragrant. Riding parties, improving every hour left them before their departure from Santa Barbara, scoured the country in search of new places of interest, or went once more to the cañons and other favorite haunts. By the first of May the "winter season" was over. The hotels had room at last for those who came, and one by one the rented cottages were given up.

But still there was not utter desertion. All who could stay did so, well knowing that beautiful as Santa Barbara is during the winter, one should know her in her summer dress to realize how great is her charm.

"I prefer the months from May until autumn," said Goodnow. "You have seen for yourself what May is, and June is nearly its equal. As for July and August, they are wonderfully cool and comfortable. There is never a night that a blanket isn't necessary. Of course it's dusty. There's no rain, and all the fields are parched. But you'll get used to that, and I like the brown hills as well as the green."

Before their departure, Reginald had planned a week's trip to the Ojai Valley, a park-like retreat about forty miles from Santa Barbara, nestled among the mountains of the Santa Ynez. Its elevation is nearly one thousand feet above sea-level, and the climate is radically different from that of Santa Barbara, being drier and more bracing. Many whose health does not improve at the sea-side go to the Ojai, and are quickly benefited. The mountains entirely surround the valley, which is about thirty miles long by from three to six wide, and the only entrance to the beautiful amphitheatre of oak-grown fields and long grassy levels is by the Casitas Pass, which leads from Carpenteria over the range to the little town of Nordhoff, the only village there.

To save trouble, Reginald engaged the regular four-horse stage that runs between Santa Barbara and the Ojai. Early in the season as it was, the day when they started was June-like in its bright freshness — clear, mild, and beautiful. For the first two hours the way led down the coast through El Montecito and Carpenteria. The fields of green grain and blue-flax, the live-oaks and wild flowers, the orange groves and nut orchards, gave, with the sea and sky, a coloring rich and varied. In Carpenteria the road ran near the beach, past a line of sand-dunes, now overgrown with trailing vines and flowers thrown into bold relief against the background of ocean. To the left, reaching the mountains, were open fields, some frilled with walnut orchards and fruit trees, others freshly ploughed and ready for their crop of Lima-beans, of which the Carpenteria Valley is the home. At the mouth of the pass the road turned abruptly northward and entered a narrow, winding cañon, guarded by steep hill-sides overgrown with oaks and tangled brushwood. Down the centre of the ravine flowed a noisy creek; and on both banks was a net-work of ferns and morning-glory vines. Before reaching the steepest part of the pass an hour's rest was taken in a spot shaded by large oaks, a short distance from which ran the brook. In every direction there was nothing but verdure—the green of the ferns intensified by the oaks, and that of the trees by the shrubs on the mountain slopes.

As the top of the pass was neared the oaks disappeared, and in their place were wild wastes of sage and chaparral, and patches of wild flowers of a hundred different shades—blue, gold, and red. Some of the distant hills appeared on fire, so thickly were they carpeted with the flowers, and so brilliant was their hue. Edith counted over seventy different varieties without leaving the wagon. When the crest of the range was reached the driver halted, and the little party gazed upon the mountains whose broken contour extended as far as the eye could see. Northward, guarded by tree-grown hills, and resting in the very lap of rugged mountains, lay the Ojai, a filmy haze softening

its outlines, and groves of live-oak. But most admired was the pass itself, winding in narrow coils around the many hills, and the view beyond it of the Santa Barbara Valley, blue, softly outlined and girded by the yellow beach, upon which the waves could be plainly seen breaking in masses of foam. With a glass the houses were visible, and with the naked eye all could see a steamer ploughing its way across the bay to the wharf. Few, perhaps no other passes in California, have the varied beauty of the Casitas; none, certainly, has its views of mountain, valley, and ocean combined in one harmonious whole.

It was nearly sundown when the Ojai was reached, and the tired but delighted travellers alighted at the Oak Glen cottages. The last half of the ride had been as interesting as the first. The road led down the mountain-side by easy grades, and through dense forests of oak and sycamore. Several streams were crossed—wide, shallow rivers of clear water into which men were casting their flies for trout. Beyond the last ford in the Ojai the wild flowers grew thicker than ever, and the air was of the mountains, crisp and invigorating. None, save Goodnow, who had made the trip before, had ever seen such oaks, so many, or so large, as those which now were passed. They made veritable forests, and beneath their widespreading branches, festooned with swaying clusters of gray Spanish-moss, were groups of resting cattle. Years ago all the southern California valleys were choked with oaks. But to-day many have been cut down, and it is only in the Ojai that one can find them in abundance.

There is little to do in the Ojai but to admire and study nature. The little town of Nordhoff is as quiet as the grave. The Oak Glen cottages stand by themselves just off the highway, and are equally as quiet. For a day after her arrival Anna sat on the veranda, shaded by a large oak, gazing listlessly down the valley beyond its trees and fields to the chain of mountains at the western end. But after she had rested there followed days of exploration. Kate was in her element. The horses were low-spirited beasts, but the country was too beautiful to ride across rapidly, so no one complained. The first excursion was down the valley to the Matilija Cañon, which extends several miles into the range, and from being wide and brush-grown, soon becomes a narrow pathway bordered by rough, rocky cliffs, washed by a swift little stream dashing headlong over a bowlder-strewn bed. At the extreme end of the cañon is a spring of strong sulphur water. Kate and Goodnow rode on to this, but the others halted at an interval for luncheon. Reginald

of continual summer, but now I think I never should."

What Edith's opinion of California life was, Goodnow had not been able to discover. That she enjoyed all she saw, he felt positively sure. But she was never enthusiastic in her expressions, and it was only lately that Goodnow had tried to

ADOBE HOUSE.

went trouting, and after an hour's casting returned with a basket of fish, which Goodnow cooked over a bed of coals.

"It's like Colorado here," said that young man of general information. "Shouldn't know it from a cañon of the Rocky Mountains. Wonderful variety of scenery we have in California. Half an hour's ride from this cañon, and we're in a park of trees."

"Spoken like a true Californian," said Edith.

"Yes; but then I am one now, you know. It's dangerous staying long in this State. There's an old legend about seeing the Rio Grande. See it once, and you'll never rest until you see it again, or live near its waters; the same might be told of California. Come, now, does any one here think he will ever be satisfied without coming back to the scenes we've been enjoying so long?"

"I should never be," said Kate. "I'm sure never to cease thinking what a California winter is like. I might get tired

fathom her thoughts. But since one quiet evening alone with her he had found that his regard had changed to love. She had read much and talked well, and to be with her gave Goodnow mental refreshment. He always asked her opinion now, and came to her with all his doubts. Reginald had noticed the change in his friend, but said nothing.

While at the Ojai, Edith and Goodnow were more often thrown together. Kate rode with them, to be sure, but was generally rushing off into side paths or dashing far ahead of her two soberer companions. She was the life of the party, and her red jacket was sure to be seen on all the highest hill-sides and isolated peaks. Reginald intended to leave the Ojai sooner than he did, but Kate had heard of Sulphur Mountain, and said she would not go away until she had climbed it.

"Perhaps you won't be able to leave then," said Goodnow, "for there isn't much of a trail, and the climb would be hard even if there were."

"But isn't the view grand from the top?"

"Oh yes, wonderfully so. We may as well try it. I know the way, and will be responsible for our safety."

Just back of the cottages a high ridge of land runs across the valley, dividing it into two nearly equal parts, known as the Upper and Lower Ojai. Making an early start, Goodnow and the girls rode over this to the Upper Ojai. The road led through a succession of wide fields of grain and past groves of orange-trees, now putting forth fresh young leaves. The region was like a bit of Scotland, not too wild or rugged, nor yet lacking in grandeur. To the right of the valley were densely wooded hills, and high above them the bare crest of Sulphur Mountain. For hours the trail was through the forests that covered the steep sides of the peak. At times it seemed impossible to proceed. Deep ravines and beds of soft asphaltum, thickets of live-oaks and chaparral, blocked the way. But Kate, determined and persevering, would stop at nothing. Goodnow rarely left Edith's side. "I can manage," Kate had said. "You look after Edith."

Once the trail was utterly lost. High overhead towered the mountain; below was a deep wide gorge. Edith was tired out, and Goodnow insisted upon her resting. Kate pushed on ahead, and in a few moments was lost to view among the wildgrowing bushes. Presently, however, Goodnow caught the bright gleam of her jacket. She had reached a point high above her companions. Her voice as she called to them could scarcely be heard, but Goodnow understood that he and Edith were to go in the direction she pointed. Riding in a zigzag course up a slope that grew steeper every moment, Kate was reached at last, and the three, getting off their horses, sat down by the side of a hardy oak.

"We can see the top now," said Kate, "and it can't be far off. What air this is! I could climb all day and not be tired."

When the crest of the mountain was reached, the country seemed to the delighted lookers-on to lay spread at their very feet. Southward, thirty miles away, but seemingly not a quarter of that distance, was the ocean, with its islands and curving shore of yellow sands; the Santa Clara Valley, watered by a river that shone in

the sunlight like a thread of silver; and nearer at hand, the sharp bare hill-tops, reaching upward like fingers of a giant hand, and holding miniature levels in their strong embrace. To the north was the Ojai, now a mere depression among the mountains; and in the distance, their slopes a deep dark blue and their summits capped with snow, rose the peaks of the Sierra Madre range. There is a small lake on the top of Sulphur Mountain—a shallow pool left by the rains of winter. It disappears in summer, but was now full of water. By its side Kate spread the luncheon which Goodnow had brought in his saddle-bags, and while they rested the tired party ate, and studied at their leisure the beauty of the view. After luncheon Edith read aloud and Goodnow smoked, while Kate, restless as ever, roamed about the place, trying from what point she had the better view. When Edith finished reading, she and Goodnow walked to where they could look afar off to the Santa Barbara Valley. It was flooded with sunshine, and its coloring was exquisite. Under the inspiration of the moment Goodnow spoke. It was a simple question that he asked, and it was as simply answered. Kate had not heard it, but knew when she came to where they stood what had been said.

"Enraptured with the view?" she asked, laughingly.

"Yes; and is our sister pleased?" said Goodnow.

"Immeasurably. But what *would* have happened, Edith, if you couldn't have answered 'yes'? Think how disagreeable the going home this afternoon would have been!"

That night the news was told Reginald and Anna. "You have my permission only on one condition," said Anna. "You must invite us to visit you at least once a year."

By the middle of May the summer season at Santa Barbara is well under way. On their return from the Ojai the bathhouses, near the wharf, were open, and every day a gay party of lookers-on gathered beneath an awning stretched over the sands to see the bathers go in. There is no better bathing in the world than that at Santa Barbara. The beach slopes gradually into deep water, and there is little surf; the temperature of the sea is much warmer than that of the Atlantic, and there is rarely any undertow. Goodnow had bathed at least once a week all through the winter, and Kate had gone in at Christmas. She now took a swim nearly every day, going with Goodnow to the end of the wharf, or taking Edith, not so strong as her companions, to the raft which is anchored a short distance from the shore. There were always twenty or thirty people in at once, and the beach was the liveliest part of the town from eleven until twelve o'clock in the morning.

Whatever Santa Barbara had done for the others, it had certainly cured Anna. No one would have recognized her in May as the woman whom they had seen in December. In his report to Dr. Kimball, Reginald said that her cough had entirely disappeared, and that she had gained strength and flesh ever since her arrival. "In fact," he wrote, "the climate of Santa Barbara is phenomenal. I have heard of many remarkable cures. Of course every one coming here is not benefited, but the majority are. All miasmatic and pulmonary diseases are greatly helped, and the place is gaining a wide reputation as a natural sanitarium. The air is wonderfully dry for a sea-side resort, and the temperature varies but slightly throughout the year, the average being about 70° for winter and 80° for summer. From May to November there is never any rain, and during the so-called 'wet season,' lasting from November to the middle of April, the rains are only occasional, and stormy days are succeeded by clear, bright, warm ones, during which it is a delight to be out-of-doors. The town has been full of invalids all winter. Many have come to stay. The accommodations—hotels, boarding-houses, and rented cottages—are excellent; in fact, there is every modern comfort. The cost of living is very reasonable; the climate excels that of Nice; the scenery is varied and beautiful. If you have any more such patients, send them out. I'll guarantee they have the best time they ever had, and will get well as rapidly as Anna has."

In nearly the centre of Santa Barbara is a quarter known as Spanishtown, which was once a good copy of villages in Spain. So late as 1836, when Richard Henry Dana, then a sailor before the mast, visited Santa Barbara, the Spaniards were almost the only people in the valley, and their thick-walled adobe houses with red-tiled roofs were huddled closely together midway between the beach and the Mission. To-day the quarter has been relegated to side streets, and a part of it given over to the Chinese.

It was not long before Kate found Spanishtown. Her first visit was made alone, but on the second she went with Edith and old Juan, the one to sketch and the other to show the more interesting features of the settlement. Juan was in his element, acting as guide and interpreter, and returned the Spanish salutations with much grace and dignity, and consumed any number of cigarettes as he walked through the narrow streets. His first stop was made before the remnant of an old thick adobe wall still standing. "It is the only part of the old presidio left," he said. "I can remember when the whole wall was up. It was too high to climb over, and inside was a large square which the soldiers used, and where there was a chapel and barracks. At the four corners were four brass cannon. And outside the walls, protected by the guns, were the houses of our people. There was nothing then between here and the beach, so that we could sit in our doorways and look out upon the bay and the mountains."

Then he told of the fête-days, when mass was said at the Mission, and there were races on the beach and dancing at the presidio. Every one had work then, for the rich Spaniards owned large ranches and had many servants.

"Sometimes it does not seem Santa Barbara any more—the new houses and strange people and hotels. Some of us have little to do now, and our own town is no longer beautiful or gay. Even our houses are being pulled down, as you can see, and in a few years, I think, there will be no Spanishtown."

One of the houses visited was that which Dana describes as the scene of the wedding festivities that took place when he was at Santa Barbara. It answers perfectly to his description, and is still owned by the same family whose daughter Dana saw married. Juan took the girls into its large court-yard and to the veranda. Near the De la Guerra Mansion, as the house is called, Juan pointed out the old Noreaga garden, once a famous place, but now overgrown with grass, and containing only a few scrubby peach-trees and neglected grape arbors. On one side of it was found the best preserved Spanish house the girls had yet seen. It was a long low building, one story high, and had a roof of bright red tiles. Around the house extended a deep veranda, shaded by overhanging eaves which rested on a row of time-stained pillars. It was still inhabited by Mexicans, whom Juan knew, and who invited him and his party in. The garden fronting the little cabin was filled with rose-bushes, and in its centre was an old well, its wooden frame nearly hid by vines.

It requires several visits to know Spanish town thoroughly. There are many interesting corners and by-ways, and in all are pictures of a life gradually dying out in Santa Barbara. Some of the cottages are in groups, and face upon the street; and others are by themselves, and have their own bit of garden and vineyard.

Chinatown always seemed an incongruity to Edith, who disliked finding the Spanish adobes peopled by so foreign a race; yet she often went there, in company with either Goodnow or Reginald, and visited the shops of Chung Wah and Sing Lee for Chinese curios. On the days when their New-Year is celebrated Chinatown is overrun with visitors, who are expected to call at the different stores and partake of the refreshments that are there spread out upon little tables. All the houses are decorated with lanterns, and long strings of Chinese crackers and bombs are exploded at regular intervals.

The marriage of Edith and Goodnow was to take place at Christmas, so that Edith might return to Santa Barbara for the last half of the winter. The two sisters, with Goodnow and other friends who might happen to go, rode nearly every day. There was nothing about Santa Barbara which they did not see. One of their rides was through El Montecito Valley to the Hot Springs Cañon. From the bath-house at the head of this gorge is a view of all Montecito and the bay, and from a spur of the range near by one can see for miles up and down the coast. The springs contain strong sulphur water, which is drank and bathed in with great bodily benefit. They have been known for years, and were widely famous among the Indians who inhabited the region. Still another ride was over the hills of the Hope Ranch to a tiny lake lying in a grove of oaks. The trail follows the edge of the cliffs after leaving the beach, and for a few miles before the lake is reached commands a view of the channel, valley, and mountains of which Kate never tired.

"But you can't decide which ride you like best," she wrote home. "Never was there such a place as this. We are always finding something new. There are a dozen or more cañons among the mountains, and we go first to one and then to another, spending the day, or just riding up the trails and home again, in time for luncheon or dinner. Last week we rode over to the San Marcos Pass, which crosses the range to the west of Santa Barbara, and went to the Santa Ynez Valley. In it are many farms and an old church, something like the one we have here, only not nearly so well preserved. The San Marcos is not so beautiful a pass as the Casitas, but is wilder, and from its top you can see from one end of the Santa Barbara Valley to the other. I like the cañons: they are always so cool and green. When we get tired of the sea or the town, we go into the mountains. Everybody tries camping for a week, and we have done as the rest.

The night before all except Goodnow were to say good-by to Santa Barbara, Kate gave a picnic on the beach. Twenty or more young people rode out to the place of meeting, while others came in carriages. Supper was served on the veranda of an old weather-beaten bath-house standing under the brow of the cliffs a mile to the east of the wharf. Some of the men built a fire of drift-wood, and as darkness came on all gathered around it, and listened to Edith, who played on the guitar and sang some quaint old Spanish songs which Juan the gardener had taught her. As she sang, the moon came up, out of the sea it seemed, and its light, with that of the fire, threw a weird soft glow over the long stretch of sands, and the faces of the picturesquely grouped listeners. It was hard to realize that this was the last evening at Santa Barbara. The time had passed all too rapidly. And when the farewells had been said on the following day, and Goodnow, the picture of woe, was left standing alone on the wharf, Edith was the only one who, looking back upon the beach, did not think of the picnic of the night before—that perfect ending of a perfect time. In her mind was present the memory of Sulphur Mountain. There, she knew, had been found the perfection of her winter's happiness; the music of the words said there was sweeter than that of the guitar she had played, and was more full of brightness than were the moonbeams on the waters.

COLORADO AND ITS CAPITAL

IF its people had not already called it
"the Centennial State" and "the
Scenic State," I might have done better
by it. I would have called it the Palace-
car State, because it is the only one in the
West where palace-cars are run all over
the tallest mountain ranges, and to the
gold and silver mines as fast as they are
discovered, and because the general style
and finish of the cities and pleasure resorts
are of palace-car luxury and thorough-
ness, while nature provides an endless
gallery and museum of gorgeous scenery
and magnificent curios that would seem
extravagant anywhere else, yet are in
keeping there.

Colorado is sufficiently settled and developed to form a valuable object-lesson
for the study of the early results of the
forces we see at work in the brand-new
commonwealths near by. They are seizing the water rights in Montana, Wyoming, and Washington, but in Colorado
the water is being sold and used. In the
newer States wiseacres are prophesying
what will be done with imperial reaches
of bunch-grass and sage-brush land, but
in Colorado county fairs are being held
upon such lands. In Montana the leaders are wishing for an agricultural battal-
ion of neighbors to the miners, but in Colorado agriculture has already distanced
mining as a wealth-producing factor.

Denver's peculiarity and strength lie
in its being all alone in the heart of a
vast region between the Canadian border

and the Gulf of Mexico; but it has been
brought suddenly near to us. Not all the
fast railway riding is done in the East in
these days. The far Western steeds of
steel are picking up their heels in grand
fashion for those who enjoy fast riding.
On a palace-car train of the Union Pacific Railroad between Omaha and Denver
the regular time is nearly fifty miles an
hour, and the long run is made in one
night, between supper and breakfast.
Denver is only fifty-three hours of riding-
time from New York as I write—twenty-
five hours from New York to Chicago,
and twenty-eight hours from Chicago to
Denver.

I am going to ask the reader to spend
Saturday and Sunday in Denver with me.
Instead of dryly cataloguing what is
there, we will see it for ourselves. I had
supposed it to be a mountain city, so
much does an Eastern man hear of its
elevation, its mountain resorts, and its
mountain air. It surprised me to discover
that it was a city of the plains. There is
nothing in the appearance of the plains
to lead one to suppose that they tilt up
like a toboggan slide, as they do, or that
Denver is a mile above sea-level, as it is.
But a part of its enormous good fortune
is that although it is a plains city, it has
the mountains for near neighbors—a long
peaked and scalloped line of purple or
pink or blue or snow-clad green, according to when they are viewed. There are
200 miles or more of the Rockies in sight

in clear weather. As there are but fifty-six cloudy days in the year, and as these mountains elevate and inspire even the dullest souls, I think we can forget that it is a city of the plains, and ever associate it with the mountains hereafter. I plighted my troth to the sea near which I was born, but in Denver and Salt Lake City, loveliest of all our inland cities, I felt a straining at my loyalty; and when I saw in the dining-room of Mr. W. N. Byers the great square window that his charming wife ordered made so that she might frame 200 miles of the Rockies as in a picture, I admitted to myself that there was much to be said for "t'other dear charmer," and that, in the language of Denver's poet, Cy Warman, "God was good to make the mountains."

We have looked on Denver's patent map, and know where we are. Every Western city has its own patent map, usually designed to show that it is in the centre of creation, but Denver's map is more truthful, and merely locates it in the middle of the country west of the Mississippi. It shows the States east of that river without a single railroad, while a perfect labyrinth of railroads crisscross the West in frantic efforts to get to Denver. Gravely a Denver man says to us afterward, as he holds the map in his hand, "If those Dutchmen and Puritans and things who settled the East could have landed out here on the plains, the thirteen original colonies would have been a howling wilderness filled with savages to-day." And that in turn reminds me of the remark of a man in Utah, a Mormon, who was a member of a colony that pre-empted an alkali lake, washed out the salt with a system of ditches, and succeeded in growing crops. "Eastern people make a great mouth about irrigation and farming in the arid belt," said he, "but we folks 'd rather scoop out a ditch than have to clear out forest stumps and blast rocks to get room for farming." The moral of both these tales is that we may have our own opinion of the West, but we can't prevent the West's having its own opinion of us.

In all other respects the patent Denver map is reliable. It shows that this city of 135,000 souls stands all alone, without a real rival, in a vast rich region. It is 1000 miles from Chicago, 400 from Salt Lake City, 600 from Kansas City, and the same distance from the Missouri River. If you drew a circle of 1000 miles diameter, with Denver in its centre, you would discover no real competitor; but the people have adopted what they call their "thousand-mile theory," which is that Chicago is 1000 miles from New York, and Denver is 1000 miles from Chicago, and San Francisco is 1000 miles from Denver, so that, as any one can see, if great cities are put at that distance apart, as it seems, then these are to be the four great ones of America.

Denver is a beautiful city—a parlor city with cabinet finish—and it is so new that it looks as if it had been made to order, and was just ready for delivery. How the people lived five years ago, or what they have done with the houses of that period, does not appear, but at present everything — business blocks, churches, clubs, dwellings, street cars, the park—all look brand-new, like the young trees. The first citizen you talk to says: "You notice there are no old people on the streets here. There aren't any in the city. We have no use for old folks here." So, then, the people also are new. It is very wonderful and peculiar. Only a year ago Mr. Richard Harding Davis was there, and commented on the lack of pavements in the streets, and I hear that at that time pedestrians wore rubber boots, and the mud was frightful. But now every street in the thick of town is paved with concrete or Belgian blocks as well as if it were New York or Paris. The first things that impress you in the city are the neatness and width of the streets, and the number of young trees that ornament them most invitingly. The next thing is the remarkable character of the big business buildings. It is not that they are bigger and better than those of New York and Chicago—comparisons of that sort are nonsensical—but they are massive and beautiful, and they possess an elegance without and a roominess and lightness within that distinguish them as superior to the show buildings of most of the cities of the country. The hotels are even more remarkable, from the one down by the impressive big depot, which is the best-equipped third-class hotel in the country, to the Brown's Palace and the Métropole, both of steel and stone, which are just as good as men know how to make hotels.

The residence districts are of a piece with the rest. Along the tree-lined streets are some of the very prettiest villas it is

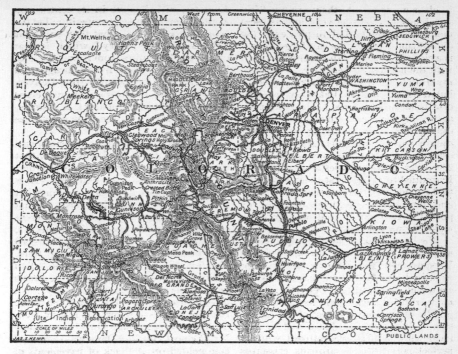

MAP OF COLORADO.

any man's lot to see at this time. They are not palaces, but they are very tasteful, stylish, cozy, and pretty homes, all built of brick or stone, in a great variety of pleasing colors and materials, and with a proud showing of towers, turrets, conservatories, bay-windows, gables, and all else that goes to mark this period, when men build after widely differing plans to compliment their own taste and the skill of originating draughtsmen. The town spreads over an enormous territory, as compared with the space a city of its size should take up, but we must learn that modern methods of quick transit are so cheap that they are being adopted everywhere, and wherever they are used the cities are spreading out. Denver has cable and electric cars, but it is the electric roads that are the city-spreaders. They whiz along so fast that men do not hesitate to build their homes five or six miles from their stores and offices, where they can get garden and elbow room. We are going to see all our cities shoot out in this way. It promotes beauty in residence districts, and pride in the hearts of those who own the pretty homes. It car-

ries the good health that comes with fresh air. But it entails a great new expense upon modern city government, for the streets and the mains and sewers and police and fire systems all have to be extended to keep pace with the electric flight of the people, who, in turn, must stand the taxes. Not that they are high in Denver, or in those other electric-car-peppered capitals, Minneapolis and St. Paul, but they are higher than they would be if the people were crowded into smaller spaces. In Denver the government has spared itself and the people one source of anxiety by ordering that, no matter where the houses reach to, it shall be a fire-proof city. The fire lines follow the extension, and every house must be of brick or stone.

As we walk about the town, noting the theatres that are absolutely gorgeous, observing that the Methodist church is a quarter-of-a-million-dollar pile of granite, seeing the crowded shopping stores that are almost like our own in New York, heeding the bustle of people and vehicles, stopping to look at the precious Colorado stones that are heaped in the jewellers' windows, and the museums of Indian curios that are peculiar to the town, a marked and distinctive secret of the place is forced upon our attention. It is that though the signs of great wealth and liberal outlay are in every view, there is no over decoration, no vulgar display, no wasteful ostentation (except in that saloon that has silver dollars sunk in the floor, and that other one where the mosaic floor slabs are set with double eagles). There is upon the show-places of the town that restraint which we call "taste." To be sure, the barrooms cost the price of a prince's ransom, and the walls and bars are made of onyx. But there they stop. A little spray of silver arabesquerie, necessary to save such a room from bareness, is all the ornament one sees. In the high-class hotels, for some reason that appears inscrutable to an American who has been surfeited with bold paintings and dubious bric-à-brac from Madison Square to Nob Hill, there is the same extraordinary good taste. The walls of all the rooms, both public and private, rely on the harmonious blending of soft tints, and on mere lines of fine beading on the hardwood fittings. Why that taste which makes the apartments of the Japanese our marvel and delight should reappear in Denver, and nowhere else out West, is certainly remarkable.

"There is in Denver," says a man who meets me in the Hôtel Métropole, "what is shockingly called 'the one-lunged army.' I am a member of it, and may repeat the nickname without shame, for we are proud of ourselves. This army comprises 30,000 invalids, or more than one-fifth of the population of Denver. Not by any means is this a host of persons with pulmonary ailments, but of men in physical straits of many sorts, who find the rare air of a place a mile on the road to heaven better than medicine. These are men of wealth, as a rule, and of cultivation and of taste. They have been more important factors in the making of this unique city than most persons, even in Denver, imagine. The stock and oil and gold and silver millionaires point to their operations as the cause of Denver's importance; and they are right. But importance is one thing, and good taste, good society, and progressiveness are quite different things. It was not mining that begot the taste which crowds our

residence quarter with elegant dwellings, or that created a demand for clubs like the Denver Club. It was not oil that gave us college-bred men to form a 'Varsity Club of 120 members, or that insisted upon the decoration of the town with such hotels as ours. The influence of the invalids is seen in all this. They are New-Yorkers, Bostonians, Philadelphians, New Orleans men, Englishmen — the well-to-do and well-brought-up men from all over the country—architects, doctors, lawyers, and every sort of professional men being among them."

After that we caught ourselves constantly looking for invalids, but without success. Even those who told us that they were members of the strange army of debilitated æsthetes did not look so. But we came upon many queer facts regarding them, and the air, and the customs of the place. One very noticeable peculiarity of the people was their habit of speaking of the East as "home." "At home in the East we call that Virginia-creeper," said one. "I go home to New York every few months," said another. "We long to go back East to our homes, but when we get there the climate does not agree with us, and we hurry back to Colorado." Thus was revealed the peculiar tenure the place has upon thousands of its citizens. But among them are very many who say that it is customary for Eastern folks to let their regard for the East keep warm until the moment comes when they seriously consider the idea of leaving Colorado. At that juncture they realize for the first time the magic of the mountain air and the hold it has upon them. Few indeed ever seriously think of leaving it after one such consultation with themselves. But I must say it is a very queer air. It keeps every one keyed up to the trembling-point, inciting the population to tireless, incessant effort, like a ceaseless breathing-in of alcohol. It creates a highly nervous people, and, as one man said, "it is strange to fancy what the literature of Colorado will be when it develops its own romancers and poets, so strong is the nervous strain and mental exaltation of the people." One would suppose alcohol unnecessary there; but, on the contrary, there is much drinking. It is a dangerous indulgence. Among the dissolutes suicides are frequent. "If you stay here a week you will read of two," said a citizen. And I did. It was found that when the saloons were allowed to remain open all night, violent crimes were of frequent occurrence. Drinking too deep and too long was the cause. The saloons were therefore ordered shut at twelve o'clock, and a remarkable decrease of these crimes followed.

We shall see that on its worst side the city is Western, and that its moral side is Eastern. It will be interesting to see how one side dominates the other, and both keep along together. But in the mean time what is most peculiar is the indifference with which the populace regards murder among those gamblers and desperadoes who are a feature of every new country, and who are found in Denver, though, I suspect, the ladies and children never see them, so well separated are the decent and the vicious quarters. It is said that not very long ago it was the tacit agreement of the people that it was not worth while to put the county to the cost or bother of seriously pursuing, prosecuting, and hanging or imprisoning a thug who murdered another thug. It was argued that there was one bad man less, and that if the murderer was at large another one would kill him. The axiom that "only bad men are the victims of bad men" obtained there, as it did in Cheyenne and Deadwood, and does in Butte. To-day a murder in a dive or gambling-hell excites little comment and no sensation in Denver, and I could distinctly see a trace of the old spirit in the speech of the reputable men when I talked to them of the one crime of the sort that took place while I was there.

The night side of the town is principally corralled, as they say; that is, its disorderly houses are all on one street. There is another mining-town characteristic—wide-open gambling. The "hells" are mainly abovestairs, over saloons. The vice is not flaunted as it is in certain other cities; but once in the gaming-places, the visitor sees them to be like those my readers became acquainted with in Butte, Montana—great open places, like the board-rooms in our stock exchanges, lined with gambling lay-outs. They are crowded on this Saturday night with rough men in careless dress or in the apparel of laborers. These are railroad employés, workers from the nearest mines, laborers, clerks—every sort of men who earn their money hard, and think to make more out of it by letting it go easily. Rou-

lette, red and black, and faro are the games. Behind each table sits the imperturbable dealer—sometimes a rough cowboyish-looking young man, who has left off his necktie so as to show his diamond stud; sometimes a man who would pass for a gray-bearded deacon in a village church. By each dealer's side sits the "lookout," chewing a cigar, and lazily looking on in the interests of such fair play as is consistent with professional gambling. All around each table, except on the dealer's side, crowd the idiots, straining and pushing to put their chips where luck will perch. These places are orderly, of course. It is the rule with them everywhere. There is very little conversation. Except for the musical clink-link-link of the ivory chips, the shuffling of feet, and the rattle of the roulette marbles, there is little noise. But the floor boards hold small sea-beds of expectoration, and over each table is enough tobacco smoke to beget the fancy that each lay-out is a mouth of the pit of hell.

Queer characters illustrate queer stories in these places, just as they do in the mining regions, but with the difference that all the stories of luck in the mines are cast with characters who are either rich or "broke," while in the hells they seem never to be in luck when you happen on them. They were flush yesterday, and will be to-morrow — if you will "stake" them with something to gamble with. The man who once had a bank of his own and the one who broke the biggest bank in Leadville were mere ordinary *dramatis personæ* when I looked in, but the towering giant of the place was the man who at twenty-six years of age had killed twenty-six men, all so justly, however, that he never stood trial for one episode. This is part of the "local color" in any picture of Denver; but, on the other hand, the best of that color is, as I have hinted, of the tone of lovely firesides, elegance, wealth, and refinement.

From the gaming to the fruit fair, that happens to be in progress, we are eager to go. The fruit or orchard exhibition was an unlooked-for consummation in so new a State. It was a sight of the dawn of the fruit industry where the best orchards were not five years old. Indeed, some of the finest fruit was plucked where Indians were guarded not long before. There were apples, pears, peaches, plums, quinces, grapes, and ground-cherries. It was too late in the year (October) for berries, but they are grown in Colorado in great abundance, and the strawberries are said to be big and most delicious. The fruits I saw displayed at the fair were of large though not Californian size. Their most remarkable quality to the eye was their gorgeous coloring—the richest and deepest I ever saw except in paintings. I found afterwards that all the fruit grown in the valleys of the Rockies is equally gorgeous. But of more practical import is the fact that this Colorado fruit is of delicious flavor. In Denver and in other parts of the State I tasted every product of the orchards. I cannot recall my experience in California clearly enough to say more than that they pick their fruit green to ship it away, and so they miss the credit they deserve abroad as growers of luscious fruit. I would like to encourage the Coloradans in their boast that theirs has higher flavor than the west-coast product (if it were true, and I had both kinds to prove it by), and I will say that I think I never enjoyed any fruit more than most of that which I ate in Colorado. The only melons at the show were muskmelons, but it is a great State for melons, particularly for watermelons. One place, Rocky Ford, in Otero County, is celebrated for its observance of what is called "melon day" every year, when the idle people, tourists, and pleasure-seekers gather there to eat free melons in a great amphitheatre built for that purpose. This affair is not altogether unique. At Monument, in Douglas County, the exuberant villagers dig a great trench and cook potatoes—as the Rhode-Islanders do clams—for the multitude, without charge. The fruit at the Denver show was grown in the following counties: Arapahoe, Boulder, Delta, Grand, Jefferson, Larimer, Mesa, Montrose, Otero, and Weld.

The wild flowers at this show were very interesting. No account of Colorado would be complete if it omitted at least some mention of these gorgeous ornaments which Nature litters with lavish hands all over the State — far up the mountain-sides, where the very rocks are stained with rich colors, and up and down the valleys, where even man's importation, the alfalfa, turns the ranches into great blue beds of thickly clustered blossoms. It may have been the flowers, or it may have been the beautifully stained rocks, or, as some say, the color of the water in the Colorado River, that gained the State the Spanish name it bears, but whichever it was, the flowers alone were sufficient to justify the christening, so multitudinous, lovely, varied, and gay are they. Fortunately for the fame of the flowers, certain Colorado ladies are skilled in pressing them so as to reproduce and preserve the natural poses of all the flowering plants, as well as to make them retain their colors unimpaired. The work of these women is now known in every part of the civilized world.

It was interesting to read the progress of Denver in the remarks of those who were presented to me during that visit to the fruit show. One gentleman was interested in the electric-light plant, and said that it is so powerful that during a recent decoration of the streets in honor of a convention that was held there, no less than 22,000 incandescent and four 5000 candle-power search-lights were used in the display. In few cities in the world, he said, is this light so generally and so lavishly used. He added that few of the dwellings, except in the poorest quarter, are without telephones.

A public official volunteered the information that since 1870 the percentage of increase of population has been greater in Denver than in any other city of the land, it being something more than 2000 per cent. A bevy of smiling young women was pointed out as representative art students; for there is a Denver Art League which has sixty members, and aims to maintain classes in oil and water-color work and sculpture. Two of the classes, one for each sex, pursue the practice of drawing and painting from the nude. This institution is the pride and care of the leading business and professional men of the city, who give it ample funds, and are encouraged by the eagerness of the youth of the State, as well as of the city, to enjoy its advantages. A merchant spoke of the Chamber of Commerce, to the enterprise and kindness of which, and especially of the secretary, I was afterward indebted. I learned that this watchful organization of promoters of the commercial welfare of the city maintains a fine free library, containing a collection of books that now numbers 20,000 volumes, and is constantly increasing. No less than 77,000 volumes were read in the homes of its patrons last year. The reading-room is kept open on all the days of the year, and the city government has passed an ordinance appropriating $500 a month, from the fines imposed by the police magistrates, for the benefit of this valuable institution. Another new acquaintance urged me to see the public schools of the city. The high-school building cost $325,000, and is the second most costly and complete one in existence. Many of the ward or district schools cost a fifth, and some cost more than a fifth, of that large sum. I could not then nor there farther insist upon the opinions that have engendered the only criticisms that have passed between myself in these papers and the new West which I am describing. The report of the Denver Board of Education is before me, and if I read it aright, it declares that the common-school system embraces a course of twelve years of study, eight in the common schools and four in the high-school. Drawing, music, physical culture, and German are mentioned as among the studies in the grammar grades, while the wide gamut between algebra and Greek, with military training for the boys, comprises the high-school course. The 700 high-school pupils are said to be of the average age of seventeen years. I reiterate that this is education for the well-to-do at the expense of the poor. If Denver is like any other town of my acquaintance, the poor cannot release their children from toil during twelve years after they are of an age to be sent to school. The disparity between the sum of 9500 in the common schools and the sum of 700 in the high-school makes it appear that Denver is no exception to the rule. I will not dwell upon my belief that the wide range of studies in these latter-day schools gives children a mere but dangerous smattering of many things and no thorough grounding in any study, and that the result is to produce a distaste for honest labor and an unfitness for anything above it. It is unpleasant to criticise at all where a community is so enthusiastic as this, but I believe the whole system, whether we find it in New York and Boston, as we do, or in Denver, is undemocratic, unjust, and unwise. The "little red school-house on the hill," which has been glorified as the chief pride of Puritan New England, is the seed that has grown into the $300,000 palace of learning for 700 children, at

the expense of the parents of more than 9000 other children. The little red schoolhouse was grand indeed. It taught the "three R's" thoroughly, and when a boy or girl wanted more, he or she managed to get it, at such pains and in such a way as to cause him or her to value all that was acquired. Honest work was the portion of all but the rich, who paid for their children's higher schooling. However, the spirit in which Denver maintains and elaborates her school system is beyond all criticism; it is, indeed, creditable and wonderful. If we do not agree about the result, I can at least testify to the impression I received—that the whole people are honestly and enthusiastically proud of their schools, and that of their elaborate kind they are among the best in the country.

Denver has other than her public schools—the (Methodist) University of Denver, the (Catholic) St. Mary's Academy, the (Episcopal) St. John's College for boys; an Episcopal school for girls, called Wolfe Hall; the Woman's College, and the Westminster University, the first a Baptist and the second a Presbyterian institution. I should have mentioned the fact that a second fine public library is maintained in connection with the public-school system. It goes without saying, in a study of a city like Denver, that musical, dramatic, literary, and kindred coteries are numerous.

Away from the fruit display, out in the brightly lit streets, were the crowds of Saturday-night shoppers. Of these many more were persons employed in manufacturing industries than those would imagine who know no more of Denver than I have told. The fine and varied building stones that will yet become a great asset in Colorado's inventory of wealth are cut and dressed in more than one establishment. The notable buildings of Denver are built of Colorado red sandstone, granite, and other beautiful materials found in the mountains. The main or parent range of the Rockies loses its striking configuration soon after leaving Colorado in the south. Then it becomes a broken, ragged chain. They have some good stones in the territories to the southward, but not the assortment found in Colorado. Already Colorado stones are shipped to Chicago, the Nebraska and Kansas towns, and Texas. These are brownstones, granite, a so-called lava or metamorphic stone of great durability and beauty, and a variety of sandstones. Some red sandstone that I saw being quarried in the Dolores Valley, where it is abundant beyond calculation, is said to be well adapted for fine interior decorative uses. Others in the crowds were workers in the cotton factory; in a knitting-mill that has been removed there from the East; in the three large establishments where preserves, fruit pickles, and sauces are made; in the making of fire-brick, drain-pipe, jugs, jars, churns, and other coarse pottery; in the manufacture of the best mining machinery in the world, whole outfits of which have been shipped to China and South Africa, to say nothing of Mexico and our own mining regions, which are all supplied from Denver. Other operatives work upon the hoisting machinery and pumping machines, of which the Denver patterns are celebrated. Still others in the streets work at the stock-yards, where there are two large packing companies, and where nearly 200,000 hogs, cattle, and sheep were slaughtered last year. A mill for the manufacture of news paper has been in operation for a year, and now (October, '92) three other paper-mills are about to be erected, the aim being to make book and letter paper, Manilas, coarse wrapping-paper, and flooring and roofing papers, as well as to produce the pulp used in these manufactures.

The three smelting-works employ nearly 400 men, and handled 400,000 tons of ore, producing $24,500,000 in gold, silver, lead, and copper, last year. In addition to the twenty foundries and machine shops of whose work I have spoken, there are thirty other iron-working establishments, making tin and sheet-iron work and wire-work. In another year a barbed-wire factory and a wire and nail making plant will be in operation. There are sixty brick-making firms. Leather-workers are numerous, but all the leather is imported; there is no tannery there. Paint and white-lead making are large industries; there are six breweries; and eight firms engage in wood-working and the making of building material. In a sentence, this busy metropolis is manufacturing for the vast territory around it, with 339 manufacturing establishments, employing 9000 operatives, and producing $46,000,000 worth of goods.

The Chamber of Commerce advertises the need of woollen mills, stocking factories, tanneries, boot and shoe factories, glue factories, and potteries, but declares that Denver will give no subsidies to get them. "The natural advantages of the centre of a region as large as the German Empire, without a rival for 600 miles in any direction, combined with cheap fuel, fine climate, abundant supply of intelligent labor at reasonable prices, unutilized local raw materials, a good and ever-growing local market, protected against Eastern competition by from 1000 to 2000 miles of railroad haul—these are the inducements that Denver offers to new manufacturing plants."

And now we will fancy it is Sunday in Denver. The worshippers are coming out of the churches. But in the streets rush the cable cars with their week-day clanging of bells. On the car roofs are the signs, "To Elitch's Gardens," where, according to the papers next day, there are "music and dancing and bangle-bedizened women." Other cars rush toward the City Park, where the State Capital Band is to play. "Oho!" thought the critical Eastern visitors; "we are in the presence of the usual American Sunday, with the gin-mills and the gambling-places all wide open." Not so. So far as I could see, not a bar-room was open. The shades were up, and the desolate interiors were in plain view from the streets. The gambling-saloons were tight shut. No one loitered near them. Here, then, had reappeared the Sunday of the Atlantic coast, for the local ordinances are enforced, and require the closing of the saloons and "hells" from Saturday midnight until Monday morning.

Except for the cling-clang of the street cars, an Eastern-Sunday hush was upon the town. Just as we see them in New York, country couples, strangers there, walked arm in arm in the business quarter, looking in the shop windows; German families, children and all, in stiff Sunday best, streamed along in queues behind the fathers; idle young men with large cigars leaned against the corners and the corner lamp-posts, and the business streets were nine-tenths dead. Thousands gathered in the park, just as they do on such a Sunday in New York. Beyond that the silence and stagnation of Sunday were on the town. In the Denver Club the prosperous men loafed about, and looked in at the great round table in the private dining-room with thoughts of the grand dinners it had borne. In the pretty homes were many circles wherein the West was discussed just as it is in New York, with sharp words for its gambling, its pistol-carrying, and its generally noisy Sundays. It was strange to hear in the West such talk of the West. It was easy to see the source of the influence that brought about that quiet day of worship. Yet in the same homes, in the same circles, was heard the most fulsome lauding of Denver and Colorado—praise that seemed to lift those altitudinous places even nearer to the clouds. With only the happiest memories and kindest wishes, then, adieu to Denver.

I made a journey of more than two thousand miles in Colorado without seeing half of it, for it is as large as New England and New York. Upon the famous "Scenic Route" (the Denver and Rio Grande Railroad) I rode from Denver to the New Mexican border, through southern Colorado, and back through the middle of the State, over the famous Marshall Pass. I took in, on the way, the full lengths of the Silverton and the Rio Grande Southern railways, which, in quest of mining towns and agricultural settlements, are laid amid some of the most gorgeous, stupendous, and varied scenery in the State. It will surprise the reader to hear that on these mountain railroads rock ballast, heavy steel rails, and gas-lighted palace-cars are provided. Yet the greatest surprise comes with seeing how the railroad-builders have flung their steel in loops upon the mountain sides and tops, where one would suppose no engines could ever haul a train, or trains could ever yield a profit, and where it is no uncommon thing to see three and even four lengths of the same railway above or below your car, as the rails "tack" to and fro toward the top of a steep mountain. "Yachting round the Rockies" was what the party on the trip with me resolved to call our journeying. There is not room in an entire paper such as this for a description of the scenery of Colorado. I had not supposed that, after enjoying the mountain scenery of British Columbia, I would find anything to delight me as much in any other part of the Rocky Mountain chain. Even now I think there are grander views in the North, but they are not as numerous, nor as beautiful and warm and full of color

and variety, as the mountain scenes in Colorado. The railway tourist in British Columbia merely crosses the mountains, whereas in Colorado it is possible to start from Denver and, riding only by daylight, to spend a week of nearly continuous mountaineering. At the end it will be difficult to determine which is the prettiest scene that memory retains for the mind's eye to return to. Perhaps it will seem that, taken altogether, the wondrous cañons were most worth seeing; those of the Rio de las Animas Perdidas, of the Grand, of the Dolores, of the Rio Grande, and that at Toltec, in New Mexico. Perhaps the surprising views of innumerable far-reaching, snow-clad mountain-peaks—seen at many points when the cars cross a divide—will be most delightfully remembered. Or it may be that the choicest recollection will be of the superb region between Trout Lake and the Cathedral Peaks, followed by a valley view of great beauty beyond. Then strangely beautiful mining towns, built in blind valleys between towering mountains, will come to mind, and Telluride, Pandora, Ouray, and other villages will seem the most enchanting bits of the grand experience. Their neat houses, shaded streets, and glorious surroundings gain much from the added novelty of mining paraphernalia in action. The pack-trains of long-eared burros, which the people call "Colorado canaries," the trolley railways, the heaps of ore, the Welsh miners—all these lend added value to the scenes. Each day is crowded with views of fearful gorges, of mountain-sides stained red and blue and green, of valleys cultivated to the degree of an Illinois prairie, of vast irrigation-works gridironing the plains with silver threads, of Mexicans and their huts and villages of adobe, of myriads of sheep on southern ranges. It is not necessary to go to Europe for scenery or for unfamiliar peoples and conditions.

I shall say even less about the mining than about the scenery. Colorado is generally known to possess both in abundance. Let it be my part to show that already the surer, more lasting resource of agriculture is the heaviest asset of the State. The Denver smelteries treated four and a quarter millions of pounds of Colorado copper, 100,000 tons of Colorado lead, twelve million ounces of silver, and 120,000 ounces of gold. The total value of all this was fifteen and three-quarter millions of dollars; but much of the Colorado ore is of the free-milling variety not treated at the smelteries; and besides, there are other smelteries at Pueblo, Rico, Leadville, and Durango. The total revenue from mining in 1891 was thirty-three and a half millions of dollars. And yet the Denver Chamber of Commerce estimates the income from agriculture at forty millions, derived from the cultivation of two millions of acres of land. If the value of the live-stock were added as a farm product, the sum would be increased by at least $15,000,000. A wonderful showing for so new a State.

It is estimated that at the end of another hundred years Colorado will boast a population of four millions of souls. Her stone quarries, her petroleum, her mineral paints, her cement, which is already classed as equal to the best, her clays, found in tremendous banks, and suitable for the production of fine china, as well as pottery of all the coarse grades, her coal and iron, her natural parks, scenic wonders, mineral waters, farm and fruit and pasture lands, her vast stores of metals—all these, and many resources that I have not mentioned, will more than support a population of that magnitude.

The range cattle business and civilization, with its fences and farms and towns, cannot exist together, and as Colorado is civilized, this rude business is almost at an end there. Cattle are being held in small bunches and with winter corrals—an infinitely more practical and humane industry. The present grade of cattle is higher than before. Every farmer sells a few head each year, and thus makes a little money where a few used to make (or lose) large sums.

One-third of the State is plains land, and two-thirds are cut up by mountains. These are separated by valleys of varying degrees of value for farm land, and the mountains are not so rocky as to be to any great extent unavailable for pasturage. Farming and orchard culture are making great headway in Larimer, Arapahoe, Boulder, Jefferson, and Weld counties, in eastern Colorado. Farmers are pushing into the valleys of southern Colorado, especially those in the southwest, that were once thickly peopled and well cultivated by the cliff-dwellers. The Mormons and other thrifty folk are taking up valley lands in the western part of the State.

Colorado's 66,560,000 acres of land lie upon either side of the continental divide and upon many secondary ranges, forming mountains, parks, and valleys, of which not five per cent. is bare of vegetation. Long ago the Mexicans began, with petty irrigation-works, to borrow from the eight principal rivers and their tributaries the water that came down from the mountains in those channels. The mean yearly precipitation west of the mountains is but 25 inches; east of them it is only 18.7 inches. At Denver the highest rainfall was in 1891, and amounted to $21\frac{4}{10}$ inches. The lowest was in 1890, and was $9\frac{1}{4}$ inches. All over the State irrigation companies have been formed, or farmers have banded together as ditch-owners, and, as we shall see, a vast acreage is under irrigation or ready for it. The destruction of the forests, and consequent loss of water, through its unequal distribution, have hurried the necessary building of reservoirs, of which there are many, and some very large ones, in use. Colorado is forward in this respect. The importance of reservoirs where water is scarce will be seen when the reader understands that the winter's stores of snow, and even the heavy rainfalls, are apt to rush away in one great flood, robbing the State of a large fraction of the too little water that comes upon it. The gauge records of the Cache la Poudre River show that 82 per cent. of the total annual discharge passes down the river in May, June, and July, whereas in August the discharge is only 6.6 per cent., and in September it is only 2.6 per cent.

Artesian wells add comparatively little to the wealth of the State, although this source of supply has been so successfully tried in the San Luis Valley that there are now more than 2000 wells there.

On the eastern slope, out to the eastern boundary of Colorado, there are nearly thirty millions of acres of arable land, of which four millions of acres are "under the ditch," and only a million and a half are actually cultivated. Of what remains unditched it is difficult to say how much may be redeemed. It depends upon the situation of the land and the extent of the water supply, and the latter factor is dependent on future developments.

For one thing, the irrigable land is constantly being extended and increased by the storage of the water of spring freshets in reservoirs that are usually formed out of natural depressions at the base of the mountains. The custom is to use the stored water on the near-by land, while the stream carries its own quota, undiminished, to distant fields. Thus the area of irrigable territory is greatly increased. Moreover, time has demonstrated the strange but important fact that, after three or four years, water used in irrigation goes twice as far as it did when the work was begun. The ground under the ditches becomes a vast reservoir, from which the water that sinks into it "seeps" or drains back into the natural waterways. Mr. Maxwell, the State Engineer of Colorado, finds that at the eastern line of the State, far beyond the ranches and farms which drain the river, the Platte carries 600 cubic feet of water per second as against the 200 cubic feet it brings out of the mountains. There is, therefore, a far better supply in the eastern plains country than formerly, and this will increase as reservoirs catch the spring floods, for it is certain that however much water be spread on the land, none is lost except by evaporation. The least hopeful outlook in eastern Colorado is for the land on the divide between the Platte and the Arkansas. There is no water there; the land is higher than the distant rivers, and wells have not succeeded there.

West of the Rocky Mountains there are more and larger streams, but there is less rainfall than on the eastern slope. It is estimated that there is a drainage area of twenty-five millions of acres in western Colorado, but that only nine millions are arable. These nine millions are mainly irrigated, the country being the field of rapid development. The principal streams flow through well-cultivated farming districts, and these form the region already noted for choice fruit-raising.

In the celebrated Greeley colony, north of Denver, the ditches are owned by the men who own the land. They bought and pre-empted a large tract (now as rich as a typical Illinois district, by-the-way), took the water rights, constructed a large canal, and distributed the water proportionately with the various holdings of the land. Thus the water has become part and parcel of the land, and costs only the trifling sum each owner is assessed for repairs and superintendence. This is as

near to the perfect and ideal method of irrigation as mankind has come in this country. It is the method of the Mormons also. But, alas! practically the whole water treasure and irrigation-work is in the hands of speculative corporations. All the newer schemes are of that sort. In the San Luis Valley, the Arkansas Valley, and along the Platte River corporations have built the ditches, appropriated and diverted the water, and are selling the liquid to farmers with a superimposed annual tax for repairs — a tax of such proportions that the plan may be justly described as making the farmers pay down at the outset for the privilege of having water afterward by paying for it over again every year. Like cows who come home to be milked at nightfall, the settlers of Colorado must "give down" each year or go dry. The first payments vary between five, eight, and ten dollars an acre for the land—usually eight to ten dollars—and the annual dues (for "maintenance," as this Colorado method of producing water-barons is called) are from a dollar to two dollars and a half an acre.

In each State I have visited where irrigation is necessary (and this is the case in something like one-fifth of the land of the United States) the conditions are about the same, and their unjustness causes thinking men to predict excessive irritation and trouble in the future. An eminent lawyer in Denver has reached the same conclusion that I announced in one of my papers on the new States in the Northwest. "Eventually and surely," said he, "the States must control the water supply within their borders. They will have to take the water by right of eminent domain, and pay the present owners for it. They must pay a great deal, for the owners count on becoming wealthy and on bequeathing Fortunatus purses to their descendants. Once in the possession of the government, the water must be distributed for the benefit of the greatest possible number. It will not be in our time, but it will be done, and it will result from the very great discontent, and perhaps even violent disorder, that are certain to breed out of the present unjust, selfish, and primitive methods."

The coal of eastern Colorado extends the whole width of the State in a belt that reaches an average distance of twenty miles out into the plains. It is an accompaniment of the Rocky Mountains, and has been thought to extend from the Gulf of Mexico to Alaska. An equal field lies to the west of the mountains, and is worked in Utah, Wyoming, and elsewhere. It is by no means uninterrupted or continuous. Glaciers and floods have worn away great reaches of it, and other lengths are overlaid by such thicknesses of rock that they are unworkable. But there are vast fields of it in Colorado—thirty thousand to forty thousand square miles, one official report declares. It is bituminous or lignite, and varies in quality, but even that which shows the lowest of these stages of development is valuable. The southern coal area is the better. There the coal is firm, does not slack, or slacks but slightly, breaks up into large blocks, is freer from impurities, and is found in thicker veins than elsewhere, as a rule. It is to get this coal and supply it to Kansas, Nebraska, New Mexico, and other States and Territories that several railways have extended their lines into Colorado, to the incalculable benefit of the State. A remarkable and indubitable "find" of anthracite coal is the gem of this vast double field of fuel. It is mined at Crested Butte, in Gunnison County, in the Elk Mountains. By the fossil remains found with it geologists determine it to be of the same origin as the lignite of the foothills and plains, altered by heat into anthracite. It is now known to occur in more than one large bed, and close to it are beds of semi-anthracite, as well as much bituminous coal. There is a great deal of coking-coal here, and other coking-coal in large quantities is found in the Trinidad region—a plateau of 750 square miles in southern Colorado and New Mexico. It is also found in lesser quantities near Durango, in the San Juan district. The field of petroleum oil in the State is in Fremont County, near Cañon City. The supply of oil is reported to be practically unlimited, and the wells are called more prolific than any others of the same number and size in the United States, yet the production of the whole field is kept down to the requirements of a very limited market. I found but one opinion in Denver, and that was that the Colorado output of oil is limited to the demands of Colorado, Wyoming, Montana, Utah, and New Mexico.

Along the entire foot-hills are geolo-gical conditions more or less similar to those at Florence, and it is not at all certain that the present wells are in the best place. That is the general opinion in Colorado, and it is also believed that natural gas will prove a factor in the State's assets some day. With varying success, nearly ninety wells have been drilled in the Florence oil-field. Fifty-two and a half per cent. have proved productive in greater or lesser degree, and some have produced constantly for five years. Out of the 30,000 barrels produced up to October, 1891, one-third of the amount was refined into oil, and 5000 barrels of lubricating oil were made, both products being excellent, for the oil is rich in illuminant and lubricating qualities.

There is among Colorado capitalists a project for operating a four-million-dollar iron and steel producing company, and this company has for a long time kept experts in the field in an endeavor to find suitable coal and iron in such proximity to one another as to warrant the establishment of furnaces for the making of pig to blend into the Bessemer product afterward. I went to the chief personage in this great prospective industry and asked him as to the quantity and kinds of iron that were supposed to exist in the State. With rare tact, and a quality of courtesy not often met with in the West, he said that exactly what I wished to know was precisely what I should not find out. What was vouchsafed to me by this custodian of the bad manners and the knowledge of the iron deposit in Colorado was as valuable as it was churlishly given.

There is, it seems, but little development-work in iron in the State, though the iron is found scattered in large fields on both sides of the mountains, some being magnetic and some hematite, not to speak of the more or less worthless ores. For twelve years iron has been made at Pueblo of ore from the San Luis Valley, Leadville, and other points. There is in the State a great deal of ore free from phosphorus and sulphur to make Bessemer steel, ore of good quality being found in many places, the only question about any of it being with regard to its quantity and availability. "But," said the gruff sage who told me this, "there is not a pound of fuel east of the Rockies that is fit to use in making iron, and to use what there is would bankrupt whoever did it."

Iron is going into Colorado from Alabama at seventeen dollars a ton, ten dollars being the market price and seven dollars the freight charge. In another year Lake Superior pig-iron will enter the Colorado market. The problem in Colorado, then, is to find iron to market at a less price. Fifteen-dollar iron would do, on a basis of thirteen dollars cost, leaving a margin for profit and interest on the plant. There is required a combination of the right ore, the right fuel, and satisfactory transportation facilities, and that combination is yet to be made. An exhaustive, energetic investigation is going forward, and the men interested hope to work at many points to produce mixtures for Bessemer. They believe that there is a good prospect of success at an early day. They are looking into the fuel question in Wyoming, where the iron supply is no longer debatable.

Second to Denver among Colorado's cities is Pueblo, in the county of that name. It claims 40,000 population, and is a substantially built and very busy town, with a banking capital of a million, and mercantile operations that amount to $35,000,000 a year. Its three smelteries produce $14,000,000 a year. It has five railroads running through it, a $400,000 opera-house, a public library, immense iron and steel works, oil-refineries, thirty miles of electric street railway, and a solid, orderly, and prosperous appearance. It is 4700 feet up in the air, and surrounded by a delightful country, either cultivated or naturally picturesque. The mineral palace for the display of the mineral resources of the State, the artesian magnetic mineral baths, the near-by lake-side summer resort, and the really fine hotels of the city have attracted tourists and invalids in great numbers.

Colorado Springs is another important place, of which it has been said that it presents the anomaly of a bustling town of fine buildings, banks, clubs, palatial hotels, and yet manufactures nothing at all, and does no business except with itself. The place has 12,000 inhabitants, and is a winter and summer resort, 6000 feet above sea-level. Residence there is advertised as a "sure cure" for consumption, which explains the mystery of its size and character. The town has electric cars, a college, the Childs-Drexel Printers' Home, hospitals, churches, schools, banks, clubs, an opera-house, and a casino, which includes a fine restaurant and an orchestra. The place is surrounded by resorts and scenic points that have been widely advertised. Pike's Peak, Manitou (another resort famed for its springs), the latest sensational mining camp, called Cripple Creek, and many other noted places are all close to Colorado Springs, which is perhaps the most finished and elegant health resort west of the Mississippi.

Colorado is dotted with springs of medicated water of various kinds—hot, cold, sulphur, soda, iron, magnetic — a great variety, and existing in almost every county. At Glenwood Springs, an especially beautiful resort, hot springs are utilized to fill an open-air bath 600 feet long, in which men and women may bathe in midwinter without being chilled while in or beside the bath. A hotel to cost $400,000 is building there.

The southwestern part of the State, called the San Juan country, has for its capital a place named Durango, which is sufficiently far from any competitor, is in a sufficiently rich country, and has a sufficient reputation for "hustling" to make it a very promising place. It is 6000 feet above the sea-level, in the Animas Valley, and includes some fine buildings, good hotels, several banks and churches, a free-and-easy, electric lights, gambling layouts in all the saloons, and, indeed, everything that goes with a high-spirited Western town. The United States land-office there has sold 102,000 acres of land, at $1 25 an acre, and has given away 50,000 acres to homesteaders. It has issued receipts for about 3000 gold and silver mining claims, and has sold 7000 acres of coal land. Here is the San Juan Smeltery, which cokes its own coal, and a smeltery that treats ore from Red Mountain and Rico. The Porter Coal Company, whose mines are near by, turned out 70,000 tons last year. The San Juan Company mines 150 tons a day; the Ute Coal Company mines twice as much; and there are still other companies in the business. The place supports three banks and a savings-bank, an iron foundry and machine shop, two flour-mills, saw-mills, a brick-yard, a lime company, a stone-quarrying company, and the inevitable brewery. Timber for charcoal, gypsum for plaster of Paris, fire-clay, and fine building stones are found near by. The farm land yields, in the local parlance, "everything from peanuts to persimmons," viz., wheat, oats, apples, pears, cherries, plums, melons, grapes, and many sorts of berries. Over in New Mexico peaches are said to do well, and they raise thirty-five varieties of grapes. There are many streams, and irrigation-works are numerous. Montrose is the likely town at the northern end of the San Juan country. Montrose County has 500 miles of ditches, and is rich in the production of wheat, corn, potatoes, hay, and very fine fruit. Here again flour-mills, lumber-mills, banks, an opera-house, a club, and the other monuments of a prosperous community are to be found.

It would be interesting to glance all over the State in this way, but since I must choose, I have told of this region—distant and backward until very lately—to illustrate what is true of the whole State.

Aspen and Leadville are no longer bold, bad mining camps. Both are solid, sober places. Creede has moved out of the original gulch to what was "Jimtown," and is also an earnest, orderly town. Greeley is a thrifty, prosperous, and beautiful farming centre; and Grand Junction, in western Colorado, is an ambitious and inviting place.

ANCIENT PEOPLES OF THE PETRIFIED FOREST OF ARIZONA

THE Petrified Forest of Arizona would alone be enough to absorb the entire attention of any visitor. When one has the opportunity likewise of scouring the region for traces of the ancient peoples who once lived there, he is doubly fortunate, especially if the quest be successful. It happened, as the result of journeys through the forest and around its borders, in the interest of the United States National Museum, last summer, that to the marvels which expand the fifth sense of wonder we may now add the needed touch of human interest.

* Published by permission of the Secretary of the Smithsonian Institution.

For here lived and loved, builded, fought, starved, and perhaps at times dined on one another, tribes of the ancient pueblo-dwellers. From the relics that remain it is found that four different stocks of Indians have lived here. No other section of the Southwest can show so many, and this in a locality without permanent springs. One of these tribes may unhesitatingly be identified as Hopi —perhaps a clan on its northward migration to Tusayan; another, with less sureness, may be related to Zuñi. The remainder are at present enigmas, and belong to peoples in a low state of advancement as compared with the former.

The reconnoissance of these ruins led

to an acquaintance with the Petrified Forest and its surroundings that well repaid the labor.

The little station of Adamanna, on the Santa Fe, whose name is a tribute to the grizzled genius of the forest, is the introduction. If the traveller but knew it, a short walk from Adamanna would bring him upon a fine ruin, one hundred and fifty feet square, well laid out, and exhibiting on the rocks below it as interesting a picture-gallery of the ancient petroglyphs as one might hope to find. Standing also at the Petrified Bridge—a colossal shaft of chalcedony spanning a chasm—one may see, with the aid of a glass, a conical hill to the southwest, crowned with a ruin, beyond the streak of tawny wash where horses paw for water. The ancient builders of this ruin were connoisseurs of stone and adepts at its working, if they were not strong in pottery. On the flanks of the butte and along the ravines are circles of large slabs of stone standing upright, many of the stones worked out as metates or corn-grinding slabs, and hence the ruin was called "Metate Ruin." Not the least interesting feature of this ruin is that it is an enigma; the people who once lived here were not related in any way to the others of this region. Even the group of three small pueblos, not a thousand feet away, on the ruin above Metate Ruin, were homes of a different people, and perhaps of a different time.

Following the road among the mesas, one passes through a canyon, emerges into the third or great forest, and sees a chaos of broken trunks of Triassic Araucarioxyla, winnowings of ages from the rock bed above, the ground strewn with splinters of lovely colors, with the glint of rock-crystal and amethyst, the setting of strange sculpture forms around a basin of sand and sage-brush, and, above, the unclouded sun and clear blue sky.

In the basin of the forest the rapid erosion has played havoc with the ruins, leaving them mere heaps of stones; the cemeteries, with their pottery and relics, have been washed away by the cloud-bursts and fierce winds. Frequently on the edge of a mesa will be found remaining a narrow fringe of a pueblo, soon to go down the gullies among the round-backed "bad lands," and the site of what must once have been a sizable village looks now as though it had been only a camping-place. So there is little left for the archæologist, who must content himself with noting the location of the ruin and the character of the potsherds scattered about, for pottery furnishes the clew as to the people.

The tribes that held the region of the

Photographed by A. C. Vroman

PETRIFIED BRIDGE

AN ANCIENT SHRINE

Petrified Forest built no large pueblos, but were content to live in small villages, forming the homes of larger families of blood relatives called clans, moving about in common when they migrated, and building not far from one another. These clusters of pueblos are familiar to one who knows the Southwest; usually, when a ruin is located, others may be found near by. The Seven Cities of Cibola illustrate this.

When the first men crept into this gorgeous but inhospitable land they found black lava-capped mountains, fantastic hills carved from the tinted marls, lofty stone-girdled mesas, wide plains, and treacherous sand rivers, which became at times raging torrents of tawny water. Game there was—of antelope, deer, and other smaller animals—more than now, and desert plants were available for food. But greater than these precious means of subsistence were the seeds they cherished, and greatest was "the seed of seeds"—corn. The secret of the peopling of the semi-arid Southwest is corn.

On the northern rim of the forest is a high, rolling prairie, broken on the east by mesas dotted with a few scattered junipers. Here were discovered four low, shard-strewn mounds of former villages and the remains of several small house sites. This proved to be virgin soil for the explorer, no "pottery-digger" having rifled the ancient sites.

The ancients of the forest rim built their pueblos to face their east, corresponding to our northeast, while to the southwest the villages presented a blank wall of two or more stories. Before the eastern opening may be traced the low mound of débris beneath which are ranged the dead, lying at length to face northeast, having their treasures of finest pottery, beads, and other things regarded as precious and of use to them. Looking toward the eastern horizon, one is struck by the sky-line, diversified with blue mesas stretching from Escudilla Peak of the White Mountains, low in the southeast, to the high mesas standing along the Puerco River on the northeast. This formed a splendid dial, along which the sun-worshippers traced the seasonal course of the sun, and for this reason they oriented their villages to face the rising of the "Father" at the winter solstice. To this day the indented horizon is the calendar of the Hopi, Zuñi, and other pueblo tribes.

Here and there without the villages remain shrines, consisting of either heaps of stones, odd in color or shape, gathered from far and near, like some of the shrines at Zuñi, or a section of petrified wood set upright over against spheres of red granite and weathered volcanic rock. Stones of strange forms are believed by the Zuñi to be the shrivelled remains of monsters of the early time, destroyed by the great fire of the Twin Gods, and are valued as fetiches, having still the magic power of those animals.

Near one of the ruins a large heap of these fetiches was found, and among the stones were a number of tubular pipes, skilfully made of lava. A few feet from this altar was a square fire-hole, lined with slabs of sandstone, containing many pieces of calcined rock. This spot was no doubt a meeting-place of the priests, probably surrounded with a hedge of juniper boughs, like a Navajo medicine-lodge.

Fascinating as were these superficial examinations of the ancient towns, the shovels of the Mexican laborers soon revealed matters of surpassing interest beneath the ground. The location of the cemetery was a comparatively easy matter, as these tribes had placed their dead to the northeast of the pueblos. When the trenches had reached about four feet, large, smooth slabs of sandstone were encountered. Beneath the slabs, which were set slanting, to keep the weight of the earth from the body, careful digging uncovered the skeleton, and about the head would be found a bowl or two, a vase, a cooking-pot, and a dipper. In the bowls frequently remained squash seed, corn, or traces of other food, provision for the journey to the underworld. Awls, hammers of fossil wood, knives, and arrow-heads were frequently encountered. Fragments of coiled baskets, matting, and fabric having a warp of twisted cord sometimes survived in the dry soil. Beads of stone and seashell and ornaments of lignite and white stone were plentiful, showing that these

Photographed by L. Bernie Gallaher

ANCIENT POTTERY

pueblos by modern Indian standards would be accounted rich in the things valued by Indians and the chief incentive for their primitive commerce.

It was evident in the cemeteries that the spot due northeast of the pueblos was an area of special significance, as here were interments of people of consequence, with rich belongings, while towards the southeast and on the edges were placed the poor, in shallow earth, with their meagre belongings.

Northeast of the largest pueblo of the group, at a depth of seven feet, the workmen came upon a fine upright slab of sandstone, measuring three by five feet, smoothed, and with rounded edges. After much labor in excavation the slab was removed, and a cist, neatly cut in the white gypsum underlying the soil, was uncovered. The cist contained a skeleton surrounded with ten pieces of pottery, several of them of fine and unique ware, thousands of small beads of white stone, shell beads, a bracelet of shell, a large awl of worked deer bone, fragments of matting and basketry, and a few sticks painted green, to which feathers had been attached. The last are the feathered prayer-sticks, called by the Hopi *pahos,* an invariable accompaniment of the Zuñi and Hopi ceremonies. Shells of the egg of the eagle were also found. When the cist had been cleared out the marks of digging implements, probably sharpened sticks, were visible on its walls, and it was seen that this remarkable sepulture had required an excavation through four feet of hard gypsum before the cist could be scooped out from the face—quite an undertaking with the simple tools possessed by the Indians.

Not far from this spot two rare and splendid bowls were taken out, one of dark red ware, with coiled exterior, over which was painted a meander pattern in white; the interior black, with a lustrous polish. The other is of black and white, thin, and well made, the design key frets in mosaic effect, and in the bottom of the bowl is admirably painted the figure of a frog, one of the sacred animals of the people of the arid country, through its connection with water.

The ruin second in size of this group is most picturesquely situated on a high cliff overlooking a deep basin scooped from the purple marl. Among the rocks a few juniper-trees, shrubs of the cowania, or cliff-rose, and the berry-bearing aromatic sumac give a touch of life not found in the other ruins on the arid stretches. The bare valley below also looks desolate and forbidding, and the surroundings seem depressing when one has learned that this is the pueblo of the cannibals.

A tragedy of long ago came to light during excavations around this village. In the cemetery, among other orderly burials, was uncovered a heap of broken human bones belonging to three individuals. It was evident that the shattered bones had been clean when they were placed in the ground, and some fragments showed scorching by fire. The marks of the implements used in cracking the bones were still traceable. Without doubt this ossuary is the record of a cannibal feast, and its discovery is interesting to science as being the first material proof of cannibalism among our North-American Indians.

Hard by were taken out over fifty objects belonging to the paraphernalia of a medicine-man: bone tubes; white, black, and green paint; a paint-grinder; quartz, amethyst, carnelian, and topaz crystals; cones, cylinders, and tablets, highly polished, worked from chalcedony; pebbles and concretions of strange form and color; a fossil; beads of stone and shell; a chipped flint drill; a flint knife; and two finely worked bone awls. This remarkable collection is interesting as it gives a clew to the relationships of the inhabitants of these pueblos. Pottery especially, if it bears symbolism, is the best means of identifying the ancient pueblos, and all ethnologists in this field are under obligations for the vessels which were deposited with the dead. In this case the paraphernalia of the medicine-man unearthed is the counterpart of that employed by the priests of Zuñi.

It is remarkable that these people should have located where there is no water. Evidently when the water, collected in natural basins from rainfall, failed, they carried it a long distance from holes dug in the bed of the wash in the Petrified Forest.

MAIN STREET, LOS ANGELES.

SOUTHERN CALIFORNIA.

III.

FROM THE TEHACHAPI PASS TO THE MEXICAN FRONTIER.

ONCE over the striking Tehachapi Pass, we are in Southern California proper. We had come a long way south already, it is true. We had met with settlements of pretty Spanish names, with old missions, with Mexican leather breeches and jingling spurs, with vineyards, and raisin-making, and occasional orange and palm trees ; but when the dividing mountain range, four thousand feet above the sea at Tehachapi, is passed, all these things are found in their utmost development. The country is older, the Spanish names more musical ; the orange and lemon are not grown in fear and trembling, for ornament simply, but as a principal crop. The climate is of a genial mildness which draws hither the greater number of all those who seek California for health.

It is a section that promises no ordinary entertainment. The widely famed Los Angeles, the City of the Angels, is the terminus of the first day's journey. The watering-place of Santa Monica and the important points of San Buenaventura and Santa Barbara are not far distant to the west, while San Diego lies at a moderate remove to the southward, by the Mexican frontier. In the intervals are scattered colonies of vine and orange growers, the number and dimensions of which are being rapidly increased.

The mountain barrier across the State is deemed by some to be of such importance that it should be a political as well as a natural division. They call for the construction of a distinct new State, to be called South California. Its proposed capital is Los Angeles.

"We are different peoples," maintains one of these separatists in the *Californian* magazine. "We are different in pursuits, in tastes, manner of thought and manner of life;....our hopes and aspirations for the future are different. The restless, uneasy population of the north, ever drifting, without local attachments, has no counterpart in Southern California; neither has the wild spirit of mining speculation ever flourished here. With this peaceable life, possibly in part as a result of it, there has grown up in the people an intense love of their land.

"And it is for their own section of the State," he goes on, "that this love exists. They call themselves, not Californians, but Southern Californians. The feeling is intense. I can only liken it to the overmastering love of the old Greek for the sunny shores that lay around the Ægean.

"For myself, I feel more and more each time that I visit the upper portion of the State that I am going into a strange land. And the impression never leaves me till upon my return I look down from the crest of the Tehachapi over the warm southland."

I have thought it worth while to quote this passage, partly because it is amusing, partly because it may serve to accentuate the topographical situation, and because it attributes a character to the section almost exactly the opposite of that which exists. Everywhere is found bustle, enterprise, push. The people will sell you a corner lot or a quarter-section of land with the greatest gusto in the world, and at its full value. Whatever effects the lapse of time may have, the present inhabitants, few of them born here or drafted from indolent climes, are certainly lotus-eaters of a very hardy type.

But meanwhile we are waiting without the gates of Los Angeles, and I, for one, had much too warm a curiosity on arriving to wait there long.

The City of the Angels is, in general effect, another San José, only upon a more hilly site. Its population must be about fourteen thousand. The long thoroughfare of Main Street proceeds, from the dépôt, at first through a shabby Spanish quarter, locally known as "Sonora," consisting of one-story, whitewashed, adobe houses. But presently—after passing a small Spanish plaza set out with sharp-pointed cypresses, and the principal hotel, the Pico House—it is lined with excellent buildings of the modern pattern, and becomes the principal street of the town. The handsome Baker Block is particularly notable. Continuing on to the ornate Los Angeles Bank, it is found that Spring Street diverges at this point at a small angle, and contributes, with Main Street, to give to what may be called the commercial skeleton of the town the shape of a Y with a very long stem. On Spring Street you find the common little post-office, the municipal offices, and a brown Dutch-looking brick building, standing free, which was originally constructed for a market, and is now the County Courthouse. You may also look into the lobby of a small adobe jail, which lobby some leisurely prisoner of the frescoer's trade has been allowed to convert into a resemblance to the dungeon scene at a theatre. These two streets, with another shorter one, Los Angeles Street, parallel to Main, and containing fruit and other produce, commission houses, comprise all of the commercial portion of the city worth mentioning.

New buildings are going up. The shops are large and well-appointed. On all sides are read placards offering goods in the usual shibboleth of enterprising traders: "To Reduce Stock!" "At a Wholesale Slaughter," and "For the Next Sixty Days." A serious depression afflicted Los Angeles in 1875, at the time of the general depression throughout the State, but that has been succeeded by a new reign of activity. Trim large residences for the more prosperous merchants are seen in the outskirts of the town. Further out yet they become villas, set down in the midst of plantations of orange and lemon, which are ruled off into formal plots by the ditches for irrigation. The class of more modest means are housed along the side streets in frame cottages. The German Turn-hall serves as the principal theatre.

It is held that Los Angeles, with its port of Wilmington, thirty miles away, should be, and will be, now upon the completion of the Southern Pacific Railroad, the entrepôt and Pacific terminus respectively of a new commercial system. San Francisco has too long sat at the Golden Gate, as it is picturesquely put, "levying toll on every pound of freight that passes through." This selfish greed on the part of San Francisco is to be properly rebuked by the diversion of a part of its trade to the places named. Enthusiastic San Diego too expects to have its share. The wickedness seems to depend largely upon who it is that takes the toll. Los Angeles, it is held, is to be the Lyons, and San Diego the Marseilles, of the State, this theory still leaving San Francisco its Paris.

The pepper-tree with its scarlet berries and fern-like leaves forms the leading-shade and ornament along Los Angeles streets. Apart from this I recollect a clump of well-grown palms on San Pedro Street, and a Mexican *nopal*, or cactus, in front of a curious octagon house on Main Street, which had attained the dimensions of a good-sized apple-tree. In the court-yard of the principal hotel droops a single ragged-looking banana. Tropical features in the vegetation are very scarce, but it is evident that this is not the fault of the climate, but of failure to encourage them. The castor-oil plant grows a tall rank weed in neglected places. In the door-yards are the Mexican aloe and the Spanish bayonet, from the adjacent deserts of Mohave and Arizona. The extraction of castor-oil was at one time an industry of the place, but is now abandoned.

We had not expected to find Los Angeles wholly foreign, but we were surprised to find it in so many respects very much like other towns in the United States. There is Spanish Town, however, and that should be important. Come, let us go through Sonora.

The Mexican element must be something like one-third of the entire population of the place. In Sonora the recollection of Mexico is revived, but of a very shabby and provincial Mexico. You may find *mescal* and *tequila*—the two varieties of intoxicating liquors distilled from the *maguey*, or aloe—to drink. The dingy little adobe shops contain dingy little stocks of goods, samples of which are set in the shuttered loop-holes of windows. A few swarthy, lantern-jawed old-timers hang about the corners, gossiping in a bad patois, and women with black shawls over their heads pass by. Much of the quarter is in a ruinous condition. There remain in the vestiges of an arcade system of the kind known in some form to travellers in most tropical or semi-tropical countries. The arcades in Sonora are not of massive brick and stone, but wooden roofs, such as are sometimes put out by our corner grocers, supported on light posts. Here and there only the battered skeletons of these awnings remain attached to the ruinous houses. Most California municipalities have borrowed something of this Spanish idea. At Sacramento, for instance, the thriving but flat and not overattractive capital of the State, one can walk nearly all over the business part of the town under cover.

There is a very respectable-looking Mexican restaurant—a vine-embowered cottage—opposite the Pico House, where the familiar *tortillas*, or pancakes, and *frijoles*, or stewed beans, may be had. Alongside it is an adobe church, quaint in pattern, but modern and devoid of interest, with a belfry, from which chimes

DON PIO PICO.

jangle several times a day in true Mexican fashion. Out of Sonora, too, emerges on the 15th of every September a military company, the Juarez Guard. It escorts a triumphal car bearing the national tricolor of red, white, and green. There is an escort also of dark little maids in white muslin and slippers. The whole proceed to celebrate with appropriate ardor the anniversary of Mexican independence.

But this is a people which has gone to the wall. They wear no very pathetic aspect in their adversity. They are for the most part engaged in the coarser kind of work; they are improvident, and apparently contented with their lot. It is only here and there that a Spanish name—a Pacheco, Sepulveda, Estudillo—rises into prominence in the State of which they were once owners. Old Don Pio Pico, the last of the Spanish Governors, resides here, impoverished, in a little cottage, in sight of property of much value which was formerly his, and of the plaza which was once the centre of his authority.

Don Pio is one of the picturesque sights of Los Angeles. With his history and circumstances, he would be esteemed an interesting figure anywhere. Above eighty now, with his stocky figure, square head, and bright eye, contrasting with his bronzed skin and close-cropped white hair and beard, he has a certain resemblance to Victor Hugo. He has a rather florid taste in jewelry, and carries himself about town, in his short overcoat with velvet collar and cuffs, with a bearing still erect and stately. It seems strange to tell, but it is true, and evidence of the conservatism and lack of adaptability in this peculiar race, that the old gentleman, though once Governor of the State, and a continuous resident in it as an American citizen ever since he surrendered it to Fremont and Stockton in 1847—strange to tell, I say, that he does not speak a syllable of anything but his own language. The talk of this historic personage suggests but a rude picture of the advantages to be enjoyed in the state of society existing during his youth. Was there anything in the world so remote as the California of the years 1810–30, or thereabouts?

"I am a plain person," the old man says, "who had the chance to learn but little from books. My father did not leave me a mule nor a vara of ground. I worked for the fathers at the old San Gabriel Mission when I was a boy."

He disclaims even being an authority on the events of his fall and the encroachments of the conquering Americans. "There are many," he says, "who have a better head for all these things than I, who will tell you better than I. I was a just man, however," he naïvely admits. "I aimed to judge a rich man who came before me no better than if he were poor. When it was asked who should be Governor, who was lo mas justo y honrado— the most just and honest man—for that place, it was answered that it was I, Don Pio Pico."

There are differences of opinion about these old Spanish officials. I do not cite the controversy here with the purpose of disparaging Don Pio. Let such an intention be far from this cursory account of the salient aspects of things in a new country. But it has a bearing upon the situation of landed property in the State to know that these officials are charged with a wholesale issue of patents to lands after the American occupation, which patents apparently belonged to the periods of their respective administrations. Edwin M.

Stanton, sent out for this service, reported to the Attorney-General of the United States that "the making of false grants, with the subornation of false witnesses to prove them, has become a trade and a business."

The treaty of Guadalupe Hidalgo, in 1847, by which the war with Mexico was concluded, secured as valid and of full force whatever had been done before the American occupation. Spanish Governors were numerous in those last days, and went in and out of office, besides, with extraordinary frequency, by reason of plots, counterplots, and the inability of the home government to enforce its authority. Alvarado, Carillo, Micheltorena, and Pio Pico reigned separately, or together, or by turns, in a revolutionary, confused, and overlapping way, which furnished afterward excellent opportunity for fraud. One would much prefer, however, not to touch upon such unpleasant suspicions, but to esteem these fallen dignitaries, not many of whom now survive, according to their misfortunes and romantic character.

Even the Chinese, singularly enough, show a greater enterprise than the Spanish population. Perhaps they may be conceded a better warrant here than elsewhere, since a Chinaman is found in the list of the twelve original settlers of the town in the year 1781. They have pushed into the very best of the old Spanish adobes, the residences which were once the best of their kind in the State. They occupy all those which flank the little plaza and an entire street extending from it. The populace are not, however, or at least have not always been, better reconciled to the hapless Mongolians here than elsewhere. One is shown a street corner where, in an outburst of deadly prejudice, in the year 1871, after having been dragged out of their old Spanish houses, they were hung to lamp-posts, to wagon tongues, and their own doorways. They were thus put to death to the number of eighteen, of all ages and sizes. An informant has described them to me as hanging like bunches of carrots. Just at present they were putting up by the plaza an ornate open-air theatre or temple, in anticipation of a triennial religious festival to last a week or more.

I shall call one of my pleasantest days at Los Angeles that which was devoted to a drive with the Zanjero.

What is a Zanjero?

His title is derived from the Spanish word *zanja* (ditch). It has been continued down from the original settlement into the present times. He is the official overseer of the water and irrigation system. He took me about with him to observe this very important and entertaining part of the economy of civilized existence in these thirsty regions. Not that Los Angeles is so dry a place by comparison, for it has thirteen inches of annual rain-fall as against two at Bakersfield above, but it is in need of abundant irrigation, for all that.

The Zanjero is elected by the City Council annually. Six deputies are given him to aid him in summer, but the force is reduced to three in winter, when the rains render artificial irrigation hardly necessary. All are invested with the authority and badges of policemen.

The city, we learn as we ride along, controls in its corporate capacity all the waters of the Los Angeles River. The Los Angeles River is a Southern California stream of the typical sort. It is a wide, shallow, almost dry bed at the moment, but in spring and winter it brawls in dangerous fashion, and carries away its bridges as often as it can. We ride up to the point near a certain railroad bridge where the water is first diverted. It is taken out by two small canals, one for the city proper, one for the thriving suburb of East Los Angeles. We find that the dam by which the river is checked for this purpose is constructed of earth, with a facing of stout posts and planking. At the beginning of winter the planking is removed, and the rushing stream allowed to sweep away the rampart of earth, to be replaced by a new one in the succeeding spring. Chain-gangs of convicts are brought out from the prison for this labor.

An earlier canal, however, is taken out of the same river twelve miles above. This supplies a pure drinking water for the city, and also water for irrigating the higher level. There are two very decided levels in the configuration of the city, one rising from the other with great abruptness, as at the sea-port town of Santa Cruz, glanced at heretofore.

Let us stop and look off from the vantage-ground of the highest level when we have reached its top. Upon this height are remains of the fort which Fremont threw up when he entered the city. Down below, directly at its foot, is the cottage of Pio Pico; the big hotel, still bearing his name, in which he sunk a handsome share of his fortune; the little cypress-studded plaza; and the shabby white quarter of Sonora. The mass of the city lies to the right, without striking features. Beyond it, toward the river, stretch breadths of a russet bloom which we know to be vineyard; and formal lines and parallelograms of orange and eucalyptus trees, set down as formally as the stiff little trees accompanying boxes of German toys. Across the river, again, "Brooklyn Heights" and "Boyle Heights" rise to a level, which becomes then a wide rolling table-land (*mesa*), which extends back to the blue Sierra Madre Mountains. Reaching out toward most of the horizons on the other sides are patches and expanses of a garden-like vegetation which have a mysterious and attractive quality. They are our dreamed-of orange groves. The supply is unstinted enough to gratify the most ardent imagination.

The city has created a considerable part of its debt by its water system, having spent probably $200,000 on the whole. The works are of an ephemeral character as yet, which will in time be replaced by something more substantial. The simple trenches and wooden flumes permit waste, and are, besides, costly to keep in repair. One of the principal ditches, however, is carried through a hill some three-quarters of a mile by a tunnel six feet in section, and there have been formed also numbers of durable reservoirs or artificial lakes for the storage of additional water in winter to supplement the river when it is low.

We ride out among the outlying villas and gardens and observe the distribution of the water in its practical application. The main ditches are three feet by two, the more ordinary sort two by one. The "head" is the nominal standard of measurement for the cheery, babbling fluid. The head should be a section of one hundred square inches, delivered under a certain uniform pressure, but it is in practice much more loosely administered. "The irrigators want their work *done*," says the Zanjero; "that is the main point. Some land takes more, other takes less, according as it is sandy or holds the water. A head of fifty inches on the east side will do as much as one hundred and twenty around the city."

Fan-palms, India-rubber-trees, and groups of tall plume-like bananas grow freely on the lawns where a little pains has been taken with them. One stops to exclaim with delight at a comfortable home embowered in myrtle, oranges, and vines, the dark glossy foliage starred with the golden fruit and with red roses. It is a spot for any tender romance. Again we come to one which has a long arcade or temple of arched windows clipped out of high arbor vitæ extending across the whole front of its garden. In the arches are framed delicious views of the distant blue mountains, their tops now powdered with snow.

What a place it should be, this land of running brooks, for the youngsters to play at sailing their boats in, though as a matter of fact we never see them doing it. Perhaps there is a law against it. There are laws for stealing the water, or for wantonly raising a gate to waste it, or for transferring it to other irrigators outside the city limits. These latter are entitled to it only upon an extra payment and after those within the city have been supplied. As all the irrigators can not be supplied at once, the manner of serving out the water is as follows: Application has to be made in the last week of each month by those who need it. The Zanjero apportions the supply so that it may pass around among the several applicants in the most convenient way. The complete circuit takes about twenty days. The applicant receives a ticket, on the payment of his fee, entitling him to receive the water at such a day and such an hour, and the right to that time is exclusively his. The rates are so fixed as to reimburse the public treasury, and are not intended as a source of profit. The average charge for the use of the water is about fifty cents by the hour, two dollars a day, or a dollar and twenty-five cents if taken during the night.

The subscriber receives the water from the deputy at his own connecting gate. At all other times the gate must be kept fastened with its secure padlock. The little gate with its handles is like a wooden shovel. Or again, as it slides smoothly downward in its grooves, it recalls the guillotine.

Chop! goes the little guillotine down upon the stream, and off goes its head. Then the surprised current, thus checked on its way among the orchards and gardens, writhes and twists in its box, but presently comes to life again, mournfully

accepts the situation, and is ready for a new career at a higher level.

Los Angeles is the metropolis of the orange trade, but the greater part of the culture itself is in numerous tracts in the surrounding country, each of which has a thriving settlement of its own as a nucleus. The lands have usually been laid out and subdivided by capitalists under the "colony" system, as described in a former article. Ten or even five acres in the valuable crops here cultivated are a comfortable property. It may be remembered that along the Italian Lake Guarda so small a piece as half an acre in lemon cultivation is found sufficient for the maintenance of a family. It is in evidence that a return of from $500 to $1000 an acre annually is frequently reaped in Southern California from the orange, lemon, and lime, after the trees have arrived at full bearing. But it will be more charming to gather our information on the spot from the orange-planters themselves. Their piazzas command attractive views; the perfume of rose and heliotrope hangs round them; and specimens of all the fruits are brought forth for our tasting, both with a lavish hospitality and an honest pride in their perfection.

We may begin with Pasadena, which is reached by a drive of ten miles from Los Angeles, or take the train and drop down in the village of San Gabriel at once. Pasadena, the Indiana Colony, San Gabriel, the Lake Vineyard tract, the Alhambra, Santa Anita, and Sierra Madre tracts, and others, all of the same general character, adjoin one another. The dwellings in them are those of people of means and a certain taste. Even the least show ambition. There are pretty chapels in the Gothic style, and neat school-houses. Well-dressed children of a city air are seen going along the roads. The roads themselves are excellent. There are no violent storms or thawing snows in this climate to tear them up, and they are kept in order with little trouble. The better yards are inclosed with hedges of lime, arbor vitæ, or rose-bushes. Some curious circles on the places from time to time attract attention. They are either filled with water, or dry, with the appearance of those rings left behind by a departed circus. These are found to be small reservoirs, used to supplement the all-pervading irrigation system. They are usually filled by the Artesian well, which flows

PARADISE.—[SEE NEXT PAGE.]

from an iron pipe rising a few feet above the ground. The water overspreads the top in a thin film, like a globe of glass, and reflects neighboring objects. These sparkling films from the pipe of an Artesian well can be seen at a considerable distance, and are a frequent item in the prospect in Southern California. As there has never been any forest, there are no unsightly stumps to indicate recent clearings. The country, in consequence, does not look new. Where settled at all, it has a surprisingly "old-fashioned" and civilized air.

The temperature, this late November day—on which there are telegrams in all the papers of snow-storms at the north and east—is perfection. It is neither hot nor cold. A sybarite would not alter it. Bees are humming in the heliotrope, climbing high upon the porches. A lovely Jacqueminot rose on its tall stem, an imperious beauty whose sway will not be gainsaid, makes its vivid crimson felt by the eye from a long distance. When we arrive among the older estates, this is pointed out as the home of Don Benito, that of Don Tomas, so and so, the family name being usually American. Audacious in love as in other things, enterprising Americans have married into the Spanish families, both before and since the conquest, and succeeded to their acres. Very few of the genuine Spanish stock still retain any properties of note.

If there be or ever existed any real earthly paradise, I think it might bear some such complexion as that of a place called the Sierra Madre Villa, which is a small hotel on the first bold rise of the mountains. I can not vouch for it as a hotel, but I can vouch for it as a situation. The air was heavy with the fragrance from extensive avenues of limes as we came up to it. The orange-trees were propped, to prevent their breaking under their weight of fruit. Forty oranges on a single bough, so close together as to touch—I have seen it with my own eyes. Some of the trees, by a freak of a recent gale, had been denuded of all their leaves, and only the golden fruit was left hanging, with a lovely decorative effect, on the bare stems. Turning round, a view of thirty miles was had across the garden of the San Gabriel Valley. A strip of blue sea closed the horizon. On the strip of blue sea rests a slight brown spot—one can not fairly call it a jewel—which is Santa Catalina Island.

Flowering vines clustered along the piazza, part of which was inclosed with glass. In a warm nook on the greensward a young couple, reclining in extension chairs, were reading a novel—one reading aloud to the other with a gentle murmur. I trust they were a young couple of recent date, for as a place for the honey-moon it seems ideal. The orange-tree bears a close resemblance to the formal idealized plant, with its symmetrical fruit, which the mediæval painters were accustomed to construct for that momentous "tree of the knowledge of good and evil" of the first chapter of Genesis. It is an appropriate place, therefore, in the earthly paradise.

Hist! The young woman who has been reading the novel aloud rises and places herself at one side of such a tree. The young man who has been listening to it rises also, with a slight yawn, and takes his stand at the other. Oh, what is this? Is she a new Eve? She reaches forth to pluck a fruit, and extends it to him. Oh, this is terrible! Is there to be a new fall in Eden, with all its direful consequences? Why does she tempt him? There should be a Cranach, a Dürer, or Raphael here to take down once more the particulars of this distressing scene. One does not see

the serpent, it is true, who should be coiled about the tree, his head half hidden among the foliage. He is more artful in these modern days; he hides himself entirely. What does Eve wish this Adam to do? Perhaps she wishes him to buy lands which have been recommended to her above their value, and go into orange-planting. Alas! he will probably be lost forever to the higher financial life on the San Francisco Stock Board. Perhaps Satan may be figured as the real-estate man whose insidious counsels—But really there may be no pressing need for such a display of fancy upon the basis of a young matron's recommending her husband a fresh orange from the tree before his dinner.

Beware of taking sides hastily on the many controverted points that arise, and are argued with warmth on the piazzas. See too some of the drawbacks that may attend an injudicious entering into this fascinating kind of life. The orange-tree grows all the time. That is to be thought of. It calls for the frequent cares which are its due as well in winter as in summer. Not a few persons of the invalid class who had looked upon its culture as a mere pastime have been broken down through this cause, and having taken up more land than they could manage. The lesson of such cases is not to attempt too much, but to keep to the five or ten acres perhaps within one's personal capacity. Nor has it been politic to put everything into the single crop of oranges. The smaller fruits, peaches, plums, and especially apricots, for canning, which come into bearing quickly, are useful in tiding over the rather tedious period of waiting for the orange-trees to mature, and are always in profitable demand. To start existence comfortably here the new-comer should have a capital of from five to ten thousand dollars. Peculiar energy of course will do with less.

It requires about nine years to bring an orange-tree from the seed into full bearing. On the other hand, it is found that by deftly inserting an orange bud into a small shoot of lemon-tree slitted in an X shape, and setting this in the ground, a tree can be obtained which bears marketable fruit after the second year. The controversy rages as to whether it is worth while to do this, since the product is but a dwarf, like the dwarf pear-tree, and though it yields early it can never yield much, and its fruit does not stand shipment as well as that of the seedling. Against this it is maintained that it lives longer than the seedling, yields choicer varieties of fruit, more uniform in size and quality, and not subject to the singular form of destruction which sometimes overtakes the seedling, that of being dashed against its own thorns.

In the same way conflicting theories of irrigation prevail. A person who bought grapes in large quantities for the purpose of making them into wine told me that overirrigation was rendering them too watery and insipid. He proposed to meet this by establishing a standard. He would pay twenty dollars a ton for all such grapes as contained twenty-three per cent. of sugar, but if they did not come up to this standard, he would not pay as much. Plentiful irrigation, however, is relied upon to counteract that fatal pest of the vine, the phylloxera. Some advocate the theory of irrigation in the winter or rainy season only. All the water possible is to be conducted upon the land at the time it naturally falls, leaving the soil to act as its own reservoir, and store up a portion for the dry season ahead. Others, again, are found to deny the necessity of irrigation altogether. They write to the papers that all that is needed is to keep the surface well scratched with a cultivator, and that thereupon a supply of moisture will always be found a few inches below. It is certain that crops both of grapes and the cereals have been produced from unirrigated ground, often for a series of years. But then has come a dry year, in which everything, animals as well as plants, has been scorched from the face of the earth.

"No," says a brisk informant, "certainty is what is wanted. You may not need a water supply, as you may not need a revolver all the time, but when you do want it, you want it awful bad."

In the plain, just under the edge of the mountains, lies the old village and mission church of San Gabriel. The mission dates from 1761. It was founded, like all the other missions of California, by friars sent out from

IRRIGATING AN ORANGE GROVE.

VINTAGE AT SAN GABRIEL.

the college of San Fernando, in the city of Mexico. I well recollected the ecclesiastical buildings of this college of San Fernando. They stand yet on the principal street which was the scene of Cortez's disastrous retreat from the city, and are marked, I believe, with an inscription commemorating the site of the famous Leap of Alvarado. The buildings founded from this picturesque source are thoroughly worthy of it. The same massiveness, the same taste for bright color, the same quaint rococo details, including the peculiar battlement, which was a kind of Spanish horn of dominion. At this one six green old bronze bells hang in as many niches together. The fern-like shadows of a line of pepper-trees print themselves in the sunshine against the time-stained white wall. No more than the church now remains, the great agricultural establishments connected with these missions having been swept away years before the American occupation by edict of the Mexican government. Some bits of broken aqueduct, and a few orange-trees above a hundred years old, in what was once the mission garden, are the only vestiges of former prosperity. The interior of the church contains a few battered old religious paintings, always of the worst type of their kind. It is doubtful if the luxury of good pictures was ever superadded in these establishments to the excellent architecture, for which there seems to have been a natural instinct.

The village is piquantly foreign. Its single street is composed entirely of white adobe houses. One of them, with a tumbling red-tiled roof, is so full of holes that it looks as if it had been shelled. All the signs are in Spanish. Here is the Zapatero, or shoemaker, and here the Panadería, or bakery. The south walls are hung with a drapery of red peppers drying in the sun to prepare the favorite condiment. The population are a humble class who gain their livelihood for the most part by day-labor on the surrounding estates. They are not too poor, however, to retain their taste for festivity still. On the occasion of some notable wedding among them they will manage to mount on horseback, and surrounding a bridal carriage driven postilion-fashion, return from the ceremony at the old mission whooping and firing pistols in the air in the most gallant and hilarious fashion.

Near by here is the large estate known as Sunny Slope, one of the most successful instances of the actual putting in practice of the sanguine representations about the capacity of the country. It has been entirely acquired and developed by its owner from very small beginnings. It consists of some nineteen hundred acres of land, most of it in vineyard and oranges. There is a large wine and brandy making establishment on the place. Eight thousand boxes of oranges and lemons, with four hundred thousand gallons of wine and one hundred thousand of brandy, have been produced at this place in a year.

The dwelling-house was approached up a stately double avenue of orange-trees, three-quarters of a mile in length. The road to the large substantial buildings of the winery was bordered by a deep orchard of oranges on one side and of olives on the other. The vineyards were seen stretching out below, in effect at a distance like vast reddish-tawny meadows. At the winery, blacksmithing and coopering were going on on a large scale, and a deft Chinaman was constructing the light orange boxes. The rich juice of the grape poured in floods, and the more concentrated essence which makes distilled spirits came from its still as clear as water. It appears that it is naturally colorless, and the color which it obtains for market is given it by burned sugar, to gratify an artificial taste.

The hands are both Chinamen and Mexicans. The superintendent tells us that the former do the most work and get less pay, but that there are certain things which they can not do. They can not plough, for instance, nor prune the vines, and they are awkward at the management of all animals. Indeed, a Chinaman on horseback, owing probably to their lack of experience in their own country, or even in a wagon, seems almost as incongruous as Jack Tar. We visited one evening the quarters in which they have their abode. It would be hard to find a more cleanly and domestic-looking interior among men of any other nationality in the same circumstances of life. They seemed much more orderly in their arrangements than their Mexican confrères, either those who came from the village or those who had a settlement on the estate itself, on the slope above.

There is much native Indian blood among these latter. We found their dwellings half wigwams, patched up out of rubbish. Mongrel dogs, a donkey, and a foundered horse wandered about among them. A reddish-brown urchin of large liquid eyes came out from one of them to look at us.

"*Cor-r-re, demonio de muchacho!*" (R-r-run, demon of a boy!) cried his slatternly mother, who appeared behind him, endeavoring to urge him upon some expeditious errand.

But the demoniac boy, exemplifying the traits of his race, had no idea whatever of being in a hurry. On the con-

A MEXICAN WEDDING.

MONGOLIAN AND MEXICAN.

trary, having removed himself to a safe distance, he dawdled in the most exasperating way, and continued to stare round-eyed at the strangers who had arrived near his abode on their critical tour of inspection.

The work of the year now was the pruning of the vines. Stripped of all superfluous runners, the rugged little stocks, regimented like veterans, were to stand bare and brown till the exuberance of a new spring should start forth in them. Faustino, Gaetano, Incarnacion, and the rest of their picturesque companions appear to good advantage in this work. Their swarthy faces are framed in slouching sombreros. They wear red and blue shirts, and handkerchiefs about their necks. They move forward in line, each with a pruning-knife in his hand, and a small saw at his belt for the tougher knots. The bright spots of color stand out upon the russet of the vineyard; the pruning-knives flash as they turn to the sun; the ground has a gentle, agreeable fall; and the splintered granite mountains, with a promise of attractive cañons among them for ex-

ploration, softened by a veil of atmosphere, back up the whole.

The orange-tree, even at a great age, is not found as large as one may have expected. Those in the old mission garden are not above two feet in diameter. It is gratifying to be at full liberty to examine this attractive kind of vegetation, which one may have known before only in its tub in the conservatory, or on the staircase at a ball. There seems but one drawback to an orange grove, and that is that it can not have a greensward below it. It is very exacting; it requires all the nourishment the soil can give. No other crop, not even grass, can be permitted between. The soil must be kept loosened and free around its roots. It must be irrigated about once a month, and the surface gone over with a cultivator afterward to prevent its baking.

The orange grove is lovely at all times. It has a mysterious air when the long alleys are dark against the red of sunset. At twilight the fruit glimmers on its boughs like a feast of lanterns not yet fully lighted. Or in the free pleasant mornings we watch the sparkle of the yellow globes among the glossy dark leaves, and catch, perhaps, the perfume of some few blossoms heralding in a new crop while the last still hangs. Here and there an enormous shad-dock, resembling the orange in appearance but the lemon in character, varies the uni-formity. The lemon itself, less hardy in rearing than the orange, is not cultivated on the same large scale. The Chinamen, with ladders and baskets, are seen gathering the fruit, and chattering to one another from the trees like magpies. It is irriga-tion-day. All at once the water is let on. Twisting and turning it runs out eagerly upon the land from its con-duit. Chinamen with hoes follow it, throwing up little dams before it, which it tries to dodge and evade. Else-where, when it runs too sluggish, they open little channels before it, and lead it where it should go. The whole surface of the orchard is soon babbling musically with running waters, and in train to be efficiently soaked.

PRIVATE RESIDENCE AT RIVERSIDE.

These and kindred scenes are to be met with in fifty, and I know not how many more, localities, towns, hamlets, "colo-nies," of a similar sort. San Fernando, Florence, Compton, Downey City, West-minster, Orange, Tustin City, Centralia, Pomona, and Artesia, in various direc-tions, may be mentioned as among lead-ing examples. The "colony" govern-ment is of a simple sort, consisting of a justice of the peace, constable, water over-seer, and school trustees. Anaheim, set-tled by Germans, one of the first estab-lished colonies, has become a town of im-portance. Santa Ana has a special bustle of its own just at present, as the terminus for the time being of the railroad build-ing from Los Angeles to San Diego.

Perhaps, however, the greatest air of general distinction is worn by Riverside. This colony seems to have been sought to an exceptional degree by persons in good circumstances. It is fifty-seven miles lower down than Los Angeles, and is reached by a drive of seven miles south-ward from the Southern Pacific Railroad station at Colton. Four miles northward from Colton takes us to San Bernardino, an important place of six thousand peo-ple, originally settled by Mormons. The real Mor-mons were withdrawn to Utah by order of Brigham Young on the threat of co-ercive war in 1857, and only a few "Josephites" now re-main, whose practices do not differ greatly from oth-er people's.

At Riverside is found a continuous belt of settle-ment and cultivation twelve miles long—to be twenty when it is finished—by two miles in average width. The population is not large, but it requires, as is seen, a

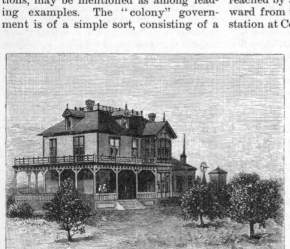

COTTAGE AT RIVERSIDE.

A SYLVAN GLIMPSE, RIVERSIDE.

great deal of room. The general situation is a valley of about forty miles square, and an elevation of twelve hundred feet above the sea. The only access to this valley is by four several passes, one each to the north, south, east, and west, as if so many doors had been providentially left in the encompassing mountain ranges. The settlement forms an oasis in the midst of the desert, as before described. Its fresh greenness and clear water canals, along which sylvan glimpses, almost English, are to be met with, derive an added charm and interest from the contrast. The rest of the high quadrangular valley, capable, no doubt, of as great development if water could be brought upon it, as yet remains in its natural condition.

A lovely drive, called Magnolia Avenue, planted with double rows of pepper and eucalyptus trees, extends through the whole length of the place from north to south. It is bordered with homes, many of which make pretensions to much more than comfort. The best of these are at the division called Arlington, located four miles below the post-office of Riverside proper. The native adobe, or sun-dried brick, supplemented with ornamental wood-work, has been used as material with excellent effect. In the interiors are found rugs, portières, Morris's wall-papers, and all the paraphernalia of Eastern civilization. Arlington rejoices, besides, in an archery club and a "German." Invalidism is heard of with considerable frequency as an excuse for the migration hither. Certainly many advantages are offered the invalid. The climate permits him to be almost constantly out-of-doors. The sky is blue, the sun unclouded nearly every day in the year, and he can go into his orchard and concern himself about his Navel or Brazilian varieties, his paper-rind St. Michaels, and his Tahiti seedlings, without let or hinderance. Orange culture affords him both a career and a revenue. If the unchanging blue of the sky grows sometimes monotonous, there are other distractions to turn to in the noble mountains on the horizons. Riverside has from this source a touch of the charm so attractive in Switzerland. Your entertainer points out to you from his piazza the great peaks of Greylock, San Bernardino, and San Jacinto, from ten to twelve thousand feet in height, and crowned with snow for a considerable part of the year, just as the Jungfrau is pointed out from Interlaken and Mont Blanc from Geneva.

To say a word further as to the climate, it is a description that applies to all of Southern California, that however great may be the heats by day, which in midsummer often rise to a hundred and five in the shade, the nights are always cool and refreshing. Neither is sun-stroke known. Nor are the violent thunderstorms with which nature with us endeavors to restore the equilibrium after having exhausted its utmost efforts in the way of oppressive warmth. The great drawback here—as there must be some drawback from perfection everywhere—is occasional heavy winds, the "northers." The northers sometimes gather up the dust from the dry surfaces over which they pass, and produce painful dust-storms of two or three days' duration.

In autumn and winter the temperature is chilly enough to make fires a necessity morning and evening, and even all day long in apartments shut off from the influence of the sun. I was astonished to find the air so keen at these times, and the thin scum of ice forming upon water in the mornings so formidable even as far down as San Diego and its vicinity. The cold has a penetrating quality far beyond that of its register by the thermometer. This is usually overlooked, and it is important to be understood, since fuel is very scarce and correspondingly dear. Fagots made from prunings of the cottonwoods, sycamores, and mesquit-trees along the beds of the streams are the principal resource. Such coal as can be obtained is both costly and of wretched quality.

The water for the irrigation of Riverside is taken from the swift little stream of the Santa Ana River, which falls so rapidly within a short compass that it has been found feasible to take out two separate canals with a difference of thirty-five feet in their levels. On all sides lands are held at $200 and $300 per acre, and when the orange-trees have come into good bearing, at $1000 per acre, which but a few years ago were purchased at one dollar and a quarter.

All these places have their local rivalries, though the section of Southern California, as a whole, is ready to unite jealously, on any point involving the validity of its claims, against the outside world. All have their pamphlets to distribute, their tables of mean temperatures and altitudes, their analyses of soils, and their claims to regard based upon nearness to or absence from some particular natural feature. Thus the coast counties pride themselves upon the genial average at which their temperature is kept by the sea, free from the extremes of heat and cold afflicting those which are shut in behind the mountain barriers. The inland counties, on the other hand, congratulate themselves on their lot that the mountains form a charming defense against the raw fogs and stormy gusts blowing in directly from the chill ocean.

These petty rivalries are a part of the history of new countries, and will pass away with the development of population and trade. There seems no need of jealousies, since there is encouragement enough for all in their several ways. The Territories of Arizona and New Mexico have just been opened to transportation by rail from this quarter. The lands suitable for the cultivation of the "citrus fruits," too, are limited in extent. The market is much more likely to improve than decline, even when the production shall have increased greatly over its present scale. High railroad freights were at one time a cause of alarm. The making of "orange wine" was proposed as a resource for using up the surplus crop. This was not a success, and fortunately it is not likely to be needed. Railroad freights have declined, and will decline more still with the building of the new roads. Shipments of oranges have been successfully made from this section as far away as Denver, Chicago, and St. Louis.

Great things are predicted of Wilmington, a little port twenty-two miles to the southwest of Los Angeles. The extensive works undertaken there by the railroad and the United States government are still incomplete, and it is but a dreary little place in its present condition. However, great ports have never been selected primarily for picturesqueness, but in accordance with such commercial necessities as short lines of transit, easy grades, and convenience for shipping. Wilmington had few natural conveniences to offer. There were originally but eighteen inches of water on its bar. This has been increased to ten feet. An enormous jetty 6700 feet long, extending out to what is called Dead Man's Island, is in progress of construction. It is to force the tide itself to do the duty of scouring out the bottom, so that a ship channel several miles long will eventually be utilized. Santa Monica is another small port at the end of a branch railroad from Los Angeles, sixteen miles directly west. It is somewhat famed as a sea-side resort. It has a hotel of considerable size, and a bold situation on a pretty horseshoe bay. The beach is of a fine hard sand, and the temperature admits of bathing, if one be inclined for it, all the year round. The hopes which were at one time entertained here also by capitalists like Senator Jones, of Nevada, of making the place a great shipping point, have been for the present abandoned. It was to have been the Pacific terminus of a new through line from the East, coming by way of the Cajon Pass. A wharf 1500 feet long was built, and a breakwater proposed.

From here, or from Wilmington, one sails up the coast to San Buenaventura and to Santa Barbara—favored of invalids. These places have as yet no railroad, but must before long become connected with the general system. Both are on that sheltered stretch of the coast which from Point Conception makes a sharp turn to the eastward, and has the direct southern exposure and a view of the islands of the Santa Barbara Channel. Santa Barbara, considered on its practical side, has devoted more attention than most places to the culture of the olive—an industry, however, which is still in its infancy. Some of the cultivators have provided themselves with a machinery, which costs about a thousand dollars, for expressing the oil. As a condiment the fruit is not pickled green here, like the Spanish olive, but ripe and black. It may be that a special education is needed for liking each variety of olives, as it is to acquire the taste in the beginning. Those in cultivation here are of a small variety, descending from the old mission times, and it is hard not to find them just at present either insipid or bitter. A leading industry of the county of which San Buenaventura is the capital—Ventura County—is the raising of honey. A product of one million pounds per annum is not an unusual quantity.

We sailed from Wilmington to San Diego. We embarked in the evening at this place in a small tug, which steamed down the tortuous windings of the channel, past black lighters that Whistler would have liked to etch, and past Dead Man's Island, and transferred us on board the coast steamer waiting without. Next morning we were at our destination, a hundred miles below. San Diego, rising on a gentle slope, makes a pretty appearance from the water. A United States barracks of yellow buildings, with a flag-staff rising in the centre, is the most prominent detail of the foreground. We rounded an immensely long narrow sand-spit of a peninsula, which contributes to form the excellent small harbor, and made fast to the long mooring wharf. It is a feature of California ports to have an immensely long wharf. To the left is "Old Town," its *playa*, the beach where Dana once loaded his hides in his "hide drogher," now become the site of a Chinese fishing village. To the right is the brand-new "National City," the location of the shops and extensive dépôt grounds for the new railway. In the centre, at a distance of about four miles from each, lies "New Town," or San Diego proper. All together have a population of about five thousand.

As we came up to the wharf a locomotive and tender, starting out from National City, made, on the new track, the whole circuit of the water-front with a formidable noise. Its whole progress was one long shrill scream, which was taken up by the hills and echoed back with terrific effect. Gods and men could no longer remain ignorant that San Diego had at last its railroad—had at last, to this extent, overtaken its future. It was cruelly disappointed once before when it was to have been the terminus of the Texas Pacific, transcontinental, road, and the panic of '73 prevented the capitalist "Tom Scott" from negotiating the foreign loan which was needed for its completion. That enterprise was abandoned, and a half-mile of graded road-bed alone remains as a sort of tumulus erected to the blighted hopes and bitter memories of the time. The name of "Tom Scott"—perhaps happily since defunct—has remained a by-word and reproach. Now, however, the "California Southern" is actually at work, and under contract to complete the one hundred and sixteen miles necessary to meet the Southern Pacific, at a point near San Bernardino, within a very short time. This road is to be a link in the new "Atlantic and Pacific," which is to follow the thirty-fifth parallel, and become a transcontinent-

PLAZA AT SAN DIEGO, OLD TOWN.

al road by means of connection with the Atchison, Topeka, and Santa Fe.

The capital and management of the California Southern are largely supplied from Boston. It is important to know that the same parties have leading interests in works under the new railway era which is revolutionizing Mexico, particularly in the Mexican Central, from El Paso, in Texas, to the city of Mexico. They have also the line from the Mexican port of Guaymas, on the Gulf of California, to the Arizona frontier at Calabasas. A further road is projected by them eastward from San Diego to Calabasas, passing through Port Ysabel, at the head of the Gulf of California. This could be built more cheaply just below the Mexican frontier than on this side of it, owing to special exemptions from taxation, and the lower rates of labor there prevailing. It is thought that the Southern Pacific will be compelled by competition to build across from Yuma. Hopes, it may be said, are still entertained of the derelict Texas Pacific. With all this in prospect, it may be seen that San Diego has at present justification for making a good deal of stir over the facts that it is many hundreds of miles nearer than San Francisco

to New Orleans and New York on the one hand, and to the Orient on the other, and for being correspondingly cheerful.

A low hand-car running on a track upon the long wharf conveys our baggage up into the town while we walk beside it. The town on being reached is found to be a place of loose texture. It has a disproportionately large hotel, the Horton House, which was built in anticipation of future greatness, and proved a loss to its proprietor. The blue shades are down and the plate-glass windows dusty also in much of the "Horton Block," opposite, which still wears an expectant look. After '73, it is said, half the shutters in San Diego were nailed up. They have now come down, however, no doubt to stay. There is a charming view of the harbor and of deep blue ocean beyond from the upper slope. A part of the view is a group of Mexican islands, particularly the bold Coronado— a solid mass of red sandstone, which American prospectors have tried to get a cession of as a quarry, but without success. Yes, there is old Mexico again close by; we have come back to it. A high flat-topped peak, Table Mountain, of the type of those we used to see in our geographies, rises out of it as if to distinguish it without fail.

DON JUAN FORSTER.

It is common to drive down from here to "the Monument," set up to mark the dividing line from the Mexican province of Baja (Lower) California.

The chronic condition of shutters in San Diego "Old Town" is to be nailed up—that is to say, so far as it can be said to have shutters still remaining. It dates from 1769. Having been found disadvantageously situated as regards the bay, it began to be deserted in favor of the newer site about ten years ago. Nothing is more desolate now. The usual old mission, with a few palms and olives about it, stands in a valley up the pretty San Diego River, and the earth-works of Commodore Stockton, who threw them up one night before the enemy knew he was ashore, are seen on the hill. Rents should be cheap in Old Town, and yet, according to the few gossips who still sit around under the piazzas by the decayed old plaza, they are not. The owners hold them stiffly, on what theory Heaven knows. The plaza has a toppling flag-staff, a decayed music stand, and vestiges of a number of burned-down edifices which it has never been worth anybody's while to build up again. The broken "Merchants' Exchange" will never supply cocktails to thirsty souls again; the Cosmopolitan Hotel, though wrecked only financially, is without a guest; whole rows of weather-beaten adobe houses—whole quarters of them—

stand vacant. It should be a famous place for ghosts, provided they care for one another's society. The children of the place, all Spanish apparently, coming home from school—for there is yet, it seems, a school—knock loudly at the vacant doors, peer in at the window-panes, and run away.

Instead of leaving San Diego by more conventional way, we traversed the surveyed line of the new railroad, the direction of which is almost due northward. The journey, after the thirty-mile section of railroad already built, was made chiefly by wagon, with an occasional half-day's pedestrianism, for which the dry, smooth surface of the ground is well adapted. It afforded an opportunity of making the acquaintance in a leisurely way of some of the ranchmen, small and great, of the old school. The principal one of these was old Don Juan Forster, a man (deceased since this visit) very well known in his section. He was an Englishman by birth, but came out when a youth with his father in a trading vessel, and became a Mexican subject and a resident of California long before the American conquest. It was so long before that he had well-nigh forgotten his English, and had to learn it over again when they arrived. His señora, a sister of old Governor Pio Pico, never learned it more than her conservative brother. Don Juan's estate, called the Santa Margarita Ranch, comprised an area of twenty-seven miles by fourteen, or one hundred and forty-five thousand acres

SEÑORA FORSTER.

FORSTER'S RANCH.

of land. There is one fence seventeen miles in length, and another of ten. The late owner made two distinct efforts to colonize a portion of this land, but without great success. He offered in London to give forty acres and the use of three cows and two horses to whoever would put upon the land improvements in the shape of houses, vineyards, etc., to the amount of $1000.

The Santa Margarita ranch-house was of adobe, very thick walled. It was approached by a terrace, and had an interior court-yard. The waiting at table was done by a broad-faced Indian woman in calico. All the domestic service was performed by those same mission Indians, except the cooking, for which a Chinaman had lately been secured, with the view of having meals on time. The manner of living on these great places was found comfortable, but without the "princely" features attributed to it by some imaginative narrators.

The greater part of the available land in the section through which we passed was devoted to pasture. The cereals were cultivated, but not as yet much fruit. Barley is the favorite cereal, since it is less liable to "rust" than wheat. Hay is made, not of grass, but of wheat and barley straw, cut green, with the milk in it. Bee-culture is an important industry. A number of varieties of wild sage, with wild buckwheat and sumac, furnish bees an exceptionally good support. The rows of square hives, painted of different colors, are seen districted into regular streets upon some hill-side, or at the mouth of a small cañon, like a miniature city.

Before reaching Don Juan Forster's, the old mission of San Luis Rey, at a hamlet of the same name, is met with. It is almost Venetian in aspect. The whole exterior was at one time faced with a decorative diagonal pattern resembling that of the ducal palace. The pile was ruined by a Mormon contingent of the American force encamped there during the invasion. Parts of the heavy adobe walls and buttresses, fallen in, have resolved themselves back into their original elements, and become mere earth heaps. Within, the images have been shot and hacked down, and a yawning cavern excavated behind the battered altar in search of fancied treasure. Upon a floor strewn with such débris and fragments of red tiles from the roof a quaint daylight falls from holes in the broken dome.

The railroad traverses some striking natural scenery, notably the Temecula Cañon —a gorge of the wildest and grandest description, some ten miles in length, through the Coast Range. A brawling stream runs down its centre. The gorge was filled with a busy force of men when we passed through it. They were terracing up the track, sometimes along the natural rock, sometimes upon a cyclopean retaining-wall, composed principally of immense bowlders. Toward evening daily the firing of heavy blasts reverberated up the defile like cannonading. The main part of the laboring force consisted of Chinamen. They had utilized the shelving ledges and random nooks by the stream for their tents and cooking ovens with great ingenuity. The Mexican and Indian laborers, who formed the next contingent in importance, were in every way less provident. The surveyors were found pleasant and hospitable fellows, as surveyors when met with on the scene of their cyclopean labors are apt to be. Their tents were small, but compactness and convenience had been reduced in them to

ant of somewhat uncommon pretensions. This was a certain "Charley"—a shock-headed boy of fourteen, a son of the last Tichborne claimant, who has strangely

SAN DIEGO.

SANTA BARBARA.

SAN LUIS REY.

sprung up at San Diego. Though condemned to a menial capacity while his father (who claims to have good and sufficient reasons for keeping silent till the present time) is taking the necessary steps with his lawyer to secure the long-lost title and fortune, our "Charley" is deaf to all banter on the subject, and superciliously firm in the faith that he too is Tichborne, "and don't you forget it."

their lowest terms, and a pleasant existence seemed quite possible. A Chinese cook was attached to each camp, and the provisions were excellent. Coming up with the engineers in the construction train over the first section of completed road, we had the distinction of being waited on by a serv-

Coming out of the cañon at the van of the construction work, we were on the Temecula Plains, a part of the Upper Santa Ana Valley. The course of the road was marked henceforth only by an occasional surveyor's stake. We rode along it through fifty miles of absolutely treeless and verdureless desert. It was desert, however, with a certain fascination in its utter sterility. It had, too, a distinct beauty of coloring. The brown, drab, and blackish waste, catching some sparkles of light on its flinty surface, shimmered in the warm sunshine. A gentle breeze tempered the heat. Crags of black waterworn rock, which had once been the reefs of an inland sea, rose boldly out of it in fantastic shapes. Noble mountain ranges stood up along the distant horizons, their native harshness deliciously softened into the blues and purples of veiling atmosphere.

Half-way across we fell in with the one sign of human life, in the shape of an abandoned pine shanty. On going around to the rear, the boards constituting that side were found to have been knocked out of it, though from the front it looked quite presentable. Some former travellers, halting here like ourselves, had occupied their leisure in covering its walls with inscriptions. Under some direction by one about obtaining drinkable water, another had written vigorously, "Lyor!!" The sole piece of furniture remaining was a rusted cooking-stove on three legs. It had a

YOUNG TICHBORNE.

quaintly diabolic and knowing air; one suspected it of holding high carnival with the coyotes, the gophers, tarantulas, and lizards that dropped in to pay it visits.

EVOLUTION OF THE COW-PUNCHER

TWO men sat opposite me once, despising each other so heartily that I am unlikely to forget them. They had never met before—if they can be said to have met this time—and they were both unknown to me. It happened in a train by which we journeyed together from Leamington to London. The cause of their mutual disesteem was appearance; neither liked the other's outward man, and told him so silently for three hours; that is all they ever knew of each other. This object-lesson afterward gained greatly by my learning the name and estate of one of these gentlemen. He was a peer. He had good rugs, a good umbrella, several newspapers—but read only the pink one,—and a leather and silver thing which I took to be a travelling - bag beside him. He opened it between Banbury and Oxford, and I saw, not handkerchiefs and ivory, but cut - glass bottles with stoppers. I noticed further the strong sumptuous monogram engraved here and there. The peer leisurely took brandy, and was not aware of our presence. But the point of him is that he garnished those miles of railroad with incomparably greater comfort than we did who had no rugs, no cut glass, no sandwich-box, no monogram. He had understood life's upholstery and trappings for several hundred years, getting the best to be had in each generation of his noble descent.

The enemy that he had made, as a dog makes an enemy of a cat by the mere preliminary of being a dog, sat in the other corner. He wore a shiny silk hat, smooth new lean black trousers, with high boots stiff and swelling to stove-pipe symmetry beneath, and a tie devoid of interest. I did not ascertain if the pistol was in his hip pocket, but at stated intervals he spit out of his window. By his hawk nose and eye and the lank strength of his chin he was a male who could take care of himself, and had done so. One could be sure he had wrested success from this world somehow, somewhere; and here he was, in a first-class carriage, on a first-class train, come for a first-class time, with a mind as complacently shut against being taught by foreign travel as any American patriot of to-day can attain or recommend, or any Englishman can reveal in his ten-day book about our continent and people. Charles Dickens and Mark Twain have immortalized their own blindness almost equally; and the sad truth is that enlightenment is mostly a stay-at-home creature, who crosses neither ocean nor frontier. This stranger was of course going to have a bad time, and feel relieved to get home and tell of the absence of baggage-checks and of the effete despot who had not set up the drinks. Once he addressed the despot, who was serenely smoking.

"I'll trouble you for a light," said he; and in his drawl I heard plainly his poor opinion of feudalism.

His lordship returned the drawl—not audibly, but with his eye, which he ran slowly up and down the stranger. His was the Piccadilly drawl; the other made use of the trans-Missouri variety; and both these are at bottom one and the same —the Anglo-Saxon's note of eternal contempt for whatever lies outside the beat of his personal experience. So I took an observation of these two Anglo-Saxons drawling at each other across the prejudice of a hundred years, and I thought it might come to a row. For the American was, on the quiet face of him, a "bad man," and so, to any save the provincial eye, was the nobleman. Fine feathers had deceived trans-Missouri, whose list of "bad men" was limited to specimens of the cut of his own jib, who know nothing of cut-glass bottles. But John gave Jonathan the light he asked, and for the remainder of our journey ceased to know that such a person existed.

Though we three never met again, my object-lesson did not end when we parted at Paddington. Before many seasons were sped the fortunes of the nobleman took a turn for the scandalous. He left cut glass behind him and went to Texas. I wish I could veraciously tell that he saw the stranger there—the traveller between whose bird-of-freedom nostrils and the wind his luxurious nobility had passed

so offensively. But I do know that his second and more general skirmish with democracy left both sides amicable. In fact, the nobleman won the Western heart forthwith. Took it by surprise: democracy had read in the papers so often about the despot and his effeteness. This despot vaulted into the saddle and stuck to the remarkably ingenious ponies that had been chosen with care to disconcert him. When they showed him pistols, he was found to be already acquainted with that weapon. He quickly learned how to rope a steer. The card habit ran in his noble blood as it did in the cowboy's. He could sleep on the ground and rough it with the best of them, and with the best of them he could drink and help make a town clamorous. Deep in him lay virtues and vices coarse and elemental as theirs. Doubtless the windows of St. James Street sometimes opened in his memory, and he looked into them and desired to speak with those whom he saw inside. And the whiskey was not like the old stuff in the cut-glass bottles; but he never said so; and in time he died, widely esteemed. Texas found no count against him save his pronunciation of such words as bath and fancy—a misfortune laid to the accident of his birth; and you will hear to-day in that flannel-shirted democracy only good concerning this aristocrat born and bred.

Now, besides several morals which no pious person will find difficult to draw from the decline and fall of this aristocrat, there is something more germane to my democratic contemplation: after all, when driven to flock with Texas, he was a bird of that wild feather. That is the object-lesson; that is the gist of the matter. Directly the English nobleman smelt Texas, the slumbering untamed Saxon awoke in him, and mindful of the tournament, mindful of the hunting-field, galloped howling after wild cattle, a born horseman, a perfect athlete, and spite of the peerage and gules and argent, fundamentally kin with the drifting vagabonds who swore and galloped by his side. The man's outcome typifies the way of his race from the beginning. Hundreds like him have gone to Australia, Canada, India, and have done likewise, and in our own continent you may see the thing plainer than anywhere else. No rood of modern ground is more debased and mongrel with its hordes of encroaching alien vermin, that turn our cities to Babels and our citizenship to a hybrid farce, who degrade our commonwealth from a nation into something half pawn-shop, half broker's office. But to survive in the clean cattle country requires spirit of adventure, courage, and self-sufficiency; you will not find many Poles or Huns or Russian Jews in that district; it stands as yet untainted by the benevolence of Baron Hirsch. Even in the cattle country the respectable Swedes settle chiefly to farming, and are seldom horsemen. The community of which the aristocrat appropriately made one speaks English. The Frenchman to-day is seen at his best inside a house; he can paint and he can play comedy, but he seldom climbs a new mountain. The Italian has forgotten Columbus, and sells fruit. Among the Spaniards and the Portuguese no Cortez or Magellan is found to-day. Except in Prussia, the Teuton is too often a tame, slippered animal, with his pedantic mind swaddled in a dressing-gown. But the Anglo-Saxon is still forever homesick for out-of-doors.

Throughout his career it has been his love to push further into the wilderness, and his fate thereby to serve larger causes than his own. In following his native bent he furthers unwittingly a design outside himself; he cuts the way for the common law and self-government, and new creeds, polities, and nations arise in his wake; in his own immense commonwealth this planless rover is obliterated. Roving took him (the Viking portion of him) from his Norse crags across to Albion. From that hearth of Albion the footprints of his sons lead to the corners of the earth; beside that hearth how inveterate remains his flavor! At Hastings he tasted defeat, but was not vanquished; to the Invincible Armada he proved a grievous surprise; one way or another he came through Waterloo—possibly because he is inveterately dull at perceiving himself beaten; when not otherwise busy at Balaklava or by the Alma, he was getting up horse-races, ready for sport or killing, and all with that silver and cut-glass finish which so offends our whistling, vacant-minded democracy. Greatest triumph and glory of all, because spiritual, his shoulders bore the Reformation when its own originators had tottered. Away from the hearth the cut-glass stage will not generally have been attained by him, and in

Maine or Kentucky you can recognize at sight the chip of the old rough block. But if you meet him upon his island, in the shape of a peer, and find him particular to dress for dinner seven days of the week, do not on that account imagine that his white tie has throttled the man in him. That is a whistling Fourth-of-July misconception. It's no symptom of patriotism to be unable to see a man through cut glass, and if it comes to an appraisement of the stranger and the peer, I should say, put each in the other's place, and let us see if the stranger could play the peer as completely as the nobleman played the cowboy. Sir Francis Drake was such a one; and Raleigh, the fine essence of Anglo-Saxon, with his fashionable gallant cloak, his adventure upon new seas, and his immediate appreciation of tobacco. The rover may return with looted treasure or incidentally stolen corners of territory to clap in his strong-box (this Angle is no angel), but it is not the dollars that played first fiddle with him, else our Hebrew friends would pioneer the whole of us. Adventure, to be out-of-doors, to find some new place far away from the postman, to enjoy independence of spirit or mind or body (according to his high or low standards)—this is the cardinal surviving fittest instinct that makes the Saxon through the centuries conqueror, invader, navigator, buccaneer, explorer, colonist, tiger-shooter; lifts him a pilgrim among the immortals at Plymouth Rock, dangles him a pirate from the gallows' on the docks of Bristol. At all times when historic conditions or private stress have burst his domestic crust and let him fly out naturally, there he is, on Darien's peak, or through Magellan, or across the Missouri, or up the Columbia, a Hawkins, a Boone, a Grey, or a nameless vagrant, the same Saxon, ploughing the seas and carving the forests in every shape of man, from preacher to thief, and in each shape changelessly untamed. And as he has ruled the waves with his ship from that Viking time until yesterday at Samoa, when approaching death could extract no sound from him save American cheers and music, so upon land has the horse been his foster-brother, his ally, his playfellow, from the tournament at Camelot to the round-up at Abilene. The blood and the sweat of his jousting, and all the dirt and stains, have faded in the long sunlight of tradition, and in the chronicles of romance we hear none of his curses or obscenity; the clash of his armor rings mellow and heroic down the ages into our modern ears. But his direct lineal offspring among our Western mountains has had no poet to connect him with the eternal, no distance to lend him enchantment; though he has fought single-handed with savages, and through skill and daring prevailed, though he has made his nightly bed in a thousand miles of snow and loneliness, he has not, and never will have, the "consecration of memory." No doubt Sir Launcelot bore himself with a grace and breeding of which our unpolished fellow of the cattle trail has only the latent possibility; but in personal daring and in skill as to the horse, the knight and the cowboy are nothing but the same Saxon of different environments, the nobleman in London and the nobleman in Texas; and no hoof in Sir Thomas Mallory shakes the crumbling plains with quadruped sound more valiant than the galloping that has echoed from the Rio Grande to the Big Horn Mountains. But we have no Sir Thomas Mallory! Since Hawthorne, Longfellow, and Cooper were taken from us, our flippant and impoverished imagination has ceased to be national, and the rider among Indians and cattle, the frontiersman, the American who replaces Miles Standish and the Pathfinder, is now beneath the notice of polite writers.

From the tournament to the round-up! Deprive the Saxon of his horse, and put him to forest-clearing or in a counting-house for a couple of generations, and you may pass him by without ever seeing that his legs are designed for the gripping of saddles. Our first hundred years afforded his horsemanship but little opportunity. Though his out-of-door spirit, most at home when at large, sported free in the elbow-room granted by the surrender of Cornwallis, it was on foot and with an axe that he chiefly enjoyed himself. He moved his log cabin slowly inward from the Atlantic, slowly over the wooded knolls of Cumberland and Allegheny, down and across the valley beyond, until the infrequent news of him ceased, and his kinsfolk who had staid by the sea, and were merchanting themselves upwards to the level of family portraits and the cut-glass finish, forgot that the prodigal in the backwoods belonged to them, and was part of their United States, bone of their bone. And thus did our wide country become as a man whose East hand knoweth not what his West hand doeth.

Mr. Herndon, in telling of Lincoln's early days in Illinois, gives us a complete picture of the roving Saxon upon our continent in 1830. "The boys . . . . were a terror to the entire region—seemingly a necessary product of frontier civilization. They were friendly and good-natured. . . . They would do almost anything for sport or fun, love or necessity. Though rude and rough, though life's forces ran over the edge of their bowl, foaming and sparkling in pure deviltry for deviltry's sake, . . . yet place before them a poor man who needed their aid, . . . a defenceless woman, . . . they melted into sympathy and charity at once. They gave all they had, and willingly toiled or played cards for more. . . . A stranger's introduction was likely to be the most unpleasant part of his acquaintance. . . . They were in the habit of 'cleaning out' New Salem." Friendly and good-natured, and in the habit of cleaning out New Salem! Quite so. There you have him. Here is the American variety of the Saxon set down for you as accurately as if Audubon himself had done it. A colored plate of Robin Hood and the Sheriff of Nottingham should go on the opposite page. Nothing but the horse is left out of the description, and that is because the Saxon and his horse seldom met during the rail-splitting era of our growth. But the man of 1830 would give away all that he had and play cards for more. Decidedly nothing was missing except the horse—and the horse was waiting in another part of our large map until the man should arrive and jump on his back again.

A few words about this horse — the horse of the plains. Whether or no his forefathers looked on when Montezuma fell, they certainly hailed from Spain. And whether it was missionaries or thieves who carried them northward from Mexico, until the Sioux heard of the new animal, certain it also is that this pony ran wild for a century or two, either alone or with various red-skinned owners; and as he gathered the sundry experiences of war and peace, of being stolen, and of being abandoned in the snow at inconvenient distances from home, of being ridden by two women and a baby at once, and of being eaten by a bear, his wide range of contretemps brought him a wit sharper than the street Arab's, and an attitude towards life more blasé than in the united capitals of Europe. I have frequently caught him watching me with an eye of such sardonic depreciation that I felt it quite vain to attempt any hiding from him of my incompetence; and as for surprising him, a locomotive cannot do it, for I have tried this. He relishes putting a man in absurd positions, and will wait many days in patience to compass this uncharitable thing; and when he cannot bring a man to derision, he contents himself with a steer or a buffalo, helping the man to rope and throw these animals with an ingenuity surpassing any circus, to my thinking. A number of delighted passengers on the Kansas Pacific Railway passed by a Mexican vaquero, who had been sent out from Kansas City to rope a buffalo as an advertisement for the stock-yards. The train stopped to take a look at the solitary horseman fast to a buffalo in the midst of the plains. José, who had his bull safely roped, shouted to ask if they had water on the train. "We'll bring you some," said they. "Oh, I come get," said he; and jumping off, he left his accomplished pony in sole charge of the buffalo. Whenever the huge beast struggled for freedom, the clever pony stiffened his legs and leaned back as in a tug of war, by jumps and dodges so anticipating each move of the enemy that escape was entirely hopeless. The boy got his drink, and his employer sent out a car for the buffalo, which was taken in triumph into Kansas City behind the passenger train. The Mexican narrated the exploit to his employer thus: "Oh, Shirley, when the train start they all give three greata big cheers for me, and then they give three mucha bigger cheers for the little gray hoss!"

Ah, progress is truly a wonder! and admirable beyond all doubt it is to behold the rapid new square miles of brick, and the stream rich with the contributions of an increased population, and tall factories that have stopped dividends just for the present, and long empty railroads in the hands of the receiver; but I prefer that unenlightened day when we had plenty of money and cheered for the little gray hoss. Such was the animal that awaited the coming of the rail-splitter. The meeting was a long way off in 1830. Not the Mexican war, not the gold on the Pacific

in '49 (though this, except for the horse, revealed the whole Saxon at his best and worst, and for a brief and beautiful moment waked once more the American muse), not any national event until the war of the rebellion was over and we had a railroad from coast to coast, brought the man and his horse together. It was in the late sixties that this happened in Texas. The adventurous sons of Kentucky and Tennessee, forever following the native bent to roam, and having no longer a war to give them the life they preferred, came into a new country full of grass and cattle. Here they found Mexicans by the hundred, all on horses and at large over the flat of the world. This sight must have stirred memories in the rail-splitter's blood, for he joined the sport upon the instant. I do not think he rode with bolder skill than the Mexican's, but he brought other and grittier qualities to bear upon that wild life, and also the Saxon contempt for the foreigner. Soon he had taken what was good from this small, deceitful alien, including his name, *Vaquero*, which he translated into Cowboy. He took his saddle, his bridle, his spurs, his rope, his methods of branding and herding — indeed, most of his customs and accoutrements—and with them he went rioting over the hills. His play-ground was two thousand miles long and a thousand wide. The hoofs of his horse were tough as iron, and the pony waged the joyous battle of self-preservation as stoutly as did his rider. When the man lay rolled in his blankets sleeping, warm and unconcerned beneath a driving storm of snow, the beast pawed through to the sage-brush and subsisted; so that it came to be said of such an animal, "A meal a day is enough for a man who gets to ride that horse."

The cow-puncher's play-ground in those first glorious days of his prosperity included battle and murder and sudden death as every-day matters. From 1865 to 1878 in Texas he fought his way with knife and gun, and any hour of the twenty-four might see him flattened behind the rocks among the whiz of bullets and the flight of arrows, or dragged bloody and folded together from some adobe hovel. Seventy-five dollars a month and absolute health and strength were his wages; and when the news of all this excellence drifted from Texas eastward, they came in shoals — Saxon boys of picked courage (none but plucky ones could survive) from South and North, from town and country. Every sort and degree of home tradition came with them from their far birthplaces. Some had known the evening hymn at one time, others could remember no parent or teacher earlier than the street; some spoke with the gentle accent of Virginia, others in the dialect of baked beans and codfish; here and there was the baccalaureate, already beginning to forget his Greek alphabet, but still able to repeat the two notable words with which Xenophon always marches upon the next stage of his journey. Hither to the cattle country they flocked from forty kinds of home, each bringing a deadly weapon.

What motlier tribe, what heap of cards shuffled from more various unmatched packs, could be found? Yet this tribe did not remain motley, but soon grew into a unit. To begin with, the old spirit burned alike in all, the unextinguished fire of adventure and independence. And then, the same stress of shifting for self, the same vigorous and peculiar habits of life, were forced upon each one: watching for Indians, guarding huge herds at night, chasing cattle, wild as deer, over rocks and counties, sleeping in the dust and waking in the snow, cooking in the open, swimming the swollen rivers. Such gymnasium for mind and body develops a like pattern in the unlike. Thus, late in the nineteenth century, was the race once again subjected to battles and darkness, rain and shine, to the fierceness and generosity of the desert. Destiny tried her latest experiment upon the Saxon, and plucking him from the library, the haystack, and the gutter, set him upon his horse; then it was that, face to face with the eternal simplicity of death, his modern guise fell away and showed once again the mediæval man. It was no new type, no product of the frontier, but just the original kernel of the nut with the shell broken.

This bottom bond of race unified the divers young men, who came riding from various points of the compass, speaking university and gutter English simultaneously; and as the knights of Camelot prized their armor and were particular about their swords, so these dusty successors had an extreme pride of equipment, and put aside their jeans and New York suits for the tribal dress. Though each

particle of gearing for man and horse was evoked from daily necessity, gold and silver instantly stepped in to play their customary ornamental part, as with all primitive races. The cow-puncher's legs must be fended from the thorny miles of the Rio Grande, the thousand mongrel shrubs that lace their bristles together stiff over the country—the mesquite, the shin-oak, the cat's-claw, the Spanish-dagger; widespreading, from six inches to ten feet high, every vegetable vicious with an embroidery of teeth and nails; a continent of peevish thicket called *chaparral*, as we indiscriminately call a dog with too many sorts of grandfathers a cur. Into this saw-mill dives the wild steer through paths and passages known to himself, and after him the pursuing man must also dive at a rate that would tear his flesh to ribbons if the blades and points could get hold of him. But he cases his leg against the hostile *chaparral* from thigh to ankle in chaps—leathern breeches, next door to armor: his daily bread is scarcely more needful to him. Soon his barbaric pleasure in finery sews tough leather fringe along their sides, and the leather flap of the pocket becomes stamped with a heavy rose. Sagging in a slant upon his hips leans his leather belt of cartridges buckled with jaunty arrogance, and though he uses his pistol with murderous skill, it is pretty, with ivory or mother-of-pearl for a handle. His arm must be loose to swing his looped rope free and drop its noose over the neck of the animal that bounds in front of his rushing pony. Therefore he rides in a loose flannel shirt that will not cramp him as he whirls the coils; but the handkerchief knotted at his throat, though it is there to prevent sunburn, will in time of prosperity be chosen for its color and soft texture, a scarf to draw the eye of woman. His heavy splendid saddle is, in its shape and luxury of straps and leather thongs, the completest instrument for night and day travel, and the freighting along with you of board and lodging, that any nomad has so far devised. With its trappings and stamped leather, its horn and high cantle, we are well acquainted. It must stand the strain of eight hundred sudden pounds of live beef tearing at it for freedom; it must be the anchor that shall not drag during the furious rages of such a typhoon. For the cattle of the wilderness have often run wild for three, four, and five years, through rocks and forests, never seeing the face of man from the day when as little calves they were branded. And some were never branded at all. They have grown up in company with the deer, and like the deer they fly at the approach of the horseman. Then, if he has ridden out to gather these waifs from their remote untenanted pastures and bring them in to be counted and driven to sale, he must abandon himself to the headlong pursuit. The open easy plain with its harmless footing lies behind, the steep valley narrows up to an entering wedge among the rocks, and into these untoward regions rush the beeves. The shale and detritus of shelving landslides, the slippery knobs in the beds of brooks, the uncertain edges of the jumping-off place, all lie in the road of the day's necessity, and where the steer goes, goes the cow-puncher too — balancing, swaying, doubling upon his shrewd pony. The noose uncoiling flies swinging through the air and closes round the throat—or perhaps only the hind leg—of the quarry. In the shock of stopping short or of leaning to circle, the rider's stirrups must be long, and his seat a forked pliant poise on the horse's back; no grip of the knee will answer in these contortions; his leg must have its straight length, a lever of muscle and sinew to yield or close vise-like on the pony's ribs; and when the steer feels that he is taken and the rope tightens from the saddle horn, then must the gearing be solid, else, like a fisherman floundering with snapped rod and tangled line, the cow-puncher will have misfortunes to repair and nothing to repair them with. Such a thing as this has happened in New Mexico: The steer, pursued and frantic at feeling the throttle of the flung rope, ran blindly over a cliff, one end of the line fast to him, the other to the rider's saddle horn, and no time to think once, much less twice, about anything in this or the next world. The pony braced his legs at the edge, but his gait swept him onward, as with the fast skater whose skate has stuck upon a frozen chip. The horse fell over the mountain, and with him his rider; but the sixty-foot rope was new, and it hooked over a stump. Steer and horse swung like scales gently above the man, who lay at the bottom, hurt nearly to death, but not enough to dull his appreciation of the unusual arrangement.

It is well, then, to wear leathern armor and sit in a stout saddle if you would thrive among the thorns and rocks; and without any such casualty as falling over a mountain, the day's common events call for uncommon strength of gear. Not otherwise can the steer be hooked and landed safely, and not otherwise is the man to hoist resisting beeves up a hill somewhat as safes are conducted to the sixth story, nor could the rider plunge galloping from the sixth story to the ground, or swerve and heavily lean to keep from flying into space, were his stirrup leathers not laced, and every other crucial spot of strain independent of so weak a thing as a buckle. To go up where you have come down is another and easier process for man and straps and everything except the horse. His breath and legs are not immortal. And in order that each day the man may be hardily borne over rough and smooth he must own several mounts—a "string"; sometimes six and more, either his own property, or allotted to him by the foreman of the outfit for which he rides. The unused animals run in a herd—the *ramuda*; and to get a fresh mount from the ramuda means not seldom the ceremony of catching your hare. The ponies walk sedately together in the pasture, good as gold, and eying you without concern until they perceive that you are come with an object. They then put forth against you all the circus knowledge you have bestowed upon them so painfully. They comprehend ropes and loops and the law of gravity; they have observed the errors of steers in similar cases, and the unattractive result of running inside any enclosure, such as a corral, they strategize to keep at large, and altogether chasing a steer is tortoise play to the game they can set up for you. They relish the sight of you whirling impotent among them, rejoice in the smoking pace and the doublings they perpetrate; and with one eye attentive to you and your poised rope, and the other dexterously commanding the universe, they will intertangle as in cross-tag, pushing between your design and its victim, mingling confusedly like a driven mist, and all this with nostrils leaning level to the wind and bellies close to the speeding ground. But when the desired one is at last taken and your successful rope is on his neck, you would not dream he had ever wished for anything else. He stands, submitting absent-mindedly to bit and blanket, mild as any unconscious lamb, while placidity descends once more upon the herd; again they pasture good as gold, and butter would not melt in the mouth of one of these conscientious creatures. I have known a number of dogs, one crow, and two monkeys, but these combined have seemed to me less fertile in expedient than the cow-pony, the sardonic cayuse. The bit his master gave him, and the bridle and spurs, have the same origin from necessity and the same history as to ornament. If stopping and starting and turning must be like flashes of light, the apparatus is accordingly severe; and as for the spurs, those wheels with long spikes cease to seem grotesque when you learn that with shorter and sharper rowels they would catch in the corded meshes of the girth, and bring the rider to ruin. Silver and gold, when he could pay for them, went into the make and decoration of this smaller machinery; and his hat would cost him fifteen dollars, and he wore fringed gloves. His boots often cost twenty - five dollars in his brief hour of opulence. Come to town for his holiday, he wore his careful finery, and from his wide hat-brim to his jingling heels made something of a figure—as self-conscious and deliberate a show as any painted buck in council or bull-elk among his aspiring cows; and out of town in the mountains, as wild and lean and dangerous as buck or bull knows how to be.

As with his get-up, so it went with his vocabulary; for any manner of life with a rule and flavor of its own strong enough to put a new kind of dress on a man's body will put new speech in his mouth, and an idiom derived from the exigencies of his days and nights was soon spoken by the cow-puncher. Like all creators, he not only built, but borrowed his own wherever he found it. *Chaps*, from *chapparajos*, is only one of many transfers from the Mexican, one out of (I should suppose) several hundred; and in *lover-wolf* is a singular instance of half - baked translation. *Lobo*, pronounced *lovo*, being the Spanish for wolf, and the coyote being a sort of wolf, the dialect of the southern border has slid into this name for a wolf that is larger, and a worse enemy to steers than the small coward coyote. Lover - wolf is a word anchored to its district. In the

Northwest, though the same animal roams there as dangerously, his Texas name would be as unknown as the Northwest's word for Indian, *siwash*, from *sauvage*, would be along the Rio Grande. Thus at the top and bottom of our map do French and Spanish trickle across the frontier, and with English melt into two separate amalgams which are wholly distinct, and which remain near the spot where they were moulded; while other compounds, having the same Northern and Southern starting-point, drift far and wide, and become established in the cowpuncher's dialect over his whole country. No better French specimen can be instanced than *cache*, verb and noun, from the verb *cacher*, to conceal. In our Eastern life words such as these are of no pertinent avail; and as it is only universal pertinence which can lift a fragment of dialect into the dictionary's good society, most of them must pass with the transient generation that spoke them. Certain ones there are deserving to survive; *cinch*, for instance, from *cincha*, the Mexican girth. From its narrow office under the horse's belly it has come to perform in metaphor a hundred services. In cinching somebody or something you may mean that you hold four aces, or the key of a political crisis; and when a man is very much indeed upper-dog, then he is said to have an air - tight cinch; and this phrase is to me so pleasantly eloquent that I am withheld from using it in polite gatherings only by that prudery which we carry as a burden along with the benefits of academic training. Besides the foreign importations, such as *arroyo* and *riata*, that stand unchanged, and those others which under the action of our own speech have sloughed their native shape and come out something new, like quirt—once *cuerta*, Mexican for rawhide—is the third large class of words which the cowboy has taken from our sober old dictionary stock and made over for himself. Pie-biter refers not to those hailing from our pie belt, but to a cowpony who secretly forages in a camp kitchen to indulge his acquired tastes. Western whiskey, besides being known as tonsil varnish and a hundred different things, goes as benzine, not unjustly. The same knack of imagery that upon our Eastern slope gave visitors from the country the brief, sure name of hayseed, calls their Western equivalents junipers.

Hay grows scant upon the Rocky Mountains, but those seclusions are filled with evergreens. No one has accounted to me for *hobo*. A hobo is a wandering unemployed person, a stealer of rides on freight-trains, a diner at the back door, eternally seeking honest work, and when brought face to face with it eternally retreating. The hobo is he against whom we have all sinned by earning our living. Perhaps some cowboy saw an Italian playing a pipe to the accompaniment of the harp, and made the generalization: oboe may have given us hobo. Hobo-ken has been suggested by an ingenious friend; but the word seems of purely Western origin, and I heard it in the West several years before it became used in the East. The cow-puncher's talent for making a useful verb out of anything shows his individuality. Any young strong race will always lay firm hands on language and squeeze juice from it; and you instantly comprehend the man who tells you of his acquaintances, whom you know to be drunk at the moment, that they are *helling* around town. Unsleeping need for quick thinking and doing gave these nomads the pith of utterance. They say, for instance, that they intend *camping on a man's trail*, meaning, concisely, "So-and-so has injured us, and we are going to follow him day and night until we are quits." Thus do these ordinary words and phrases, freshened to novelty by the cow-puncher's wits, show his unpremeditated art of brevity, varying in aptness, but in imagination constant; and with one last example of his fancy I shall leave his craft of word-making.

It is to be noted in all peoples that for whatever particular thing in life is of frequent and familiar practice among them they will devise many gradations of epithet. *To go* is in the cattle country a common act, and a man may go for different reasons, in several manners, at various speeds. For example:

"Do I understand you went up the tree with the bear just behind you?"

"The bear was not in front of me."

Here the cowboy made ordinary words suffice for showing the way he went, but his goings can be of many sorts besides in front of and behind something, and his rich choice of synonyms embodies a latent chapter of life and habits. To the several phases of going known to the pioneer as vamose, skip, light out, dust, and

git, the cowboy adds, burn the earth, hit, hit the breeze, pull your freight, jog, amble, move, pack, rattle your hocks, brindle, and more, very likely, if I knew or could recall them; I think that the observer who caught the shifting flicker of a race or a pursuit, and said brindle first, had a mind of liveliness and art.

It may be that some of these words I have named as home-bred natives of our wilderness are really of long standing and archaic repute, and that the scholar can point to them in the sonnets of Shakespeare, but I, at least, first learned them west of the Missouri.

With a speech and dress of his own, then, the cow-puncher drove his herds to Abilene or Westport Landing in the Texas times, and the easy abundant dollars came, and left him for spurs and bridles of barbaric decoration. Let it be remembered that the Mexican was the original cowboy, and that the American improved on him. Those were the days in which he was long in advance of settlers, and when he literally fought his right of way. Along the waste hundreds of miles that he had to journey, three sorts of inveterate enemies infested the road—the thief (the cattle-thief, I mean), who was as daring as himself; the supplanted Mexican, who hated the new encroaching Northern race; and the Indian, whose hand was against all races but his own immediate tribe, and who flayed the feet of his captives, and made them walk so through the mountain passes to the fires in which he slowly burned them. Among these perils the cow-puncher took wild pleasure in existing. No soldier of fortune ever adventured with bolder carelessness, no fiercer blood ever stained a border. If his raids, his triumphs, and his reverses have inspired no minstrel to sing of him who rode by the Pecos River and the hills of San Andreas, it is not so much the Rob Roy as the Walter Scott who is lacking. And the Flora McIvor! Alas! the stability of the clan, the blessing of the home background, was not there. These wild men sprang from the loins of no similar father, and begot no sons to continue their hardihood. War they made in plenty, but not love; for the woman they saw was not the woman a man can take into his heart. That their fighting Saxon ancestors awoke in them for a moment and made them figures for poetry and romance is due to the strange accidents of a young country, where, while cities flourish by the coast and in the direct paths of trade, the herd-trading interior remains mediæval in its simplicity and violence. And yet this transient generation deserves more chronicling than it will ever have. Deeds in plenty were done that are all and more than imagination should require. One high noon upon the plains by the Rio Grande the long irons lay hot in the fire. The young cattle were being branded, and the gathered herd covered the plain. Two owners claimed one animal. They talked at first quietly round the fire, then the dispute quickened. One roped the animal, throwing it to the ground to burn his mark upon it. A third came, saying the steer was his. The friends of each drew close to hear, and a claimant thrust his red-hot iron against the hide of the animal tied on the ground. Another seized it from him, and as they fell struggling, their adherents flung themselves upon their horses, and massing into clans, volleyed with their guns across the fire. In a few minutes fourteen riders lay dead on the plain, and the tied animal over which they had quarrelled bawled and bleated in the silence. Here is skirmishing enough for a ballad. And there was a certain tireless man in northern New Mexico whose war upon cattle-thieves made his life so shining a mark that he had in bank five thousand dollars to go to the man who killed the man who killed him. A neighborhood where one looks so far beyond his own assassination as to provide a competence for his avenger is discouraging to family life, but a promising field for literature.

Such existence soon makes a strange man of any one, and the early cow-punchers rapidly grew unlike all people but each other and the wild superstitious ancestors whose blood was in their veins. Their hair became long, and their glance rested with serene penetration upon the stranger; they laughed seldom, and their spirit was in the permanent attitude of war. Grim lean men of few topics, and not many words concerning these; comprehending no middle between the poles of brutality and tenderness; indifferent to death, but disconcerted by a good woman; some with violent Old Testament religion, some avowing none, and all of them uneasy about corpses and the dark. These hermited horsemen would dismount in camp at nightfall and lie looking at the stars, or else squat about the fire conversing with crude sombreness of brands and horses and cows, speaking of *humans* when they referred to men.

To-day they are still to be found in New Mexico, their last domain. The extreme barrenness of those mountains has held tamer people at a distance. That next stage of Western progress—that unparalleled compound of new hotels, electric lights, and invincible ignorance which has given us the Populist—has been retarded, and the civilization of Colorado and silver does not yet redeem New Mexico. But in these shrunk days the cow-puncher no longer can earn money to spend on ornament; he dresses poorly and wears his chaps very wide and ungainly. But he still has three mounts, with seven horses to each mount, and his life is in the saddle among vast solitudes. In the North he was a later comer, and never quite so formidable a person. By the time he had ridden up into Wyoming and Montana the Indian was mostly gone, the locomotive upon the scene, and going West far less an exploration than in the Texas days. Into these new pastures drifted youths from town and country whose grit would scarcely have lasted them to Abilene, and who were not the grim long-haired type, but a sort of glorified farm hand. They too wore their pistols, and rode gallantly, and out of them nature and simplicity did undoubtedly forge manlier, cleaner men than what our streets breed of no worse material. They galloped by the side of the older hands, and caught something of the swing and tradition of the first years. They developed heartiness and honesty in virtue and in vice alike. Their evil deeds were not of the sneaking kind, but had always the saving grace of courage. Their code had no place for the man who steals a pocket-book or stabs in the back.

And what has become of them? Where is this latest outcropping of the Saxon gone? Except where he lingers in the mountains of New Mexico he has been dispersed, as the elk, as the buffalo, as all wild animals must inevitably be dispersed. Three things swept him away—the exhausting of the virgin pastures, the coming of the wire fence, and Mr. Armour of Chicago, who set the price of beef to suit himself. But all this may be summed up in the word Progress. When the bankrupt cow-puncher felt Progress dispersing him, he seized whatever plank floated nearest him in the wreck. He went to town for a job; he got a position on the railroad; he set up a saloon; he married, and fenced in a little farm; and he turned "rustler," and stole the cattle from the men for whom he had once worked. In these capacities will you find him to-day. The ex-cowboy who set himself to some new way of wage-earning is all over the West, and his old courage and frankness still stick to him, but his peculiar independence is of necessity dimmed. The only man who has retained that wholly is the outlaw, the horse and cattle thief, on whose grim face hostility to Progress forever sits. He has had a checkered career. He has been often hanged, often shot; he is generally "wanted" in several widely scattered districts. I know one who used to play the banjo to me on Powder River as he swung his long boots over the side of his bunk. I have never listened to any man's talk with more interest and diversion. Once he has been to Paris on the proceeds of a lengthy well-conducted theft; once he has been in prison for murder. He has the bluest eye, the longest nose, and the coldest face I ever saw. This stripe of gentleman still lives and thrives through the cattle country, occasionally goes out into the waste of land in the most delicate way, and presently cows and steers are missed. But he has driven them many miles to avoid live-stock inspectors, and it may be that if you know him by sight and happen to be in a town where cattle are bought, such as Kansas City, you will meet him at the best hotel there, full of geniality and affluence.

Such is the story of the cow-puncher, the American descendant of Saxon ancestors, who for thirty years flourished upon our part of the earth, and, because he was not compatible with Progress, is now departed, never to return. But because Progress has just now given us the Populist and silver in exchange for him, is no ground for lament. He has never made a good citizen, but only a good soldier, from his tournament days down. And if our nation in its growth have no worse distemper than the Populist to weather through, there is hope for us, even though present signs disincline us to make much noise upon the Fourth of July.

THE RIGHT HAND OF THE CONTINENT

AS has been said before, on no better
authority,* any one who will look
a map of America in the face may
perceive that California is the right hand
of the continent. If this shall seem, to
such as see only the map, a mere poetic
figure or accident of a peninsula, it is to
be proved that this anatomy is no metaphor, no freak, no inconsequent brachial
process on the opposite side of the body
from the heart. In sober fact, it is the
right hand, with all the name implies;
and with triceps, biceps, forearm, wrist,
fist, and fingers full sinewed for its office.
The passing prophecy, five years ago, that
in time this member must come to be
realized of the rest—"tho' to this day
the self-sufficient left hand outscriptures
scripture, and as little cares as it little
knows what the right hand doeth"—has
had fulfilment sooner than should have
been expected. We have decided (offi-
cially, at least) to be a " world-power."
Whether we conclude that the Influence
which in one century has modified every
other civilized government on earth, and
been direct model for every constitution
in the New World, is world-power, or
that there can be no strength without a
club and some alien head to prove it
upon—in either alternative the right
hand has come suddenly to the threshold
of his own, and quite regardless of what
we may be ripe to admit. The law of
gravitation does not pass around an asy-
lum of the blind, and Destiny halts as
little for the wilful deaf as for them who

* This Magazine for February, 1895.

listen so hard for her that they hear many
things she never said. All the blindfold
habit, all the local investments or local
pride of seventy-four million people, cannot lastingly outweigh a handful, and
—the "shortest line." To paraphrase
(not ignobly, I hope) Garrison's magnificent word, it is a case where one man
and the geography are a majority.

From California we have reached out
to pocket the Hawaiian orphans and the
Philippine rebels (begging the dictionary's pardon); from California we shall
continue to administer them, at their
proper cost, in so far as we shall carry
out the contract. Even should a certain
rather American reaction from emotion
to figures, and from the voice of the siren
to the voice of the Fathers, serve to put a
hitch in our gallop, we can never again
forget (though it may take us some time
fully to remember) our actual national
anatomy. Nothing can put us back so
left-handed as we were in 1897.

There are many people still smitten
with surprise that harbors generally happen near cities—the bigger the city, the
better the harbor. By a like providential
coincidence, the easiest grades pursue railroads; and where the ships are gathered
together a short curve of the earth tags
obedient in their wake. Perhaps we are
too used to plane geography, whereupon
the rest of the world is mere unimproved
paper, and only the United States glows
with lithographic life. This is not always
conducive to roundness of ideas. Certainly he is no typical American who can

beset a globe awhile and not begin to get a glimmering of what the Pacific means besides wastefulness of papier-maché. So many and so greatly larger prophets have foretold it the coming chief theatre of the world's activities that only sheer impudence could here insist upon it with the detail of an inventor. At present I desire to suggest this ocean merely as a facility for getting somewhere — almost anywhere, in fact, since it is a spacious way. And the relation of the Pacific Ocean to the world's imminent commerce once grasped, it is not far to begin to discern the relation of our Pacific coast to the Pacific Ocean. Yonder is the stage upon which the world's chief drama is to be played. Here, so far as the leading lady (we trust) is concerned, is the stage entrance. Here is our door to India, China, Japan, Australia, the South Seas, the west coast of South and Central America and Mexico and Alaska—in fact, to the richest of the Old World and the New, with a tolerably overwhelming majority of the world's population and productivity, and a range in each to which human knowledge writes not one addendum. This in itself might suffice to justify some more sober consideration of our outlet.

Yet it would be, of course, a gross ignoring of history to think of this right hand as a mere organ wherewith to reach and grasp, or yet as a

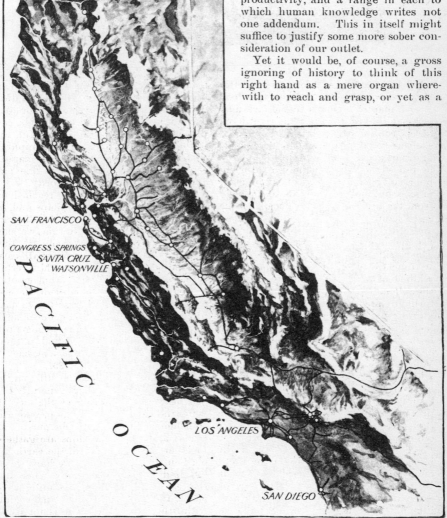

A RELIEF MAP OF CALIFORNIA.

SAN FRANCISCO, FROM ALCATRAZ.

potentiality rather than a fact. If it be needed now (as it is) to get into others' pockets, it has already gone down into its own, and filled therefrom the complacent left. California has, indeed, already performed the dexter functions, and rather overwhelmingly. I seriously mean to demonstrate that no one State, no six States, no census division even, has so vitally meddled with the nation. If this be treason, we will proceed to make the most of it. First, by a glance along some major lines of history; later, by such significant detail as shall commend itself as most illuminative. There is nowhere else in history a chapter of the proportionate wagging of a nation by a frontier, though in history generally the tail has been dominant. Rome was not on the seven hills, and England is not the British Isles. Peru, the South-American California of three centuries earlier, did not a half so much subvert Spain; and Australia, with respect to England, barely suggested the parallel, whether we reckon commercially or sociologically.

We may gather from trustworthy sources, for instance, that "sound money" has now some importance in our national economies. Well, California put the United States on a gold basis, and has kept it there. And California only; though her legitimate children, whom we may count in the States and Territories born directly of California men and money, are nowadays sharing the burden, and for the moment carrying the butt end of it, as Colorado is just now producing more gold than her mother, but has not in total produced a tenth as much.

The proof is as simple and as sure as in anything else which depends on the comforting multiplication table. Up to the civil war, the whole United States in its whole history had produced less than twenty-five millions in gold and silver put together, outside of California — a figure eloquent enough when we remember our shinplasters and wild-cat banks. In five years from its discovery by us, California multiplied the hard money of the country by ten—and more. The whole stock of gold in the United States to-day—coin and bullion — is considerably less than California contributed in thirteen consecutive years. If by some adventitious luck we had had an equal gold stock before California, all the mines then in the country could hardly have made good the abrasion alone on such an amount. Of all the gold produced by the United States to

ALCATRAZ ISLAND, SAN FRANCISCO HARBOR.

this very day, California has given more than one-half from her own pockets. Of the remaining fraction she is demonstrably responsible for at least seven-tenths. Possibly there is some significance in the fact that the United States now produces more gold per year, by 70 per cent., than the whole world produced before California; and that California itself, even at its lowest ebb, turns in annually two-fifths as much of the reliable metal as the whole round of earth dug before the California awakening.

Thirteen hundred millions in gold from one State has been in itself of some import to the finances of a nation which even now transacts its business with half that sum. But it is only a beginning in the commercial consequence of the State. California not only invented the gold-fever, but made it contagious. She precipitated Australia, the only continent which ever rivalled our own State as a gold-producer. It is of course notorious that Australia had been "discovered" and suppressed until men from California and with the California itch made suppression impossible—for Hargreaves went to school to us. So in five years a yellow fleck picked up from a California tail-race had revolutionized the money-markets of the world, at once and forever.

It is stress that brings about great things. Solomon was already a gold-bug; and the priest of far-shooting Apollo came with a ransom, not of greenbacks, nor yet of silver. But since before Ophir the world had been content to gopher for its little gold. For much gold (after an apprenticeship of human stupidity) California made mining for the first time a business, and has taught the world. From a faro game unprecedented in history, nor yet paralleled, she reduced it to science; from brute, though gigantic, retail to dexterous wholesale; from shopkeeping to commerce. As she became less pick-upable with loose nuggets, and bent her back to serious quartz veins, her vagabond graduates turned back a thousand miles on their own tracks and developed the lesser but adequate bonanzas of Colorado and its peers. Her scholars are to-day the first men wherever there is gold—in the Black Hills or the Rand. The vast majority of Western Argonauts would never have been in the West at all, nor at all gold-seeking, but for California. Shaft-mining nor low-grade ore ever yet made a stampede. People do not buy lottery tickets for the dollar prizes, nor yet for a chance to make a livelihood by hard work. The one sanity of the mining craze is that the capital prize attracts people, and finally diverts them to sober work on enlarged lines. It seems to be a generic wisdom of Nature to gain her ends by dazzling the vision. She adorns sex that posterity shall not fail. She would rather trust the peahen's eyes than its forethought—or a man's. She peoples the wilderness by showing us not a moral obligation nor a civic advantage, but a glitter. Yet she has a sane antidote. It is the history of all these madnesses that they promote sanity. The beauty of women increases crime, no doubt, but it also perpetuates humanity. Somewhat so, the wild lusts of a gold-rush vastly accelerate and vastly broaden sober progress.

Our real West dates from California. It is not enough to remember that Minnesota, Oregon, Kansas, Nevada, Nebraska, Colorado, the two Dakotas, Montana, Washington, Idaho, Wyoming, Utah, have been admitted as States, and New Mexico, Arizona, Oklahoma, and Alaska organized as Territories, since California came into the Union. The pertinent question is, how many of them we should have if there had been no California. If only a Pathfinder and a few score trappers had seen the intervening waste between Independence and the coast; if nothing seismic enough had befallen to fetch into California more people in a tide than there were in all the country between California and the older States as late as 1860 (for we must remember that when the war broke out California was the only State west of the Missouri, except a part of Texas): if the ready money of the country had not been doubled several times, and the spirit of adventure increased by a still larger multiplicand—who will pretend that by now we should have a full-growing West, already big enough to feed the old folks? No one, certainly, who knows East and West; nor even any one for whom the census has not been in vain.

Particularly since time was an element of the contract. The Pacific Slope did not need to go begging. There were other hands reached out for it—above all, it was leaning to other hands. It was more by good fortune than by general wit that our fist closed upon it first. We had not many Jeffersons and Bentons. The United States was mostly content to remain a narrow huddle of provinces when California, suddenly and almost empirically, unrolled our trivial halfway map to another ocean and gave us

a national span, and pulled along population enough to vindicate the map. To this day there are many excellent people who never reflect what Uncle Sam's stature would have been if he had slept on with Canada at his head, Mexico for a foot-board, and his back against a British wall somewhere about the Platte.

I fear no smiles from any whose smile is seriously discouraging when I venture

40 FEET UP A REDWOOD-TREE, MILL VALLEY.

the suggestion that, if there had been no California in 1848, there could have been no civil war in 1861; nor for at least a decade—and probably a generation—later. In grammar-school, war can be defined with a word; later we find it complicated. Conscience may be concerned in it; but it involves also politics, money, and the fighting temper. It is hardly necessary to remark that, without a California, the United States could not have been by '61 in any financial position to afford the luxury of its convictions. As to the last straw which breaks a patient man to impatience, California had certainly contributed more than its share. Men who have fought Indians and claim-jumpers are on the average more ripe to fight strangers than

WHITE OAK.

confirmed farmers are; and as their touchiness spreads even to the farmers of their acquaintance, a nation with this leaven comes to blows sooner than a nation without it. As to politics (which are most of any war), California made the States (*in posse*) which largely made the issue. It was no more a question of slavery than of the extension of slavery that brought the rupture.

Yet that great cleavage along the line of human rights had to come some time. We of this generation, at least, are entitled to thank California that it came so soon. Without the new problems, the new money, and the new pugnacity bred of '49, that deadliest struggle in history would only by now be ending or by now begun. As it is, tall trees are risen upon its graves, its widows are past the heartbreak of youth, and North and South are grown one. Not by any means *because* of a new war, but by the slow "intention" of time and the blood; merely evidenced when a crisis pulls on the old wound and finds hardly a scar left.

It would be rather long than difficult to trace, along many other largest lines of the material development of the nation, the like influence of California, and

to clinch wholesale assertion by retail and statistical proof (as I purpose to prove all large premises herein). Without being at the outset too tedious to those who forget that even American progress has to have reasons, and that even American character is woven of more threads than the one stout one of birth, it may still be well to recall a few other typical and generic truths in the material category.

California first invented a serious need of steamboats in the United States, and for a generation practically monopolized them. By a poetic injustice, she has to this day very nearly the worst steamboats. She invented long-distance railroading—indeed, one may probably say the American railroad system. There was not, nor has been, any other reason for mileages over three thousand. California called for a railroad three times as long as the world had ever seen; and getting it, gave back the sinews to vein the East with railroads—the sinews and the impetus. It is hardly necessary to remark that transcontinental railroading is a technic by itself; and that precisely as American methods actually direct Continental ones, so the long, lean, single-track, sand-ballasted railroads across our continent are still tutors to the short, fat, perfected road-beds of the narrow States.

CALIFORNIA SYCAMORE.

MOUNT TAMALPAIS, NEAR SAN FRANCISCO.

At the head of any profession stands the man who has to solve the most problems, not the man who inherited the largest practice. Incidentally, too—not of vainglory, but as a matter of history not without use in the final analysis—it is to be noted that even in the year of grace 1900 California, with one exception, is the only country any one ever cared to build three thousand miles of rail to get to, and it is the only land a hundred thousand men ever walked two thousand miles sooner than stay away from.

There must be some, also, who remember American machine-shops in the forties. There were American mechanics. The grasshopper engines they builded were *good* grasshoppers of their time, else these men could never have jumped to building leviathans. For it was almost between two days that the demand came for such engines as even Yankee mechanics had not seen in their nightmares. In this large activity, as in many others, California was the first commanding voice. And perhaps as striking a hint as any of what she had done for the United States in this line is the fact that at ten years old she was already com-

petent to build her own unprecedented Comstock in the same shop that now turns out the *Oregon* engines; and that to-day she can and does build bigger and better machineries than any portion of the Union built twenty years ago. I am quite prepared to learn that it was "an age of progress." True. But what made it so? Did new wealth have anything to do with new desires? Were new desires provocative of new invention?

But the engines were for bigger mechanisms than themselves. California took scientific mining unborn and made a man of it. No mining so big nor so corrupting has ever since been seen— though we have striven vigorously after both goals. As if gold were not enough, the Argonauts invented silver—as a factor big enough to be an unrest. Only a certain unacquaintance can compare Cerro de Pasco or Potosi or Guanajuato with Virginia City. They are not comparable in our idiom. The Peruvian, Bolivian, and Mexican bonanzas have outranked ours in dollars; but they count by half-centuries where we count decades, by labor whose wage would not have bought the Comstock miner his

LOOKING NORTHWEST FROM MOUNT TAMALPAIS.

cigar, by the very absence of what we call "business method." Knowing both well, I have no lingering doubt that the Potosino or Pasqueño "got more out of it," and gave more; lived, on the average, more happily and more beloved. But we wiser people do not mine precisely to live; we are rather more in the way of living that we may mine. The benighted Don never knew what a mining-stock was. He was content with silver. Whereas we have made our shadow bigger than his substance. Stock-gambling was a California invention; for before that even our progressive blood had not risen to the fine game of throat-cutting by ticker. There could be no sharper proof of racial superiority. Our rude prototype made a fair fling so long as he had bullion to pave the street —as he literally did, *pro tem.*, in cases of exhilaration—but had to stop when his last coin rang on the counter. A smarter generation learned to take that coin and weigh it against a quire of paper, put on four bits' worth of printer's ink, cut the pile into ten thousand pieces, and sell each piece for the value of the original coin. Nor was it all the "epoch of progress," for it has not yet been "gone better." Our best efforts are rather

crude now beside the stiff game of the frontier inventor—when stocks on the San Francisco board rose in value a million dollars a day for months, and the sales in one year in one small city were 120 millions; when a certain stock went from nothing to $1570 a share, and back to $33, all within eight months; when two silver-mines produced 105 millions in five years, and the valuation of one lode was nearly 400 millions; when 250 millions were spent in "developing" one little huddle of hills, and, though thousands got rich by what "stuck to their fingers," there were bigger dividends than all the mills or all the railroads in the United States ever paid. By some illogic of the map, the Comstock is in Nevada; but it must always be borne in mind that the Comstock was as distinctively a California affair as Bunker Hill belongs to Massachusetts. California money, California brawn, California brains, California madness, made it—and to later boot gave us Leadville, Tombstone, and all the other giants. Rich as the nation is, if only the original money from between the boundaries of California were bewitched out of our pockets and our enterprises, we should go hopelessly bankrupt—without insisting at all upon California's equity in the investments built upon that money, nor upon a royalty in the mineral output of other States that can be proved definitively to be a specific consequence of California, nor yet counting at all the many other industries whereby the State of Bewilderment has enriched the Union and herself in the half-century.

Nor is it by any suggestion a mere case of "*has* done." California sowed her wild oats royally, and taught her timidest sister to tipple. No State was ever before so drunken — nor so contagious in her cups — and none is to-day more sober. I knew once every county in New England by sight, but if there is any New England town of about 8000 which beats a peace record of one arrest per month, it has grown up since I came away. And in all seriousness that is typical. There is no State comparable in population and wealth freer to-day from the gambling spirit than this ex-gambler to whose once vast game even Chicago city must stand in the relation of neophyte. Of this phase there is much to be said later. At present we must "cut" only the "main trail." Here is a modern State of good American manners and morals ; with more than one-twenty-second of the area of the United States (Alaska inclusive), and one-sixtieth of the population; with a quarter as many people as New England, and two and a half times as many acres. It raised in 1897 two hundred and ninety-three times as much wheat as New England, eighteen times as much barley, half as much corn. It has two million acres more forest than New England—forests not only incomparably nobler but incomparably more valuable. It has, indeed,

one-twenty-fourth of all the forests in the United States ; and the densest forests (in "merchantable lumber") in the world. It has more horses, more milch-cows and oxen, more swine, than all New England, and over four times as many sheep. It has more acres in grapes than New England has in corn, and produces more wine than all the rest of the Union put together. It is the only raisin-maker, and turns out thirty-nine thousand tons of raisins a year. With less than a fifth of the total coast-line of the United States, it has (by value) one-fourteenth of the

PORT HARFORD.

fisheries. It raises many times as much fruit as New England, of many times the variety, and of at least double the market rating. With a third of Ohio's population (and no President-making nor natural gas), it manufactures as much as Ohio in value. It has more money in savings-banks per depositor than any other State in the Union—double the New England average, more than seven times the average of Great Britain. And it is not the lucky few. Its savings-bank deposits mean not only $110 or so for every man, woman, and child in the State, Chinese and Indians included, but that one in

EL RANCHO DEL POZO DE VERONA.
Mrs. Phoebe A Hearst's country house, Pleasanton.

every seven of this entire population is a depositor. Its State indebtedness per capita is a quarter that of Massachusetts; not far above a third that of New York—and it has got quite as much for its money. Its assessed valuation per capita is 30 per cent. above that of New York, more than four times larger than that of Illinois, and in the whole Union is equalled only by Massachusetts and Rhode Island.

Possibly from the material stand-point this suffices for the present to indicate that one may be less frivolous than one looks in speaking of California as the right hand, and that the heretic suggestion may be worth following up. This is but a beginning of the fact, and if these truths seem seditious, the wrath be not upon my head, but upon that of the Census Bureau and its fellow-conspirators.

The most vital influence in shaping American character (for we will drop the pocket awhile) radiated first and longest from the stingy littoral of our hostile ocean. The Puritan conscience is dominant to-day in California as it is in New England and many States between. On neither verge is it nowadays in majority

of numbers; on both it is the backbone minority that stiffens—and in the long run controls—every democracy. In both (if unequally) its surface asperities have been rubbed and weathered, to their possible betterment; but the oaken core perdures, unspoiled in fibre by the "finish."

Now back to the peevish ocean from the serene one, from the generous to the "close" fields, there is (and growing daily more momentous) a sociologic reaction as little to be disregarded in any sober analysis of national character. The frontiersman has counted as many per cent. in evolving the present American culture type as the Puritan himself. We are great not alone because of our keen sense of the immorality of other people. The compelling a continental wilderness would have given us moral muscle if we had started without any to speak of, and has very visibly enlarged and given new suppleness to the generous stock of our heredity. The Puritans themselves would have presently become "impossible" if they had landed in the Garden of Eden, and we can never be too thankful that California was beyond them. They were near enough to impossible as it stood, but the wilderness is a wonderfully sane thing. Only death matches it as a corrective. New England was counter-irritant enough even for its pioneers. California, by a curious partnership of circumstances, intrinsic and extrinsic, was frontier plus a still more inevitable influence. I believe it as possible to prove, and as conclusively, that California made over the American mind as that it made over American finances, and am now headed thitherward, after a merely introductory fashion.

Here was our first (and still largest) national romance, the first wild flower of

California was also the nation's first taste of "big money"—alias, the unearned increment. Far be it from me to pretend that this was an unmixed blessing. Very likely it was not a blessing whatever. But I speak to a common standard, and the challenged party has the choice of weapons. Forty-eight was, to a sturdy, sober land, the first giant unrest, the first epidemic temptation. We had never before dreamed of being—well, as we are. It changed the temper of the American mind forever—though by no means every American mind at once. It taught

A BERKELEY HOME IN WINTER.

mystery, the first fierce passion of an uncommonly hard-fisted youth. To this day it persists the only glamour between the covers of our geography. For more than fifty years its very name has been a witchcraft, and its spell is stronger now than ever, as shall be coolly demonstrated. This has meant something in the psychology of so unfanciful a nation. The flowering of imagination is no trivial incident, whether in a farm-boy's life or in a nation's. It may be outgrown, and even forgotten, but it shall never again be as if it had never been. Without just that flower we should not have just this fruit.

a generation aiming point-blank at slow competency to raise the sights for riches on the wing, and we have forgotten how to shoot low. It bred more discontent and more widely shifted the social viewpoint than any other event or condition in our history before or since, slavery and steam not excluded—for steam we tie, and we have untied slavery; but no nation ever yet rebottled the afrit of its own imagination and desire. I know, indeed, in all history, no comparable transubstantiation of mind in a people; for of course the easy parallel is not yet by a long way history.

VALLEY OF SAN LUIS REY.
Mission of San Luis Rey de Francia in the distance.

Very possibly the patient student nowadays realizes, more broadly than any Argonaut even, how swift, how unforeseen, how irreluctably, that galvanic pulse ran through the narrow nation, and how fiercely possessed its very capillaries. Slavery itself was never so stirring a question in so many hearts—for when the men of 200,000 homes were facing danger our concern was for something more complicated than the abstract question, just as the California fever took on new complications when it involved the absence of so many scores of thousands of loved ones. I make the comparison between the two agitations by their intrinsic depth, so far as such simplification is possible. The files of the New York, Boston, Philadelphia, Baltimore, and other newspapers, of every periodical, little and big, warming (from a conservatism whereof no large residue is anywhere left us) to the first colossal sensation in American journalism; the popular songs (and only a collector dreams how as the sands of the sea for multitude were the "California songsters" which flooded the country—of the span of a dime novel, but rainbow-covered with the saddening lithographies of the day)—these are straws of how the wind blew. To say nothing of the passenger-lists. The United States has over four times the population it had in '48, but it has never since duplicated that shifting of population.

And the books! Without final data at hand, I incline to believe that by the time the war came along to give us a new text, California had already, in a dozen years, doubled the volume of American literature. In the same way, of course, that it was then doubled again—for our war-literature was not mostly written upon the battle-field. In half a century this current has not ceased. It is a lean month even now which does not see somewhere some sort of a book about California. It is certain that as much literature (using the word as it is used) has been written of California as of all the other States together. This means, of course, only matter in which the State is an essential, not an incident. It is surprising, too, what a proportion of the best of this literature of California was published by one publishing-house; and there is to me a certain special pleasure that these latter words come to light under the same old imprint.

It was given to the Argonauts of '49 to

weigh more per capita, and for a longer
term, than any other class of citizens.
Whether they staid at the rainbow's end
or reverted at last to the old home,
whether they "made their pile" or
"went broke," they had a disproportion-
ate influence upon whatsoever society
they touched—even by their rare letters.
It is perfectly true that California has
not even yet given birth to one man of
the largest national stature, nor even returned an adopted son so tall as the very
giants of the States that mothered her.
That is not unexpected in history. Homer
could hardly have come the day after
Cadmus. It does not in the least diminish our patriotic head that the Gladstones
and Tennysons and Bismarcks refrain at
home from the better side of the world,
nor that our actual immigrants are not
largely Websters by the time they are
ready for naturalization papers. What
we do expect is that, given the like blood
and a fair start, we can trust time to work
out for us better average results than tired
monarchies may look for. That is the
United States against the field. The in-
itiate Californian has precisely the same
conviction as against the rest of the
world, the Eastern States inclusive. If
with as definable and as defensible logic,
may be decided later.

These over-average men who made, and
were made by, California—and they were
visibly above average who braved the

A MADROÑO-TREE IN BLOOM.

2000-mile tramp, or six months' voyage,
and the hardships and dangers of way-
side and goal—were all stamped forever
with a new seal. Such a school never
graduates even its dunces unchanged.
Every man of that unprecedented migration lost something in California, and
found something; things worse lost, and
better; things it was well to find, and
things that were a pity. Some that had
been strong so long as environment
crutched them, turned weak when they
tried to stand alone; and some, weakling
by disuse, turned giants under exercise.
Some "good men" became bad, and some
"bad men" became good. It was the
Circe that bewitched a man to his true
inner shape—of fox or wolf or hog or
man. And so is the frontier always.
Cold storage is not righteousness, nor a
plaster jacket character.

But every man jack of those men was
changed—grown along his line of least
resistance. Somehow, too, he was larger,
in one dimension if not in all. He had
learned vastly in self-reliance, self-con-
trol, observation, independence, beyond
the man that had never overstepped the
native township. He might be no better
man; he was certainly different. He had
swapped horizons, and for the bigger.
Travel (and not by Pullman), contact

AN OLD SPANISH CALIFORNIA VERANDA.

with Nature—in larger, fiercer, yet nobler maturity than her corseted under-study knows who lags in gardens—the attrition of men, no longer circumscribed but as broken loose to individuality as himself—these had opened him.

Above all, the having had to shoulder for himself the burden of human responsibility, which the social machine had mostly borne for him before; the having to begin back toward the beginning, with no better tools than his shrewdness and his vague concept of history, to build new in the wilderness that strange compromise of do and do not which we agree to call civilization. That experience made him not a man alone, but a figure. He was impossible to be dodged, and no one cared to dodge such an excitement. His face, his attitude, his step, his money (if he brought any), so "easy" earned, so royal spent—a farm's crop

THE KITCHEN CHIMNEY.
Mission San Juan Capitano.

in a panful of gravel—even his frontier-made vices, were interesting. They were all big, and even in this sore world nothing has yet got so little as to be proof against bigness. He infected not only potential imitators in roving, but as truly (and perhaps more deeply) those who never had a serious peril of leaving their saner shoe-shops or stone pastures—and that those *are* saner than the first pathologies of a gold-fever only those may deny who do not much care what they say. No Easterner ever looked at the world through unchanged glasses after contact with a Californian Argonaut, and doubtless no Easterner endowed with the organs of listening ever escaped that confident voice altogether.

One should always have learned something from each of one's schoolmasters, even the rudest, and it is an axiom of a now bygone school to which I shall never be so ungrateful as to deny my debt, never to empty your six-shooter, and never to fire in the air. This is nothing more

than a beginning even of the generic truth about a topic which seems to me one of the largest and most interesting that it has ever been given to Americans to see upon their own blackboard. Nor do I plan to exhaust the subject.

As also has been said before, and sometimes on still worse authority, California is above all others the land of contrasts. It is true; but truth is a club too heavy to be used unmercifully. We need not conjure up contradictions for smartness' sake, since nothing is really cheaper. There is no virtue in "boom" superlatives. There is no ambition in me to insist on 300-pound squashes, and on 150-pound watermelons, and beets a farmer cannot hump into his cart unaided, and occasional thousand-dollar-an-acre crops. These things be, and a thousand circus side-shows like them. But if the Easterner is not tired of hearing of them, some of us are. I would rather deal with California as a figure in the market than in the museum, to see if it really means something—big, perhaps, but sane—in its own and the nation's development, and if so, why; to analyze—with what skill I can find, but, at any rate, with accuracy, which I never need lose—how it comes to be evolving (as it unquestionably is) a civilization unique in the United States, and what this new sociologic trend may mean and is likely to mean for California and for the rest of the federal family. In fine, to discuss it as a factor, not as a freak.

Freak, indeed, it may superficially seem to our average experience. Yet I would rather think of it as Nature's true normal, and of the peevish climate temper of my native coast as it were her neuralgia. For it is not good to think ill of our descent. If Mother Nature is indeed as we see her here, broad-browed and broad-bosomed, strong and calm—calm because strong—swaying her vain brats by unruffled love, not by fear; by wise giving, not by privation; by caresses and gentle precepts, not by cuffs and scoldings and hysterics — why, then she shall better justify our memories and the name we have given her. It is well that our New England mothers had a different climate in their hearts from that which beat at their windows. I know one Yankee boy who never could quite understand that his mother had gone *home* till he came to know the skies of California.

As a sane and actual, though exceptional, State of the Union, then, let us reckon with California. Even so we must depart from many conventions, and face many paradoxes without undue timidity. The superlative is a degree no ticklish person (whether in conscience or in vanity) can afford to take in vain, though one may prefer the things that merit superlatives. Nor yet is it a thing to skulk from. A scientific maximum is as true as a scientific minimum. The only rule is never to use the degree wantonly, nor of guess-work, nor of emotion.

Any study of California at this date must be, to be justified, a little broader, a little deeper, a little more intimate, a little more comparative. My one apology for daring to try the unequal task must be that no one does the thing which seems to need doing. In place of the genius such a theme should engage, I can hope only to give larger patience and more drudgery; for brilliant intuition, an acquaintance of fifteen years; for a few books to lean on, every book, I believe, in Spanish, English, or French, from the beginning; for the railroad travel and a couple of cities, residence, study, and wide pursuit; and all re-enforced by more than two hard years of special review and many thousand miles of inland travel for the one object. No one who knows California well enough to write about her can pretend indifference; and here is an unabashed lover. But not because she is the first and only fair one. I shall compare her face and figure, her temper, mind, manners, and the color of her eyes, knowing all her Union sisters and nearly all her New World cousins; hoping also that no one better knows her infirmities.

MODERN DWELLINGS IN SANTA BARBARA.
After the Spanish.

What is hereinafter to be said of her will not be Western braggadocio, for the witness is but an Easterner emancipated; nor merely because it is true (since truth is often impudent); nor at all because the truth is good to California, which needs no help of me; but solely because it seems to me a theme interesting to any real mind whatever, and of literal concern to the whole nation that California is proud to be some part of. Unless the basic idea is an egregious blunder, there will be some sober worth as well as some interest in this series of studies of the real California—what it is, why it is so, and what it all means to American business, American thought, American character. And it is not to be reckoned folly to count as of some big import in all these lines a State which has twice been populated faster than any other on the continent, with classes respectively as unlike as buccaneers from professors; which was the most Western, and is now the most Eastern, State in the Union; the most foolish once, and now, I believe, the wisest—in every event, the most potent. Nor can there fail to be, aside from economics, a certain human interest in the State which was our only transient hotel, and is now the most ineradicable home; the only State so many Americans ever sought in fever, and so few ever leave in any temperature.

THE HEART OF THE DESERT

I WENT to it with reluctance. I shrink from attempting to say anything about it. If you knew that there was one spot on the earth where Nature kept her secret of secrets, the key to the action of her most gigantic and patient forces through the long eras, the marvel of constructive and destructive energy, in features of sublimity made possible to mental endurance by the most exquisite devices of painting and sculpture, the wonder which is without parallel or comparison, would you not hesitate to approach it? Would you not wander and delay with this and that wonder, and this and that beauty and nobility of scenery, putting off the day when the imagination, which is our highest gift, must be extinguished by the reality? The mind has this judicious timidity. Do we not loiter in the avenue of the temple, dallying with the vista of giant plane-trees and statues, and noting the carving and the color, mentally shrinking from the moment when the full glory shall burst upon us? We turn and look when we are near a summit, we pick a flower, we note the shape of the clouds, the passing breeze, before we take the last step that shall reveal to us the vast panorama of mountains and valleys.

I cannot bring myself to any description of the Grand Cañon of the Colorado by any other route, mental or physical, than that by which we reached it, by the way of such beauty as Monterey, such a wonder as the Yosemite, and the infinite and picturesque deserts of New Mexico and Arizona. I think the mind needs the training in the desert scenery to enable it to grasp the unique sublimity of the Grand Cañon.

The road to the Yosemite, after leaving the branch of the Southern Pacific at Raymond, is an unnecessarily fatiguing one. The journey by stage—sixty-five miles—is accomplished in less than two days—thirty-nine miles the first day, and twenty-six the second. The driving is necessarily slow, because two mountain ridges have to be surmounted, at an elevation each of about 6500 feet. The road is not a "road" at all as the term is understood in Switzerland, Spain, or in any highly civilized region—that is, a graded, smooth, hard, and sufficiently broad track. It is a makeshift highway, generally narrow (often too narrow for two teams to pass), cast up with loose material, or excavated on the slopes with frequent short curves and double curves. Like all mountain roads which skirt precipices, it may seem "pokerish," but it is safe enough if the drivers are skilful and careful (all the drivers on this route are not only excellent, but exceedingly civil as well), and there is no break in wagon or harness. At the season this trip is made the weather is apt to be warm, but this would not matter so much if the road were not intolerably dusty. Over a great part of the way the dust rises in clouds and is stifling. On a well-engineered road, with a good road-bed, the time of passage might not be shortened, but the journey would be made with positive comfort and enjoyment, for though there is a certain monotony in the scenery, there is the wild freshness of nature, now and then an extensive prospect, a sight of the snow-clad Nevadas, and vast stretches of woodland; and a part of the way the forests are magnificent, especially the stupendous growth of the sugar-pine. These noble forests are now protected by their inaccessibility.

From 1855 to 1864, nine years, the Yosemite had 653 visitors; in 1864 there were 147. The number increased steadily till 1869, the year the overland railroad was completed, when it jumped to 1122. Between 4000 and 5000 persons visit it now each year. The number would be enormously increased if it could be reached by rail, and doubtless a road will be built to the valley in the near future, perhaps up the Merced River. I believe that the pilgrims who used to go to the Yosemite on foot or on horseback regret the building of the stage road, the enjoyment of the wonderful valley being somehow cheapened by the comparative ease of reaching it. It is feared that a railway would still further cheapen, if it did not vulgarize it, and that passengers by train would miss the mountain scenery, the splendid forests, the surprises of the way (like the first view of the valley from Inspiration Point), and that the Mariposa big trees would be further off the route than they are now. The traveller sees them now by driving eight miles from Wawona, the end of the first day's staging. But the romance for the few there is in staging will have to give way to the greater comfort of the many by rail. The railway will do no more injury to the Yosemite than it has done to Niagara, and in fact will be the means of immensely increasing the comfort of the visitor's stay there, besides enabling tens of thousands of people to see it who cannot stand the fatigue of the stage ride over the present road. The Yosemite will remain as it is. The simplicity of its grand features is unassailable so long as the government protects the forests that surround it and the streams that pour into it. The visitor who goes there by rail will find plenty of adventure for days and weeks in following the mountain trails, ascending to the great points of view, exploring the cañons, or climbing so as to command the vast stretch of the snowy Sierras. Or, if he is not inclined to adventure, the valley itself will satisfy his highest imaginative flights of the sublime in rock masses and perpendicular ledges, and his sense of beauty in the graceful water-falls, rainbow colors, and exquisite lines of domes and pinnacles. It is in the grouping of objects of sublimity and beauty that the Yosemite excels. The narrow valley, with its gigantic walls, which vary in every change of the point of view, lends itself to the most astonishing scenic effects, and these the photograph has reproduced, so that the world is familiar with the striking features of the valley, and has a tolerably correct idea of the sublimity of some of these features. What the photograph cannot do is to give an impression of the unique grouping, of the majesty, and at times crushing weight upon the mind, of the forms and masses, of the atmospheric splendor and illusion, and of the total value of such an assemblage of wonders. The level surface of the peaceful park-like valley has much to do with the impression. The effect of El Capitan, seen across a meadow and rising from a beautiful park, is much greater than if it were encountered in a savage mountain gorge. The traveller may have seen elsewhere greater waterfalls, and domes and spires of rock as surprising, but he has nowhere else seen such a combination as this. He may be fortified against surprise by the photographs he has seen and the reports of word painters, but he will not escape (say at Inspiration Point, or Artist Point, or other

lookouts) a quickening of the pulse and an elation which is physical as well as mental, in the sight of such unexpected sublimity and beauty. And familiarity will scarcely take off the edge of his delight, so varied are the effects in the passing hours and changing lights. The Rainbow Fall, when water is abundant, is exceedingly impressive as well as beautiful. Seen from the carriage road, pouring out of the sky overhead, it gives a sense of power, and at the proper hour before sunset, when the vast mass of leaping, foaming water is shot through with the colors of the spectrum, it is one of the most exquisite sights the world can offer; the elemental forces are overwhelming, but the loveliness is engaging. One turns from this to the noble mass of El Capitan with a shock of surprise, however often it may have been seen. This is the hour, also, in the time of high-water, to see the reflection of the Yosemite Falls. As a spectacle it is infinitely finer than anything at Mirror Lake, and is unique in its way. To behold this beautiful series of falls, flowing down out of the blue sky above, and flowing up out of an equally blue sky in the depths of the earth, is a sight not to be forgotten. And when the observer passes from these displays to the sight of the aerial domes in the upper end of the valley, new wonders opening at every turn of the forest road, his excitement has little chance of subsiding. He may be even a little oppressed. The valley, so verdant and friendly with grass and trees and flowers, is so narrow compared with the height of its perpendicular guardian walls, and this little secluded spot is so imprisoned in the gigantic mountains, that man has a feeling of helplessness in it. This powerlessness in the presence of elemental forces was heightened by the deluge of water. There had been an immense fall of snow the winter before, the Merced was a raging torrent, overflowing its banks, and from every ledge poured a miniature cataract.

Noble simplicity is the key-note to the scenery of the Yosemite, and this is enhanced by the park-like appearance of the floor of the valley. The stems of the fine trees are in harmony with the perpendicular lines, and their foliage adds the necessary contrast to the gray rock masses. In order to preserve these forest trees, the underbrush, which is liable to make a conflagration in a dry season, should be re-

1. COAST OF MONTEREY.　2. CYPRESS POINT.　3. NEAR SEAL ROCK.

moved generally, and the view of the great features be left unimpeded. The minor cañons and the trails are of course left as much as possible to the riot of vegetation. The State commission, which labors under the disadvantages of getting its supplies from a Legislature that does not appreciate the value of the Yosemite to California, has established a model trail service. The Yosemite, it need not be said, is a great attraction to tourists from all parts of the world; it is the interest of the State, therefore, to increase their number by improving the facilities for reaching it, and by resolutely preserving all the surrounding region from ravage.

This is as true of the Mariposa big tree region as of the valley. Indeed, more care is needed for the trees than for the great chasm, for man cannot permanently injure the distinctive features of the latter, while the destruction of the sequoias will be an irreparable loss to the State and to the world. The *Sequoia gigantea* differs in leaf, and size and shape of cone, from the great *Sequoia semper virens* on the coast near Santa Cruz; neither can be spared. The Mariposa trees, scattered along on a mountain ridge 6500 feet above the sea, do not easily obtain their victory, for they are a part of a magnificent forest of other growths, among which the noble sugar-pine is conspicuous for its enormous size and graceful vigor. The sequoias dominate among splendid rivals only by a magnitude that has no comparison elsewhere in the world. I think no one can anticipate the effect that one of these monarchs will have upon him. He has read that a coach and six can drive through one of the trees that is standing; that another is thirty-three feet in diameter, and that its vast stem, 350 feet high, is crowned with a mass of foliage that seems to brush against the sky. He might be prepared for a tower one hundred feet in circumference, and even four hundred feet high, standing upon a level plain. But this living growth is quite another affair. Each tree is an individual, and has a personal character. No man can stand in the presence of one of these giants without a new sense of the age of the world and the insignificant span of one human life; but he is also overpowered by a sense of some gigantic personality. It does not relieve him to think of this as the Methuselah of trees, or to call it by the name of some great poet or captain. The awe the tree inspires is of itself. As one lies and looks up at the enormous bulk, it seems not so much the bulk, so lightly is it carried, as the spirit of the tree, the elastic vigor, the patience, the endurance of storm and change, the confident might, and the soaring, almost contemptuous pride, that overwhelm the puny spectator. It is just because man can measure himself, his littleness, his brevity of existence, with this growth out of the earth, that he is more personally impressed by it than he might be by the mere variation in the contour of the globe which is called a mountain. The imagination makes a plausible effort to comprehend it, and is foiled. No, clearly it is not mere size that impresses one; it is the dignity, the character in the tree, the authority and power of antiquity. Side by side of these venerable forms are young sequoias, great trees themselves, that have only just begun their millennial career—trees that will, if spared, perpetuate to remote ages this race of giants, and in two to four thousand years from now take the place of their great-grandfathers, who are sinking under the weight of years, and one by one measuring their length on the earth.

The transition from the sublime to the exquisitely lovely in nature can nowhere else be made with more celerity than from the Sierras to the coast at Monterey. California abounds in such contrasts and surprises. After the great stirring of the emotions by the Yosemite and the Mariposa, the Hotel del Monte Park and vicinity offer repose, and make an appeal to the sense of beauty and refinement. Yet even here something unique is again encountered. I do not refer to the extraordinary beauty of the giant live-oaks and the landscape-gardening about the hotel, which have made Monterey famous the world over, but to the sea-beach drive of sixteen miles, which can scarcely be rivalled elsewhere either for marine loveliness or variety of coast scenery. It has points like the ocean drive at Newport, but is altogether on a grander scale, and shows a more poetic union of shore and sea; besides, it offers the curious and fascinating spectacles of the rocks inhabited by the sea-lions, and the Cypress Point. These huge uncouth creatures can be seen elsewhere, but probably nowhere else on this coast are they massed in greater numbers. The trees of Cypress Point are unique, this species of cypress having been found nowhere else. The long, never-ceasing swell of the Pacific incessantly flows up the many crescent sand beaches, casting up shells of brilliant hues, sea-weed, and kelp, which seems instinct with animal life, and flotsam from the far-off islands. But the rocks that lie off the shore, and the jagged points that project in fanciful forms, break the even great swell, and send the waters, churned into spray and foam, into the air with a thousand hues in the sun. The shock of these sharp collisions mingles with the heavy ocean boom. Cypress Point is one of the most conspicuous of these projections, and its strange trees creep out upon the ragged ledges almost to the water's edge. These cypresses are quite as instinct with individual life and quite as fantastic as any that Doré drew for his "Inferno." They are as gnarled and twisted as olive-trees two centuries old, but their attitudes seem not only to show struggle with the elements, but agony in that struggle. The agony may be that of torture in the tempest, or of some fabled creatures fleeing and pursued, stretching out their long arms in terror, and fixed in that writhing fear. They are creatures of the sea quite as much as of the land, and they give to this lovely coast a strange charm and fascination.

CHURCH AT LAGUNA.

tarium as well as a pleasure resort. The Hot Springs have much the same character as the Töplitz waters in Bohemia, and the saturated earth—the *Mutterlager*—furnishes the curative "mud baths" which are enjoyed at Marienbad and Carlsbad. The union of the climate, which is so favorable in diseases of the respiratory organs, with the waters, which do so much for rheumatic sufferers, gives a distinction to Las Vegas Hot Springs. This New-Mexican air—there is none purer on the globe—is an enemy to hay-fever and malarial diseases. It was a wise enterprise to provide that those who wish to try its efficacy can do so at the Montezuma without giving up any of the comforts of civilized life.

It is difficult to explain to one who has not seen it, or will not put himself in the leisurely frame of mind to enjoy it, the charms of the desert of the high plateaus of New Mexico and Arizona. Its arid character is not so impressive as its ancientness; and the part which interests us is not only the procession of the long geologic eras, visible in the extinct volcanoes, the *barrancas*, the painted buttes, the petrified forests, but as well in the evidences of civilizations gone by, or the remains of them surviving in our day—the cliff dwellings, the ruins of cities that were thriving when Coronado sent his lieutenants through the region three centuries ago, and the present residences of the Pueblo Indians, either villages perched upon an almost inaccessible rock like Acamo, or clusters of adobe dwellings like Isleta and Laguna. The Pueblo Indians, of whom the Zuñis are a tribe, have been dwellers in villages and cultivators of the soil and of the arts of peace immemorially, a gentle, amiable race. It is indeed such a race as one would expect to find in the land of the sun and the cactus. Their manners and their arts attest their antiquity and a long refinement in fixed

The traveller to California by the Santa Fe route comes into the arid regions gradually, and finds each day a variety of objects of interest that upsets his conception of a monotonous desert land. If he chooses to break the continental journey midway, he can turn aside at Las Vegas to the Hot Springs. Here, at the head of a picturesque valley, is the Montezuma Hotel, a luxurious and handsome house, 6767 feet above sea-level, a great surprise in the midst of the broken and somewhat savage New-Mexican scenery. The low hills covered with pines and piñons, the romantic glens, and the wide views from the elevations about the hotel, make it an attractive place; and a great deal has been done, in the erection of bath-houses, ornamental gardening, and the grading of roads and walks, to make it a comfortable place. The latitude and the dryness of the atmosphere insure for the traveller from the North in our winter an agreeable reception, and the elevation makes the spot in the summer a desirable resort from Southern heat. It is a sani-

dwellings and occupations. The whole region is a most interesting field for the antiquarian.

We stopped one day at Laguna, which is on the Santa Fe line west of Isleta, another Indian pueblo at the Atlantic and zontal ledges in the distance. Laguna is built upon a rounded elevation of rock. Its appearance is exactly that of a Syrian village, the same cluster of little, square, flat-roofed houses in terraces, the same brown color, and under the same pale

TERRACED HOUSES, PUEBLO OF LAGUNA.

Pacific junction, where the road crosses the Rio Grande del Norte west of Albuquerque. Near Laguna a little stream called the Rio Puerco flows southward and joins the Rio Grande. There is verdure along these streams, and gardens and fruit orchards repay the rude irrigation. In spite of these watercourses the aspect of the landscape is wild and desert-like—low barren hills and ragged ledges, wide sweeps of sand and dry gray bushes, with mountains and long lines of hori- blue sky. And the resemblance was completed by the figures of the women on the roofs, or moving down the slope. erect and supple, carrying on the head a water jar, and holding together by one hand the mantle worn like a Spanish *rebozo*. The village is irregularly built, without much regard to streets or alleys, and it has no special side of entrance or approach. Every side presents a blank wall of adobe, and the entrance seems quite by chance. Yet the way we went over, the smooth slope was worn here and there in channels three or four inches deep, as if by the passing feet of many generations. The only semblance of architectural regularity is in the plaza, not perfectly square, upon which some of the houses look, and where the annual dances take place. The houses have the effect of being built in terráces rising one above the other, but it is hard to say exactly what a house is—whether it is anything more than one room. You can reach some of the houses only by aid of a ladder. You enter others from the street. If you will go further, you must climb a ladder, which brings you to the roof, that is used as the sitting-room or door-yard of the next room. From this room you may still ascend to others, or you may pass through low and small doorways to other apartments. It is all hap-hazard, but exceedingly picturesque. You may find some of the family in every room, or they may be gathered, women and babies, on a roof which is protected by a parapet. At the time of our visit the men were all away at work in their fields. Notwithstanding the houses are only sun-dried bricks, and the village is without water or street commissioners, I was struck by the universal cleanliness. There was no refuse in the corners or alleys, no odors, and many of the rooms were patterns of neatness. To be sure, an old woman here and there kept her hens in an adjoining apartment above her own, and there was the litter of children and of rather careless house-keeping. But, taken altogether, the town is an example for some more civilized, whose inhabitants wash oftener and dress better than these Indians.

We were put on friendly terms with the whole settlement through three or four young maidens who had been at the Carlisle school, and spoke English very prettily. They were of the ages of fifteen and sixteen, and some of them had been five years away. They came back, so far as I could learn, gladly to their own people and to the old ways. They had resumed the Indian dress, which is much more becoming to them, as I think they know, than that which had been imposed upon them. I saw no books. They do not read any now, and they appear to be perfectly content with the idle drudgery of their semi-savage condition. In time they will marry in their tribe, and

the school episode will be a thing of the past. But not altogether. The pretty Josephine, who was our best cicerone about the place, a girl of lovely eyes and modest mien, showed us with pride her own room, or "house," as she called it, neat as could be, simply furnished with an iron bedstead and snow-white cot, a mirror, chair, and table, and a trunk, and some "advertising" prints on the walls. She said that she was needed at home to cook for her aged mother, and her present ambition was to make money enough by the sale of pottery and curios to buy a cooking stove, so that she could cook more as the whites do. The house-work of the family had mainly fallen upon her; but it was not burdensome, I fancied, and she and the other girls of her age had leisure to go to the station on the arrival of every train, in hope of selling something to the passengers, and to sit on the rocks in the sun and dream as maidens do. I fancy it would be better for Josephine and for all the rest if there were no station and no passing trains. The elder women were uniformly ugly, but not repulsive like the Mojaves; the place swarmed with children, and the babies, aged women, and pleasing young girls grouped most effectively on the roofs.

The whole community were very complaisant and friendly when we came to know them well, which we did in the course of an hour, and they enjoyed as much as we did the bargaining for pottery. They have for sale a great quantity of small pieces, fantastic in form and brilliantly colored—toys, in fact; but we found in their houses many beautiful jars of large size and excellent shape, decorated most effectively. The ordinary utensils for cooking and for cooling water are generally pretty in design and painted artistically. Like the ancient Peruvians, they make many vessels in the forms of beasts and birds. Some of the designs of the decoration are highly conventionalized, and others are just in the proper artistic line of the natural—a spray with a bird, or a sunflower on its stalk. The ware is all unglazed, exceedingly light and thin, and baked so hard that it has a metallic sound when struck. Some of the large jars are classic in shape, and recall in form and decoration the ancient Cypriote ware, but the colors are commonly brilliant and barbaric. The designs seem to be indigenous, and to betray

little Spanish influence. The art displayed in this pottery is indeed wonderful,
and, to my eye, much more effective and
lastingly pleasing than much of our cultivated decoration. A couple of handsome jars that I bought of an old woman,
she assured me she made and decorated
herself; but I saw no ovens there, nor
any signs of manufacture, and suppose
that most of the ware is made at Acoma.

It did not seem to be a very religious
community, although the town has a
Catholic church, and I understand that
Protestant services are sometimes held in
the place. The church is not much frequented, and the only evidence of devotion I encountered was in a woman who
wore a large and handsome silver cross,
made by the Navajos. When I asked
its price, she clasped it to her bosom, with
an upward look full of faith and of refusal to part with her religion at any
price. The church, which is adobe, and
at least two centuries old, is one of the
most interesting I have seen anywhere.
It is a simple parallelogram, 104 feet long
and 21 feet broad, the gable having an opening in which the bells hang. The interior is exceedingly curious, and its decorations are worth reproduction. The floor
is of earth, and many of the tribe who
were distinguished and died long ago are
said to repose under its smooth surface,
with nothing to mark their place of sepulture. It has an open timber roof, the
beams supported upon carved corbels.
The ceiling is made of wooden sticks,
about two inches in diameter and some
four feet long, painted in alternated colors—red, blue, orange, and black—and so
twisted or woven together as to produce
the effect of plaited straw, a most novel
and agreeable decoration. Over the entrance is a small gallery, the under roof
of which is composed of sticks laid in
straw pattern and colored. All around
the walls runs a most striking dado, an
odd, angular pattern, with conventionalized birds at intervals, painted in strong
yet *fade* colors—red, yellow, black, and
white. The north wall is without windows; all the light, when the door is
closed, comes from two irregular windows,
without glass, high up in the south wall.
The chancel walls are covered with frescoes, and there are several quaint paintings, some of them not very bad in color
and drawing. The altar, which is supported at the sides by twisted wooden pil-

lars carved with a knife, is hung with ancient sheepskins brightly painted. Back
of the altar are some archaic wooden images, colored; and over the altar, on the
ceiling, are the stars of heaven, and the
sun and the moon, each with a face in it.
The interior was scrupulously clean and
sweet and restful to one coming in from
the glare of the sun on the desert. It was
evidently little used, and the Indians who
accompanied us seemed under no strong
impression of its sanctity; but we liked to
linger in it, it was so *bizarre*, so picturesque, and exhibited in its rude decoration so much taste. Two or three small
birds flitting about seemed to enjoy the
coolness and the subdued light, and were
undisturbed by our presence.

These are children of the desert, kin in
their condition and the influences that formed them to the sedentary tribes of upper
Egypt and Arabia, who pitch their villages
upon the rocky eminences, and depend
for subsistence upon irrigation and scant
pasturage. Their habits are those of the
dwellers in an arid land which has little
in common with the wilderness—the inhospitable northern wilderness of rain and
frost and snow. Rain, to be sure, insures
some sort of vegetation in the most forbidding and intractable country, but that
does not save the harsh landscape from
being unattractive. The high plateaus of
New Mexico and Arizona have everything
that the rainy wilderness lacks—sunshine.
heaven's own air, immense breadth of
horizon, color and infinite beauty of outline, and a warm soil with unlimited possibilities when moistened. All that these
deserts need is water. A fatal want?
No. That is simply saying that science
can do for this region what it cannot
do for the high wilderness of frost—by the
transportation of water transform it into
gardens of bloom and fields of fruitful-
ness. The wilderness shall be made to
feed the desert.

I confess that these deserts in the warm
latitudes fascinate me. Perhaps it is because I perceive in them such a chance
for the triumph of the skill of man, seeing how, here and there, his energy has
pushed the desert out of his path across
the continent. But I fear that I am not
so practical. To many the desert in its
stony sterility, its desolateness, its unbroken solitude, its fantastic savageness,
is either appalling or repulsive. To them
it is tiresome and monotonous. The vast

INTERIOR OF THE CHURCH AT LAGUNA.

plains of Kansas and Nebraska are monotonous even in the agricultural green of summer. Not so to me the desert. It is as changeable in its lights and colors as the ocean. It is even in its general features of sameness never long the same. If you traverse it on foot or on horseback, there is ever some minor novelty. And on the swift train, if you draw down the curtain against the glare, or turn to your book, you are sure to miss something of interest—a deep cañon rift in the plain, a turn that gives a wide view glowing in a hundred hues in the sun, a savage gorge with beetling rocks, a solitary butte or red truncated pyramid thrust up into the blue sky, a horizontal ledge cutting the horizon line as straight as a ruler for miles, a pointed cliff uplifted sheer from the plain and laid in regular courses of Cyclopean masonry, the battlements of a fort, a terraced castle with towers and esplanade, a great trough of a valley, gray and parched, enclosed by far purple mountains. And then the unlimited freedom of it, its infinite expansion, its air like wine to the senses, the floods of sunshine, the waves of color, the translucent atmosphere that aids the imagination to create in the distance all architectural splendors and realms of peace. It is all like a mirage and a dream. We pass swiftly, and make a moving panorama of beauty in hues, of strangeness in forms, of sublimity in extent, of overawing and savage antiquity. I would miss none of it. And when we pass to the accustomed again, to the fields of verdure and the forests and the hills of green, and are limited in view and shut in by that which we love, after all, better than the arid land, I have a great longing to see again the desert, to be a part of its vastness, and to feel once more the freedom and inspiration of its illimitable horizons.

There is an arid region lying in northern Arizona and southern Utah which has been called the District of the Grand Cañon of the Colorado. The area, roughly estimated, contains from 13,000 to 16,000 square miles—about the size of the State of Maryland. This region, fully described by the explorers and studied by the geologists in the United States service, but little known to even the travelling public, is probably the most interesting territory of its size on the globe. At least it is unique. In attempting to convey an idea of it the writer can be assisted by no comparison, nor can he appeal in the minds of his readers to any experience of scenery that can apply here. The so-called Grand Cañon differs not in degree from all other scenes; it differs in kind.

The Colorado River flows southward through Utah, and crosses the Arizona line below the junction with the San Juan. It continues southward, flowing deep in what is called the Marble Cañon, till it is joined by the Little Colorado, coming up from the southeast; it then turns westward in a devious line until it drops straight south, and forms the western boundary of Arizona. The centre of the district mentioned is the westwardly flowing part of the Colorado. South of the river is the Colorado Plateau, at a general elevation of about 7000 feet. North of it the land is higher, and ascends in a series of plateaus, and then terraces, a succession of cliffs like a great stairway, rising to the high plateaus of Utah. The plateaus, adjoining the river on the north and well marked by north and south dividing lines, or faults, are, naming them from east to west, the Paria, the Kaibab, the Kanab, the Uinkaret, and the Sheavwitz, terminating in a great wall on the west, the Great Wash fault, where the surface of the country drops at once from a general elevation of 6000 feet to from 1300 to 3000 feet above the sea-level—into a desolate and formidable desert.

If the Grand Cañon itself did not dwarf everything else, the scenery of these plateaus would be superlative in interest. It is not all desert, nor are the gorges, cañons, cliffs, and terraces, which gradually prepare the mind for the comprehension of the Grand Cañon, the only wonders of this land of enchantment. These are contrasted with the sylvan scenery of the Kaibab plateau, its giant forests and parks, and broad meadows decked in the summer with wild flowers in dense masses of scarlet, white, purple, and yellow. The Vermilion Cliffs, the Pink Cliffs, the White Cliffs, surpass in fantastic form and brilliant color anything that the imagination conceives possible in nature, and there are dreamy landscapes quite beyond the most exquisite fancies of Claude and of Turner. The region is full of wonders, of beauties, and sublimities that Shelley's imaginings do not match in the "Prometheus Unbound," and when it becomes accessible to the tourist it will offer endless field for the delight of those whose minds can rise to the heights of the sublime and the beautiful. In all imaginative writing or painting the material used is that of human experience, otherwise it could not be understood, even heaven must be described in the terms of an earthly paradise. Human experience has no prototype of this region, and the imagination has never conceived of its forms and colors. It is impossible to convey an adequate idea of it by pen or pencil or brush. The reader who is familiar with the glowing descriptions in the official reports of Major J. W. Powell, Captain C. E. Dutton, Lieutenant Ives, and others, will not save himself from a shock of surprise when the reality is before him. This paper deals only with a single view in this marvellous region.

The point where we struck the Grand Cañon, approaching it from the south, is opposite the promontory in the Kaibab Plateau named Point Sublime by Major Powell, just north of the 36th parallel, and 112° 15′ west longitude. This is only a few miles west of the junction with the Little Colorado. About three or four miles west of this junction the river enters the east slope of the east Kaibab monocline, and here the Grand Cañon begins. Rapidly the chasm deepens to about 6000 feet, or rather it penetrates a higher country, the slope of the river remaining about the same. Through this lofty plateau—an elevation of 7000 to 9000 feet—the chasm extends for sixty miles, gradually changing its course to the northwest, and entering the Kanab Plateau. The Kaibab division of the Grand Cañon of the river, is 220 miles; by a median line between the crests of the summits of the walls with two-mile cords, about 195 miles; the distance in a straight line is 125 miles.

TOURISTS IN THE COLORADO CAÑON.

is by far the sublimest of all, being 1000 feet deeper than any other. It is not grander only on account of its greater depth, but it is broader and more diversified with magnificent architectural features.

The Kanab division, only less magnificent than the Kaibab, receives the Kanab Cañon from the north and the Cataract Cañon from the south, and ends at the Toroweap Valley.

The section of the Grand Cañon seen by those who take the route from Peach Springs is between 113° and 114° west longitude, and, though wonderful, presents few of the great features of either the Kaibab or the Kanab divisions. The Grand Cañon ends, west longitude 114°, at the Great Wash, west of the Hurricane Ledge or Fault. Its whole length from Little Colorado to the Great Wash, measured by the meanderings of the surface

In our journey to the Grand Cañon we left the Santa Fe line at Flagstaff, a new town with a lively lumber industry, in the midst of a spruce-pine forest which occupies the broken country through which the road passes for over 50 miles. The forest is open, the trees of moderate size are too thickly set with low-growing limbs to make clean lumber, and the foliage furnishes the minimum of shade; but the change to these woods is a welcome one from the treeless reaches of the desert on either side. The cañon is also reached from Williams, the next station west, the distance being a little shorter, and the point on the cañon visited being usually a little further west. But the Flagstaff route is for many reasons usually preferred. Flagstaff lies just southeast of the San Francisco Mountain, and on the great Colorado Plateau, which has a pretty uniform elevation of about 7000 feet above the sea. The whole region is full of interest. Some of the most remarkable cliff dwellings are within 10 miles of Flagstaff, on the Walnut Creek Cañon. At Holbrook, 100 miles east, the traveller finds a road some 40 miles long, that leads to the great petrified forest, or Chalcedony Park. Still further east are the villages of the Pueblo Indians, near the line, while to the northward is the great reservation of the Navajos, a nomadic tribe celebrated for its fine blankets and pretty work in silver—a tribe that preserves much of its manly independence by shunning the charity of the United States. No Indians have come into intimate or dependent relations with the whites without being deteriorated.

Flagstaff is the best present point of departure, because it has a small hotel, good supply stores, and a large livery-stable, made necessary by the business of the place and the objects of interest in the neighborhood, and because one reaches from there by the easiest road the finest scenery incomparably on the Colorado. The distance is 76 miles through a practically uninhabited country, much of it a desert, and with water very infrequent. No work has been done on the road; it is made simply by driving over it. There are a few miles here and there of fair wheeling, but a good deal of it is intolerably dusty or exceedingly stony, and progress is slow. In the daytime (it was the last of June) the heat is apt to be excessive; but this could be borne, the air is so absolutely dry and delicious, and breezes occasionally spring up, if it were not for the dust. It is, notwithstanding the novelty of the adventure and of the scenery by the way, a tiresome journey of two days. A day of rest is absolutely required at the cañon, so that five days must be allowed for the trip. This will cost the traveller, according to the size of the party made up, from forty to fifty dollars. But a much longer sojourn at the cañon is desirable.

Our party of seven was stowed in and on an old Concord coach drawn by six horses, and piled with camp equipage, bedding, and provisions. A four-horse team followed, loaded with other supplies and cooking utensils. The road lies on the east side of the San Francisco Mountain. Returning, we passed around its west side, gaining thus a complete view of this shapely peak. The compact range is a group of extinct volcanoes, the craters of which are distinctly visible. The cup-like summit of the highest is 13,000 feet above the sea, and snow always lies on the north escarpment. Rising about 6000 feet above the point of view of the great plateau, it is from all sides a noble object, the dark rock, snow-sprinkled, rising out of the dense growth of pine and cedar. We drove at first through open pine forests, through park-like intervals, over the foot-hills of the mountain, through growths of scrub cedar, and out into the ever-varying rolling country to widely extended prospects. Two considerable hills on our right attracted us by their unique beauty. Upon the summit and side of each was a red glow exactly like the tint of sunset.

We thought surely that it was the effect of reflected light, but the sky was cloudless and the color remained constant. The color came from the soil. The first was called Sunset Mountain. One of our party named the other, and the more beautiful, Peachblow Mountain, a poetic and perfectly descriptive name.

We lunched at noon beside a swift, clouded, cold stream of snow water from the San Francisco, along which grew a few gnarled cedars and some brilliant wild flowers. The scene was more than picturesque; in the clear hot air of the desert the distant landscape made a hundred pictures of beauty. Behind us the dark form of San Francisco rose up 6000 feet to its black crater and fields of spotless snow. Away off to the northeast, beyond the brown and gray pastures, across a far line distinct in dull color, lay the *Painted Desert*, like a mirage, like a really painted landscape, glowing in red and orange and pink, an immense city rather than a landscape, with towers and terraces and façades, melting into indistinctness as in a rosy mist, spectral but constant, weltering in a tropic glow and heat, walls and columns and shafts, the wreck of an Oriental capital on a wide violet plain, suffused with brilliant color softened into exquisite shades. All over this region Nature has such surprises, that laugh at our inadequate conception of her resources.

Our camp for the night was at the next place where water could be obtained, a station of the Arizona Cattle Company. Abundant water is piped down to it from mountain springs. The log house and stable of the cow-boys were unoccupied, and we pitched our tent on a knoll by the corral. The night was absolutely dry, and sparkling with the starlight. A part of the company spread their blankets on the ground under the sky. It is apt to be cold in this region toward morning, but lodging in the open air is no hardship in this delicious climate. The next day the way part of the distance, with only a road marked by wagon wheels, was through extensive and barren-looking cattle ranges, through pretty vales of grass surrounded by stunted cedars, and over stony ridges and plains of sand and small bowlders. The water having failed at Red Horse, the only place where it is usually found in the day's march, our horses went without, and we had recourse to our canteens. The whole country is essentially arid, but snow falls in the winter-time, and its melting, with occasional showers in the summer, creates what are called surface wells, made by drainage. Many of them go dry by June. There had been no rain in the region since the last of March, but clouds were gathering daily, and showers are always expected in July. The phenomenon of rain on this baked surface, in this hot air, and with this immense horizon, is very interesting. Showers in this tentative time are local. In our journey we saw showers far off, we experienced a dash for ten minutes, but it was local, covering not more than a mile or two square. We have in sight a vast canopy of blue sky, of forming and dispersing clouds. It is difficult for them to drop their moisture in the rising columns of hot air. The result at times was a very curious spectacle —rain in the sky that did not reach the earth. Perhaps some cold current high above us would condense the moisture, which would begin to fall in long trailing sweeps, blown like fine folds of muslin, or like sheets of dissolving sugar, and then the hot air of the earth would dissipate it, and the showers would be absorbed in the upper regions. The heat was sometimes intense, but at intervals a refreshing wind would blow, the air being as fickle as the rain; and now and then we would see a slender column of dust, a thousand or two feet high, marching across the desert, apparently not more than two feet in diameter, and wavering like the threads of moisture that tried in vain to reach the earth as rain. Of life there was not much to be seen in our desert route. In the first day we encountered no habitation except the ranch-house mentioned, and saw no human being; and the second day none except the solitary occupant of the dried well at Red Horse, and two or three Indians on the hunt. A few squirrels were seen, and a rabbit now and then, and occasionally a bird. The general impression was that of a deserted land. But antelope abound in the timber regions, and we saw several of these graceful creatures quite near us. Excellent antelope steaks, bought of the wandering Indian hunters, added something to our "canned" supplies. One day as we lunched, without water, on the cedar slope of a lovely grass interval, we saw coming toward us over the swells of the prairie a figure of a man on a horse. It rode to us straight as the

crow flies. The Indian pony stopped not two feet from where our group sat, and the rider, who was an Oualapai chief, clad in sacking, with the print of the brand of flour or salt on his back, dismounted with his Winchester rifle, and stood silently looking at us without a word of salutation. He stood there, impassive, until we offered him something to eat. Having eaten all we gave him, he opened his mouth and said, "Smoke 'em?" Having procured from the other wagon a pipe of tobacco and a pull at the driver's canteen, he returned to us all smiles. His only baggage was the skull of an antelope, with the horns, hung at his saddle. Into this he put the bread and meat which we gave him, mounted the wretched pony, and without a word rode straight away. At a little distance he halted, dismounted, and motioned toward the edge of the timber, where he had spied an antelope. But the game eluded him, and he mounted again and rode off across the desert—a strange figure. His tribe lives in the cañon some fifty miles west, and was at present encamped, for the purpose of hunting, in the pine woods not far from the point we were aiming at.

The way seemed long. With the heat and dust and slow progress, it was exceedingly wearisome. Our modern nerves are not attuned to the slow crawling of a prairie wagon. There had been growing for some time in the coach a feeling that the journey did not pay, that, in fact, no mere scenery could compensate for the fatigue of the trip. The imagination did not rise to it. "It will have to be a very big cañon," said the Duchess.

Late in the afternoon we entered an open pine forest, passed through a meadow where the Indians had set their camp by a shallow pond, and drove along a ridge, in the cool shades, for three or four miles. Suddenly, on the edge of a descent, we who were on the box saw through the tree-tops a vision that stopped the pulse for a second, and filled us with excitement. It was only a glimpse, far off and apparently lifted up — red towers, purple cliffs, wide-spread apart, hints of color and splendor; on the right distance, mansions, gold and white and carmine (so the light made them), architectural habitations in the sky it must be, and suggestions of others far off in the middle distance, a substantial aerial city, or the ruins of one, such as the prophet saw in a vision. It was only a glimpse. Our hearts were in our mouths. We had a vague impression of something wonderful, fearful, some incomparable splendor that was not earthly. Were we drawing near the "City"? and should we have yet a more perfect view thereof? Was it Jerusalem, or some Hindoo temples, there in the sky? "It was builded of pearls and precious stones, also the streets were paved with gold; so that by reason of the natural glory of the City, and the reflection of the sunbeams upon it, Christian with desire fell sick." It was a momentary vision of a vast amphitheatre of splendor, mostly hidden by the trees and the edge of the plateau.

We descended into a hollow. There was the well, a log cabin, a tent or two under the pine-trees. We dismounted with impatient haste. The sun was low in the horizon, and had long withdrawn from this grassy dell. Tired as we were, we could not wait. It was only to ascend the little steep, stony slope — 300 yards—and we should see! Our party were straggling up the hill. Two or three had reached the edge. I looked up. The Duchess threw up her arms and screamed. We were not fifteen paces behind, but we saw nothing. We took the few steps, and the whole magnificence broke upon us. No one could be prepared for it. The scene is one to strike dumb with awe, or to unstring the nerves; one might stand in silent astonishment, another would burst into tears.

There are some experiences that cannot be repeated — one's first view of Rome, one's first view of Jerusalem. But these emotions are produced by association, by the sudden standing face to face with the scenes most wrought into our whole life and education by tradition and religion. This was without association, as it was without parallel. It was a shock so novel that the mind, dazed, quite failed to comprehend it. All that we could grasp was a vast confusion of amphitheatres and strange architectural forms resplendent with color. The vastness of the view amazed us quite as much as its transcendent beauty.

We had expected a cañon—two lines of perpendicular walls 6000 feet high, with the ribbon of a river at the bottom. But the reader may dismiss all his notions of a cañon, indeed of any sort of mountain or gorge scenery with which he is familiar. We had come into a new world. What

we saw was not a cañon, or a chasm, or a gorge, but a vast area which is a break in the plateau. From where we stood it was 12 miles across to the opposite walls —a level line of mesa on the Utah side. We looked up and down for 20 to 30 miles. This great space is filled with gigantic architectural constructions, with amphitheatres, gorges, precipices, walls of masonry, fortresses terraced up to the level of the eye, temples mountain size, all brilliant with horizontal lines of color—streaks of solid hues a few feet in width, streaks a thousand feet in width— yellows, mingled white and gray, orange, dull red, brown, blue, carmine, green, all blending in the sunlight into one transcendent suffusion of splendor. Afar off we saw the river in two places, a mere thread, as motionless and smooth as a strip of mirror, only we knew it was a turbid boiling torrent, 6000 feet below us. Directly opposite the overhanging ledge on which we stood was a mountain, the sloping base of which was ashy gray and bluish; it rose in a series of terraces to a thousand feet wall of dark red sandstone, receding upward, with ranges of columns and many fantastic sculptures, to a finial row of gigantic opera-glasses 6000 feet above the river. The great San Francisco Mountain, with its snowy crater, which we had passed on the way, might have been set down in the place of this one, and it would have been only one in a multitude of such forms that met the eye whichever way we looked. Indeed, all the vast mountains in this region might be hidden in this cañon.

Wandering a little away from the group and out of sight, and turning suddenly to the scene from another point of view, I experienced for a moment an indescribable terror of nature, a confusion of mind, a fear to be alone in such a presence. With all this grotesqueness and majesty of form and radiance of color, creation seemed in a whirl. With our education in scenery of a totally different kind, I suppose it would need long acquaintance with this to familiarize one with it to the extent of perfect mental comprehension.

The vast abyss has an atmosphere of its own, one always changing and producing new effects, an atmosphere and shadows and tones of its own—golden, rosy, gray, brilliant, and sombre, and playing a thousand fantastic tricks to the vision. The rich and wonderful color effects, says Captain Dutton, "are due to the inherent colors of the rocks, modified by the atmosphere. Like any other great series of strata in the plateau province, the carboniferous has its own range of colors, which might serve to distinguish it even if we had no other criterion. The summit strata are pale gray, with a faint yellowish cast. Beneath them the cross-bedded sandstone appears, showing a mottled surface of pale pinkish hue. Underneath this member are nearly 1000 feet of the lower Aubrey sandstones, displaying an intensely brilliant red, which is somewhat marked by the talus shot down from the gray cherty limestone at the summit. Beneath the lower Aubrey is the face of the Red Wall limestone, from 2000 to 3000 feet high. It has a strong red tone, but a very peculiar one. Most of the red strata of the west have the brownish or vermilion tones, but these are rather purplish-red, as if the pigment had been treated to a dash of blue. It is not quite certain that this may not arise in part from the intervention of the blue haze, and probably it is rendered more conspicuous by this cause; but, on the whole, the purplish cast seems to be inherent. This is the dominant color of the cañon, for the expanse of the rock surface displayed is more than half in the Red Wall group."

I was continually likening this to a vast city rather than a landscape, but it was a city of no man's creation nor of any man's conception. In the visions which inspired or crazy painters have had of the New Jerusalem, of Babylon the Great, of a heaven in the atmosphere with endless perspective of towers and steeps that hang in the twilight sky, the imagination has tried to reach this reality. But here are effects beyond the artist, forms the architect has not hinted at. And yet everything reminds us of man's work. And the explorers have tried by the use of Oriental nomenclature to bring it within our comprehension, the East being the land of the imagination. There is the Hindoo Amphitheatre, the Bright Angel Amphitheatre, the Ottoman Amphitheatre, Shiva's Temple, Vishnu's Temple, Vulcan's Throne. And here indeed is the idea of the pagoda architecture, of the terrace architecture, of the *bizarre* constructions which rise with projecting buttresses, rows of pillars, recesses, battlements, esplanades, and low walls, hanging gardens, and truncated pinnacles. It is a city, but a city of the imagination. In many pages I could tell what I saw in one day's lounging for a mile or so along the edge of the precipice. The view changed at every step, and was never half an hour the same in one place. Nor did it need much fancy to create illusions or pictures of unearthly beauty. There was a castle, terraced up with columns, plain enough, and below it a parade-ground; at any moment the knights in armor and with banners might emerge from the red gates, and deploy there, while the ladies looked down from the balconies. But there were many castles and fortresses and barracks and noble mansions. And the rich sculpture in this brilliant color! In time I began to see queer details: a Richardson house, with low portals and round arches, surmounted by a Nuremberg gable; perfect panels 600 feet high, for the setting of pictures; a train of cars partly derailed at the door of a long low warehouse, with a garden in front of it. There was no end to such devices.

It was long before I could comprehend the vastness of the view, see the enormous chasms and rents and seams, and the many architectural ranges separated by great gulfs, between me and the wall of the mesa twelve miles distant. Away to the northeast was the blue Navajo Mountain, the lone peak in the horizon; but on the southern side of it lay a desert level, which in the afternoon light took on the exact appearance of a blue lake; its edge this side was a wall thousands of feet high, many miles in length, and straightly horizontal; over this seemed to fall water. I could see the foam of it at the foot of the cliff; and below that was a lake of shimmering silver, in which the giant precipice and the fall and their color were mirrored. Of course there was no silver lake, and the reflection that simulated it was only the sun on the lower part of the immense wall.

Some one said that all that was needed to perfect this scene was a Niagara Falls. I thought what figure a fall 150 feet high and 3000 long would make in this arena. It would need a spy-glass to discover it. An adequate Niagara here should be at least three miles in breadth, and fall 2000 feet over one of these walls. And the Yosemite—ah! the lovely Yosemite! Dumped down into this wilderness of gorges and mountains, it would take a guide who knew of its existence a long time to find it.

The process of creation is here laid bare through the geologic periods. The strata of rock, deposited or upheaved, preserve their horizontal and parallel courses. If we imagine a river flowing on a plain, it would wear for itself a deeper and deeper channel. The walls of this channel would recede irregularly by weathering and by the coming in of other streams. The channel would go on deepening, and the outer walls would again recede. If the rocks were of different material and degrees of hardness, the forms would be carved in the fantastic and architectural manner we find them here. The Colorado flows through the tortuous inner chasm, and where we see it, it is 6000 feet below the surface where we stand, and below the towers of the terraced forms nearer it. The splendid views of the cañon at this point given in Captain Dutton's report are from Point Sublime, on the north side. There seems to have been no way of reaching the river from that point. From the south side the descent, though wearisome, is feasible. It reverses mountaineering to descend 6000 feet for a view, and there is a certain pleasure in standing on a mountain summit without the trouble of climbing it. Hance, the guide, who has charge of the well, has made a path to the bottom. The route is seven miles long. Half-way down he has a house by a spring. At the bottom, somewhere in those depths, is a sort of farm, grass capable of sustaining horses and cattle, and ground where fruit trees can grow. Horses are actually living there, and parties descend there with tents, and camp for days at a time. It is a world of its own. Some of the photographic views presented here, all inadequate, are taken from points on Hance's trail. But no camera or pen can convey an adequate conception of what Captain Dutton happily calls a great innovation in the modern ideas of scenery. To the eye educated to any other, it may be shocking, grotesque, incomprehensible; but "those who have long and carefully studied the Grand Cañon of the Colorado do not hesitate for a moment to pronounce it by far the most sublime of all earthly spectacles."

I have space only to refer to the geologic history in Captain Dutton's report of 1882, of which there should be a popular edition. The waters of the Atlantic once overflowed this region, and were separated from the Pacific, if at all, only by a ridge. The story is of long eras of deposits, of removal, of upheaval, and of volcanic action. It is estimated that in one period the thickness of strata removed and transported away was 10,000 feet. Long after the Colorado began its work of corrosion there was a mighty upheaval. The reader will find the story of the making of the Grand Cañon more fascinating than any romance.

Without knowing this story the impression that one has in looking on this scene is that of immense antiquity, hardly anywhere else on earth so overwhelming as here. It has been here in all its lonely grandeur and transcendent beauty, exactly as it is, for what to us is an eternity, unknown, unseen by human eye. To the recent Indian, who roved along its brink or descended to its recesses, it was not strange, because he had known no other than the plateau scenery. It is only within a quarter of a century that the Grand Cañon has been known to the civilized world. It is scarcely known now. It is never twice the same, for, as I said, it has an atmosphere of its own. I was told by Hance that he once saw a thunder-storm in it. He described the chaos of clouds in the pit, the roar of the tempest, the reverberations of thunder, the inconceivable splendor of the rainbows mingled with the colors of the towers and terraces. It was as if the world were breaking up. He fled away to his hut in terror.

The day is near when this scenery must be made accessible. A railway can easily be built from Flagstaff. The projected road from Utah, crossing the Colorado at Lee's Ferry, would come within twenty miles of the Grand Cañon, and a branch to it could be built. The region is arid, and in the "sight-seeing" part of the year the few surface wells and springs are likely to go dry. The greatest difficulty would be in procuring water for railway service or for such houses of entertainment as are necessary. It could, no doubt, be piped from the San Francisco Mountain. At any rate, ingenuity will overcome the difficulties, and travellers from the wide world will flock thither, for there is revealed the long-kept secret, the unique achievement of nature.

THE JOHN DAY FOSSIL BEDS

DURING the last three or four decades some of the most notable contributions that American investigators have made to science have been based on the study of fossil remains exhumed in the Bad Lands of the western United States. In these strange formations there have been found, scattered through a great thickness of strata, the remains of race after race of ancient animals, all differing more or less widely from the existing inhabitants of the earth. Through a study of these fossils many previously existing gaps in the history of life have been closed up; a flood of light has been thrown upon innumerable scientific problems; and so many new creatures have been discovered that it has been necessary to modify the scheme of zoological classification considerably in order to accommodate them.

Most of these great fossil fields have received more or less careful attention from the traveller and the scientist, but, strangely enough, one of the longest known and most productive of them, tl John Day Basin, of eastern Orego which furnishes, perhaps, the most r markable chapter in the ancient histo of the earth, has remained practically u known, excepting to the few who ha actually visited it.

Like many another rich field for scie tific investigation, these fossil beds we discovered by a military expedition. 1861 a number of fossil rhinoceros teet in the hands of army officers returnii from a campaign against the Indians, a tracted the attention of Professor Thom Condon, then pastor of the Congregatio al church at The Dalles, Oregon. He pe ceived that a great discovery had bee made. In the following spring he obtai ed permission to accompany a party g ing out to re-enforce troops that had wi tered in the field, and under military pr tection he made a reconnoissance toi through the principal fossil localities, b was prevented by marauding Indi bands from collecting many specimens.

Some time after the discovery of the field a number of bones and teeth were sent by Condon to Professor Marsh, of Yale, with the result that Marsh came out post-haste, and having satisfied himself of the importance of the discovery, engaged several collectors, who were employed by him interruptedly for many years. Following the example set by Professor Marsh, many prominent institutions of this country and of Europe have worked over the beds, obtaining the remains of a large number of strange and interesting animals previously unknown.

But for the existence of the John Day River, we would know little regarding the ancient life of eastern Oregon, for great lava floods have covered almost the entire country, burying thousands of feet deep all but the later geological formations. As the result of long ages of erosion, the John Day has cut a deep and narrow valley, which passes through the lavas, and exposes to view, layer upon layer, in almost diagrammatic arrangement, the formations above and below them. In the strata of this section we find entombed the remains of those venerable creatures which attract the scientist to this field; and written, as it were, upon the walls of the great mausoleum, we discover the record of a remarkable series of changes in the physical geography of the country, that occurred in the ages during which these animals inhabited it.

In the erosion of their cañons the John Day and its tributaries have uncovered about ten thousand feet of strata, comprising eight or more geological formations, which represent as many distinct periods in the history of the country. At the bottom of this enormous pile are masses of ancient crystalline rocks the age of which is yet unknown. The lowest well-known strata are two almost inseparable formations, aggregating not less than 3500 feet in thickness. They contain numerous fossil remains which are all of marine animals, and demonstrate the existence of the sea over this region at the time they were being deposited. The lower formation is mainly hardened mud, indicating rather deep water, while the upper one is principally sand and coarse gravel, showing that the sea was shallowing as it accumulated.

The Cretaceous period, to which this, the first legible record in the history of this region, is carried back by these lower formations, though by no means early in geological time, is so remote from the present that it is difficult to measure its distance, except by the magnitude of the changes in the earth and its inhabitants which have taken place since it began. Perhaps the best illustration of this, from the physical stand-point, is found in the fact that at the beginning of Cretaceous time a considerable portion of the strata which now form the Himalayas, the Alps, and the Rocky Mountains were not yet even deposited, as gravel, sand, and mud, on the floor of the ocean; while to the long period required for their accumulation we must add the time necessary for the elevation and sculpturing into their present form of these enormous masses of material.

Though we find no remains of land animals in the Cretaceous beds of the John Day, we know from a study of other

SKULL OF THREE-TOED HORSE

DIGGING OUT A CAMEL SKULL

deposits of the same age that the dominant animals of this period were gigantic, fantastic, reptilian forms, quite unlike anything living at the present day; and that the mammalia, which played such an important rôle in the later John Day life, were represented in the Cretaceous very sparingly by insignificant creatures.

Following the close of the Cretaceous period, during which the fires of the earth were slumbering, there was inaugurated in the John Day region a long era of vulcanism, extending almost up to the present day. In this age volcanic and other igneous activity seems to have been almost continuous in or around the basin, and there were accumulated about 6000 feet of strata, consisting principally of lava and volcanic ashes. The four or five hundred feet of hardened ash and tufa at the bottom of the section are known as the Clarno formation, of Eocene age, and constitute one of the unique scenic features of the valley. Wherever they are exposed, these strata weather very unevenly, producing numberless grotesque balanced rocks and mock statues. Resting upon the Eocene in the river cañon are nearly two thousand feet of soft, fancifully sculptured and pinnacled, and often beautifully colored, ashy beds, designated as the John Day Miocene. Upon the crumpled surface of this formation lie the great Columbia lava beds, three thousand feet thick. Above the lavas are eight hundred feet of tilted ashy strata, the Cottonwood formation, of Pliocene age; and upon these, in nearly horizontal position, are about four hundred feet of coarse gravel and volcanic tufa, the Rattlesnake beds. In the river valleys, which are necessarily younger than the strata into which they are cut, we find, on terraces about fifty to seventy-five feet above the stream, the ashy and gravelly remnants of the last deposits formed before the present period.

All the formations of this age of fire contain fossils, but in none of them do we find shells or skeletons of marine animals. The remains are all of land or fresh-water forms, which signifies that the shallowing Cretaceous sea disappeared entirely from the region before the beginning of the following period, and that the later strata were deposited either in fresh water or as ash drifts or flows of mud and lava upon the land. Judging from the character of these deposits, they are generally considered as having originated in large lakes. We have evidence of the existence of four of these inland seas, in which showers of volcanic ash, streams of volcanic mud, and the natural wash from the land, heaped up, layer upon layer, great deposits, the remains of which we now recognize as fossil lake beds in the Clarno, the John Day, the Cottonwood, and the Rattlesnake formations.

Some of the lakes seem to have extended over large areas. Scattering outcrops of these deposits are found over a great portion of eastern Oregon, indicating at least a correspondingly wide extension of the ancient seas. The relations of the strata of successive deposits to each other show that the bed of the Eocene lake had apparently been dry some time before the waters of the John Day lake began to gather. We know also that the second, in turn, was dried up before the first eruption of the Columbia lavas, for we often find in the bottom of the lower lava beds the charred remains of forest trees, which thickly covered the upper surface of the John Day formation when they were overwhelmed and buried by the first flows.

The Columbia lava formation, as we find it here, is one of the most remarkable products of igneous activity which the world has known. Varying from fifteen hundred to three thousand feet in thickness over an area of approximately 200,000 square miles, it represents an enormous mass of molten material removed from beneath the earth's crust and poured out upon its surface. It was not, as has sometimes been supposed, due to a single great volcanic outburst, but is composed of a large number of small flows that were apparently poured out at intervals during a long period.

Little is known as yet regarding the sources from which the immense quantity of lava and ashes in eastern Oregon has been derived, or of the vents through which it came to the surface. The magnificent volcanic cones of the Cascade Range to the west, which would naturally be considered as the source, are not of sufficient calibre to furnish all this erupted material, and are, moreover, of later age than part of it.

Beneath the lava the strata are in many places broken or faulted by many great fractures, and into some of these the molten basaltic material has been squeezed, forming dikes. The Davis dikes, crossing the main John Day River near the junction of the North and South forks, extend, with some slight interruptions, for about fifteen miles as a well-marked wall of basalt many feet in height. Though it has not yet been possible to connect the dikes with the flows above, it is pretty certain that the great lava masses are the result of what are known as fissure eruptions, or the squeezing out of vast bodies of molten material through wide cracks in the earth's crust.

Where it has not been cut through by streams, the Columbia lava now covers the whole of the John Day country north of the East Fork as a nearly horizontal sheet. Along the northern side of this valley it bends down sharply, passing beneath the river-bed, and in this depression rest the strata which give us the next chapter in the history of the region, namely, the deposits of the Cottonwood lake. These beds, as well as those of the Rattlesnake formation just above them, are tilted in the same direction as the lava, indicating that the sinking of the lake floor was continued through a long period, the last subsidence having given a slight slope to the uppermost strata. Deposits similar to those of the Cottonwood and Rattlesnake lakes are found at other localities in eastern Oregon, and a number of large bodies of water probably existed here on a wide lava plain in Pliocene time.

One incontestable proof of the great antiquity of even the uppermost strata of the John Day section is furnished by the cañon-cutting of the rivers, which is perhaps the most striking thing in the average landscape of the basin. Everywhere the narrow valleys show on either side the edges of similar beds that were evidently once connected. This means that the great gorges have been formed since the deposition of the uppermost strata through which they cut. That many millenniums would be required by the streams in scouring their way through the adamantine lavas and into the formations below, at the most rapid rate at which they wear, is evident to any one who looks into the chasms that are the result of their work. An interesting confirmation of the evidence supplied by erosion is found in the occurrence of remains of the mammoth, and other animals now long extinct, in the terraces near the bottom of the valley. These deposits, with the included remains, are stranded remnants of stream wash, formed when the excavation of the gorge had advanced almost to the present stage.

The purely physical history of the John Day Basin is in itself a subject of absorbing interest. The kaleidoscopic changes in the geological record present to us in succession over the same area the deep waters of an open sea, an alterna-

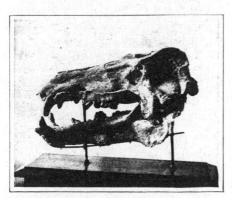

ELOTHERIUM SKULL, BRIDGE CREEK. LENGTH OF SKULL ABOUT THIRTY INCHES

tion of great lakes and dry plains, an ocean of molten stone, a second series of alternating lakes and plains, and finally the existing landscape, cut by persistent abrading of the streams out of the débris accumulated in preceding ages. All this shows plainly that the physical

features of the earth's surface, which serve as our symbols of the everlasting and unchangeable, only appear permanent because the range of human observation is limited to a mere moment in the long stretch of geological time.

To a student of living things, these physical revolutions are, however, only changes of scene in the history of the creatures which have inhabited this region. His chief interest centres on those living beings which kept the flame of life alive through these long ages.

The history of the ancient inhabitants of the country is furnished us by the remains entombed in the strata of successive periods at the time of their accumulation. The majority of the fossils found are single bones and teeth, or parts of skeletons which apparently lay for a long time upon the land before the scattered and decayed fragments were carried into the lakes, a few at a time, by stream or rain wash, and buried in the slowly accumulating deposits. In many instances the bones have evidently been torn apart and broken by beasts of prey; in other cases they were almost gnawed to pieces by small prehistoric rodents, which left indubitable evidence of their work in the innumerable marks of their sharp incisor teeth. Occasional entire skeletons discovered are probably the remains of animals which were drowned or mired in the lake, or perhaps were overtaken and buried upon the land by ashes or mud from volcanic eruptions.

The collecting of fossils in this region has about it a fascination that is, in a manner, a combination of the passions of the hunter and the miner with the natural inborn desire to learn of something entirely new. The danger that one experiences in climbing over steep and treacherous places on the cliffs in search of specimens, and the unquenchable hope that each projecting fragment encountered may prove to be a part of some fine skeleton, are sufficiently strong to raise the otherwise tedious and laborious occupation far above the level of drudgery. Whole skulls or portions of skeletons are occasionally found almost freed from the rock by erosion, and the pleasurable excitement felt in coming suddenly upon such treasure, after perhaps many hours of fruitless search, is not exceeded in the securing of any other variety of game. Usually there is exposed only a very small portion of a bone, which has, through weathering, come to look so much like the surrounding rock that only the most careful scrutiny of the exposed strata will result in its discovery. When the large Elotherium skull now in the museum of the University of California was found, only a portion of a single dingy front tooth was in sight; and not until several days of hard labor had been expended in cutting away the surrounding rock with pick and chisel was it at all certain that the whole cranium was present. The skull was situated in an almost inaccessible place near the top of a steep bluff about two hundred feet high, and in order to get standing - room from which to work, it was necessary to cut foot-holes. To make matters worse, the cranium ran straight back into the cliff, necessitating so much excavation that a number of loose blocks above were almost certain to fall and damage it. To avoid all possibility of accident, steps were cut to a pinnacle about twenty feet above the specimen, and from that point the face of the cliff was systematically torn down till a working space was uncovered. The whole operation of excavating occupied for two weeks as many persons as could conveniently work at the same time, and resulted in the discovery of the most important parts of the animal's skeleton. The lower jaw was found intact some distance away from the cranium, one of the fore limbs and a few scattered bones were beneath the head, and close behind it were all of the neck vertebrae.

So many specimens would seem to be discovered by pure accident that one learns to examine the rocks with all manner of possible occurrences in mind. Although digging blindly into a cliff for fossils is generally about as fruitless an expenditure of energy as would be harpooning at random into the sea for

whales, the collector never neglects to explore for some distance around the hole from which a skeleton has been removed, as many of the finest specimens known have come to light in this way.

On one of the California expeditions

SKULL OF LARGE OREODON

the writer discovered a nearly perfect head of a three - toed horse resting on the brink of an excavation made by some earlier expedition. Probably the picks of the first collectors had cut within a few inches of the skull, which was not then uncovered by erosion. After removing the horse head, a stroke into the surrounding matrix jerked a perfect wolf skull entirely free from the rock.

The explanation of finds of this character is found in the fact that the skeletons seem actually to be in pockets or nests, where they may have been brought together by currents in the lake.

The remains found in the lake beds represent the most common animals of their time. Then, as now, only one skeleton out of many thousand would be buried, even in part, in such a way as to insure indefinite preservation, and the chances of rarer forms being thus entombed would be very slight. The fossils in the John Day beds proper, where they are more abundant than elsewhere, pretty certainly furnish us a fair picture of the dominant life of eastern Oregon in Miocene time. Probably the total variety of animals that have so far been found there is about what a prehistoric hunter would have encountered in the flesh on an excursion of a fortnight's duration about the John Day lake.

The known remains from John Day strata include the leaves of a few types of trees, a number of snail and clam shells, many large tortoises, a few birds, a snake, a lizard, and a large number of mammals. These last forms are by far the most abundant as well as the most interesting fossils. Compared with the existing fauna of this continent, the mammalia from these beds are indeed a strange assemblage of creatures. None of the species are living now, and even the majority of the sub-families are extinct.

At least three-fourths of all the material collected consist of remains of certain peculiar hoofed animals known as Oreodons, curious forms which do not closely resemble anything now living, though they are related to the deer and the hogs. Possessing grinding teeth somewhat similar to those of the deer, they had also prominent tusks developed on both the upper and lower jaws as weapons of defence. The numerous species varied in size from that of a dog to the dimensions of a small cow. Several skulls of the giants of this group, that have been examined by the writer, are at least seventeen inches in length, and must certainly have belonged to large and powerful animals. The Oreodons probably roamed over the hills and along the shores of the lake in small herds like the deer or sheep of later ages.

Not so common as the Oreodon bones are those of a small horse, about as large as a sheep, which, from the absence of any visible means of defence, must have trusted to his slender, three-toed limbs to keep him out of danger. In constantly standing or running on the tips of his longest or middle toes, he was obtaining from his limbs the highest possible degree of elasticity and speed, and was at the same time losing the use of the side digits, and developing the one-toed type of foot which we find in his living relatives.

The largest animals yet discovered in the John Day beds are the giant Elotheres, relatives of the living hog, ranking among the largest known mammals. The skull of the specimen at the University of California measures about thirty inches in length, and numerous fragments of other skeletons indicate the existence of much larger individuals. Judging from what we know of the skeleton, the Elotheres must have attained a length of over ten feet and a height of six or seven feet. Probably few animals have ever existed that were better able to protect themselves than these huge Miocene boars; yet they have long since disappeared from the earth, leaving no direct descendants.

No less strange than the creatures that have been mentioned, appear to us the ancient representatives of several groups of animals which now inhabit parts of the earth remote from Oregon. Remains of near relatives of the rhinoceros, the camel, the tapir, and the peccary are well known from these deposits. The rhinoceros is now confined to the Eastern Hemisphere, the camel tribe is represented in the Eastern Hemisphere and in South America, tapirs are found in southeastern Asia and South America, and peccaries are at home in South America, though they range into southern United States. All this goes to show that the present distribution of animals has no more been permanent from the beginning than were the physical conditions in any given locality.

Preying upon the weaker hoofed animals were numerous flesh-eating forms, of which we find remains not uncommon. Wolves are represented by more than a dozen species, and the cat tribe by eight forms belonging to the family of sabretooths. In these cats the upper canine teeth were greatly elongated, flattened, and serrated along the edges, making the most formidable weapons ever possessed by any carnivore. Some of the sabretooths were much larger than the living puma, and probably preyed upon all the other mammals, excepting the larger species of Elotherium.

The teeth of these carnivores, as well as of all the other mammals, are usually preserved to us practically unchanged, not only in form, but in the materials which compose them. The worn surfaces which we find on the murderous teeth of ancient wolves and sabretooths are the actual surfaces which clicked together when they tore through quivering nerves and muscles. The glistening enamel surface which we find on the sabres of the great cat is the same that dripped with the blood of Oreodons and three-toed horses so long ago that the mountains of eastern Oregon have no recollection of the day, because they were then unborn.

The fossil forms of the Cottonwood lake beds are not only very different from the animals living at the present time, but they are also unlike those of the John Day period. So far as the writer is aware, not a single species of John Day mammal survived the period of Columbia lava flows and left remains in the deposits of the Cottonwood lake. This does not necessarily mean that every living thing was overwhelmed and buried in the lava, though doubtless many perished in that way, but rather that the time which elapsed between the two lake periods was so long that before its close the accumulated changes by evolution and the immigration of new types of animals from other regions had resulted in the complete alteration of the mammalian fauna.

In the interval during which the paleontological record was interrupted, the pigmy three-toed horses had become very rare, their place being taken by a larger form, in which the side toes were relatively much smaller. In the ashy beds at Cottonwood we find teeth and scattered bones of this interesting animal quite common. In the museum of the University of Oregon there is from this locality a perfect foot, which served as a basis for part of Professor Marsh's famous work on the evolution of the horse. The little camels of the John Day are also replaced by much larger forms, which are more common than their predecessors. The Oreodons had nearly disappeared, and their bones form only a small part of our collection. Elotherium remains are unknown in these strata, but in their place we find another giant, the mastodon, the oldest representative of his race in this country.

In the strata of the next section of the geological record, the Rattlesnake beds,

we find fossils of a still higher type than those from the Cottonwood lake beds, but the change in the fauna is not so great as that which occurred during the period of Columbia lava flows.

Along the John Day and other rivers of Oregon, in the many remnants of an-

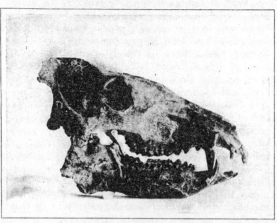

SKULL OF PECCARY FROM JOHN DAY FOSSIL BEDS

cient stream deposits left stranded on the sides of the valley as the river channel deepened, we find fossil remains which tell of still another, later, but distinct, period, in which the life of this region was different both from that of the age preceding and from the fauna of the present day. In these terraces are found foot bones of horses closely resembling the existing domestic animal, but still a distinct species. In the same deposits are fragmentary skeletons of gigantic cattle, compared with which our Texas steers would seem quite diminutive. Associated with the remains of these animals, which foreshadow the fauna of our own time, are the bones of a gigantic sloth, a grotesque creature entirely different from any beast now living. Some years ago there was found in these deposits, near Cañon City, Oregon, a nearly complete skeleton of an extinct elephant, with tusks, skull, limbs, and vertebrae in almost perfect condition.

The occurrence of the great sloth and the elephant in these deposits shows us that as late as is this period, compared with the many preceding, it is still so remote from the present as to be entirely beyond the range of human history and tradition.

The few typical examples that have been given of the fossil contents of consecutive formations present, as it were, the record of a succession of organic worlds, each specifically distinct both from those preceding and those following it. Early investigators in Europe concluded, from a study of faunas similarly related, that the geological history of the earth was made up of a series of periods of quiet with abundant life, alternating with universal catastrophes in which everything organic was destroyed. Each period was, in a manner, an experiment of the Creator in His search for the highest types of creatures. The general aspect of the life of each formation is, however, more like that of the present than is that of the beds below it, showing a gradual advance along definite lines. In some cases, as illustrated by the horse and camel tribes, the stages are of such a character as to leave no room for doubt that a blood relationship existed between forms of succeeding periods. We find, further, that in each formation the fossils of the uppermost beds differ materially from those in the lower ones, which means that considerable changes were taking place while the record was being made. The physical history of the region, as already indicated, shows us that the strata of the successive formations are not a continuous record, but that long intervals may have elapsed between the periods of their origin. The fossils of consecutive formations we therefore consider as recording *stages* in the history of an uninterrupted chain of living forms stretching from early geological time to the present day. The remains in a given series of formations are not necessarily all in a direct line of descent, for shifting currents of migration frequently changed the entire fauna of each region, bringing to it new life from other lands. The conclusion of each cycle, however, always finds the average life higher than at its beginning.

Although there are other geological sections, particularly in western United States, which furnish as remarkable a history as that which has been barely outlined, there are probably none in which the relations of the various chapters to each other are more evident than they are in the record inscribed on the walls of the John Day Cañon. The deciphering of the geological story of most regions is accomplished through the enthusiastic labors, over wide areas, of men taught to see things which escape the notice of untrained observers. The John Day section tells its story so plainly that to one who sees the record a comprehension of its meaning is unavoidable. Standing above the Picture Gorge, a magnificent cañon near Cottonwood, one may see, marking out with almost diagrammatic clearness upon the valley slopes, nearly the entire series of formations. From these strata were obtained the greater number of the fossils mentioned in this outline, together with many others no less interesting, and the succession of faunas is here splendidly illustrated. Probably nowhere in the world does the scientist work amid more impressive surroundings than in this valley, where every cliff has blazoned upon it the proof of such immeasurable antiquity of the entombed remains. To one who reads this record as it stands, an undisputed work of the Creator, there is made a revelation no less magnificent in its expression of historic fact than that in the creation story of the books of Moses.

SKULL OF SABRE-TOOTH TIGER

THE MORMON SITUATION

FOR an American to study the situation of affairs in Utah is a task which brings only a reward of grief and indignation, and these feelings increase as the subject is more and more investigated and understood. One is grieved over the welding of such a superstition upon thousands of people, incensed at the degradation of poor women, and indignant that in the United States a system is being encouraged and strengthened annually which kills the clear sense of right in young minds, and taints childhood with errors which can never be eradicated. The system was founded in the most transparent fraud of the century; the men who first gave it prominence were creatures whose brutal impulses were the only guide to their lives; the prominent leader who in Utah for thirty years was hailed as a prophet of the Lord was simply a despoiler of his people, and the most obscene and brutal of men; while the present chiefs are men whose lives are covered with falsehood and guile. And still while this thing called the Mormon Church is revealing a record as dark as that of the Thugs, reducing woman to the condition she occupied before the Saviour's teachings emancipated her, offering the reward that Mohammed offered to men's lusts, debasing the tender and plastic minds of childhood, and while the leaders of this system, through the lusts and superstition of their followers, are able to enthrall the minds and absorb the earnings of tens of thousands of deluded mortals, the men and authorities of this republic stand by and watch with apparent indifference the cloud which is rising among the mountains of mid-continent, which if let alone will break at last in tears and blood, and drench the whole land.

To give a clear understanding of the present position of the Mormon people and the influences which control them, together with the outlook for the future under that control, is a most difficult task. I can tell what I know, what ten thousand people around me know, and while knowing that it is all true, often find it almost impossible to support the statement with the proofs which a legal or prejudiced mind would demand. Hence in what I shall say below only facts perfectly well known will be stated. A writer on this theme is in the same position that the courts in Utah are when they attempt to punish a man for the offense of having at the same time two or twenty wives. Every resident may know the fact, the children of the different "wives" may be seen daily at play about the streets, the Mormons themselves will tell what the maiden names of the women were; and still, arraign that man and charge him with the crime, and those very women will come into court and on oath declare that they were never married to the man, and if necessary (as they have before now) swear that they do not know who is the father of their own children. Of course the court is baffled, and justice is defeated. The Mormons will prove by their "sacred" books that they may not lie or commit violence, that a good Mormon can not help but be a truthful, God-fearing man. But such things always have with them a double meaning. With them it means simply that to a brother Mormon they must be true, while to an outsider the rule does not apply. In private the more candid of them will admit this, and will cite examples by the score from the Bible to prove how from the first it has been the rule for God's people to deceive and spoil the heathen. There is a double meaning or a chance for a reservation everywhere in their professions and statements. Their Church itself is a *double entendre*. They went to Utah poor; they have sought no way to acquire wealth except from the products of the soil; the coming of strangers was a signal for the most cruel persecutions by them, those persecutions taking the form of ostracism, of open murder, and secret assassination. For years Gentiles carried their lives in their hands; the prayers in the churches on the Sabbath were that the Gentiles might be destroyed; Governors and judges and other United States officials were driven away; to prospect for minerals in the hills of Utah was death; and though the Gentiles, against this opposition, and while wronging no one, opened the mines and made a market for Mormon produce, gave employment to Mormon laborers, paying in gold, and making the present wealth of Utah except the value of the naked land, within the last three months the Premier of the Mormon Church, a man who claims to be an apostle of the Lord, furnished to a distinguished magazine of the East an article in which he directly claims that not only against the barbarism of the wilderness, but against the most merciless and continued persecutions, the pa-

tient and long-suffering Mormons have builded for themselves homes in the desert. As this man is really the controlling spirit of the Mormon Church, a brief reference to some of his statements will give the reader a fair estimate of the worth of any Mormon's statement concerning Mormon affairs.

He says of Joseph Smith: "He had the courage of his convictions, and did all that mortal man could do to prove to the world that he knew that his teachings were true—he died for them."

The truth is, Smith was arrested as any other culprit might be, and died as any criminal might, and certainly as much against his own will or intention as ever did felon of greater or less degree at the rash hands of an outraged community.

Of Brigham Young this man says: "The man who had the courage to lead an expatriated people through the wilderness, the statesmanship to found a great commonwealth, and the truthfulness and probity to make his word among business men have the value of a bond, can not be injured by malicious envy." The courage of going to Utah was nothing more than thousands of others dared, the statesmanship displayed was simply in claiming divine power, and making some hundreds —and later some thousands—of people work for him; and while his word was good where he could not afford to break it, Salt Lake City is full of people of both sexes whom he deliberately robbed. The writer of the foregoing extract was the man who delivered the funeral eulogy over Brigham Young's remains. In that culogy he declared his full belief in the integrity and divinity of the dead "prophet." Within a few days afterward, however, he was one of the parties to a suit which compelled the heirs of the "prophet" to make restitution of more than one million dollars stolen from a deluded people. Again, this writer denies that the Mormons in Idaho were ordered how to vote last year. At the time, a Mormon bishop stated that against their will they were ordered to vote, and the result of the election showed that every Mormon obeyed.

The same writer asserts that the Mormons are attached to the Constitution of the United States, and claims, therefore, that they are good Americans. They do claim that under the Constitution polygamy, or any other cant or fraud under the name of religion, is allowable, and thus far and no farther are Mormons Americans. When the civil war was raging, Brigham Young, in the Tabernacle one day at Salt Lake City, said: "The men of the South pray to God for the destruction of the men of the North; the men of the North beseech God to bring destruction upon the men of the South; I say amen to both prayers." These words reveal fully the love which the Mormon people bear to the people and government of the United States.

Further on in his article the Mormon Premier says: "Every person was at liberty to do as he pleased about prospecting and opening mines." The truth is that Lawrence and Godbe were cut off from the Church for advocating mining. Men who tried to prospect were murdered or driven away, and the first mines opened in Utah were only opened under guard of United States soldiers. He claims that in the early days of Utah there were no liquor or gambling saloons or prostitutes in the Territory. Brigham Young early engaged in the manufacture of liquor, and it was openly sold (a most vile compound) in Mormon stores that bore the sign of "Holiness to the Lord" and "the all-seeing eye" over the doors. There were no houses of public prostitution, for such houses can not exist where there is no money; but that there were ample materials to supply such houses is manifest from Brigham Young's old sermons, one of which is before this writer as he writes, but which by its obscenity is preserved from reproduction.

He praises the Mormon schools of Utah, when the testimony of Gentile teachers is unanimous that they are of the very lowest type.

He further says: "From the time when travel across the continent to California commenced, it has been a constant custom in Utah to invite ministers of repute of every denomination who were passing through to preach in the various places of worship." It has been the custom occasionally to ask ministers to preach one sermon in Salt Lake City; these sermons have been themes for ridicule on the succeeding Sabbaths. But to show the real Mormon spirit I will cite one case. A young Presbyterian minister came to Utah a few years ago to try to regain his lost health. He went to San Pete Valley, where there were no schools,

where there were boys and girls nearly grown to manhood and womanhood who were totally ignorant of the rudiments of an education, and opened a school. Hearing of it, Brigham Young and his nearest counsellors repaired to San Pete, and before a full congregation on the Sabbath day Young instructed his hearers to kill the offending minister. George Q. Cannon, who made the above statement of Mormon liberality, sat by and heard Young's order, as did also the Rev. Mr. McMillan, against whom the order was directed, and who, despite three attempts upon his life, still lives and continues to teach and preach in San Pete. Mr. Cannon also tries to charge the Mountain Meadows Massacre upon John D. Lee and the Indians. There is nothing better known in Utah than that Lee was but a mere instrument in the hands of his superiors, that he would not have dared to act without orders, that the murders were planned in Salt Lake City, and that many of the effects of the victims were carried to that city and sold. More, in a meeting of the seventies in Salt Lake City, Brigham Young justified the massacre.

I have cited the above extracts to show just how much a Mormon's word is worth to the outside world. The man I have quoted from is second in place in Mormon authority, claims to be an apostle of the Lord, and to speak with an inspiration received direct daily from God. His brother, who is also high in authority in the Church, but a few days since, under oath, declared that he did not know that his brother was living in polygamy, and that he knew the names of no women who claimed to be his brother's wives except his first wife. There is hardly a child in Salt Lake City who does not know four women who are Cannon's wives, and their children.

Mr. Cannon denies that in Utah there is any union of Church and state, while under date of January 6, 1881, John Taylor, President of the Mormon Church, in a communication to Henry Randall Waite, special United States Census Agent, admits that the Mormon Church has full control over the temporal as well as the spiritual affairs of the Mormon people. This same thing is preached weekly in the Mormon churches.

The first colony that went to Utah was composed of only a few hundred people; now the Church claims that it rules some one hundred thousand followers in the

Territory. The first comers had a large percentage of Americans, who were drawn into the toils before the full enormities of the institution were divulged, but of those who have connected themselves with the Mormon Church during the past thirty years quite nine-tenths have been from Europe, and from the very lowest classes of European society. The immigration has increased from a few hundreds annually to a few thousands. Last year more than three thousand came, and this year a heavy increase over that number is expected. The children of school age, as returned by the Mormon authorities, number forty thousand. Those too young to attend school, together with those above school age and still under the age of twenty-five years, must number quite thirty thousand more. It is clear that the Mormon kingdom in Utah is composed of foreigners and the children of foreigners. It is necessarily so. It is an institution so absolutely un-American in all its requirements that it would die of its own infamies within twenty years, except for the yearly infusion of fresh serf blood from abroad. Few Americans could ever be made to bear the unquestioned and unquestioning obedience which is exacted from this people. The government is an absolute despotism. Every ward in the city, every small precinct in the country, is under the control of a bishop. To him the people have to submit all their affairs, temporal as well as spiritual. His advice amounts to a command, and a command which must be obeyed. The bishops report to the elders, the elders to the seventies, the seventies to the high priests, the high priests to the presidents of stakes, they to the patriarchs, they to the twelve apostles, and they to the president and his high counsellors. Down the same scale the orders are sent. These leaders are the same as God to the blinded thousands of Utah. At the last October conference the burden of the harangues to the people was to impress upon them that the chiefs, being daily and regularly inspired by God, could make no mistake, could do no wrong. The discourse of Elder Orson Pratt is full of this business, and he did not fail to warn all who doubted that they would be damned. At the same conference another elder explained that the people must obey their leaders in financial as well as spiritual affairs, even as the people did in the days of Moses.

Through such a system it is easy to see how an ignorant and fanatical people are held under absolute control by the heads of the organization. In Brigham Young's time, he was a more absolute ruler than was ever the Czar of Russia. Since his death, the president, John Taylor, and his first counsellor, George Q. Cannon, make the controlling power, and give direction to the whole system. Both are Englishmen. A favorite expression of Brigham Young's used to be, "We follow the forms of a republic, but this is a kingdom." It is a kingdom, or rather a despotism, so all-embracing that intelligent Americans at a distance do not believe the truth about it when it is told.

The sentiment throughout the country is that however misguided the Mormon leaders may be, they are entirely sincere, that their religious convictions are a part of their lives, and that in treating with them this fact must never be lost sight of. There are many among the ignorant followers who are sincere, and there are many who, at the command of John Taylor, would go out with only staves and pitchforks, against a fully armed and disciplined army corps, and expect to conquer, for they are thorough fanatics, and are steeped in superstition. The fact that for years they have worked uncomplainingly, while their leaders have absorbed all the profits of the toil, is a convincing proof of their sincerity. But with the leaders, that is, with four-fifths of them, the case is altogether different. With them their Church is simply a colossal political and commercial machine through which a few leaders may hold control over the minds and earnings of the followers, through steady appeals to their fanaticism and superstition, by holding over them the terrors of excommunication, and the promises of sensual indulgences in this world, and a Mohammedan paradise after death if they are but faithful. It is an absolute theocracy; it holds itself above the government of the United States, or any other government; teaches its adherents that "all governments founded merely by men are illegal"; claims that its founder was a prophet inspired by Omnipotence; that as he died his mantle descended upon his successors, with all its divine powers; that as he could do no wrong, they, in his place, and the direct custodians of his powers, can do no wrong, and that when men, poor and weak, and groping in the darkness of this world, make laws which are contrary to their desires, or which conflict with their plans, they are not only not under the slightest obligations either to obey or respect them, but have a perfect right to commit perjury or any other crime to avoid obeying them. So, while within the republic, claiming all its protection and advantages, these leaders are teaching their followers steadily to look forward to the time, in the near future, when the dominion of the whole land shall be theirs—not only the spiritual dominion, but the political and commercial dominion. Their contempt for the government of the United States has been and is being shown in a hundred ways. Their election law giving the ballot to women is a sample. Under that law girls under age, and alien women with the odor of the emigrant ship still upon their clothes, without ever having taken an oath of allegiance to the United States, without the slightest idea of the meaning of the act they are performing, or what is intended by it, cast their votes as they are instructed to, in some tongue unknown to ordinary Americans, and go away dazed. During the past eighteen months more polygamous marriages have been consummated in Utah than ever before in the same length of time. Every day, in Salt Lake City, can be seen women, still girls in years, carrying in their arms infants the fathers of which they would not, under torture, reveal. The Mormon leaders and Mormon journals take the ground that a person can not be punished for the crime of polygamy until his guilt is established by direct proof in a court of competent jurisdiction, and jeeringly defy the authorities to obtain the proof. Daniel H. Wells, one of the oldest leaders and highest officers of the bogus Church, and the chief custodian of the Endowment House records at Salt Lake City, swore in court there that he knew of no record of Mormon marriages. Brigham Young, when arraigned, swore that he had but one wife, that he never was but once married. Every Mormon knows how desperate was the perjury which these men committed, and every one of them justifies their acts.

A few years ago, in Salt Lake City, late at night, a physician was called from his home, as he was informed, to attend upon a wounded man. He was met a few steps from his own gate by a body of men, and murdered. Next morning Brigham Young headed a subscription with $500 as a reward for the arrest and conviction of the murderers. Other prominent Mormons signed large sums. On that same morning Brigham Young could have had those murderers brought before him in five minutes, had he so desired. A few days later, in a public assemblage, Young bewailed the murder, and declared that he would give a large sum to have the perpetrators brought to justice; all the time the murderers were smiling up at him from the congregation, and he knew them, and knew what they had done. The physician's offense had been the location of a few acres of land and some springs that the Mormons wanted. Crimes as open as this have been somewhat relinquished during the past few years in the main centres of Utah, but the old spirit remains just the same. The present policy of the organization is to put on the outward forms of peace, tó assume before the world the mien of martyrs and non-combatants, and to tell of the cruel persecutions they have suffered, and of the slanders that are hurled at them. In secret they are as aggressive as of old, and are only waiting for strength to make their purpose too pronounced to be mistaken. Joe Smith wanted to imitate Mohammed—to raise his flag and go out and conquer a kingdom. He was persuaded by his more prudent followers to relinquish a plan so rash; but the mixed Puritanism and Mohammedanism in the soul of Smith, and which gave origin and direction to the Mormon institution, still control the spirit of affairs in Utah. By Puritanism we mean, above, that kind that burned witches, and compelled men to worship God one way. It is but a little while ago, in a village but a few miles from Salt Lake City, that a woman was shot for being "a witch." With a spirit as full of fanaticism as ever warmed a Thug to kill bodies in order that souls might be saved, the first years of Utah, after the coming of the whites, were full of assassinations and cruelties to all that were outspoken in opposition to the Mormon faith, or who questioned the divinity of the Mormon religion. The presence of the United States flag over Camps Douglas and Cameron, the soldiers garrisoning those posts, the knowledge that in case of trouble the Gentile miners in Utah would be a difficult element to manage, together with the present facilities for concentrating a government force there, have changed the outward bearing of the Mormons, but the old spirit is still the moving principle. Great as is the effort to conceal it, now and then it breaks out in muttered threats, or in exclamations of open defiance. At the last October conference Apostle Cannon defied all the powers of earth and of hell to interfere with the Mormon Church or its customs. He was talking to the assembled thousands in the Salt Lake Tabernacle, and he meant that his words should have full effect upon the fanatics before him.

The superb organization of the Church is held complete in all its details; nothing is permitted to be neglected. No general ever held an army under more perfect control than Taylor and Cannon hold the whole body of the Mormon people. Through tithes a tremendous fund is secured annually, with which the priests strengthen any weak spot in their position. Their lines are solid from within, and toward the world the organization bristles everywhere with the defiance of disciplined strength. More and more missionaries are sent out annually, and the annual increase of bigoted, priest-enslaved foreign creatures to join the "kingdom" in Utah is very great. From Utah colonies are selected, and sent wherever a place presents itself. In this way the valleys of Colorado, and Arizona, Idaho, Wyoming, Montana, and Washington Territories, are being swiftly appropriated, and wherever these colonists go, they carry with them joyfully their badge of slavery to a few men in Salt Lake City who, as they believe, are the vicegerents on earth of the living God.

Another feature of the system is that the people are taught that the whole Gospel was not revealed to Joseph Smith, but that those who follow in his footsteps, like him, are inspired, and liable, even as Joseph was, to receive covenants and laws from Heaven at any time. No mortal man can tell when the Mormon religion will be fully completed, or what new jugglery may be added to it before the final patent shall be applied for. It is now nearer what the Mohammedan Church was at the time of Mohammed's death than anything else ever was. Its aim is universal dominion. Its leaders contemplate the time when they will absolutely direct, over whole States, the political, commercial, religious, and social affairs

of the people, in utter defiance of the laws of the country. More: they believe that in the near future the control of the republic itself will pass into their hands, and this they are careful to keep impressed upon their people. This is preached from every Mormon pulpit; this is the settled belief of the Mormon thousands. Some little time before Brigham Young died he announced from his pulpit that before twelve years he would dictate the person who would be elected President of the United States. They are but waiting until they can gain political control of one State. With that accomplished, the country would soon understand what Mormonism means. Polygamy would be legalized, the offices would be distributed exclusively among polygamists, free thought would be strangled, a free press would not be permitted to exist for a day, and within six months from the time that full power was placed in Mormon hands all the region within the lines of that State would be as absolutely foreign as are the Barbary States to-day; that is, it would be so if no violent resistance were to be interposed by resident Gentiles. There are impetuous Gentiles in Utah who, understanding the Mormon system thoroughly, as well as the ways and purposes of the Mormon leaders; who have been lied about, traduced, and wronged; who have watched as the government, year after year, has trifled with this mighty wrong; who have seen men high in authority, civil and military, lend their sympathy and encouragement to the men who in Utah are defying the laws and plotting the overthrow of the republic—who would welcome Statehood to Utah if the government would but agree to keep its hands off, and leave the people to adjust the differences which would follow. In that case there would be a speedy surrender by the Mormons of the two baneful features of their creed, polygamy and Church rule, or there would be a repetition of what transpired in Missouri or Illinois some years ago. Otherwise, the Mormons would make laws which would render the presence of Gentiles in Utah impossible; and if resisted, they would, as the legal authorities, call for help from the Federal government. Politicians already pander to them. They understand perfectly the art of managing corporations to keep them friends. It is their expectation that members of Congress who are also railroad attorneys will prevent in the future, as in the past, any legislation hostile to them. The railroad press of the country is preaching conciliation, kindness, and the extending of schools as the only means through which to subdue or change the spirit of the Mormon people. While pretending to be horrified at polygamy and Church rule, the moment that anything is proposed which threatens to be a real blow at either, the cry is raised that force, violence, or harsh means never were effective in influencing men's religious convictions, and never can be. They ignore the fact that the Mormon Church is merely a gross political machine; that it is changed, expanded or contracted, at any time, to suit its leaders; that kindness and conciliation are lost upon its members; that their purpose is perpetually aggressive; that they mean to destroy free government in the United States, and reproduce in this country such a state of affairs as rules in Mohammedan countries; and that there is but one thing they respect, which is irresistible power. The masses of the Mormon people are kept so poor, and their minds are so enslaved with the teachings of their leaders, that they can not be reached by the usual means of enlightenment, except in a most limited degree. The great mass can not read English books or newspapers; they would not if they could. Out of the slums of Europe they have been brought to a land which supplies them with fresh vegetables, meats, and comfortable clothing, and the change to them seems so nearly a miracle that they do not wish to question its genuineness. So steeped are they in superstition and ignorance that they obey without question all orders from the heads of the organization. But for the steady influx of foreigners—low, base-born foreigners, hereditary bondsmen—the two dreadful features of the Mormon Church, polygamy and the exalting of the church over the state, would die out in America in two generations. As it is, not half of the daughters of Mormons who have grown up amid a large population of Gentiles will ever enter into polygamy, but among the masses in the country districts fanaticism is as strong as ever.

It may safely be affirmed that there never was an institution so demoralizing to the religious sentiments of humanity as this Mormon Church. The spectacle of one hundred thousand people in the midst of this republic who believe implicitly that some cunning rogues are real priests and apostles of the Lord, who believe they can cure the sick by touching them, that repeated miracles have been performed by them since the days of Joe Smith, who heed none of the teachings of the past eighteen hundred years, on whom modern progress makes no impression, may well make men ask, if all this is possible under the electric light, with the magnetic telegraph clicking, with the powerpress sounding, with the locomotive whistling, with the world full of books and daily journals, what might not cunning priests eighteen hundred or three thousand years ago have concocted?

And while this system is spreading and being daily strengthened, while something is going on in Utah which, if left exclusively to itself, would, in a generation, bring women to the auction block, and utterly brutalize men, the people of the East do not seem to be greatly worried. Though the Gentiles of Utah never wronged the Mormons, though they have given to Utah its prosperity and accumulated wealth, though they own quite two-fifths of the property of the Territory, and though they have never asked anything of the Mormons except that they obey the laws, still, the sentiment of the East is that they are a predatory set, and that the Mormons are entitled to peculiar and tender consideration, because they, when their presence and customs had become intolerable to the people among whom they dwelt, started out into the wilderness and established a thriving Territory.

While doing this the Mormons have shrunk from no crime, recoiled at no falsehood, have murdered and robbed Americans in secret, and laid the crime to savages, and still, while despoiling Americans, have shed crocodile tears over their own extreme sufferings. They have disobeyed and derided the laws, and still continue to do so; they have insulted and driven away United States officials for no offense except that of trying to do their duty under their oaths, and all this has been performed by the orders of less than thirty men, who, in the mean time, have absorbed so much of the earnings of the people that they possess more money and property than five times twenty thousand of their dupes possess. Worse than all, they have again forged the chains of an ignominious slavery on the wrists of women; what they call their religion offers a perpetual premium for men's lusts; their teachings kill the germ of chastity in the hearts of childhood before it is ever warmed into life, and destroy the honor and sacredness of home.

The men of the East should consider these things, and should remember that once before there was an institution in this country around which there was a shield of sympathy; its divine rights were declared from a thousand pulpits; Congress was too sordid and too cowardly to deal with it; wholesale merchants and great corporations lent their influence to perpetuate it, and a venal press rang with anathemas against any who dared to de-nounce it. But there came a day at last when men had to choose which should live and rule, that institution or this nation.

The history of what followed is fresh in all minds; and little as the masses believe it now, there will come a time, if this monster in Utah is left to grow, when there will be another call for volunteers and for money; and, as before, tens of thousands of brave young men will go away, never to return; as before, there will be an enormous debt incurred; as before, the country will be hillocked with graves, and the whole land will be moistened by the rain of women's tears.

A STUDY OF A 'DECREED' TOWN

ABRAHAM LINCOLN and Charles Kingsley have presented two strikingly contrasted views of individual destiny in economic affairs. Abraham Lincoln, in his message to Congress on December 3, 1861, said: "There is not in necessity any such thing as a free, hired laborer being fixed to that condition for life. Many independent men, everywhere in these States, a few years back in their lives were hired laborers. The prudent, penniless beginner in the world labors for wages a while, saves a surplus with which to buy tools and land for himself, then labors on his own account another while, and at length hires a new beginner to help him. This is the just and generous and prosperous system, which opens the way to all— gives hope to all, and consequent energy and progress and improvement of condition to all."

Charles Kingsley, on the other hand, in one of his books, utters these words: " I do not think the cry ' Get on ' to be anything but a devil's cry. The moral of my book [*Alton Locke*] is that the workman who tries to get on, to desert his class and rise above it, enters into a lie and leaves God's path for his own. . . . . Second, I believe that a man might be as a tailor or a costermonger every inch of him a saint and a scholar and a gentleman, for I have seen some few such already. . . . I believe from experience that when you put workmen into human dwellings and give them a Christian education, so far from wishing discontentedly to rise out of their class, or to level others to it, exactly the opposite takes place. They become sensible of the dignity of work, and they begin to see their labor as a true calling in God's church."

Far apart as the two ideals are, may not each be true in its own way, the one the voice of the Old World, the other the voice of the New? "Be content; accept your station. If you are a carpenter, be the best carpenter you possibly can, with the employment of all your powers; improve your mental and spiritual faculties; be, if possible, a ' saint and a scholar and a gentleman.'" The other ideal bids the humble wage-earner aspire to the loftiest position, and never rest content with any present achievement.

This latter ideal has, unquestionably, been the American ideal, and is, perhaps, still a true expression of the American spirit. Those who live in our own East, and seldom go one hundred miles west of the Atlantic coast, may be inclined to doubt this statement; and certainly they can scarcely understand the forces which underlie the Americanism of this continent. The vast prairies of the Mississippi Valley, and the arid far West, are an essential part of America, and only those who come in contact in a real, vital way with the millions inhabiting this immense territory understand the American people. The typical American spirit is the spirit of the newer sections of the country, which are but slightly removed from the frontier. He who would understand this sentiment fully must examine it in the concrete, and perhaps the whole American continent affords no better place for this kind of sociological study than Greeley, Colorado. Here events have moved rapidly, and within the short period of thirty years we may see an economic development which has elsewhere frequently required a century.

Between three and four thousand people live in Greeley in comfort, a large proportion with an adequate supply of wealth for the satisfaction of all rational, economic wants, while those whose condition, for a place of this kind, must be described as one of affluence, are a

A BUSY DAY IN GREELEY

considerable body; and substantially all this wealth has come into existence since 1870. Moreover, it has come directly and indirectly from agriculture, and this renders the progress of Greeley all the more instructive for the American, because, in the past, it is agriculture which has shaped American thought and formed American ideals.

In 1869 Nathan C. Meeker, at that time associated with Horace Greeley on the New York *Tribune,* conceived the idea of establishing a colony in the West which should, through co-operation and carefully thought-out plans, afford all who might participate in the movement substantially equal opportunities for improvement of their own individual resources, while at the same time enabling them to provide themselves with the advantages of long-established communities. When the project was broached to Horace Greeley, it received from him both sympathy and support. The plan was to gather together men of high moral character and intelligence and some little property. It was hoped that a considerable number would join the colony having as much property as $10,000 each; that there would be twice as many with $5000, and that others would have prop-

erty varying in amount from $200 to $1000. Mr. Meeker's call, which appeared in the New York *Tribune* late in 1869, begins with these words:

" I propose to unite with the proper persons in establishing a colony in Colorado Territory. . . . The persons with whom I would be willing to associate must be temperance men and ambitious to establish a good society. . . . Whatever professions and occupations enter into the formation of an intelligent and educated and thrifty community should be embraced by this colony, and it should be the object to accept what is best in modern civilization. In particular should moral and religious sentiments prevail, for without these qualities man is nothing. At the same time tolerance and liberality should also prevail. One thing more is equally important. The happiness, wealth, and glory of the state spring from the family, and it should be the aim and high ambition to preserve the family pure in all its relations, and to labor with the best force life and strength can give to make the home comfortable, to beautify and adorn it, and to supply it with whatever will make it attractive and loved."

These lofty ideals of Mr. Meeker are,

in Greeley, still ideals, and only partially realized. Yet they are now, as they always have been, a living force in this community.

It was the plan of Mr. Meeker, and one which has been quite largely carried out, that the people should live in the village and cultivate holdings outside the village, as well as gardens within it. The aim was to avoid the isolation of American farm life and to secure the advantages of associated effort. By way of explanation, I cannot do better than to quote two paragraphs from his circular:

" My own plan would be to make the settlement almost wholly in a village, and to divide the land into lots of ten acres, and to divide these into eight lots for building purposes; and then to apportion to each family from forty to eighty, even 160, acres, adjoining the village. Northampton, Massachusetts, and several other New England towns and villages were settled in this manner, but some improvements are suggested. Since some outlying tracts will be more desirable than others, a preference may be secured by selling them at auction, and the proceeds of such appropriated to the use of the colony; and all the lots of the village should be sold, that funds may be obtained for making improvements for the common good—such as the building of a church, a town hall, a school-house, and for the establishment of a library, by which means the lots will be worth five or ten times more than they cost; and one of the very first public institutions should be a first-class school, in which not only the common, but the higher branches should be taught, including music. The town of Lincoln, the capital of Nebraska, adopted this plan on a large scale, and several hundred thousand dollars have already been obtained.

" Some of the advantages of settling in a village will be—easy access to schools and public places, meetings, lectures, and the like; and society can be had at once. In planting, in fruit-growing, and improving homes generally, the skill and experience of a few will be common to all, and much greater progress can be made than where each lives isolated. It seems to me that a laundry and a bakery could be established, and the washing and baking could be done for all the community; but other household work should be done by the families. In all this the separate household and the ownership of property should be without change; and I only propose that if there are any advantages in co-operation, they should be secured by a colony. Cheap rates of freight and passage could be secured, while many things which all will want in the commencement can be bought at wholesale. There are some other advantages which I think such a town will possess, and they are important; but in this commencement I do not think proper to mention them; and there are besides, of course, disadvantages."*

The Union Colony of Colorado was thus established and a committee appointed to secure a location. After considerable investigation and careful scrutiny of various proposed locations, a most wise selection was made, namely, the territory now occupied by the city of Greeley and the surrounding country. This was the beginning of the most successful colony with which Horace Greeley was ever associated. Colonies, socialistic and semi-socialistic in nature, which he more or less actively helped organize, have long since disappeared; but Greeley, based upon private property and private industry, still flourishes.

After early trials, after many mistakes inevitable in all such undertakings, after the plague of grasshoppers for four years, after a destructive blizzard and a devastating hail - storm, and after other misfortunes, the colony began to move forward in the acquisition of wealth; and then, notwithstanding bad years now and again, prosperity finally came to the people of Greeley by " leaps and bounds."

It is important to bear in mind the fact that Greeley is one of the many *a priori* or " decreed " cities in the United States. American cities have been of two classes, those which have simply " grown up," like Topsy, and those which have been carefully planned in advance. Among the latter, in the West, we may instance Grinnell, Iowa, with its reservation for Iowa College; Colorado Springs, of which Colorado College also seems to

* *A History: Greeley and the Union Colony of Colorado.* By David Boyd. pp. 32–33.

THE STATE NORMAL SCHOOL

have been a part in the original plan; Salt Lake City, and also the other Mormon settlements.

Greeley is a type of this class of American cities, and an examination of them will convince us that human forethought counts for as much in city building as it does elsewhere, and the only inclination to find fault is in the fact that those who make the plans do not look a little farther ahead and make still more generous provision for common needs. Rugby, Tennessee, established quite largely through the instrumentality of the revered author of *Tom Brown at Rugby,* affords an illustration of a colony with generous provision for common needs, but which shows that even wise plans, without the right kind of material to carry them out, accomplish very little.

It is interesting and instructive briefly to contrast Rugby and Greeley. In 1883 I accepted an invitation from Judge Hughes to meet him at Rugby and discuss with him the English Christian socialism of the '50's. I was glad while there to make an examination of the conditions existing in Rugby. I found that Rugby was a "decreed" community. Evidently the *a priori* plans were quite as well thought out as in Greeley, and possibly more ample provision was made for common needs, in reservations of property for public use. The importance of beauty was appreciated, as shown by the selection of the site of the colony, along high, beautifully wooded banks of

a river, with an abundance of wild flowers and magnificent shrubbery. The village itself was attractive in its neat, homelike-looking cottages, surrounded by flowers, suggesting romantic love in a cottage, and all that sort of thing. I remember in particular the charm of the cottage occupied by the aged mother of Judge Hughes. Everywhere in Rugby one met evidences of superior refinement and culture.

As was to be expected, there was a co-operative store, and the original plans contemplated a large measure of co-operation along with private property and private industry. There was just one thing lacking, and that was the right kind of men to carry out the finely planned and carefully elaborated colony scheme. First of all, it may be mentioned that, on account of the absence of experienced men in the committee on location, the land selected seemed to be somewhat indifferent in quality for agricultural purposes. In the second place, the natives seem to have been too shrewd at bargaining with the purchasers of their land, and an unduly high price appears to have been paid for it. Then the colonists were, almost altogether, sons of English gentlemen—fine fellows, to be sure, but men who wanted to live the life of country gentlemen. A man who is at all acquainted with pioneering in this country must smile at the idea. In Rugby I met one workingman, an English gardener, and he and his wife were contented, happy, and prosperous, raising vegetables and selling them at a profit. I also heard about a hard - working young Englishman who was a sheep - raiser and was making money. I saw in the billiard-room of the hotel, and elsewhere, amusing themselves, young men who appeared to be typical colonists. Although sheep were raised in Rugby, there was not one individual there who knew how to slaughter a sheep, and when the hotel desired fresh mutton the manager was obliged to send for it to Cincinnati, a hundred miles or more away.

In Greeley, on the other hand, the colonists were ' men of large previous experience in various walks of life, and men, moreover, who did not consider themselves superior to any honest labor. Some of those who became farmers had had no more previous experience in farming than the colonists of Rugby, but they were willing to work hard and eager to learn from the experience of others. We see, then, in Rugby, Tennessee, and in Greeley, Colorado, that the highest measure of success implies well - devised schemes carried out by men strong in body and mind, and men industrious and resourceful. First of all, and above everything else, success depends upon the character of the individual man. It is well to emphasize this, but it is possible to go too far in the emphasis which we lay upon the individual, and so to neglect the importance of wise social plans and contrivances. No one who studies American economic history in the concrete can fail to see the truth of this proposition.

We have already seen that in Mr. Meeker's circular he had in the beginning planned the sale of lots, with the use of the proceeds " for making improvements for the common good," special mention being made of a church, town hall, and school-house, and the establishment of a library. The school is especially emphasized. Ten acres were set aside in the heart of the city for a public park, now called Lincoln Park, and a most attractive feature of Greeley. Provision has also been made for a larger outlying park, and something like fifty acres have been reserved near the city; but this has as yet never been improved. Efforts were made, only partially success-

ful, to prevent any person from seizing more than a fair share of the opportunities. In other words, speculation was discouraged, and it was desired to give every one a fair opportunity to carve out his own fortune, with the aid of neighbors and friends.

While the wealth of Greeley is connected with agriculture, it should not be forgotten that this is irrigated agriculture, and that irrigation brings with it its own problems, and that it produces more or less peculiar effects in the kind of cultivation which it develops. The construction of irrigating-ditches is by no means an altogether simple engineering undertaking, and novices are bound to make mistakes, as did the pioneers of Greeley. Their ditches were too small, and before they could be enlarged and made adequate they had cost twentyfold more than was originally anticipated. This delayed the coming of prosperity, and exhausted the strength and resources of many who had not staying-power. But this is not all. Irrigation implies comparatively small farms, an eighty-acre farm being one of very fair proportions, and it necessitates a very close association of all those who live " under " ditches belonging to one system, and, indeed, a considerable degree of co-operation and association between the various systems. There is a close solidarity binding together those who pursue an irrigated agriculture, and this comes ultimately to embrace even those who live in different States. The individualist must unlearn his individualism and become a co-operative man before he can succeed in irrigated agriculture. This means many a hard knock for obstinate human nature.

Tradition and environment made the American farmer of early days an individualist. His economic life was, relatively speaking, an isolated one. He entertained strong prejudices against corporations and their methods, and was reluctant to adopt any highly developed form of co-operation. Irrigation must change all this, and until the farmer adjusts himself to new habits of thought and action he is involved in perpetual difficulties. Litigation has been, and still is, the curse of the irrigated regions of the United States, and while irrigation

SOME OF THE BETTER CLASS OF HOMES IN GREELEY

draws men together, there arises an antagonism of interests which breeds suspicion and hatred among neighbors, and between sections, and even States, all of which can be avoided only by a very strong hand regulating economic relations. There must be a vigorous government of some sort, giving to each man his due and assuring each man that no one will take that from him, in order to bring peace and prosperity to those regions which depend for prosperity upon irrigation. Where there is an absence of forceful regulation of relations, the unscrupulous will take advantage of the scrupulous, and action which begins with the less conscientious will, in self-defence, be followed by those who are naturally right-minded and right-acting, until general suspicion replaces general confidence.

We see in Greeley the process going on which we can observe everywhere in the United States. As men come into close economic relations with each other, they learn that a condition of prosperity and of industrial liberty is found in the regulation of economic relations by a superior power representing all impartially. There is no choice in regard to this, and it is a condition imposed by stern necessity. Consequently we witness everywhere in the United States, as well as elsewhere in modern civilization, a change of attitude with respect to the nature and functions of government.

The history of irrigation in the United States is still young. Its modern phases in this country began with the settlement of Utah by the Mormons, and a second great historic step was taken when Greeley was founded. As Professor Mead finely says in his recent book on *Irrigation Institutions**: " As Utah is the result of a religious emigration, so Greeley is the creation of the New England town meeting transplanted to the far West. Its founding marked the beginning of a new and different industrial development in Colorado. Before the colony became noted, the wealth of the mines and the migratory and adventurous life of the range live-stock men had been the chief magnets in attracting settlement. Greeley represented an

* Chap. III.

effort of home-making people to enjoy both landed independence and social and intellectual privileges equal to those of the towns and cities they had left. Among its first buildings was Colony Hall, and among its first organizations the Lyceum, in which all the affairs of the community were debated with a fervor and fearlessness quite worthy of Horace Greeley's following. The wisdom and justice of making common property of the town site, where beauty and value could be created only by the enterprise and public spirit of all, were recognized and put into practice with satisfactory results. The best methods, both of irrigation and of cultivation, were sought out through numberless experiments, until Greeley and its potatoes grew famous together. The homes and civic institutions of the colony became the pride of the State, and the hard-won success of the community inspired numerous similar undertakings, and furnished an impulse which resulted in the reclamation and settlement of northern Colorado. Boulder, Longmont, Loveland, and Fort Collins were the outgrowth of this success, and each adopted many of the ideas and tendencies of the parent colony."

Greeley is in Weld County, some fifty miles north of Denver. It is strange that in 1870 this particular location should have been selected for the new colony. It did not look, to be sure, quite so desolate as the cactus-covered sands of the valleys of Utah, but to all appearances it was a barren waste. Apart from a limited supply of prairie-grass, the principal vegetable products of the plateau were the sage-brush and the cactus, and the animals most found were the rattlesnake, the prairie-dog, the horned toad, and the wolf. On the other hand, there were some small streams traversing the county, of which the principal are the Cache la Poudre, the Big Thompson, and the South Platte rivers. Doubtless Mr. Meeker and the other members of the committee saw the vegetation along the borders of the streams; and then they had also the experience of the Mormons in Utah to encourage them. They had the belief that the apparently barren soil would be found fruitful if it could be covered with water. This proved literally true, while other theories of a change of

climate by cultivation have proved wholly illusory. Six feet beyond the irrigation ditches the soil produces no more than it did a generation ago. The soil is fertile, and in some places has a depth of twenty or thirty feet, so that the dirt thrown up from the bottom of the wells is fruitful. The colonists had many things to learn, and many obstacles to overcome. Notwithstanding the productivity of the soil, it is unlike the dark, rich soil surrounding the "decreed" Iowa city which has been mentioned—namely, Grinnell,—in that it requires constant fertilization. The discovery of one single crop has proved the salvation of Greeley, and of a large part of our Western territory, and that is alfalfa. Three crops of alfalfa and four or five tons to the acre can be harvested yearly; but that is not the main thing in Greeley. The main thing is the value of the alfalfa for fertilizing purposes, its roots extending three feet and more underground. After alfalfa was discovered, another invention was still required to enable the farmers to utilize the alfalfa for purposes of fertilization by turning it under. The long, hard, intertwined roots could not be ploughed until a peculiar plough for that express purpose had been invented. After the irrigating-ditches had been enlarged suitably, and the colonists had learned how large a supply of water is needed for irrigation, and learned also how to apply the water, after the cultivation of alfalfa had been introduced and suitable tools for ploughing the alfalfa under had been invented, the initial steps had been taken for a marvellous production of agricultural wealth. Four years of the grasshopper plague, from 1873 through 1876, were a period during which the struggle for existence was a severe one. Writing of this period, one of the colonists says, " Some of us were pretty well pegged out in the contest, and some of us were already dead."

The chief source of wealth in Greeley up to the present time has been the potato—or, as they frequently say in Colorado, the spud. In Greeley " Potato is king." " Potato is king " does not sound so poetical as " Cotton is king," or even " Corn is king," but one who has never seen the broad fields of Greeley in potatoes cannot imagine their beauty.

I have never seen the cotton-fields in their full glory, but I have frequently admired immense areas covered with Indian corn in Illinois, Iowa, and Nebraska. But no corn-field which I have ever seen equals in beauty, in my opinion, the potato-fields of Weld County, Colorado. They stretch away for long distances towards the horizon, in long, straight rows, covered with the richest green and dotted with the beautiful potato blossoms. Here and there towards the horizon one sees the cottonwood-trees, sometimes looking like stately elms, sometimes like sturdy, broad-branched oaks; and I may remark that the cottonwood-tree, often despised, has a beauty which is rarely appreciated by those who live where it flourishes and is the main reliance for shade. Occasionally one sees a long avenue of cottonwood-trees which can compare in beauty with the elms of a New England town.

It is claimed that nowhere else in the United States is there so large a production per acre of potatoes of high quality as in Weld County, of which Greeley is the county-seat and the principal city. An eighty-acre farm has been known to produce as high as $10,000 worth of potatoes in a single year. In recent years the price of land has become high, say from $75 to $150 per acre, but it has again and again happened that a man has paid for his farm in one crop.

As the cultivated area has extended out from Greeley, an increasingly large number of people live outside the city, although many farmers cling to the old plan of living in the city and going out to their work in the country. Every one in Greeley, whatever profession or calling he follows, has an interest in potatoes. It is said that a Greeley banker would not stand well if he did not own a potato farm. It is customary in various parts of Colorado to have an annual celebration, which has some of the features of the Harvest Home. It is connected in each case with the harvesting of the crop which, in the particular section, plays the chief rôle. At Rocky Ford we have a melon day; in Boulder, the strawberry day; in Grand Junction, the peach day; and in Greeley, the potato day. All the world is invited to participate in the celebration, and a great picnic with free food is held, the chief article being the product which is celebrated. The Greeley day was a fitting observance of the harvesting of the tuber for the country in which potato

is king. Curiously enough, potato day has ceased to be celebrated in Greeley, and that for a reason which is short-sighted, and does not reflect the greatest credit upon her people. It was feared the celebration of the potato day would attract too great attention to the potato and lead to competition which would decrease the value of their product.

Stock-raising has from the beginning been one of the chief industries of the colonists. At first there were vast public ranges where free pasturage could be had. Cattle and sheep roamed over these, and the cowboy and the herdsman played their part in the life of this new country. As has always been the case from time immemorial, there was, and still is, strife between the cattlemen and sheep-raisers, —the sheep destroying the pastures for cattle. At times it was simply a question who could first reach his six-shooter and, as they say in the West, "get the drop" on the other. But such conditions fast disappeared, and as irrigation has extended and the public ranges have continued to decrease in size, conditions have changed. Herds are smaller, but still the aggregate production of sheep and cattle is as large as ever before. The accompanying illustration showing the sheep feeding about Greeley suggests a man rich in flocks.

Recently beet-culture has been introduced, and a great beet-sugar factory was finished in Greeley in the fall of 1902. The production of the sugar beet has introduced various changes in Greeley and elsewhere. The inhabitants of this section have been largely of American birth, and have been men mainly of New England traditions. Work has been done chiefly by machinery, and the hoe culture of the potato and other crops, so painfully familiar to many of us brought up in the East, is regarded as antiquated. The hoe may be used to some little extent to cut down stray weeds, but that is about all. Beet-culture requires more hand labor, and has brought in a great many Russian families, who cultivate the beets at so much per acre. It is feared that this will change the complexion of the city disadvantageously.

Greeley has become a wealthy city, in which people have means for the satisfaction of their wants. The circum-

stances under which it has grown up produce many striking effects. Manual labor receives a very high rate of remuneration, and land is abundant. The two are closely related. Five hundred dollars is a high price for a lot in Greeley which is well located and has an area of 100 by 190 feet. Many a good lot can be bought for $200. I saw one fine corner lot, 175 by 90 feet, covered with fruit trees, which had recently been sold for $300 — the highest-priced lot which I found outside the central business section of the city. Manifestly it is easy, under such conditions, to own a home, as most of the people living in Greeley do. Carpenters, machinists, janitors of public buildings, and people of that economic class occupy very attractive homes, which appeal to the æsthetic sense of culture. The accompanying illustration affords a type of a working-man's home which is common enough in Greeley.

The "helpers" of the skilled mechanics who were working on the extension of the Normal School building in Greeley while I was there were receiving $3 a day. Twenty cents an hour is the common price for a working-woman, and sometimes when they come early and stay late they receive more than $2 for a day's work. A maid of all work in the kitchen receives $20 or $25 a month. An unmarried farm-laborer will receive perhaps $30 a month and board. It is curious that farm labor in the West, where labor is very high, receives a comparatively low rate of remuneration, as I found to be particularly the case in Montana with the sheep-herders, and is something which no one whom I met seemed able to explain to me.

How natural it is to think that every one can rise in life under conditions such as those which have obtained in Greeley, and again and again we see precisely that sort of thing which Abraham Lincoln described.

When we examine a little more closely into the lot of those who originally settled Greeley and have come since, we find a large chance element in individual fortunes which has never received adequate scientific attention. Good health has much to do with the acquisition of a competence, and death frequently

THE CHIEF SOURCE OF WEALTH IN GREELEY

comes just at the time to prevent the fruition of well-founded hopes. It is not merely good health in general, but it is having sufficient strength and a sufficient degree of good fortune in respect to good health at a critical juncture. Many a Greeley colonist could now withstand the adversity of poor health on his own part, or that of his family, who would have been ruined by one year's bad health with attendant expenses and attendant incapacity at a critical juncture.

"Blood will tell," and men of the ancestry of the Greeley people are sure to love intellectual pursuits, and to provide themselves with educational opportunities. The original New-Englander is somewhat akin to the Greek in his intellectual activity, although he does not spend all his time in "seeking some new thing." The Lyceum played a large rôle in the early days of Greeley, and national and local problems were zealously debated. There was a common, active, intellectual life in which all shared. The first thought was to provide good schools, and I do not think that I have ever been in a place of the size of Greeley which has, on the whole, better educational opportunities. In addition to the ward schools, there is a high school, and one

of the best Normal schools in the United States. Even in the country districts, in marked contrast to the conditions which I found in the South, the schools are maintained for nine months of the year, and the teachers receive as high as $75 a month. The High School enrolment is said to be relatively the largest which can be found in the United States. The total school population, including all between six and twenty-one, residing in the district, is 1376. The total enrolment of the public schools, outside of the Normal School, is 955, and the High School enrolment is 175. It must be borne in mind also that in the Normal School there is a high-school department, which draws quite largely on the same territory for its pupils. It is said that in the West there have been seven stages in the evolution of the school-house, as follows: first, the dugout; second, the sod or adobe school-building; third, the log cabin; fourth, the slab house; fifth, the frame building; sixth, the little brick school-house; and seventh, the magnificent ward school-house, costing as high as $150,000. The Greeley school-houses in the country districts are in the fifth and sixth stages, and in the city itself the seventh stage has been reached.

As another illustration of intellectual

life the Greeleyites make the claim that, according to the Post-office reports, the post-office business of Greeley has in times past been larger than that of any other city of its size in the Union. We find in Greeley what we find in every other American city of that size—and what we find perhaps to a greater extent in the West than in the East—religious sectarianism. The great number of religious bodies makes each one weak, and divides the spiritual resources of the city. Greeley has, as already stated, a population something like 3500, and approximately a dozen different denominations. Fortunately, however, one notices in Greeley, as elsewhere, the breaking down of denominational bitterness and increasing inclination to come together to promote common interests and civic righteousness. In this particular, as in others, we witness in Greeley, in a small, concrete way, a great national movement.

The farther West one goes, the more democratic becomes society. I must confess that I did not understand true Americanism, in one of its phases at least, until I got far away from the Atlantic coast. Coming to Madison, Wisconsin, from Baltimore, Maryland, the freedom of intercourse between all economic classes and men of the widest divergence of wealth and intellect attracted my attention; but there are social differences even in Madison which would be scorned in a place like Greeley. Anything like aristocracy seems to be absolutely unknown in Greeley, unless it is the aristocracy of personal merit.

A curious fact in the evolution of civilization is this—that individuals, as they swarm from their early homes and form new settlements, may take with them their individual acquisitions, but to only a limited extent do they carry with them their social acquisitions. They lose in a large part the results of social experience, and have to begin by slow and painful processes the formation of a civilized society. What they precisely lose in a great measure is what we must term a social consciousness and a social conscience, and without both a high grade of civilization is not possible. This explains the civic backwardness and, in some cases, the civic corruption in new cities. It also explains in some measure,

I believe, the fact that in our civic life we Americans are in many particulars still behind the older countries of the world. One reason for this is that in a new city men expect to stay for a short time, make just as much money as they possibly can, and then leave. Consequently one frequently finds a most shocking but deliberate sacrifice of the future to the present. When the public-utility franchise question came up in Seattle, Washington, not long ago, one of the citizens, voicing the sentiments of others, said:

"I don't care about the future. What I want is to make money now."

But apart from such crass materialism, there is the absence of social consciousness. The men in a new city come together from various places, and they have to learn to act together, and ties among them must be formed. They must also learn who among them are trustworthy and suitable leaders. It was only within a few years that the ten acres reserved for Lincoln Park in Greeley, now so attractive, were improved. The civic spirit is growing rapidly in Greeley now, and they have a Civic Improvement Society, which, among other things, provides baskets for waste paper and rubbish—a small thing, but indicative of much. All this is especially noteworthy in Greeley, because a deliberate effort was made to carry thither the acquisitions of an older civilization, and because there was a larger measure of success than one usually finds. There was some public provision for public needs—common funds were provided for irrigation ditches; land was reserved for parks, for school-houses, and churches. There is a small reservation about the water-works which belongs to the city. Citizens gave forty acres of land to the Normal School, and a small sum of money was raised for it. The spirit of individualism is still rife, however, and, on the whole, the public provision for public needs is less than one would probably find in a New England city. The spirit of giving for public purposes is one which is gradually developed, and has not received a very high grade of development in Greeley.

One of the main features of Greeley is that there they have prohibition which actually prohibits. This is a part of the

TYPICAL COTTAGE OF GREELEY WORKING-PEOPLE

original plan. Only "temperance people" were invited in the beginning to join the community. In all the deeds it is provided that land shall be forfeited if in any way it is connected with the traffic of intoxicating beverages. Among the people there is a sentiment—indeed, a practically unanimous sentiment—against the sale of intoxicating beverages in Greeley, and measures have been taken once or twice to suppress the so-called "blind pig" which show that a man incurs a serious risk both to his person and his property if he attempts to violate the prohibitory regulations of the city.

The development which has begun in Greeley will continue. Many of the early pioneers have passed away; the others will quickly join "the great majority"; but Greeley will continue to be a monument to Nathan C. Meeker, and in lesser degree to Horace Greeley. Mr. Meeker was one of those idealists who knew better how to help others than to help themselves. He himself was massacred while an Indian agent, endeavoring to elevate the Indians, and had little property to leave. He left his family a noble memory, and a grateful country has pensioned his widow. Mr. J. Max Clark tells us that toward the close of Mr. Meeker's life he was one day driving with him through the country surrounding

Greeley to which permanent prosperity had come. Mr. Meeker had been speaking to Mr. Clark about his own financial difficulties, and perhaps it was at this time that he spoke about his own mistake in not "taking up" a good-sized tract of farming-land, inasmuch as he had not believed in the speculative ownership of land. He had come to see that the social institutions are not individual creations, and that individuals must act in accordance with institutions which have been established by society. The only result of his abstinence from land-ownership was that he did not share in the increasing value of land which had come to others. Mr. Meeker also spoke about his increasing troubles in the management of the Indians; but as they reached a bluff from which they could overlook the city of Greeley, with its many happy homes, and with the dense foliage of the trees which had replaced the former bleak outlook, he said to Mr. Clark: "After all, Max, although the enterprise yielded me nothing in return, in a worldly sense, yet I am proud to have been the leader in such a movement; it will be counted an honor to every man who took part in the settlement of Greeley. I am more than compensated in the grand success of the undertaking itself, and I have nothing to regret."

SOUTHERN CALIFORNIA

A BIT OF OLD MONTEREY.

WONDERFUL things are always a long way from home. This is so well understood that something like regular ratios might no doubt be established. Thus a locality three thousand miles distant is more extraordinary than one but two; six thousand miles is twice as marvellous as three; while if a traveller will but go twelve, he may assure us, with little dispute, that the inhabitants there are accustomed to breakfast at midnight, and have never heard of walking matches, defaulting bank cashiers, or five-o'clock teas.

This reverential attitude toward distance has had its sway not less with travellers themselves than the readers of their accounts. But in these perverse later times a tendency arises to doubt and question, to find things otherwise than as represented, and even sometimes less wonderful than what has been left behind at home, this having now in its turn attained the due remoteness. Such a questioning frame of mind will have to be struggled against to some extent by him who arrives in California, as I did on coming from Mexico, in the months of the year known as the dry season. The conception has gone out about the country, and particularly about Southern California, of which it is to be my pleasure to speak, that it is an earthly paradise. Enthusiastic writers have so pictured it. Proprietors of transportation routes, lands, and "pleasure resorts" have modestly agreed with the truth of this estimate. I declare, for my part, that it is charming; but at the first blush it is an earthly paradise very unlike the best idea of it one has been able to attain by a good deal of previous investigation.

Southern California, especially in the dry season—which comprises a large part of the California year—is perhaps like those friendships which are the best worth having and endure the longest—it makes its way to favor subtly and gradually.

It is not easy to decide on the instant just what Southern California should be deemed to comprehend. A very large part of the State outside of the mining and lumbering districts displays some of those tropical characteristics in which its charm to the Eastern imagination consists. One sees orange, fig, and pomegranate trees environing pleasant homes at Sonoma, well to the north of San Francisco; there is an important raisin district around Sacramento and Marysville to the northwest; and at Calistoga, seventy-five miles north of San Francisco, is to be found a group of as fine palms as any in California. At the same time, one safely assumes that all this will be found in its greatest perfection as the distinctively low latitudes are approached.

San Francisco lies not far from midway in the State, and forms a convenient point of division. Southern California may be taken to comprise all that part of the State lying south of the famous seaport and metropolis. It is upon the area just below the city, at the Gates, that the Rev. Starr King has lavished the most laudatory sentences of his polished style, describing the "flowers by the acre, flowers by the square mile," which he saw in a ride around the bay. It was to the vicinity of San José, but fifty miles down, that Bayard Taylor (if he should live to be old, and note his faculties failing) proposed to retire in order to recover his lost youth. Seventy-five miles further south yet are the popular summer resorts—and winter resorts as well—of Santa Cruz and Monterey.

I set out upon my travels from the metropolis in mid-autumn, the season of county fairs, when, if ever, the products of an agricultural country should be seen to advantage. There was being held at San José the combined fair of the counties of Santa Clara and Santa Cruz. There is no means of exit from San Francisco by land except to the southward, the long narrow peninsula on which it lies being surrounded on all other sides by water. One may cross, however, by ferry to Oakland, its Jersey City as well as Brooklyn—as he must do for all the greater journeys—and go around the bay on that side by a branch road which brings up at San José also. In doing so he traverses Alameda County, which raises nearly a million bushels of wheat (from Murray Township alone), a vast number of tons of sugar-beets, and more hay than any other county in the State. It comes third in rank for grape-vines, and has tropical pretensions of its own besides, making no small exhibit of orange and lemon trees in certain favored nooks. But the most direct way is to take the coast division of the Southern Pacific Railway, and so I took it and went with it to the important places whither it leads.

If topography may be glanced at a moment, California is fenced into valleys by two long up and down ranges of mountains, the Sierra Nevadas, of immensely the higher elevation, and the Coast Range. These meet in acute points, north at Shasta, and south at the Tejon Pass, and thereafter become one. They inclose between them the vast central space known in its upper portion as the Sacramento Valley, and below as the San Joaquin Valley, from the two main rivers by which it is drained. It is the granite Sierra Nevadas that contain the peaks of from thirteen to fifteen thousand feet elevation which have obtained so extensive a fame in the world. The Coast Range averages only from two to six thousand feet, and is of softer material. The Sierra Nevadas do not much divide their strength; but the Coast Range throws out frequent spurs parallel to itself, which get separate names, as Sierra Morena, Santa Clara, and Santa Cruz mountains, and are the means of making numerous long narrow valleys, and also benches of table-land left between them and the Pacific Ocean. It is down the large Santa Clara Valley, in this last diversified region, that the first excursion takes us.

It is no ordinary moment, this opening venture into an earthly paradise, and one settles himself luxuriously back in his seat to enjoy it. By the time the long files of freight cars that constitute the immediate approach to American cities are passed, we are running through a tract of small vegetable gardens and windmills in the suburbs. Clusters of white buildings in white inclosures, that have looked from a distance on their hills like Mexican haciendas, prove to be "institutions" of various sorts. A long arm of San Francisco Bay, which accompanies us thirty miles south, is seen at a distance to the left, with a wide, dismal stretch of marsh between. White ark-like houses on piles, placed at intervals along the water's edge, are found to be keeping guard over oyster beds. The small California oyster has never yet been either coaxed or driven into a development commensurate with the general grandeur of things about it.

Our guide-book promises, "after a few minutes' ride, orchards, vineyards, elegant farm-houses, prospects to charm all who love the beauties of nature." But, really, one is inclined to rub his eyes. The ground is bare and brown, bare to the skin. Hardly a tree or a bush; not a green blade of grass. At length some trees begin to appear. They are scrub oaks, a small-leaved variety, at a little distance resembling the olive. Farm-houses are few, and not strikingly elegant. The hills are of the color of a camel's hide, and not unlike its humps in shape and texture. At Millbrae there is a glimpse of some wooden towers, in the American style, rising from a villa; and there is a large dairy barn. At Belmont we come closer to the low hills than at any other point. At Menlo Park a charming flower bed is cared for, close by the track, as is seen at some foreign railway stations. We are at the chosen site for villa residences of the San Francisco millionaires. The surface is flat, and with its growth of oaks recalls scenery in the outskirts of Chicago, as Hyde Park or Riverside.

The valley widens till the hills are distant enough to be veiled in blue, and fills up with tawny grain fields. The combination of buff and blue is pleasing, but there is no verdure. And where are the wild flowers? One hardly expected them now by the acre and by the square mile, since it is autumn. But of all the primroses, the larkspurs, the lupins, and pop-

PALO ALTO.

pies of tradition, not one ? Not a narcissus ? not a chrysanthemum ? Oh, predecessors !

It is in the spring or rainy season only
that the flowers bloom, and then, indeed,
they carpet the earth as the grass carpets
it elsewhere. In the spring the eulogists
have not said a word too much. But it
is my originality to have seen Southern
California in the autumn and winter, to
have seen it as it is for seven months in
the year, and as it is, in exceptionally dry
seasons, the whole year through. The
leaves fall here as elsewhere, and are not
renewed till another year. The whole
face of nature is parched and sad.

Not to make mention of this bareness
and dryness would be to omit a most essential feature of the aspect of California.
The annual rains begin in December, January, or February, and continue till June,
greatly diminishing in May, which is
sometimes also a dry month. It must
not be thought that the rainy season is a
continual down-pour. It is simply
that in which there are occasional
rains, as with us, while during the rest
of the year there are none at all.

At the same time, however, it must
be borne in mind that the brown season
is to be contrasted with our own winter. The mere dryness of surface, always pleasant to the tread, and in time
to the eye also, under a uniformly
genial temperature, is to be compared
with our own fields of sheeted white
under their howling blasts, and our quag-
mires of mud and slush in alternate par-
oxysms of thawing and freezing.

"But you set up to be a land of perpetual summer, you know," one argues with
the resident Californian, in this first state
of surprise.

"So we are," he replies; "but that does
not necessarily mean perpetual verdure
without a more liberal use of water in irrigation than we have yet been able to
arrive at. But look at the thermometer!
look at the fertility of the land! Nothing
is scarce with us but the water." And
then perhaps he will add, with a dignity
well justified by the facts of the case:
"California sets up to be a land which by
the enormous extent of all its relations,
commercial, agricultural, mineral, and social, has become a power in the world. It
has revolutionized values, struck the key-
note of new social conditions, and is to be
the point of departure of a new commercial era in a trade with the Orient and the

isles of the sea, the extent of which no man can estimate. California has arrived at a point where she takes her place on equal terms with the States of the Union, and no longer depends for favor upon narratives of astounding beauties and eccentricities—though of all this, too, it has no lack, as you will find."

San José, a city of twenty thousand people, is described as contending with Sacramento for the honor of being third in importance in the State. One alights at the small station, in the vicinity a horse-car line, a blacksmith's shop, and some flat rail fences painted with the usual advertisements. These have a very American look to begin with, for a place with so pretty a Spanish name, a place to which Bayard Taylor wished to retire in the failing of his powers to find the elixir of youth. And so have the small picket fences an American look, and so have the comfortable little clapboarded wooden houses behind them, with the scroll-sawed ornaments in their piazzas. With the exception of an unusual number of French and Italian names on the sign-boards, and some large clean tuns in front of the shops of dealers in native wines, it is as downright a little Yankee town as ever was. There is much shade in the streets, and on a public green or common, from trees that are small and low as yet.

It is a clean, prosperous little city, the centre of a rich agricultural district. It has excellent schools and all the other conveniences of life. A good deal of money has been spent for show on the principal business buildings. Like those of many other small capitals throughout the State, they are of a neat, bay-window architecture, which might be described as the San Francisco style. There was an iron trestle-work tower or pharos going up at the intersection of two important streets, which was to rise to a height of two hundred feet, and contain an electric light to illuminate the entire town. The white court-house, in the classic style, though not large, is agreeably proportioned, and quite a model of its kind.

The week's doings at the Fair Grounds had resolved themselves chiefly into trotting matches. I was told that the combined display of the two counties was poorer than either had been in the habit of making alone. The most interesting thing was racing and ornamental riding, one day, by young women. Those who took the premiums, such as a handsome saddle and whip, were girls of but fourteen and sixteen years of age. A popular feature of this with other county fairs of the time was a "firemen's tournament," in which different companies had contests of speed, equipped with all the paraphernalia of their craft.

Games of chance went on freely in the refreshment-rooms under the grand stand. There was but a scattering display of live stock, and little or no fruit. I did not see the two-hundred-pound squash, the twenty-six-pound turnip, nor the beet which is five feet in length and a foot through, nor the apples and pears commensurate with these. I had seen them before, however, and did not so much regret their absence. I have a secret suspicion that there is a proper standard of the vegetable as of the human kind, and that the Tom Thumbs and General Bateses of the one are hardly more happy in their departure from it than those of the other.

The capacity of the country to produce fruits of fine quality as well as of abnormal size — always excepting the apple, which seems to require extremes of heat and cold, and in this even climate remains comparatively insipid—has perhaps been too well tested to need the stimulus of competitive exhibitions. What better county fair is needed than the daily display of fruits and vegetables in the San Francisco market? The regular season for any and all of them is twice as long as on the Atlantic coast at corresponding latitudes.

I traversed the much-eulogized "Alameda," an avenue of willows and poplars, three miles long, set out in 1799 by Spanish friars. These founded a mission among the Indians at Santa Clara, to which town the avenue extends. There remains at Santa Clara the chapel of this early mission, with its adobe walls five feet thick, and flat wooden ceiling, rudely painted. It is now a part of a flourishing collegiate institution. Across the way is a clump of ruinous old adobe cottages of the same date—a genuine bit of picturesqueness. But I am adjured to pay no heed to these, since we are going to Monterey, and Monterey makes, as it were, a grand specialty of all that kind of thing.

The Alameda's poplars and willows make but a moderate showing for their age, and could hardly be rated as equal,

say, to an avenue of New Haven elms.
Behind them, along both sides of the
road, are houses of the same *bourgeois*
air of comfort as in the town.　There are
said to be many residents of wealth and
leisure who have been attracted here by
the climate to pass the remainder of their
days in peace.　The Coast Mountains are
thought to cut off something of the fogs
and winds of the ocean, and a higher
range on the other side to bar out the
heats of the country eastward.　You en-

One had been inclined to expect a good
deal of novelty and picturesqueness from
these towns of romantic Sans and Santas
and Loses and Dels, and feels rather ag-
grieved not to get it.　The absence of
Spanish picturesqueness is explained by
the fact that there were rarely any original settlements corresponding to the present names, which were taken from ranches, springs, or mines in the neighborhood.
On the arrival of the Americans there
were but thirteen thousand Spanish or

RALSTON'S COUNTRY PLACE.

deavor to divine, in some superior refinement of taste, which the abodes of these
may be.　It is a poetic conception, that of
living for the pure physical delight of it,
and makes them highly interesting.　Perhaps there should be at the gates some
young women, their daughters, with a re-
pining air mingled with their superior distinction, as if, for their part, they had not
so willingly consented to abandon a world
of larger opportunities.　But after all,
the desire to live for the pure pleasure of
living does not imply a cultivated taste in
architecture and landscape gardening.

Mexicans in all California—a territory as
large as New York, Pennsylvania, and
the six New England States put together.
Let us believe, however, that their pleasing designations will act as a subtle stimulus, and that all these communities will
live up to their names with an artistic development which they never could have
attained had they been simply Smithvilles
and Jonesvilles.

　　The impressions resulting, both at San
José and the country at large, from a second visit a month later, were much more
agreeable.　Something like the proper

point of view had now been attained. I knew that the face of nature was brown, and the towns were not quite strikingly picturesque; but I had begun to note the continued cloudlessness of the sky, the quality of the air, and to experience the pleasure that may reside in climate pure and simple.

The district containing the villa residences of the San Francisco millionaires when penetrated into gains much in attractiveness. There are white and chestnut oaks, as well as scrub oaks, which in groups give a park-like appearance, and live-oaks with the long gray Spanish moss depending from them.

If there be no wild flowers, there are plenty of the cultivated sort, carefully gardened, and lawns kept green by spraying fountains and rubber hose furnish a proper background. We take lesson number one in the uses of water. Where there is water enough, and as far as it goes, the winter, or brown season, need never extend. As a rule, long stretches of white picket-fence surround the places, and the houses themselves are painted white. These are the dwellings—some for the summer only, some throughout the year—of the great railway and banking and bonanza kings, the stories of whose sudden and vast accumulations of fortune in these late years read like fables of the *Arabian Nights.*

Even the bonanza kings, it seems, have been invested with a somewhat greater magnificence than really belongs to them. Their places have cost them immense sums, it is true, but a reduction should be made to Eastern standards. The outpouring of untold millions from the mines and other sources of wealth put up the prices of land, labor, and every commodity entering into the result, so that less was obtained for the money than an equal expenditure would have procured here. As a parallel exhibit, the Menlo Park district is inferior to Llewellyn Park, Englewood, Irvington, and others in the neighborhood of New York.

The builders have struck out a kind of style of their own, being perhaps in too great haste to wait for imported ideas. The houses, as at San Francisco, are chiefly of wood. Flood, of the famous firm of barkeepers, Flood and O'Brien, who owned the Consolidated Virginia Mine when the astonishing bonanza was struck, had just completed at the time of my visit one of great size on his estate of five hundred

acres at Menlo Park. There is a terrace, with a fine bronze fountain in front. The main steps were of polished marble with bronze sphinxes on them, and there were bronze dragons on the equally ornate stables. The whole is glaringly white and gorgeous, and affects one like the playing of a brass band.

There are, to be sure, some gentler, more home-like places, painted in the quieter tones of, and recalling the best rural life at, the East. Such a one is ex-Governor Leland Stanford's, at Palo Alto, a breeding farm for horses, which is one of the most complete establishments of the kind in the world. Of the seventeen hundred acres in the place, one hundred are occupied by the stables, barns, and small paddocks. The buildings, at the foot of a gentle rise of ground, make a small city by themselves, inhabited by a population of nearly five hundred, who return hither from their business on the pastures and race-tracks, and have two hundred persons employed in their domestic service. The spacious barns are uniformly floored and ceiled up with redwood—a handsome material, which resembles cedar in effect. They are strewn with the freshest straw, and kept as neat as the most unexceptionable drawing-rooms.

Scions from the stock here raised, which represents the best thorough-bred and trotting strains in the country, are likely to be a most important influence in improving the breed of horses throughout the Pacific coast. It was here that curious experiments were conducted, at the expense of Governor Stanford, for arriving at a better understanding of the speed of horses by photographing them in rapid motion. The photographer, Muybridge, of San Francisco, succeeded by an ingenious arrangement of electrical wires, communicating at the touch of the animal with cameras already prepared, in securing twelve distinct views of the different stages of a single stride. The attitudes are of the most unexpected and curious sort, some of them highly comic.

Great pains are taken in the raising and training of the young colts. From the time of foaling the colts are handled gently and constantly, and are made as familiar with the touch of harness as they are with that of human hands. As a natural consequence they are perfectly tame, gentle, and even affectionate, and never need breaking. The effect of this system of training has been apparent in the performances of some of the colts which have been publicly speeded against time. The first notable exhibition of speed by a Palo Alto colt was made on the Bay District Association track at San Francisco in 1880, when the two-year-old colt Fred Crocker lowered the record for a one-mile trot to 2′ 25¼″. Last year Bonita, a two-year-old filly from Palo Alto, cut the record down to 2′ 24½″; and later, at the same trotting exhibition, Wildflower, another two-year-old from the same farm, made the mile in 2′ 21″;

At the Mills house, for an example, at Millbrae, the residence of a well-known banking and railway magnate, now become a citizen of New York, are seen all the portières and Oriental rugs and Christmas-card patterns of decorations, and bedchambers done in fine woods, and silken hangings of the latest Eastlake taste; a picture-gallery of the choice works of Gérôme, Detaille, and Bouguereau; and vistas through all the windows of fan-palms, flower beds, greensward, and bronzes.

The Ralston house, at Belmont, now in the possession of Senator Sharon, is that,

A BRANDY CELLAR.

and Hinda Rose, a yearling filly, on the same day, added to the fame of the farm by cutting down the yearling record to 2′ 36½″. It is asserted that there are colts on the farm which can do even better.

The interiors of these millionaires' dwellings are, as a rule, better than the exteriors.

perhaps, having the greatest interest of all. The remarkable man who built it was of the traditional California type in its most astonishing development. Starting from a humble origin, he became a forwarder of every brilliant scheme of improvement, public and private, and conducted

CHAMPAGNE-MAKING.

a hundred projects to success which in other hands would have been sheer folly. He arrived thus at an unbounded confidence in his star. Entangled finally while cashier of the Bank of California, he handed in his resignation to the directors one day, and went down to the public baths near the Potrero. A strong. athletic man, in the prime of life, he swam out half a mile into the bay—for refreshment in his troubles, as some say, but, as the general opinion is, with the deliberate purpose of suicide—and was never again seen alive.

The house that was his is notched into a hill-side, in a rolling country, much pleasanter than the plain at Menlo Park. A pretty gorge behind it is dammed at a certain level to furnish the water-supply. There are gas-works, a bowling-alley, and an elaborate Turkish bath among the outbuildings, and a grange-like barn of solid stone, ivy-grown now, which cost $80,000. As to the immense residence itself, that is of wood, white, in the usual fashion. With its numerous stories and windows, it is not unlike a large country hotel without; but its peculiar arrangements and great spaciousness within make it quite palatial. The principal rooms open into one another by glass partitions, which can be rolled away. There is no crowding through doorways. There is an arcade in the story above, around the grand staircase, with a balustrade, and tribunes pro-

FROM THE OLD FORT, MONTEREY.

jecting from the balustrade, in which young women in pink and corn-color at an evening party must look particularly houri-like. What in any other house would be the ordinary veranda is here a delightful promenade, glazed in, provided with easy furniture and a parquetry floor. Then comes a tier of such main apartments as a drawing-room and library; then a parallel tier, of which one is a great gallery, entirely faced with mirrors. There are a piano, mantels, and stair-posts of California laurel. This was a new industry that he encouraged among others.

We drove from Belmont back through a succession of cup-like dells in the lower mountains, a number of them dammed to form pretty lakes, the sources of supply for the Spring Valley Water Company—a corporation of great prominence at San Francisco. The slopes at first were tawny with grain stubble; then scattered with the stiff thick brush known as chaparral; then bare. We passed an occasional lonely "milk ranch," or a "chicken ranch." There are no farms, so called, in California; no matter how small, they are always ranches.

In the strong warm sunshine any chance object on the bare rolling slopes casts an intense shadow. The spot under a distant tree is as purplish dark as if a pit were dug there. The shadow of a large bird flying low is followed as distinctly along the ground as the bird itself. One becomes reconciled at last to the brown tone. It is like what the painters show us of Algeria. White stands out brilliantly against it, only it should be a more solid white than that of wooden houses. The falconry parties of Fromentin, or a conference of rival Arab chiefs by Pasini, might be held in these hills.

It was the mature vintage season now in the country around San José. Santa Clara County, of which San José is the business venture. Here there are about one hundred and seventy-five thousand vines set out—a thousand, perhaps, to the acre. The large cheerful farm buildings are upon a gentle rise of ground above the area of vines, which is nearly level. An Alsacian foreman shows us through the wine-cellars. A servant-maid bustling about the yard is a thorough French peasant, only lacking the wooden shoes.

CEDARS AT MONTEREY.

county seat, boasts of a number of acres of grape-vines under cultivation (something over eleven thousand) larger than any but one other in the State, that of Sonoma. Napa, however, also to the north, and Los Angeles, to the south, greatly surpass it in the number of gallons of wine and brandy made.

We visited the Le Franc vineyard, which dates from 1851, and was the pioneer in the way of making wine-growing a regular The long tables, set for the forty hands employed in the vintage-time, are spread with viands in the French fashion. Scarcely a word of English is spoken. At other places the surroundings are as exclusively Italian. One feels very much abroad in the scenes of this new industry on American soil. A certain romantic interest attaches to it wherever found. The great tuns in the wine-cellars, and all the processes, seem delightfully clean. It

THE HOTEL DEL MONTE.

is re-assuring to see the pure juice of the grape poured out in such floods, and to know that at this source of supply there is to be no need, founded in scarcity at least, of adulteration.

Heavy loads of grape are driven up, across a weighing scale, and lifted to an upper story, and put into a hopper, where the stems come off, and the fruit falls through into a crusher. It is lightly crushed at first. It is something of a discovery to find that the first product of grapes of every variety is white wine. Red takes its hue from the coloring matter in the skins, which are utilized in a subsequent rougher treatment. It is not necessary to describe all the various processes of the work, the racking off, clarifying, and the like, though, having been favored with so much of the company of persons who spoke with authority on these matters, and were continually holding up little glasses to the light with gusto, like the figures in certain popular chromos, I consider myself to yield in knowledge of the subject to but few. Immense upright casks containing a warm and audibly fermenting mass, and others lying down, neatly varnished, and with concave ends, are the most salient features in the dimly lighted wine-cellars.

They are not cellars, properly so called.

They are wholly above-ground, and the casks rest on wooden sills upheld by short brick posts. Those of General Naglee, a successful maker of excellent brandy on a large scale, are really charming from an artistic point of view. The cobwebs have been allowed to increase till they hang like tattered banners. Through these the light penetrates dimly from above, or it makes a white glare through a latticed window, upon which the patterns of vine leaves without are defined. The buildings are brown, gray, vine-clad, and covered with quaint Dutch-pavilion-looking roofs, with dove-cotes attached ; and the lofty windmill water-tank—a feature of every California rural homestead—is of a more tower-like pattern than usual. Round about are long avenues of eucalyptus and pine, tamarinds with their black, dry pods, the willow-like pepper-tree with its scarlet berries, large clumps of the *nopal* cactus, and an occasional maguey or century-plant. Among the plantations autumn is hardly less warm-colored here than elsewhere. Poplars and cottonwoods turn yellow, and peach and almond trees, the Lawton blackberry, and the vineyards themselves, touched by the frost, supply scarlet and crimson. The country is bathed in fixed sunshine, or steeped in the hues of its own wines.

The vines, short, thick, and needing no stakes for support, bear, each at the head of its stalwart stock, an incredible number of purple clusters, all growing from the same point. They quaintly suggest those uncouth little men of Hendrik Hudson's *Half-Moon*, who stagger up the mountains in the play of *Rip Van Winkle*, each with his keg of spirits. No especial attention is given to the frosts now, but those occurring in the early spring are the object of many precautions. The most effectual of these is to kindle smudge fires about the vineyard toward four o'clock in

lesser yield excel them in quality. The best results here, we were told, are secured from such vines as the Mataro, Carignane, and Grenache, imported cuttings from the French slope of the Pyrenees. There are on the Le Franc place not less than sixty different varieties under probation, many others of which will, no doubt, give an excellent account of themselves in time. They are from Greece, Italy, Palestine, and the Canary Islands, the remotest sections of the earth, and each has its own interest, historical as well as botanical. Every phase of the subject, too, has its at-

THE CHINESE FISHING QUARTER, MONTEREY.

the morning. The smoke envelops it and keeps it in a warmer atmosphere of its own till the sun be well risen.

Three to four tons of grapes to the acre are counted upon here; while further south, where irrigation is used, it is from eight to twelve. But it is claimed, in the standing controversy on the subject, that the irrigated grapes are watery, while those of the

tractions, from the rude preparation of a few hundred gallons each for their own use by the Italians and Portuguese to the manufacture of American champagne on a great scale by the Hungarian, Arpad Haraszthy, at San Francisco. The pure American families have not yet acquired the habit of looking upon wine as a necessity.

CHINESE FISH-DRYING HOUSE, MONTEREY.

But with so much attention for the present to an alluring theme, we leave it to drive along the dry, shallow bed of the Guadalupe River to the Guadalupe Quicksilver Mine, a more remote and less visited companion of the New Almaden. The mine is in a lovely little vale, with a settlement of Mexican and Chinese boarding-houses clustered around it, some bold ledges of rock jutting out, and the superintendent's house surrounded with flowers hanging on the hill-side. Above the works a weird-looking flume conveys the sulphurous acid from the calcining furnaces to a hill-top, upon which its poison blasts every trace of vegetation.

Then we make a little tour by rail further southward through the immense "Murphy" and "Miller and Lux" ranches, a grain country as flat as a floor. We turn west through the fertile little Pajaro Valley, whose emporium, both for produce and the fine redwood lumber, cut in great quantities on the adjoining Santa Cruz Mountains, is the thriving town of Watsonville. We run along the rugged coast, past the wooded gorges and white sea-side cottages of Aptos and Soquel, to Santa Cruz. Santa Cruz has bold variations of level, new and commonplace buildings, a noble drive along cliffs eaten into a hundred fantastic caverns by the waves, shops for the sale of shells, and plenty of summer boarders, a part of whom are now turned winter boarders. Thence we come down finally to the old Spanish capital of Monterey.

Here at last is something to commend from the point of view of the picturesque, without mental reservation. Monterey has a population which still, in considerable part, speaks Spanish only, and retains the impress of the Spanish domination, and little else. When one is told in his own country that anybody with whom he is about to have dealings "does not speak English," he infers naturally that it is brokenly, or only a little. But at Monterey it means absolutely not a word. There are Spanish signs on the shops, and Spanish advertisements, as the *Wheeler & Wilson Maquinas á Coser*, on the fences. "*Las rosas son muy secas*" (the roses are very dry), says the Señorita Cualquiera, apologetically, as we enter her little garden, laid out in numerous equal parallelograms, behind an adobe wall topped with red tiles. We have come to call, and to admire, though they are falling to pieces in the wind, the large yellow and red roses, and her long low white adobe house.

She is one of those who speak no English. It seems as if it were some willful perversity, after all these years (since 1846) of having been a part of the most bustling State of the most active country in the

PORTUGUESE WHALE-MEN AT MONTEREY.

world. It seems as if it must be due to some lingering hatred of the American invader. But the señorita is far too gentle and friendly in her manners to be suspected of that. Whatever the reason be, if there be any beyond the mental apathy through which the Mexican survivors have suffered all their property interests as well to go by the board, it is not hatred.

The señorita is a little thin old lady of fifty now, who had a romance with an American officer, so it is said, thirty years ago. The roses are indeed very dry at Monterey.

As seen from a distance, scattered loose and white on the forest-crested slope of the fine crescent-shaped bay of Monterey, the little city, which has now perhaps two thousand inhabitants, hardly shows at once its real dissimilarity to other places. But when entered it is found to consist almost exclusively of whitewashed adobe houses, and straggling mud-colored adobe walls, forming inclosures, known as "corrals," for animals and the like. Plenty of them are abandoned; and at frequent intervals is encountered some abandoned old adobe barracks, or government house, or military prison of historic fame, with its whitewash gone, holes in its walls, and some bits of broken grating and balcony hanging aimlessly from it, only waiting the first opportunity to let go.

The travellers of my youth, I recollect, had a fashion of talking glibly of adobe, without ever explaining what adobe is. Let me not be guilty any longer of the same fault. Adobe is a building material used in the same manner as brick. One adobe is about twice the size of an ordinary brick. It is brick, only dried in the sun, and not baked. Walls are made of great thickness of it in order that, even though the outside and inside crumble off, there may be a good deal left. Like a number of other things, it stands very well while it is not assailed; and in this climate it is supposed, with reason, that it will rarely be assailed by any violent extremes of temperature.

The typical adobe house of the best class is stuccoed and whitewashed, large on the ground, two stories in height, with verandas. Again it is of but one story, and has an interior court-yard. It has green doors and shutters, and green turned posts in what we should now call the Queen Anne style, and is a comfortable and home-like edifice to look at. One of them —whither I was taken to see the first piano ever introduced into California, and to call upon a lady whose husband had

THE DAY OF SAN CARLOS.

made haste to sell out his all at San Francisco and invest it here, in order to reap
the prosperity thought to be waiting upon
Monterey at an early date—has two old
iron guns planted as posts at the corners.
In front of others are walks neatly made
of the vertebræ of whales. The whales
are taken by the Monterey Whaling Company, a band of hardy, weather-beaten
men, chiefly Portuguese from the Azores.
They have a lookout station on the hill
under the ruined fort, a barracks lower
down, and pursue their avocation from
the shore in boats, with plenty of adventure and no small profit.

Monterey, which is now not even a
county seat, was the Spanish capital of
the province from the time it was first
thought necessary to have a capital, after
the landing here of the missionary father
Junipero Serra in the year 1770. It was
next a Mexican capital under eleven successive governors. Then it became the
American capital, the first port of entry,
the scene of the first Constitutional Convention of the State, and an outfitting
point for the southern mines. Money
in those early days was so plenty, as I
have heard tell, that store-keepers hardly
stopped to count it, but threw it under the
counter by the bushel-basketful. A secret
belief in some ultimate revival and recovery of prestige seems always to have survived in certain quarters, corresponding,
as it were, to that of the re-appearance of
Barbarossa from the Kylfhäuser Berg, or
the restoration of the Jews to Palestine.
Breakwaters are ambitiously talked of, to
make the bay a harbor, and the town a
shipping point and a rival of San Francisco.

The only step toward such revival as
yet, however, has been the establishment
of a great hotel, which will probably make
it, instead of Santa Cruz, across the bay,
the leading sea-side resort of the Pacific
coast. Though not so grandiose a direction, this is really the one for the present
in which the peculiar conditions of the
old capital are most likely to tell. The
summer boarder can revel among its historic remains and traditions of greatness
when they are good for nothing else. The
Hotel del Monte is a beautiful edifice, not
surpassed in its kind at any American
watering-place, and not equalled, I think,
at any of them in its charming groves of
live-oaks and pines, the profusion of cul-

tivated flowers by which it is surrounded, and the air of comfort existing at the same time with its elegant arrangements. That is the way with our friends of the Pacific coast. If they do not always stop in their zeal to follow Eastern ideas and patterns, when they really do attempt something in the same line, they are more likely than not to surpass us.

The local climate at Monterey, according to statistical tables, is remarkably even. The mean temperature is 52° in January and 58° in July. This strikes one as rather cool for bathing, but the present mode is to bathe in the tanks of a large bath-house, to which sea-water is introduced artificially warmed, instead of in the sea itself. In other respects the place seems nearly as desirable a resort at one time of the year as another. The quaint town is always here; so are the wild rocks with their gossiping families of gulls and pelicans, and the romantic drives through extensive forests of pine and cypress. There are varieties of these two trees—the latter of which is like the Italian stone-pine—peculiar to Monterey alone. They are hoary with age and hanging moss. They are contorted into all the fantastic shapes imagined in Doré's illustrations to the "Inferno," and they stand by the most savage points of rock, where the breakers toss up handfuls of white spray to them, forty feet in the air, as if in amity and greeting.

Along the beach at this remote point of the great Pacific Ocean is a lonely Chinese settlement. The veritable Celestials, with hardly a word of English among them, paste crimson papers of hieroglyphics on their shanty residences, burn tapers before their gods, and fish for a living in such junks and small boats as are seen at Hong-Kong and Canton. They prepare, too, the avallonia meat and avallonia shells for their home market. We shall find that the Chinese element, which one had thought of as confined to San Francisco, constitutes a feature of exceeding quaintness and picturesqueness throughout all of Southern California as well.

At Monterey, too, one sees his first old mission of the delightfully ruinous sort. It is in the little Carmel Valley, bare and brown again, after the great woods are passed, and four miles from the town. The mission fathers once had 90,000 cattle, and everything else to correspond, on the mission they founded here among the Indians. There are now only some vestiges, resembling earth-works, of their extensive adobe walls, and on a rise overlooking the sea the yellowish, low, Spanish rococo church of San Carlos.

The design and proportions of the edifice are good, as is almost invariably the case as to style, but the workmanship is curiously rude, and speaks of the disadvantages under which it was built. A dome of concrete on the bell tower has one half bulged more than the other. A star window in the front has points of many sizes. The interior does not yield, as a picture of sentimental ruin, to Muckross Abbey, or any broken temple of the Roman Campagna. The roof, open now to the sky, with grasses and wild mustard growing against it out of the crevices, was originally made of stone arches, supplemented with timber-work tied together with rawhides. The whole body of the church—pilasters, capitals, frieze, and all—forms part of a curve springing from the floor, a peculiarity I have never elsewhere remarked. There are grasses growing within, sculptured stones tumbled down, vestiges of a tile pavement, tombs, bits of fresco, and over all the autograph scribblings in pencil of a myriad of A. B. Smiths and J. B. Joneses, who have been here as visitors, like ourselves.

Once a year, on St. Charles's Day, which comes in early November, a memorial service is held here, which is attended by all the shabby Spanish-Indian life remaining in the country round about. The place is a unique spectacle, full of incitement to reflection. Nothing is more conducive to a gentle pensiveness of the pleasant sort than to lie within this ruined inclosure, and listen to the splash of the sea on the shore.

II.

FROM MONTEREY TO THE TEHACHAPI PASS.

THE Yosemite Valley, currently spoken of as the "Valley" simply, is included in a belt formed by drawing lines across the State from San Francisco and Monterey respectively. It is a wild, strange nook, far to the eastward among the wintry Sierras. It perhaps hardly comes within the scope of our inquiry, yet I can not refrain from making mention of it as a place not only not disappointing, but worthy of even more praise than has ever been bestowed upon it. It is like one of those dimly mysterious spots situated on the outskirts of the fairy-land or paradise described in the story-books. It is a standing diversion and field of adventure to all who come to California, either temporarily or to take up a permanent abode. I reached the Yosemite by a stage ride of sixty miles from the Southern Pacific Railroad, at Madera, to Clark's Station, and thence by a stage and horseback journey of twenty-five miles further.

The autumn days were lovely there. The foliage, turned by a local climate quite as severe as that of New England, glowed with a vivid richness. A gentle stream, pausing in mirror-like pools, meanders among it, along the bottom of the valley, which is as level as a floor. Walls of rock rise on either hand to an incredible height. The place is rather a chasm than a valley. At night a full yellow moon irradiated it and invested its wonders with heightened enchantment. The cliffs here are what it seems that cliffs should be, but seldom are. They are of the hardest granite, pleasantly gray in color, and terminate in castle and dome like forms. The precipices are sheer and unbroken to the base. They have almost none of those slopes of débris that detract from the height of precipices in general. It is a little valley that would have been suitable, without a hair's-breadth of alteration, to the purposes of any giant, enchanter, or yellow dwarf of romance. This is the kind of quaint impression to which it gives rise. It is such scenery as that which Doré has imagined for the "Idyls of the King," and one should be Sir Lancelot or Sir Gawain riding in on his charger in search of adventure along this lovely and majestic mountain trail. He should wear chain-mail, and a

MAP OF SOUTHERN CALIFORNIA.

winged helmet on his head, and a good sword by his side, upon the cross of which he had sworn to do deeds of redoubtable valor.

It was the coast valleys and some coast towns, it will be remembered, that we explored in our first journey. This time we have come down the main line of the Southern Pacific Railway along the great central basin of the State. The railway is traced along the great central valley known as the San Joaquin, on a line nearly midway between the Sierra Nevadas to the east and the Coast Range to the west. The road is still comparatively new, and the settlements along it have not yet attained great dimensions. It did not as a rule touch at the older towns already existing, but pursued a direct route through a country where all had to be opened up, and town sites established from the beginning. As some of the places thus passed by were of considerable size, no little dissatisfaction ensued, of which some mutterings are still heard. Very frequent mention of this grievance is heard by the traveller through Central and Southern California. Some of the neglected places even maintain that they would have been better without any railroad at all. References are thrown out to their former possession of glories of quite a dazzling sort. It is sometimes difficult to credit these stories, though a railroad naturally effects great innovations in the course of trade. The complaints occasionally come from persons who have an exaggerated idea of the speed with which it is their natural right to make a fortune, and who are unable to understand any benefits in which they are not personally very much included. To an ordinary observer it would appear that the introduction of such a splendidly equipped railway, even if in the natural imperfection of all things human it distribute its blessings a little unequally at first, and its tariff be high, must inevitably be a great and permanent advantage to everything in the State near to it, as well as remote. For the first time an adequate means is afforded for the transportation of immigrants and supplies through the whole length of the country. The Central and Union Pacific railways across the continent are most notable instances in point. Who can have seen the chain of towns and cities that have sprung up across the once barren waste, and the stir of activity branching out from every one of them into adjacent mining and stock-raising and agricultural districts, without the warmest feeling of admiration for the means that can produce such marvels, and without deeming it cheap at almost any cost?

The Southern Pacific Railway has completed connections which give it a transcontinental route from San Francisco, across Arizona, New Mexico, and Texas, to New Orleans. It is promised that this is to introduce a new era in the prosperity of the State. Immigrants are to be brought in by steamer from Liverpool to New Orleans, and thence by rail at a rate not higher than that which it costs to reach the central West. The fares to California heretofore have been almost prohibitive of immigration. We find a wonderfully rich country, equal in extent, it is estimated, to New York, Pennsylvania, and all of New England put together, but containing as yet less than a million of people. The languid movement hither of the same valuable class of immigration which pours so rapidly into the West is ascribed by some alarmists to the presence of the Chinese. It is much more probably due to the heavy cost of travel across the continent, and, large as the territory is, to the lack of cheap lands suitable for settlement. The Chinese are not rivals in the matter of taking up the land. They acquire little or none of it. As to wages, the prices of white labor, even with Chinese competition, remain higher on the Pacific slope than at the East.

The new opportunities opened in the way of transportation, the depression of the mining interests, and the rapid increase in numbers of the Chinese, have awakened an exceptional interest in the subject of white immigration. A committee, comprising some of the most prominent men in the State, has been appointed, and has opened an inquiry into the most effectual means of promoting it. It will no doubt set forth more clearly than it has ever been done before an account of such territory as is open to settlers, whether it is offered by the government, the railroads, or the great ranches, and its advantages and the methods of reaching it. It seems a little singular at first sight that a lack of suitable lands can be adduced as a principal reason for the lack of population in so vast a region, of the climate and other natural advantages of which so much has been said the world over. It can only be understood when we take into account the unusual atmospheric dryness, and the important part which has to be played by water brought upon the soil by artificial and costly means. The locations where there is sufficient natural moisture for the maturing of crops are of comparatively small extent. They were among the first taken up. In much of the central and southern portions of the State the annual rainfall is almost an infinitesimal quantity.

At Bakersfield, the capital of Kern County—whither our journey southward will presently lead us—it is no more than from two to four inches. It is found that light crops of grain and pasturage for stock may occasionally be got even under these conditions. The only certain reliance in cultivation, however, is in artificial irrigation. Works of the requisite importance would heretofore have been beyond the means of a simply hard-working and thrifty class of immigrants like those who have gone into Iowa, Wisconsin, or Minnesota.

The springs and small streams in the country were early appreciated at their full value, and seized upon by persons who control with them great tracts of the surrounding country, almost valueless except as watered from these sources of supply. These tributary tracts are used chiefly as cattle and sheep ranges. A person owning five thousand acres of land will often have for his stock the run of twenty thousand. Cultivation is confined about the springs and water-courses, and is seen in a succession of charming oases in the midst of a desert the superficial sterility of which is something phenomenal. The tenure of land in tracts of thousands of acres under a single ownership is a tradition descending from Spanish and Mexican times. It has been much decried as a great evil. It is said that the State would be much more prosperous if divided into a series of small farms. This is probably true, and the system as it exists may be ascribed in part to the overweening greed of individuals. At the same time it arises in considerable part, as we have seen, out of the natural features of the country. The wealth and enterprise of the large farmers, too, enable them to undertake works of improvement, such as canal-making, drainage, and tree-planting, on the only scale that could be effectual. It may be that the State will have to lend its assistance, and establish a public system of irrigation and drainage, before the land to any very great extent can be prepared for the purposes of the small settler. Water! water! water! How to slake the thirst of this parched, brown country, and turn it over to honest toil and thrift, is everywhere the great problem as we go southward. The processes of irrigation, and its distinctive marks upon the landscape, are the most salient peculiarities that greet the eye.

It is in early November that we begin to traverse the long San Joaquin Valley from Lathrop Junction, just below Stockton, southward. The side tracks of the railroad are crowded with platform-cars laden with wheat for the sea-board. The "elevator" system is not yet in use, and the grain is contained in sacks for convenient handling. Hereabouts are some of the largest of the famous wheat ranches. A man will sometimes plough but a single furrow in a day, but this may be a furrow fifteen or twenty miles long. There is sufficient rain-fall for the cereals, but not enough for the more exacting crops. The land gives but few bushels to the acre under the easy system of farming, but there are a great many acres. The stubble of the grain fields is whitened now with flocks of wild fowl. At a way-station we see a small rustic in an immense pair of boots go over to a pool and blaze away with a shot-gun. Presently he returns, dragging by the necks an immense pair of wild-geese, almost beyond his strength to pull. The tawny color of the fields, and the great formal stacks of straw looming up in them, recall some aspects of the central table-land of Mexico. Many and capacious barns and out-buildings are not necessary in the mild, dry climate of California. The prosperous ranches have, in consequence, a somewhat thin and unfurnished appearance as compared with Eastern farms.

The most prominent object at each successive railroad station is a long, low warehouse provided by the company for the accommodation of grain. Like the station buildings generally, it is painted of a dark Indian red, in "metallic" paint. The station of Merced is one of the two principal points of departure for the Yosemite Valley, Madera the other. At Merced an immense wooden hotel for the accommodation of travellers bound for the valley quite overshadows the small town. It rises close beside the track, while the town is scattered loosely back on the plain. At Madera is seen the end of a curious V-shaped wooden aqueduct, or flume, which brings down lumber from the mountains fifty miles or more away, and terminates in a planing-mill. Some of the hands employed in this work occasionally come down the flume also in temporary V-shaped boats. As the speed is prodigious, these voyages abound in excitement and peril. The structure, supported on trestles of greater or less height, according to the formation of the ground, stretches away in an interminable perspective toward the mountains. These mountains turn to rose-pink, and then to solemn purple, at sunset. The scene is somehow suggestive of the Roman Campagna, with this slight and essentially American work as a whimsical parody upon its broken aqueducts and temples of

to a very recent period, was known as the San Joaquin Desert. One should alight here by all means. There is no better place for examining the really marvellous capabilities of a soil which appears at first sight inhospitable and unfruitful to the last degree. Fresno is in the hands of enterprising persons, who push and advertise it very actively. We heard at San Francisco of the Fresno Colony,

COUNTY COURT-HOUSE, FRESNO.

solid masonry. The lumber flume, however, is a very bold and costly enterprise, though we appear to smile at it.

By degrees we draw away from the wheat ranches, and journey more and more on the uncultivated plain. The town of Fresno, two hundred miles below San Francisco, and about midway between two important streams, the San Joaquin and Kings rivers, is in the midst of a particularly desolate tract, which, up

Central Colony, the American Colony, the Scandinavian Colony, the Temperance Colony, the Washington Colony, and of others of similar names clustered around Fresno. It was advertised as one of those genial places, alluring to the imaginations of most of us, where one could sit down under his own vine and fig-tree, secure from the vicissitudes of rigorous Northern climates. It was promised, too, that he could find a profitable

CHINESE QUARTER, BAKERSFIELD.

career open to him in the cultivation of the fruits of the soil, and need not live a mere life of indolence; and furthermore, that all could be secured at a moderate cost. The promise seems strictly true. The aspect of things is very different from what had been expected, as is so often the case, but all the substantial advantages claimed are found within the reach of moderate purses. The process of founding a homestead and a tenure and position in the world may be witnessed in all its stages.

The town has a population of two thousand, most of which it has gained in the past five years. It is set down on the east side of the railroad highway, with but a thin scattering of foliage to veil the squareness of its outlines. It consists of a few streets of two-story wooden and brick buildings. The streets cross one another at right angles, and have planked sidewalks. A slight eminence above the general level has been chosen as the site of the county court-house, which some-

what resembles an Italian villa in design, and has Italian cypresses in front of it. The court-houses of half a dozen counties down the line from Modesto, the capital of Stanislaus, to Bakersfield, are identical with this in pattern, so that it is both typical of its kind and evidence of a conservative and economical spirit. A sharp distinctness of outline is characteristic generally of these cities of the plain. Separated from the main part of Fresno, as by a wide boulevard, is seen a long row of low wooden houses and shops, as clearly cut out against the encompassing desert as a row of bathing-houses on a beach. This is the Chinese quarter. Its isolation tells the story of the peculiar people who tenant it; and of the feeling of social ostracism entertained toward them on the one hand, and their own unconquerable clannishness on the other.

There is now hardly any hamlet so insignificant, even down in the wastes of Arizona, that the Chinese have not penetrated to it, in search of labor and opportunities for profit. Almost every settlement of the Pacific slope has its Chinese quarter, as mediæval towns had their Ghetto for the Jews. It is not always set without the rest of the place, as at Fresno; but wherever it be, it constitutes a close corporation and a separate unit, unencroached upon by any other. Its people, in dress, language, and habit of life, adhere as closely to Oriental tradition as their new conditions will permit.

Whoever is gifted with an eye for the picturesque very soon puts the Chinese in the foreground in almost every prospect in California. They have not introduced a national style of architecture, and build little but shanties themselves. They rather adapt what they find to their own purposes, distinguishing their handiwork with such emblems and devices that the character of the dwellers within can not thereafter be mistaken. There is a great incongruity between the common little Yankee wooden dwellings tenanted by the Chinese in this rural life and the tasselled lanterns, gilded signs, and hieroglyphics upon red and yellow papers with which they are so profusely overspread. Here are Ah Coon and Sam Sing, keeping laundries like the usual Chinese laundry the world over. Yuen Wa advertises himself as a contractor for laborers. Hop Ling, Sing Chong, and a dozen others have miscellaneous stores. In their windows are junk-shaped slippers, opium pipes, bottles of saki (a rice brandy), dried fish, goose livers, gold and silver jewelry, and packets of face-powder, and hair ornaments for the women. The pig-tailed merchants sit within on odd-looking chests and budgets, and gossip in an animated cackle with friends, or figure gravely in brown-paper books, using a pointed brush as a pen. Some women—who are much more numerous in proportion to the men than is commonly supposed—occasionally waddle by. Their black hair is very smoothly greased, and kept in place by long silver pins. They wear wide jackets and pantaloons of cheap black " paper cambric," which increase the natural awkwardness of their short and uncomely figures.

Upstairs in some unpainted, cobwebby second stories are found the joss-houses or temples, which the rustic Chinamen, even with the disadvantages under which they labor, do not neglect to establish. Here the hideous but, it must be confessed, extremely decorative idols grin as serenely as if in the centre of their native Tartary, and as if there were no snug little spires of Baptist and Methodist meeting-houses rising in severe reproach across the way. There are pastilles burning before these idols, and some crimson banners draped about; and there are usually a few pieces of antique bronze upon which the eye of the connoisseur can not but rest enviously.

Other interiors are cabarets, which recall those of the French working classes in the great air of animation reigning within. The air is thick with tobacco smoke of a peculiar Chinese odor. Games of dominoes are being played with a magpie-like chatter by excited groups of men clustered around long stout wooden tables. Most of those present wear the customary blue cotton blouse and queer little black felt hat, and all have queues, which either dangle behind them or are coiled up like the hair of women. Some, however—teamsters perhaps from place to place, and here only temporarily—are dressed in the slop clothing and cowhide boots of ordinary white laborers. The Chinamen are servants in the camps, the ranches, and the houses of the better class; they are track-layers and section hands on the railroad, and laborers in the factories and fields. What Southern California, or California generally, could do without them just at this time it is difficult to see. They are found, for the most part, capable, industrious, honest, and neat. One divests one's self rapidly of any prejudice against them with which he may have started. Let us hope that laborers of a better class, by whom they are to be succeeded, may have at least as many praiseworthy traits.

Fresno town is as yet chiefly a supply dépôt and market point for the numerous colonies by which it is environed. These colonies straggle out in various directions, beginning within a mile or two of the town. The intervening land still lies in its natural condition, held for settlement. It is difficult to convey an idea of the arid and seemingly hopeless barrenness of the plain. Instead of complaining of a dry and brown vegetation here, one would be grateful for so much as a blade of grass of any kind. The surface is like that of a gravelled school-yard. It is even worse, for it is undermined with the holes of countless gophers, owls, jack-rabbits, and squirrels, who here form sociable communities. To ride at any speed is certain.

to bring one to grief through the entangling of his horse's legs in these pitfalls. As the traveller passes, there is a scampering movement on all sides. The gray squirrels speed for their holes with flying leaps, the jack-rabbits with long kangaroo-like bounds. They even run toward us as we approach, if they chance to have been absent from home in an opposite direction. Not one considers himself safe from our clearly malicious designs till he has dived headlong into his own proper tenement.

Here and there tracts are seen powdered white with alkali. Flakes of this substance, at once bitter and salt to the taste, can be taken up in an almost pure condition. Elsewhere for variety we pass through some tracts of wild sunflower, a weed growing tall, and quite charming when in flower, but now, in the long dry season, thoroughly desiccated, and rattling its stalks together like the bones of skeletons. It is not abusive nor ungenerous to present this picture of the condition of the land as it really is. It is a description that applies, for the greater part of the year, not only to the vicinity of Fresno, but in an almost equal degree to that of Bakersfield, Los Angeles, and the whole of Southern California down to San Diego at the Mexican frontier. Nothing less would be just and fair either to the region itself or the intending visitor. And nothing less would adequately explain the marvels and wonders which have been produced upon the late San Joaquin desert and its like by human agency. The face of nature in all this district was a blank sheet of paper. Everything was to be put upon it. The cultivator had absolutely everything to do. Fortunately he discovered on trial that he had a soil of remarkable capacity, and that with the aid of water and the genial climate he could draw from it whatever he pleased.

Water is the salvation of the waste places, and makes the desert blossom like the rose. One's respect for this pleasant element in nature is, if possible, increased upon seeing what it is here capable of. It almost seems that, if used with sufficient art, it might draw forth a crop from a surface of cast iron. The vegetation of Southern California is mainly artificial. It consists, as has been said, of a series of scattered plantations created by the use of water. In these the traveller may find his flowers, his palms, his vineyards, and orange groves. Ensconcing himself among them,

like the ostrich when it buries its head in the sand, he may refuse to recognize the existence of everything else; but it seems that at this stage in the development of California a franker policy is in every way more desirable. What has been done in the past is but an earnest of what can be done in the future. It is found that, according as irrigation is practiced, the land stores up part of the water used, so that less is needed each succeeding year. In wells, too, the water is found nearer the surface, proving that the soil acts as a natural reservoir. As time goes on, and canals and vegetation increase, no doubt important climatic changes are to be looked for in this part of our country. In the end Southern California may be as different from what it is at present as can possibly be conceived.

The several Fresno colonies for the most part join one another, and form a continuous belt of cultivation. On entering their confines, the change in the appearance of things is startling. Close alongside the desert, the home of the gopher and jack-rabbit, and only separated from it by a narrow ditch of running water, are lovely vineyards, orchards of choice fruits, ornamental flowers and shrubs, avenues of shade trees, fields of corn, and refreshing green pastures of alfalfa—a tall and strong clover, which gives half a dozen crops a year. Embowered among these are the homes of happy families. Here and there larger establishments for the drying of fruits and the converting of the munificent crops of grapes into wine arise. Many of these homes are as yet but modest wooden cottages. Others, of a better sort, are built of adobe, or sun-dried brick, which is treated in an ornamental way with wooden piazzas and Gothic gables. The best is that of a late member of the San Francisco Stock Board, who has taken up his residence here for the cultivation of grapes on a large scale as a speculation. It is a handsome villa that would do credit to any older town priding itself upon dwellings of the sort. The improvements on this, the Barton place, were in but an incipient state at the time of our visit. A great acreage of young vines brightened the recently sterile soil with a timid smile, as if not quite certain of approval. Young orange and lemon trees in the door-yard were muffled in straw till they should have gained a greater hardihood to withstand the autumn frosts. Elsewhere water was being run out from the irrigating ditches over fields in course of preparation for the first time. It is the custom to soak them thus in order that they may be perfectly levelled. Knolls or any other inequalities must not be left which might hinder the equal distribution of moisture to the crop when planted. A wide canal stretched back from the rear of the numerous out-buildings toward the horizon. On the verge of the wide plain were visible the blue Sierras, veiled by a slight chronic dustiness in the air.

In the more established portions of the colonies some charming bits of landscape are found. The Chinese farm hand, in his blue blouse and a wide basket hat which he calls *mow* (and pronounces, with a grin, "heap good," if complimented upon it), is such as we see him in representations of his native tea fields. His occupation is to prune the vines or collect the generous clusters of grapes they bear. Or he weeds a vegetable garden by the side of a canal in which he, his vegetables, his cabin, a row of poplar-trees, and the blue sky overhead are all reflected together. Poplars, willows, and cottonwoods are planted along the canals to strengthen their banks. At Eisen's wine-making place, for a considerable distance, oleanders in flower are seen spaced between the trees. The water runs clear and swift. At Eisen's it turns a mill. No doubt devices for bathing in it might be managed.

The long symmetrical lines of trees have a foreign, or at least an un-American, air. It is not difficult to recall to mind the rows of mulberries and elms that bend over the irrigating canals of Northern Italy, and drop their yellow leaves upon them in the autumn in the same way. One might persuade himself that it was Lombardy again, and the glimpses of blue through the pleasant vistas were the Alps and not the Sierras. The locks, gates, and division works for the water are of an ephemeral structure as yet. They are made of slight planking instead of the substantial brick and stone in use in Lombardy. The smaller ditches are often stopped with bits of board let down piece-meal into grooves, instead of with gates with regular handles. It is urged in excuse for the practice that handles offer too much inducement to idlers to lift up the gates out of pure mischief, waste being caused thereby.

The colonies are not colonies in the usual sense of the term. That is to say, they were not founded by groups of persons who combined together and went out at one and the same time. The lands which they occupy were originally distributed into parcels by the owner or owners, and after being provided with water facilities by an irrigation company, were put upon the market at the disposal of whoever might wish to buy. No doubt a certain general consistency has been adhered to through the influence of the names in the make-up of the several settlements, but it is not rigorous. Probably nothing need prevent a native American from joining the Scandinavian Colony, or a Scandinavian the American Colony, should either desire to do so. As to the Temperance Colony, its principle of organization would constitute in it a valid difference. It must be sorely tried in a spot of which the most liberal and profitable yield is the wine grape. It seems hardly a propitious place to have chosen. Scoffers say that in some of these temperance colonies, while certain settlers will not consent to make wine directly, they sell their grapes to establishments for the manufacture of wine. This, if true, would seem a distinction with but a very slight difference.

The standard twenty-acre piece or lot, as prepared for market in the Fresno district, is bordered with a main irrigating ditch of perhaps four feet in width, connecting with the general irrigating system. For a payment of twelve and a half dollars a year this land receives a water-right entitling it to the use of whatever water it may need. The buyer must make his own minor ditches, and prepare his ground from this point. He usually aims to establish in his fields a number of slightly differing levels, that the water may be led to one after the other. For ground in the preliminary condition described, about fifty dollars per acre is demanded. Most of the earlier settlers bought for less, and the price named strikes one as high, considering the newness of the country, and that excellent farming land is to be had in all the older States of the Union for less. Prices are lower here than in the Los Angeles and Riverside districts or at San Diego, all much further south. It is argued in answer to objectors everywhere throughout Southern California that if the land be

PRIVATE RESIDENCE IN FRESNO.

not nominally cheap, it is really cheap in consideration of its extraordinary productiveness. It is held that an investment here gives much better returns than elsewhere, and that at the same time the climate and other conditions promise a much more pleasurable existence than could be enjoyed elsewhere. This Fresno land, for instance, gives four and five crops of alfalfa a year. Vineyards planted but two and a half years are shown which already produce five tons of grapes to the acre. Five years is the period required to bring the vines into full bearing. It is estimated that an acre of vines arrived at this condition will have cost one hundred and twenty-five dollars, allowing fifty dollars as the price of the ground. But it is then counted upon for an annual yield of ten tons of grapes, and these find a ready sale at twenty dollars a ton. The rate of growth in vegetation is one of the important things to note. Fruit trees are said to advance as far in three years in this earthly paradise as in seven at the Eastern sea-board.

The personal stories of some of the colonists are interesting, as the stories of colonists of intelligence, who have generally had some previous hard experience of the world, are apt to be. Such a man, whom we saw working sturdily in the fields preparing the ground around a brand-new cottage, had once been a person of large fortune. He had lost it on the San Francisco Stock Board. The funds for his present enterprise were provided by a devoted wife, who had turned her talent to the keeping of boarders. She was sending him her small profits each month until he should have made ready the place by the work of his own hands for their joint occupancy. Some instances were heard of where nice properties had been secured with no other original capital than the labor of brawny hands. These, however, were exceptional instances. The country appears to be one where it is desirable that the new-comer should begin with some small capital.

In the Central Colony a comfortable estate is owned by four spinsters of San Francisco, who are school-teachers by occupation. They have combined in the purchase of eighty acres. One of them lives on the place, and manages it. The others contribute from their earnings, or were in the habit of doing so until it had arrived upon a paying basis—the needed money for its proper development. They come and pass their vacations only at present, but look forward to their property as an ultimate retreat. The idea seems both a praiseworthy new departure in the direction of female emancipation and a charming enterprise in itself. I had the pleasure of making the acquaintance of the resident manager of this experiment. Her detailed experiences, if written out, would, I think, be interesting and instructive. There was an open piano in the pleasant

MOONEY'S BREWERY, VISALIA.

cottage interior, and late books and maga-
zines were scattered about, showing the
occupations indulged in during the intervals of active labor.   It was a bit of refined civilization dropped down into the
very midst of the desert.

This lady manager had come, she said,
because she desired rest.   She took pleasure in the country, and in seeing things
grow.   She thought she had made mistakes in her management at first, mainly
through trusting to others, but now had
everything in good control.   Four farm-
hands — Chinamen — were employed on
the place.   The eighty acres were distributed into vineyard, orchard, and alfalfa
patches.   About one-half was devoted to
the vineyard.   Its product was turned not
into wine, but raisins.   Apricots and nectarines had been found up to this time the
most profitable orchard fruits.   Almonds
were less so, owing to the loss of time in
husking them for market.   There was a
field of veritable Egyptian corn.   This is
a variety which grows tall and slender,
and runs up to a bushy head instead of
forming ears.   The sight of it carries one
back to the Biblical story of Joseph and
his brethren, and to the picture-writing
in the Pyramids.   The grapes for raisin-
making were of the sweet Muscat variety.
There was a "raisin-house" piled full of the
neat boxes in which this delicacy is tradi-
tionally bestowed.   The process of raisin-
making is very simple.   The bunches of
grapes are cut from the vines, and laid
down in trays in the open fields.   They
are left here, being properly turned at intervals, for a matter of a fortnight.   There

are neither rains nor dews to dampen them
and delay the curing.   Then they are removed to an airy building known as a
"sweat-house," where they remain possibly a month, till the last vestiges of moisture are extracted.   Hence they go to be
packed and shipped to market.   It is a
simple process, this raisin-making, but it
requires climate and proper fruit.

One must walk rather discreetly at
Fresno just at present not to discern
through the young and scattering plantations the bareness beyond, but in another
ten years the scene can hardly fail to be
one of rich and far-extending luxuriance.
The site is flat and prairie-like.   Some
might prefer to locate their earthly paradise, if possible, nearer to the hills.   Still
the fancy of the times runs toward earthly paradises which are at the same time
shrewd commercial ventures, and it is
well known that the cultivation of the
soil is easier on the plain than the slopes.

Visalia, capital of Tulare County, thirty-four miles south of Fresno, is one of the
older towns which existed at the advent
of the railroad, and were left aside by it.

AN OLD-TIMER.

It is reached now from a junction at Goshen by a short branch road of its own. It is larger than Fresno, but less animated. It has perhaps twenty-five hundred people. Patriotic Visalians, however, asseverate that it is not Visalia that has been left out by the railroad, but the railroad that has been left out by Visalia. So, they say, in the sequel it will prove. Visalia has a court-house of the pattern described already, and a United States land office. When the epithet "old" is used of any California town not of Spanish origin it simply means an approximation toward the year 1849. The building of the most hoary antiquity in Visalia dates from the year 1852. It has been a government house, a jail, and store in turn, and is now decorated with the sign of Mooney's Brewery. The town was founded by one Vise, an erratic person who came across the plains from Texas. He followed in his life various other professions besides that of pioneer, such as preacher, trader, gambler, foot-racer, and jockey. It happened, as the story goes, that the quarter section of land upon which he settled was at the time unsurveyed, and not legally open to pre-emption. This irregularity was not discovered till some years later, when the town had grown up on this site. It was brought to light by an ingenious employé in the land-office, who thereupon undertook to pre-empt the ground in due form for his own benefit. "And what came of this attempt upon vested interests?" you inquire.

"The party was fired out of town immediately," a citizen explains, "and that put an end to the scheme."

Visalia is a rather prolific place in stories. If an "old-timer" of the right sort can be got hold of, he will be sure to

have a fund of interesting reminiscences to draw upon. Certain ex-cattle kings, whose sway was enjoyed at a time when the whole San Joaquin Valley was filled with herds little less than wild, have retired here from business. The old-timer will tell you, perhaps, how Cattle King "Pat Murray" won his wife. She was a fascinating person, it seems, in her youth. She was the daughter of the landlady with whom Pat Murray, then a struggling and impecunious person, boarded in company with a number of his mates. There was a great aspiration and rivalry among

LOGGING BACK OF VISALIA.

the boarders for the hand of the land-lady's daughter, but Pat Murray stole a march upon the rest in this wise. As he was setting off with a number of them upon some expedition, he took occasion to say at the last moment: "The trip is to be a rough and dangerous one, boys. I propose that we leave our money and val-uables with the old lady for safe-keeping." The rest agreed, and handed over to him as agent their property of the kind de-scribed. The shrewd Pat Murray, how-ever, represented the whole budget to be his own. He obtained in this way such consideration in his landlady's eyes as a person exceptionally well to do in the world that she advised her daughter to "set her cap" at him above all the others. This counsel being followed, the matter was happily concluded before the ruse was discovered.

On another occasion, whether during the same courtship or not, Pat Murray disposed of a number of rivals, who vis-ited in their leisure evenings a comely damsel of the general acquaintance. It is said that he soft-soaped a log serving as a bridge on which they were accus-tomed to cross a small stream to her cabin. Having thus arranged the approach, he sat calmly enjoying the fair one's socie-ty, and listened with appreciative ears to the splashes and profanity as the successive rivals slid off into the stream.

Stories are told of Spanish bandits, and treasures of the precious metals in the mountains, and the wild administration of justice in early times, when offenders were occasionally executed first and sen-tenced by a form of trial afterward. The first treasurer of the county is said to have been without an office, and to have carried his official records in his hat. Being a person much given to travel, and of a somewhat absent-minded habit, he scattered these documents behind him as far as the confines of Utah and Arizona.

At Visalia we have our first view of "Spanishtown," a community which be-gins to appear regularly alongside of "Chinatown" as we go southward in the State. It is composed of persons of Mex-ican blood and appearance, who are poor, shiftless, and not always of the most rep-utable character. Charming views of the high Sierras, now powdered with the first snows of winter, are had from this place. The surface is more rolling than at Fresno, and is strewn with fine clumps of chestnut oaks. There are big trees back in the great mountains equalling in size those in the vicinity of the Yosemite. Lumbermen at work there cut down numbers which, though insignificant as compared to the very largest, are monstrous in themselves.

The water for the irrigation of this dis-trict is drawn out of Kings, Tule, and Kaweah rivers by companies who give to their principal canals such names as the People's Ditch, the Last Chance Ditch, the Mussel Slough Ditch, the Lower Kings River Ditch, and the like.

The main ditches or canals range from twelve up to forty feet in width. Wing dams set up at the points of junction con-fine and direct into them portions of the wide, meandering rivers. A California river of the southern plains is something of a curiosity. It is extravagantly wide, but then in compensation it is preposterously shallow. Only a few of the most exuber-ant last over the dry season at all; the rest evaporate and wholly disappear. Their dry beds then, only variegated by a few islets studded with sycamores, are more like wagon-roads than the beds of rivers. Sometimes these exhausted water-courses differ in color from the surrounding soils, and are seen stretching as rivers of gray or silvery sand through the yellow desert.

Though irrigation is yet in its infancy, its belongings have attained great dimen-sions. There are three hundred miles of canals of the requisite size in Tulare County, and in all California more than three thousand miles. One main canal, the San Joaquin and Kings River, has a length of seventy-four miles by a width of nearly seventy feet.

A branch road westward from Goshen, a continuation of that going eastward to Visalia, conveys the traveller to the bus-tling, fast growing little towns of Hanford and Lemoore, in the Mussel Slough coun-try. This district, adjoining Tulare Lake, was recently part desert and part swamp. It has been redeemed so as to rank now among the best farming land in Califor-nia. Its chief product is wheat. The in-habitants hardly raise the vegetables need-ed for their own use. Malaria is known, but it is said to arise, as in many other irrigated districts, from the careless use of the water rather than the fundamental constitution of things. The water, in-stead of being carefully drained off, is too often allowed to lie in stagnant pools on the soil. This district was the theatre of

GYPSY CAMP, BAKERSFIELD.

a bloody conflict in May, 1880, which has become famous throughout the State. Officers of the law, acting for claimants under a railroad title, attempted to dispossess actual settlers who conceived themselves to have pre-empted the land. Legally in the wrong, though perhaps morally in the right, the settlers organized to resist. They threw out stirring manifestoes, which read like declarations of oppressed peoples struggling for liberty, and they called on gods and men to bear witness to the justice of their cause. In the fight in question five of the settlers lost their lives, all, singularly enough, at the hands of one man. This person, one Crowe, a United States marshal, displayed a prowess and a coolness under fire not surpassed in any of the narratives of sensational literature. He was himself dispatched in the end. A number of the surviving settlers were tried for their part in the affair, and condemned to eight months' imprisonment. They served out their term in Santa Clara jail. They had been released about a month before our arrival, and received by their brethren and well-wishers on their return home with an ovation the noise of which was yet in the air.

Bakersfield, the capital of Kern County, seventy-five miles further south, and somewhat smaller than Visalia, could boast at one time the unusual distinction of a malady peculiar to itself. The Bakersfield type of malarial fever, whatever the fine difference was that distinguished it from others, had a position apart in the medical works.

The sanitary condition of the place, however, has been greatly improved by the extension of drainage and irrigation works, and can no doubt be made still better. Of the three lakes, Tulare, Buena Vista, and Kern, which make so large a showing on the map, the latter two, with their surrounding marshes, have been dried up, and the former is on its way to extinction also. These lakes have worn on the map a mysterious as well as important air. One is glad to seize the first opportunity to penetrate their mystery, which little has been done by former travellers to dispel. We ride down to Tulare Lake on horseback. We find that we can not approach the margin for fear of miring. Nor is the approach much easier on foot. The tules, or rushes, rise high above our heads, and the tules are infested with a dangerous breed of wild hogs, strayed originally from the droves on the ranches. In what fragmentary glimpses are had between and over the tules an expanse of dreary surface is seen which may either be water or simply the alkali-whitened bed from which the water has receded. The vicinity swarms with wild fowl. Their multitudinous chatter has a kind of metallic clang in it. Now white, now dark, according as they are before or against the sunlight, they rise and fall above the tawny rushes and stubble fields like floating leaves.

The drying up of the lakes has been occasioned by the diversion of the surplus waters of the Kern River above for the redemption of lands which were formerly desert. This gave rise to a controversy which has lately been settled by a decision which is an important step toward the crystallization of a system of water jurisprudence for California. The great firm of real-estate owners and ranchmen, Miller and Lux, owned the lands below; the almost equally great firm of Haggin, Carr, and Tevis, those above, for the improvement of which the water was taken out. The former proprietors complained of the diversion of the waters as a detriment to their lands, and an infringement of the doctrine of riparian right. This is the English common law doctrine, which declares that the resident on a stream has the right to have it flow as it was wont through his grounds without diminution or alteration.

The contest was at first a show of physical force. Men were sent up by Miller and Lux with orders to close the sluices by which the water was taken out. The retainers of Haggin, Carr, and Tevis were mustered in opposition. They were the hardy *vaqueros*, or herdsmen, whose business it is to look after the great droves of cattle with which the ranches abound. They had orders to lasso and throw into the canal anybody who should dare interfere with the gates. When the case came into the courts it was held that the doctrine of riparian right is not that which prevails in California, but the doctrine of "prior appropriation for beneficial uses." That is to say, the tendency is to consult the greatest good of the greatest number. The same point had been raised before in controversies about the diversion of water for mining purposes. In these cases the ruling had been that the doctrine of riparian right is "inapplicable, or applicable only in a very limited extent, to the necessity of miners, and inadequate for their protection," and furthermore that all of the English common law is not in force in California, but only such portions of it as are adapted to the peculiar conditions of the State. The agricultural and mining interests, therefore, are now to be put in this respect on the same footing.

Bakersfield takes its tone from live stock, and not from farming operations. The town has special resorts for drovers and sheep-herders. Its streets are generally full of horses, caparisoned in the Spanish style, tied to the hitching posts, and awaiting their owners in the stores and taverns. The sheep-herders are a lonely class, who become morose and melancholy through long wanderings with their flocks far from the habitations of men and human speech. They are far enough removed, indeed, from the type of shepherds of Boucher and Watteau. Some of them are said to go insane through the monotony of their lives. It is an occupation only taken up as a last resort, and which unfits its pursuer for any other. Strangely enough, there is a rather English tone among the herders, and young prodigals of good family are found in it, who have come here after trying their fortunes in Australia and India, and they eat their husks of repentance in true Scriptural fashion.

The principal shops in Bakersfield, as throughout the greater part of the area of our travels, are kept by Jews. Chinatown is a district of compact little streets, of an extent that indicates for it a population almost equal to that of the rest of the place. An irrigating ditch surrounds it like a moat. The cabins along this, and picturesquely reflected in it, are gray and weather-beaten, variegated with patches

A TYPICAL RANCH-HOUSE.

of bright-colored Orientalism, and over-shadowed by a line of tall poplar-trees. Spanishtown, close by, is a cluster of small dance-houses and corrals, in which a swarthy José and Juanita or two are seen lounging about.

As if this were not foreignness enough, we stumble upon a camp of strolling gypsies, who have pitched their tents on the borders of Spanishtown, resting briefly from their travels. They are English, and have come last from Australia, dropping their "h's" all along the way no doubt. The figures are like types in Cruikshank's illustrations to Dickens. There is an apple-faced, Mrs.-Jarley-looking woman in a large bonnet with plumes. There is a very tightly dressed, slender individual with a weed on his hat, who might pass for Sam Weller, but proves to be a horse-tamer and jockey. At his heels follows a belligerent-looking bull-dog. Behind a tent a child of nine, one Cassie by name it appears, who has fine large dark eyes, is making her toilet before a bit of cracked mirror. She is pasting down her wetted hair into a semblance of the "water waves" of fashionable society. When interrupted with a compliment upon the arrangement, she tosses her black locks all abroad again, but it is with a native coquetry and not displeasure. The Mrs.-Jarley-looking woman tells fortunes. She declares with a professional blarney that there are persons whose fortunes she would not tell for twenty—no, not for fifty—dollars; but ours, on account of a fancy she has taken to us, she will tell for two.

The possessions of some of the great land-owners of this section are prodigious. It is a favorite story that certain men are able to drive a herd of cattle from the northern counties of the State to San Diego at its extreme southern limit, and quarter the animals every night upon their own territory. Haggin, Carr, and Tevis, whose property I was privileged to examine considerably in detail, have some four hundred thousand acres. Much of this was secured for a mere trifle while in the condition of waste land, and after-

A RODEO.

ward redeemed. A neighbor who had acquired a great estate of a similar kind, mainly while holding the post of survey-or-general of the United States, drew forth one of the best *bonmots* of President Lincoln. "Let me congratulate you," said Lincoln, as this gentleman was retiring from office under his administration. "You have become monarch of about all you have surveyed."

The owners do not often live upon their estates, but leave them in the hands of managers, and draw the revenues. The Haggin, Carr, and Tevis property is divided into a number of separate ranches, each with its resident superintendent. The Bellevue Ranch, so called, is the centre and focus of authority for the whole. Here is the residence and office of the general manager, and here are assembled a force of book-keepers, engineers, and mechanics, who keep the accounts, map, plan, supervise, construct, and repair, and give to the whole the clock-work regularity of a great commercial enterprise. The numerous buildings constitute a considerable settlement. There is a "store" of general merchandise and supplies. A dormitory and a dining-hall have been erected for the laboring hands. A tower-like water-tank, surmounted by a windmill, and accommodating a milk-room below, rises at one side. There are shops for the

mechanics, capacious barns, and long sheds filled with an interminable array of agricultural implements. It is worth while to take a walk past this collection of reapers, threshers, sulky ploughs, and rakes, and study out their uses. The immense "header and separator" rises from the rest like some awe-inspiring leviathan of the deep. A whole department is devoted to the "road scrapers," "buck scrapers," and ploughs of various sorts used in the construction and dredging out of the irrigating ditches. The soil is fortunately free from stones, and the work is for the most part quite easy. One enormous plough is seen which was designed to be drawn by sixty yoke of oxen, and to cut at once a furrow five feet wide by four deep. Like the famous steamship *Great Eastern*, it has defeated itself by pure bulk, and is not now in use.

More than $500,000 has been expended on the great estate in the item of fencing alone. An average of four hundred laborers is employed, and in the harvest season seven hundred. The rate of wages is quoted at from two and a half to three dollars per day to mechanics, and one dollar per day to common hands. This seems low as compared with information from other sources, and that which appears in the chronic complaints of the scarcity of farm labor in the California papers.

No great portion of this domain appears to be now in the market at the disposal of settlers of small means, though the intention is avowed of offering some of it in this way when all shall have been thoroughly reclaimed. Numerous tracts, however, are occupied on very favorable terms by renters, as they are called. They take from 120 to 600 acres. Very many of them

The division superintendents and upper employés on the place are found to be largely Southern. California, it will be remembered, was a favorite point for Southern immigration before the war —so much so that the course of the State in the great civil conflict, under the lead of such once well-known names as Judge Terry and Senator

THE TEHACHAPI PASS.

are Portuguese and Italians. They are usually unmarried, work in companies of from six to fifteen persons, and wear the red Garibaldi shirt. The renter is provided by his landlords with a house, an artesian well, a credit to a moderate amount at the general store, and the use of some cows. He has the milk of the cows, but must give their increase to the estate. His lease runs three years, and he pays as rent one-third of his crop. Instances of large profits are frequent among these persons, and no doubt the same opportunities are open to others who may wish to follow their example.

Gwin, was at one time considered problematic. These, however, are hardly of

SAN LUIS OBISPO.

that time. They are gentlemen who have come here to repair their fortunes at a later period. They have titles from the land and naval service of the extinct Confederacy, and they speak in the gentle voices and conduct themselves with the friendly courtesy characteristic of the best Southern type.

The typical ranch-house of the best class, such as that of our friend Major McClung, with whom we pass a night on his section of the subdivided property, is a long two-story dwelling, painted of the Indian-red tone which seems so popular throughout the country. It is raised on posts considerably above the ground, to allow a free circulation of air underneath. There is left an open space through the centre for the same purpose. An irrigating ditch resembling a moat passes in front, and is crossed by a little rustic bridge. Traces of alkali yet show white in the soil of the orchard and garden, but this does not prevent a plentiful growth of oleanders, roses, pear, peach, cherry, almond, and apricot trees. The young orange-trees are now put up in their mufflings of straw for the winter. The weather is very hot at noonday, but so cool at morning and evening that wood fires are burned. The chill in the air is of a kind that penetrates to the marrow, being felt the more by contrast with the heat of the rest of the day, and fire is imperatively necessary. The servants in the house are clean, white-aproned Chinamen, those out-of-doors Mexicans. One of these latter had trained a tame goose—Dick—which followed him about as a pet dog might have done, strutting with a ridiculous air of pride and content in his servitude.

Cattle-raising is the leading industry on the estate. Alfalfa, for carrying the stock over periods of scarcity in pasture, is the leading crop. Stacks of alfalfa of great size, one containing as much as seven hundred tons, are scattered about. It is of the ordinary color of hay externally, but when cut into, though completely dry, is found green. A successful experiment has been made in the raising of cotton. We see the hands in the fields going among the white pods for a second picking. It is out of the season, but a *rodeo* is organized for our benefit, that we may see the method of handling the roving cattle on a large scale. A number of vaqueros ride out in various directions till they are lost to sight. Presently there are traces of dust on the several horizons. The plain, on which but a few cows were peacefully feeding, begins to fill up with stamping and lowing herds, driven in by the careering vaqueros, and urged toward a central rendezvous. When they are gathered in sufficient numbers, feats of lassoing, either by the horns or leg, separating out special animals or classes of animals, and the like, are undertaken, and carried through with marvellous dexterity. As a culmination, we are treated to the sight of hats and ropes picked up from the ground while the rider goes at full speed. A silver half-dollar, placed on edge, is finally seized by a swarthy Aztec from the dust of the road, under the same conditions. The herders are usually Mexicans, that is to say, of the original population of the State before its conquest by the Americans. They are equipped in the Mexican style, with the greater part of the finery, however, left out. Their bosses, who often even excel them in horsemanship, are generally pure Americans.

The ranch known as the Livermore borders Kern and Buena Vista lakes, and is the southernmost in the series. The herds are gathered here in early spring, and driven hence to the ranch of San Emidio, in the mountains to the westward. They pick up their subsistence at San Emidio till the middle of September, when they are conducted back again. This transmigration from plain to mountain pasture recalls the movements in Norwegian peasant life described in Boyesen's charming pastoral romance of *Gunnar*.

When at the Livermore Ranch we had come to the apex of the San Joaquin Valley. Here the Sierra Nevada and the Coast Range effect a junction, and become henceforth one. They form a natural barrier to further progress. The railroad crosses this barrier by a wonderful piece of engineering over the Tehachapi (pronounced Te-*hatch*-a-pi) Pass. At the most unique place five different lengths of track are seen passing and repassing each other at as many different levels. In the famous Loop the road enters a tunnel, and then

emerging and twisting spirally around the mountain, re-appears directly above itself.

At San Emidio we are on the line of San Luis Obispo County, and might make our way to its pretty mountain-encompassed capital. This is more easily reached, however, as is the attractive point of Santa Barbara, in the county below, by steamer, or the stage-road along the coast.

Returning to Bakersfield, we ride west to the wild cañon of the Kern River, and toward the mining towns of Kernville and Havilah. The mining industry has never taken the same development south of the San Joaquin River as to the north of it. It is probable both that there is less ore and that the ventures have been managed with less skill. At Kernville is found a quartz mill provided with a hundred

IN THE KERN RIVER CAÑON.

stamps, which after many vicissitudes has fallen into the hands of its former workmen for debt, and is now run by them on the co-operative principle.

The rolling country over which the Kern River cañon is approached is, if possible, more desolate than the plain below. There seems almost a necessary connection between hills and trees, so that when foliage is missing from hills, the lack of it is doubly notable. The utterly baked, verdureless, brown and yellow surface, with a texture like that of gravel, extends over all the inequalities of the ground, up hill and down dale, to the savage, splintered granite rocks of the river gorge.

We fall in with an isolated sheep ranchman, one Captain Jack Barker, an enterprising person, who has already created a garden spot in the waste, and shown what it is capable of. He is engaged upon a great project, that of conveying water, by means of a flume and ditches, from the high level of the river at the cañon's mouth, several miles above his place, and thus bringing some thousands of acres of land under cultivation. In the brief spring-time all this bare ground is hidden from sight by wild flowers, notably a certain small orange-scarlet poppy, which makes it a delight to the eye.

The Kern River comes tumbling in alternate falls and rapids down the bottom of its gorge for four miles in length, between granite walls of an average height of six hundred feet. Its waters are here of a translucent green in some deep untroubled pools, and again churned into floods as white as milk among its black bowlders. The cañon is dark, gloomy, and all but impassable. It acts like a funnel, and produces a violent commotion in the atmosphere. While all around is still, a column of air is driven out of it, which, striking the table-land like a cannon-ball a quarter of a mile away, raises a chronic dust-cloud. Driving across the front of the pass in a wagon at this place, the wind assails us furiously, and all the while we are passing seems likely to upset the vehicle. Upon this experience we go back to Captain Jack Barker, and dine upon ribs of his Angora goats. Then we return again to Bakersfield, take the railway, and cross the picturesque Tehachapi Pass.

A CALIFORNIAN OBSERVATORY

AFTER ten years of preliminary work, including not only the discussion of plans, but the settlement of the legal complications growing out of the disposition of Mr. Lick's estate, the great Lick Observatory of California now seems fairly on the road to success. With the interest which naturally attaches to this new institution must be combined a curiosity to know something of the character, motives, and object of the founder. Mr. Lick's whole life was that of a modest and retiring man of business, as far removed from all contact with the intellectual world as a member of a civilized community well could be. His career, though checkered, had little to specially distinguish it from that of the typical Californian. He was born in Pennsylvania, in 1796, of a German family. His first occupation, after growing up, was that of a piano-maker. From early manhood until the age of fifty he lived mostly in South America, slowly gaining a competence by successful trade. He removed to California, and became a resident of San Francisco, shortly before the gold discoveries of 1848. He had the sagacity to see that that city was destined to be the great *entrepôt* of our Pacific coast, and therefore invested all the money he could gain in real estate. His general policy was to purchase for cash, rarely selling or speculating. For several years he was known only as a shrewd and safe investor, holding his money with a grasp not usual among California adventurers.

In 1854 he surprised his fellow-citizens by a venture entirely out of keeping with his previous character. This was the erection of the largest flouring mill that had yet been built in the State, and its completion in a style which for extravagance of expenditure had nothing to approach it. The interior was finished in solid mahogany, and the structure was marked in every part by the elegance of a palace. A quarter of a million of dollars was said to have been expended on the building alone, and as much more on the grounds and accessories, while the owner himself occupied a building in the neighborhood little better than a hovel. It is said in his behalf that this extravagance was not merely the play of an eccentric humor, but was intended as a protest against the cheap and flimsy style of building which then prevailed in California. He wished to show that there was at least one Californian who

REAR VIEW OF THE OBSERVATORY.

could erect a building regardless of expense. But the enterprise told against his good judgment yet more strongly than against his reputation as a hoarder of wealth. The ground occupied by the mill was subject to inundation almost every year, and he finally had to abandon the place. He now went on yet another tack, which he had been least of all expected to take, by presenting the mill and grounds to the Paine Memorial Society of Boston, which sold the entire property for $18,000 in cash. This sale was effected without the knowledge of Mr. Lick, who was extremely dissatisfied with the proceedings, as he would willingly have given $50,000 himself for the property.

It would seem that, with all his eccentricities and his penuriousness of character, Mr. Lick was a man of real public spirit, whose apparent narrowness of view arose from the life which he had led, and from his personal experience of human nature as exhibited in California at that time. Being a man of sterling integrity, who had made his fortune by hard work and business enterprise, he could not tolerate the spirit of men who sought to command more for their labor than it was legitimately worth. He was particularly averse

to paying what seemed to him extravagant prices for personal services of any kind, and could never be made to understand that there were some kinds of work which he could not get in any other way. Shortly after the completion of his mill he erected the Lick House, one of the most substantial buildings which had then been seen in the State. The peculiarities of the founder were well shown in its noted diningroom. In magnitude and architectural effect it surpassed anything which had before been known in the West. He showed his appreciation of what was appropriate in art by having its walls decorated with paintings of California scenery. But the artistic qualities of the work may be judged from what we have already said of his views of personal services. Better specimens of art were the carved rose-wood frames of the mirrors, which were in part the work of Mr. Lick's own hands.

Up to the year 1873 Mr. Lick was known publicly only as a wealthy and eccentric Californian, the proprietor of the Lick House and of the mahogany mill, a supporter of the California Academy of Sciences, and one of the founders of the Society of California Pioneers. In that year he made his name widely known to the world by an expressed intention of giving his entire fortune to a board of trustees, the interest to be expended for scientific and public objects. Among the latter was a monument to Francis S. Key, author of the "Star-spangled Banner." It is also said that he would have erected a monument to Thomas Paine, of whose works he was a great admirer, but that he was dissuaded by the assurance of his friends that it would not do to outrage public opinion in this way, and that such a monument would not be allowed to stand. Other beneficiaries of his trust were to be the societies already mentioned. But the object to which he devoted the largest sum, $700,000, and which was nearest of all to his heart, was the construction of a telescope "larger and more powerful than any ever before made," together with an observatory which should be connected with it. But he evidently regarded the observatory as an appendage of the telescope.

One question which will naturally arise in the mind of a visitor will be, Why did the eccentric founder take such interest in the foundation of a scientific institution, the work of which should be so far removed from everything with which he was concerned during his life? It is highly probable that Mr. James Lick never saw a large telescope, and certain that he knew nothing more of astronomical instruments or their uses than the average California gold-digger. We search in vain through the record of his life to find any traces of astronomical knowledge, or any unusual taste for that science. But astronomy is a science which seems to have the strongest hold on minds which are not intimately acquainted with its work. The view taken by such minds is not distracted by the technical details which trouble the investigator, and its great outlines are seen through an atmosphere of sentiment, which softens out the algebraic formulæ with which the astronomer is concerned into those magnificent conceptions of creation which are the delight of all minds, trained or untrained.

It is worthy of note that Mr. Lick's movement followed close upon the construction of the great Washington telescope, and upon a discussion in some papers devoted to diffusing scientific knowledge of the possibility of constructing a "million-dollar telescope." It is said that one of the parties who had taken some interest in the latter enterprise went so far as to visit the shop of Messrs. Alvan Clark and Sons with a view of learning whether it was really possible to make a million-dollar telescope.

"Suppose we make 'em a telescope—charge 'em a million dollars for it—then they'd have a million-dollar telescope," was the sententious but conclusive reply.

The subject was not again heard of in the East, but it is not impossible that it reached Mr. Lick in the newspapers. Whatever may have been the source of Mr. Lick's interest, it is certain that he did not begin by mastering the conditions of the problem. All that he said and wrote on the details of the observatory was, from a scientific point of view, of the crudest kind, and showed that he had no idea of the practical difficulties involved in the task which he was about to undertake. To his mind the problem of making a telescope of any required power was purely one of enterprise and money, like that of building a hotel of any required size, and, once pointed at the sky, he evidently thought that discoveries would be made by merely the looking. One can not but suspect that if he had but known a little more of practical astronomy he would never have given money to found an observatory.

His first public act was the appointment of a board of seven trustees, comprising some of the leading business men of San Francisco, to whom he executed a deed of gift of his entire fortune, making no reservation for himself except an annual sum for his own support during his life. The first thing he desired was the construction of the telescope, and he probably hoped to see its completion himself. The smallest aperture which he could be induced to think of for his telescope was forty inches, which would admit more than double the light of the Washington telescope; but he constantly strove for a much larger size —four feet or upward.

A spot of great natural beauty was chosen near Lake Tahoe as the future site of the observatory, on the recommendation of a consulting engineer, Mr. Von Schmidt. But, as the location was afterward changed, no interest now attaches to this site.

None of the trustees had before been connected with so great a scientific enterprise, and they naturally felt some embarrassment respecting their proper course. The business of investigating what arrangements should be made was placed in the hands of one of their number, Mr. D.

VIEW FROM THE OBSERVATORY.

O. Mills, the well-known financier, who was about making a visit to the East. He consulted with the leading astronomers as to how the rough glass could be obtained, and what opticians could make the telescope. It was desired to have the instrument made by the most competent person, regardless of what part of the world he lived in, and the necessity of a complete investigation of the subject was increased by the fact that Mr. Lick had suddenly taken an antipathy to the only American firm who could undertake so great an instrument. As Mr. Mills found it impossible to get the detailed information required without personal intercourse with European mechanicians, a special agent was sent abroad to gather information on the subject. In Germany the most renowned firm was that of Merz, in Munich, but neither he nor any other German mechanician who could give satisfactory guarantees was willing to undertake the work. It would have been not merely to do more than they had themselves undertaken, but more than the English or Americans, who had made far larger telescopes than those of the Germans, had undertaken. Although the French had not actually succeeded in completing a telescope of the largest size, they had been working in that direction for a number of years, and Paris was next visited. The firm of Eichens were then at work on the mounting of the great four-foot reflector for the Paris Observatory, and were ready to accept Mr. Lick's commission. But when their written proposals were received it was quite clear that the prospect

of lightening the burden of a successful gatherer of California gold, anxious to get rid of a large surplus accumulation, was higher in their minds than the scientific glory they might acquire by constructing the largest telescope ever made. The agent assured them that it was absolutely useless to submit their proposition to the trustees. Although they then made a considerable reduction in their price, it was still above a reasonable limit. The general result of the inquiry was that the European with whom it was best worth while to negotiate was Mr. Howard Grubb, of Dublin. The latter was favorably known as co-laborer with his father in the construction of the great reflector mounted at Melbourne, Australia, and had made several objectives for the English astronomers, which had given great satisfaction. He was then negotiating for the construction of the great Vienna telescope, which has recently been completed and put into operation, and was quite ready to undertake the Lick telescope in addition on reasonable business terms.

But before the telescope could be even commenced, the glass disks from which the objective must be made had to be obtained. The difficulties in the way of getting the rough glass were about equal to those of constructing the telescope. The largest disks of proper quality which had ever been successfully completed were those of the Washington telescope, and they had required more than a year in the manufacture. It was very doubtful whether the minimum size satisfactory to Mr. Lick—forty inches—could be practically reached. Only two firms could undertake the work—Chance and Co., of Birmingham, and Feil, of Paris. The former had the advantage of the capital and responsibility of a great firm; the latter, of especial skill and enthusiasm. It was difficult to choose between them.

Before the trustees had time to reach a conclusion on the report of their agent, Mr. Lick suddenly took a course which threatened destruction to the whole project. He became distrustful of his board of trustees, and especially of the president, whose resignation he finally demanded. The board was not composed of men who were willing to be trifled with in this way, and the resignation was refused. Mr. Lick thereupon revoked his gift, thus throwing the whole project into utter confusion from the doubt cast upon the title to his own landed estate. Whether the board of trustees abandoned the case or fought him, the result might have been equally disastrous. They therefore adopted the dignified and public-spirited course of filing a bill in equity, in which they asked the court to accept their resignation, and appoint a new board to perform their duties. This gave the court the opportunity to transfer all the rights, duties, and responsibilities of the old board upon the new one which had been selected by Mr. Lick, and thus to legalize the changed course which things had taken.

Mr. Lick died before his affairs could be settled up, and his death was followed by a course of litigation between the different beneficiaries and his son and heir, which was not finally settled until 1880. The new president of the board was Captain Richard S. Floyd, of San Francisco, who, from the time of his entering upon the active administration of the trust in 1876, devoted great attention to the subject both at home and abroad. Being a graduate of the United States Naval Academy, he had a basis of practical experience in the use of astronomical instruments which served him a good purpose in his work. The question of greatest difficulty was whether the telescope should be a reflector or a refractor. Theoretically there was no limit to the size of the former, and, as a matter of fact, great reflectors like that of the Earl of Rosse far exceeded in size any refracting telescope which it was possible to construct. But the practical difficulties in the way of their successful use

were such that not even the largest of them had exceeded the largest refractors in performance. The problem for the solution of which the trustees were waiting was whether success could be obtained with a great reflector. Up to the time when a decision had to be reached no satisfactory evidence was developed that the requirements could be fulfilled by any form except that of a refracting telescope. It was therefore finally adopted.

Before Mr. Lick changed his board of trustees he grew distrustful of the site which had been selected on the border of Lake Tahoe, and chose another on what is now known as Mount Hamilton. The latter is a prominence in the Coast Range of California, forty-four hundred feet above the level of the sea, and some fourteen miles in a straight line east of San José.

The view from the summit is one of the most commanding in the United States. Through a ravine toward the west the spectator sees the city of San José, its buildings dotting with white the beautiful plain in which it is situated. The view of the Pacific Ocean beyond is cut off by a range of mountains. Toward the north the eye takes in a vast region, covered with innumerable hills, half mountain and half field. In very clear weather the peak of Mount Shasta may be seen at a distance of more than two hundred and fifty miles. On the east, above the neighboring hills, a fine view of the outlines of the Sierra Nevada range, one hundred and thirty miles distant, may be obtained at sunrise. On the south the view is bounded by another peak about the same height as Mount Hamilton. Between the two mountains lies a ravine more than a thousand feet deep. Snow and glaciers are wanting, so that the views do not compare in magnificence with those obtained in the Alps, but the clearness of the atmosphere partially compensates for this by the extent and variety of the field which the eye takes in.

The astronomer is not concerned with the earth, but with the heavens; and an elevated station is of no use to him unless it brings some advantage in looking upward. Other circumstances come into play to such an extent that the mere gain of going above a mile of the atmosphere is comparatively slight, and, as a matter of fact, many of the finest observations have been made at the sea-level. Notwithstanding the clearness of the air, doubt was thrown upon the suitability of the site for astronomical observations. Observers had reported a current of warm air rising up the side of the mountain during the night sufficiently strong to carry a sheet of tissue-paper out of sight. Such a current would be fatal to astronomical observations, and it became important, before commencing the building, to have a thorough trial of the atmospheric conditions made by a competent observer.

The astronomers who were consulted united in commending S. W. Burnham, of Chicago, as the best available judge in the case. This gentleman, although an amateur in the science, had gained a world-wide reputation by the discovery, with an eight-inch telescope, of a great number of double stars which had escaped the scrutiny of the Herschels and the Struves. Long practice at Chicago in all sorts of atmospheric conditions fitted him to recognize good conditions more quickly and certainly than one who had devoted himself to more widely extended branches of the science.

In the summer of 1879 Mr. Burnham accepted a proposal to proceed to California with his telescope, and spend several weeks in surveying the heavens from the top of Mount Hamilton. The month of August found him installed in a little observatory which had been designed and erected by Captain Floyd. The results of his examination exceeded all expectations, and an astronomer has seldom had occasion to make so enthusiastic a report as that of Mr. Burnham. Not only were the atmospheric conditions of the finest kind, but night after night the astronomer enjoyed such views of the heavenly bodies as Chicago offered him only a few nights in the year. The general experience of observers is that the very finest nights for seeing are few in number; the man who can secure a dozen in a year would be considered extremely fortunate. Even one of these favorable nights might not remain so for an hour. But at Mount Hamilton that steadiness of view which is so rarely to be found at less favored spots generally continued through the whole night. Whether the future astronomer who shall scan the heavens from this unsurpassed spot with an unrivalled telescope will enjoy during the whole year such weather as occurs during summer and autumn can not be foreseen;

but even if he does not, he will be more than satisfied with the year's work which he can perform during the favorable season.

As bearing on this subject we may cite the observations and photographs of the transit of Venus taken at the Lick Observatory in 1882 by Professor D. P. Todd. These proved to be the finest photographs of the transit ever taken. The skill of the astronomer was indeed a very essential requisite to the work; but this would have availed nothing had the condition of the atmosphere been unfavorable. Altogether, we may assume that, so far as mere looking is concerned, no existing observatory is so favorably situated as that now being erected by the Lick trustees.

With the legal complications all adjusted and the site assured, the trustees were prepared to commence the actual negotiations for making the telescope and erecting the necessary buildings. The first was really the most tedious and difficult work. In 1880 a contract was made with Messrs. Alvan Clark and Sons to furnish an objective of thirty-six inches clear aperture. This was six inches greater than the glass they had just arranged to make for the Russian government, and thus the telescope would fulfill the condition of being the largest and most powerful ever made. The result has proved the old rule, that the larger the glass, the more difficult it is to make it. In this connection there is a curious contrast between our present experience and that of the opticians in the early part of the century. At that time the making of the crown-glass for the double lens offered comparatively little difficulty; it was the flint-glass with which the trouble was found. The latter contained lead, a substance of great specific gravity, which persisted in settling toward the bottom of the pot in which the glass was melted, and thus producing a difference between the two sides of the glass which was fatal to its performance. But this difficulty has been so completely overcome that all the trouble now arises with the crown-glass. The method of making the best flint was long supposed to be a secret in the hands of a Swiss named Guinand and his family; but it is now believed that the supposed secret involved nothing more than the very simple device of continuously and vigorously stirring the molten glass until it became too cool and stiff to permit the heavier material to settle. However this might be, Feil, of Paris, who has been most successful in making large disks, supplied a satisfactory flint in a reasonable time. But so much delay was met with in casting the crown-glass that it has not yet reached the hands of the optician. The cause of his failure is one so simple that one can not but wonder that it should offer any trouble after being once detected. We call to mind that when the founder has succeeded in casting his lump of glass, weighing several hundred pounds, the clay pot in which it is contained is broken away. The outside portions of the glass itself, being impregnated with the clay and other impurities, have to be cut away. This is a most tedious process. If any ordinary cutting tool were used, the glass would be apt to fly to pieces. It has to be sawed by a wire working in sand and water. The process of cutting away the outside is one, therefore, involving weeks, if not months, of labor. When it is done, the mass must be pressed into the shape of a disk, like a very thin grindstone, and in order to do this the lump must first be heated nearly to the melting-point, so as to become plastic. But when Feil began to heat his large mass it flew to pieces. In successive attempts he took more and more time for the heating, but broke a dozen or more pieces before he at last succeeded. In February, 1884, he reported that a glass was actually moulded without having been broken, and would soon be ready for shipment. But it has not been shipped up to the time of sending these pages to press, and no one this side of the Atlantic knows what the state of things in the Paris foundry really is.

All this refers only to the great objectglass of the telescope, which, though the one vital organ of the instrument, is really a very small portion of the whole. The construction of the delicate yet powerful machinery by which the tube sixty feet long is to be pointed toward any region of the heavens, and kept in motion by clock-work, has not yet been commenced. In fact, the question who shall construct this "mounting," as it is called, is a difficult one to decide. In size and weight it is a piece of very heavy machinery, and would naturally be made in some great shop devoted to the construction of steam and other engines of the largest size. But the great masses of metal which form the axes and supports of the instrument have to be moved by a system of mechanism some parts of which are as delicate as those of a watch. The micrometer alone will, if made in the most approved way, be a piece of mechanism far more intricate than an ordinary astronomical instrument. In all this an astronomical instrument maker is required. Finally, what is more important, a multitude of provisions must be made for the handling and pointing of the instrument, for illuminating the different portions, and for enabling the observer to read off the fine lines by which he knows at each moment exactly at what star his instrument may be pointed. The difficulty of this last problem is one that is very slightly appreciated by those not accustomed to the use of telescopes. When using a power of one thousand, the whole field of view of the telescope is only a little spot of the heavens not one-hundredth of the apparent surface of the sun or moon. Within this little spot is contained all that the observer sees when he looks into the telescope. Yet by being magnified a thousand times it seems to fill a fourth of the sky. Since the observer can not see anything outside of this little spot, he has no knowledge which way to turn his telescope by mere sight of the heavens. He must therefore have a delicate arrangement of circles by which he finds out where he is looking, not by what he sees, but by looking into microscopes attached to various parts of the instrument itself. All this requires the combined skill of the astronomer, the astronomical mechanician, and the engineer.

After a decision is reached, it will probably require two years to complete the instrument. The trustees are apparently delaying the decision in order to be free to choose the best course when the completion of the object-glass is assured. Meanwhile the erection of the buildings and the construction of the other instruments are being pushed forward. The astronomers with whom the trustees consulted were unanimous in counselling them against any unnecessary expenditure upon buildings. The really important part of the observatory is its instruments; the buildings serve no purpose except to protect the instruments from the weather, and to furnish the necessary office rooms for the astronomers and their books. It was also urged upon them that no piece of pretentious architecture should be attempted, but that each instrument should, so far as possible, have its own little building. The observatory has been constructed on these ideas. At one end is the dome which is to contain the great telescope, at the other end is a smaller dome with a much smaller telescope, to be hereafter described. Between these two domes extends the observatory proper, which consists mainly of a corridor with a row of rooms opening out on each side. On the front is a piazza, commanding, as we have already described, one of the most imposing terrestrial views in the world. In the back is a level plain hardly a hundred yards in extent, formed by blasting off the peak of the mountain. Here is mounted the great meridian circle made by the Repsolds, a transit instrument by Facctt, of Washington, and a photoheliograph, which, as its name implies, is an instrument for obtaining photographs of the sun. With this instrument was taken the photographs of the transit of Venus already alluded to.

In the small dome is a twelve-inch telescope which has a curious history. Some eight years ago Messrs. Alvan Clark and Sons made a contract with the Portuguese government for a photographic telescope. When the telescope was done, the Portuguese were duly informed of the fact, but although an advanced payment had been made, no directions respecting the disposition of the instrument could be obtained. Repeated applications having failed to elicit any reply, or to secure the completion of the payment, the constructors were at liberty to dispose of the instrument. The objective was, however, one made not for the best sight of celestial objects, but to take the best photographs. It was therefore unfit for ordinary observations. It happened, however, that Professor Henry Draper, the lamented astronomer, of New York, had a visual objective of nearly the same size, which he wished to replace by a photographic one. Accordingly a change of glasses was made. Dr. Draper's objective was fitted to the mounting of the Portuguese telescope, and the latter sold to the Lick trustees. It was mounted in 1881, under the direction of Professor E. S. Holden, who went out to Mount Hamilton in company with Mr. Burnham to inspect the observatory, and make observations on the transit of Mercury in November of that year.

It will be seen that although the Lick Observatory is still in an unfinished state, it is in a position to do excellent work. Unfortunately, however, the terms of Mr. Lick's donation are such as to prevent the trustees from inaugurating a course of observations. They have authority only to erect the observatory and mount the instruments. Until this is done they can not relieve themselves of the charge. When finished, the institution is to be turned over to the Regents of the University of California, who are to appoint an astronomer, and put the institution into operation. The trustees having no authority to appoint an astronomer, the work which has been done there has been incidental to the completion of the building. One bad effect of this is that the trustees are unable to make arrangements with a view to any special line of research. The astronomer who is to take charge finally must make the best use he can of the appliances furnished him, and depend for their improvement upon the current income of the establishment.

It will be seen that the prospects for contributions to astronomy of an important and interesting kind are good. If we could get the frank opinion of the ablest astronomers of to-day, it would no doubt be that the making of great telescopes had already been pushed beyond the requirements of science, and that current solid work must mostly be done with smaller instruments. Yet no one would object to the completion of a single instrument to surpass all others, provided it was placed in a position corresponding to its superior power. This being, as is hoped, the case with the Lick telescope, its completion will be welcomed everywhere.

Yet it is not to be denied that the efficiency of an institution like that we are considering is liable to be impaired by a multitude of causes. Few people are alive either to the difficulty or importance of getting the proper man as astronomer of the institution. From the popular point of view, that the principal business of the astronomer is to make good use of his eyes, the difficulty can not be seen at all. The plain fact is that upon him more than upon the instruments the reputation of the observatory must depend.

THE CALIFORNIAN'S TALE

THIRTY-FIVE years ago I was out prospecting on the Stanislaus, tramping all day long with pick and pan and horn, and washing a hatful of dirt here and there, always expecting to make a rich strike, and never doing it. It was a lovely region, woodsy, balmy, delicious, and had once been populous, long years before, but now the people had vanished and the charming paradise was a solitude. They went away when the surface diggings gave out. In one place, where a busy little city with banks and newspapers and fire companies and a mayor and aldermen had been, was nothing but a wide expanse of emerald turf, with not even the faintest sign that human life had ever been present there. This was down toward Tuttletown. In the country neighborhood thereabouts, along the dusty roads, one found at intervals the prettiest little cottage homes, snug and cozy, and so cobwebbed with vines snowed thick with roses that the doors and windows were wholly hidden from sight—sign that these were deserted homes, forsaken years ago by defeated and disappointed families who could neither sell them nor give them away. Now and then, half an hour apart, one came across solitary log cabins of the earliest mining days, built by the first gold-miners, the predecessors of the cottage-builders. In some few cases these cabins were still occupied; and when this was so, you could depend upon it that the occupant was the very pioneer who had built the cabin; and you could depend on another thing, too—that he was there because he had once had his opportunity to go home to the States rich, and had not done it; had later lost his wealth, and had then in his humiliation resolved to sever all communication with his home relatives and friends, and be to them thenceforth as one dead. Round about California in that day were scattered a host of these living dead men—pride-smitten poor fellows, grizzled and old at forty, whose secret thoughts were made all of regrets and longings—regrets for their wasted lives, and longings to be out of the struggle and done with it all.

It was a lonesome land! Not a sound in all those peaceful expanses of grass and woods but the drowsy hum of insects; no glimpse of man or beast; nothing to keep up your spirits and make you glad to be alive. And so, at last, in the early part of the afternoon, when I caught sight of a human creature, I felt a most grateful uplift. This person was a man about forty-five years old, and he was standing at the gate of one of those cozy little rose-clad cottages of the sort already referred to. However, this one hadn't a deserted look; it had the look of being lived in and petted and cared for and looked after; and so had its front yard, which was a garden of flowers, abundant, gay, and flourishing. I was invited in, of course, and required to make myself at home—it was the custom of the country.

It was delightful to be in such a place, after long weeks of daily and nightly familiarity with miners' cabins—with all which this implies of dirt floor, never-made beds, tin plates and cups, bacon and beans and black coffee, and nothing of ornament but war pictures from the Eastern illustrated papers tacked to the log walls. That was all hard, cheerless, materialistic desolation, but here was a nest which had aspects to rest the tired eye and refresh that something in one's nature which, after long fasting, recognizes, when confronted by the belongings of art, howsoever cheap and modest they may be, that it has unconsciously been famishing and now has found nourishment. I could not have believed that a rag carpet could feast me so, and so content me; or that there could be such solace to the soul in wall-paper and framed lithographs, and bright-colored

* Originally printed for private circulation

tidies and lamp-mats, and Windsor chairs, and varnished whatnots, with sea-shells and books and china vases on them, and the score of little unclassifiable tricks and touches that a woman's hand distributes about a home, which one sees without knowing he sees them, yet would miss in a moment if they were taken away. The delight that was in my heart showed in my face, and the man saw it and was pleased; saw it so plainly that he answered it as if it had been spoken.

"All her work," he said, caressingly; "she did it all herself—every bit," and he took the room in with a glance which was full of affectionate worship. One of those soft Japanese fabrics with which women drape with careful negligence the upper part of a picture-frame was out of adjustment. He noticed it, and rearranged it with cautious pains, stepping back several times to gauge the effect before he got it to suit him. Then he gave it a light finishing pat or two with his hand, and said: "She always does that. You can't tell just what it lacks, but it does lack something until you've done that—you can see it yourself after it's done, but that is all you know; you can't find out the law of it. It's like the finishing pats a mother gives the child's hair after she's got it combed and brushed, I reckon. I've seen her fix all these things so much that I can do them all just her way, though I don't know the law of any of them. But she knows the law. She knows the why and the how both; but I don't know the why; I only know the how."

He took me into a bed-room so that I might wash my hands; such a bed-room as I had not seen for years: white counterpane, white pillows, carpeted floor, papered walls, pictures, dressing-table, with mirror and pin-cushion and dainty toilet things; and in the corner a wash-stand, with real china-ware bowl and pitcher, and with soap in a china dish, and on a rack more than a dozen towels—towels too clean and white for one out of practice to use without some vague sense of profanation. So my face spoke again, and he answered with gratified words:

"All her work; she did it all herself—every bit. Nothing here that hasn't felt the touch of her hand. Now you would think— But I mustn't talk so much."

By this time I was wiping my hands and glancing from detail to detail of the room's belongings, as one is apt to do when he is in a new place, where everything he sees is a comfort to his eye and his spirit; and I became conscious, in one of those unaccountable ways, you know, that there was something there somewhere that the man wanted me to discover for myself. I knew it perfectly, and I knew he was trying to help me by furtive indications with his eye, so I tried hard to get on the right track, being eager to gratify him. I failed several times, as I could see out of the corner of my eye without being told; but at last I knew I must be looking straight at the thing—knew it from the pleasure issuing in invisible waves from him. He broke into a happy laugh, and rubbed his hands together, and cried out:

"That's it! You've found it. I knew you would. It's her picture."

I went to the little black-walnut bracket on the further wall, and did find there what I had not yet noticed—a daguerreotype-case. It contained the sweetest girlish face, and the most beautiful, as it seemed to me, that I had ever seen. The man drank the admiration from my face, and was fully satisfied.

"Nineteen her last birthday," he said, as he put the picture back; "and that was the day we were married. When you see her—ah, just wait till you see her!"

"Where is she? When will she be in?"

"Oh, she's away now. She's gone to see her people. They live forty or fifty miles from here. She's been gone two weeks to-day."

"When do you expect her back?"

"This is Wednesday. She'll be back Saturday, in the evening—about nine o'clock, likely."

I felt a sharp sense of disappointment.

"I'm sorry, because I'll be gone then," I said, regretfully.

"Gone? No—why should you go? Don't go. She'll be so disappointed."

She would be disappointed—that beautiful creature! If she had said the words herself they could hardly have blessed me more. I was feeling a deep, strong longing to see her—a longing so supplicating, so insistent, that it made me afraid. I said to myself, "I will go straight away from this place, for my peace of mind's sake."

"You see, she likes to have people come and stop with us—people who know things, and can talk—people like you. She delights in it; for she knows —oh, she knows nearly everything herself, and can talk, oh, like a bird—and the books she reads, why, you would be astonished. Don't go; it's only a little while, you know, and she'll be so disappointed."

I heard the words, but hardly noticed them, I was so deep in my thinkings and strugglings. He left me, but I didn't know it. Presently he was back, with the picture-case in his hand, and he held it open before me and said:

"There, now, tell her to her face you could have stayed to see her, and you wouldn't."

That second glimpse broke down my good resolution. I would stay and take the risk. That night we smoked the tranquil pipe, and talked till late about various things, but mainly about her; and certainly I had had no such pleasant and restful time for many a day. The Thursday followed and slipped comfortably away. Toward twilight a big miner from three miles away came—one of the grizzled, stranded pioneers—and gave us warm salutation, clothed in grave and sober speech. Then he said:

"I only just dropped over to ask about the little madam, and when is she coming home. Any news from her?"

"Oh yes, a letter. Would you like to hear it, Tom?"

"Well, I should think I would, if you don't mind, Henry!"

Henry got the letter out of his wallet, and said he would skip some of the private phrases, if we were willing; then he went on and read the bulk of it—a loving, sedate, and altogether charming and gracious piece of handiwork, with a postscript full of affectionate regards and messages to Tom, and Joe, and Charley, and other close friends and neighbors.

As the reader finished, he glanced at Tom, and cried out:

"Oho, you're at it again! Take your hands away, and let me see your eyes. You always do that when I read a letter from her. I will write and tell her."

"Oh no, you mustn't, Henry. I'm get-

ting old, you know, and any little disappointment makes me want to cry. I thought she'd be here herself, and now you've got only a letter."

"Well, now, what put that in your head? I thought everybody knew she wasn't coming till Saturday."

"Saturday! Why, come to think, I did know it. I wonder what's the matter with me lately? Certainly I knew it. Ain't we all getting ready for her? Well, I must be going now. But I'll be on hand when she comes, old man!"

Late Friday afternoon another gray veteran tramped over from his cabin a mile or so away, and said the boys wanted to have a little gayety and a good time Saturday night, if Henry thought she wouldn't be too tired after her journey to be kept up.

"Tired? She tired! Oh, hear the man! Joe, *you* know she'd sit up six weeks to please any one of you!"

When Joe heard that there was a letter, he asked to have it read, and the loving messages in it for him broke the old fellow all up; but he said he was such an old wreck that *that* would happen to him if she only just mentioned his name. "Lord, we miss her so!" he said.

Saturday afternoon I found I was taking out my watch pretty often. Henry noticed it, and said, with a startled look,

"You don't think she ought to be here so soon, do you?"

I felt caught, and a little embarrassed; but I laughed, and said it was a habit of mine when I was in a state of expectancy. But he didn't seem quite satisfied; and from that time on he began to show uneasiness. Four times he walked me up the road to a point whence we could see a long distance; and there he would stand, shading his eyes with his hand, and looking. Several times he said:

"I'm getting worried, I'm getting right down worried. I know she's not due till about nine o'clock, and yet something seems to be trying to warn me that something's happened. You don't think anything has happened, do you?"

I began to get pretty thoroughly ashamed of him for his childishness; and at last, when he repeated that imploring question still another time, I lost my patience for the moment, and spoke pretty brutally to him. It seemed to shrivel him up and cow him; and he looked so wounded and so humble after that, that I detested myself for having done the cruel and unnecessary thing. And so I was glad when Charley, another veteran, arrived toward the edge of the evening, and nestled up to Henry to hear the letter read, and talk over the preparations for the welcome. Charley fetched out one hearty speech after another, and did his best to drive away his friend's bodings and apprehensions.

"Anything *happened* to her? Henry, that's pure nonsense. There isn't anything going to happen to her; just make your mind easy as to that. What did the letter say? Said she was well, didn't it? And said she'd be here by nine o'clock, didn't it? Did you ever know her to fail of her word? Why, you know you never did. Well, then, don't you fret; she'll *be* here, and that's absolutely certain, and as sure as you are born. Come, now, let's get to decorating—not much time left."

Pretty soon Tom and Joe arrived, and then all hands set about adorning the house with flowers. Toward nine the three miners said that as they had brought their instruments they might as well tune up, for the boys and girls would soon be arriving now, and hungry for a good old-fashioned breakdown. A fiddle, a banjo, and a clarinet—these were the instruments. The trio took their places side by side, and began to play some rattling dance-music, and beat time with their big boots.

It was getting very close to nine. Henry was standing in the door with his eyes directed up the road, his body swaying to the torture of his mental distress. He had been made to drink his wife's health and safety several times, and now Tom shouted:

"All hands stand by! One more drink, and she's here!"

Joe brought the glasses on a waiter, and served the party. I reached for one of the two remaining glasses, but Joe growled, under his breath:

"Drop that! Take the other."

Which I did. Henry was served last. He had hardly swallowed his drink when the clock began to strike. He listened till it finished, his face growing pale and paler; then he said:

"Boys, I'm sick with fear. Help me —I want to lie down!"

They helped him to the sofa. He began to nestle and drowse, but presently spoke like one talking in his sleep, and said: "Did I hear horses' feet? Have they come?"

One of the veterans answered, close to his ear: "It was Jimmy Parrish come to say the party got delayed, but they're right up the road a piece, and coming along. Her horse is lame, but she'll be here in half an hour."

"Oh, I'm *so* thankful nothing has happened!"

He was asleep almost before the words were out of his mouth. In a moment those handy men had his clothes off, and had tucked him into his bed in the chamber where I had washed my hands. They closed the door and came back. Then they seemed preparing to leave; but I said: "Please don't go, gentlemen. She won't know me; I am a stranger."

They glanced at each other. Then Joe said:

"She? Poor thing, she's been dead nineteen years!"

"Dead?"

"That or worse. She went to see her folks half a year after she was married, and on her way back, on a Saturday evening, the Indians captured her within five miles of this place, and she's never been heard of since."

"And he lost his mind in consequence?"

"Never has been sane an hour since. But he only gets bad when that time of the year comes round. Then we begin to drop in here, three days before she's due, to encourage him up, and ask if he's heard from her, and Saturday we all come and fix up the house with flowers, and get everything ready for a dance. We've done it every year for nineteen years. The first Saturday there was twenty-seven of us, without counting the girls; there's only three of us now, and the girls are all gone. We drug him to sleep, or he would go wild; then he's all right for another year—thinks she's with him till the last three or four days come round; then he begins to look for her, and gets out his poor old letter, and we come and ask him to read it to us. Lord, she was a darling!"

AN AMERICAN-INDIAN COMPOSER

"WHAT has the Pahana* come for, how long is she going to stay, and what are in all those boxes?" My hostess was peppered with questions by the group of curious Hopi Indians who had gathered to witness my arrival in their village after a two days' drive across that Arizona wilderness of beauty known as the "Painted Desert."

What was in those boxes? Ah, thereby hung the tale! They held the cause and purpose of my visit to the Indian reservation—a phonograph. Many have said truly that the songs of the negro and the American Indian contain a wealth of musical material for the composer. But I sought the Indian songs solely that I might reverently record and preserve what I could of an art that is now fast passing away beneath the influence of the Moody and Sankey hymn tunes and patriotic songs taught the Indians in the government schools.

Before coming West, I had the vague idea that all Indian music was a monotonous, barbaric chanting without form, with no beginning and no end. I shared too the ignorance regarding the Indian that makes us class all tribes together as a race of savage people in the same primitive grade of development. Not until I saw with my own eyes the vast differences even in tribes who are close neighbors could I realize the absolute truth of the authoritative statement that there are as great differences between the tribes of North-American Indians as there are between Norwegians and Spaniards among Europeans.

Certainly no people could be more unlike than the peace-loving Hopis and their warlike neighbors the Navajos. And yet their reservations lie side by side in the deserts and table-lands of northeastern Arizona. The Hopis are commonly known as "Moquis," a word of their

*The Hopi word for American.

own language, signifying "dead." It is thought that it was derisively applied to them by the Navajos, for they call themselves the Hopis, which means the "quiet" or "good people." It was to escape the ravages of the Ute and Apache that the agricultural Hopis fled to the very summit of the rocky plateaus that rise 600 feet abrupt and sheer from the level sands. On inaccessible craggy heights they built their villages, seven in number, of which Oraibi is the largest and most characteristic.

Every one has seen pictures of the Moqui villages. The square stone houses are built close together around open courts, in which are sunk the "kivas," or underground council-chambers, of the different clans. It is here that the sacred ceremonies and secret rites are performed, and here the Hopi men assemble to talk over grave matters or to indulge in friendly intercourse. The kiva of each clan is to its members what the club is to the white man.

The scarcity of water can hardly be conceived by those who have not been there. Every drop used in Oraibi has to be brought for a distance of two miles, one-half of which is up the steep trail, and carried all that long way in heavy earthen jars on the backs of toiling women.

And so the Hopi prays for rain. His ceremonial dances are all for rain; it is the great need, the great want, the one cry. I had heard since I had come West much of these village-dwelling Indians, and I expected to see in them a higher grade of culture than that of the nomad Navajos or the Indians of southern Arizona. But I was not prepared to find a people with such definite art-forms, such elaborate and detailed ceremonials, such crystallized traditions, beliefs, and customs.

Their music astounded me. I felt that I had come in search of gold and had found diamonds. The Hopis' every act of life seems to be a ceremonial rite, containing a symbol, a poetic significance known only to those outsiders who have dwelt long in Hopi land and are deep-versed in Hopi lore. "We have songs for everything," my little Hopi neighbor exclaimed, when I caught her singing as she combed her baby's hair. "We have songs for dancing, songs for planting, songs for grinding the corn, for putting the babies to sleep, even for combing the baby's hair." She laughed as she continued the refrain which my visit had interrupted.

These songs for different purposes are different in character. They are all definite in form, with forceful, graceful, or poetic words. The Katcina dance songs consist of an introduction on vowel syllables, then the song itself, also interspersed with vowel refrains, and lastly a sort of coda, again on vowel syllables.

And the Hopis *sing*. Theirs is no crooning over a camp-fire, no monotonous chanting, no nasal droning. The men have fine, clear voices, and the women sing softly with a "breathy" tone, the quality of which sounds often just a little sharp in pitch. The gentle lullabies, the pretty, graceful basket-songs of the women, and the melodies to which they grind their corn are as different from the rugged, rhythmic Katcina songs as are the cliffs of the mesa from the blossoms in the fields below.

There are three great elements in music—rhythm, melody, and harmony. The rhythmic quality of the Hopi Katcina songs is, in its intensity and variety of syncopation, unlike anything I ever heard. And it must be heard to be realized, for to me the Hopi sense of rhythm seems far to surpass ours. In Japanese music also I had found a wonderful variety of rhythm. Here again the rhythmic forms seem more complex and interesting than ours. But the Japanese have no harmony, and their melodies are monotonous, so that they rely chiefly on their ever - changing rhythm for variety of musical effect. Not so the Hopi. Though he too lacks harmony, his melodies are rich and full of beauty. And so Japan, with its written language and advanced civilization, is still behind our American village In-

dian in the art of music. Indeed, it is a question whether in their free use of unusual intervals the Hopis do not surpass in melodic variety not only the Japanese, but the European as well. Rhythm and melody are essential in any music, no matter how crude; but harmony, being a later development, is naturally absent in primitive forms of music. For this reason, though we may compare them, we cannot place Japanese or Hopi music on the same plane with our own. Our system of polyphony and harmony, with its instrumentation, its combination of choral and instrumental effects, and its wealth of tone-color, is a world of which the Hopi, who sings always in unison, does not dream. He has but one really musical instrument, the flute, and marks the rhythm of his songs with the rattle, the drum, and the crude scraping of wooden sticks.

Ruskin says that a people writes its character in its art, and I was interested to observe how Hopi music reflects Hopi life. The music of the European is the language of the soul. In it thoughts and feelings find expression transcending the power of words. But Hopi music is decorative rather than expressive. I use the word in the sense in which it is technically applied to drawing. Indeed, in his art generally the Hopi shows this characteristic, that instead of reproducing an object he symbolizes it only. This is speaking broadly, and my meaning is best illustrated in the form of Hopi art-work most familiar to Americans,—pottery and basketry. In the designs on jug and woven plaque there is no attempt to produce an exact image of an object. The Hopis do not make a picture of cloud, water, bird, flower, or feather in the way that we would. They make a sign which stands for that thing. For instance, a wavy line, a symbol so common among Indians, is not intended to depict water; it simply *means* water. If we laugh at this method of delineation, it is because we do not understand it. So, in Hopi poetry, a single word may stand for an idea that would take a sentence to express fully. Thus even those who speak the language may not understand the poetry, because they do not know the thought suggested by the word.

In Hopi music there is no attempt to represent in sound the meaning of the words. The songs are songs above all else. Whether in a given song the Hopi sing of rain or thunder, or whether he sing simple vowel refrains of " o-ho," " a-ha," and the like, the listener would never know from the quality of the music that one part of the song had more significance than the other. In fact, a word is often drawn out in true decorative style over bar after bar of music. For instance, the word " Yoe," meaning rain, may be prolonged as follows, *Yo-o-o-o-o-ho-ho-e,* thus forming a melodic phrase by itself. Such music is as unemotional as the conventionalized cloud forms and feather symbols on baskets and pottery. Yet, like all true art, the Hopi music reflects the people's life. It is essential to all their ceremonials, sacred and other, and accompanies their every act. But of the music of emotion, of the longings of the spirit, of joy, grief, or love, the Hopi has no idea. This may be because he is still living on what we may call the external plane.

That intensity of mental and spiritual experience that makes the inner life, with its moral struggles, its emotions, and aspirations, is unknown to the Hopi. So no matter how rich their music in form, rhythm, and melody, it will ever be barbaric in quality so long as it speaks not of the soul. Yet it was a revelation to me; for our music, though it expresses much, has by no means exhausted all the forms of expression. I had not been in Oraibi twenty-four hours before my mental picture of the scope of music faded like desert mirage, revealing a new and far-off horizon stretching boundless as the desert itself—a new world of art.

My workshop, as I called it, was one of the " government houses " at the foot of the mesa. The government builds the foundations, and furnishes materials for walls and roof, thus seeking to induce the Indians to leave their homes on the mesa for dwellings nearer the water-supply. In one of these houses I had my phonograph, and here the Indians collected daily with true Hopi curiosity to peek in at the windows, to stare at the " Pahana," and to join in the fun and excitement of singing into the machine.

Indeed, I had but to be seen issuing from the house where I lived, to be followed by a stream of Hopis—women with babies on their backs, men on their way to the fields, children just off to school. The Indians opened my door and entered my little house as unceremoniously as they did each other's. I always welcomed them, and offered them the customary empty boxes to sit on. There were never enough to go around, and half my visitors sat on the floor. But this was Hopi style; boxes are an innovation of civilization.

One morning, early, before any other Indians had come, the door opened noiselessly, and a graceful Hopi youth entered the room, and stood with folded arms quietly watching me. It was Koianimptiwa, known to the white people as " Thompson "—a name which had been given to him at the government Indian school. He spoke English and wore American clothing, and was thus considered a " civilized " Indian. After watching me quietly a while, my visitor announced, simply, " I want to sing," and pointed to the phonograph.

" I am delighted," I answered. " What will you sing?"

" I want to sing *my song,*" said he.

" Your song?" I asked. " Why, what do you mean?"

" My own song," he answered. " I make a song—yesterday; nobody heard my song yet. I like to sing it in that "—pointing again to the phonograph—" before anybody hear it."

" Why, Koianimptiwa," I exclaimed, thoroughly surprised and very much interested, " can you make songs—can you make the words and the music too?"

" Yes," he answered, with a quick smile, " I make songs; I make new song yesterday for next Katcina dance."

I gazed at Koianimptiwa and saw him in a new light. I had often watched him hauling wood, but now I wondered that I had never before thought of him as a poet.

His slanting eyes had a dreamy charm, his face was thoughtful almost to gravity; the easy good nature and ready joke of the Hopi seemed foreign to him. His cheeks were hollow, his shoulders high, and his whole appearance delicate and spiritual. He was, as I said, dressed in American clothing, but for all that he was a picturesque figure as he took his seat upon an upturned box before the phonograph. His thick hair was parted in the middle and hung on either side. It was not long enough to tie up behind in true Hopi fashion, for Koianimptiwa worked at road-making, and the government employs only those Indians who are willing to cut their hair. But he was still beautiful in spite of the government's decree, for his black locks, instead of being sheared off short, like those of so many Indians, hung below his ears in a glossy sweep, making an oval frame for his thin face. He was a study in black and white for an artist. His high, broad shoulders, lithe frame, and slim, sinewy muscles were sharply outlined beneath a tight-fitting black jersey. He wore duck overalls and a broad black felt hat, which fastened under his chin with a cord. He resembled more a study by Velasquez than our common idea of an American Indian. His face had a particularly earnest look to-day. The singing of his new song was a matter of moment to him. I knew that, like all Katcina songs, the rhythm would be one of the distinguishing features, and I also knew that I never could catch it unless I could record in my phonograph the sound of the rattle which marks the rhythm. So before Koianimptiwa began I placed in his hand the *éia,* as they call it, and told him to shake it just as he would if he were dancing.

The singing was indeed a solemn event to Koianimptiwa, and we both awaited with keen interest the result on the phonograph. It was a great success. Koianimptiwa flashed a smile as we listened, and I was delighted, for I had been struck with the beauty of the song, and felt that with its associations it would always be one of my most prized records.

"Will you make that sing for the other Indians and not say nothing? I like to hear if they like my song," said the young poet.

This was easily done. By noon the room was full of Hopis. I placed the song upon the machine. Koianimptiwa stood with impassive face.

"Do you know that song?" I asked of an old man who sat near me on the floor. "Can you tell me what it is?"

He thought a minute; then said, "It is a Katcina song."

Yes, all Katcina songs have the same general character—the genus is easily recognizable.

"Can you sing it for me?" I asked. "Is there anybody here that knows it?"

The old man thought; a look of embarrassment came over his face; then he answered, truthfully, "It seems I do not know that song."

All the Indians became quite thoughtful. I could see that they were puzzled.

"Do you like it?" I asked. "Is it a good Katcina song?"

"It is a fine song," the old man exclaimed. "Lolomai, pas lolomai!" (splendid, splendid), and the others echoed, "Lolomai!"

Koianimptiwa and I exchanged a glance of satisfaction; then he stole from the room.

What is a Katcina song? This had been one of my first questions in regard to Hopi music. The Katcina is a mythical being, a semi-deity, a creature between the gods and man, who intercedes with the gods in man's behalf. The Katcinas bring to the gods the Hopi's prayers. They are strange beings with extraordinary heads, some with beaks, some with colored faces, all monstrous and all decorated with tufts of feathers. The Indians themselves impersonate Katcinas, and dance "Katcina dances" in supplication for rain. When the chief proclaims a dance he orders new songs to be made, choosing the composers from the village poets.

A few days after making his song Koianimptiwa consented to give me the words thereof. Slowly he dictated, while I strove to record in written symbols the strange melody of the Hopi speech, for the language has the vowel music of the Samoan, and yet the soft guttural strength of the Greek.

Koianimptiwa folded his arms and leaned upon the table with fixed, intent face. The most difficult part of his task was now before him, that of putting into the white man's tongue his Hopi poem.

"My song," he began, "is about the butterflies flying over the corn-fields and over the beans. They are blue and they are yellow; their faces are bright; and I cannot explain in English how that is.

A Portion of Koianimptiwa's Song

FIRST AND SECOND VERSES WITH REFRAIN

Allegro: with marked rhythm. (MM ♪ = 176.)

Rattle.

Voice.

Ah - ha ha - ah i - hi hi - i, ah - ha ha - ah i - hi hi - i

(♪ = 108.) *in time* (♪ = 176.)

1. Se - kya vo - li - mu - u - u - uh Hö - mi - si ma - na - tuh yu - u - u - u -
2. Sa - kwa vo - li - mu - u - u - uh Mo - ri - si ma - na - tuh yu - u - u - u -

u - i Ta - la - si yam - muh yu Pit - zang - wa - a ti - ma - kiang Tö - ve -
u - i Ta - la - si yam - muh yu Pit - zang - wa - a ti - ma - kiang Tö - ve -

nang - uh yi - ma - ni...... ah - ha.. i - hi....)
nang - uh yi - ma - ni...... ah - ha.. i - hi....} O - ho o - o -

o... o........ o - ho - é............. é.... hé.. yé.. é - é - é - lo -

i o - o - o.... ah é - yé - hé.. loi o....... o - ah é......

.... yé.. hé - yé loi...... hi ai - ya - ha - ya ya - ow lo - lo - si......

* Bracketed bars to be taken nearly twice as slowly as the original time: ♪ = 108.

One butterfly is running after the other like the hunt, and there are many. But I cannot say that just in English, either. The second part is about the bees. They are flying over the corn and over the beans and singing. And I must explain: it is not the big corn and the big beans; my song is about the corn and beans when they are little. Then comes the thunder in the cloud, and that is hanging over the corn-field. Then comes the rain; and I cannot tell you just how that is in English. It first comes afar off, a little bit—drops, —then lots of them falling very fast. That is what the song means, but I cannot say it right." He passed his hand over his forehead. "This is very hard for me," he sighed; then added, "That is the end; that is all."

I was filled with the poetry of the song, and I looked at my Indian guest with something like awe. I longed to know how the creative impulse had stirred his poet fancy to activity. I longed to know the workings of the Indian mind when roused by the call of genius.

"Will you tell me one thing more, Koianimptiwa?" I said. "I would like to know just how you made your song. Did you go away where it was quiet and think about it for a long time, or did it come to you suddenly when you were not thinking about it? Tell me how it was!"

"It was like this," he answered. "Yesterday I go all day with my burro to load wood, and while I load my wood I make my song."

"Did you make the words first and then the music, or how was it?" I asked. The Indian looked puzzled, as though not understanding the question. Then he said, simply: "I do not make first words, then music. I make a *song*. My song has words and music."

"And did you make it all at once?" I said, "or did you make a little bit, and then think about something else, and then make a little more?"

He pointed to the east. "The yellow light," he said (for so the Hopis call the dawn),—"the yellow light just coming when I start with my burro, and then I begin my song. The sun was there" — he pointed slantingly above his head —"when I had finished."

"You finished it, then, about two hours before midday?" I asked.

"Yes," he answered, with a quick smile, "about two hours before midday."

He rose to go. "To-morrow I go to the kiva to teach the men my song." He paused in the doorway, looking off to the sandy wastes, which his fancy had seen already in blossom, with blue butterflies flying over them and wild bees singing above them all day long.

The sun was setting, and the evening light fell on the grave, dreamy face. Through the open door I saw a group of Hopis, who passed us with their burros to begin the steep ascent to the mesa top. They were returning from their fields, singing as they came. Had they, too, been making songs as they planted their corn? The voices drifted faint and fainter down the trail; the sun dipped low and lower; the mountains were pink

---

KOIANIMPTIWA'S SONG

(*Translation*)

Yellow butterflies
With pollen-painted faces
Chase one another in brilliant throng
Over the blossoming virgin corn.

Blue butterflies
With pollen-painted faces
Chase one another in brilliant streams
Over the blossoming virgin beans.

Over the blossoming virgin corn
The wild bees hum:
Over the blossoming virgin beans
The wild bees hum.

Over your field of growing corn
All day shall come the thunder-cloud:
Over your field of growing corn
All day shall come the rushing rain.

NOTE.—"Pollen-painted faces." The Hopis paint their faces for a ceremonial dance. So here the idea is that the butterflies, for their flight, paint their faces with pollen.

"Blossoming virgin corn." The Hopis call the corn-plant "virgin" until it bears fruit. Then they call the ears its children.

and lavender against the sky. Slowly came the stars. I wondered not that Koianimptiwa was a poet.

"Koianimptiwa, will you teach me your song, just as you taught it to the men in the kivas?" We were driving across the desert, for I had begun my homeward journey, and Koianimptiwa's mules were to bring me to the camping-place where I should find friends and shelter.

The sand stretched dazzlingly before us. It seemed to breathe and palpitate like a living thing as the hot air quivered over it in layers of light. Only the desert, Koianimptiwa, and I — solitude and desert silence save for the jolting of the cart and the fresh young voice that rang out across the wastes. Again and again the Indian youth sang his song, and again and again I strove to imitate, but the subtle, shifting rhythm baffled me, and I cried at last,

"Ah, Koianimptiwa, I am stupid, and your song seems very difficult to me!"

"Yes," he answered, gently, and with something of commiseration in his tone. "It is too hard for you."

"It is not easy for Pahanas to learn the Hopi songs," I said: "is it as difficult for the Hopis to learn the American music in the schools? Do the teachers have to sing the hymns and march tunes many times?"

"No," my companion answered. "Some things we try to learn in the school are hard, like arithmetic, but the singing is all easy."

Indeed, I had myself noticed that not Hopis only, but Indians of many tribes, have but to hear a melody once or twice to know it perfectly. Never have I found such extraordinary musical aptitude. So quickly indeed do the Indians absorb our music that I fear the coming generation will never hear the song that drifted down the trail to me at evenfall,—the poet will have vanished from the pueblo.

Morning grew noon—the sun burned, then the shadows lengthened, and still Koianimptiwa sang. He sang song after song, and again and again he sang his own, shaking an imaginary *éia* in the air, or marking the rhythm with a shrill cut of his long whip. It seemed as though the very spirit of the desert spoke through his voice.

By evening I had learned the song. The sands had grown purple, and the sun had dropped below the mountains as we neared the camp. I took Koianimptiwa's hand in parting. "I have learned your song," I said, " and I am going to take it to my home in the East. I shall sing it for my people, the Pahanas, who live near the great, great water. I want them to know that the Indian songs are beautiful. They have never heard any Hopi music; you have never seen the great waters near which my people live. The Pahanas will listen to your song, and it will be as new, as strange, as wonderful to them as the big salt ocean would be to you. And when they have listened and wondered, I will say to them: 'This is Koianimptiwa's song. May it bring rain to his fields!'"

NOTE.—For assistance in the translation of this song, and for much information regarding the Hopi Indians, I am indebted to the Rev. H. R. Voth, the eminent Hopi authority.